ADVANCED ANIMATION AND RENDERING TECHNIQUES

Theory and Practice

ADVANCED ANIMATION AND RENDERING TECHNIQUES

Theory and Practice

Alan Watt
University of Sheffield

Mark Watt
Xaos, San Francisco

ACM Press
New York, New York

Addison-Wesley Publishing Company
Wokingham, England · Reading, Massachusetts · Menlo Park, California
New York · Don Mills, Ontario · Amsterdam · Bonn · Sydney · Singapore
Tokyo · Madrid · San Juan · Milan · Paris · Mexico City · Seoul · Taipei

Cover designed by Crayon Design of Henley-on-Thames.
Typeset by Colset Private Ltd, Singapore.
Printed and bound in Great Britain by
William Clowes Limited, Beccles and London

First printed 1992. Reprinted 1993 and 1994.

British Library Cataloguing in Publication Data
A catalogue record for this book is available from the British Library.

Library of Congress Cataloging in Publication Data
Watt, Alan H., date
    Advanced animation and rendering techniques / Alan Watt, Mark
Watt.
        p.   cm.
    Includes index.
    ISBN 0-201-54412-1
    1. Computer graphics.   2. Computer animation.   I. Watt, Mark.
II. Title.
T385.W378   1992
006.6—dc20   92-17651
                                                        CIP

To our mother and grandmother
who died while this book was being written

Preface

Aim of the book

This text is an exposition of state of the art techniques in rendering and animation. It is aimed at advanced undergraduates, postgraduates and professional computer graphicists or implementors. The motivation of the text is to explain the many and various techniques that have evolved, with sufficient theoretical rigour and in enough detail to enable implementation, without the reader having to refer to the research literature.

We make certain assumptions about the existing computer graphics and mathematical knowledge of our readers. Elementary knowledge of vector theory such as the concept of dot and vector products and normalization is assumed. We also assume that you are familiar with linear transformation in three-dimensional space.

In most advanced rendering algorithms the complexity is embedded in geometric and logical relationships and very few graphics utilities are required to implement the algorithms. We have not, therefore, attempted to deal with graphics utilities *per se*, with the exception of RenderMan.

Structure of the book

Computer Graphics is a relatively new area, particularly the topics with which we are dealing. It borrows concepts from a number of scientific disciplines and there is no convenient theoretical umbrella that can be used as a general framework. It is difficult to categorize topics rigorously and we have decided to split the book into four parts.

Part I: Basics This contains everything you need to know to write or understand a simple renderer that deals with polygonal objects. It describes a particular, but very popular, rendering philosophy based on the Z-buffer algorithm.

Part II: Theoretical foundations This part deals with the important theoretical topics that underline many computer graphics algorithms. First, we outline aspects of reflection theory that are used in computer graphics reflection models. In many advanced applications parametric representation is used and much space is devoted to this important topics. Finally, an attempt is made to treat anti-aliasing theory comprehensively.

Part III: Advanced rendering techniques   This part is a detailed and comprehensive treatment of modern rendering techniques. The coverage is intended to build on the theory described in Part II and it deals with algorithms in sufficient detail to enable implementations. We start with the two major 'add-ons': shadows and texture mapping. Next, global illumination algorithms are described. Volume rendering, an exciting new area, is dealt with in some detail and, finally, we look at approaches that enable a user to specify the way in which various subtle effects can be combined in image synthesis.

Part IV: Advanced animation   This part begins with a theoretical foundation chapter for animation. The following three chapters are concerned with mainstream approaches in computer animation. Again much implementation detail is included. Case studies are built around commercial animation sequences.

Listings

Throughout the text we have presented extracts of sample code. These are meant to be examples and no attempt is made at consistency, in that only a subset of the algorithms that we discuss are implemented as code. Well known topics such as standard (polygonal object) rendering and forward ray tracing are generally not given. On the other hand, you will find a routine that can produce soft shadows. Generally, interesting algorithms, with implementation details other than those given in the text, are presented. Also, when it is possible to isolate critical parts of an algorithm in a procedure, this is done. Occasionally we have presented complete implementations. For example, the marching cubes algorithm does not lend itself to example extracts and we have given a suite of programs.

Our overall philosophy is to present examples of code writing practice for new and advanced areas, where implementation details are often not easily extractable from the literature.

Acknowledgements

Much of this book is based on work done over several years at Digital Pictures, one of Europe's leading computer graphics houses, based in London. The authors would like to thank the following individuals, many of whom have subsequently left DP while some still carry the torch, for their invaluable contributions which either directly or indirectly have benefited this work:

Chris Briscoe for his vision and direction in setting up and establishing DP; David 'Fat Boy' Lomax especially for producing many images specifically for this book; Simon 'A million pounds is not a lot of money these days' Rooms who wrote the animation software; Sheila Dunn for the animation; Chris 'Basher' Barret for his balding pate; the very, very beautiful Julian Woodfield; Alec 'Cream Bun' Knox; Nigel Hardwidge; Jan 'Tenacity Vaseline' Pinkava and Damian Steel.

We would like to thank the University of Sheffield for the use of certain invaluable facilities when writing this book.

For use of their illustrations the authors are indebted to:

James Arvo   Plate 33
Sabine Coquillart   Plates 59, 60, 61, 62
William Latham and S. Todd   Plate 30
David Lomax   Plates 1, 25, 26, 27, 28
Karl Sims   Plate 31
Steve Maddock   Plate 56
Archie Moore   Plates 38, 39, 40, 41
Mark Fuller   Plates 42, 43, 44, 45, 46(a)
Klaus de Geus   Plate 46(b) and (c)
Euan Macdonald   Plate 7
Jan Pinkava   Plate 8
Damian Steel   Plate 54
D. Greenberg, S. Feldman and J. Wallace   Plate 73
Pixar   Plate 5
Muybridge Collection, Kingston upon Thames Museum   Plate 68 (black and white)

The authors would like to acknowledge the following agencies, designers and others who variously designed, directed or produced sequences, realized at DP, that are used to illustrate the text:

Robinson Lambie Nairn for the 'Access Percentages' sequence featured in Plate 9;
Richard Dean and Collet, Dickenson, Pearce for the 'Yoplait' sequence featured in Plates 16, 64, 65, 66;
Matt Forest and Snapper Productions for the 'Wired' sequence featured in Plates 49, 50, 51, 52, 53;
Digital Productions and Evans, Hunt and Scott for the 'Commodore' sequence featured in Plate 55;
Liz Friedman and BBC Graphics for the 'Korea' sequence featured in Plate 21;
Digital Productions and Salon Films for the 'Hong Kong Airport' sequence featured in Plate 47;
Enigma Films for the 'Cola' sequence featured in Plate 48;
Dick Burns and TVS for the 'TVS' sequence featured in Plate 12.

Finally, we should acknowledge Addison-Wesley for their care and uncomplaining patience over last minute changes; in particular Sheila Chatten and Lynne Balfe.

Alan Watt
Mark Watt
July 1992

Contents

PART I

Basics

1 ‖ Rendering polygonal objects

This chapter deals with a basic renderer for polygonal objects. Chapter 4 contains a description of more advanced rendering strategies that incorporate anti-aliasing. Chapter 3 describes how objects represented by a net of bicubic parametric patches can be converted into polygons for input to a standard renderer such as the one described in this chapter.

Introduction

For a number of years the workhorse of three-dimensional graphics has been a basic system that renders objects represented by a set of polygons. The 'traditional' approach to rendering three-dimensional objects is to build a basic renderer then add on various enhancements. Usually a basic renderer is one that incorporates a local reflection model, such as the Phong model (Chapter 2), into a Phong incremental shader (described in this chapter). Most renderers work with objects that are represented by a set of polygons. This approach solves a number of problems:

1. Modelling objects using polygons is straightforward (although tedious). Piecewise linearities in the polygonal structure are rendered invisible by the shading technique (except on silhouette edges).

2. Geometric information is only stored at the polygon vertices, and information required for the reflection model that evaluates a shade at each pixel is interpolated from this vertex information. This makes for fast shading and this rendering approach is the one

that is incorporated in fixed program hardware in many graphics workstations.

A polygon-based renderer can also be used to render objects that are made up of a set of bicubic patches (see Chapter 3). An easy way to deal with such objects is to subdivide the patches and convert the subdivision products into a set of planar polygons, injecting these into the polygon renderer.

On the other hand, polygonal objects are subject to certain disadvantages. For example, it is difficult to map textures from a two-dimensional domain onto the surface of an object. Shadow algorithms that are based on polygonal objects generally have high coding complexity and produce hard-edged shadows. Polygons are expensive – a single complex object that is to be represented to a high level of detail can generate a very large number of polygons (for example, the head shown in Plate 1 has around 400 000 polygons).

At this stage we should mention that although we are concerned with the detailed workings of an entire polygon-based renderer, it is likely that nowadays graphics software developers may already have a basic renderer at their disposal. This may be in the form of a fast workstation with polygon shading hardware that is accessed from a graphics standard such as PHIGS

3

[PHIG88] which supports shading. More exotic rendering facilities are likely to be found within various manufacturers' rendering and animation software.

The main steps in rendering a polygonal object are (see Figure 1.13):

1. Polygons representing an object are extracted from the database and transformed into the world coordinate system using linear transformations such as translation and scaling.

2. A scene constructed in this way is transformed into a coordinate system based on a view point or view direction.

3. The polygons are then subjected to a visibility test. This is called 'backface elimination' or 'culling' and removes those polygons that face away from the viewer. Typically half the polygons in an object are removed by this test (generally a convex object of any shape will tend to have half of its surface invisible to a viewer) and these do not have to be dealt with by a general (and more expensive) hidden surface removal algorithm.

4. Unculled polygons are clipped against a three-dimensional view volume.

5. Clipped polygons are then projected onto a view plane or image plane.

6. Projected polygons are then shaded by an incremental shading algorithm. This algorithm runs three processes in parallel. First, the polygon is rasterized, or those pixels that the edges of the polygon contain are determined (usually in scan line order). Second, a depth for each pixel is evaluated and a hidden surface calculation is performed. Third, the polygon is shaded. Both the second and third processes use geometric information from three-dimensional world or view space, but overall the process is driven from, or controlled by, screen space. By this we mean that the algorithm processes pixels consecutively.

Steps 1 to 5 are standard for most renderers and involve geometric operations on vertex information. The sixth step involves the combination of rasterization, hidden surface removal and shading. In this phase many different methodologies are possible. The major options are the choice of a hidden surface removal algorithm and an anti-aliasing method. The particular approach we have described in step 6 depends in practice on using a Z-buffer algorithm to solve the hidden surface removal problem. The Z-buffer has low complexity but high memory requirements. It has become the most popular hidden surface removal algorithm and many graphics terminals offer a hardware Z-buffer.

1.1 Polygonal representation of three-dimensional objects

Objects that possess curved surfaces have these surfaces approximated by polygonal facets. Thus, for example, a cylinder could be represented by a set of n rectangles for the curved surface, together with a pair of n-sided polygons for the end faces (Figure 1.1). The error in the representation – the difference between the real surface and the polygonal approximation – is visually diminished by using interpolative shading algorithms, and the success of such algorithms, together with the general ease of setting up a polygonal object, are the reasons for the popularity of this approach. The major visual defect of polygonal models is the visible piecewise linearity exhibited by silhouette edges (see, for example, Figure 3.20). The only way in which this can be improved is by increasing the polygonal resolution – using more and more polygons to represent areas of high spatial curvature. For complex objects, as we have already remarked, a number of polygons in excess of 10^5 is not uncommon. This has major ramifications in database access time and rendering time (see Section 3.2.1 for a comparison between polygonal and parametric representation). A connected problem occurs when objects are scaled up. An object adequately approximated at one projected size may degrade when the object is enlarged. This has been called 'geometric aliasing'.

Polygonal representations can be generated manually from a designer's abstraction, or automatically from real objects by using devices such as laser rangers in conjunction with the appropriate software. Also, they can be generated automatically from implicit descriptions by such strategies as sweeping a cross-section around an axis and generating a solid of revolution.

In general, polygonally represented objects are not particularly suitable for interactive manipulation or free form sculpting. It is difficult, when altering the shape of a polygonal object, to ensure that the adequacy of the representation is maintained.

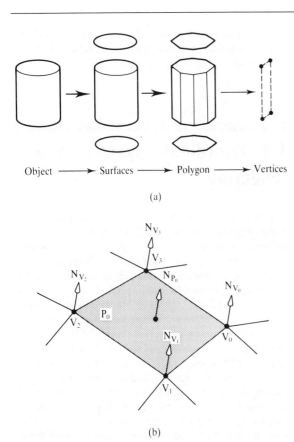

(a)

(b)

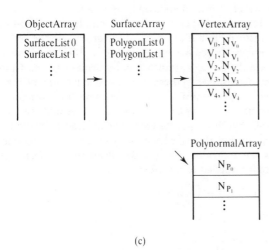

(c)

Figure 1.1 (a) Object as a hierarchy. (b) Polygon information. (c) Embedding it in a hierarchical data structure.

Complete information necessary to shade a polygon, given that it is part of a set of polygons representing a surface, is usually stored in a hierarchical data structure, the general principles of which are shown in Figure 1.1(a). (In practice the structure usually contains another level so that polygon vertices are stored once only.) Each surface is defined by pointers into a list of polygons, and each polygon by pointers into a list of vertices.

The information that we need to store for each polygon is also shown in Figure 1.1. This consists of:

1. A list of the polygon vertices – each vertex is a three-dimensional coordinate in a local coordinate system associated with the object.

2. A list of vertex normals – these are required by the shading algorithm; their geometric nature is described in Section 1.6.1. Vectors are stored as three components in the same local coordinate system.

3. A polygon normal – the true geometric normal to the plane containing the polygon. This is required in the culling operation.

There is a disadvantage in this approach: the fact that edges are shared between adjacent polygons is not explicitly contained in the data structure. This leads to rendering strategies where edges are processed twice. We now discuss this point in more detail.

1.1.1 Polygon-based representation versus edge-based representation

The conventional approach to rendering polygonal objects is to treat polygons as independent entities. This is the easiest way to deal with polygons and classic algorithms, such as the Sutherland–Hodgman re-entrant polygon clipper and the full screen Z-buffer hidden surface removal algorithm (described in Section 1.5) deal with polygons as isolated entities.

An alternative approach that offers certain advantages is edge-based rendering, described in [MITC90]. The representation of object data is based on polygon edges rather than the polygons themselves and each edge is represented in the data structure as shown in Figure 1.2. The four indices within each element in the edge array point to the two appropriate vertices and the two polygon normals associated with the edge. (There is a special dummy polygon 0, which is treated as a second polygon by edges which are adjacent to only a single polygon.)

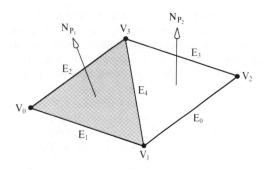

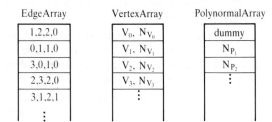

Figure 1.2   An edge-based representation.

This approach can be more efficient and will result in a simpler data structure to represent each object. For example, while a polygon may have an arbitrary number of vertices, an edge has exactly two end points and is shared (mostly) between two polygons. Shared edges are stored once in the data structure and are processed once only. A rendering approach that treats polygons as independent entities effectively deals with each shared edge twice for such nontrivial processes as clipping and rasterization.

The obvious disadvantage to using an edge-based approach is that it implies the use of a scan line based algorithm in the organization of the rendering process. Scan line based algorithms simultaneously process all the polygons that are intersected by the current scan line. This places an upward limit on scene complexity that is determined by the largest number of polygons that can be held in memory and processed simultaneously. However, this is easily overcome by using a full screen Z-buffer to render objects and a scan line algorithm for polygons within objects. We can, for each object, render polygons in scan line order, allowing us to make use of the shared edge structure.

The maximum number of polygons which can be active simultaneously on a single scan line is now determined by the maximum object complexity, not the maximum scene complexity. Thus no limit is placed on scene complexity and full use can be made of shared information.

1.2 Coordinate systems and rendering

One view of the geometric part of the rendering process is that it consists of the application of a series of coordinate transformations that takes an object database through a series of coordinate systems. These coordinate systems are common to all rendering systems and are fundamental to the understanding of three-dimensional computer graphics. A series of operations fundamental to the construction of a computer generated image is associated with each space (see Figure 1.13). It is often necessary when rendering to move from one system to another and good rendering software architectures should provide routines to facilitate this. The notation used to describe the transformations in these systems is now firmly established, namely the 4 × 4 homogeneous transformation matrix, and it is the one that we shall use here. Before discussing these processes in more detail, however, a brief digression is necessary.

In general, when transforming an object we need to transform both the vertices of the object and the vertex normals – since it is generally more efficient to transform the normals, rather than recalculating them from the transformed vertices. Naively we might expect that, for a given transformation, the same transformation matrix can be applied to both the vertices and the normals, but this is not the case when the transformation is anisotropic, that is, when it is not equal in all directions, as the following example will demonstrate. Consider scaling applied to a vertex:

$$(x', y', z') = (S_x x, S_y y, S_z z)$$

where generally

$$S_x \neq S_y \neq S_z$$

If the same scaling is applied to the normal components, the incorrect results are obtained as shown in Figure 1.3.

Working in homogeneous coordinates it can be shown [GLAS90] that the transformation matrix for the nor-

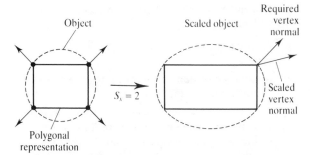

Figure 1.3 Errors occur if differential scaling is applied to vertex normals.

mals, M_n, is derived from the transformation matrix of the vertices M in the following two steps:

1. Remove the components of the matrix M that are responsible for translation. In practice this means setting M_{30}, M_{31} and M_{32} to zero. This gives us M_T, the transformation matrix for the tangential directions of the object.

2. Using the fact that the relation between the untransformed tangent and normals, $T \cdot N = 0$, must also hold for the transformed tangents and normals, $T' \cdot N' = 0$, the matrix for the normals is obtained by taking the transpose of the inverse of the tangent's transformation matrix, that is:

$$M_n = \left(M_T^{-1} \right)^t$$

Returning to our scaling example and working through the above procedure, we see that the correct transformed normal is given by:

$$\left(n_x', n_y', n_z' \right) = \left[\frac{n_x}{S_x}, \frac{n_y}{S_y}, \frac{n_z}{S_z} \right]$$

Finally, note that transformations applied to vertex normals do not in general preserve the length of the vector. Consequently, a normalized vector, after undergoing a transformation, will have to be renormalized.

1.2.1 Local coordinate systems

For ease of modelling and application of local transformations it makes sense to store the vertices of an object with respect to some point conveniently located in or near the object. In PHIGS this is called the 'modelling coordinate system'. For example, we may locate the origin for a cube at one of the cube vertices, or we may make the

axis of symmetry a polygonal object, generated as a solid of revolution, coincident with the z-axis. As well as storing the polygon vertices in a coordinate system that is local to the object, we would also store the polygon normals and the vertex normals. When local transformations are applied to the vertices of an object, the corresponding transformation (derived in the previous section) is applied to the normals.

1.2.2 World coordinate system

Once an object has been modelled, the next stage is to place it in the scene that we wish to render. All objects that together constitute a scene each have their separate local coordinate system. The global coordinate system of the scene is known as the 'world coordinate system'. In fact, the definition of a scene can be thought of as constructing a world coordinate system from the various local coordinate systems. All the objects have to be transformed into this common space in order that their relative spatial relationships may be defined. The act of placing an object in a scene defines the transformation required to take the object from local space to world space. If this object is being animated then the animation system provides a time-varying transformation that takes the object into world space on a frame-by-frame basis.

The scene is lit in world space. Light sources are specified, and if the shaders within the renderer function in world space then this is the final transformation that the normals of the objects have to undergo. The surface attributes of an object – texture, colour and so on – are specified and tuned in this space.

1.2.3 Eye or camera coordinate system

The eye or camera coordinate system is a space used to establish viewing parameters and a view volume. A virtual camera is often used as a conceptual aid in computer graphics. The camera can be positioned anywhere in world space and point in any direction. The analogy of the film plane in computer graphics is the view plane – the plane on which the scene is projected. The viewing system in PHIGS is called the 'view reference coordinate system' or the (U, V, N) system. PHIGS discarded the notion of an eye point, view point or camera point in favour of a completely general (and cumbersome) viewing system that uses a view reference point as any arbitrary point in world coordinate space to establish the view reference coordinate system. In your authors' opinion the generality afforded by such a system is more than outweighed by its complexity and, as a result, many manufacturers' systems use a more constrained specification for a space we shall call eye or camera coordinate space. Thus we explain how to implement a minimal practical system. The best treatment of how to implement a general viewing system, using a PHIGS type model, is given in [FOLE89].

For example, Pixar's RenderMan [PIXA88] uses an eye point or virtual camera position requiring that:

1. The origin of eye space and the centre of projection are the same point.

2. The view plane normal, the viewing direction, is coincident with the z-axis in eye space.

3. The viewing direction is such that with the camera looking towards positive z-values, increasing values of z are further from the eye, x is to the right and y is up giving a left-handed coordinate system (PHIGS uses a right-handed coordinate system).

Adopting such a system and using the virtual camera analogue we have a camera that can be positioned anywhere in world coordinate space and pointed in any direction – the view direction. Additionally, we allow the camera to be rotated about the view direction. Using

a treatment by Fiume [FIUM89], we can specify this (redundantly) by three vectors and a position (Figure 1.4):

1. A camera position C. This point is also the centre of projection.

2. A viewing direction vector N (the positive z-axis) – a vector normal to the view plane.

3. An 'up' vector V that orients the camera about the view direction and establishes with N the orientation of the view plane window within the view plane.

4. An (optional) vector U to denote the direction of increasing x in the eye coordinate system. This establishes a right- or left-handed coordinate system.

Fiume derives a vector E using simple vector calculus, where the transformation from a point in world coordinate space to a point in camera coordinate space is given by[†]:

$$[x_e \ y_e \ z_e \ 1] = [x_w \ y_w \ z_w \ 1]E$$

E splits into a translation T and a change of basis B:

$$E = TB$$

where:

$$T = \begin{bmatrix} 1 & 0 & 0 & 0 \\ 0 & 1 & 0 & 0 \\ 0 & 0 & 1 & 0 \\ -C_x & -C_y & -C_z & 1 \end{bmatrix}.$$

B rotates any vector expressed in the world coordinate system into the camera system. In particular, the three axis vectors of the camera system (expressed in world coordinates) are transformed into camera system coordinates as $(1,0,0)$, $(0,1,0)$ and $(0,0,1)$. That is, B maps:

U to $(1,0,0)$
V to $(0,1,0)$
N to $(0,0,1)$

[†] We have in this text adopted the convention of using row vectors to represent three-dimensional points. This was, until fairly recently, the de facto standard in computer graphics. The de jure standard, adopted by PHIGS and, for example, [FOLE89] is to use column vectors; this is of course the convention used by mathematicians. We have decided to stick with the traditional computer graphics convention for the eminently sensible reason that when transformation matrices are concatenated the left to right order in which they appear in the concatenation product is the order in which the corresponding transformations are applied to the points.

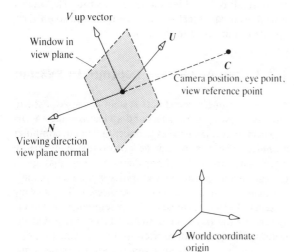

Figure 1.4 Establishing an eye coordinate system in world space.

or in matrix form:

$$[U_x \ U_y \ U_z \ 1]B = [1 \ 0 \ 0 \ 1]$$
$$[V_x \ V_y \ V_z \ 1]B = [0 \ 1 \ 0 \ 1]$$
$$[N_x \ N_y \ N_z \ 1]B = [0 \ 0 \ 1 \ 1]$$

Because U, V and N are unit vectors, we know that:

$$U_x^2 + U_y^2 + U_z^2 = 1$$

and similarly for V and N. Also U, V and N are mutually orthogonal, therefore:

$$U_x V_x + U_y V_y + U_z V_z = 0$$

and similarly for other coordinates. Thus B is given by:

$$B = \begin{bmatrix} U_x & V_x & N_x & 0 \\ U_y & V_y & N_y & 0 \\ U_z & V_z & N_z & 0 \\ 0 & 0 & 0 & 1 \end{bmatrix}$$

The only problem now is specifying a user interface for the system and mapping whatever parameters are used by the interface into U, V and N. A user needs to specify C, N and V. C is easy enough. N, the viewing direction or view plane normal, can be entered, say, using two angles in a spherical coordinate system:

θ the azimuth angle

ϕ the colatitude or elevation angle

where:

$$N_x = \sin\phi \ \cos\theta$$
$$N_y = \sin\phi \ \sin\theta$$
$$N_z = \cos\phi$$

V is more problematic. For example, a user may require 'up' to be the same sense as 'up' in the world coordinate system. However, this cannot be achieved by setting:

$$V = (0, 0, 1)$$

because V must be perpendicular to N. A sensible strategy is to allow a user to specify an approximate orientation for V, say V' and have the system calculate V. Figure 1.5 demonstrates this. V' is the user-specified up vector. This is projected onto the view plane:

$$V = V' - (V' \cdot N)N$$

and normalized. Finally, if U is unspecified, it is obtained from:

$$U = N \times V$$

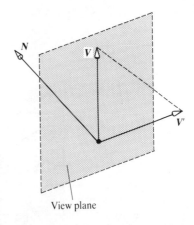

Figure 1.5 *V* can be calculated from an 'indication' given by *V'*.

resulting in a left-handed coordinate system.

A user interface for a viewing system is difficult. As we have hinted, an interface into a completely general viewing system (as recommended by the two major graphics standards GKS and PHIGS) is impossibly confusing. We have given an absolutely minimum system. A neat idea for an interface is suggested by Figure 1.14 (see Section 1.2.4). In a separate window to the main display you can have a view of the viewing system itself. This indirect abstraction can reinforce a user's sense of perception of the selected viewing parameters. In the end, it's all a matter of taste and how well a user can feel three-dimensional space.

The eye space is the most convenient space in which to 'cull' polygons and we now look at this problem.

Backface elimination or culling

This operation removes entire polygons that face away from the viewer. If we are dealing with a single convex object, culling completely solves the hidden surface problem. If an object contains a concavity, or if it is only one of a number of objects in a scene, we need a general hidden surface removal algorithm as well as culling. (A general hidden surface removal algorithm will deal with the case where only part of a polygon is hidden; culling deals with polygons as single entities.)

Determining whether a polygon is visible from a view point involves a simple geometric test. The geometric normal to the polygon is calculated and the angle between this and the line-of-sight vector is determined. The line-of-sight vector is the vector from the polygon to the

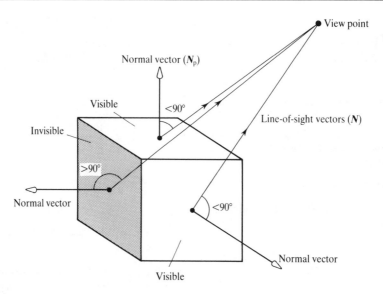

Figure 1.6   Culling or backface elimination.

view point. If this angle is greater than 90° then the complete polygon is invisible to the viewer and the database is tagged accordingly (Figure 1.6). Thus:

$$\text{visibility} := N_p \cdot N > 0$$

where:

N_p is the polygon normal
N is the line-of-sight vector

A polygon surface normal can be calculated from three noncollinear vertices. We define two vectors contained in the plane of the polygon, the cross-product of which gives the surface normal (Figure 1.7). The normal must point away from the surface and not into the object. For this to happen the vertices must be ordered in a counterclockwise direction when looking from the outside.

If we perform the operation in screen space things become much simpler. Because the centre of projection is removed to $(0, 0, -\infty)$ (see Figure 1.12) the line-of-sight vectors become parallel and equal to the viewing direction vector. That is:

$$N = (0, 0, 1)$$

In this case the visibility comparison is very simple – it reduces to

$$N_{pz} > 0$$

However, from an efficiency point of view, we need to perform the test that gets rid of most polygons before we

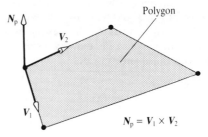

Figure 1.7   Calculating the normal vector to a polygon.

embark on the far more expensive clipping test – which must be performed in eye space. Thus we tolerate a more expensive culling test and perform the operation in eye space.

1.2.4   Screen space

The final space into which we transform the data is the least intuitive. It is the process that describes the method of viewing the scene and is concerned with projective geometry, or how to define those light rays that reach the eye (or virtual camera).

The fundamental transformation that takes us into screen space is the perspective transformation, which takes a point in the scene and projects it onto a view plane or screen positioned at distance D away from the view point and oriented normal to the viewing direction. (The terms 'screen' and 'view plane' mean slightly different things. Strictly, screen coordinates may be derived from view plane coordinates after a device-dependent transformation.) Referring to Figure 1.8 we can see that the calculation is trivial. Using similar triangles we can see that the screen coordinates (x_s, y_s) of the point P' – the projection of the point P – are given by:

$$x_s = D\frac{x_e}{z_e}$$

$$y_s = D\frac{y_e}{z_e}$$

Although trivial, this calculation has behind it a distinguished history. The origins of this transformation can be traced back as far as the fifteenth century to the artist's society in Florence, where artists struggled to find a way of evoking three-dimensional space and depicting solid form in a way that was systematic and consistent. The first appearance of such a system is usually credited to Filippo Brunelleschi who around 1413 invented, or discovered, linear perspective. His system was a simple geometric construction. However, full-scale mathematicization of perspective, into what we could recognize as the perspective projection, did not occur until 1600. The first application of perspective science can be seen in religious pictures dating from that time, where figures are depicted against geometrically constructed buildings and tiled floors. For a full and fascinating account of the progress of perspective as an artistic technique the reader is referred to [KEMP90].

Screen space is defined to act within a closed volume called the viewing frustum, that delineates the volume of space which is to be rendered. Objects that lie outside the viewing frustum are not rendered. The view volume can be specified as follows: suppose we have a square window, the view plane window, of size $2h$, arranged symmetrically about the viewing direction. The four planes defined by:

$$x_e = \pm\frac{hz_e}{D}$$

$$y_e = \pm\frac{hz_e}{D}$$

together with the two additional planes, called the near and far clipping planes respectively (perpendicular to the viewing direction) defined by:

$$z_e = D$$
$$z_e = F$$

make up the definition of the viewing frustum as shown in Figure 1.9. Suppose we make the view plane and the near clip plane coincident. We can see that the view volume is formed, for a perspective projection, by constructing lines from the window corners to the centre of projection. This is a much simpler specification than that adopted by the graphics standards GKS and PHIGS. It is based on a treatment given in [NEWM73].

We should digress for a moment to examine the nature of these constraints. Returning to our camera analogy, we can see that allowing a view plane to have other than a normal orientation (with respect to the viewing direction) is equivalent to allowing the film plane in a real camera to tilt. This effect is actually used in certain camera designs to correct for perspective distortion in such contexts as photographing a tall building from the ground. Thus constraining the view plane to be normal to the viewing direction and symmetrical about its centre results in a virtual camera that corresponds to the design of most modern cameras.

An alternative virtual camera specification and one that is closer to a real camera is adopted in the Render-Man specification [PIXA88]. To avoid a user specification of D, the distance of the view plane from the eye point, RenderMan fixes the view plane (RenderMan uses the term 'image plane') one unit in positive z away from the view point. The view volume is then determined entirely by the view plane window (RenderMan uses the confusing term 'screen window') which determines the field of view angle (Figure 1.10).

Returning to our simple viewing frustum, we shall now discuss the transformation of the third component of

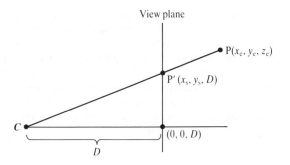

Figure 1.8 Perspective transformation.

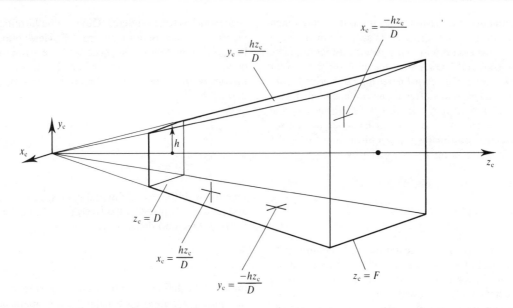

Figure 1.9 Definition of view frustum through six planes.

screen space, namely z_s – ignored so far because the derivation of this transformation is somewhat subtle. Now, the bulk of the computation involved in rendering an image takes place in screen space. In screen space polygons are clipped against scan lines and pixels, and hidden surface calculations are performed on these clipped fragments. In order to perform hidden surface calculations (in the Z-buffer algorithm), depth information has to be generated on arbitrary points within the polygon. In practical terms this means, given a line and plane in screen space, being able to intersect the line with the plane, and to interpolate the depth of this intersection point of the line from the depth of the two end points. This is only a meaningful operation in screen space providing that, in moving from eye space to screen space, lines transform into lines and planes transform into planes. It can be shown [NEWM73] that these conditions are satisfied provided the transformation of z takes the form:

$$z_s = A + \frac{B}{z_e}$$

where A and B are constants. These constants are determined from the following constraints:

1. Choosing $B < 0$ so that as z_e increases then so does z_s. This preserves our intuitive Euclidean notion of depth. If one point is behind another, then it will

have a larger z_e value, if $B < 0$ it will also have a larger z_s value.

2. Normalizing the range of z_s values so that the range $z_e \in [D, F]$ maps into the range $z_s \in [0, 1]$.

The full perspective transformation is given by:

$$x_s = D \frac{x_e}{hz_e}$$

$$y_s = D \frac{y_e}{hz_e}$$

$$z_s = F \frac{1 - D/z_e}{F - D}$$

where the additional constant, h, appearing in the transformation for x_s and y_s ensures that these values fall in the range $[-1, 1]$ over the square screen. Now this transformation is different to the others that we have encountered so far in that it is nonlinear and so cannot be put into matrix notation. This is inconvenient and in order to get round this problem, convention separates the transformation into two steps; a linear part followed by a nonlinear part by introduction of a fourth coordinate, w. The separation is:

$$x = x_e$$

$$y = y_e$$

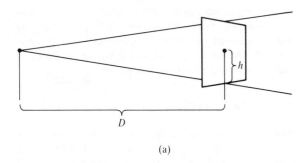

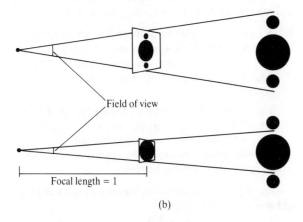

Figure 1.10 Alternative ways of defining a view window. (a) Simple viewing system: D and h are varied. (b) RenderMan: D is fixed at one unit and h is varied.

$$z = \frac{hFz_e}{D(F-D)} - \frac{hF}{F-D}$$

$$w = \frac{hz_e}{D}$$

followed by the nonlinear so-called perspective divide essential to generating a perspective image:

$$x_s = \frac{x}{w}$$

$$y_s = \frac{y}{w}$$

$$z_s = \frac{z}{w}$$

The coordinates (x, y, z, w) are called 'homogeneous coordinates'. The fourth coordinate, w, can be thought of as carrying the perspective information necessary to

generate an image. The purpose of this separation is that it enables us to represent the linear part of the transformation, which contains all the parameters of the perspective transformation, as a 4×4 matrix – the perspective matrix P. Transformation from eye space to perspective space can thus be treated in the same way as transformations from earlier spaces, and the perspective matrix is simply concatenated with all the other preceding transformation matrices in the rendering pipeline. P is defined as:

$$[x\,y\,z\,w] = [x_e\,y_e\,z_e\,1]\,P$$

where:

$$P = \begin{bmatrix} 1 & 0 & 0 & 0 \\ 0 & 1 & 0 & 1 \\ 0 & 0 & hF/(D(F-D)) & h/D \\ 0 & 0 & -hF/(F-D) & 0 \end{bmatrix}$$

Note that the perspective matrix differs from the standard transformation matrices M_{ij} such as scale, translate and rotate, in the fourth column – the standard transformations have the element M_{33} set to 1. This is because although these standard transformations act on homogeneous coordinates, w is redundant. It is always set equal to 1 and M_{33} will stay 1 after such a transformation. The perspective transformation is the only one in the rendering that uses w nontrivially. The need to incorporate perspective into the rendering pipeline explains why Euclidean space has to be represented homogeneously.

It is instructive to consider the relationship between z_e and z_s a little more closely; although as we have seen by construction, they both provide a measure of the depth of a point, interpolating along a line in eye space is not the same as interpolating this line in screen space. Figure 1.11 illustrates this point. The upper line is marked off at equal intervals of z_e, the line beneath it shows what happens to these intervals after the transformation into screen space. As z_e approaches the far clipping plane, z_s approaches 1 more rapidly. Objects in screen space thus get pushed and distorted towards the back of the viewing frustum. This difference can lead to errors when interpolating quantities, other than position, in screen space. (This point is further discussed in the next section and in Section 1.5.2).

In spite of this difficulty, by its very construction screen space is eminently suited to perform the hidden surface calculation. All rays passing through the view

Figure 1.11 The upper line is equal intervals of z_e. The lower line shows the intervals after transformation into screen space.

point are now parallel to the z_s-axis because the centre of projection has been moved to negative infinity along the z_s-axis. This can be seen by putting $z_e = 0$ into the above equation giving $z_s = -\infty$. Making those rays that hit the eye parallel, in screen space, means that hidden surface calculation need only be carried out on those points that have the same x_s, y_s-coordinates. The test reduces to a simple comparison between z_s values to tell if a point is in front of another. The transformation of a box with one side parallel to the screen is shown in Figure 1.12. Here light rays from the vertices to the view point in eye space become parallel in screen space.

The overall precision required for the screen depth is a function of scene complexity. For most scenes 8 bits are insufficient and 16 bits usually suffice. The effects of insufficient precision is easily seen when, for example, a Z-buffer algorithm is used in conjunction with two

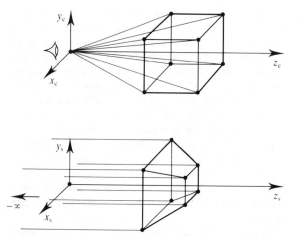

Figure 1.12 Transformation of box and light rays from eye space to screen space.

intersecting objects. If the objects exhibit a curve where they intersect, this will produce aliasing artefacts of increasing severity as the precision of the screen depth is reduced. The related problem of Z-buffer resolution is dealt with in more detail in Chapter 4.

The clipping process

Now that our description of screen space is complete we now describe how to process the object data before transforming it from eye space to screen space. This involves testing the object against the viewing frustum and is necessary for the following two reasons:

1. A view point or camera position is an arbitrary point initially specified in world space. Clearly we do not wish to deal with objects that do not contribute to the final image, such as objects that are behind the view point.

2. The screen space transformation is ill-defined outside the viewing frustum. There is a singularity at $z_e = 0$. Moreover, a mirrored region in homogeneous space, corresponding to negative w, also maps into the viewing frustum.

A given object in relation to the viewing frustum can fall into one of three categories:

1. The object lies completely outside the viewing frustum, in which case it is discarded.

2. The object lies completely inside the viewing frustum, in which case it is transformed into screen space and rendered.

3. The object intersects the viewing frustum, in which case it is clipped against it and then transformed into screen space.

The clipping operation must be performed on the homogeneous coordinates before the perspective division. Translating the definition of the viewing frustum above into homogeneous coordinates gives us the clipping limits:

$$-w \leqslant x \leqslant w$$
$$-w \leqslant y \leqslant w$$
$$0 \leqslant z \leqslant w$$

The clipping algorithm (later in this section) clips all four of the homogeneous coordinates – w is treated no differently to any other component.

This completes that part of the rendering process which deals with the geometric transformations. The

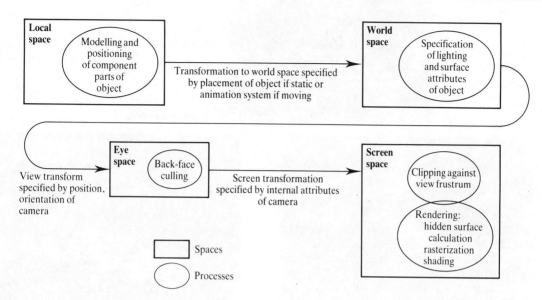

Figure 1.13 The rendering pipeline.

remaining processes, which are carried out concurrently in screen space, are rasterization, hidden surface removal and shading. Figure 1.13 summarizes the overall process.

We now present a pictorial overview of the geometric processing involved in going from eye space to screen space. Figure 1.14(a) shows a simple scene in world space; Figures 1.14(b), (c) and (d) show the scene as it gets processed through the rendering pipeline. The sequence in Figures 1.14(e), (f) and (g) show the same scene from a different view point and field of view. The first image in each of the sequences shows the eye, the viewing frustum (drawn as lines) with the scene clipped to the viewing frustum, and the rendered image projected onto the screen. The second image in each sequence shows the clipped objects in screen space rendered as if they were normal three-dimensional objects within the viewing frustum which now, by definition, is a rectangular box. This is how the renderer 'sees' the objects internally (the screen corresponds to the rightmost face of the box). Note the distortion of the objects and how they are crowded towards the back end of the viewing frustum as we discussed. Note also the greater the field of view, the greater is this distortion. Of course this distortion is only visible because we are taking an unusual view point of screen space – the standard view point looking down the z-axis will give us the final image in the sequence – the goal of the entire process – the rendered image, which is the final figure in each sequence.

Wireframe objects and clipping space

Sometimes scenes do not need to be fully rendered – mere wireframe representation will suffice. This is a common approach in developing an animation sequence. A sequence in wireframe is all that is necessary to test the dynamics of the animation and with modern workstations real-time interaction is possible. Traditional animators use a similar system of uncoloured drawings to test their animation. This is known as a line test or pencil test. Under such circumstances we do not need to use the full screen space transformation. We can make do with a simple transformation into clipping space involving a trivial multiplication of the x_e and y_e coordinates that makes the clipping operation straightforward. Since we are only concerned with clipping edges the depth information needed for solid rendering becomes redundant. The clipping transformation is defined as:

$$[x_c\, y_c\, z_c\, 1] = [x_e\, y_e\, z_e\, 1]\, C_l$$

where:

$$C = \begin{bmatrix} D/h & 0 & 0 & 0 \\ 0 & D/h & 0 & 0 \\ 0 & 0 & 1 & 0 \\ 0 & 0 & 0 & 1 \end{bmatrix}$$

(a) A view of the scene.

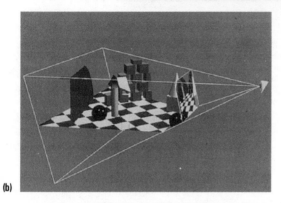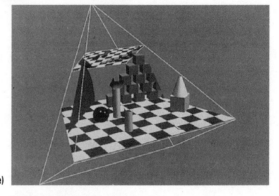

(b) (e)

A view of the viewing system showing the viewing frustum and the view plane.

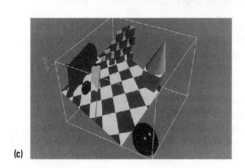

(c) (f)

Three-dimensional screen space.

(d) (g)

Contents of the view plane window.

Figure 1.14 Proceeding from eye space to screen space.

Translating the definition of the viewing frustum above into clipping space gives us the simple clipping limits:

$$-z_c \leqslant x_c \leqslant x_c$$
$$-z_c \leqslant y_c \leqslant z_c$$
$$D \leqslant z_c \leqslant F$$

which is just a straightforward comparison between coordinates. Once an edge has been clipped, the perspective divide discussed in the previous section is applied to get the screen coordinates (x_s, y_s). Note that clipping must be performed before the perspective divide.

A clipping algorithm

We now discuss clipping in more detail. Although these algorithms are described in terms of clipping coordinates, they can also be applied to the four homogeneous coordinates of screen space described above. First, we consider that before the clipping process is entered, it is possible to perform a simple test that will reject objects wholly outside the view volume and accept those within. This can be achieved by calculating a bounding sphere for the object and testing this against the view volume. The radius of the bounding sphere of an object is a fixed value and this can be precalculated and be part of the object database. When an object is processed by the three-dimensional viewing pipeline, its local coordinate system origin (the bounding sphere is deemed to be disposed about this origin) is also transformed into clipping space. To test an object, its bounding sphere radius is multiplied by the maximum of the scaling factors s_x, s_y, s_z and then by the maximum of the factors used to scale x and y when going from eye space to clipping space.

If (x, y, z) is the transformed local coordinate system origin in clipping space, r is the scaled bounding radius and z_{near} and z_{far} are the distances of the near and far planes then the object is completely within the clipping volume if all the following conditions are satisfied:

$$z > x + (2)^{1/2} r$$
$$z > -x + (2)^{1/2} r$$
$$z > y + (2)^{1/2} r$$
$$z > -y + (2)^{1/2} r$$
$$z > r + z_{near}$$
$$z > -r + z_{far}$$

and totally outside the volume if any of the following conditions are satisfied:

$$z < x - (2)^{1/2} r$$
$$z < -x - (2)^{1/2} r$$
$$z < y - (2)^{1/2} r$$
$$z < -y - (2)^{1/2} r$$
$$z < -r + z_{near}$$
$$z > r + z_{far}$$

If the object is completely outside the view volume it can be discarded, if it is entirely within the view volume it does not have to be clipped and is passed down the pipeline. Only if neither of these conditions applies, that is, it straddles a clipping boundary, does the object need to be passed through the clipping algorithm. One of the disadvantages of using an 'easy' object, such as a sphere, as a bounding volume is that it depends on the shape of the object as to whether the bounding volume is 'efficient' or not. For example, a long, thin object enclosed in a sphere could be entirely outside the view volume even if the sphere straddled a view volume boundary. This point is explored in more detail in Chapter 9.

Objects that need to be clipped are most easily dealt with by the Sutherland–Hodgman re-entrant polygon clipper [SUTH74a]. In this approach each polygon is tested against every clipping rectangle in the view volume. A polygon is tested against a clip boundary by testing each polygon edge against a single infinite clip boundary. This structure is shown in Figure 1.15. In clipping a polygon against a three-dimensional view volume, the clip boundaries form either a rectangle or a quadrilateral. However, the algorithm is completely general and will allow any (concave or convex) polygon to be clipped against any convex clipping polygon.

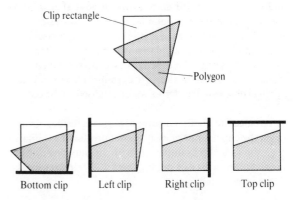

Figure 1.15 Sutherland–Hodgman clipper clips each polygon against each edge of each clip rectangle.

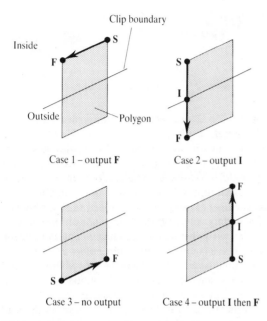

Figure 1.16 Sutherland–Hodgman clipper – within the polygon loop each edge of a polygon is tested against each clip boundary.

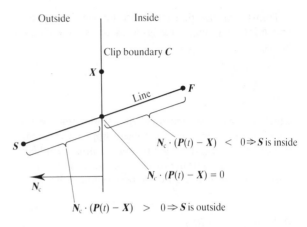

Figure 1.17 Dot product test to determine whether a line is inside or outside a clip boundary.

$$0 \leqslant t \leqslant 1$$

We define an arbitrary point on the clip boundary as X and a vector from X to any point on the line. The dot product of this vector and the normal allows us to distinguish whether a point on the line is outside, inside or on the clip boundary. In the case shown in Figure 1.17:

$$N_c \cdot (S - X) > 0 \Rightarrow S \text{ is outside the clip region}$$
$$N_c \cdot (F - X) < 0 \Rightarrow F \text{ is inside the clip region}$$

and

$$N_c \cdot (P(t) - X) = 0$$

defines the point of intersection of the line and the clip boundary. Solving Equation (1.1) for t enables the intersecting vertex to be calculated and added to the output list.

In practice the algorithm is written recursively. As soon as a vertex is output the procedure calls itself with that vertex and no intermediate storage is required for the partially clipped polygon. This structure makes the algorithm eminently suitable for hardware implementation.

We consider the innermost loop of the algorithm, where a single edge is being tested against a single clip boundary. In this step the process outputs zero, one or two vertices to add to the list of vertices defining the clipped polygon. Figure 1.16 shows the four possible cases. An edge is defined by vertices S and F. In the first case the edge is inside the clip boundary and the existing vertex F is added to the output list. In the second case the edge crosses the clip boundary and a new vertex I is calculated and output. The third case shows an edge that is completely outside the clip boundary. This produces no output. (The intersection for the edge that caused the excursion outside is calculated in the previous iteration and the intersection for the edge that caused the incursion inside is calculated in the next iteration.) The final case again produces a new vertex which is added to the output list.

To calculate whether a point or vertex is inside, outside or on the clip boundary we use a dot product test. Figure 1.17 shows a clip boundary C with an outward normal N_c and a line with end points S and F. We represent the line parametrically as:

$$P(t) = S + (F - S)t \qquad \text{(1.1)}$$

where:

1.3 Pixel-level processes

Rasterization, hidden surface removal and shading are three processes carried out in the inner loops of the renderer. These processes operate on one polygon at a time and they are organized around spans and pixels. A span is the intersection of a scan line with two (notional) edges of a polygon that is converted into a run of consecutive pixels (see Figures 1.20 and 1.23).

A subsidiary problem is how to derive the appropriate pair of edges from the data structure for a particular scan line. The edges are interpolated from the two pairs of vertices that define the edge. This is usually achieved by constructing an 'edgelist' for each polygon. In principle, this can be carried out using an array of linked lists with an array element corresponding to each scan line. Initially all the elements are set to nil. Each edge of the polygon is rasterized in turn, and the x-coordinate of each pixel generated by this process is inserted into the linked list corresponding to its y-value. Each of the linked lists is then sorted in order of increasing x.

We can view the three processes of rasterization, hidden surface removal and shading as three two-dimensional linear interpolation processes. Rasterization consists of interpolating between vertices to find the x-coordinates that define the limits of a span, and then finding the pixels between these limits. Hidden surface removal consists of interpolating screen space z-values to obtain a depth for each pixel from the vertex depth values. Shading implies interpolating from vertex intensities to find an intensity for each pixel. To perform the interpolation we use the same equations and inject either vertex coordinates (rasterization), vertex depth values (hidden surface removal) or vertex intensities (shading). The interpolation equations are given once only (see Equations 1.2) for the case of shading. The interpolations are embedded in a simple nested loop structure which should be compared with Figure 1.13. Finally, the overall structure of the rendering process is:

for each polygon
    perform geometric transformations into screen space
    for each scan line within a polygon
        find spans by interpolation and rasterize span
        for each pixel within the span
            perform hidden surface removal and shade

1.4 Rasterization

Rasterization is the process of finding out which pixels a polygon projects onto in screen space. The process of rasterization is intimately connected with anti-aliasing methods, but rather than attempt to discuss both these issues at once, we have dealt with the aliasing problem in Chapter 4. This approach is in line with treating anti-aliasing as an option and the most common anti-aliasing method, supersampling, simply leaves all the rendering methodology unaltered and calculates a solution in a virtual screen space that is at a higher resolution than real screen space.

There are a number of general issues that need to be addressed concerning rasterization and we shall deal with these first before looking at how we find which pixels the edge of a projected polygon lies on.

At one level rasterization is simple – we calculate, for each scan line within a polygon, by linear interpolation, the x-values of the edge pixels, x_{start} and x_{end}. This results in a span of pixels between two edges that have to be rendered. There are, however, a number of problems. For example, where exactly does an edge start and end? Where within a pixel should the sample point – the real value used in rasterization calculations – be? Should screen coordinates be rounded to integers or stored to fractional precision? Incorrect solutions to these questions can lead to holes between polygons, overlapping polygons (disastrous when transparency is being used), discontinuities on surfaces which have a mapped texture and inaccuracies in anti-aliasing. Such annoying small flaws occur surprisingly often when rendering software is being written (they are not unknown in commercially available renderers). A lot of these flaws are due to incorrect rasterization.

Consider first the problem of screen coordinates. Clearly if they are rounded to integers polygons will have their shape changed slightly. Each vertex will be 'snapped' to the nearest grid point as shown in Figure 1.18. Anti-aliasing by supersampling cannot then be carried out. Also, the slight shape change can produce a

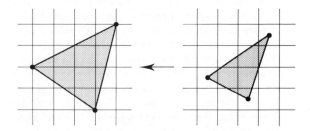

Figure 1.18 Integer rasterization: rounding screen coordinates to integers results in a slight shape change.

'wobble' if the projection is changing in an animation sequence.

Another subtle effect of integer coordinates arises when there is a step in a nearly vertical edge. If integers are being used in the rasterization with shading interpolation, this will introduce a pixel discontinuity in the shading values between two scan lines. For interpolative shading this does not matter, but it can be disastrous in texture mapping. Figure 1.19 illustrates this point where the x-coordinate of the left-hand side of the polygon suddenly jumps a unit. Thus precision in rasterization is of the utmost importance.

The next point to consider is the position of a sample point within a pixel. This applies to point sampling rendering strategies such as the one we have adopted here. A rendered image is calculated at a set of sample points distributed in the form of a two-dimensional array. Most authors consider sample points at the centre of the pixel (for example [ROGE85]). This leads to unnecessary complications such as scan line intersection calculations at $y + 0.5$ rather than integer y. It does not matter where the sample point is in a pixel as long as we are consistent. Using a sample point on only one of the pixel corners means that the entire rendered image will be displaced up to half a pixel from its correct position.

For a sample point on the bottom left-hand corner of the pixel we now consider rasterization in two parts. First we consider, given a left-hand and a right-hand (high precision) value for a horizontal span across a scan line, how to round these values to integer screen coordinates. (The equivalent problem occurs vertically with y scan line values.) Second, we consider how to detect those edge values that define the span.

1.4.1 Rasterizing spans and scan lines

A span is the intersection of the plane formed by the scan line and the polygon currently being rasterized. Figure 1.20 shows a visualization or model of this process considered as a plane in three-dimensional screen space that moves down through screen space producing scan line intersections with polygons. In a Z-buffer algorithm a span is simply the line between the points x_{start} and x_{end} – the intersection of the scan line plane and the polygon edges. For other hidden surface removal algorithms a span may be defined as just part of this line.

For horizontal spans, if we are using real numbers,

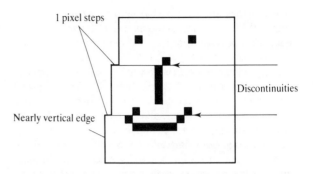

Figure 1.19   Integer rasterization can introduce discontinuities in texture mapping.

then given x_{start} and x_{end} as the start and end points of the scan, the strategy is:

- round x_{start} up;
- round x_{end} down;
- if the fractional part of x_{end} is 0 then subtract 1 from it.

Alternatively, for efficiency, we can use integer arithmetic and, for precision, we should scale all integers up by some factor (we have found a multiple of 16 to be sufficient). Using integers we:

- round x_{start} up to the next multiple of 16;
- round x_{end} down to the next multiple of 16;
- if x_{end} is already a multiple of 16, subtract 16 from it.

Thus integer screen coordinates are generated for every multiple of 16 between x_{start} and x_{end} inclusive. The working of these rules is shown in Figure 1.21. This shows five possibilities, each consisting of three horizontal spans, which collectively cross three sample points, and which do not overlap but form a continuous line. The spans are all on the same scan line but each span is displaced vertically for clarity. The black dots indicate the integer screen coordinates generated by each span. As an example, the first diagram shows three spans, with ranges of 5–20, 20–25 and 25–50, say. After rounding, this gives span end points of 16–16, 32–16 and 32–48. The first span yields a screen coordinate at location 16, the second yields nothing (because $x_{start} > x_{end}$) and the third yields screen coordinates at 32 and 48. From these diagrams it can be seen that:

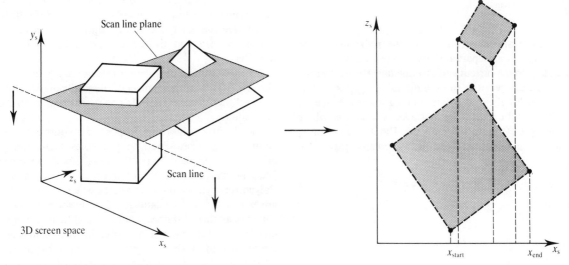

Figure 1.20 A visualization of the rasterization process.

1. Each time all three (consecutive) screen coordinates or pixels are generated – there are no holes.

2. No more than three pixels are generated – there is no overlap.

3. A pixel generated by a span always lies within the bounds of that span. This would not be the case if, for example, end points were rounded to the nearest multiple of 16.

Figure 1.21 Five possibilities involving three horizontal spans (separated vertically in the diagram but all part of the same scan line) that illustrate the span rounding strategy.

1.4.2 Rasterization and interpolation

As we have discussed, most of the flaws resulting from rasterization occur from rounding x-values in spans or rounding y-values over the scan line extent of the polygon. Successful rasterization mostly depends on dealing with these issues properly. The remainder of the rasterization problem is quite straightforward. It is appropriate also to discuss the interpolation of shading information at the same time for reasons that will shortly be apparent.

For each pair of edges we have to find the values of x_{start} and x_{end}. We do this by linear interpolation, incrementally scan line by scan line, by dividing the difference between the x-coordinates of the end points by its height in scan lines. This increment is added to the previous x_{start} and x_{end} values to obtain the current values. We deal with the interpolation of the shading parameters in exactly the same incremental way and at the same time. For Gouraud shading there will be an intensity associated with each vertex to be interpolated. And for Phong interpolation there will be three vector components to be interpolated (specific details on both these interpolative shading schemes are given in Sections 1.6.1 and 1.6.2).

Also interpolated from vertex values is the screen depth, and this is supplied on a pixel-by-pixel basis to the hidden surface removal algorithm.

The interpolation of x-values and shading parameters (we will call the shading parameters p for the moment) will be carried out at enhanced precision as we discussed in the previous section and the Δp values along a scan line are given by:

$$\Delta p = \frac{p_{end} - p_{start}}{x_{end} - x_{start}}$$

In the example introduced in the previous section pixels are 16 units apart and for each pixel generated we add $16\Delta p$ to the current value to calculate the next value.

We should generally not use the value p_{start} as a starting value for the interpolation along a span. Since we always round up x_{start}, the first pixel will be somewhere to the right of the start of the span. The start value of p, that is p_0, is calculated from the interpolated edge value as:

$$p_0 = p_{start} + k\Delta p \qquad \text{for some } k; \ 0 \leqslant k < 15$$

where:

$$k = x_{st}^r - x_{start}$$
x_{st}^r is the rounded value of x_{start}

1.5 Hidden surface removal algorithm

The full screen Z-buffer algorithm has become a de facto standard in computer graphics. It is a low complexity (virtually a single if statement) high memory-cost algorithm, and modern graphics terminals tend to have a dedicated Z-buffer memory.

Many hidden surface removal algorithms have been developed (mainly in the 1970s) and most of these are described and categorized in a classic paper by Sutherland *et al.* [SUTH74b]. We will confine ourselves in this text to the Z-buffer algorithm (and its anti-aliasing descendant – the A-buffer algorithm, described in Section 4.4.1). An excellent and comprehensive treatment of hidden surface algorithms is to be found in [FOLE89].

The Z-buffer algorithm is best viewed as operating in a three-dimensional screen space. Each pixel is associated with a two-dimensional screen coordinate (x_s, y_s), together with a depth or z-value interpolated from the vertex eye space z-depth at the same time as shading values are interpolated and rasterization is performed. The Z-buffer is initialized to the depth of the far clipping plane. For each pixel we compare its interpolated depth with the depth already stored in the Z-buffer (x_s, y_s). If

this value is less than the stored value then the pixel is nearer the viewer than previously encountered pixels, in which case the current shading value is written to the screen memory and the current depth placed in the Z-buffer.

The algorithm is equivalent in effect, but not in execution, to a search, for each pixel, through all polygons that intersect that pixel to find the one that is nearest to the view point.

The Z-buffer algorithm imposes no constraints on database organization and, in its simplest form, can be driven on a polygon-by-polygon basis, with polygons being presented to the rendering process in any order. Polygons appear on the screen in the order in which they are extracted from the database. Clearly some polygons will appear then disappear and this highlights a major inefficiency of the algorithm, in that shading calculations are performed on (hidden) pixels that are subsequently overwritten. Because the algorithm deals with one polygon at a time, it imposes no constraints on scene complexity and this is another reason for its popularity in a decade that has seen a steady increase in modelling resolution or object complexity.

Depth precision is important and very complex scenes or objects may require 32-bit precision. In this case a full screen Z-buffer will occupy more memory than a corresponding frame buffer. Perspective projections increase the problem – objects that are at a different (distant) depth may transform into the same z-value after the perspective divide.

Finally, we note that the algorithm operates with units that are shaded pixels. It does not necessarily require polygons and can be used with any object representation.

1.6 Interpolative or incremental shading algorithms

A major reason for the growth of popularity of polygon-based renderers is the existence of two interpolative or incremental algorithms known usually as Gouraud shading and Phong shading. These are simple schemes that calculate shading parameters at the vertices of polygons and then interpolate across the entire polygon surface. Gouraud shading or interpolation [GOUR71] is faster than the other method but cannot produce accurate highlights. It is usually used in applications where speed is important; for example, in flight simulators or in interactive applications in CAD. Phong shading [PHON75] gives higher quality images but is more expensive. Gouraud shading calculates intensities at polygon vertices only, using a local reflection model, and interpolates these for pixels within the polygon. On the other hand, Phong shading interpolates vertex normals and applies a local reflection model at each pixel.

The motivation of both schemes is efficiency and the 'convincing' rendering of polygonal objects. This means that as well as giving an impression of solidity or three-dimensionality to the model, the shared edges in adjacent polygons, that approximate a curved surface, are made invisible.

Although both these methods have become almost standard (Gouraud shading is to be found in direct programmed hardware in most modern graphics work-stations; Gouraud and Phong shading are included in GKS3D and PHIGS) they were not the first shading schemes to emerge. Earlier methods were developed by Bouknight in 1970 [BOUK70] and by Wylie *et al.* in 1967 [WYLI67]. These are further discussed in Section 2.3.2. Wylie *et al.* used a crude approximation to a local reflection model to calculate vertex intensities (for triangles) based on distance. These were then interpolated. Bouknight's work concentrated on hidden surface removal and the polygons were 'constant' shaded. This method calculates a single intensity for each method and uses this over the entire area of the projected polygon. This gives an impression of three-dimensionality but leaves the underlying polygon mesh structure clear. It is still sometimes used when a very fast impression is required, but hardware advances are diminishing its role.

1.6.1 Gouraud shading

Here we take the approach of discussing the interpolation of intensities before discussing how these intensities are calculated. Generally, we make the intensity of light at a polygon vertex a function of the orientation of vertex normals (described shortly) with respect to both the light source and the eye. This function is called a reflection model and is discussed at length in Chapter 2.

Gouraud shading [GOUR71] applies a local reflection model at each vertex of a polygon to calculate a set of vertex intensities. These intensities are linearly interpolated across the polygon interior on a scan line basis.

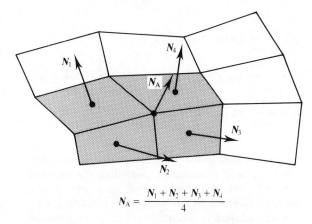

$$N_A = \frac{N_1 + N_2 + N_3 + N_4}{4}$$

Figure 1.22 The vertex normal N_A is the average of the normals N_1, N_2, N_3 and N_4, the normals of the polygons that meet at the vertex.

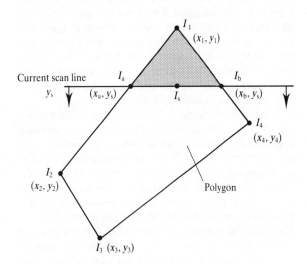

Figure 1.23 The notation used for the intensity interpolation equations.

A normal is calculated at a vertex and used in the reflection model. This normal attempts to approximate the normal that the unpolygonalized surface would have exhibited at that point and this is achieved by averaging the normals to the polygons that share the vertex (Figure 1.22 and Plate 2). The process is easily integrated with rasterization as discussed in the previous section. The intensities along an edge are interpolated from pairs of vertex intensities and this produces a start and finish intensity for each scan line (Figure 1.23). The interpolation equations are:

$$I_a = \frac{1}{y_1 - y_2} \left[I_1 (y_s - y_2) + I_2 (y_1 - y_s) \right]$$

$$I_b = \frac{1}{y_1 - y_4} \left[I_1 (y_s - y_4) + I_4 (y_1 - y_s) \right]$$

$$I_s = \frac{1}{x_b - x_a} \left[I_a (x_b - x_s) + I_b (x_s - x_a) \right]$$

(1.2)

As we discussed in the previous section, we can implement the third equation by calculating the increment between pixels and, for a current pixel, obtaining its value by adding it to the value of the previous pixel.

Gouraud shading is usually used only in conjunction with the diffuse component of a local reflection model (see Chapter 2 for a discussion of reflection models that contain diffuse and specular components). It does not cope well with highlights. An obvious example is the case of a highlight that should appear within a polygon and whose variation is such that it does not produce any effect at the vertices (Figure 1.24). The specular component in the reflection model equation evaluated at the vertices will evaluate to zero and, of course, the highlight will not appear in the interpolation.

A more subtle defect is Mach banding. Although the use of vertex normals ensures that there is no numerical discontinuity across adjacent polygon boundaries, the eye produces a classic optical illusion and the boundaries are annoyingly perceived as light lines or Mach bands. The psycho-physical explanation for this is as follows. If we consider the intensity change across a boundary between polygons, this will exhibit a piecewise linear profile – there is no first-order continuity. The human visual system enhances the second derivative of intensity changes – reputedly because of our need to detect and enhance edges – and the discontinuity at the shared edges of polygons results in these apparent bands.

Gouraud in his landmark paper states:

> The linear interpolation which has been used here produces a shading which is continuous in value but not in derivative across polygon boundaries. The resulting Mach band effect can be observed mostly in the vicinity of silhouette curves and where the surface bends sharply. Interpolation schemes more powerful than the linear interpolation could probably be used . . .

This leads us into the next interpolative shading scheme – Phong interpolation.

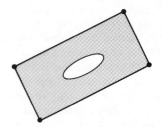

Figure 1.24   A polygon that 'contains' a highlight – there is no highlight component at the vertices. Gouraud shading will miss the highlight.

1.6.2 Phong shading

Phong shading [PHON75], also known as normal-vector interpolation shading, overcomes the disadvantages associated with Gouraud shading at the cost of substantially increased overheads. The highlight problem is solved and the Mach band effect is reduced (but not completely eliminated). A linear interpolation scheme, integrated with rasterization, is still used. This time the vertex normals, calculated exactly as before, are interpolated and the reflection model is applied *at each pixel* using the interpolated normal (Figure 1.25). (Note that this implies that a reflection model which is solely a function of the surface normal must be used.) In the figure, N_s is the interpolated vector at the current pixel. The general idea is illustrated in Figure 1.26 which shows that the vector interpolation tends to restore the underlying curvature of the surface approximated by the polygonal approximation.

Compared with Gouraud interpolation we now have an interpolation involving three vector components so this phase of the method is at least three times as expensive. In addition, we have to evaluate a shading equation for each and every pixel – a processing extra that is a linear function of the area of the polygon.

Plate 2 is a comparison of the shading options used in standard renderers – flat or constant shaded polygons, Gouraud shading and Phong shading. Note the piecewise linearities on the silhouette edges. These are particularly visible on the teapot spout.

Speedup techniques for Phong shading

The expense of Phong shading has motivated a number of speedup techniques. These can be generally cate-

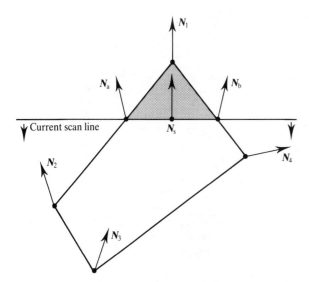

Figure 1.25 In the Phong method vector interpolation replaces intensity interpolation.

gorized as numerical or geometric. Before discussing these, we point out that in a large number of practical contexts the interpolation can be approximated and the reflection model applied only at every other pixel, the values for intermediate pixels being calculated from simple averaging. This double-step interpolation results in virtually no loss in image quality in most contexts. The scheme is equivalent to Gouraud shading where each polygon projects onto a three-pixel-wide screen area and at this polygonal resolution the defects of Gouraud shading disappear. This gives an immediate saving in total rendering time, which is reduced by a factor of about 0.3.

Numerical optimizations have been investigated by Bishop [BISH86] and by Duff [DUFF79]. Duff com-

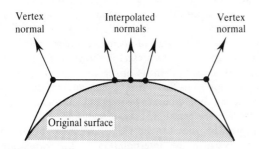

Figure 1.26 Vector interpolation tends to 'restore' curvature.

bined the interpolation and shading equations into one expression which he then evaluated using forward differences, reducing the calculation to three additions, one division and one square root per pixel. Bishop adopted the same strategy but used a two-variable Taylor series to approximate the shading equation. Claiming that the approximation produced results that were indistinguishable from those obtained by the accurate version, Bishop produced a method that evaluates a diffuse component with two additions per pixel and a specular component with five additions and one table access per pixel.

Geometric approaches are investigated by Bergman *et al.* [BERG86c] and Harrison *et al.* [HARR88]. Both approaches depend on detecting or predicting where highlights are going to occur. In [HARR88] Gouraud interpolation is used to shade the entire object. Those polygons that contain a highlight have a specular component evaluated and superimposed. The price paid for the considerable increase in efficiency (most objects exhibit a small highlight area) is a toleration of Mach banding.

The highlight detection is based on a hierarchy of simple tests that predict the value of the highlight function on the line between two vertices. For there to be a contribution from the specular term which is a function of $(N \cdot H)$ (vector H relates to the orientation of the surface with respect to the light source and the eye and is fully described in Section 2.3.4) we can say:

$N \cdot H \geq T$, a threshold term

The value of this term is examined at pairs of vertices to predict the variation in its magnitude along the edge. A hierarchy of five simple tests performs this prediction:

(A)   Determines whether $N \cdot H$ at any vertex is greater than the threshold value.

(B)   Determines if $N \cdot H$ reaches a maximum along any polygon edge.

(C)   Determines whether the maximum of test B is greater than zero.

(D)   Determines if this maximum is greater than the threshold value.

(E)   Is performed once per polygon, and determines if a polygon has a maximum along each of its edges.

Figure 1.27 shows the four distinct highlight possibilities for a polygon:

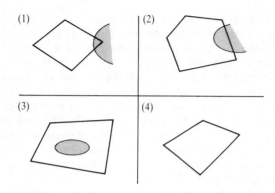

Figure 1.27 Highlight possibilities with respect to a single polygon.

1. a highlight can cover one or more vertices, intersecting the lines between this vertex and its two neighbouring vertices;
2. a highlight can spread over a single line between two vertices, but not over any vertices;
3. a highlight can be contained within a polygon; or,
4. there is no highlight associated with the polygon.

The five tests, A to E, are used to ascertain which of the four highlight cases has occurred. The way in which the tests are organized to do this is shown in Figure 1.28.

Defects in Phong interpolation

We recall that the interpolation scheme is an efficient method for specularly shading polygonal objects, while at the same time reducing the visibility of shared polygon edges. There are a number of inaccuracies or shortcomings that are built into the method which, to a greater or lesser extent, result in visual defects.

Edge silhouettes

This is the most obvious visual defect when shading polygonal objects. It is, of course, due to the object representation rather than the Phong interpolation and it is most easily dealt with in a brute-force manner by ensuring a sufficient polygonal resolution to start with. This, however, raises a contradiction. The *raison d'être* of Phong interpolation is to ensure a convincing shading effect of an object that is inaccurately represented by polygons. Using finer and finer polygons makes the method less and less efficient. When the projected size of

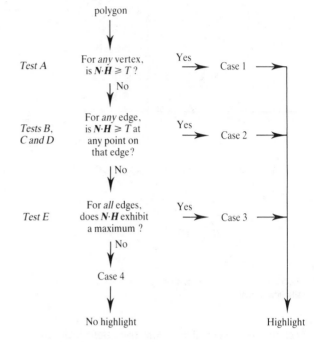

Figure 1.28 Testing for highlights.

a polygon begins to approach a few pixels the costs of setting up the interpolation outweigh its savings.

Interpolation inaccuracies

There are a number of inherent defects associated with the interpolation of vertex normals. First, we recall that the interpolation is controlled from screen space (although it operates on vectors in world or eye space). Consider a polygon in perspective. Interpolating using equal intervals between scan lines means that the distance incremented in world space is greater for areas of the polygon further from the viewer. Perspective foreshortening means that we are calculating a shading intensity in world space as a function of an interpolated normal, but are using nonuniform steps in the interpolation. The nature of this defect is shown in Figure 1.29.

Second, even if there is no perspective error in the interpolation steps there are still inaccuracies due to the fact that we should be using equal angular increments to interpolate vectors along, say, a scan line.

A problem that can be made visible by animation occurs because the interpolation is not orientation independent. This results in visible differences between

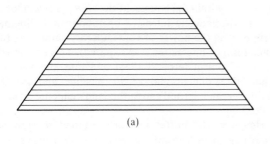

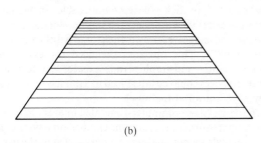

Figure 1.29   Linear interpolation using scan line increments is incorrect. (a) Linear interpolation using scan line increments. (b) 'Perspective' interpolation using nonuniform increments.

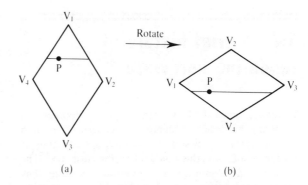

Figure 1.30   P is the same interior point in a rotated polygon but interpolates from different vertex sets in each case.

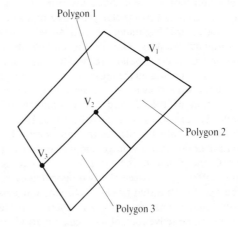

Figure 1.31   Neighbouring polygons with an unshared vertex.

successive frames when polygons rotate. It is caused because the interpolation always proceeds, irrespective of the polygon orientation, along a scan line and from scan line to scan line. The point P interpolates in Figure 1.30(a) from V_1, V_4 and V_2. In Figure 1.30(b) the polygon has been rotated and the same point interpolates from V_1, V_4 and V_3. Again the only easy solution to these problems is to increase the polygonal resolution.

Vertex normal inaccuracies
To function correctly over all polygons the interpolation scheme requires a net of polygons where, for example, for four-sided polygons, each vertex forms a junction between four polygons. If the situation shown in Figure 1.31 occurs and vertex V_2 is not in the vertex list of polygon 1 then this polygon will interpolate values between V_1 and V_3 and shading discontinuities will occur between polygon 1 and polygons 2 and 3.

Another vertex normal problem occurs if the orientation of adjacent polygon normals changes rapidly. Figure 1.32 shows a case where using the averaging scheme to calculate the vertex normals results in a set of (erroneously) parallel normals.

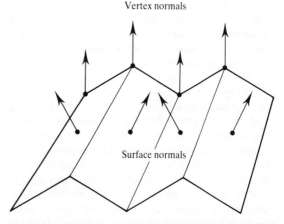

Figure 1.32   A regularly corrugated surface producing identical vertex normals from non-identical surface normals.

1.7 A brief history of rendering hardware

In this section we shall review the major developments in rendering hardware. Although, of course, there is a parallel development strand in rendering techniques or rendering software, this would take up an entire text. The hardware developments are important because they made it possible to produce shaded images economically. Also, the hardware developments have had a greater influence on how the field has evolved.

The emergence of the cathode ray tube (CRT) as a device for displaying computer-generated imagery probably marks the beginning of specialized hardware for computer graphics. One of the earliest items of specialized hardware to be adopted was line interpolation circuitry. This facilitated the creation of vector displays, where lines were drawn on the screen by the direct manipulation of the X- and Y-axis controls of the cathode ray beam in a standard oscilloscope. This was an analogue device which generated the appropriate linearly increasing or decreasing voltage ramps that were applied to the X- and Y-plates. These signals were based on the relative difference between the two coordinates of the end points of the line that was to be plotted, and a visible line was traced out on the screen. The scheme allowed for very simple interactive control – the coordinate values of the vertices could be modified, and the display updated. The earliest device with a CRT display was the Whirlwind computer at MIT.

This was precisely the technology used by the acknowledged pioneer of interactive graphics – Ivan E. Sutherland – who published a thesis in 1963 entitled 'Sketchpad: A Man–Machine Graphical Communications System' [SUTH63].

With this technology in place in the early 1960s, it was soon realized that it could be used to display three-dimensional imagery. What was required was the ability to transform three-dimensional coordinates according to a viewing system, then to project the results onto a view plane. The resulting two-dimensional coordinates were then entered into the hardware for the vector display. Allowing arbitrary views of three-dimensional data created the problem that transformed vertices would sometimes be projected outside the limits of the display device. Thus it was necessary to clip lines such that they always lay within the bounds of the view plane window. The mathematically intensive operations and clipping were beyond the power of contemporary computers (if some form of interaction was required). This prompted the development (around 1968) of Evans and Sutherland's three-dimensional vector pipeline and matrix multiplier, and Sproull and Sutherland's clipping divider [SPRO68].

However, the buffer memory required to store a wireframe picture of any complexity was expensive and a costly processor was required to refresh the display in a reasonable time. Only a few thousand vectors could be displayed before flicker became noticeable. In the late 1960s the direct view storage tube was developed. In this device a line image was drawn and stored within a special type of CRT. This obviated the need for expensive refresh facilities and graphics took a major leap forward as these devices could be interfaced to a minicomputer (as they were known at the time).

The desire to use computer-generated imagery in flight simulators, in order to replace the cumbersome system of physical scale models and servo cameras, led to the need for solid-shaded imagery rather than wireframe pictures. Vector-type displays were unsuitable for this, so raster or television-type displays were adopted. Initially, the systems were designed to produce pixels in scan line order, which were then sent out to the display monitor: at the time, a full screen frame buffer would have been prohibitively expensive. This caused problems because the pixels needed to be generated in a steady stream, while the processing workload might vary wildly in different parts of the screen, depending on the image.

Hidden surface removal was initially a problem. At first this was resolved by using the Watkins algorithm [WATK70], which divided scan lines up into spans, within which the nearest polygon segment could be rendered.

With memory prices plummetting, a full screen frame buffer soon became a practical proposition. This led to the development of the 'painter's' algorithm [NEWE72], in which polygons were sorted in increasing depth and then rendered in reverse order, with pixels in near polygons overwriting those generated by more distant polygons. The algorithm relied on the fact that, with a frame buffer, it was possible to produce pixels in a random order, and to overwrite pixels. However, it suffered from the twin problems that the sorting of polygons was nontransitive, that is to say polygon A can overlap polygon B which can overlap polygon C which can overlap polygon A – providing polygons are allowed to intersect. This problem was overcome by the introduction of further per-pixel storage capacity in the form of a depth or Z-buffer. Now visibility conflicts could be resolved at the pixel level, at the cost of an extra 16 or so bits per pixel.

One of the next milestones was the implementation of the clipping of polygons using a custom integrated circuit. This was the so-called geometry engine [CLAR82], which forms the heart of the IRIS family of workstations. A pipeline constructed from geometry engine chips allows the coordinates of a polygon to be entered at one end, and to emerge transformed and clipped at the other end.

Similar steps forward have been taken to implement, in custom silicon, the process of generating pixels from the transformed and clipped polygons. Probably the most famous examples of this are Pixel-Planes [FUCH85] and its successor, Pixel-Powers [GOLD86]. Here a two-dimensional array of 1-bit ALUs is used, in conjunction with a tree of adders, to decide in parallel whether each pixel lies inside or outside a polygon, and if inside, what shading value it should have. Other more conventional approaches to pixel generation have also been taken and an overview can be found in [MYER84].

PART II

Theoretical foundations

2 | The theory and practice of light/ object interaction

Chapter 1 dealt with integrating the local reflection models described in this chapter into an interpolative shading scheme. Local reflection models are also used in ray tracing (Chapter 8). In Chapters 8 to 12 we look at the restrictions of local reflection models and how global reflection can be simulated in computer graphics.

Accurate colour treatment is dealt with in this chapter; it should be read in conjunction with colour aliasing (Chapter 4). More detailed treatment of colour in computer graphics is given in [HALL89].

Introduction

Considerable research efforts in computer graphics have been devoted to simulating the reflection of light from objects. Some knowledge of the theory on which these models are based is thus necessary to understand fully the simulations and their limitations.

This chapter deals with the simulation of first-order (or local) reflection models used in computer graphics. We categorize first-order models as those in which only the direct or first reflection of light from a surface due to a light source is considered. The models that we shall consider in this chapter are:

- a completely empirical model – the Phong model,
- a hybrid scheme that uses a physical model based on surface roughness to calculate the intensity of reflections and a wave theory model to account for cer-

tain colour effects – the Cook and Torrance model [COOK82],

- a model based completely on a physical surface roughness simulation [CABR87], and
- a model based completely on wave theory [KAJI85].

In conjunction with an interpolative scheme for polygonal objects the Phong model has become a de facto industrial standard.

In computer graphics we generally consider objects that reflect, transmit and emit light. The six main phenomena that arise from light–object interaction, that is, those that give rise to colour by modifying or filtering the energy distribution of the incident light, are: reflection, transmission, absorption, diffraction, refraction and interference. Although all of these phenomena have been modelled to some extent in computer graphics, most attention has been paid to reflection.

Reflection models in computer graphics are motivated, not so much by the imitation of reality, as by the simulation of certain aspects of reality that are computationally possible within the constraints of the application and the equipment available. The general workhorse of reflection – the Phong model – is an empirical imitation of specular and diffuse reflection that approximates more precise theoretical models to an extent that produces visually acceptable results across a wide variety of applications.

First-order or local models are inherently limited in their ability to simulate illumination within a complete environment. Basically they treat objects as if they were floating in free space and interacting only with a light source. We shall return to this theme in later chapters when we look at the development of global reflection models. Established global models that simulate reflection are ray tracing and radiosity. Ray tracing selects one particular aspect of light–object interaction – specular reflection and transmission – approximates this and excludes other considerations. The radiosity method, which in one sense is the converse of ray tracing, favours the interaction of diffusely reflecting surfaces to the exclusion of specular reflection.

We start off with some definitions. These are based on work in *Thermal Radiation and Heat Transfer* by Siegel and Howell [SIEG84] and is material pertinent to computer graphics reflection models.

A theoretical foundation is necessary to understand the limitations and approximations inherent in computer graphics reflection models, and will enable the reader to form a comparative basis for different models.

2.1 Theory: intensity and energy

We describe the effect of a coloured object by defining a directional intensity. That is, the radiation that emanates in a particular direction from a surface is defined as the sum of the reflected and the emitted intensity. In simple computer graphics models, reflection is usually dealt with entirely separately from emission. Objects are entities to which reflection models are applied and light sources, usually approximated to point light sources, are separate entities that initially supply the energy. However, in the radiosity method (Chapter 11), all surfaces whether they are emitters or reflectors (or emitters and reflectors) are incorporated into the same

model. Such surfaces obey the general equation for reflected and emitted intensity:

$$I(\theta_r, \phi_r) = I_{\text{emitted}}(\theta_r, \phi_r) + I_{\text{reflected}}(\theta_r, \phi_r)$$

where:

(θ_r, ϕ_r) is an outgoing direction specified by two angles (Figure 2.1)

In this section we will be concerned with reflection and we define reflectivity in a number of ways. The particular definitions that are chosen are those most commonly used in computer graphics. In most methods that are described in the text such definitions tend to be approximated by being embedded in some algorithmic method, rather than being used as a precise mathematical formula. Nevertheless it is important to understand the different ways in which reflected intensity can be related to incident light.

Consider initially the ratio:

$$\rho'' = \frac{I_r(\theta_r, \phi_r, \theta_i, \phi_i)}{E_i(\theta_i, \phi_i)}$$

This relates the incoming energy to the outgoing intensity where:

I_r is the reflected intensity in the outgoing direction

E_i is the energy in the incoming direction

ρ'' is a spectral reflectivity coefficient. The double prime indicates that it depends on both the incoming and the outgoing directions

(θ_r, ϕ_r) is the outgoing direction

(θ_i, ϕ_i) is the incoming direction (Figure 2.1)

In computer graphics the directions are usually referred to as unit vectors:

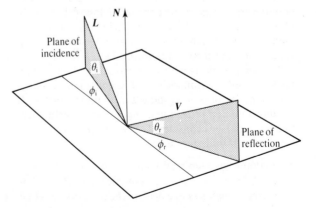

Figure 2.1 Conventions used in reflection.

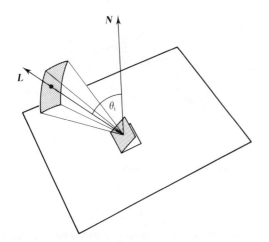

Figure 2.2 Intensity is measured with respect to projected area normal to its direction.

$L = (\theta_i, \phi_i)$ the light direction vector (when the subscript is omitted this generally means we are considering incoming radiation from any (or all) directions, rather than a particular direction

and:

$V = (\theta_r, \phi_r)$ the viewing vector or the outgoing direction vector of interest

Note that (θ_r, ϕ_r) is *not* the mirror direction. The use of the word 'reflected' is somewhat confusing because it is sometimes used to indicate the mirror direction. We will generally use the word 'reflected' to mean the viewing direction – the reflected direction of interest, and 'mirror' to mean the direction in which light is specularly reflected.

The incoming energy $E_i(\theta_i, \phi_i)$ is related to the incoming intensity by (Figure 2.2):

$$E_i(\theta_i, \phi_i) = I_i(\theta_i, \phi_i) \cos\theta_i \, d\omega_i \qquad (2.1)$$

This relates the incoming energy to the incoming intensity, the solid angle $d\omega_i$ in which the energy is contained and the projected differential area. The solid angle ω of a surface element, as seen from a given point, is defined as the area of the surface element divided by the square of the distance from the point.

2.1.1 Bidirectional spectral reflectivity

Energy reflected from a point on a surface depends on the angle of the incident energy and also on the angle that

is being considered for the reflected energy. Hence we can define a bidirectional spectral reflectivity. The definition is described as spectral because we recognize that in all practical cases this reflectivity will be a function of wavelength.

Consider incident spectral radiation in a particular incoming direction (θ_i, ϕ_i). Some of this radiation will be reflected in the (θ_r, ϕ_r) direction and we can refer to a reflected intensity as:

$$I_{\lambda,r}(\lambda, \theta_r, \phi_r, \theta_i, \phi_i)$$

which is a function of wavelength, λ, and the reflected and incident directions. Another way of defining reflectivity is to consider the total magnitude of $I_{\lambda,r}$ due to all incident radiation. This is a function of wavelength and the reflected direction only

$$I_{\lambda,r}(\lambda, \theta_r, \phi_r)$$

is obtained by summing the contributions from all the incident energy in all possible directions over the hemisphere centred on the point on the surface.

To define the bidirectional spectral reflectivity we consider an element dA on the surface. The energy received from any incoming direction (θ_i, ϕ_i) per unit area per unit wavelength is:

$$I_{\lambda,i}(\lambda, \theta_i, \phi_i) \cos\theta_i \, d\omega_i$$

This can be seen by considering a line from dA in the direction (θ_i, ϕ_i) which passes through an element dA_h on the surface of the hemisphere. The incident intensity passing through dA_h is:

$$I_{\lambda,i}(\lambda, \theta_i, \phi_i)$$

and this is the energy per unit area of the hemisphere, per unit solid angle $d\omega_h$ per unit time. The energy incident on dA is:

$$I_{\lambda,i}(\lambda, \theta_i, \phi_i) dA_h \, d\omega_h \, d\lambda$$

where:

R is the radius of the hemisphere and

$d\omega_h = \dfrac{dA\cos\theta_i}{R^2}$ is the solid angle subtended by dA when viewed from dA_h (Figure 2.3(a)).

It is more convenient to use the solid angle $d\omega_i$ centred at dA (Figure 2.3 (b)) since energy incident from more than one direction can be measured relative to the same origin, namely dA. From Figure 2.3 it can be seen that

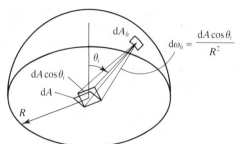

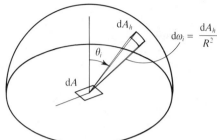

(a) Solid angle as seen from surface of
hemisphere

(b) Solid angle as seen from centre of
hemisphere

Figure 2.3

$$dA_h\,d\omega_h = \frac{dA\,dA_h\cos\theta_i}{R^2} = dA\,d\omega_i\cos\theta_i$$

from which it follows

$$I_{\lambda,\,i}\left(\lambda,\,\theta_i,\,\phi_i\right)dA_h\,d\omega_h\,d\lambda = I_{\lambda,\,i}\left(\lambda,\,\theta_i,\,\phi_i\right)d\omega_i\cos\theta_i\,dA\,d\lambda$$

and the energy per unit area per unit time is:

$$I_{\lambda,\,i}\left(\lambda,\,\theta_i,\,\phi_i\right)\cos\theta_i\,d\omega_i$$

which simply states that the incoming energy has to be
weighted by $\cos\theta_i$ because that determines the amount
of energy intercepted by dA.

We can now define the bidirectional spectral reflectivity as the ratio of the outgoing intensity in a particular
direction $(\theta_r,\,\phi_r)$ to the incoming intensity:

$$\rho_\lambda''\left(\lambda,\,\theta_r,\,\phi_r,\,\theta_i,\,\phi_i\right) = \frac{I_{\lambda,\,r}\left(\lambda,\,\theta_r,\,\phi_r,\,\theta_i,\,\phi_i\right)}{I_{\lambda,\,i}\left(\lambda,\,\theta_i,\,\phi_i\right)\cos\theta_i\,d\omega_i} \qquad \textbf{(2.2)}$$

The numerator is that part of the reflected intensity in the
$(\theta_r,\,\phi_r)$ direction that is provided by the energy incident
in the $(\theta_i,\,\phi_i)$ direction. The entire magnitude of $I_{\lambda,\,r}$
would be obtained by considering *all* the radiation inci-
dent over the hemisphere that is reflected in the $(\theta_r,\,\phi_r)$
direction.

For a diffusely reflecting surface, an incoming inten-
sity $I_{\lambda,\,i}(\lambda,\,\theta_i,\,\phi_i)$ is reflected equally in all directions
(Figure 2.4(a)). A surface that exhibits some mirror-like
or specular properties will tend to have a largish reflected
component in the 'mirror' direction (Figure 2.4(b)). The
phenomena of diffuse and specular reflection and their
importance in reflection models in computer graphics
will be more fully discussed later in this chapter.

It can be shown [SIEG84] that the bidirectional spec-
tral reflectivity exhibits reciprocity. That is ρ_λ'' is symmetric with respect to the reflection and incidence angles.
The energy outgoing from direction $(\theta_r,\,\phi_r)$, due to
incoming energy in direction $(\theta_i,\,\phi_i)$, is related by
the bidirectional spectral reflectivity. This reflectivity
remains identical if the outgoing energy is in direction
$(\theta_i,\,\phi_i)$ due to energy incoming in direction $(\theta_r,\,\phi_r)$. We
write

$$\rho_\lambda''\left(\lambda,\,\theta_i,\,\phi_i,\,\theta_r,\,\phi_r\right) = \rho_\lambda''\left(\lambda,\,\theta_r,\,\phi_r,\,\theta_i,\,\phi_i\right)$$

That is, we can place the light source at the eye and the
eye at the light source and get the same result.

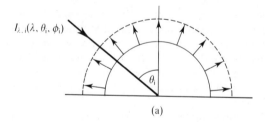

(a)

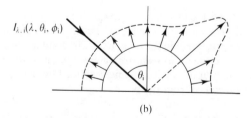

(b)

Figure 2.4 (a) A perfect diffuse surface 'spreads' reflected intensity
equally in all outgoing directions. (b) A surface with a specular or
mirror-like reflectivity will tend to produce a high component in the
'mirror' direction.

Reciprocity relationships are used in important computer graphics algorithms. For example, in ray tracing (see Chapter 11), rays are traced from the eye into the scene; that is the reverse of the direction of light propagation (Figure 2.5). This scheme, usually implemented for specular reflection and transmission, presupposes that the reflection coefficient is symmetric with respect to the incident and reflected angles. Reciprocity relationships are also exploited in the radiosity method (Chapter 11).

Figures 2.4(a) and 2.4(b) imply a directional spectral reflectivity obtained by integration over the reflecting hemisphere. This is termed the directional-hemispherical spectral reflectivity. It is directional rather than bidirectional because it depends only on the direction of the incoming intensity. The directional-hemispherical spectral reflectivity is related to the bidirectional spectral reflectivity by a summation over all reflected angles as follows:

$$\rho_\lambda'\left(\lambda, \Theta_i, \phi_i\right) = \int_\Omega \rho_\lambda''\left(\lambda, \Theta_r, \phi_r, \Theta_i, \phi_i\right) \cos\Theta_r \, d\omega_r \qquad (2.3)$$

where Ω denotes integration over the solid angle of the entire hemisphere

This relationship specifies how light incident in one direction is reflected into all directions over the reflecting hemisphere.

Conversely, we can define a relationship between the reflected intensity in a single direction that is due to the incident radiation that arrives from all directions onto the hemisphere. This is known as the hemispherical-directional reflectivity. When the incident intensity is uniform over the hemisphere it is given in terms of the bidirectional reflectivity by summing over all incident angles:

$$\rho_\lambda'\left(\lambda, \Theta_r, \phi_r\right) = \int_\Omega \rho_\lambda''\left(\lambda, \Theta_r, \phi_r, \Theta_i, \phi_i\right) \cos\Theta_i \, d\omega_i$$

Comparison of these two integrals in conjunction with the reciprocity of the bidirectional spectral reflectivity above shows that they are in fact equal. That is, the reflectivity of a material subject to incoming radiation at a particular angle of incidence measured over the entire reflecting hemisphere is equal to the reflectivity for a single outgoing angle due to uniform incoming radiation. That is:

$$\rho_\lambda'\left(\lambda, \Theta_i, \phi_i\right) = \rho_\lambda'\left(\lambda, \Theta_r, \phi_r\right)$$

2.1.2 Diffuse and specular surfaces

Perfect diffuse and perfect specular surfaces are two special cases that have simplified versions of the above definitions. These extremes are of particular interest in computer graphics because common empirical reflection models represent a surface as some combination of a perfect diffuse and a perfect specular surface.

A perfect diffuse surface reflects radiation equally in all directions and appears equally bright from any viewing direction. (However the amount of energy reflected may vary as a function of the incident angle (Θ_i, ϕ_i).)

The bidirectional spectral reflectivity is thus independent of (Θ_r, ϕ_r):

$$\rho_\lambda''\left(\lambda, \Theta_r, \phi_r, \Theta_i, \phi_i\right) = \rho_\lambda''\left(\lambda, \Theta_i, \phi_i\right)$$

and Equation (2.3) gives

$$\rho_{\lambda, \text{ diffuse}}'\left(\lambda, \Theta_i, \phi_i\right) = \rho_\lambda''\left(\lambda, \Theta_i, \phi_i\right) \int_\Omega \cos\Theta_r \, d\omega_r$$

$$= \pi\rho_\lambda''\left(\lambda, \Theta_i, \phi_i\right)$$

which means that for a diffuse surface the directional-hemispherical spectral reflectivity is equal to π times the bidirectional reflectivity.

Generally the reflected intensity into any outgoing direction (Θ_r, ϕ_r) in terms of bidirectional reflectivity is given by:

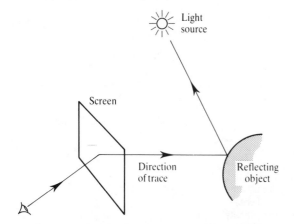

Figure 2.5 Reciprocity in ray tracing: showing that rays are traced in a direction that is opposite to the direction of light propagation.

$$I_{\lambda,\,r}\left(\lambda,\,\theta_r,\,\phi_r\right)$$

$$= \rho_\lambda''(\lambda,\,\theta_r,\,\phi_r,\,\theta_i,\,\phi_i)\,I_{\lambda,\,i}\left(\lambda,\,\theta_i,\,\phi_i\right)\int_\Omega \cos\theta_i\,d\omega_i$$

For a diffuse surface with a bidirectional reflectivity independent of the incoming angle (θ_i, ϕ_i) and incident intensity uniform for all angles, this reduces to:

$$I_{\lambda,\,r}\left(\lambda\right) = \rho_{\lambda,\,\text{diffuse}}''\left(\lambda\right) I_{\lambda,\,i}\left(\lambda\right)\int_\Omega \cos\theta_i\,d\omega_i$$

$$= \pi\rho_{\lambda,\,\text{diffuse}}''\left(\lambda\right) I_{\lambda,\,i}\left(\lambda\right)$$

A perfect mirror surface reflects light in a single direction if the incident radiation is confined to a single direction.

The angle that the reflected radiation makes with the surface normal is equal to the angle of the incident radiation with respect to the surface normal and both beams are in the same plane:

$$\theta_r = \theta_i \quad\text{and}\quad \phi_r = \phi_i + \pi$$

If the mirror is perfect then there is no outgoing radiation in any other direction and

$$\rho_{\lambda,\,\text{specular}}''\left(\lambda,\,\theta_r,\,\phi_r,\,\theta_i,\,\phi_i\right) = \rho_{\lambda,\,\text{specular}}''\left(\lambda,\,\theta_i,\,\phi_i\right)$$

is a function only of the direction of the incoming radiation and wavelength.

The above definitions are summarized in Table 2.1.

Table 2.1 Summary of reflectivity definitions.

Name	Symbol	Definition	Aide-mémoire
Bi-directional spectral reflectivity	$\rho_\lambda''(\lambda,\,\theta_r,\,\phi_r,\,\theta_i,\,\phi_i)$	Ratio of the outgoing intensity in direction (θ_r, ϕ_r) to incoming intensity in direction (θ_i, ϕ_i)	
Directional-hemispherical reflectivity	$\rho_\lambda'(\lambda,\,\theta_i,\,\phi_i)$	Ratio of outgoing intensity over all directions to incoming intensity in a single direction	
Directional-hemispherical reflectivity for a diffuse surface	$\rho_{\lambda,\,\text{diffuse}}'(\lambda,\,\theta_i,\,\phi_i) = \pi\rho_\lambda''(\lambda,\,\theta_i,\,\phi_i)$	Special case of directional-hemispherical reflectivity for a diffuse surface	
Hemispherical-directional reflectivity	$\rho_\lambda'(\lambda,\,\theta_r,\,\phi_r)$	Ratio of outgoing intensity in one direction (θ_r, ϕ_r) to incoming intensity in all directions (when the incoming intensity is uniform in all directions)	

2.2 Aspects of reflection

This section is a wordy discussion of the phenomenon of reflection and addresses those points that are important to computer graphics' practitioners and which do not necessarily emerge easily from the mathematical models.

Radiation incident on a surface is reflected according to well-known laws. Many factors are involved in determining the magnitude and the direction of the reflected radiation.

One of the ways in which computer graphics attempts to simulate the fact that objects of different material behave differently when illuminated is to simulate surface properties in some way and then interact this model with environment geometry. A surface attribute that is commonly modelled in computer graphics is the surface roughness. A perfectly smooth surface reflects incident radiation in a single direction. A rough surface tends to scatter incident radiation in every direction although certain directions may contain more reflected energy than others. This behaviour also depends on the wavelength of the radiation; a surface that is smooth for certain wavelengths may be rough for others. For example, oxidized or unpolished metal is smooth for radio waves (say $\lambda = 10^{-2}$ m) and rough for radiation in the visible part of the spectrum (0.4–0.7 μm). In general, metals can be diffuse or specular reflectors in the visible spectrum depending on whether they are polished or not. So reflection is not predominantly dependent on the material but on its surface properties.

Reflected intensity may also depend on the angle of the incident radiation. A black road surface, manifestly a rough surface, produces glare or a high reflected intensity when the sun is low on the horizon. At noon a black asphalt surface will reflect virtually no light.

Any reflection from a practical surface, that is, a surface that is neither a perfect mirror nor a perfect diffuse reflector, is considered as the sum of a specular component and a diffuse component. The existence of these two components has been shown experimentally and is not a consequence of the choice of a particular model. A mirror reflects light according to well-known classical laws. A surface such as powdered glass diffusely scatters light in all directions. Materials can exhibit both phenomena. Glossy paper viewed from above appears white and unglossy. When viewed at a low angle, it is glossy and reflects objects. However, an image reflected in the paper appears hazy because specular and diffuse reflections are occurring simultaneously.

The colour of most objects in our environment is due to the selective absorption of incident light by the object. Most objects in manmade environments and natural environments do not emit light of their own. Their colour is due to the re-emission of selected parts of the spectrum of the incident light. The amount of reflected light depends, in classical theory, on the refractive index and if this varies significantly with wavelength then an object will appear coloured. However, things are not quite as simple as that. Polished glass is a colourless reflecting and transmitting surface because it is extremely smooth. When it is powdered it appears as a white, diffusely reflecting surface because it exhibits no selective absorption.

2.2.1 Multiple reflections

The multiple reflection problem is addressed, but only partially solved, in computer graphics by global reflection models. These are described in later chapters. In this chapter we will restrict ourselves to a qualitative discussion.

Many subtle second-order effects, that are due to multiple reflections, are important to our perception of our environment. Multiple reflecting surfaces tend to exist more in manmade environments and objects than in natural scenes. Most of these effects are either not modelled or are only partially modelled in computer graphics; but they should be considered as a kind of backdrop against which computer graphics reflection models can be qualitatively evaluated. Such knowledge goes some way to answering the question: why is it that I know this is a computer-generated image and not a photograph of a real scene?

Multiple reflections are important because of the way in which illumination in a scene is modified as light is reflected from one surface to another. Interactions between diffuse surfaces are important but are a phenomenon that we tend to take for granted. Consider a room illuminated by a window in one wall. Apart from the wall immediately opposite the window, all the surfaces are illuminated by secondary illumination. This problem is addressed in computer graphics by two theoretically related, but algorithmically different, approaches: the radiosity method (Chapter 11) and backwards ray tracing (Chapter 10).

Another important aspect of diffuse interaction concerns shadows with soft edges – called soft shadows in computer graphics. Traditionally, computer graphics has dealt with shadows by considering the geometric interaction between the object and the light source. This approach gives the projection of the shadow but not its intensity. Intensity within a shadow is a function of diffuse interaction. A surface in shadow emits some light – shadows are not usually completely black – and the intensity of this light is due to diffuse interaction.

A more subtle consequence of interaction between surfaces is given the somewhat exotic name 'colour bleeding' (see Chapter 11 where this is incorporated into a computer graphics model).

Probably the most common manifestation of interreflection of light in an environment is the tendency for object colours to become desaturated when illuminated by nondirect diffuse light. A room illuminated by an incandescent light will produce, after successive reflections from say, cream-coloured walls, light that becomes progressively redder as a function of the order of the reflection. Objects illuminated by such light have their colours desaturated.

In practice, however, the effect of the alteration of the colour of an object by nondirect illumination is not perceived, except in very degenerate conditions. An object will be viewed either in a direct light or in a nondirect light. The overwhelming effect of colour constancy (the ability of the human visual system to perceive the colour of an object as a *constant* attribute of the object under a wide variety of illuminating conditions) means that the differences can be perceived only by some kind of instrumental intervention, such as spectrophotometry. (The colour-change effect is easily seen if an object is photographed under the two extreme lighting conditions – indirect diffuse light and direct diffuse light, and the photographs displayed side by side.)

So what are we to make of this in our ongoing pursuit of realism in computer graphics? Is it necessary to simulate such effects in colour-critical applications, such as CAD in interior or textile design? It can certainly be simulated with the radiosity method (see Chapter 11). Colour constancy operates generally in a natural environment and it may be that a computer graphics monitor should produce identical images (as far as colour is concerned) of an object under different lighting conditions, thus simulating colour constancy.

Multiple reflections also occur in objects that have received a partially transparent coating, such as varnish, and this phenomenon accounts for the significant change

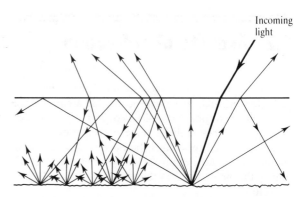

Figure 2.6 Showing what happens to a ray of light striking a diffusing surface covered by a thin coat of varnish or wax.

in the appearance of materials such as wood when they are varnished or polished. Figure 2.6 shows the possibilities that may occur for light incident on such a surface. A diffuse surface covered with a transparent layer will exhibit multiple reflections. Light passing through the layer will be selectively absorbed by the inner surface, partially reflected by the outer surface and selectively absorbed again when it is reflected internally by the outer surface. The viewer receives an additive mixture of a fraction of the light that has been selectively absorbed once, twice and so on, and this effect accounts for the

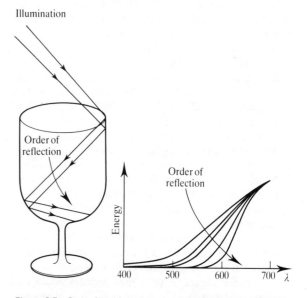

Figure 2.7 Deepening colour change as a function of the order of reflection in a multiple reflecting metallic object.

quality of the perceived light that finally leaves the surface.

A similar effect can occur in self-multiple reflections in objects. This is particularly noticeable in gold. Inside a gold goblet, it is possible to get multiple reflections of a high order because gold has high reflectivity and low absorption. The reflected light gradually changes to deep red as a function of the order of the reflection (Figure 2.7).

Of course reflection, as a mechanism, accounts for only part of our overall perception of a scene. Light interacts with objects in many different ways as we have discussed. An important contribution comes from shadows, which are a function of the nature and the geometry of the light source. Shadows are important because they give information on the position and nature of the light sources that are illuminating an object, which may be invisible to the viewer. They are also important in perceiving depth and the general spatial relationships between objects. Shadows are properly part of global reflection as we shall discuss later.

2.3 Reflection models in computer graphics

2.3.1 Introduction

The purpose of reflection models in computer graphics is to render three-dimensional objects in two-dimensional screen space such that reality is mimicked to an acceptable level. As we saw in Chapter 1, it is an operation that involves geometric transformations, hidden surface removal and the application of a reflection model.

The first reflection models developed in computer graphics, and the most frequently used 'standard' reflection model – the Phong model – dealt with primary reflections of light from an object with uniform surface properties. None of the second-order effects discussed in the previous section are dealt with. Thus most of the reflection models in three-dimensional computer graphics only model one aspect of light–object interaction and within this constraint only simulate primary or first-order reflections. The variety or richness of computer graphics images, using this standard model as a basis, derives from a number of ad hoc techniques, such as shadows and texture, that have been grafted onto the basic model.

The phrase 'reality is mimicked to an acceptable level' depends on the context of the application. More effort is expended on add-on techniques if a higher degree of reality is required. Reality also depends on the accuracy of the geometric model that represents the object.

One of the important practical considerations in computer graphics is the relationship between the complexity of the model and the processing time that it demands. For example, simple models are used in computer-generated imagery for flight simulators. Even with large multiple processors, the prodigious demands of such systems constrain the accuracy of the reflection models and the geometric representation of the solids. Also, an accurate shading model in a flight simulator may not be as important as texturing a surface. Textures are important depth cues in flight simulators and texture mapping may place as heavy a demand on the processor as reflection. On the other hand a television commercial comprising a short animated sequence may demand, for aesthetic reasons, a much richer reflection model and tens of minutes may be spent in generating each frame in the sequence on a single processor. Somewhere between these two extremes is the shading of solid models in CAD packages. Here a machine part may be designed interactively using a solid modelling capability. In the design loop a user of such a system may operate with wireframe models. To visualize the finished object most three-dimensional CAD systems have a shading option. This uses a basic reflection model to shade the surfaces of the object. Such a process, running on a CAD workstation, may take from tens of seconds to a few minutes to complete.

The above is not meant to imply that an image generator can simply select a reflection model of arbitrary complexity, in the degree to which it can imitate reality, constrained only by the available computing resources. There are, at the moment, only a few models that have been developed and all of these have immediate and noticeable defects. Generally, reflection models in computer graphics are a metaphor for reality that invoke a small number of the dominant variables which exist in any lit environment.

A reflection model, not as basic as those used in flight simulation, nor as rich as the current research models in image synthesis, has been in use in computer graphics since the mid-1970s. It is with this model that we begin, but first a brief historical digression involving two models, really two variations of the same model, out of which the Phong model developed.

2.3.2 A historical digression: early computer graphics reflection models

The first reflection models developed are no longer used in mainstream computer graphics. But in a text with some pretension to comprehensiveness we should include these. Like the reciprocating engine it may seem obvious now but it surely wasn't then. 'Then' was pre-1970.

One of the first appearances of shaded objects came in a paper by Wylie *et al.* [WYLI67]. The model shaded points on the surface of an object using a (monochromatic) intensity inversely proportional to the distance of the point from the light source. (Warnock [WARN69] also used a distance attenuation effect.) This means that parallel planes at different distances exhibit different intensities. Interestingly, this distance dependence is now more or less ignored for most standard applications. Distance effects are now only used in special applications and tend to be modulated by a simulation of atmospheric haze (see Chapter 5). Certainly, distance dependence over the extent of an object is not worth the computation.

The other (obvious in retrospect) development was the consideration of the orientation of a planar surface or surface facet with respect to the light source. Bouknight [BOUK70] used a Lambertian diffuse term (the $\cos\Theta$ dependence of Equation 2.4) to evaluate a constant intensity for a polygon or facet of an object represented as a polygon mesh. An ambient term was also included to illuminate parts of an object that are visible to the viewer but invisible to the light source. Bouknight's model can be described by:

$$I_{\lambda, r} = I_{\lambda,\,\text{ambient}}\, k_{\text{ambient}} (\lambda) + k_{\text{diffuse}} (\lambda)\, (N \cdot L)$$

where:

$I_{\lambda,\,\text{ambient}}$ is a term that models the ambient light in the environment. Otherwise scenes illuminated by just a point light source are unnatural and hard – like illuminating a scene at night with a thin flashlight beam. This is usually approximated by a constant as discussed in the next section.

k_{ambient} is a reflection coefficient for ambient light. This should be a function of wavelength as we implied in the previous section.

k_{diffuse} is a diffuse reflection coefficient (also discussed in the next section).

L is the unit vector from the surface point to the light source.

N is the unit surface normal at the point of interest

Note that this statement is a generalization to wavelength dependence to make the model consistent with the definition of the Phong model in the next section. Bouknight's original equation was

$$I = R * \text{range} * \cos\Theta + \text{back} \qquad (2.4)$$

where:

R is the reflection coefficient
range is $256 - \text{back}$
back is the ambient term
Θ is the angle between N and L

The next major development was the Gouraud model [GOUR71] and this led into the standard shading methodology used in computer graphics – the Phong reflection model and interpolative scheme. Both of these interpolative approaches address the dual problem of shading and dealing with intensity variations in the context of a polygon mesh model. When constant shading (allocating a single intensity across the interior of a facet in a polygon mesh model) is applied to the polygon mesh its faceted appearance is retained. The Gouraud and Phong approaches reduce or eliminate this faceted look. The Phong reflection model (for a single point) is discussed in the next section and the Gouraud and Phong interpolative schemes for polygon mesh models were dealt with in Chapter 1. (It is common now to use the same reflection model (Phong) in both Gouraud and Phong interpolative shading, selecting one shading/ interpolation scheme or the other according to the desired image generation time. Thus the term 'Gouraud shading' applies to an interpolative scheme only. On the other hand, the term 'Phong' is used to describe both a reflection model and a shading scheme or even both.)

2.3.3 The Phong reflection model

This classic reflection model, the most commonly used model in computer graphics, divides the reflectivity into a diffuse component and a specular component. The bidirectional spectral reflectivity is given by:

$$\rho_\lambda'' (\lambda, \Theta_r, \phi_r, \Theta_i, \phi_i) = k_{\text{diffuse}} + k_{\text{specular}} \cos^n\Phi$$

k_{diffuse} is the fraction of energy diffusely reflected

k_{specular} is the fraction of energy specularly reflected

Φ is the angle between the mirror direction R and the viewing direction V (Figure 2.8)

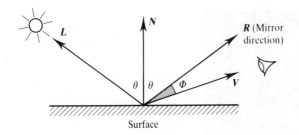

Figure 2.8 Vectors used in Phong reflection model.

In his original paper [BUIT75] Phong gives:

$$k_{\text{specular}} = W(i)$$

implying a dependence on the incidence angle i. However, no details are given on the nature of $W(i)$ and most implementations now ignore this and reduce the bidirectional reflectivity to a reflectivity that depends only on the outgoing angle of interest:

$$\rho''_{\lambda, \text{phong}}(\lambda, \Theta_r, \phi_r, \Theta_i, \phi_i) = \rho'_\lambda(\lambda, \Phi)$$

where the material is assumed to be isotropic. Although there is nothing to prevent an anisotropic dependence of reflectivity on both the outgoing angles the Phong model is most often implemented as above. The empirical spread of the highlight about the mirror direction was Phong's important innovation, giving a cheap but effective way of calculating the geometry of the specular highlight.

The common implementation of Phong's model is usually given in terms of unit vectors associated with the geometry of the point under consideration. Shortening the ambient, diffuse and specular subscripts to a,d and s respectively we have:

$$\begin{aligned} I_{\lambda, r}(\lambda, \Phi) = I_{\lambda, a} k_a(\lambda) &+ I_{\lambda, i}\,(k_d(\lambda)\,(L \cdot N) \\ &+ k_s\,(R \cdot V)^n) \end{aligned} \quad (2.5)$$

where:

$I_{\lambda, a}, k_a(\lambda), I_{\lambda, i}, k_d(\lambda)$, **L** and **N** are as before
R is the unit reflection vector
V is the unit vector from the surface point to the viewer
n is an index that controls the 'tightness' of the specular highlight

Note that k_s is independent of wavelength making the colour of the highlight the same as that of the source. Figure 2.9 shows the variation in light intensity at a point on a surface calculated using this equation. The intensity variation is shown as a profile that is a function of the viewing vector **V** as it rotates in all possible orientations, in the plane of the paper, about the point of interest. The semicircle represents the constant diffuse and ambient contribution and the specular contribution is shown for varying values of n.

If more than one light source is used, then Equation (2.5) becomes:

$$\begin{aligned} I_{\lambda, r}(\lambda, \Phi) = I_{\lambda, a} k_a(\lambda) &+ \sum_m I_{\lambda, i, m}(\lambda)\,(k_d(\lambda)\,(L_m \cdot N) \\ &+ k_s\,(R_m \cdot V)^n) \end{aligned}$$

where:

m is the number of separate light sources
L_m is the vector from the point to the mth light source
R_m is the reflection vector associated with the mth light source

There are thus a number of attributes that we can vary in the Phong reflection model and Figure 2.10 is a stan-

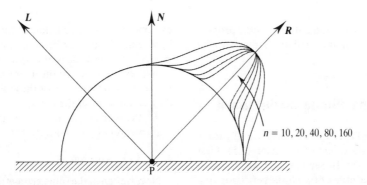

Figure 2.9 The light intensity at point P as a function of the orientation of the viewing vector **V**.

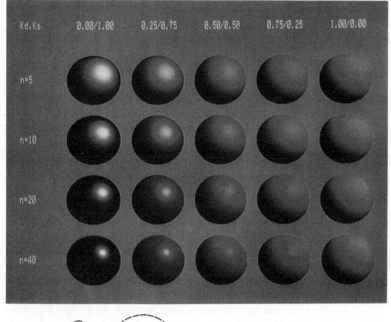

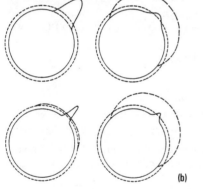

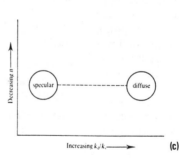

(a)

(b)

(c)

Figure 2.10 (a) and (b) The 20 spheres example (after an illustration by Roy Hall). (b) Slices through the specular bump showing the variation in magnitude of the diffuse, specular and ambient components over the surface of each of the following spheres: top row, spheres 1 and 4; bottom row, spheres 1 and 4.

dard example that shows the effect of varying the proportion of the diffuse-to-specular contribution together with the value of n.

2.3.4 Making the Phong model work

The coded-up version of the Phong model is usually some way from the elegant statement of Equation (2.5). First consider the ambient term. In Section 2.2.1 we discussed the subtle second-order effect of multiple reflection in a room on the perceived colour of an object. This is an extremely complex function of interacting surfaces and light and, with current resources, is almost impossible to model. Not only does the spectrum of ambient light change as a function of the interaction between surfaces, but so does the intensity of the ambient light vary according to position in the room.

All these problems are 'neatly' circumvented by most implementors by making the entire product a constant:

$$I_{\lambda, a} k_a (\lambda) = \text{constant}$$

Next we can make some geometric simplifications that reduce the expense of Equation (2.5). If the light source

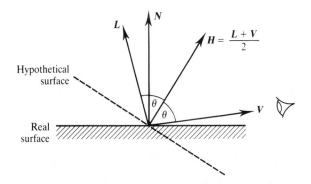

Figure 2.11 *H* is the unit normal to a hypothetical surface oriented in a direction that bisects the angle between *L* and *V*.

and the view point are considered to be at infinity then *L* and *V* are constant over the domain of the scene. The vector *R* is expensive to calculate and although Phong gives an efficient method for calculating *R*, it is better to use a vector *H*. This appears to have been first introduced by Blinn [BLIN77]. The specular term then becomes a function of $(N \cdot H)$ rather than $(R \cdot V)$. *H* is the unit normal to a hypothetical surface that is oriented in a direction halfway between the light direction vector *L* and the viewing vector *V* (Figure 2.11).

$$H = \frac{L + V}{2}$$

This is the required orientation for a surface to reflect light maximally along the direction *V*. It is easily seen that the angle between *R* and *V* is twice the angle between *N* and *H* but this can be compensated for, if necessary by adjusting *n*. Equation (2.5) now becomes:

$$I_{\lambda, r}(\lambda, \Phi)$$
$$= \text{constant} + I_{\lambda, i}(\lambda)\left(k_d(\lambda)(L \cdot N) + k_s(N \cdot H)^n\right)$$

This now means that the reflected intensity is solely a function of the surface normal *N* (and wavelength) for a particular light source. If *L* and *V* are constant vectors then so is *H*.

The next factor to consider is wavelength dependence.

2.3.5 Wavelength dependence in the Phong model

To control the colour of an object we evaluate the Phong equation at a number of wavelengths. The standard com-

puter graphics paradigm is the RGB model and we evaluate the Phong reflection model at three wavelengths. k_d is varied amongst the equations to control the colour of the diffuse component. For example, to render a pure red object we set:

$$k_d(R) = \text{constant}$$
$$k_d(G) = 0$$
$$k_d(B) = 0$$

In general we use three equations:

$$I_{\lambda, r}(\lambda, \Phi)$$
$$= \text{constant} + I_{\lambda, i}\left(k_d(\lambda)(L \cdot N) + k_s(N \cdot H)^n\right)$$
$$\text{for } \lambda = R, G \text{ and } B \qquad (2.6)$$

Three samples suffice in most applications because the colour of objects on a computer graphics monitor is, within certain context-dependent constraints, an arbitrary choice of the designer. For colour-critical applications more samples are required of both the energy distribution of the light source and the variation of reflectivity as a function of wavelength in the object. Inadequacies of the above scheme can be seen by referring to Figure 2.12. The energy distribution of reflected light is a wavelength-by-wavelength product of the energy distribution of the light source and the reflectivity. Three uniform samples of the spectral energy distribution of a light source will not simulate the variations, obviously.

The same situation exists in the variation of the reflectivity with wavelength. What is happening in Equation (2.6) is that three sample points, widely spaced in colour space, are being used to compute three reflected intensities that are then additively mixed in the computer graphics monitor to produce a coloured pixel. The technique amounts to severe undersampling in colour space and leads to colour aliasing artefacts, just as spatial undersampling produces spatial aliasing artefacts. This effect is described in experiments conducted by Hall in [HALL83], who simulated a pair of overlapping filters that have light passed through them. Filters have spectrally distributed transmissivities that exhibit much steeper variations than the spectral distribution of reflectivity for an opaque material. Such variations are lost by the three-sample approach. Hall was able to show, by using a control simulation with intensities evaluated at 1 nm increments, that nine samples in RGB space is a good compromise. This approach is not of course restricted to the Phong reflection model and can be applied to any model that evaluates intensity as a func-

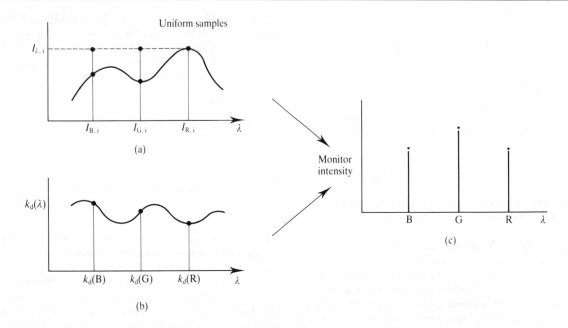

Figure 2.12 Inadequacies of the three sample/equation approach to shading. (a) Uniform samples simulate a perfect white light. Sampling any real distribution three times is inadequate. (b) Undersampling the reflectivity function. (c) The computer graphics solution: three monitor intensities computed from (a) and (b).

tion of wavelength. This important aspect of rendering is further taken up in Section 4.9.

As we have discussed, many subtle second-order effects contribute to the final look of an object in an illuminated environment, but if reasonable colour accuracy is deemed necessary then an n-sample approach ($n > 3$) has to be adopted. (Note that the use of such an approach requires the use of a calibrated and gamma-corrected monitor that is viewed under controlled conditions.) The general scheme is summarized in Figure 2.13, which shows the sequence of calculations involved. The energy distribution of the light source and the variation of spectral reflectivity are both sampled to produce an $I_{\lambda, i}(\lambda)$ and a $k_d(\lambda)$ for the reflection model. Colour aliasing and a more elaborate sampling scheme are discussed in Section 4.9. The reflection model evaluates an intensity at n discrete wavelengths and these are then subsequently converted to monitor RGB tristimulus values for a calibrated monitor. This final process is described in [HALL89].

A final point can be summed up by the standard response that students give when first implementing the Phong model: it doesn't do what it's supposed to do, or, what's happened to the specular highlight?

The idea of having a white specular highlight is that plastic-like objects reflect the colour of the incident light. However, unless the specular term is allowed to saturate, a pure green object, say, would produce, ignoring the ambient component, equal red and blue intensities together with a green intensity that was larger than the red and blue intensities by an amount equal to the diffuse component. This would result in a green-biased specular highlight. Saturation means that the curve of the variation of highlight is limited or chopped. Consider the approximation of a point light source. In reality such a source would produce a single point highlight in a glossy object because a specular highlight is just the image of the source in the object. However, the saturation plateau produces a spread highlight that looks as if it originates from a light source with geometric extent. You can see that it's all a bit of a fudge but it works.

Perhaps one of the sources of confusion is due to textbooks that term n a 'glossiness' parameter. In fact the predominant subjective effect of varying n is to make it look as if the light source is varying in size. Decreasing n makes it look as if the light source has got bigger; it does *not* decrease the glossiness of the object. Glossiness or roughness is not well simulated by the empirical specular

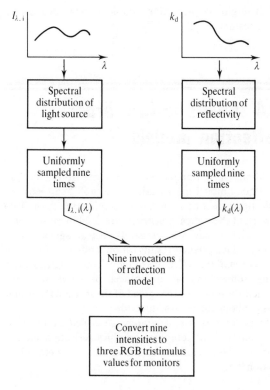

Figure 2.13 A representation of a nine sample/equation reflection model.

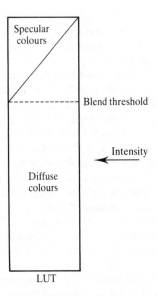

Figure 2.14 Using an LUT to blend diffuse and specular colours.

term in the Phong model. This confusion is clearly seen in Figure 2.10.

2.3.6 Postprocessing Phong rendered images

Lookup tables can be used to postprocess images of objects that have been Phong shaded using a process due to Warn and described in [WARN83]. Warn uses Phong's model but assumes that the intensity at a point on a surface consists of a diffuse and specular contribution, and that a particular intensity corresponds to exactly one combination of diffuse and specular components. (This is a simplification that appears to work in practice.) The calculated intensity is stored in a frame buffer that is then used to access a lookup table (LUT). The LUT is loaded with a set of diffuse colours of increasing intensity that blend into a set of specular col-

ours (Figure 2.14). The diagonal line in Figure 2.14 represents the transition from diffuse colour to specular colour. Both the specular and diffuse colours can be changed interactively via a suitable user interface. The 'blend' intensity, the threshold at which specular highlights start to occur, can also be changed interactively, altering the area of visible specular highlights and therefore the look of the image without having to recalculate from the shading equation.

One disadvantage of this approach is that a separate partition is required in the LUT for each surface type. This places obvious restrictions on the number of surface types and the colour range within a surface type.

2.3.7 The global/local problem

We mentioned at the beginning that we are, in this chapter, concerned with first-order reflection models. This term is used to distinguish such models from approaches that consider multiple reflecting light. In computer graphics the terms used are 'local' and 'global'.

The Phong model is a local model, that is, both the diffuse and specular terms are local. Ideally we would like to consider the interaction between diffusely reflecting surfaces, expressed in the model as an ambient term that is approximated as a constant, but this is extremely expensive and a viable model – the radiosity method (Chapter 11) – did not come onto the scene until 1984.

The locality of the specular term calculation is a severe restriction if the object is supposed to be glossy. In a real scene a glossy object should contain images of other nearby objects and this is predominantly why they look glossy (and why Figure 2.10 does not really represent objects of different glossiness). This can be overcome by ray tracing (as described in Chapter 8) but it is an expensive option compared with Phong shading.

Shadows are part of the global illumination problem. An object is in shadow if it cannot see the light source due to the effect of another nearby object. Shadows have to be separately computed if they are to be used in conjunction with Phong shaded objects. The lack of shadows makes objects look as if they are floating above instead of resting on a surface (see Figure 5.1 for a demonstration of this effect). Another important shadow effect is self-shadows in objects containing concavities. These are not only omitted but the concavities in which they should appear are, in a sense, erroneously shaded. In other words, omitting object shadows makes objects appear to float but omitting self-shadows makes objects look wrong.

2.3.8 Summary of the Phong model

The following points summarize most implementations of the model.

1. Light sources are assumed to be point sources. Any intensity distribution of the light source is ignored.

2. All geometry except the surface normal is ignored (that is, light source(s) and viewer are located at infinity).

3. The diffuse and specular terms are modelled as local components.

4. An empirical model is used to simulate the decrease of the specular term around the reflection vector, modelling the glossiness of the surface, but the variation of this term is clipped as the intensity saturates.

5. We suggest that rather than controlling the glossiness, the index n makes the light source look bigger or smaller.

6. The colour of the specular reflection is assumed to be that of the light source (that is, highlights are rendered white regardless of the material).

7. The global interaction (ambient) is modelled as a constant.

2.4 Realistic first-order reflection models

Building a reflection model that is closer to reality than the Phong model means using an established theory of reflection rather than an empirical reflection term. Two important theoretical constructs are used in more realistic models. They are: classical electromagnetic wave theory, which predicts results for optically smooth, clean surfaces; and the reflection of light from rough surfaces using some kind of microfacet distribution which predicts the nature of the spread of the so-called 'specular bump' about the mirror direction.

These aspects are separately described in the next two sections and computer graphics reflection models that use these theoretical constructs are detailed in Section 2.5.

2.4.1 Elements of classical wave theory used in computer graphics

Classical wave theory is based on Maxwell's wave equations (consult your favourite physics textbook for further details) and forms a theoretical foundation for the many technologies that rely on the propagation of electromagnetic waves through a medium. In computer graphics we are interested in what happens to an electromagnetic wave at an air/object interface, and wave theory applies because it deals with the propagation of waves through different media. However, it can only deal with certain aspects of reflection that arise from the interaction of a wave with a surface under ideal conditions and this means that the surface must be clean and optically smooth as, for example, polished metal. An important aspect of reflection – the bidirectional nature of reflectivity – discussed in previous sections, is predicted by classical wave theory. Wave theory does not deal with colour due to selective absorption. This is usually considered in a quantum mechanical framework (see, for example [WEIS68]).

Maxwell's equations are functions of the magnetic field vector H and the electric field vector E, for a transverse electromagnetic wave (Figure 2.15). The cross product of these two vectors is S, the Poynting vector. Electromagnetic waves also possess polarization properties and in this section we assume linearly polarized waves. This is where the E vector, for example, moves up and down in a straight line.

The solution of Maxwell's equations for the propagation of a wave in a perfect isotropic dielectric material gives:

$$E = E_{\mathrm{m}} \left(\cos \left(\omega \left(t - \frac{nx}{c_0} \right) \right) + i \sin \left(\omega \left(t - \frac{nx}{c_0} \right) \right) \right) \quad (2.7)$$

for the amplitude of the field vector where:

E_{m} is the maximum amplitude of E

c_0 is the speed of light in a vacuum

n is the refractive index of the material – the ratio of the speed of the wave in a vacuum to the speed in the material

x is the direction of propagation of the wave

ω is the frequency of the wave

When the wave travels through a medium of finite conductivity, it is attenuated because energy is absorbed and Equation (2.7) becomes:

$$E = E_{\mathrm{m}} \left(\cos \left(\omega \left(t - \frac{(n - i\Gamma)x}{c_0} \right) \right) \right.$$
$$\left. + i \sin \left(\omega \left(t - \frac{(n - i\Gamma)x}{c_0} \right) \right) \right)$$

where Γ is the extinction coefficient for the material that controls the attenuation. A complex refractive index:

$$n - i\Gamma$$

replaces the simple refractive index n.

We can now consider the relationships that exist at the boundary between two perfect dielectrics. To do this we consider an incident wave $E_{\parallel,\mathrm{i}}$ linearly polarized so that it exists in a plane parallel to the plane of incidence (Figure 2.16). The resultant reflected and transmitted, or refracted, waves remain parallel to the plane of incidence. The reflected wave $E_{\parallel,\mathrm{r}}$ emerges at angle θ_{r} and the transmitted wave is refracted into medium 2 at angle θ_{t}. Consideration of boundary conditions gives the well-known law of reflection, which is that the incident and reflected waves have directions symmetrical with respect to the normal at the point of incidence:

$$\theta_{\mathrm{r}} = \theta_{\mathrm{i}}$$

Derivable in the same way is the law of refraction:

$$\frac{\sin \theta_{\mathrm{t}}}{\sin \theta_{\mathrm{i}}} = \frac{n_1}{n_2}$$

where:

n_1 is the simple refractive index of medium 1 that contains the incident wave

n_2 is the simple refractive index of medium 2

If medium 1 is air ($n_1 \approx 1$) then:

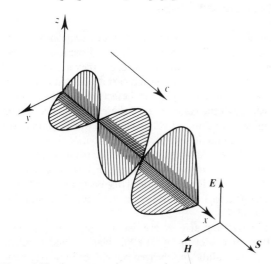

Figure 2.15 A transverse electromagnetic wave.

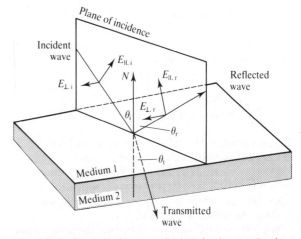

Figure 2.16 Convention for wave reflection/refraction at an interface between two media.

$$n_2 = \frac{\sin \Theta_i}{\sin \Theta_t}$$

Next we state Fresnel's coefficients which give reflected intensity in terms of incident intensity. These are defined in terms of $E_\parallel$ and $E_\perp$, the components of the E vector parallel and perpendicular to the plane of incidence:

$$\frac{E_{\perp,r}}{E_{\perp,i}} = -\frac{\sin\left(\Theta_i - \Theta_t\right)}{\sin\left(\Theta_i + \Theta_t\right)}$$

$$\frac{E_{\parallel,r}}{E_{\parallel,i}} = \frac{\tan\left(\Theta_i - \Theta_t\right)}{\tan\left(\Theta_i + \Theta_t\right)}$$

or

$$\frac{E_{\perp,r}}{E_{\perp,i}} = -\frac{\cos\Theta_t/\cos\Theta_i - n_1/n_2}{\cos\Theta_t/\cos\Theta_i + n_1/n_2}$$

$$\frac{E_{\parallel,r}}{E_{\parallel,i}} = \frac{\cos\Theta_i/\cos\Theta_t - n_1/n_2}{\cos\Theta_i/\cos\Theta_t + n_1/n_2}$$

Because the energy carried by an electromagnetic wave is proportional to the square of the amplitude of the wave, we can define an energy ratio that is equivalent to the directional-hemispherical spectral reflectivity:

$$\rho'_{\lambda,\parallel}\left(\lambda,\,\Theta_i,\,\phi_i\right) = \left(\frac{E_{\parallel,r}}{E_{\parallel,i}}\right)^2$$

and

$$\rho'_{\lambda,\perp}\left(\lambda,\,\Theta_i,\,\phi_i\right) = \left(\frac{E_{\perp,r}}{E_{\perp,i}}\right)^2$$

For unpolarized radiation we take the average of these two reflectivities, and because we consider the media to be isotropic (no dependence on ϕ) we have:

$$\rho'_\lambda\left(\lambda,\,\Theta_i\right) = \frac{1}{2}\frac{\sin^2\left(\Theta_i - \Theta_t\right)}{\sin^2\left(\Theta_i + \Theta_t\right)}\left(1 + \frac{\cos^2\left(\Theta_i + \Theta_t\right)}{\cos^2\left(\Theta_i - \Theta_t\right)}\right)$$

This is known as Fresnel's equation and we note that it defines a reflectivity with an explicit dependence on the angle of incidence as well as wavelength λ (n_1 and n_2 are both functions of wavelength for any practical material). Also note that it depends only on Θ_i. The reflected light is along the mirror direction $\Theta_r = \Theta_i$.

When the materials are not dielectrics, the reflectivities become complex quantities as the complex refractive

indices are substituted. Consider, for example, the special case of metals in air ($n_1 \approx 1$):

$$\sin\Theta_t = \frac{\sin\Theta_i}{(n_2/n_1) - i(\Gamma/n_1)} = \frac{\sin\Theta_i}{n_2 - i\Gamma}$$

where $n_2 - i\Gamma$ is the complex refractive index of medium 2

The absolute value of this complex quantity is

$$|\sin^2\Theta_t| = \frac{\sin^2\Theta_i}{n_2^2 + \Gamma^2} \leqslant \frac{1}{n_2^2 + \Gamma^2}$$

For metals, both n_2 and Γ are large and

$$\cos\Theta_t = \left(1 - \sin^2\Theta_t\right)^{1/2} \approx 1$$

and

$$\frac{E_{\perp,r}}{E_{\perp,i}} = \left(\frac{(n_2 - i\Gamma) - \cos\Theta_i}{(n_2 - i\Gamma) + \cos\Theta_i}\right)^2$$

$$\frac{E_{\parallel,r}}{E_{\parallel,i}} = \left(\frac{(n_2 - i\Gamma) - (1/\cos\Theta_i)}{(n_2 - i\Gamma) + (1/\cos\Theta_i)}\right)^2$$

Finally, note that the reflectivities obey the principle of reciprocity, and light reflected in the $(\Theta_r,\,\phi_r)$ direction from light incident in the $(\Theta_i,\,\phi_i)$ direction is the same as light reflected in the $(\Theta_i,\,\phi_i)$ direction for light incident in the $(\Theta_r,\,\phi_r)$ direction.

2.4.2 Classical wave theory and practical surfaces

The equations given in the previous section apply to clean, optically smooth surfaces. Practical surfaces depart from this ideal case, because they are rough and possibly oxidized and contain surface contaminants. At the wavelengths of light such defects become important.

Although the simulation of these effects in computer graphics is of dubious value, classical wave theory in the context of practical surfaces is used to model two effects not implemented by the Phong model: the dependence of reflectivity on incoming angle $(\Theta_i,\,\phi_i)$ as in [COOK82] and the dependence of reflectivity on the two outgoing angles $(\Theta_r,\,\phi_r)$ for anisotropic surfaces [KAJI85] and [CABR87].

Polarization effects are incorporated into a local reflection model in [WOLF90]. Natural and artificial lights are mainly unpolarized but can become polarized after reflection from a specular surface. Incorporating this effect into a computer graphics simulation, Wolff claims, can make a noticeable difference to rendered scenes.

The Rayleigh criterion

The Rayleigh criterion is an approximate quantification that defines when a smooth surface becomes rough, or when specular reflections become diffuse, in terms of λ, Θ_i and the height, h, of the roughness. Refer to Figure 2.17 which shows two rays incident on different parts of a rough, but otherwise perfect surface at angle β (where the grazing angle $\beta = 90 - \Theta_i$). The path difference between the two rays is given by:

$$\delta_p = 2h \sin \beta$$

and the phase difference by:

$$\delta_\phi = \frac{2\pi}{\lambda} \delta_p$$

$$= \frac{4\pi h}{\lambda} \sin \beta$$

The Rayleigh criterion is deduced from the following argument. If the phase difference is small the two rays will be in phase and the behaviour of the two waves will be the same as if they were reflected from a perfectly smooth surface. As the phase difference increases, interference occurs and when the phase difference is

$$\delta_\phi = \pi$$

the waves will cancel. Since the surface is deemed to be a perfect reflector exhibiting surface roughness, no

energy can be absorbed by the surface, and if it is not emitting energy in the mirror direction, it must be scattering energy into other directions. Thus we define two extreme cases:

$\delta_\phi = \pi$ the surface is rough
$\delta_\phi = 0$ the surface is smooth

Arbitrarily selecting a value of $\pi/2$ between these two limits gives:

$$h < \frac{\lambda}{8 \sin \beta}$$

Alternatively we can simply use the term

$$\frac{4\pi h \sin \beta}{\lambda}$$

and state that the conditions for a smooth surface are

$$\frac{h}{\lambda} \rightarrow 0 \text{ or } \beta \rightarrow 0$$

The second condition is equivalent to the qualitative discussion of surfaces such as asphalt, which are manifestly rough, that specularly reflect for low grazing angles.

Kirchhoff's solution

Kirchhoff's solution for rough surfaces approximates the field at any point on a surface by the field that would occur if the surface were replaced by its tangent plane (Figure 2.18) at that point. The validity of this approximation depends on the radius of curvature of the irregularities being large compared with the wavelength λ. It breaks down when the surface contains irregularities that exhibit sharp points. With this approximation we can write:

$$E = \left(1 + \rho'_\lambda\right) E_i \tag{2.8}$$

$$\frac{\partial E}{\partial N} = \left(1 - \rho'_\lambda\right) E_i \, k_1 \cdot N \tag{2.9}$$

where:

E is the scalar intensity of the electric field vector
N is the surface normal at the considered point
k_1 is the wave vector for E_i
ρ'_λ is the Fresnel factor

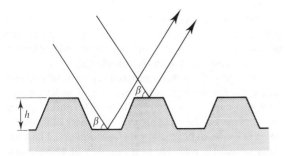

Figure 2.17 Illustrating the Rayleigh criterion for a rough surface.

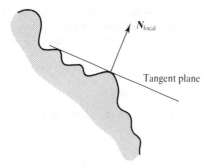

Figure 2.18   Tangent plane to local geometry.

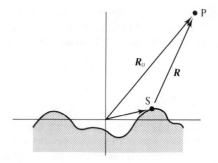

Figure 2.19   Conventions used in Equation (2.10).

The first equation says that the field at the point of interest is the sum of the incident and reflected waves. The second equation follows from the first by differentiation.

Kajiya [KAJI85] derives a form of the Kirchhoff integral:

$$E(\text{P}) = \frac{-\exp\left(\text{i}\,|\,k\,|\,|R_0|\right)}{4\pi\,|R_0|}\int_s \left(N \cdot k_2\,\text{i}E - \frac{\partial E}{\partial N}\right)$$

$$\times \exp\left(-\text{i}\,k_2 \cdot S\right)\text{d}s \qquad \textbf{(2.10)}$$

that gives the value of the field at point P as an integral over the surface, s, in terms of E and $\partial E/\partial N$ where:

P is a point far away compared with λ

k_2 is the wave vector in the direction of P $\big(|k| = |k_1| = |k_2|$ the wave number of the incident and the reflected wave$\big)$

R_0 is the vector from P to the centre of the region over which the integration is performed

R is the vector to the point S on the surface at which E and $\delta E/\delta N$ are evaluated

S is the vector from the centre of the region to the point s (Figure 2.19)

N is the surface normal at point s

Substituting Equations (2.8) and (2.9) into (2.10) Kajiya derives a reflectivity:

$$\rho''_{\lambda,\,k}\left(\text{P},\,k_1,\,k_2,\,N\right) = \frac{1}{2N_0 \cdot k_1\,A}\int_s N\big(\rho'_\lambda(k_1 - k_2)$$

$$- (k_1 + k_2)\big)\,\exp\left(\text{i}(k_1 - k_2) \cdot S\right)\text{d}s$$

$$\textbf{(2.11)}$$

where:

A is the area over which the integration is performed

$k_1,\,k_2$ are the incident and reflected wave vectors

Note that the angles used in ρ'_λ are the local angles of incidence with respect to the local normal N, a function of the 'microsurface' that is being modelled. This reflectivity is used in a complete computer graphics model described in Section 2.5.

Statistical/microfacet approaches

A common approach to modelling surface roughness is to use a so-called microfacet model, where the surface is still assumed to be clean and to consist of very small perfect microfacets oriented in various directions around the mean surface (Figure 2.20). Various statistical approaches can then be used to model the reflectivity of such a surface, and classical geometric optics is broadened by using a statistical approach. Because any small area on the surface is assumed to consist of a collection of microfacets of orientation distributed about the mean or average surface over that area, specular reflection will occur as for an optically smooth surface but will be spread about the mirror direction.

The basis of microfacet models is that the surface, represented by perfect but geometrically perturbed mirror-like elements, can be treated by using classical geometric optics, because the size of the microfacets is still small compared with the wavelength of light.

This approach has been adopted in computer graphics where the Fresnel equation is used but is weighted by a term that models surface roughness. The philosophy of this approach is shown in Figure 2.21, where the reflected beam is shown to be partially diffusely reflected and partially specularly reflected as a function of some roughness parameter. The shape of the specular 'bump' is a function of this parameter, and the nature of this varia-

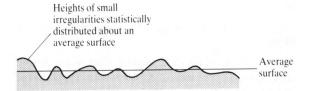

Figure 2.20 The view of a practical surface on which statistical approaches are based.

tion and the surface parameters chosen distinguish the various models.

For example, Davies [DAVI54] uses a simple statistical approach for perfectly conducting surfaces, in terms of RMS roughness. Assuming no multiple reflections between facets and a Gaussian distribution for the heights of the surface perturbations about the mean surface, Davies defines a specular reflectivity for a rough surface as:

$$D\rho'_\lambda\left(\lambda, \theta_i\right)$$

where:

$$D = \exp\left(-\left(4\pi\frac{h}{\lambda}\cos\theta_i\right)^2\right)$$

$\rho'_\lambda\left(\lambda, \theta_i\right)$ is the specular reflectivity of an optically smooth surface of the same material

h is the RMS height of the rough surface with respect to the average surface

This expression contains the Rayleigh criterion as a limit and approaches 1 for

$$\frac{h}{\lambda}\cos\theta_i \rightarrow 0$$

Blinn [BLIN77] and Cook and Torrance [COOK82] use a more elaborate scheme that incorporates a term

G – an attenuation factor due to the self-shadowing of rough surfaces, defining a spectral reflectivity as:

$$DG\,\rho'_\lambda\left(\lambda, \theta_i\right)$$

This is based [TORR67] on the notion of a reflecting surface that consists of a large number of microfacets in the form of symmetric V-shaped grooves, each with perfectly reflecting or mirror faces (Figure 2.22). The geometric extent of a surface element – the unit of surface area from which a reflected intensity is calculated – means that it is made up of a collection of such microfacets. These can be described by a distribution function of the slope or orientation of the reflecting planes of the microfacets.

The Cook and Torrance model uses a distribution proposed by Beckmann [BECK63]:

$$D = \frac{1}{4m^2\cos^4\alpha}\exp\left(-\frac{\tan^2\alpha}{m^2}\right)$$

where:

m is the RMS slope of the microfacets and D returns the proportionate area of microfacets orientated at angle α to the average normal of the surface

Lobes are shown in Figure 2.23 for Gaussian and Beckmann distributions for different values of m. The value of D is given as a distance from the surface element (to the outside of the lobe) and is a maximum along the mirror direction. The smaller the m the gentler the slopes of the microfacets and the more tightly is the distribution centred around R. G is an attenuation factor due to the effect of shadowing by the microfacets. To save unnecessary use of symbols we will use a convention consistent with the next section for the incoming and outgoing directions. That is:

$\left(\theta_i, \phi_i\right) \equiv L$ the unit light direction vector

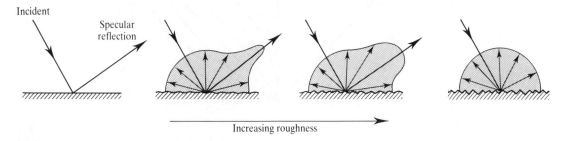

Figure 2.21 Reflectivity as a function of surface roughness.

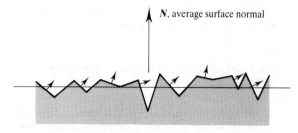

Figure 2.22   Microfacet model of a reflecting surface: a set of symmetric V-shaped grooves whose orientation can be modelled by a distribution about a particular direction.

and

$(\theta_r, \phi_r) \equiv V$ the view vector or the outgoing direction of interest

Figure 2.24 shows the three possible cases which depend on the relative positions of L and V with respect to the microfacets oriented in the H direction. The term 'shadowing' is used to describe interference in the incident light and 'masking' to describe interference in the reflected light. The degree of masking and shadowing is dependent on the ratio l_1/l_2 (Figure 2.25) which

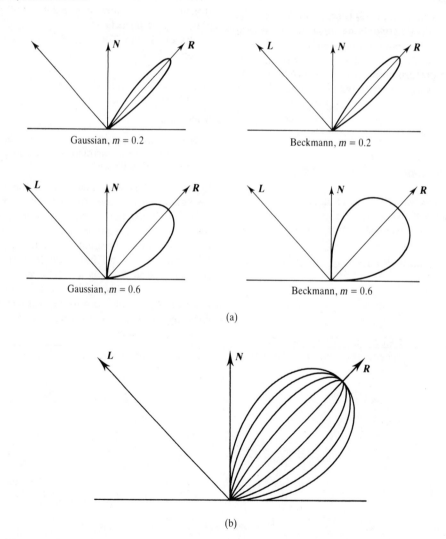

Figure 2.23   (a) Microfacet orientation distributions. (b) Gaussian distributions with m varying from 0.2 to 0.8.

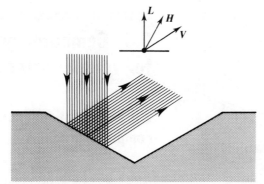

Case 1. No interference : angle between **L** and **V** is small – all light
falling on the microfacet escapes.

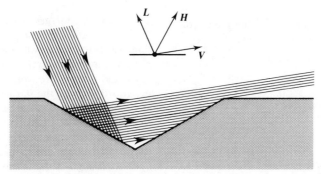

Case 2. Some reflected light is trapped – 'masking'.

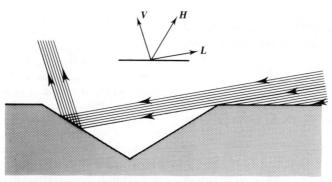

Case 3. Some incident light is 'shadowed' (inverse of case 2).

Figure 2.24   The interaction of light with a microfacet reflecting surface.

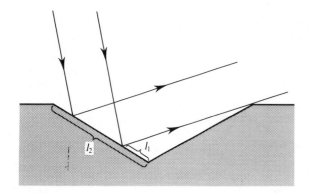

Figure 2.25   Amount of light which escapes depends on $(1 - l_1/l_2)$

describes the proportionate amount of the facets contributing to reflected light that is given by:

$$G = 1 - \frac{l_1}{l_2}$$

In the case where l_1 reduces to zero then all the reflected light escapes and

$$G = 1$$

A detailed derivation of the dependence of l_1/l_2 on L, V and H is given in [BLIN77]. For masking:

$$G_m = \frac{2(N \cdot H)\,(N \cdot V)}{V \cdot H}$$

For shadowing the situation is geometrically identical with the role of the vectors L and V interchanged. For shadowing we have:

$$G_s = \frac{2(N \cdot H)\,(N \cdot L)}{V \cdot H}$$

The value of G that must be used is the minimum of G_s and G_m. Thus:

$$G = \text{min\_of}\ \{1, G_s, G_m\}$$

From an energy point of view, incident light that is intercepted contributes its energy to the specular component of the microfacet that intercepted it. On the other hand, reflected light that is masked will, given a somewhat simplistic analysis, tend to emerge into the environment in a direction far removed from the local mirror direction, and can thus be deemed to contribute to the diffuse or ambient component.

2.5 Computer graphics models for rough surfaces

2.5.1 Statistical/microfacet models in computer graphics

Two computer graphics models incorporate a specular reflectivity term of the form:

$$\frac{DG\rho'_\lambda(\lambda, \theta_i)}{N \cdot V}$$

This definition merges three different models. The D term incorporates the statistical microfacet approximation. The G term deals with the geometry of attenuation. $\rho'_\lambda(\lambda, \theta_i)$ incorporates the dependency of the reflection along the mirror direction on wavelength. The denominator deals with the flaring effect that occurs at low angles of incidence. The models are due to Blinn [BLIN77] and Cook and Torrance [COOK82]. The difference between the models is in the choice of D and in Blinn's model there does not seem to be a dependence of ρ'_λ on wavelength λ. Blinn's model can be defined, for a single light source, as:

$$I_{\lambda, r}(\lambda, \theta_i)$$
$$= I_{\lambda, a}\, k_a(\lambda) + I_{\lambda, i} \left[k_d(\lambda)\,(L \cdot N) + \frac{k_s\, DG\, \rho'_\lambda(\theta_i)}{N \cdot V} \right]$$

and the model can be seen as the linear combination of an ambient, diffuse and specular term, where the specular term is based on the Fresnel equation for reflection at a perfect surface, modified by the terms D and G. (The inverse dependence on $N \cdot V$ is explained shortly.) In this respect, and the fact that it models light due to direct illumination only, it is similar to Phong's approach. One of the original aims of the model was to render polished metallic surfaces correctly. The Phong models gives the impression of coloured plastic surfaces. Also it is inaccurate in the specular term for illumination at low angles of incidence. Physically the amplitude of the specular 'bump' is a function of the angle the light source makes with the surface. Figure 2.26 shows the value of the reflected intensity for a light source at high and low angles of incidence obtained using the Phong model and the improved model described in this chapter.

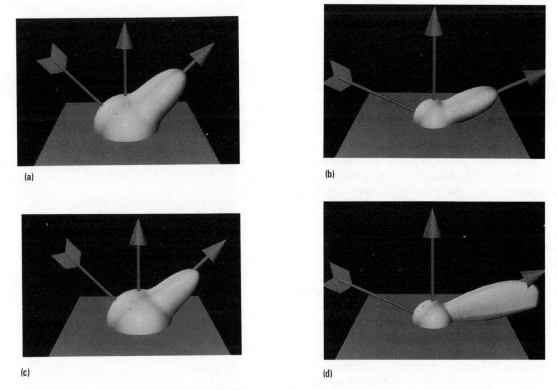

(a)

(b)

(c)

(d)

Figure 2.26   A rendered version of the solid formed by considering the reflected intensity (in all directions) for light incident from a particular direction. The arrow tail is L and the arrowhead shows the mirror direction. (a) and (b) The Phong model for high and low angles of incidence. (c) and (d) The Blinn model for high and low angles of incidence.

Figures 2.26(a) and (b) use the Phong model for the two angles of incidence. They are a three-dimensional version of Figure 2.9. The reflected intensity peaks along the mirror direction and its value is independent of the angle of incidence. (Although there is a scale change to enable Figures 2.26(b) and (d) to be compared.) Figures 2.26(c) and (d) are for the same two angles of incidence, but this time using the Blinn model. Figure 2.26(c) is virtually identical to Figure 2.26(a). However, comparing Figure 2.26(d) with (b) you can see that the lobe is much larger and is no longer coincident with the mirror direction.

The Cook and Torrance model uses an energy-based approach to derive a reflected intensity. Rewriting Equations (2.1) and (2.2) using computer graphics terminology, we have:

$$E_i = I_{\lambda, i}(L \cdot N)\, d\omega_i$$

and

$$I_{\lambda, r} = \rho_\lambda''(\lambda, \Theta_r, \phi_r, \Theta_i, \phi_i)\, I_{\lambda, i}(L \cdot N)\, d\omega_i$$

Cook and Torrance define the bidirectional reflectivity as the sum of a diffuse and a specular component:

$$\rho_\lambda'' = R = k_s R_s + k_d R_d$$

where:

$k_s + k_d = 1$ are fractions rather than coefficients
$R_d = R_d(\lambda)$ is a function of wavelength only

$$R_s = \frac{DG\, \rho_\lambda'(\lambda, \Theta_i)}{\pi\, N \cdot V}$$

Note that the specular term is equivalent to Blinn's model except that the dependence of the Fresnel term has had its wavelength dependence restored. Also note that the term is a bidirectional reflectivity. Although the Fresnel term depends only on Θ_i, G and the denominator are functions of the outgoing angle.

Thus we have, for a single light source:

$$I_{\lambda,\,r}(\lambda,\,\Theta_i) = I_{\lambda,\,a}\,k_a(\lambda) + I_{\lambda,\,i}\,d\omega\big(k_d R_d(\lambda)\,(L \cdot N)$$
$$+ k_s R_s(\lambda,\,\Theta_i)\big)$$

where:

$d\omega$ is the solid angle of the illuminating source. Note that $d\omega$ has the same 'status' as $I_{\lambda,\,i}$. Doubling the value of $d\omega$ and keeping $I_{\lambda,\,i}$ the same will have the same effect as keeping $d\omega$ unchanged and doubling $I_{\lambda,\,i}$.

We should now explain the inverse dependence of $N \cdot V$. As the angle between N and V is increased more of the surface is seen along the viewing direction. A greater proportion of the microfacets oriented in the H direction will be seen. If the surface is viewed normally then only a very small area will be seen. If, on the other hand, the surface is viewed at a low angle then a large number of microfacets will be seen along the surface. This effect is counteracted by the attenuation factor G.

Now consider colour. In reality the colour of a specular highlight depends on the physical characteristics of the material, except when the illumination is at a low angle of incidence when the colour of the highlight approaches that of the light source. In the Phong model the highlight colour is the colour of the light source, usually white, and the change from a white highlight to a region exhibiting diffuse reflection means a change of colour that depends on the relative magnitude of the diffuse and specular terms. As the specular term reduces to zero the colour surrounding the highlight would approach the colour given by the diffuse coefficients.

In the Cook and Torrance model it is possible to represent, for example, highly polished metallic surfaces with a diffuse contribution of zero. A change in both the colour and the intensity of the highlight term is controlled by the value of the specular reflection coefficient.

$\rho'_\lambda(\lambda,\,\Theta_i)$, the Fresnel term in R_s, accounts for the colour change of the specular highlight as a function of the angle of incidence of the light source Θ, reproduced here for convenience:

$$\rho'_\lambda(\lambda,\,\Theta_i) = \frac{1}{2}\frac{\sin^2(\Theta_i - \Theta_t)}{\sin^2(\Theta_i + \Theta_t)}\left(1 + \frac{\cos^2(\Theta_i + \Theta_t)}{\cos^2(\Theta_i - \Theta_t)}\right)$$

where:

Θ_i is the angle of incidence,
that is, $\cos^{-1}(L \cdot H) = \cos^{-1}(V \cdot H)$
Θ_t is the angle of refraction
$\sin\Theta_t = \sin\Theta_i / n$ where n is the refractive index of the material

$\rho'_\lambda(\lambda,\,\Theta_i)$ is minimum, that is, most light is absorbed

when $\Theta_i = 0$ or normal incidence. No light is absorbed by the surface and $\rho'_\lambda(\lambda,\,\Theta_i)$ is equal to unity for $\Theta_i = \pi/2$. The wavelength-dependent property of $\rho'_\lambda(\lambda,\,\Theta_i)$ comes from the fact that n is a function of wavelength. This dependence is not normally known and Cook and Torrance suggest a practical compromise, which is to fit the Fresnel equation to the measured normal reflectance for a polished surface.

Rewriting the Fresnel equation as:

$$\rho'_\lambda(\lambda,\,\Theta_i) = \frac{1}{2}\frac{(g-c)^2}{(g+c)^2}\left(1 + \frac{(c(g+c)-1)^2}{(c(g-c)+1)^2}\right) \qquad (2.12)$$

where:

$$c = \cos\Theta_i = V \cdot H$$

and

$$g^2 = n^2 + c^2 - 1$$

for $\Theta_i = 0$, that is normal incidence

$$\rho'_\lambda(\lambda,\,0) = \frac{(n-1)^2}{(n+1)^2}$$

giving

$$n = \frac{1 + (\rho'_\lambda(\lambda,\,0))^{1/2}}{1 - (\rho'_\lambda(\lambda,\,0))^{1/2}}$$

This then gives values for n as a function of wavelength from the measured values of $\rho'_\lambda(\lambda,\,0)$ and this can be substituted into Equation (2.12) to give $\rho'_\lambda(\lambda,\,\Theta_i)$ for any angle of incidence Θ_i. A method to approximate the colour changes in the highlight as a function of Θ_i is to proceed as follows:

1. $\rho'_\lambda(\text{red},\,0)$, $\rho'_\lambda(\text{green},\,0)$ and $\rho'_\lambda(\text{blue},\,0)$ are obtained from measured values [PURD70] giving n_{red}, n_{green} and n_{blue}.

2. These values of n are then substituted into (2.12) to obtain $\rho'_\lambda(\text{red},\,\Theta_i)$, $\rho'_\lambda(\text{green},\,\Theta_i)$ and $\rho'_\lambda(\text{blue},\,\Theta_i)$. These slices through $\rho'_\lambda(\lambda,\,\Theta_i)$ are shown in Figure 2.27.

3. These values of $\rho'_\lambda(\lambda,\,\Theta_i)$ are used in three (R, G, B) intensity equations.

In general, both R_d and $\rho'_\lambda(\lambda,\,\Theta_i)$ (and thus R_s) vary with the geometry of reflection. Cook and Torrance assume that R_d is the bidirectional reflectance for normal illumination and restrict dependence on the illuminating angle to $\rho'_\lambda(\lambda,\,\Theta_i)$. The dependence of $\rho'_\lambda(\lambda,\,\Theta_i)$ on incidence angle Θ_i and wavelength λ is shown in

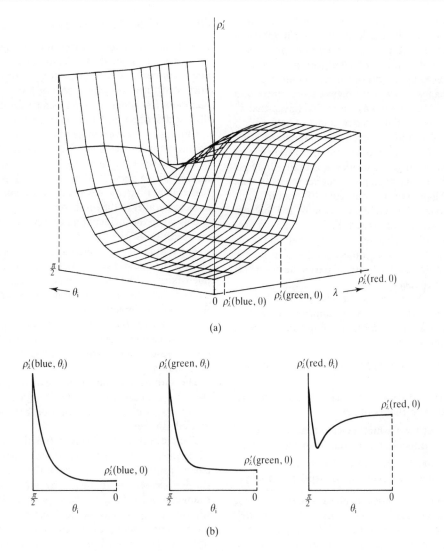

(a)

(b)

Figure 2.27 (a) Reflectance ρ'_λ as a function of wavelength (λ) and angle of incidence (polished copper). (b) The dependence of ρ_λ on θ_i for red, green and blue wavelengths.

Figure 2.27 for a polished copper surface. From this it can be seen that significant colour changes only occur when θ_i approaches $\pi/2$. Also note that it is inaccurate to attempt to model 'realistic' colour by working with three sets of coefficients at the red, green and blue wavelengths. And if no attempt is going to be made to model the colour accurately there seems little point in using a more expensive reflection model. Accurate rendering of the colour and colour changes that simulate

real metals, requires consideration of the complete spectral variation of $\rho'_\lambda (\lambda, \theta_i)$ and the spectral distribution of the light source. These considerations are described in Sections 2.3.5 and 4.9.

Plate 3 demonstrates the model using spheres of different materials. The illustrations are exaggerated to show how the model controls the rendering of shiny metallic objects. In this respect the diffuse components have been deliberately set equal to zero. In practice a nonzero diffuse contribution would produce a more 'recognizable' effect. In the illustration each sphere is illuminated by a perfect white illuminant at normal incidence and at an angle of 77°. The top sphere in each case was produced by a form of Phong shading and this exhibits no change in intensity between the centre and edge highlight. The colour was controlled (given that k_d is zero) by setting the light source colours to the object colour. The centre sphere in each case is rendered using the Cook and Torrance model, but the Fresnel term dependence on the angle of incidence is omitted. These spheres exhibit an edge highlight of higher intensity than the centre highlight which is markedly different in shape from the Phong edge highlight. Finally the bottom sphere in each case includes the Fresnel term which produces a distinct colour change – the edge highlight tends to white. Plate 1 shows an object rendered using the Cook and Torrance model. Material parameters were set for bronze and copper.

The Cook and Torrance model clearly works but the reader should bear in mind that the approach is really a linear combination of a number of completely different models and approximations:

1. An ambient term to approximate global illumination.
2. A Lambertian diffuse term that will model colour.
3. A specular term that contains:
    (i) a Fresnel term which gives the dependence of specular intensity and colour on incidence angle;
    (ii) a microfacet model term that spreads the specular intensity, giving an 'off-specular bump'.

The microfacet model is not entirely satisfactory because it is based on a one-dimensional 'cross-sectional' model. The Torrance and Sparrow model [TORR67] assumes a surface of infinitely long, symmetrical wedge-shaped grooves. This point is taken up in the next microfacet model, due to Cabral et al. [CABR87].

2.5.2 An explicit microfacet model

A microfacet model, derived by explicitly constructing a surface of triangular microfacets, is given by Cabral et al. [CABR87]. The reflection model is generated by precalculation (rather than simulation by a parametric distribution or function) and a table of reflectivities:

$$\rho_\lambda''(\lambda, \Theta_r, \phi_r, \Theta_i, \phi_i) = \rho_\lambda''(\lambda, L, V)$$

is built up and subsequently indexed by (Θ_i, ϕ_i) and (Θ_r, ϕ_r) or L and V. Thus any surface whose microstructure can be represented can be modelled. The microstructure can be isotropic or anisotropic, and the method is less restricted than using a statistical distribution as described in the previous section.

Cloth is a simple example of a surface that will exhibit an anisotropic reflection characteristic. This is because of the nature of the microstructure – a weave of parallel threads with a circular cross-sectional area. Each thread scatters light narrowly when the incident radiation is in a plane parallel to the direction of the thread, and more widely when the incident plane is parallel to the 'circular' cross-section of the thread.

The nature of the microsurface can be controlled by varying the size and vertex perturbation of the triangular microfacets. Such a triangular microsurface is most conveniently constructed from a bump map or height field – a two-dimensional array of vertex heights. These heights can be distributed in any desired way: Cabral gives an example of a surface constructed from vertices whose heights are controlled by a white noise distribution.

The authors also show how the method can be used in the context of environment mapping (Chapter 6) where the diffuse and specular reflection can be treated in a unified manner.

The bidirectional reflectivity function is generated by firing rays or beams onto a surface element that encompasses a sufficiently large area of the microsurface. The surface element is modelled by an array or grid of triangular microfacets. The rays that hit the element without being shadowed and emerge without being masked contribute a 'delta function' to the bidirectional reflectivity function. The complete function is the sum of all such delta functions. Information is built up for a reflectivity function by dividing the hemisphere, positioned on the surface element, into a number of cells or bins. Each reflected beam is assigned to a particular bin and a piecewise linear bidirectional reflectivity function is built up.

As detailed in Section 2.1, the energy received by a surface element per unit time per unit area per unit solid angle is

$$I_{\lambda, i}(\lambda, \Theta_i, \phi_i) \cos\Theta_i$$

which using computer graphics terminology is

$$I_\lambda(\lambda, L, N_i)(L \cdot N_i)$$

Cabral *et al.* consider an irradiated surface element to consist of a square array of $2m^2$ triangular microfacets and define vector U_i and V_i to be the edges of a facet S_i that projects onto the horizontal x, y-plane. The height field is a bump map of perturbations in z (Figure 2.28).

Area A_i of a triangular microfacet S_i is given by:

$$A_i = \frac{|U_i| \ |V_i|}{2}$$

and the normal of S_i is:

$$N_i = \frac{U_i \times V_i}{|U_i| \ |V_i|}$$

The mirror direction for the microfacet is:

$$R_i \equiv (\theta_{mr}, \phi_{mr})$$
$$= 2 \ (L \cdot N_i) \ N_i - L$$

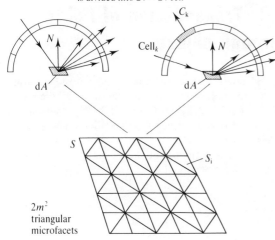

Hemisphere surrounding microsurface element is divided into 24 × 24 cell

$2m^2$ triangular microfacets

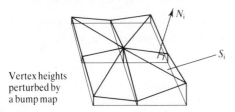

Vertex heights perturbed by a bump map

Figure 2.28 Modelling a surface with height-field perturbed triangular microfacets.

this being simply the law of reflection restated in a vector format convenient for computer graphics.

Shadowing and masking are incorporated in the model and these effects are quantified using a technique, originally developed by Max [MAX86b], called horizon mapping, that creates self-shadows on bump-mapped surfaces. This gives a factor B_i of the area A_i of the microfacet i and this is used to weight the energy incident on a microfacet:

$$E_i(L) = B_i \, D_\lambda \left(L \cdot N_i \right) \rho_\lambda' (\lambda, L, N_i)$$

where:

D_λ is the illuminating flux density
$\rho_\lambda' (\lambda, L, N_i)$ is the Fresnel factor

This is the reflected energy for a particular incoming direction L and a particular microfacet i.

The next development considers how to generate or accumulate the bidirectional reflectivity function. This is accomplished by considering the reflection of the microsurface for a number of incident and reflected directions. Cabral quotes a 'resolution' of 24 × 24 × 24 × 24. A hemisphere divided into cells is positioned on the microsurface and the total reflected energy that flows through each cell k is evaluated by accumulating contributions from all $2m^2$ facets. A single microfacet i with a reflected vector R_i will make a contribution to cell k where:

$$k = \text{nearest} \ (R_i)$$

The function nearest (R) returns the index of the cell hit by a ray fired in direction R. When this process has been repeated for all $2m^2$ microfacets, we can define the energy flowing through one cell as:

$$E_k(L) = \sum_{i=1}^{2m^2} \delta \left(k - \text{nearest} \left(R_i \right) \right) E_i(L)$$

where:

δ is the Kronecker delta function

$$\delta(i) = \begin{cases} 1 & i = 0 \\ 0 & i \neq 0 \end{cases}$$

Note that more than one microfacet is likely to contribute energy to cell k. For a cell k we then have:

$$I_{\lambda, \, r, \, k} = \frac{E_k(L)}{d\omega_k \ dA \ (C_k \cdot N)}$$

where:

$d\omega_k$ is the solid angle of cell k
C_k is its direction vector
dA is the area of the surface element
N is the normal to the surface element

and the reflectivity is given by

$$\rho_\lambda''(\lambda, L, V) = \frac{I_{\lambda, r, k}}{D_\lambda (L \cdot N)}$$

$$= \sum_{i=1}^{2m^2} \frac{\delta(k - \text{nearest}(R_i)) B_i D_\lambda (L \cdot N_i) \rho_\lambda'(\lambda, L, N_i)}{D_\lambda (L \cdot N) \, d\omega_k \, dA \, (C_k \cdot N)}$$

$$= \sum_{i=1}^{2m^2} \frac{\delta(k - \text{nearest}(R_i)) \, G_i}{d\omega_k \, (C_k \cdot N)}$$

where:

$$G_i = \frac{B_i (L \cdot N_i) \, \rho_\lambda'(\lambda, L, N_i)}{(L \cdot N) \, dA}$$

the fraction of incoming flux reflected by facet S_i

The square of the reflectivity can then be used to apply the model to a shading scheme.

2.5.3 A wave theory model

Kajiya [KAJI85] develops a computer graphics reflection model based on the reflectivity function given in Equation (2.11), which is derived using Kirchhoff's method. The computer graphics model is a direct use of this equation and the description of the model that follows is a general overview of Kajiya's implementation method.

The technique is similar in two respects to the model of Cabral *et al.* in the previous section. It sets up a table of bidirectional reflectivities, indexed by two vectors L_i and V_j and can (therefore) model anisotropic reflectivity functions. Kajiya developed the method explicitly to model the anisotropic behaviour of a cloth surface and notes that the microstructure of such surfaces can be specified by using a height field or a bump map.

The integral of Equation (2.11) is evaluated or precalculated, over a surface element that encompasses a sufficient area of the microstructure, for all pairs of incident and outgoing wave vectors k_i and k_j whose directions correspond to L_i and V_j. This is done by centring a hemisphere over the surface element and dividing the hemisphere into cells.

Each pair of cells defines a k_1 and a k_2 and a reflectivity is calculated by integrating over the surface element using these two wave directions. Kajiya uses the method of stationary phase to approximate the integral.

The square of the reflectivity for directions k_i, k_j is stored in table element i, j and linear interpolation is subsequently performed between adjacent table entries, if necessary, to obtain a reflectivity estimate from these values for values of k_i, k_j other than those precalculated. Kajiya quotes a division of the hemisphere of 100 cells giving a table size of 10^4.

To render a surface whose reflection model has been calculated in such a way, the vectors L and V are used as indexes into the table to obtain, directly or by interpolation, the square of $\rho_{\lambda, k}''$. The incident intensity is then multiplied by this coefficient to obtain the reflected intensity.

2.6 Transmission of light through objects

Except in the context of ray tracing and atmospheric scattering, computer graphics has not devoted the same effort to modelling light transmitted through transparent or semi-opaque objects as it has to modelling light reflected from a surface.

At an optically smooth boundary between two media, we have, from Section 2.4.1:

$$\frac{\sin \Theta_t}{\sin \Theta_i} = \frac{n_1}{n_2}$$

where:

n_1 and n_2 are the simple refractive indices of the media

The reflected and transmitted directions in terms convenient for computer graphics are given by:

$$R = 2(N \cdot L)N - L$$

$$T = \frac{n_1}{n_2} L - \left[\cos \Theta_t + \frac{n_1}{n_2} (L \cdot N) \right] N$$

where:

T is the transmitted direction

Because the reflectivities relate reflected and transmitted energy to incident energy, we have:

$$\rho'_{\lambda,r} + \rho'_{\lambda,t} = 1$$

where:

$\rho'_{\lambda,r}$ is the Fresnel reflectivity coefficient
$\rho'_{\lambda,t}$ is the Fresnel transmissivity coefficient

Thus:

$$\rho'_{\lambda,t} = 1 - \rho'_{\lambda,r}$$

In Section 2.5 we saw that we could model a specular reflectivity by using the Fresnel coefficient and some kind of rough surface model to spread the reflected energy about the specular direction. This analysis was based on the application of classical wave theory to (perfect) microfacets. Clearly we could apply the same analysis to the spread of a transmitted wave about T, but this is generally not considered in computer graphics. The possible reason for this is that in computer graphics we always tend to view semi-transparent objects from air, and modelled objects possess two interfaces – an air/glass interface and a glass/air interface. The second interface – the one nearer the viewer, say, will tend to predominate in most practical situations, and will itself contain reflections. There are other complications, such as internal reflections from the second interface due to illumination incident on the first interface and refractive effects. When a background is viewed through, for example, a wine glass, a viewer expects to see refractive effects. These are reasons why transmission has tended to be considered in the context of ray tracing.

2.6.1 Empirical approaches to light transmission

We mention here two empirical schemes that can be used to model certain aspects of transmitted light. The first was introduced by Hall [HALL83] and in one sense is a generalization of the Phong reflection model. It could be called a Phong transmission term and its effect is to spread the transmitted energy about the specular transmitted direction. It can be used to model the spread that a light source produces when viewed through a semi-transparent medium, but subject to the comments in the previous section. The term is:

$$k_t (N \cdot H')^n$$

where:

k_t is a transmission coefficient

N is the surface normal

H' is the orientation that the surface must have to refract light maximally

H' is analogous to H in the context of reflection, which was the orientation required to reflect light maximally. H' is thus a function of L, V and the refractive indices and is given by:

$$H' = \frac{L - \dfrac{n_1}{n_2} V}{\dfrac{n_1}{n_2} - 1}$$

A representation of this model is shown in Figure 2.29.

A second common empirical approach uses the simple device of intensity reduction of detail in the scene behind the object. If refraction is ignored then transparency can be grossly (but effectively) approximated using a linear parameter t to mix the object colour with the intensity of a single background. The object colour I_o is computed in the normal way using a reflection model. In the simplest case background colour, I_b, can be a constant. The final intensity I is given by the mix:

$$I = t I_b + (1 - t) I_o$$

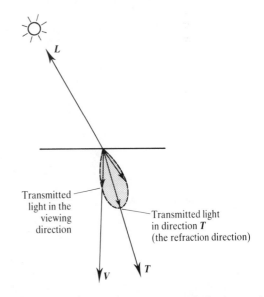

Figure 2.29 Extending the Phong model to account for the spread of transmitted light in a transparent object.

If refractive effects are to be taken into account and the scene is simple – say a single planar background – then a simple special-case ray tracing scheme (where rays terminate on the background) is easily implemented. This is dealt with in Chapter 6 where it is called 'refraction mapping'.

For partially transparent objects that are hollow, t can be 'modulated' by the z-component of the normalized surface normal of the projected object [KAY79]. We are then saying that t is a transmission factor that attenuates anything behind the object (further z) according to an amount that can be approximated by multiplying by N_z. For the paths shown in Figure 2.30, P_1 is longer than P_2 and point s on the surface of the object should exhibit a lower intensity of background colour than point r. t is given by:

$$t = t_{\min} + (t_{\max} - t_{\min})N_z$$

Finally, the main problem with this kind of 'add-on' approach to transparency is that it cannot be easily integrated with the preferred rendering method – a Z-buffer-based approach.

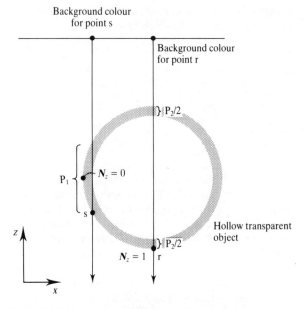

Figure 2.30 Mixing background colour and object colour as a function of N_z, the z-component of the surface normal.

3 The theory and practice of parametric representation techniques

Important applications of the material described in this chapter in computer animation are to be found in Chapters 15 and 17.

Introduction

This chapter deals with the important topics of parametric curves and surfaces and their application in computer graphics.

The theory of the parametric representation of curves and surfaces has been established for many years (see for example [FAUX79]) and the associated practical techniques are a foundation of Computer Aided Design (CAD) systems. Two major geometric modelling methods are used in CAD: solid modelling and surface modelling. Solid modelling involves representing an object by a composite of primitive solids, such as blocks and cylinders; a complex solid is built up using Boolean operations between the primitive solids. Surface modelling involves representing a complex object by a parametric description of its surface.

The surface representation is more general than the primitive solid representation. Although most engineering solids can be represented as combinations of, for example, cylinders, spheres and blocks, we are generally interested in 'free-form' surfaces, where part of a surface may not necessarily be representable as such a Boolean collection. The computer graphics discipline is not the first to address itself to parametric surfaces. The need for a more general free-form representation was first felt by the car and aeroplane manufacturers when designing prototypes. Consequently, there exists a large body of work on parametric representation due to research funded by these industries.

Within computer graphics we shall see that modelling an object using the parametric representation has certain advantages over the polygonal one. For example, for reasons explained in context, imposing shape changes on an object to implement so-called 'soft object animation' has drawbacks if the object is polygonal. These can be overcome by using the parametric form.

Leaving aside solid modelling, which is used mostly in CAD, polygonal representation and parametric representation are the two major modelling techniques in three-dimensional computer graphics. Hopefully the pluses and minuses of each representational form will become obvious in the course of this chapter.

We will also address the problem of rendering from a parametric description. Aside from parametric surfaces, parametric curves in their own right also provide an invaluable tool in animation. In Chapter 15 we set out the fundamentals of the spline-driven animation system which is one of the commonest ways of specifying animations.

The theory splits naturally into consideration of parametric curves and parametric surfaces. Curves are easier to consider and their relevant properties extend without difficulty to parametric surfaces. We will describe such operations on a curve as differentiation, degree elevation and subdivision in some detail. All of these operations have their equivalents in parametric surfaces.

3.1 The parametric representation

A parametrically defined curve in three dimensions is given by three univariate functions:

$$Q(u) = (X(u), Y(u), Z(u))$$

where:

$$0 \leqslant u \leqslant 1$$

As u varies from 0 to 1 the functions sweep out the curve. Similarly a parametric surface is defined by three bivariate functions:

$$Q(u, v) = (X(u, v), Y(u, v), Z(u, v))$$

where:

$$0 \leqslant u \leqslant 1 \text{ and } 0 \leqslant v \leqslant 1$$

As we vary u from 0 to 1 and hold v constant we again sweep out a curve in three-space. An infinity of such curves exists as we vary v from 0 to 1 and this defines a surface in three dimensions.

3.1.1 Parametric representation versus implicit representation

The parametric representation is much more useful in computer graphics than the implicit form of representing curves and surfaces which specifies them in terms of their cartesian coordinates, that is:

$$f(x, y, z) = 0$$

Both parametric and implicit forms are analytical representations. In practice this means that they are exact, and mass properties, such as surface area and volume, are extractable from such descriptions. To see why the parametric representation is more useful, let us consider the specific example of a circle of unit radius centred at the origin and lying in the x, y-plane. The parametric form is given by:

$$Q(u) = (\cos(u/2\pi), \sin(u/2\pi), 0)$$

and the implicit form by:

$$x^2 + y^2 - 1 = 0$$
$$z = 0$$

Suppose we wish to draw the circle by generating a sequential set of connected points that lie on the circle. The parametric description allows us to do this by incrementing u from 0 to 1 for equal intervals of u and we trace out the shape of the circle quite naturally.

The implicit form is more unwieldy – for each point we have to solve a quadratic – in general the implicit form forces us to solve nonlinear equations. Moreover, the ability to move along the circumference is not available to us; solving for x will give us either two roots on different parts of the circle or no roots at all (Figure 3.1).

In general, if the curve or surface is multivalued, that is, if there exists more than one solution to the equation

$$f(x, y, z) = 0$$

for a given x, y or z then the implicit form will be unable to trace out the shape – a severe disadvantage.

Derivatives are also more naturally expressed in parametric form than implicitly. Derivatives expressed parametrically describe rates of change with respect to the

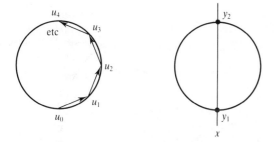

Figure 3.1 The parametric and implicit representations for a circle.

direction of the increasing parameter, that is, along the curve, rather than in the more arbitrary direction of increasing x, y or z. Consider the same example again. The parametric and implicit derivatives are given by:

$$Q_u = \left(-\sin\left(u/2\pi\right)/2\pi, \cos\left(u/2\pi\right)/2\pi, 0 \right)$$

and

$$\frac{dy}{dx} = \frac{-x}{y}$$

Consider these values at the point $u = 0$ or equivalently $x = 1$, $y = 0$. The parametric derivative is $(0, 1/2\pi, 0)$ which tells us that in the direction of increasing u the derivative is vertical, that is, y is increasing but x is momentarily constant. Compare this with the derivative from the implicit form – ∞ – a number computers have some difficulty in dealing with.

Most design applications involve complex curves (and/or surfaces) which cannot be described either by simple functions or by single parametric curves or surfaces. However, an important feature of the parametric representation is that it facilitates piecewise descriptions – a complex curve or a surface can be a set of single parametric curves or surfaces, that is, a composite curve or surface.

It is not only in comparison with the implicit representation that the parametric form is to be preferred, but also in its own right, since the parametric representation produces a rich variety of curves and surfaces useful to computer graphics. Before we examine these in detail we need to look at the general parametric form a little more closely. We consider curves only but, as usual, the extension to surfaces is straightforward. In contexts where this is not true, for example, in surface modelling and rendering, we shall consider surfaces in detail. The advantage of considering curves is that notation is minimized.

3.1.2 Parametric curves: the notion of bases and control points

The parametric curve is usually a polynomial or rational polynomial. We write a polynomial of order $k + 1$ which contains terms up to and including those of degree k as:

$$Q(u) = p_0 + p_1 u + p_2 u^2 + \dots + p_k u^k \qquad (3.1)$$

The degree of the polynomial used in computer graphics is usually 3, that is cubic. A polynomial of degree 2, a quadratic, does not offer sufficient shape flexibility. For degree greater than 3, there is a tradeoff between descriptions that are more and more cumbersome and shape flexibility. Curves of arbitrary complexity can be described by polynomials of sufficiently high degree, but large numbers of coefficients are required and unwanted oscillations may be introduced. A polynomial of degree n may have up to $n - 1$ turning points if all the solutions of $Q(u)$ happen to be real. This implies that the greater n is, the more oscillatory is the curve. Polynomials of less than degree 3 cannot be made to pass through specified end points with specified derivative properties. This is a crucial point since composite curves and surfaces, made up of distinct segments, need to be joined smoothly over segment boundaries. The cubic is the lowest order polynomial that gives us C^1 and C^2 continuity.

Whatever the degree of the polynomial, however, it is inconvenient to represent the curve directly using the coefficients p_i. The relationship between the shape of the curve and the polynominal coefficients is not clear or intuitive. In CAD it would be difficult for a designer to specify and interact with a curve shape using these coefficients. Similarly, in computer animation it would be difficult to design a script to deform the curve. Instead of having to manipulate the coefficients directly, the polynomial form can be rearranged into control points and basis functions which provide a more intuitive connection to the shape of the curve.

An analogy with three-dimensional Euclidian space, R^3, will make this clearer. A coordinate system, typically three mutually perpendicular directions, can uniquely describe any point in R^3. The three directions are said to form a basis of R^3. Formally a basis of a vector space is a collection of vectors that is linearly independent and that can express any vector in the space as a linear combination. Now as we know, more than one coordinate system can describe the same position in R^3. That is, there exists more than one basis for R^3. A different basis or coordinate system is used at different times depending on the context of the application. It would make no sense, for example, to use any coordinate system other than the camera coordinate system when describing objects relative to the camera.

Now consider the set of all $(k + 1)$th-order polynomials which includes polynomials up to and including those of degree k. This set of polynomials forms a vector space $\mathscr{P}^{k+1}$. The formulation of our curve $Q(u)$ in Equation (3.1) can be thought of as specifying a position in the vector space $\mathscr{P}^{k+1}$ via the coordinates $(p_0, \ldots, p_k)$ and the basis $(1, u, u^2, \ldots, u^k)$ which is called the power basis.

Here, our basis is not one of linearly independent directions as in the case of R^3, but a collection of linearly independent polynomials $b_i(u)$ given by:

$$b_i(u) = u^i \quad 0 \leqslant i \leqslant k$$

These are called basis functions and the coordinates p_i are called control points. We can now write Equation (3.1) as:

$$Q(u) = \sum_{i=0}^{k} p_i b_i(u)$$

Since we confine our attention largely to the cubic case, this equation reduces to a cubic segment described by four control points and four basis functions:

$$Q(u) = \sum_{i=0}^{3} p_i b_i(u)$$

Figure 3.2 shows a curve segment (actually a Bézier curve) and the associated control points. Connecting the control points together forms the control polygon also known as a convex hull, a useful device that provides an intuitive connection with the shape of the curve. The con-

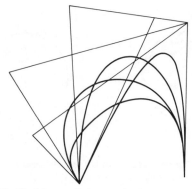

Figure 3.3   The influence of the control points on the shape of the Bézier curve.

trol polygon relates to the shape of the curve in a way that is easy to understand and manipulate. Control points are used in a variety of contexts. Because they approximate the curve that they specify (to an extent that can be controlled) they can be used in modelling, where they are derived from physical data. They are then used to produce a curve or surface that passes through or approximates the data points. They can also be used in interactive design where a user, in moving the position of these points, can cause a curve or surface to deform. Figure 3.3 shows how a curve shape is influenced by moving the control points.

3.1.3 Properties shared by most useful bases

Most of the basis functions used in computer graphics share the following two important properties:

Convex hull property

If the basis functions identically sum to 1, that is

$$\sum_{i=0}^{k} b_i(u) = 1$$

and the basis functions are not negative over the interval they are defined, which is typically $u \in [0, 1]$, then any point on the curve is a weighted average of its control points. It can be shown that under these conditions no point on the curve lies outside the polygon formed by joining the control points together. The curve is said to lie in the convex hull of the control polygon (Figure 3.4). A similar condition exists for surfaces. If the bases used

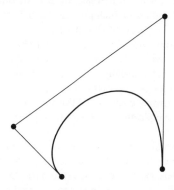

Figure 3.2   A Bézier curve, its control points and control polygon.

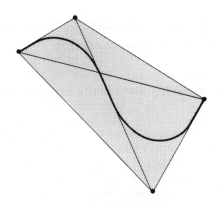

Figure 3.4 Convex hull property for a cubic spline. The curve is contained in the shaded area formed from the control points.

in the surface definition have the convex hull property, then the surface will lie inside the polyhedron formed by joining the control points.

This is an extremely useful property since it provides us with an inexpensive means for calculating the bound of a curve or surface in space. It is useful in robotics, for example, to check for collisions of paths in space. Two curves will not intersect if their convex hulls do not. It can also be used in scan line based renderers to calculate the maximum screen height for a patch. Also it can be used as a bounding volume when an object modelled from parametric surfaces is to be ray traced.

Affine invariance

Consider a curve in space evaluated at a series of points. Suppose we apply a transformation to this curve by transforming all the points in turn. If we can achieve the same result by transforming the control points and then regenerating the curve from the transformed control points – a computationally more efficient process – the curve is said to be affinely invariant. Let Φ be an affine map, of which all the typical transformations used to position or scale objects in computer graphics are examples, then the basis b_i is said to be affinely invariant, if

$$\Phi(Q(u)) = \sum_{i=0}^{k} (\Phi(p_i)) b_i(u)$$

Consider the following example that demonstrates the importance of affine invariance in this context. Suppose

we wish to scale a curve segment by scaling points on the curve. It is not clear how many points are needed to ensure smoothness when the curve is magnified. If the basis is affine invariant we can just scale the control points and this problem does not occur. Bases that are not affinely invariant are not particularly useful, thus all bases that we consider will be affinely invariant. Note here that perspective transformations are nonaffine, so we cannot map control points to screen space and compute the curve there.

3.1.4 Different bases in the parametric representation

Just as in R^3 more than one coordinate system can specify the same point in space, there exists more than one basis in $\mathscr{P}^{k+1}$ that can specify the same curve or surface. A given curve may have different representations in different bases and different bases may have certain properties that are useful in different contexts. In most cases we can move between different bases just as a coordinate transformation takes us from one coordinate system to another. (This procedure is described in more detail in Section 3.11.) The study of parametric curves and surfaces consists largely in examining and exploiting the properties of different bases. For example, we shall see that a parametric surface, from its modelling through to being rendered, may undergo several changes of basis, according to the different needs of the modelling and rendering process.

We will examine the properties of some of the most important bases used in computer graphics. It is quite easy to get lost in the wealth of theory of curves and surfaces, much of it indigestible, so we shall adopt a utilitarian approach paying particular attention to practical applications. Readers requiring more theoretical background are referred to the many texts on the subject; [FAUX79] and [FARI90] are particularly recommended.

3.2 Parametric surfaces: general considerations

A single surface element is the surface traced out as the parameters (u, v) take all possible values between 0 and

1. This element is colloquially known as a patch. Free-form surfaces are modelled by using nets of patches. For the same practical constraints that we enumerated for the case of curves, we use cubic basis functions and the patches are functions of two parametric variables. Complex surfaces are modelled using nets of individual patches analogous to the way in which complex curves are made up of individual curve segments. Bicubic parametric patches are defined over a rectangular domain in u, v-space and the boundary curves of the patch are themselves cubic polynominial curves. A point Q with coordinates (x, y, z) in cartesian space is represented by the parameters (u, v) in parametric space.

As with curves we can define all points on the surface using a summation

$$Q(u, v) = \sum_{i=0}^{3} \sum_{j=0}^{3} p_{ij} b_i(u) b_j(v)$$

where p_{ij} is a set of 16 control points:

$$\begin{array}{cccc} p_{00} & p_{01} & p_{02} & p_{03} \\ p_{10} & p_{11} & p_{12} & p_{13} \\ p_{20} & p_{21} & p_{22} & p_{23} \\ p_{30} & p_{31} & p_{32} & p_{33} \end{array}$$

Such surfaces are sometimes called cartesian or tensor product surfaces because they are formed from the product of the basis functions in u and v. Figure 3.5 shows a patch (actually a Bézier patch described in the next section) together with the net of 16 control points. The net of control points forms a polyhedron in cartesian space and the position of the points in this space controls the shape of the surface, just as the position of the control points associated with a curve controlled the shape of the curve. This effect is shown in Figure 3.6.

3.2.1 Patch representation versus polygon mesh representation

It is fair to say that when modelling, a polygon is a far simpler and more flexible building block than a patch. However, a parametric representation of an object, though in practice harder to set up, has certain significant theoretical advantages over a polygonal representation. This is why Pixar [REEV90] adopt the obvious, but none the less brave, strategy of using polygons to model only flat things. The *raison d'être* for patch representation is contained in the following two points:

1. *Conciseness* A parametric representation of a surface is 'exact' and 'economic' in that it is analytical. The concept of exactness needs further qualification: certain surfaces, for example conic sections, can be represented only by certain basis functions. That the representation is analytical means that mass properties (such as surface area) which may be required in CAD applications, can be extracted. With a polygonal object, exactness can only be approximated by increasing the polygonal resolution at the expense of increased processing and database costs. The parametric form is thus more economical on memory than its approximating polygonal counterpart. In general 16 control points making up a patch describe a far more sophisticated surface than, say, a polygon mesh made up of 16 vertices.

2. *Deformation and shape change* The need to change the shape of objects has long been a requirement for interactive CAD. More recently, soft object animation, that is, animating the deformation of surfaces and objects, has become increasingly popular in

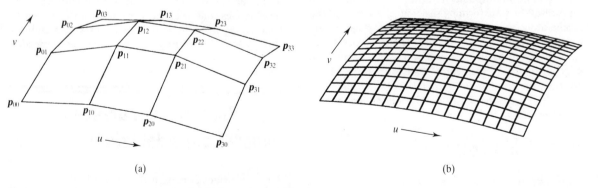

(a)   (b)

Figure 3.5   (a) A control polyhedron and (b) the resulting bicubic Bézier patch.

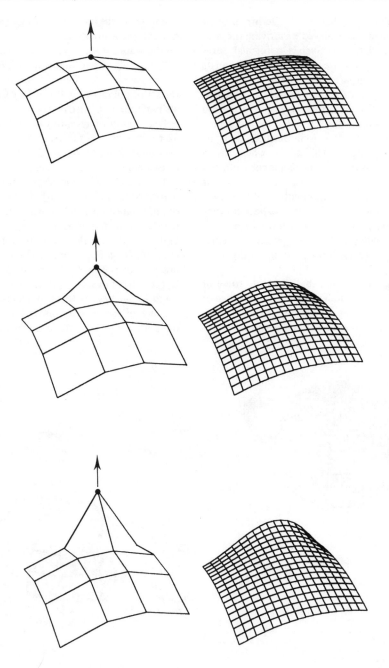

Figure 3.6   The effect of 'lifting' one of the control points of a Bézier patch.

computer graphics (see Chapter 17). Deformation of a parametric surface is achieved by moving the control points that define it. Such a deformed parametric surface is in no sense less well defined than its undeformed counterpart so the deformations will appear just as smooth and accurately represented when rendered. Compare this with a deformation acting on a polygonal object. Here the deformed object can easily be less well defined than its undeformed counterpart. This occurs when, say, a region of low curvature, and one that is consequently represented by a small number of polygons, is deformed to become a supposedly highly curved region. In order for this deformation to be accurately represented, the polygons would have to be subdivided – a difficult problem. For parametric representation, however, this 'drops out' naturally.

Two examples are now given that illustrate some of these issues. The first, the Utah teapot, is an instance of the kind of object that may be represented by bicubic parametric patches. In Figure 3.7(a) we show a wireframe where the lines are constant values of u and v. The object is made up of exactly 32 patches and a single patch on the teapot body is shown as a shaded region. Figure 3.7(b) is a wireframe made up of the boundary curves of the 32 patches and Figure 3.7(c) is an exploded view of the set of polyhedrons formed by the control points for all patches. It is instructive to consider an equivalent polygon mesh representation. In this example, whereas 32 patches gives a precise representation, at least 2048 polygons would be required to represent the surface to a reasonable degree of accuracy.

The second example shows how an object can be deformed without difficulty. It also reveals another area of importance – the relationship between the number of patches in the model and the degree of local control. In Figure 3.8(a) each face of a cube is represented by 4 patches and 16 patches respectively. Each deformation was obtained by pushing columns of control points inwards. In the second example (again consisting of a cube with 4 and 16 patches per face) control points in the centre of the face of the cube are moved inwards. The deformations 'look natural'. Attempting to do this with a polygon

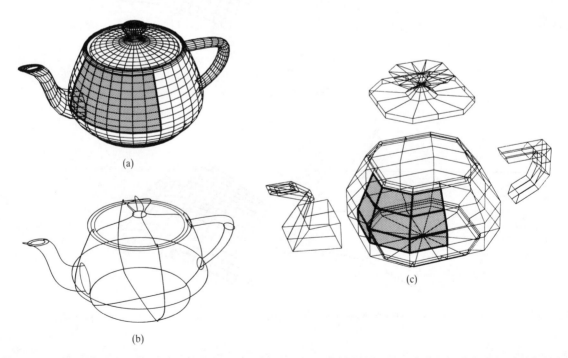

(a)

(b)

(c)

Figure 3.7   The Utah teapot. (a) Lines of constant u and v. The teapot is made up of 32 Bézier patches. A single patch is shown shaded. (b) A wireframe of the control points. The shaded region shows the control polyhedron for the shaded patch. (c) A wireframe of the patch edges.

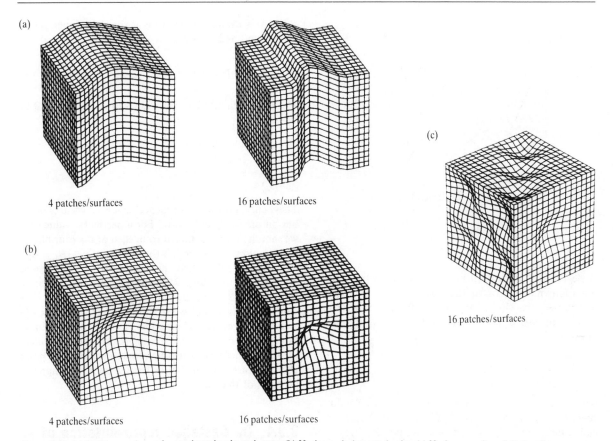

(a)

4 patches/surfaces   16 patches/surfaces

(c)

16 patches/surfaces

(b)

4 patches/surfaces   16 patches/surfaces

Figure 3.8 (a) Pushing a column of control patches in each case. (b) Moving a single control point. (c) Moving a number of single points.

mesh model of 4 and 16 polygons per face would have resulted in problems unless the polygons had been appropriately subdivided.

As already hinted, patch representation of surfaces does involve certain inherent difficulties connected with modelling and rendering. Consider a common problem: representing a real three-dimensional object given the availability of a three-dimensional digitizer (this problem of surface fitting will be dealt with in more detail later in Section 3.7). A polygonal representation is easily extracted from such data. The polygonal representation does not contain much more information than the data points themselves. Obtaining a patch representation is far more difficult. From a series of data points we have to extrapolate a complete analytical description of the entire surface. Much more information has to be constructed than actually exists. How do we interpolate through the data points? How many patches do we need? What basis shall we use for the patches?

As far as rendering is concerned, paradoxically an easy, if brute force, method of rendering is to convert the patches back into a polygon mesh representation (after an appropriate subdivision of each patch). We include a description of the problems of rendering patch surfaces along with a working example of a typical patch renderer later in Section 3.4.

3.3 Bézier curves and surfaces

The first representational form or basis we shall examine is due to Bézier [BEZI72] who was the originator of an early CAD system, UNISURF, used by Renault, the French car manufacturers. The theory of Bézier curves

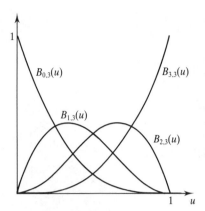

Figure 3.9   The Bézier basis functions.

is elegant and lends itself naturally to geometric interpretation, making it one of the most popular forms used.

A Bézier curve $Q(u)$ of degree n can be defined in terms of a set of control points p_i, $(i = 0, 1, 2, \ldots, n)$ and is given by

$$Q(u) = \sum_{i=0}^{n} p_i B_{i,n}(u)$$

where each term in the sum is the product of a blending function $B_{i,n}(u)$ and a control point p_i. The $B_{i,n}(u)$ are called Bernstein polynominals and are defined by:

$$B_{i,n}(u) = {}^nC_i u^i (1 - u)^{n-i}$$

where:

${}^nC_i$ is the binomial coefficient ${}^nC_i = \dfrac{n!}{i!(n-i)!}$

Consider, for example, a curve of degree 3. Figure 3.2 shows such a curve and the associated control points p_0, p_1, p_2 and p_3. We can see straight away that the curve end points are coincident with p_0 and p_3 and that the control points p_1 and p_2 are not coincident with the curve. Moving the control points around influences the shape of the curve and Figure 3.3 shows the effect of moving p_1 on the curve shown in Figure 3.2. We can see from this that it would be possible to set up an interactive program that allowed the user to move the control points, and deform the curve in a way that is intuitive, under the control of a locator device. This practical facility afforded by the control point position is the foundation of its importance and practical utility. The shape of the curve is determined entirely from the position of the control points.

We now examine the nature of the basis functions in more detail and consider the cubic curve:

$$Q(u) = \sum_{i=0}^{3} p_i B_{i,3}(u)$$

The basis functions $B_{i,3}(u)$ are shown in Figure 3.9. These are:

$$B_{0,3}(u) = (1 - u)^3$$
$$B_{1,3}(u) = 3u(1 - u)^2$$
$$B_{2,3}(u) = 3u^2(1 - u)$$
$$B_{3,3}(u) = u^3$$

These curves show the 'influence' that each control point has on the final curve form. For a particular value of u we sum the values obtained from each of the four blending functions. p_0 is most influential at $u = 0$ ($B_{1,3}$, $B_{2,3}$ and $B_{3,3}$ are all zero at this point). As u is increased 'towards' p_1, $B_{0,3}$ and $B_{1,3}$ mainly determine the curve shape, with $B_{2,3}$ and $B_{3,3}$ exerting some influence. The control points p_1 and p_2 have most effect when $u = 1/3$ and 2/3 respectively. The manner in which the basis functions affect the curve shape is the reason they are called blending functions. Note that moving any control point will influence, to a greater or lesser extent, the shape of all parts of the curve.

3.3.1 De Casteljau representation of Bézier curves

The above description of Bézier curves is based on Bernstein polynomials. De Casteljau developed an alternative representation which is geometrically more revealing and useful in computer graphics as we shall see. The de Casteljau algorithm generates points on the curve by repeated linear interpolation. Let p_0, $p_1, \ldots, p_n$ be the n control points of a Bézier curve of degree n. We define:

$$p_i^r(u) = (1 - u)p_i^{r-1}(u) + u\,p_{i+1}^{r-1}(u)$$

where:

$r = 1, \ldots, n$
$i = 0, \ldots, n - r$
$p_i^0(u) = p_i$

then a point on the curve with parameter value u is given by $p_0^n(u)$. That is:

$$Q(u) = p_0^n(u)$$

Unravelling the recursive equation by substituting for all

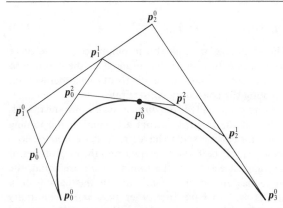

Figure 3.10 The de Casteljau algorithm – recursive linear interpolation to produce the point p_0^3 on the Bézier curve.

levels of recursion will take us back to the Bernstein representation for the Bézier curve.

Figure 3.10 shows how this algorithm works for the cubic case. Starting with the control polygon p_i^0 ($i = 0, 1, 2, 3$) the edges are subdivided in the ratio u ($u = 0.6$) as given above (the superscript corresponds to the level of recursion, starting at 0). These points, p_i^1, are then connected in order and the resultant edges subdivided to give the points p_i^2 ($i = 0, 1$). The recursion stops when only one edge remains, the subdivision of this edge producing the point on the curve $p_0^3(u)$.

Since linear interpolation is an affine map, the de Casteljau algorithm, which is just a sequence of linear interpolations and hence a sequence of affine maps, tells us that Bézier curves must be affinely invariant.

3.3.2 Bézier curves: matrix formulation

An alternative convention for specifying a Bézier curve is the matrix convention:

$$Q(u) = UM_{\mathrm{B}}P_c = \begin{bmatrix} u^3 & u^2 & u & 1 \end{bmatrix} \begin{bmatrix} -1 & 3 & -3 & 1 \\ 3 & -6 & 3 & 0 \\ -3 & 3 & 0 & 0 \\ 1 & 0 & 0 & 0 \end{bmatrix} \begin{bmatrix} p_0 \\ p_1 \\ p_2 \\ p_3 \end{bmatrix}$$

Premultiplying the power vector with the basis matrix gives us the basis functions

$$\left(B_0, B_1, B_2, B_3 \right) = UM_{\mathrm{B}}$$

A matrix formulation is useful when considering hardware implementation and different bases. Each basis or representation has a different characteristic matrix. The matrix formulation is also useful when it is desired to convert between representations. (See Section 3.11 for a description of basis conversion matrices.)

3.3.3 Bézier curves: differentiation

The first derivative of a Bézier curve $Q(u)$ of degree n is a Bézier curve of degree $n - 1$. We state without proof that

$$\frac{\mathrm{d}Q(0)}{\mathrm{d}u} = n\left(p_1 - p_0 \right)$$

$$\frac{\mathrm{d}Q(1)}{\mathrm{d}u} = n\left(p_n - p_{n-1} \right)$$

For example, for a cubic we have:

$$\dot{Q}(0) = 3\left(p_1 - p_0 \right)$$
$$\dot{Q}(1) = 3\left(p_3 - p_2 \right)$$

These derivatives are in fact the tangent vectors to the curves at the end points (Figure 3.11) and it can be seen from this that altering the position of the control points is, in effect, altering the strength (or magnitude) and orientation of the tangent vectors.

We can see then that the Bézier form can be viewed as a representation that uses the end points and two other points to indirectly specify the strength and orientation of the tangent vectors to the curve. This is generally

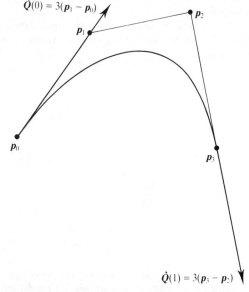

Figure 3.11 The relationship between Bézier control points and tangent vectors.

more convenient than forms that require the direct specification of tangent vectors (for example, the Hermite basis).

3.3.4 Bézier curves: degree elevation

This property implies that a curve of degree $n + 1$ can be obtained from a curve of degree n. The context in which this can be useful is when data constraints lead to Bézier curves of different degree. All curves can be made the same degree n by elevating any curves of degree less than n. We state without proof that given the set $p_0, p_1, \ldots, p_{n-1}, p_n$ of $n + 1$ control points of an nth degree curve, the corresponding $n + 2$ control points of an identical curve of degree $n + 1$ are given by:

$$p_0, \frac{p_0 + np_1}{n+1}, \frac{2p_1 + (n-1)p_2}{n+1}, \ldots, \frac{np_{n-1} + p_n}{n+1}, p_n$$

3.3.5 Bézier curves: joining

Bézier curve segments can be joined together to make a composite curve. The difficulty of connecting individual curve segments together at the end points depends on the continuity constraints to be applied. Zero-order continuity is achieved across two segments by ensuring that the end control points are coincident (Figure 3.12). If the control points are q_i and r_i then $q_3 = r_0$. First-order continuity is achieved by imposing the additional constraint that the edges of the control polygons are to be collinear, that is (Figure 3.12):

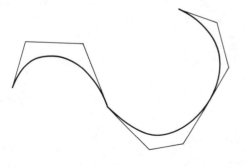

Figure 3.12 Three Bézier curve segments and their convex hulls. The second segment is zero-order continuous with the first segment and first-order continuous with the third.

$$(q_3 - q_2) = k(r_1 - r_0) \tag{3.2}$$

The advantage of being able to build a composite curve from segments is somewhat negated by the inability to move control points independently of each other without violating the continuity constraints.

More specifically if the directions, but not the magnitudes, of the tangent vectors are equal at the joining point, the curve is said to have first-order *geometric* continuity G^1. If both the directions and the magnitudes of the tangent vectors at the joining point are equal, the curve has first-degree continuity in the parameter u and is said to have first-order *parametric* continuity C^1. Thus if a curve is C^1 continuous it is also G^1 continuous.

3.3.6 The Bézier patch

The Bézier patch is defined in matrix notation by:

$$Q(u, v) = U\, M_B P_c M_B^T V$$

where:

M_B is the Bézier basis matrix
U and V are the row and column vectors for the geometry vectors for the parameters u and v
P_c is the matrix of 16 control points

and alternatively by:

$$Q(u, v) = \sum_{i=0}^{k} \sum_{j=0}^{k} p_{ij} B_{i,n}(u) B_{j,n}(v)$$

where:

$B_{i,n}(u)$ and $B_{j,n}(v)$ are Bézier basis or blending functions identical to the Bézier basis or blending functions used to formulate Bézier curves

A cubic Bézier patch and its control point polyhedron is shown in Figure 3.5. We can note that the boundary curves of a Bézier patch are themselves Bézier curves. This fact is important because it is the basis for setting up a surface made up of a set of joined patches from a mesh of cubic curves. For example the curve from p_{00} to p_{03} is given by:

$$Q(0, v) = \sum_{j=0}^{3} p_{0j} B_j(v)$$

The Bézier patch has analogous properties to and advantages of the Bézier curve.

3.3.7 Bézier patches: differentiation

It is instructive to examine the relationship between the control points and derivative vectors at the corner of a patch. For example, if we consider the point p_{00} it can be shown that the three derivative vectors are given by:

$$\frac{\partial Q(0,0)}{\partial u} = Q_u(0,0) = 3(p_{10} - p_{00})$$

similarly:

$$Q_v(0,0) = 3(p_{01} - p_{00})$$

These derivative vectors are the tangent vectors at p_{00} along the two boundary curves. Thus moving p_{10} or p_{01} will affect the shape of a boundary curve and will alter the shape of the patch.

The other derivative vector is

$$Q_{uv}(0,0) = 9(p_{00} - p_{01} - p_{10} + p_{11})$$

This is a cross derivative, sometimes called a twist vector, that specifies the rate of change of the tangent vectors with respect to u and v. The twist vector is a vector that is normal to the plane containing the two tangent vectors. A geometric interpretation of the twist vector is given later in Section 3.7.2.

3.3.8 Bézier patches: joining

Joining patches together to form a more complex surface than can be represented by a single patch is a large subject and no description of the properties of a given basis is complete without considering it. It is a topic that is inex-

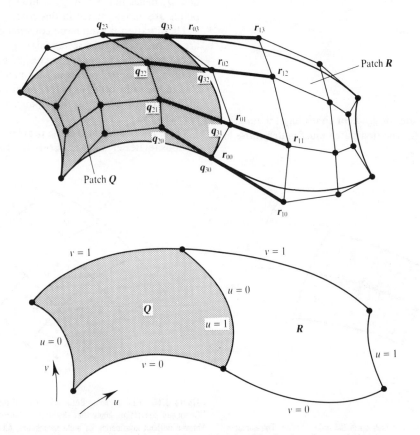

Figure 3.13 Control polyhedra of two adjacent patches under the constraint of positional and gradient continuity.

tricably connected with modelling issues and CAD methodologies such as cross-sectional design and can in itself form the topic of a textbook. In this section we will restrict ourselves to the basic points. For CAD methodologies the interested reader is referred to [CHIY88] and [FAUX79].

There are two common ways in which Bézier patches can be joined. They differ in the severity of the constraints applied. The first method is an extension of the curve segment joining approach given in Section 3.3.5. A geometric interpretation is straightforward and is given in Figure 3.13. Consider two patches Q and R sharing a common edge. For positional or zero order continuity

$$Q(1, v) = R(0, v) \qquad 0 \leqslant v \leqslant 1$$

This condition implies that the two patches require a common boundary edge characteristic polygon and if the control points are q_{ij} and r_{ij} respectively then:

$q_{33} = r_{03}$
$q_{32} = r_{02}$
$q_{31} = r_{01}$
$q_{30} = r_{00}$

or

$q_{3i} = r_{0i} \qquad i = 0, \ldots, 3$

To satisfy first-order or gradient continuity the tangent vectors at $u = 1$ for the first patch must match those at

$u = 0$ for the second patch for all v. This implies that each of the four pairs of polyhedron edges that straddle the boundary must be collinear. That is:

$$q_{3i} - q_{2i} = k(r_{1i} - r_{0i}) \qquad i = 0, \ldots, 3$$

where:

k is a positive constant – the cross boundary tangent magnitude ratio

Faux and Pratt [FAUX79] point out that this constraint is too severe in practical CAD applications. Consider, for example, constructing a composite surface by building up from individual patches. Figure 3.14 shows four patches. Say that Q_1 was the first patch and Q_2, Q_3 and Q_4 were built on in the order implied by the subscripts. We are completely free to choose any 16 control points for Q_1. Q_2 has 8 of its control points constrained by Q_1 leaving 8 free to be chosen. Similarly only 8 control points are free in Q_3. The joining constraints of both Q_3 and Q_2 mean that when Q_4 is inserted only 4 control points are undetermined in this patch.

The situation is even more constrained if the patches are constructed from a rectangular net of Bézier curves. These form the boundary curves of each patch, constraining 12 control points in each patch. Inserting patches in the same order as before means that the number of free control points in the 4 patches is 4, 2, 2 and 1 respectively.

These constraints also cause problems in deforming a composite Bézier surface. Consider Figure 3.15. Any

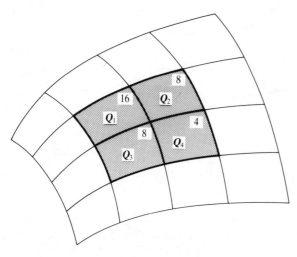

Figure 3.14 Four patches built up in the order implied. The numbers indicate the 'free' control points.

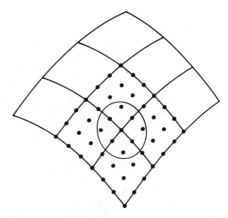

Figure 3.15 Four adjoining Bézier patches and their control points. Continuity constraints imply that the central control point cannot be moved without considering its eight neighbours. All nine points can be moved together and continuity maintained.

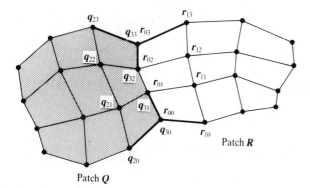

Figure 3.16 A less severe joining regime. The bold edges are coplanar.

corner point cannot be moved without controlling 8 adjacent points to maintain continuity. We could move all 9 points together as a single unit but this tends to produce a step-like deformation.

The severity of the constraint implied by Equation (3.2) can be relaxed by discarding the collinearity condition on the edges of the control point polyhedron. The justification for this is given in [FAUX79]. A geometric interpretation of this new constraint is shown in Figure 3.16. Positional continuity is maintained and the collinearity condition across the boundary is discarded. A new interpretation of gradient continuity is introduced. This is satisfied by making the tangent vectors meeting at the common patch corner coplanar. We state the relevant constraint relations without proof. These are:

$$r_{10} - r_{00} = k\left(q_{30} - q_{20}\right) + s_0\left(q_{31} - q_{30}\right)$$
$$r_{11} - r_{01} = k\left(q_{31} - q_{21}\right) + \tfrac{1}{3}s_0\left(2q_{32} - q_{31} - q_{30}\right)$$
$$\qquad + \tfrac{1}{3}s_1\left(q_{31} - q_{30}\right)$$
$$r_{12} - r_{02} = k\left(q_{32} - q_{22}\right) + \tfrac{1}{3}s_0\left(2q_{33} - q_{32} - q_{31}\right)$$
$$\qquad + \tfrac{2}{3}s_1\left(q_{32} - q_{31}\right)$$
$$r_{13} - r_{03} = k\left(q_{33} - q_{23}\right) + \left(s_0 + s_1\right)\left(q_{33} - q_{32}\right)$$

Note that if $s_0 = s_1 = 0$ then these constraints reduce to Equation (3.2).

3.4 Rendering bicubic patches

There are two major approaches to rendering patches. The most popular, and the one to which we shall devote most attention, is patch splitting. Here patches are preprocessed and approximated by planar polygons before being input to a standard rendering system. It may seem that this approach is somewhat paradoxical: what is the point of modelling with bicubic patches if their major *raison d'être* - their accuracy - is discarded in the rendering phase? The answer to this is that the subdivision is carefully controlled and can be stopped at a level that will, in conjunction with an interpolative shading strategy, ensure a high-quality rendered image.

The second approach is one that has been implemented in hardware [SHAN87], and this involves rendering *directly* from the analytical description of the patch by using forward differences - no approximation is attempted. Earlier direct rendering techniques (for example [LANE80]) used Newton iteration to compute the intersection of the patch with the scan line plane, but these techniques have not generally been taken up by the computer graphics community.

3.4.1 Recursive subdivision of Bézier curves

Let us return to the de Casteljau algorithm and Figure 3.10 showing how it works in the case of a cubic. It turns out that the de Casteljau algorithm not only computes the point $p_0^n(u)$ but it also provides the control vertices of the Bézier curve corresponding to the interval $[0, u]$. By omitting elements in Figure 3.10 we have Figure 3.17 and the reader can see that the control points of the smaller interval are given by

$$p_0^i \qquad i = 0, \ldots, n$$

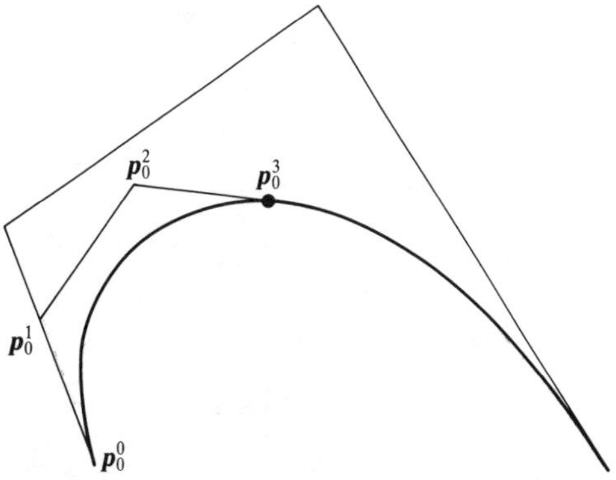

Figure 3.17 The de Casteljau algorithm provides the control points p_0^i for the segment over $[0, u]$.

Similarly, it can be verified that the control points for the segment of the curve over the interval $[u, 1]$ are given by

$$p_i^{n-i} \qquad i = 0, \ldots, n$$

So a Bézier curve can be subdivided anywhere along its length into two smaller curves, each with their respective distinct control polygons.

From Figure 3.17 the reader will note that the convex hull of the smaller section lies closer to the curve than the original convex hull. Repeated subdivision will produce a closer approximation to the curve and this is the principle of the subdivision algorithm. In order to render a curve, rather than evaluate points along a curve, it is cheaper to subdivide recursively until the convex hulls are a sufficiently good approximation to the curve. These are then drawn as straight-line segments. The termination criterion can be based on a linearity test applied to the convex hull. The test determines how far the interior control points deviate from the line connecting the two outer control points (Figure 3.18). Since in the Bézier represen-

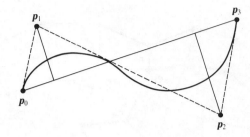

Figure 3.18   Linearity test on the convex hull of a Bézier curve.

tation the end points of the curve segments are the first and last control points, the termination criterion is particularly straightforward. This is a good reason for preferring Bézier to other bases when subdividing a curve recursively. Alternative subdivision strategies acting on other bases may require a more complicated flatness test as the end points may have to be calculated.

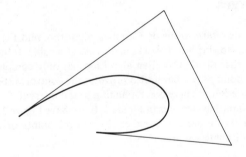

(a)

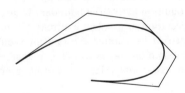

(b)

(c)

Figure 3.19   Subdivision of a Bézier curve showing how the convex hulls approach the curve as the subdivision increases (a) one segment, (b) two segments and (c) four segments.

Returning to the Bernstein representation, Lane [LANE80] derives the subdivision formulae about the midpoint ($u = 0.5$). Let the control polygon of the original be p_i and the control points of the smaller sections q_i and r_i. The point $q_3 = r_0$ is the end point of the first curve and the start of the second. The formula is

$$
\left.
\begin{aligned}
q_0 &= p_0 & r_0 &= q_3 \\
q_1 &= \frac{p_0 + p_1}{2} & r_1 &= \frac{p_1 + p_2}{4} + \frac{r_2}{2} \\
q_2 &= \frac{q_1}{2} + \frac{p_1 + p_2}{4} & r_2 &= \frac{p_2 + p_3}{2} \\
q_3 &= \frac{q_2 + r_1}{2} & r_3 &= p_3
\end{aligned}
\right\} \quad (3.3)
$$

Subdivision about the midpoint is to be preferred, since as the formula shows, it is particularly efficient involving only division by 2 and addition. Figure 3.19 shows the curve at three successive levels of subdivision and verifies that each successive subdivision produces a better approximation than the previous one.

3.4.2 Recursive subdivision of Bézier surfaces – patch splitting

Let us now consider the subdivision process applied to Bézier surfaces. Extending the formula of Equations (3.3) to the two orthogonal directions u and v enables us successively to subdivide the control polygons of a Bézier surface, producing a series of polygons that represent the Bézier surface to a given tolerance in curvature. We shall call this process 'patch splitting'. This is extremely useful since these polygons can be passed to a conventional polygonal renderer and standard polygon rendering techniques can be used to render surfaces made up of nets of patches. Moreover, the fact that any tensor product surface can be converted to the Bézier form makes it the ideal candidate base on which to build a patch splitter. The task of rendering a patch of any basis would then involve a conversion of basis to the Bézier form, and then using a Bézier patch splitter. We now describe the Bézier patch splitter that was used to render all the parametrically modelled surfaces included as illustrations in this text.

The basic splitting process is a straightforward extension of the formula given in the previous section. This is because of the orthogonality of the parametric directions u and v. That is, we can split the patch in one parameter

without considering the other. In order to split in the u direction, say, we consider a patch – an array of 16 control points p_{ij} – to be made up of four curves, the control points of which correspond to the rows of the array. So the jth curve will have control points p_{ij} ($i = 0$, ..., 3). The splitting is then applied to these curves separately yielding two sets of four curves q_{ij} and r_{ij}. Because of the orthogonality referred to above, these turn out to be the two subpatches of the original patch.

The mathematical reasoning is as follows:

$$
Q(u, v) = \sum_{i=0}^{3} \sum_{j=0}^{3} p_{ij} B_i(u) B_j(v)
$$

which may be rewritten as:

$$
Q(u, v) = \sum_{j=0}^{3} B_j(v) \left\{ \sum_{i=0}^{3} p_{ij} B_i(u) \right\}
$$

We can see that for each value of j the summation within the curly brackets is a Bézier cubic in u. We can split this into two halves and multiply through by the term outside the curly brackets which will give us two separate patches that describe the same surface as the original patch.

The code to produce the subdivision is given in Listing 3.1. *hull_split_u( )* and *hull_split_v( )* split the patch in the u and v directions respectively. The reader will note that in form it is identical to the formula given in the previous section.

How do we decide when to terminate the subdivision? A cheap strategy is simply to subdivide all patches down to the same level. Figure 3.20 shows the Utah teapot rendered by uniformly subdividing each patch into 4, 16, 64 and 256 subpatches (generating 128, 512, 2048 and 8192 polygons). This approach is generally uneconomic, however, as it will apply the same degree of subdivision to large flat areas as it does to highly curved areas. Also no account is taken of the screen space projection of the patch. There is no point in further subdivision when a patch projects onto less than a pixel. A better method is to subdivide until a flatness criterion is achieved for each subdivision product.

A given patch is subdivided down until the convex hull is deemed to be sufficiently planar and the edges sufficiently linear. Satisfaction of these two conditions enables interior control points and the middle control points along the edges to be disregarded. The patch can then be turned into two triangles by taking the four corners of the patch as triangle vertices as shown in Figure 3.21.

Listing 3.1   hull_split.c

```
void hull_split_u(P,Q,R)
float  P[4][4][3],Q[4][4][3],R[4][4][3];
{
         int  i,iv;

         for (iv=0;iv<4;iv++) {
                 for  (i=0;i<3;i++) {

                         Q[0][iv][i]  =  P[0][iv][i];
                         Q[1][iv][i]  =  (P[0][iv][i]+P[1][iv][i])/2.;
                         Q[2][iv][i]  =  Q[1][iv][i]/2.+(P[1][iv][i]+P[2][iv][i])/4.;

                         R[3][iv][i]  =  P[3][iv][i];
                         R[2][iv][i]  =  (P[2][iv][i]+P[3][iv][i])/2.;
                         R[1][iv][i]  =  R[2][iv][i]/2.+(P[1][iv][i]+P[2][iv][i])/4.;

                         Q[3][iv][i]  =  (Q[2][iv][i]+R[1][iv][i])/2.;
                         R[0][iv][i]  =  Q[3][iv][i];

                 }
         }

}
void hull_split_v(P,Q,R)
float  P[4][4][3],Q[4][4][3],R[4][4][3];
{
         int  i,iu;

         for (iu=0;iu<4;iu++) {
                 for  (i=0;i<3;i++) {

                         Q[iu][0][i]  =  P[iu][0][i];
                         Q[iu][1][i]  =  (P[iu][0][i]+P[iu][1][i])/2.;
                         Q[iu][2][i]  =  Q[iu][1][i]/2.+(P[iu][1][i]+P[iu][2][i])/4.;

                         R[iu][3][i]  =  P[iu][3][i];
                         R[iu][2][i]  =  (P[iu][2][i]+P[iu][3][i])/2.;
                         R[iu][1][i]  =  R[iu][2][i]/2.+(P[iu][1][i]+P[iu][2][i])/4.;

                         Q[iu][3][i]  =  (Q[iu][2][i]+R[iu][1][i])/2.;
                         R[iu][0][i]  =  Q[iu][3][i];

                 }
         }

}
```

1 A complex polygonal model rendered using the Cook and Torrance model. The materials simulated are bronze and copper. (See Section 13.6 for a full description on the way in which the model was produced.)

2 The Utah teapot and shading options. Note the visibility of piecewise linearities along silhouette edges since this representation contains only 512 polygons. (*top left*) Wireframe plus vertex normals. (*top right*) Constant shaded polygons. (*bottom left*) Gouraud shading. (*bottom right*) Phong shading.

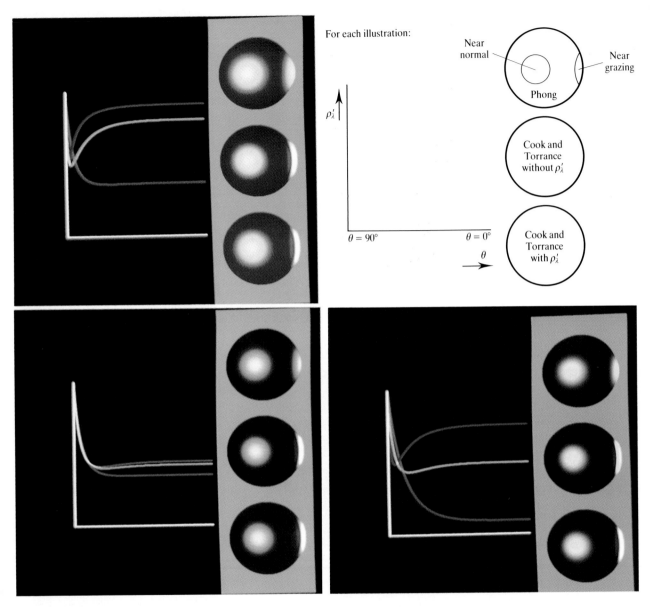

For each illustration:

Near normal

Near grazing

Phong

Cook and Torrance without ρ'_λ

Cook and Torrance with ρ'_λ

ρ'_λ

$\theta = 90°$ $\theta = 0°$

θ

3 The Cook and Torrance model used to simulate different materials. Each RGB profile shows the dependence of ρ'_λ on θ for the material: (*top left*) gold; (*bottom left*) silver; (*bottom right*) copper.

4 The mip-maps used to produce Figure 6.3.

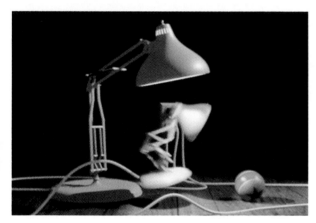

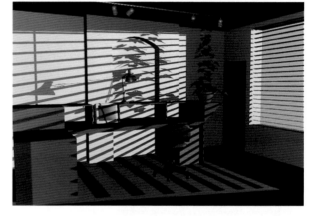

5 A frame from *Luxo Jr.* produced by John Lasseter, Bill Reeves, Eben Ostby and Sam Leffler; © 1986 Pixar; Luxo™ is a trademark of Jak Jacobson Industries. The film was animated by a keyframe animation system with procedural animation assistance, and frames were rendered with multiple light sources and procedural texturing techniques. This frame exhibits motion blur as described in Section 10.4.4.

6 A scene produced using the shadow volume technique. The scene exhibits the characteristic inadequacies of this technique, including severe aliasing problems in the shadows. These are discussed fully in the text.

7 A scene that is more suitable for the application of the shadow volume technique. Compare this with the 'Venetian blind' scene. Both scenes were produced by the same program.

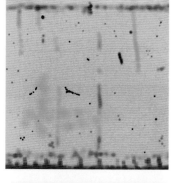

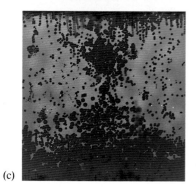

8 Practical texture mapping: texture mapping onto a standard simple object which is then distorted to make the desired object.

Texture maps.
(a) banana; (b) apple;
(c) pear

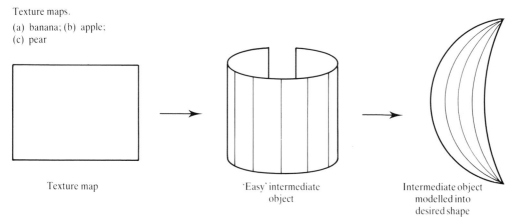

| Texture map | 'Easy' intermediate object | Intermediate object modelled into desired shape |

9 Practical texture mapping: two examples of the 'reverse projection' technique described in the text. Objects that have a plane of symmetry – the frog and duck – were texture mapped using this technique.

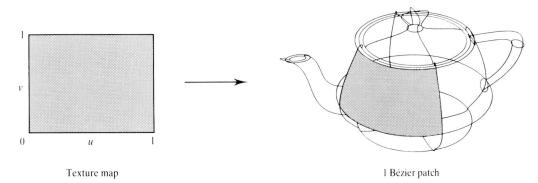

Texture map   1 Bézier patch

10 (*Left*) Texture map; (*right*) One Bézier patch; (*below*) Recursive teapot.

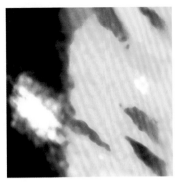

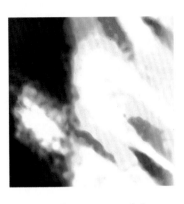

11   Chrome mapping: using two maps for different parts of the object.

12   Chrome mapping: part of a chrome-mapped animation sequence. The edges of the letter are bevelled to avoid the ubiquitous visual discontinuities that usually result when chrome-mapped block letters are animated. (*right*) The chrome map used for the sequence.

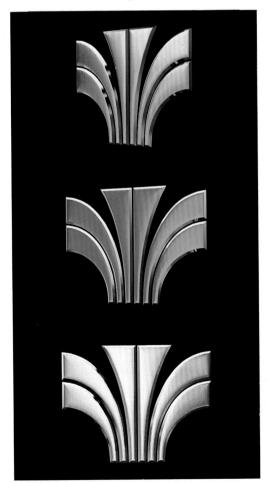

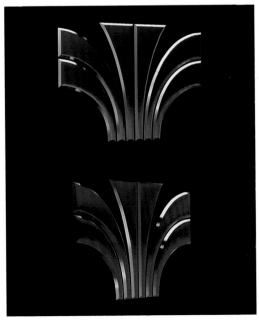

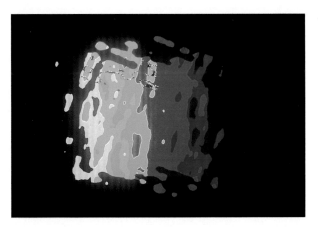 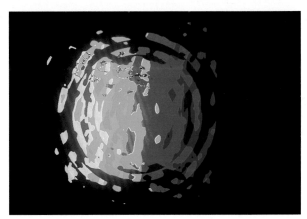

13 Refraction mapping: two examples of refraction mapping. One surface is modelled using long-crested waves; the other uses circular waves. (*below right*) The colour bar map used in the mapping.

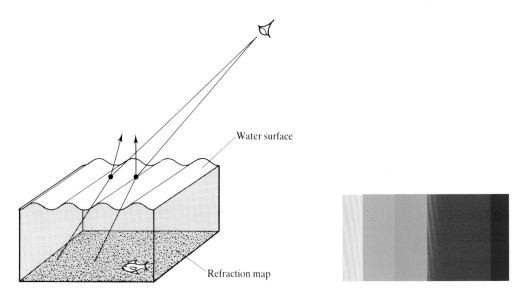

Water surface

Refraction map

14 Refraction mapping: two examples of refraction mapping used with a transparent object. These examples are less convincing than the water example. Ray tracing needs to progress to a deeper level in this scene.

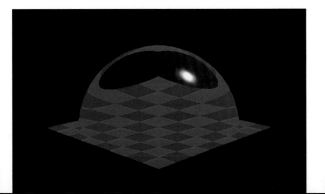 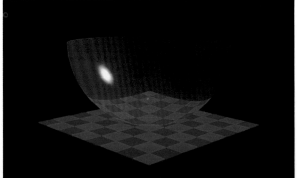

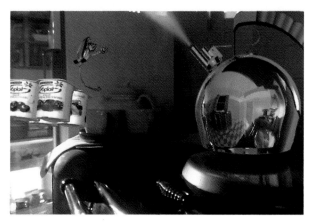

15 Environment mapping: an environment map created by frame grabbing six photographs. Notice the discontinuities that occur across the seams in the map.

16 Environment mapping: a copper kettle rendered using the photographed environment map.

17 Environment mapping: two synthetic or rendered environment maps of the same scene. The illustrations show the effect of rendering maps from different points in the scene.

18 Environment mapping: two views of a scene containing an environment-mapped teapot. Note that the reflection of the teapot in the table top is also environment mapped. This hack is explained in Section 6.3.3.

19 Environment mapping: a scene that resulted in memory thrashing due to severe random access among the six maps. The problem arises as the object that is being mapped becomes small in screen space.

20 Bump mapping: an example of a bump-mapped object and the corresponding map.

21 Fractal terrains generated using the subdivision method, showing the effect of varying the viewing distance.

22 Using fog to diminish the creasing problem described in the text.

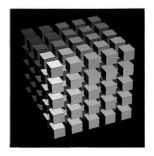

23 Three-dimensional mapping: an example of a simple mapping. The colour of each cube is obtained from an identity mapping into the RGB cube.

24 Three-dimensional mapping: the procedural definition for the wood grain was set up by using concentric cylinders perturbed by a harmonic function.

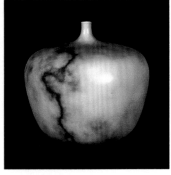

25 Turbulence: using the three-dimensional noise function to simulate turbulence – in this case a convincing imitation of marble.

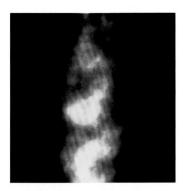

26 Turbulence: an example of simulated turbulence used to modulate transparency. A full description of the cloud effect is given in Section 7.2.2.

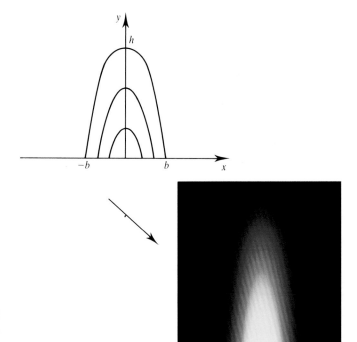

Turbulence function

27 Modelling and simulating flame using a turbulence function. (*above*) unturbulated flame; (*right*) turbulated flame.

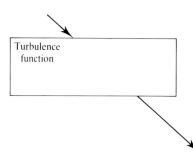

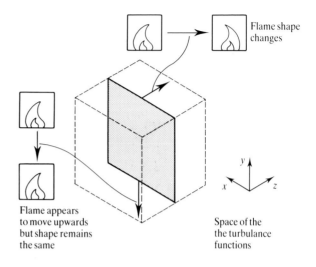

Flame shape changes

Flame appears to move upwards but shape remains the same

Space of the the turbulance functions

28 Turbulence: animating a flame. The flame is rendered using simulated turbulence in two space. The *z*-axis of the turbulence function becomes time and an animation sequence is easily achieved by moving the flame plane through the space of the turbulence function.

29 Recursive generation of tree structures: examples of the technique described in Section 7.4.

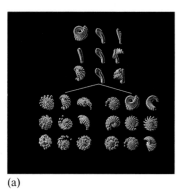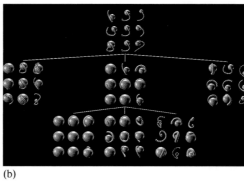

(a)   (b)   (c)

30 Evolutionary procedural modelling: results obtained from the Mutator program (courtesy of S. Todd and W. Latham, IBM UK).

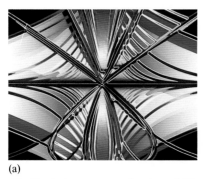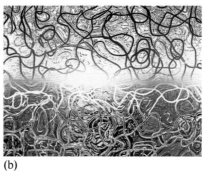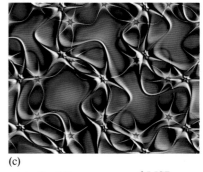

(a)   (b)   (c)

31 Evolutionary procedural modelling: images produced from geneotypes that consist of arbitrary groups of LISP expressions (courtesy of K. Sims, Thinking Machines Corporation).

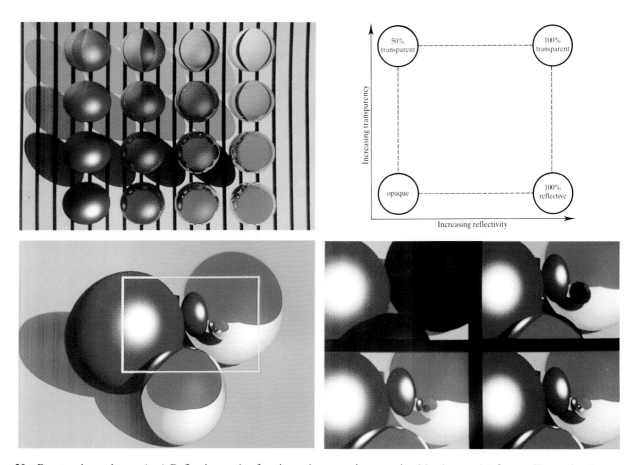

32 Ray tracing spheres. (*top*) Reflective and refractive spheres against a striped background (after an illustration by Apollo Computers). (*bottom left*) Ray tracing to a depth of 6. (*bottom right*) Part of the above image traced to a depth of 1, 2, 3 and 4.

33 An example of Arvo's method of backwards ray tracing (courtesy of J. Arvo, Cornell University).

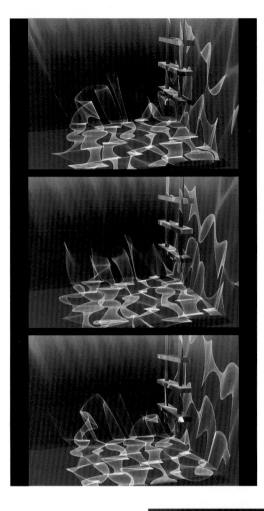

34 Caustics formed by refraction: three frames from the swimming pool animation as seen from under the surface. Note that the sides of the pool approximately tangential to the diacaustic are more uniformly lit than the sides approximately normal to the diacaustic.

35 Caustics formed by refraction: three frames from the swimming pool animation as seen from above the surface. The fourth frame is a view with the water removed. Notice the curved edge of the shadow.

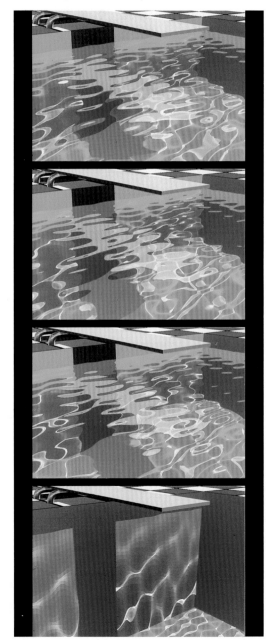

36 Caustics formed by refraction: the 'shadow sausage' effect. Caustics generated by refraction through the meniscus wash out the shadow of the pencil on the base of the container. The front of the container is removed.

37 Caustics formed by reflection: an example of caustics formed by light reflection from a perturbed water surface.

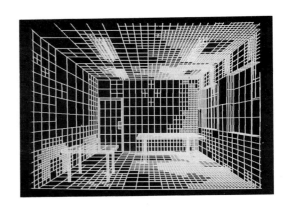

38 Radiosity method for diffuse interaction. The result from the window lit scene using subdivision of the patches to produce the elements shown in Figure 11.4.

39 Radiosity method for diffuse interaction. The same scene lit with strip lights.

40 Radiosity method for diffuse interaction. The scene is as before except that the ceiling is coloured bright red and the reflectivities are turned up. The ceiling colour transports to all other surfaces.

41 Hemicube aliasing. The scene is as before but the intensity of the strip light is turned up. Aliasing artefacts parallel to the long axis of the light are clearly visible.

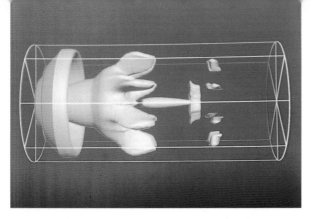

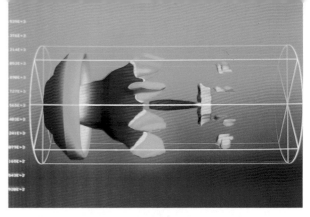

42 Marching cubes and CFD data: a Navier–Stokes CFD simulation of a reverse flow pipe combuster. Flow occurs from left to right and from right to left. The interface between these flows defines a zero velocity isosurface. The marching cubes algorithm is used to extract this surface which is then conventionally rendered.

43 Marching cubes and CFD data: a texture-mapped zero velocity surface. A pseudocolour scale that represents field temperature is combined with the colour used for shading in the previous illustration.

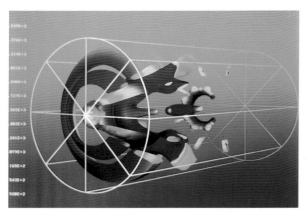

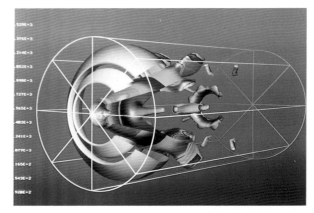

44 Marching cubes and CFD data: a cutaway view of the previous illustration.

45 Marching cubes and CFD data: using a discontinuous pseudocolour scale for the texture mapping. Note the false contouring on the lobes near the fuel jets indicating high temperature gradients in these areas.

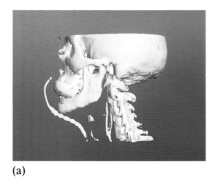

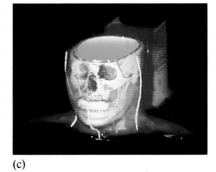

(a)   (b)   (c)

46 Skull (a): the marching cubes algorithm applied to CT data. The isosurface is defined by the X-ray absorption coefficient for bone. Skulls (b) and (c): the same data as (a) but this time rendered using a volume rendering algorithm. The first illustration is a direct comparison with the marching cubes illustration – only bone is rendered. The second shows skin and soft tissue.

Height   Sea

Forest   Concrete

47 Using texture trees. The maps 'height', 'sea', 'forest' and 'concrete' are used in the texture trees for the new Hong Kong airport.

Sand

Shallow water

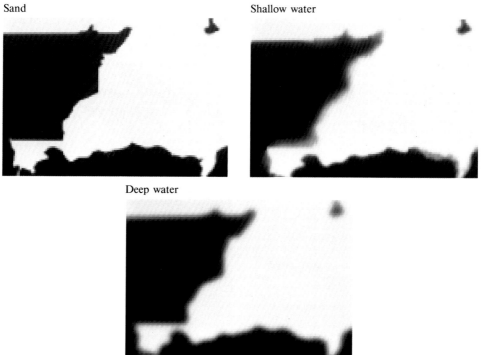

Deep water

47 *continued.* The maps 'sand', 'shallow water' and 'deep water' are used in the texture trees. They are the same map showing increasing blur.

Maps used in the texture trees
for Hong Kong airport

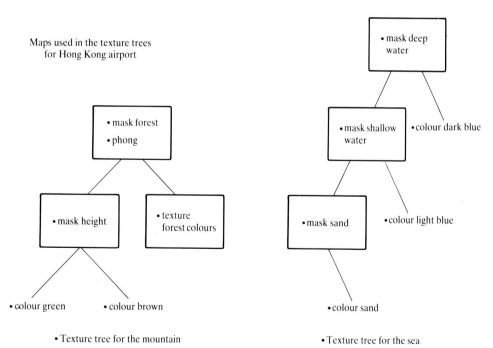

• mask deep
  water

• mask forest
• phong

• mask shallow
  water

• colour dark blue

• mask height

• texture
  forest colours

• mask sand

• colour light blue

• colour green

• colour brown

• colour sand

• Texture tree for the mountain

• Texture tree for the sea

47 *continued.*

48 Using a texture tree for a cola bottle.

Label

Drops

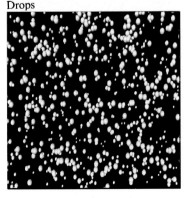

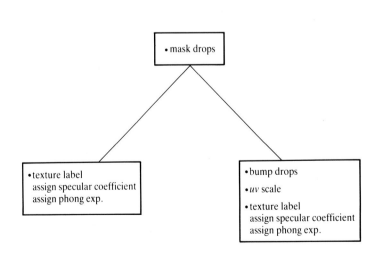

mask drops

- texture label
  assign specular coefficient
  assign phong exp.

- bump drops
- *uv* scale
- texture label
  assign specular coefficient
  assign phong exp.

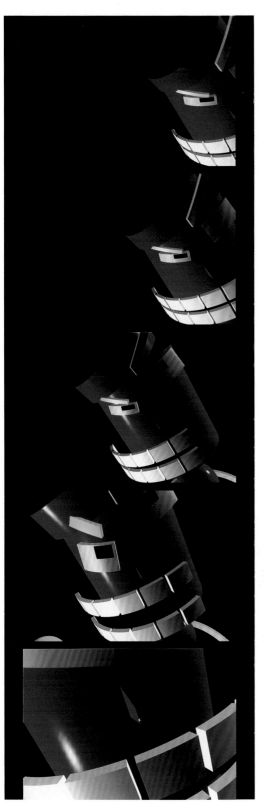

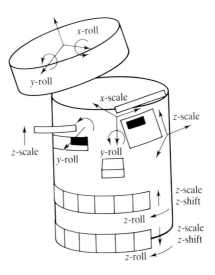

49 Explicitly and implicitly linked hierarchical structures: a sequence from the animation of an articulated model – *Mad Bastard* – made up of explicitly and implicitly linked geometric primitives. Most of the primitives are just cylinders and spheres but the paucity of the geometric forms does not detract from the vitality of the animation.

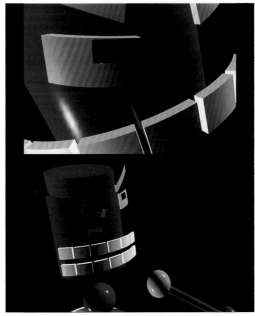

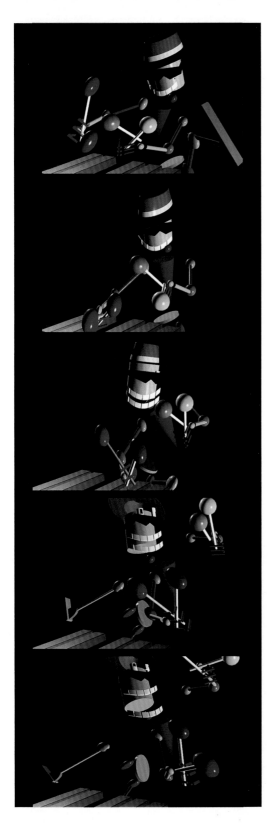

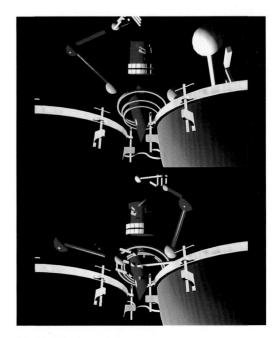

51 Interaction of structures: a sequence
illustrating the interaction between actors – in
this case the mallets and the drumskin.

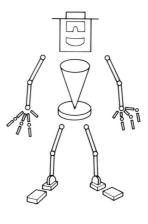

50 Linked hierarchical structures: an example
of the animation of a full figure with both
explicit and implicit links.

52 Independent manipulation of nodes in a hierarchy: selected transformations of the bass are inherited by the bass player, but the bass spins independently of the player.

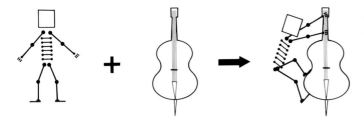

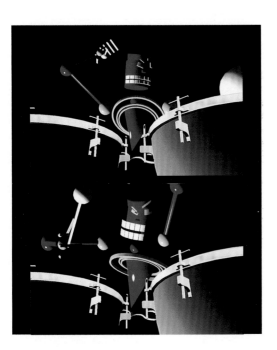

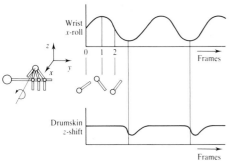

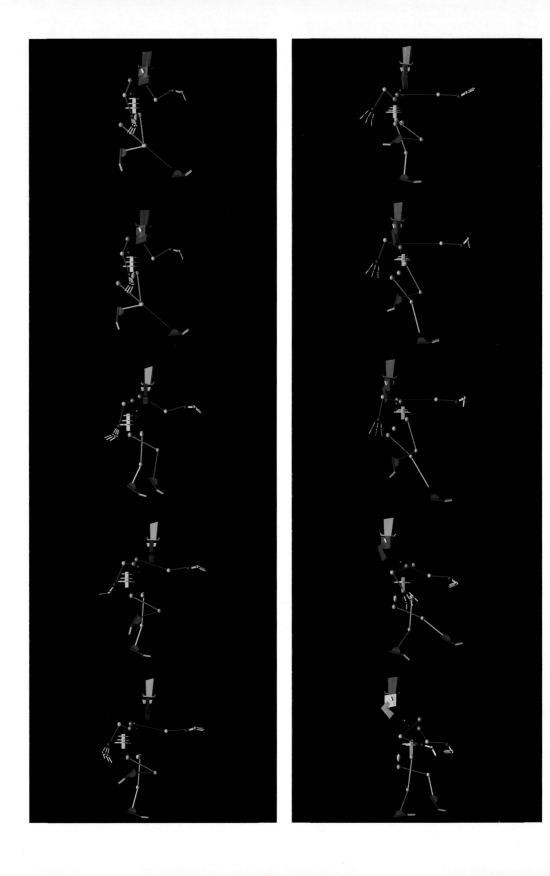

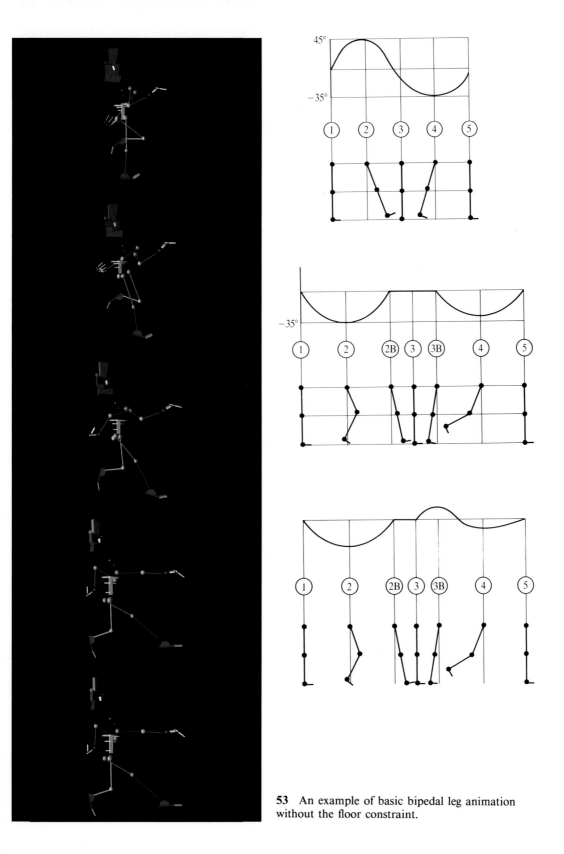

53 An example of basic bipedal leg animation without the floor constraint.

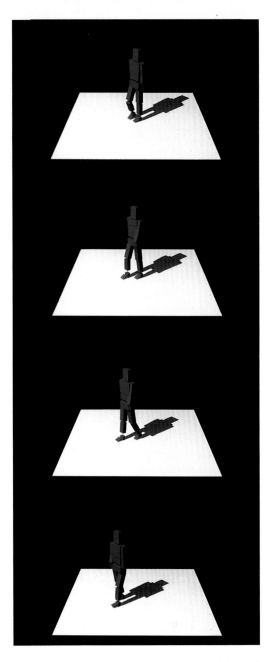

54 Using forward kinematics for bipedal leg animation: to produce this animation the hierarchy was inverted (driven by the foot). This solves the floor constraint problem.

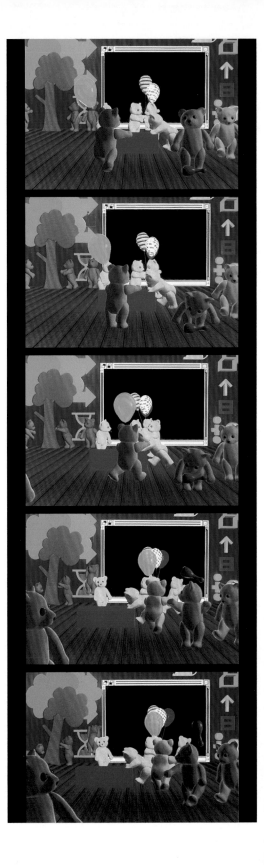

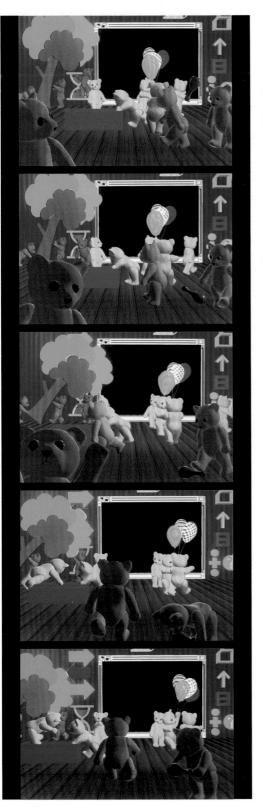

55 Interaction among articulated structures. The sequence shows various hierarchical figures interacting with each other; a bear picks up a skittle, another pushes a box along the floor, another jumps on the box and so on. If we consider the entire scene to be a single hierarchy, then each of these events corresponds to an internal detachment of a particular sub-tree and its re-attachment at some other node of the hierarchy. This is described in detail in Section 16.7.

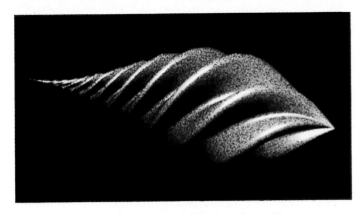

56 Global transformation on a polygon mesh model – a corrugated cylinder, twisted and tapered.

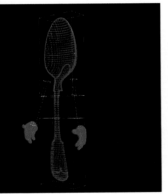 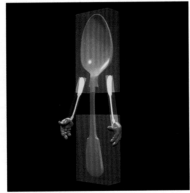

57 FFD animation and characterization: the undeformed spoon model shown in wireframe and rendered form, together with the FFD blocks. Note the polygonal resolution of the model compared with the resolution of the FFD block.

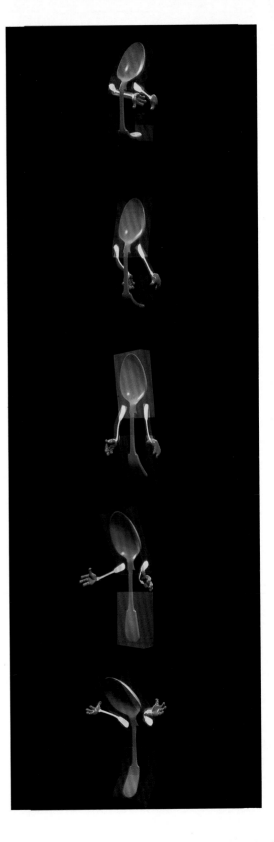

58 FFD animation and characterization: part of an animated sequence for the spoon. Basic characterization becomes possible as even the static frames demonstrate. The sequence shows the spoons jumping. Two FFD blocks are used to control the upper and lower halves of the spoon, and two FFD blocks control the shape of the arms. FFD blocks (not shown) also control the fingers.

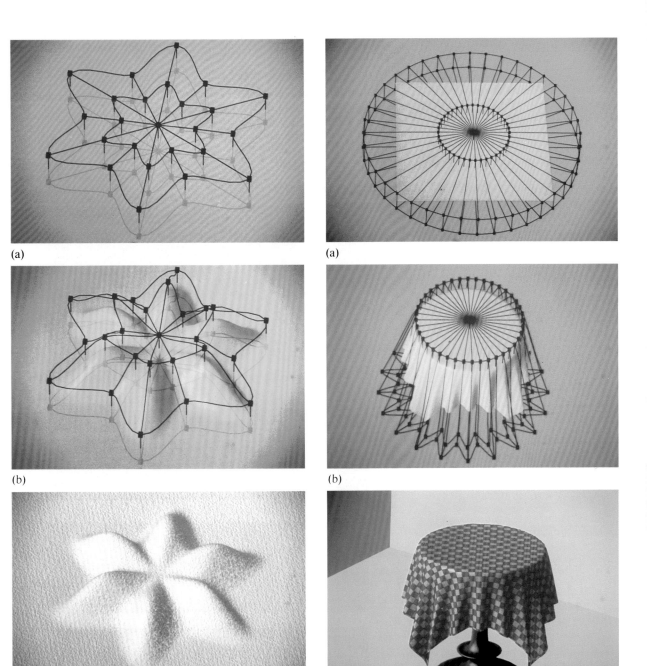

(a)

(b)

(c)

59 Extending free form deformation to include a nonparallelepiped lattice – the EFFD technique. In this example a cylindrical lattice is used (courtesy of S. Coquillart, INRIA–Rocquencourt, Le Chesnay, France). (a) a cylindrical EFFD block attached to a surface. (b) Deforming the EFFD block. (c) The deformed surface.

60 The same technique as the previous example used to deform a square tablecloth (courtesy of S. Coquillart, INRIA–Rocquencourt, Le Chesnay, France). (a) A cylindrical EFFD block attached to a surface. (b) Deforming the EFFD block. (c) The deformed surface.

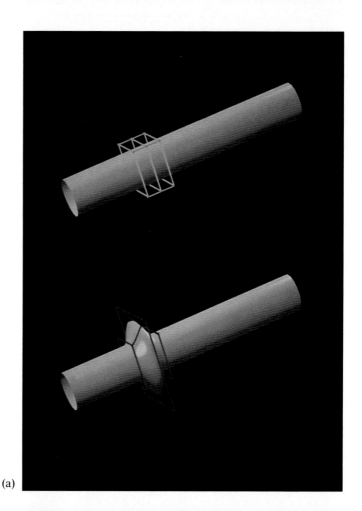

61 Independent animation of deformation and object; animating a deformation that passes along a stationary object (courtesy of S. Coquillart, INRIA–Rocquencourt, Le Chesnay, France). (a)

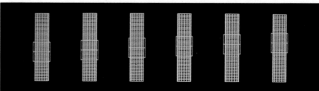

The undeformed FFD block is translated along the object. (b)

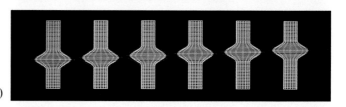

The deformed FFD block undergoes the same translation. (c)

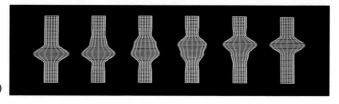

The corresponding effect using inbetweening (note that this is inferior to (c)). (d)

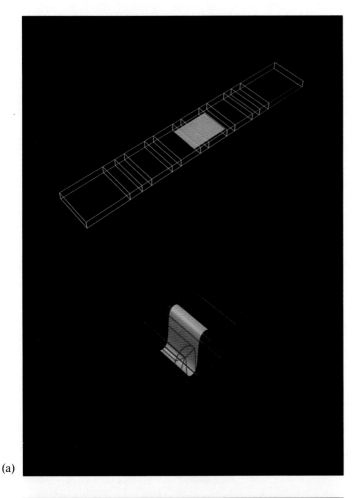

(a)

62 Independent animation of deformation and object: animating an object through a stationary FFD (courtesy of S. Coquillart, INRIA–Rocquencourt, Le Chesnay, France).

(b)

Object moving through static FFD block.

(c)

Deformation obtained as lattice space coordinates of paper are 'plugged into' deformed FFD block.

(d)

The corresponding effect using inbetweening (note that this is inferic to (c)).

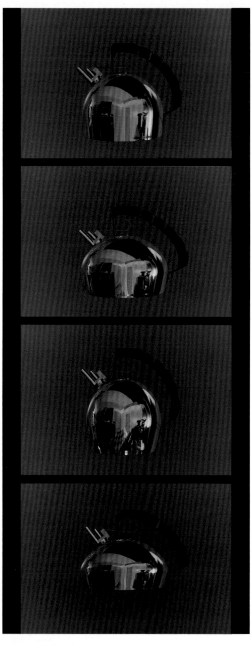

63 FFD animation: an environment-mapped kettle jumping exhibiting the classic squash and stretch technique.

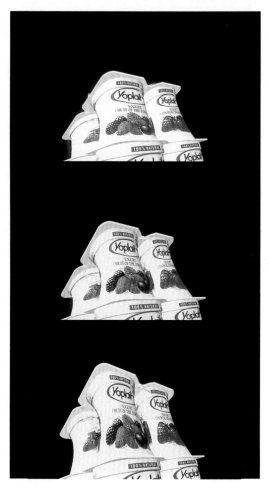

65 FFD animation: yoghurt cartons taking off and flying out of a fridge.

64 A frame from an animated sequence that contains the jumping kettle.

66 A frame from an animated sequence that contains the yoghurt cartons.

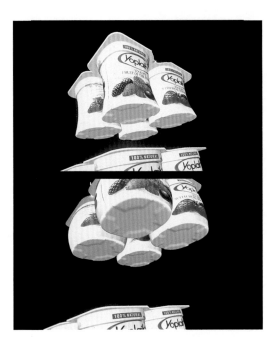

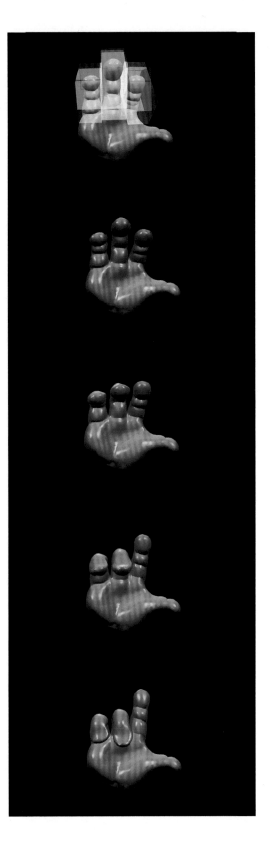

67 FFDs and articulated structures: partially overlapping FFD blocks being used to control finger bending. Here the deformation of one FFD block occurs after the deformation of another. Where FFD blocks overlap two deformations occur.

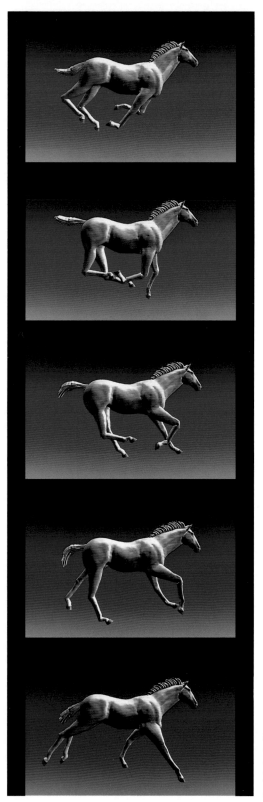

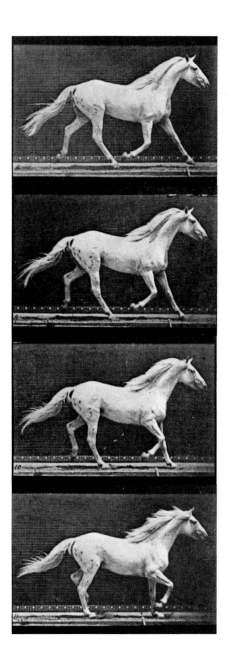

68 FFDs and articulated structures: FFD blocks were used to control the neck, head and tail of the horse. The sequence was based upon Eadweard Muybridge's classic work *Animals in Motion* (1899).

69 Simulating wind driven water waves: two frames from a chrome-mapped animation sequence showing waves approaching a beach.

70 A surface modelled from long-crested wave sets at two main orientations.

71 Adding radial waves as bump map packets.

72 The chrome map used in the water waves illustration.

73 Radiosity illustration: Simulated steel mill. The image was created using a modified version of the hemicube radiosity algorithm, computed on a VAX 8700 and displayed on a Hewlett-Packard Renaissance Display. The environment consists of approximately 55 000 elements, and is one of the most complex environments computed to date (courtesy of Stuart Feldman and John Wallace, Program of Computer Graphics, Cornell University).

74 A frame from an animated sequence that includes many of the techniques described in the text. (1) FFD blocks were used to control the movement of the ducks' necks (Chapter 17). (2) Long-crested wave model with raindrop perturbations added as bump map packets. The water surface is chrome-mapped. (3) Selective ray tracing for the reflection of the ducks in the water (see Chapter 9). The water surface was tagged to be ray traced. (4) The ducks were texture mapped using the 'reverse projection' technique described in Chapter 6.

Figure 3.20   Parametric patch rendering at different levels of subdivision (128, 512, 2048 and 8192 polygons).

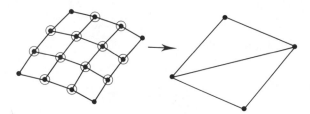

Figure 3.21   Patch to polygons by disregarding the circled control points.

3.4.3   Normals to the Bézier patch

The question of what normals to assign to these vertices now arises. As we would expect if we just assigned the plane normal to these triangles, the resultant patch surface would look faceted when shaded. A superior solution is to calculate the normals to the parametric surface at the patch corners and assign these values to the relevant surfaces. The standard trick of interpolating the normals along polygon edges will then give the patch a smoother appearance.

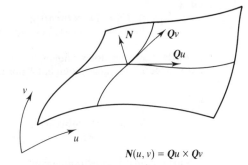

$$N(u, v) = Q_u \times Q_v$$

Figure 3.22   The surface normal to a patch.

The code fragment used, *get_patch_normals( )*, is given in Listing 3.2. It works as follows. By definition, both tangent vectors Q_u and Q_v are tangent to the surface $Q(u, v)$. The surface normal N is the cross product of these two vectors (Figure 3.22):

$$N(u, v) = Q_u \times Q_v$$

From Section 3.3.3 we know that:

Listing 3.2   get_patch_normals.c

```c
int  get_patch_normals(hull,normals)
float  hull[4][4][3],normals[2][2][3];
{
            float  utangent[3],vtangent[3];
            int  i,j;
            int  zero_vector();

            j=1;
            do {
                        if  (j==4)  return(0);
                        for  (i=0;i<3;i++)  utangent[i]  =  hull[j][0][i]−hull[0][0][i];
                        j++;
            } while  (zero_vector(utangent));
            j=1;
            do {
                        if  (j==4)  return(0);
                        for  (i=0;i<3;i++)  vtangent[i]  =  hull[0][j][i]−hull[0][0][i];
                        j++;
            } while  (zero_vector(vtangent));
            cross_product(utangent,vtangent,&normals[0][0][0]);

            j=1;
            do {
                        if  (j==4)  return(0);
                        for  (i=0;i<3;i++)  utangent[i]  =  hull[j][3][i]−hull[0][3][i];
                        j++;
            } while  (zero_vector(utangent));
            j=2;
            do {
                        if  (j==−1)  return(0);
                        for  (i=0;i<3;i++)  vtangent[i]  =  hull[0][3][i]−hull[0][j][i];
                        j−−;
            } while  (zero_vector(vtangent));
            cross_product(utangent,vtangent,&normals[0][1][0]);

            j=2;
            do {
                        if  (j==−1)  return(0);
                        for  (i=0;i<3;i++)  utangent[i]  =  hull[3][0][i]−hull[j][0][i];
                        j−−;
            } while  (zero_vector(utangent));
            j=1;
            do {
                        if  (j==4)  return(0);
                        for  (i=0;i<3;i++)  vtangent[i]  =  hull[3][j][i]−hull[3][0][i];
                        j++;
            } while  (zero_vector(vtangent));
            cross_product(utangent,vtangent,&normals[1][0][0]);

            j=2;
            do {
```

Listing 3.2   cont.

```
                    if (j==−1) return(0);
                    for (i=0;i<3;i++)  utangent[i]  =  hull[3][3][i]−hull[j][3][i];
                    j−−;
          } while (zero_vector(utangent));
          j=2;
          do {
                    if (j==−1) return(0);
                    for (i=0;i<3;i++)  vtangent[i]  =  hull[3][3][i]−hull[3][j][i];
                    j−−;
          } while (zero_vector(vtangent));
          cross_product(utangent,vtangent,&normals[1][1][0]);

          return(1);
}
```

$$Q_u(0,0) = 3(p_{10} - p_{00})$$

and

$$Q_v(0,0) = 3(p_{01} - p_{00})$$

Listing 3.2 basically calculates the tangent vectors and computes the cross product at each corner of the patch (omitting the scalar multiple of 3 since we are only concerned with directions). However, there is one important complication to which we draw the reader's attention. As we have already discussed, the original patch being rendered may have been modelled in a basis other than Bézier. In order to satisfy boundary conditions some modelling strategies may duplicate control points which would result in duplicate control points appearing in the corresponding Bézier patch. If, say, p_{00} and p_{10} are identical then the tangent vector $Q_u(0,0)$ is the zero vector. In this case the tangent vector is defined by p_{00} and the first p_{i0} along that edge that is distinct from p_{00}. Degenerate patches, where an edge has collapsed signifying a triangular patch, or where Q_u and Q_v are parallel signifying a cusp, are dealt with by returning zero.

3.4.4 Patch-splitting strategy

Listings 3.1 and 3.2 represent the lowest level routines required for a patch splitter but some overall strategy is needed to employ them. The simplest and most naive of implementations would convert the patch representation to polygons as a preprocessing step prior to rendering. If the renderer is scan line based, however, the patch itself

could be passed to it and, by virtue of the convex hull property, sorted into the relevant scan line since the maximum possible Y-value of the patch will be bound by the maximum Y-value of the 16 control points making up the convex hull. As each scan line is processed, patches that are encountered are treated for subdivision as follows.

If the termination criteria are satisfied, then convert patches to polygons, otherwise subdivide the patch down to subpatches. Take each subpatch and hang it off the end of the current scan line or the one lower depending on the projection of its convex hull onto the image plane. This process is repeated until there are no patches on the current scan line, only polygons, whereupon they are rendered.

This method of patch rendering is superior to the brute force of the preprocessing approach since it is much less demanding on memory. Maximum advantage is taken of the patch's more concise data, only downloading to its more memory intensive polygonal counterpart scan line by scan line.

3.4.5 Terminating patch splitting

The tests that are used to decide whether or not to split a patch further should be as inexpensive as possible, since they are to be applied to every patch at every level of subdivision. The most obvious termination criterion is based on object space curvature applied to the control points of the convex hull. Flatness is tested by forming a plane between three (corner) control points and measuring how far the remaining control points deviate from the plane.

Just as for curves, a measure of the linearity of the edges is to check how far the middle control points of the edge deviate from the line joining the end points.

If the patches are subdivided within the renderer as described above, then one can devise termination criteria based on the patch's projection on the screen. For example, if the area of the projection of the convex hull on the screen is less than one pixel then there seems little point in subdividing further. One can also develop heuristics for testing screen space curvature by taking the curvature in object space and dividing by the Z-depth of the control points.

The more elaborate the termination criterion, however, the more it defeats its own purpose, since the saving gained by ceasing to subdivide could be less than the effort in applying the tests to every patch at every level of subdivision. Moreover, screen-driven termination criteria have to address the problem of transition between different levels of subdivision should a patch move in an animation sequence. (This is not dissimilar to the 'bubbling' problem in fractal modelling mentioned in Chapter 7.) These considerations have led us to implement the simplest of tests based on object space curvature.

3.4.6 The cracking problem

Whatever method is employed to stop subdivision, the problem of 'cracking' needs to be solved. Cracking results from the independent subdivision of adjacent subpatches.

Consider the following example. Suppose we use linearity of patch edges as our criteria for subdivision.

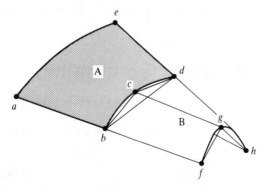

Figure 3.23 The cracking problem: the common edge between patches A and B is represented both by *bd* and *bcd*.

Let two patches A and B share a common edge as shown in Figure 3.23. Patch A is reasonably flat and so needs no further subdivision; it therefore turns into the polygon *abde*. Patch B, however, still has an edge that is not considered to be sufficiently linear and so is subdivided accordingly. Patch B then gets turned into the two polygons *bfgc* and *cghd*. The common edge is thus represented differently by the two patches. Patch A says it is the straight line *bd* whereas patch B says it consists of the two straight line segments *bc* and *cd*. This will result in a small separation appearing in the resulting polygons which may be visible from certain view points.

If this problem is not dealt with the patch splitter should be constrained to uniform subdivision – each patch is subdivided to the same level. (There is a choice here: you can avoid both the cost of the flatness test and the cracking problem by simply adopting the brute-force procedure of uniform subdivision. Generally this alternative will be more expensive but easier to implement.) The only real solution to the cracking problem that appears in the literature is due to Clark [CLAR79]. In order to overcome the problem, Clark uses a different method of subdivision that we now describe in detail. As usual we shall consider the case of curves first, generalizing later to surfaces.

Taylor's expansion is an expansion of a function into an infinite series, where the coefficients of the successive terms involve the successive derivatives of the function. Let $f^n(u)$ denote the nth derivative of u, then the Taylor expansion about the point u is:

$$f(u + du) = \sum_{i=0}^{\infty} \frac{(du)^n}{n!} f^n(u)$$

For cubics the right-hand side reduces to three terms from which it is easy to derive the following:

$$f(u + du) + f(u - du) = 2f(u) + (du)^2 \frac{f''(u)}{2}$$

where

f'' denotes the second derivative

From this we can express $f(u)$ as a central difference, that is, the value of the function $f(\ )$ at the midpoint u of the interval $[u - du, u + du]$ is obtained by averaging its value at the end points and subtracting the term containing the second derivative evaluated at the midpoint:

$$f(u) = \frac{f(u + du) + f(u - du)}{2} - (du)^2 \frac{f''(u)}{2} \qquad (3.4)$$

Figure 3.24 Parametric subdivision of [0, 1] at level k.

Replacing $f(u)$ by $f''(u)$ and repeating the above derivation allows us to express the second derivative also in terms of central differences giving:

$$f''(u) = \frac{f''(u + du) + f''(u - du)}{2}$$

Clark uses these central difference formulae to subdivide the curve recursively about successive midpoints at each level of recursion. The derivation of the recursion formulae is as follows. The curve will be represented at level k by a series, $u_{i,k}$ $(i = 0, \ldots, 2^k)$ points equispaced parametrically by a distance Δu_k as shown in Figure 3.24 where:

$$u_{i,k} = \frac{i}{2^k} \qquad i = 0, 1, \ldots, 2^k$$

$$\Delta u_k = \frac{1}{2^k}$$

From this we can deduce that:

$$u_{2i, k+1} = u_{i,k}$$

which tells us, not surprisingly, that some of the points at the next level of recursion are already calculated. These are the 'even' points and we write, trivially

$$f(u_{2i, k+1}) = f(u_{i,k}) \qquad i = 0, 1, \ldots, 2^k$$

The remaining 'odd' control points are obtained by central differencing between 'adjacent' even points. From Equation (3.4) we have:

$$
\begin{aligned}
f(u_{2i+1, k+1}) &= \frac{f(u_{2i+2, k+1}) + f(u_{2i, k+1})}{2} \\
&\quad - (\Delta u_{k+1})^2 f''(u_{2i+1, k+1}) \\
&= \frac{f(u_{i+1, k}) + f(u_{i,k})}{2} - g(u_{2i+1, k+1})
\end{aligned}
$$

where we define:

$$g(u_{i,k}) = (\Delta u_k)^2 f''(u_{i,k})$$

from which we can deduce the following recursive relationship for $g( )$

$$g(u_{2i, k+1}) = \tfrac{1}{4} g(u_{i,k})$$

Applying central differencing to $g( )$ completes the set of recursion formulae:

$$
\begin{aligned}
g(u_{2i+1, k+1}) &= \frac{g(u_{2i+2, k+1}) + g(u_{2i, k+1})}{2} \\
&= \frac{g(u_{i+1, k}) + g(u_{i,k})}{8}
\end{aligned}
$$

The initial conditions are:

$$u_{00} = 0 \qquad\qquad u_{10} = 1$$
$$f(u_{00}) = f(0) \qquad\qquad f(u_{10}) = f(1)$$
$$g(u_{00}) = \frac{f''(0)}{2} \qquad\qquad g(u_{10}) = \frac{f''(1)}{2}$$

Subdivision using central differences extended to bicubic patches is a little more involved. The Taylor expansion for two variables $f(u + du, v + dv)$ in the case of bicubics is given by:

$$
\begin{aligned}
f(u + du, v + dv) &= f(u, v) + du\, f_u(u, v) + dv\, f_v(u, v) \\
&\quad + \frac{1}{2!} \big[du^2 f_{uu}(u, v) + 2 du\, dv\, f_{uv}(u, v) \\
&\quad + dv^2 f_{vv}(u, v) \big]
\end{aligned}
$$

For a bicubic patch we split in either the u direction, with v held constant, or vice versa. In either case, $dv = 0$ or $du = 0$, the Taylor expansion for the two variables reduces to that of a single variable. Consequently the recursion formulae for splitting a bicubic in $\overline{u}$ with v constant is the same as splitting a cubic in u as derived above.

Let us consider the specific case of splitting in the direction of u along the line $v = v_0$ as shown in Figure 3.25. $f(u, v_0)$ is a cubic in u and so $f(u_{1/2}, v_0)$ is expressible as a central difference in terms of $f(u, v_0)$ and $f_{uu}(u, v_0)$. So they are split using Equation (3.4) where $f(u, v_0)$ replaces $f(u)$ and $f_{uu}(u, v_0)$ replaces

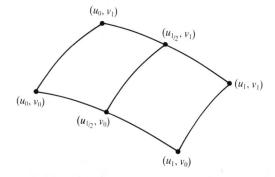

Figure 3.25 Patch splitting.

$f''(u)$. However, $f_{vv}(u, v_0)$ is also a cubic in u and so it must also be split using Equation (3.4), where this time $f_{vv}(u, v_0)$ replaces $f(u)$ and $f_{uuvv}(u, v_0)$ replaces $f''(u)$.

The initial values for splitting $f(u, v)$ setting $u_{00} = u_0$ and $u_{10} = u_1$ are:

$$f(u_{00}) = f(u_0, v_0) \qquad f(u_{10}) = f(u_1, v_0)$$

$$g(u_{00}) = \frac{f_{uu}(u_0, v_0)}{2} \qquad g(u_{10}) = \frac{f_{uu}(u_1, v_0)}{2}$$

and for splitting $f_{vv}(u, v)$ are:

$$f(u_{00}) = \frac{f_{vv}(u_0, v_0)}{2} \qquad f(u_{10}) = \frac{f_{vv}(u_1, v_0)}{2}$$

$$g(u_{00}) = \frac{f_{uuvv}(u_0, v_0)}{4} \qquad g(u_{10}) = \frac{f_{uuvv}(u_1, v_0)}{4}$$

In practice each patch corner needs only these four values:

$$f(u, v) \quad \frac{f_{uu}(u, v)}{2} \quad \frac{f_{vv}(u, v)}{2} \quad \text{and} \quad \frac{f_{uuvv}(u, v)}{4}$$

associated with it for splitting in all directions. Splitting in a given direction just involves grouping these four values into the two appropriate pairs of $f()$ and $g()$ for that direction.

Now the advantage of this method of subdivision is due to Equation (3.4), which expresses the midpoint of the edge of a patch as the average of its end points plus another term – we will call it the nonlinear term – since if this term is zero the three points are collinear and the edge must be a straight line. The nonlinear term thus provides a measure of the linearity of the patch edge. Clark suggests removing this term from Equation (3.4) during

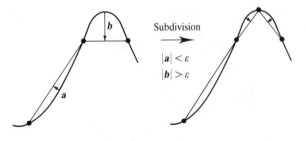

Figure 3.26 Subdivision continues if the magnitude of the vector connecting the midpoint of an interval to midpoint of the straight line joining the end-points of the interval is greater than some threshold.

the splitting process once it is less than a certain tolerance. At some point in the subdivision process, therefore, the patch edge will be treated as a straight line should the patch require further subdivision for reasons other than this edge. During subsequent subdivisions subpatches will treat this common edge in exactly the same way as an adjoining patch that has stopped subdividing hence separation between two edges is avoided and cracking disappears.

Figure 3.26 shows geometrically how this works. The nonlinear term provides a measure of the magnitude of the vector connecting the midpoint of an interval to the midpoint of the line joining the end points of that interval. If this value is sufficiently small then the interval is treated as a straight line. Returning to Figure 3.23 then, on splitting patch B, c will be made collinear with b and d.

The fact that terms measuring the bilinearity of the patch are given as a byproduct of the arithmetic of central differences is also advantageous. Using the magnitudes of these terms for our termination criteria removes the need to, and the computational expense of, providing our own. Readers should note that when splitting $f_{vv}()$ in the direction of u, or $f_{uu}()$ in the direction of v, the nonlinear term provides a measure of $f_{uuvv}()$ which tells us how flat the middle of the patch is. This term, therefore, should also be included in the termination criteria.

3.4.7 A hybrid splitter

A serious drawback to this scheme is that subdivision using central differences has nothing equivalent to the convex hull property. The four vector quantities given by Equation (3.4) do not provide us with a bound for the patch. Consequently, used in isolation this splitting scheme could not be employed to subdivide patches within the renderer on a scan line by scan line basis. Seeking to take advantage of the complementary strengths of both splitting schemes, we have found a hybrid technique to be useful, splitting the patch's convex hull in order to hang the patch off the correct scan line, but using four corner points provided by central differencing in order to avoid cracking.

Finally, beware of the fact that once a central difference scheme judges an edge of a patch to be linear, the convex hull property no longer holds good and so the patch has to be downloaded to its polygonal representation at that scan line.

3.5 B-splines

Originally a spline was a flexible strip of metal used by draughtsmen to facilitate the drawing of a curve. A curve shape was made up of a set of such strips that were pulled into shape by hanging small metal weights – called ducks – from the splines. This created a composite curve that possessed second-order continuity. We now consider cubic B-splines which are composite curves made up of several curve segments. C^2 continuity exists between these segments and we shall see that we do not have to set up any continuity conditions between segments as was the case for Bézier segments.

B-splines are commonly used in computer graphics for reasons that will shortly become apparent. The question that obviously arises is: if such a construction is available with C^2 continuity guaranteed between segments, then what is the point of ever using the Bézier basis? The main answer to this question, as far as this text is concerned, is that the Bézier basis, as we have seen, enables an efficient patch-splitting algorithm for rendering, and we can simply view the Bézier basis as the *final* basis in any modelling or animation system. Whatever basis is being used for patches or curves in the application can be finally converted into the Bézier basis and rendered using the techniques described in the previous section.

3.5.1 The uniform B-spline

We will refer to the ith segment in a cubic B-spline as Q_i. Such a curve segment possesses four control vertices that we will refer to as p_i, p_{i+1}, p_{i+2} and p_{i+3}. Using this notation Q_{i+1} has control vertices p_{i+1}, p_{i+2}, p_{i+3} and p_{i+4}, and shares control points p_{i+1}, p_{i+2} and p_{i+3} with its neighbour Q_i. This notation anticipates the fact, which we shall derive, that B-spline segments share control vertices.

A single segment of a B-spline curve is derived in the following way. Consider the following construction. Let $Q_i(u)$ be a cubic spline defined over the interval $0 \leqslant u \leqslant 1$ with basis functions $B_k(u)$, $(k = 0, \ldots, 3)$ and control vertices p_i, p_{i+1}, p_{i+2} and p_{i+3}. We write:

$$Q_i(u) = \sum_{k=0}^{3} p_{i+k} B_k(u) \tag{3.5}$$

Let $Q_{i+1}(u)$ be defined similarly. We seek the set of basis functions $B_k(u)$ such that C^0, C^1 and C^2 continuity is assured between the end of Q_i and the start of Q_{i+1}. For C^0 continuity this implies that

$$Q_i(1) = Q_{i+1}(0)$$

that is

$$\sum_{k=0}^{3} p_{i+k} B_k(1) = \sum_{k=0}^{3} p_{i+k+1} B_k(0)$$

Since the control vertices can take arbitrary values, this equation is satisfied by balancing their coefficients. This gives:

$$B_0(1) = 0$$
$$B_1(1) = B_0(0)$$
$$B_2(1) = B_1(0)$$
$$B_3(1) = B_2(0)$$
$$0 = B_3(0)$$

Similarly, satisfying the C^1 and C^2 continuity condition gives us the constraints:

$B_0'(1) = 0$	$B_0''(1) = 0$
$B_1'(1) = B_0'(0)$	$B_1''(1) = B_0''(0)$
$B_2'(1) = B_1'(0)$	$B_2''(1) = B_1''(0)$
$B_3'(1) = B_2'(0)$	$B_3''(1) = B_2''(0)$
$0 = B_3'(0)$	$0 = B_3''(0)$

This gives us 15 equations but since each of the B_k are cubics we have 16 unknowns. Therefore we need to supply an additional equation in order to reach a solution. Since we know the convex hull property to be useful let us make the basis functions sum to one at an arbitrary point, $u = 0$, say. That is:

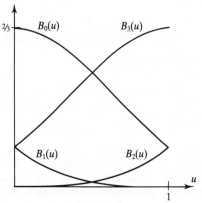

Figure 3.27 The B-spline basis functions.

$$B_0(0) + B_1(0) + B_2(0) + B_3(0) = 1$$

Solving the equations gives us:

$$B_0(u) = \frac{(1+u)^3}{6}$$

$$B_1(u) = \frac{3u^3 - 6u^2 + 4}{6}$$

$$B_2(u) = \frac{-3u^3 + 3u^2 + 3u + 1}{6}$$

$$B_3(u) = \frac{u^3}{6}$$

These are the B-spline basis functions as shown in Figure 3.27.

3.5.2 B-spline curves: matrix formulation

Considering then a B-spline as a single cubic polynomial segment controlled by a set of four vertices we can state a matrix formulation as follows:

$$Q_i(u) = UM_{BS}P$$

$$= \begin{bmatrix} u^3 & u^2 & u & 1 \end{bmatrix} \frac{1}{6} \begin{bmatrix} -1 & 3 & -3 & 1 \\ 3 & -6 & 3 & 0 \\ -3 & 0 & 3 & 0 \\ 1 & 4 & 1 & 0 \end{bmatrix} \begin{bmatrix} p_i \\ p_{i+1} \\ p_{i+2} \\ p_{i+3} \end{bmatrix}$$

and from this we can see that P is a set of four points in a sequence of control points.

3.5.3 Uniform B-spline: local and global parameters

The next step, although seemingly trivial, contains a notion, the generalization of which is basic to the theory of splines. Suppose that we have $n-2$ curve segments Q_i, where $i = 0, \ldots, n-2$, and therefore $n+1$ control points p_i, $i = 0, \ldots, n$. Now we know from our construction that all the curve segments join to form one continuous piecewise curve, so it would seem more natural to seek a parametrization of the entire curve in terms of a global parameter U. We shall adopt the nota-

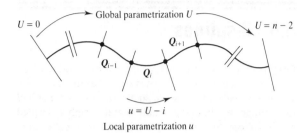

Figure 3.28   Local and global parametrization for B-spline curve segments.

tion U for the global parameter across the entire curve and u for the local parameter across an individual curve segment. Since each segment has a local parametrization our task is simple. Globally the parameter U is defined over the interval $[0, n-2]$ whereas locally the parameter u is defined over the interval $[0, 1]$, and for segment i is given by $u = U - i$. This is shown schematically in Figure 3.28.

The formulation of a global parameter enables us to examine the effect a single control vertex has on the entire curve. From Equation (3.5) we can see that each curve segment is defined by four control points; aside from the end control points, each control point influences four curve segments. p_i comes into the calculation of segments $Q_{i-3}, Q_{i-2}, Q_{i-1}, Q_i$ where it is weighted by the basis functions B_3, B_2, B_1 and B_0 respectively. Moving across a junction between segments causes p_i to switch suddenly from one basis function that weights it to another. Globally we collect these functions and intervals into one function $N_i(U)$ that is the blending function for weighting the control points p_i. This expresses how p_i is weighted as a function of the global parameter of the entire composite curve.

The curve $Q(U)$ is thus given by:

$$Q(U) = \sum_{i=0}^{n} p_i N_i(U)$$

where:

$$N_i(U) = \begin{cases} B_3(u_0) & i-3 \leqslant U < i-2 \\ B_2(u_1) & i-2 \leqslant U < i-1 \\ B_1(u_2) & i-1 \leqslant U < i \\ B_0(u_3) & i \leqslant U < i+1 \end{cases}$$

where $N_i(U)$ takes the global parameter U and converts it into the appropriate local parameter u_j relevant to that segment where $u_j = U - i + 3 - j$ ($j = 0, \ldots, 3$). Figure

Figure 3.29 The blending functions (dotted) and the basis functions (bold) for a uniform B-spline.

3.29 shows several of these control point blending functions (which somewhat confusingly are also called basis functions). The reader will note that $N_i(U)$ is nonzero over the interval $[i-3, i+1]$ and p_i exerts maximal influence at the point $U = i - 1$ corresponding to the maximum of $N_i(U)$. As can be seen from the figure, the $N_i(U)$ are all translates of each other, each one nonzero over the relevant interval. The curves, represented by the unbroken line, show how our original basis function B_i (shown in Figure 3.27) fits into the scheme.

Now the reason for such an apparently elaborate digression will be made clear. Functionally the formulation arrived at above is but a specific subset of a more general class of B-spline. The subset is the class of uniform B-splines and the superset the class of non-uniform B-splines. In order to move from the former to the latter the following generalizations have to be made.

3.5.4 The blending functions and knot vectors

A uniform B-spline, by definition, consists of curve segments the ends of which occur parametrically at equal intervals with respect to the global parameter. In the case just considered the ends are situated at $[0, 1, \ldots, n]$ of U. These values are called 'knots' and the collection of them is termed the 'knot vector'. We generalize the knots to allow for relative parametric intervals between segments that need not be the same. The spline curve then becomes a collection of knot intervals, $t_0 < t_1 < \ldots$

$< t_n$, and if the knot spacing is nonuniform then so is the B-spline.

The order k (degree $k - 1$) of the spline is allowed to vary. So far we have only considered cubics but generally our blending function $N_i(u)$ becomes $N_{i,k}(u)$ where, for cubics, $k = 4$.

We can now quote the Cox de Boor algorithm which is the recursive definition for the blending function $N_{i,k}(u)$ and is the B-spline equivalent of the de Casteljau algorithm for Bézier curves. The blending function $N_{i,k}(u)$ is defined recursively over the knot range $[t_i, t_{i+k}]$ as follows:

$$N_{i,1}(u) = \begin{cases} 1 & \text{if } t_i \leqslant u < t_{i+1} \\ 0 & \text{otherwise} \end{cases}$$

$$N_{i,k}(u) = \frac{(u - t_i)N_{i,k-1}(u)}{t_{i+k-1} - t_i} + \frac{(t_{i+k} - u)N_{i+1,k-1}(u)}{t_{i+k} - t_{i+1}}$$

The reader will note that the blending functions are no longer identical translates of each other since they now depend directly on the local knot distribution. Over the knot vector $(t_0, \ldots, t_n)$ the $N_{i,k}(u)$ have the following properties:

1. Non-negativity:

   $N_{i,k}(u) \geqslant 0$ for all i,k,u

   Partition of unity:

   $$\sum_{i=0}^{n} N_{i,k}(u) = 1$$

   These two properties taken together mean that the control polygon of a B-spline curve is the convex hull of that curve.

2. The computation of $N_{i,k}(u)$ involves only the knots from t_i to t_{i+k} and no others – we say that the support of $N_{i,k}(u)$ is $[t_i, t_{i+k}]$. (The support of a function is the region over which that function is nonzero.) $N_{i,k}(u)$ is zero outside the range $[t_i, t_{i+k}]$.

3. 0/0 is deemed to be zero – thereby allowing the possibility of defining knots with the same value – so-called multiple knots.

It is instructive to unravel this recursion for the case of cubic splines as shown by the tree of Figure 3.30. This figure provides us with the following insights into the internal workings of the recursion. Going left as we leave a node corresponds to following the first terms in the

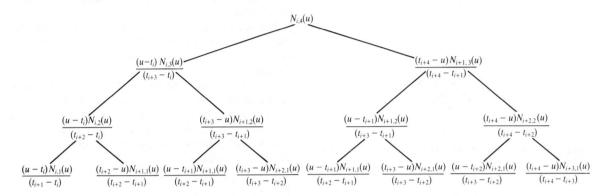

Figure 3.30   Tree illustrating recursive generation of cubic B-splines.

recursion whose support is $[i, k-1]$. Going left therefore prunes the support by removing one knot interval from the end of the support, that is, from $[i, k]$ to $[i, k-1]$. Similarly, going right prunes the support by removing a knot interval from the beginning of the support, that is, from $[i, k]$ to $[i+1, k]$. The leaves have support of only one interval and the denominator of these leaves contains the width of that interval. These observations will prove useful later when evaluating the blending function under specific conditions.

3.5.5 Nonuniform B-splines: knot vectors and control points

Now let us consider how the knot vectors and control points relate to each other by considering a B-spline curve of degree k consisting of $n+1$ control points in terms of this blending function. We write

$$Q(u) = \sum_{i=0}^{n} p_i N_{i,k}(u) \qquad (3.6)$$

Since each of the $n+1$ control points has a blending function associated with it, there are $n+1$ blending functions. Now each blending function $N_{i,k}(u)$ has support $[t_i, t_{i+k}]$. $N_{0,k}(u)$ has support $[t_0, \ldots, t_k]$ and the last blending function $N_{n,k}(u)$ has support $[t_n, \ldots, t_{n+k}]$. Therefore there must exist $n+k+1$ knots, which together make up the knot vector $[t_0, \ldots, t_{n+k}]$. In general:

Number of knots = Number of control points + order

The properties of the nonuniform B-spline follow from the properties of the blending function:

1. *Localness* $N_{i,k}(u)$ is zero outside the interval $[t_i, t_{i+k}]$. Therefore outside this interval the control point p_i has no effect. The control points of the B-splines are said to exert the property of localness. Moving control point p_i only changes the shape of the curve between knots $[t_i, t_{i+k}]$. The functions act like switches, as u moves past a knot one $N_{i,k}(u)$ function (and hence the influence of the corresponding p_i) switches off, and a new one switches on.

2. *Continuity* We have seen that C^0, C^1 and C^2 continuity for cubic B-splines is assured by virtue of the representation. We simply do not have to worry about continuity across adjacent curve segments. Compare this with composite Bézier segments where intersegment continuity requires additional constraints to be satisfied. For applications involving piecewise composite curves the B-spline basis is thus to be preferred over the Bézier basis.

Generalizing to include nonuniform knot vectors gives the curve certain advantages over the subset of uniform B-splines. We shall see later in the section on interpolation that using uniform B-splines to interpolate through a set of unevenly spaced data points gives rise to unwanted oscillations. In this context, the nonuniform B-spline gives significantly better results. In general, shape control for uniform B-splines is affected by moving control points; with the introduction of nonuniform knot vectors, however, we have additional control over shape, thereby enabling us to model a larger class of shapes.

3.5.6 Nonperiodic knot vectors

Returning to Equation (3.6); since each curve segment is defined over one interval and since a given blending function has a support over k intervals, it follows that there are at most k blending functions nonzero over a given interval. Therefore each curve segment requires k control points for its definition, the first being $(p_0, \ldots, p_k)$ and the last $(p_{n-k+1}, \ldots, p_n)$. Therefore there exist $n - k + 2$ distinct curve segments. This would imply $n - k + 2$ distinct knot intervals which implies $n - k + 3$ distinct knots. Since there are $n + k + 1$ knots in the knot vector, we have

$$(n + k + 1) - (n - k + 3) = 2k - 2$$

knots left to define.

The commonest type of knot vector, the nonperiodic knot vector, deals with this by repeating each of the first and last knots an extra $k - 1$ times. These end knots are said to have multiplicity k. The knot vector has the form:

$$T = (t_0, \ldots, t_{n+k})$$

$$= (\underbrace{0, \ldots, 0}_{k}, t_k, \ldots, t_n, \underbrace{1, \ldots, 1}_{k})$$

The uniform knot vector is given by:

$$t_i = \begin{cases} 0 & i = 0, \ldots, k-1 \\ i - k + 1 & i = k, \ldots, n-1 \\ n - k + 2 & i = n, \ldots, n+k-1 \end{cases}$$

(And the reader can verify that the formulation constructed in Section 3.5.3 is the Cox de Boor algorithm unravelled for the specific case of $k = 4$ with a uniform nonperiodic vector.) Endowing the end points with multiplicity k means that the end points and the end control points are coincident. It can be shown that:

$$Q(t_{k-1}) = p_0$$
$$Q(t_{n+1}) = p_n$$

Outside of this interval $[t_{k-1}, t_{n+1}]$ the curve is not defined since when two knots are identical $t_j = t_{j+1}$ the curve segment Q_j reduces to a single point – which brings us to a powerful facility afforded us by the B-spline representation.

3.5.7 Knot insertion

It is possible to add a new knot and control point anywhere along a nonuniform B-spline without changing the shape of the curve. This is a valuable tool. The consequences of knot insertion fall into two categories:

1. Adding a new knot to the knot vector enables easy shape modification by refinement. New knots are inserted along that section of the curve that requires changing. So a user interface to modify geometry locally can be based on knot insertion.
2. Adding a new knot by repeating an existing knot reduces parametric continuity. $Q(t_i)$ is $k - m - 1$ times differentiable at a knot t_i of multiplicity m, $t_i = t_{i+1} = \ldots = t_{i+m}$. We have seen that for a nonperiodic knot vector a knot of multiplicity k at the end points makes the curve pass through the end control points. In general, if any knot t_i has multiplicity k then $Q(t_i)$ is a control point. Finally, the reader will note that an interior knot of multiplicity k effectively splits the B-spline into two distinct B-splines since each segment has its own nonintersecting set of control points.

The general formula for inserting a single knot is as follows. Let

$$Q(u) = \sum_{i=0}^{n} p_i N_{i,k}(u)$$

be the B-spline curve with knot vector $(t_0, \ldots, t_{n+k})$. Let us insert a new knot:

$$t' \in (t_0, t_{n+k}) \qquad t_j < t' \leqslant t_{j+1}$$

The same curve is described by the new set of control points p_i':

$$Q(u) = \sum_{i=0}^{n+1} p_i' N_{i,k}(u)$$

where:

$$p_0' = p_0, p_{n+1}' = p_n \text{ and } p_i' = (1 - a_i)p_{i-1} + a_i p_i$$

$$a_i = \begin{cases} 1 & i = 1, \ldots, j-k \\ \dfrac{t' - t_i}{t_{i+k} - t_i} & i = j-k+1, \ldots, j \\ 0 & i = j+1, \ldots, n \end{cases}$$

The derivation and examples are given in [BÖHM82]. If it is required to insert more than one knot at a time, then a generalization of this algorithm called the Oslo algorithm [COHE83] should be used.

3.5.8 The Bézier B-spline connection

Consider a knot vector with no interior knots. For a spline of order k there are $2k$ knots with a knot vector given by

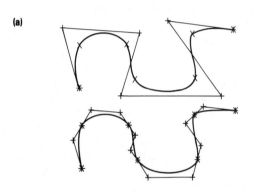

(a)

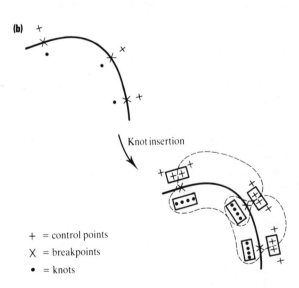

(b)

+ = control points
X = breakpoints
• = knots

Knot insertion

Figure 3.31 (a) Two representations of the same curve and their convex hulls. The upper representation is a nonuniform B-spline, the lower a Bézier generated by knot insertion. (b) Two representations of the same curve (nonuniform B-spline and Bézier) showing the relationship between control points, breakpoints and knots between the two representations.

$$t_i = 0 \quad 0 \leqslant i < k$$
$$t_i = 1 \quad k \leqslant i < 2k \qquad (3.7)$$

Consider this knot vector in relation to the function tree of Figure 3.30. A leaf of this tree will only be nonzero if its denominator $t_{j+1} - t_j$ is nonzero. We have seen (Section 3.5.4) that the support of the topmost node of $N_{i,k}(u)$ contains the support of the nodes lower down. It follows that $N_{i,k}(u)$ is nonzero only if it contains intervals $[j, j+1]$ that are nonzero. Now we started this section by defining a knot vector that is only nonzero over one interval $[k-1, k]$. It follows that $N_{i,k}(u)$ is nonzero only if its support $[i, i+k]$ contains the interval $[k-1, k]$ from which we can deduce:

$$i \leqslant k - 1$$
$$i + k \geqslant k$$

Using Equation (3.7) this implies that

$$t_i = 0 \text{ and } t_{i+k} = 1 \quad \text{for all } i,k$$

Substituting this into the Cox de Boor algorithm gives us

$$N_{i,k}(u) = u N_{i,k-1}(u) + (1-u) N_{i+1,k-1}(u)$$

which is the de Casteljau algorithm for Bézier curves. From which we can conclude that a B-spline curve with no interior knots is a Bézier curve.

Now we can take any knot vector and, via knot insertion, increase the multiplicity of all knots to have multiplicity k. As we have seen, each segment can now be considered distinctly as a curve which has a knot vector with no interior points like a Bézier curve. This result is important, as it provides us with a route for conversion from a B-spline to a Bézier representation and, by extension, from B-spline surfaces to Bézier surfaces enabling us therefore to render B-spline surfaces using our Bézier patch splitter. Others [ROCK89] follow the same route.

The reader may wonder why the standard method of converting from one basis to another, via say matrix multiplication, is not used. The answer is that for a nonuniform B-spline the basis function is not the same for each curve segment as it also depends on the local knot distribution. This method would require calculating the basis functions and then calculating the change of basis matrix for each segment in turn. It is cheaper numerically to use knot insertion.

Figure 3.31(a) shows the two different representations of the same curve. The upper curve is the nonuniform B-spline; the lower curve shows it decomposed into Bézier segments by multiple knot insertion – distinct segments are delineated by crosses which are called breakpoints.

One breakpoint is always coincident with a number of knots by definition. Schematically, the distribution of knots and control points at the breakpoints before and after knot insertion is given in Figure 3.31(b). The ringed groups of knots and control points indicate distinct Bézier segments. A group of points enclosed by a rectangle indicates that these points are coincident.

3.6 Interpolation

Interpolation finds two major applications in computer graphics. It is used as a modelling tool where a parametric surface is fitted to a set of data points that may, for example, be the output from a digitizer or scanner. In this way an internal representation of real objects can be obtained. Interpolation is also used in computer animation to imitate the classical technique of 'in-betweening'. An animator wishing to define the motion of an object, or camera, may do so by specifying certain points in space and time. A curve will then be required to interpolate through these 'keyframes'. Information for the in-between frames is then derived from these curves (see Chapter 15).

Stated baldly the problem of interpolation is, given a set of data points, to seek a curve (or surface) that passes through these points. Cubic splines are the classical tool used to solve this problem, producing twice differentiable interpolants that give a high degree of flexibility within a fairly simple mathematical framework.

As we shall see, while it may be relatively easy to find a curve that fits through the data points, it is a much trickier problem to find one whose whole shape is pleasing to the eye. The importance of this is obvious in a modelling context. In animation we also require a 'pleasing' curve otherwise eccentric motion may result. This issue has occupied a significant amount of research and it is responsible for such notions as chord length parametrization and the distinction between geometric and parametric continuity. These, and other related topics, will be covered in this section. Since, as we have seen, B-splines guarantee continuity across segments, the B-spline basis would seem a natural candidate for interpolation.

3.6.1 Interpolation using B-splines

Let us assume the knot vector is given and that it is nonperiodic and since we are concerned with cubics we let $k = 4$. Now, with nonperiodic knot vectors we have a complication at the end points. Assume that there exist $n + 1$ control points. We have seen (Section 3.5.6) that at the end-points:

$$Q(t_3) = p_0$$
$$Q(t_{n+1}) = p_n$$

and that the curve is defined over $[t_3, t_{n+1}]$ only. This implies that there exist only $n - 2$ distinct intervals and so only $n - 1$ distinct breakpoints on the curve. These breakpoints are our data points through which our curve is to interpolate. So, assuming a knot vector, the problem is to define $n + 1$ control points given $n - 1$ data points, which we shall denote as the set X_i, $i = 0, \ldots, n - 2$. The system is underdefined and for a unique solution we need to specify two further conditions at the start and the end of the curve. We shall make the two end control points coincident (although it is not the only end condition available). Our $n + 1$ equations in $n + 1$ unknowns are therefore given by the $n - 1$ equations that equate the breakpoints to the data points:

$$Q(t_{i+3}) = X_i \qquad i = 0, \ldots n - 2$$

and the end conditions

$$p_0 = p_1, p_n = p_{n-1}$$

The configuration of data points, knot points and control points is shown schematically in Figure 3.32.

The expression $Q(t_{i+3}) = X_i$ tells us we need to evaluate the blending function at knot values. The easiest way to do this is to find which leaves of our function

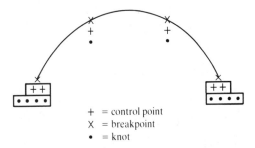

+ = control point
X = breakpoint
• = knot

Figure 3.32 Interpolation using B-splines – the configuration of data points, knot points and control points.

$$N_{i,4}(t_{i+1}) = \frac{(t_{i+1} - t_i)^2}{(t_{i+2} - t_i)(t_{i+3} - t_i)}$$

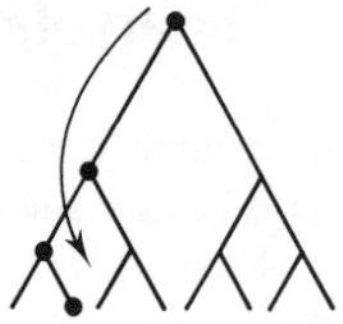

$$N_{i,4}(t_{i+2}) = \frac{(t_{i+2} - t_i)(t_{i+3} - t_{i+2})}{(t_{i+3} - t_{i+1})(t_{i+3} - t_i)} + \frac{(t_{i+4} - t_{i+2})(t_{i+2} - t_{i+1})}{(t_{i+4} - t_{i+1})(t_{i+3} - t_{i+1})}$$

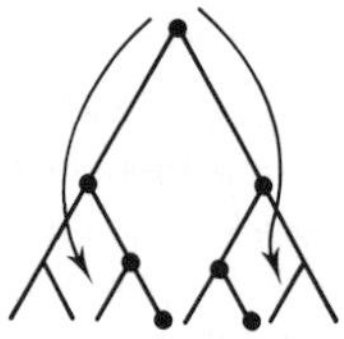

$$N_{i,4}(t_{i+3}) = \frac{(t_{i+4} - t_{i+3})^2}{(t_{i+4} - t_{i+1})(t_{i+4} - t_{i+2})}$$

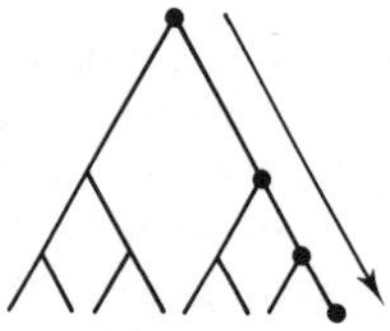

Figure 3.33   The evaluation of $N_{i,4}()$.

tree of Figure 3.30 are nonzero and work backwards ($N_{i,1}(t_j)$ is nonzero only if $i = j$). Since $N_{i,4}(u)$ has support (t_i, t_{i+4}) it has to be evaluated for the five knots contained by this support. These evaluations alongside the nonzero components of their function are shown in Figure 3.33. From this we can deduce that the only nonzero contributions to the curve at $Q(t_i)$ are given by

$$Q(t_i) = N_{i-3,4}(t_i)p_{i-3} + N_{i-2,4}(t_i)p_{i-2}$$
$$+ N_{i-1,4}(t_i)p_{i-1}$$

so:

$$Q(t_{i+3}) = N_{i,4}(t_{i+3})p_i + N_{i+1,4}(t_{i+3})p_{i+1}$$
$$+ N_{i+2,4}(t_{i+3})p_{i+2}$$

which gives:

$$X_i = \alpha_i p_i + \beta_i p_{i+1} + \Gamma_i p_{i+2}$$

where:

$$\alpha_i = N_{i,4}(t_{i+3})$$
$$\beta_i = N_{i+1,4}(t_{i+3})$$
$$\Gamma_i = N_{i+2,4}(t_{i+3})$$

In matrix formulation, the complete set of equations, relating to the data and control points, is given by:

$$
\begin{bmatrix}
1 & & & & & \\
\alpha_1 & \beta_1 & \Gamma_1 & & & \\
& & \cdot & & & \\
& & & \cdot & & \\
& & & \alpha_{n-3} & \beta_{n-3} & \Gamma_{n-3} \\
& & & & & 1
\end{bmatrix}
\begin{bmatrix}
p_1 \\ p_2 \\ \cdot \\ \cdot \\ p_{n-2} \\ p_{n-1}
\end{bmatrix}
=
\begin{bmatrix}
X_0 \\ X_1 \\ \cdot \\ \cdot \\ X_{n-3} \\ X_{n-2}
\end{bmatrix}
$$

which in the case of uniform B-splines reduces to

$$
\begin{bmatrix}
1 & & & & & \\
3/2 & 7/2 & 1 & & & \\
& 1 & 4 & 1 & & \\
& & \cdot & & & \\
& & & 1 & 4 & 1 \\
& & & 1 & 7/2 & 3/2 \\
& & & & & 1
\end{bmatrix}
\begin{bmatrix}
p_1 \\ p_2 \\ \cdot \\ \cdot \\ p_{n-2} \\ p_{n-1}
\end{bmatrix}
=
\begin{bmatrix}
X_0 \\ 6X_1 \\ \cdot \\ \cdot \\ 6X_{n-3} \\ X_{n-2}
\end{bmatrix}
$$

Listing 3.3 gives a routine *interpolate_bspline ( )* that returns the control points given a set of data points *nodata* in number and given a nonperiodic knot vector *knots*. This routine calls a specialized numerical routine *tridiag( )* that solves for points $X[\ ][3]$ given the tridiagonal linear set

$$
\begin{bmatrix}
b_0 & c_0 & & & & \\
a_1 & b_1 & c_1 & & & \\
& & \cdot & & & \\
& & & \cdot & & \\
& & & a_{n-2} & b_{n-2} & c_{n-2} \\
& & & & a_{n-1} & b_{n-1}
\end{bmatrix}
\begin{bmatrix}
X_0 \\ X_1 \\ \cdot \\ \cdot \\ X_{n-2} \\ X_{n-1}
\end{bmatrix}
=
\begin{bmatrix}
d_0 \\ d_1 \\ \cdot \\ \cdot \\ d_{n-2} \\ d_{n-1}
\end{bmatrix}
$$

Texts on numerical analysis will tell you that this system of equations is said to be tridiagonal – only the diagonal elements and the two neighbours are nonzero. By exploiting the structure of the tridiagonal matrix we can solve more efficiently and bypass the standard elimination techniques.

The basic scheme is as follows. Since any row of the matrix equation represents one linear equation of the system, and we can add any two multiples of these equations together without affecting the result, we can alter a row of the matrix by adding multiples of any other row. We perform a forward substitution sweep, where for each row ($i > 0$) we eliminate the leftmost element, that is the a_i, of that row using the row directly above, that is row $i - 1$, and then normalize the diagonal. The resulting matrix will look like this:

Listing 3.3   interpolate_bspline.c

```
interpolate_bspline(data,control,knots,nodata)
float  data[][3],control[][3],knots[];
int  nodata;
{
            int  i;
            float  *alpha,*beta,*gamma;
            float  t1,t2,t3,t4,t5;

            alpha = (float *)malloc(nodata*sizeof(float));
            beta  = (float *)malloc(nodata*sizeof(float));
            gamma = (float *)malloc(nodata*sizeof(float));

            alpha[0] = 0. ; beta[0] = 1. ; gamma[0] = 0. ;
            alpha[nodata-1] = 0.; beta[nodata-1] = 1.; gamma[nodata-1] = 0.;

            for  (i=1;i<nodata-1;i++)  {
                        t1 = knots[i+1];
                        t2 = knots[i+2];
                        t3 = knots[i+3];
                        t4 = knots[i+4];
                        t5 = knots[i+5];

                        alpha[i] = (t4 - t3)*(t4 - t3)/(t4 - t1);
                        beta[i] = (t3 - t1)*(t4 - t3)/(t4 - t1) + (t5 - t3)*(t3 - t2)/(t5 - t2);
                        gamma[i] = (t3 - t2)*(t3 - t2)/(t5 - t2);
                        alpha[i] /= (t4-t2);
                        beta[i]  /= (t4-t2);
                        gamma[i] /= (t4-t2);
            }

            tridiag(alpha,beta,gamma,data,control+1,nodata);

            for  (i=0;i<3;i++)  {
                        control[0][i] = control[1][i];
                        control[nodata+1][i] = control[nodata][i];
            }

            free(alpha);free(beta);free(gamma);
}
```

$$\begin{bmatrix} 1 & \Gamma_0 & & & & \\ & 1 & \Gamma_1 & & & \\ & & \cdot & & & \\ & & & \cdot & & \\ & & & & \cdot & \\ & & & & 1 & \Gamma_{n-2} \\ & & & & & 1 \end{bmatrix} \begin{bmatrix} X_0 \\ X_1 \\ \cdot \\ \cdot \\ \cdot \\ X_{n-2} \\ X_{n-1} \end{bmatrix} = \begin{bmatrix} \delta_0 \\ \delta_1 \\ \cdot \\ \cdot \\ \cdot \\ \delta_{n-2} \\ \delta_{n-1} \end{bmatrix}$$

So

$$X_{n-1} = \delta_{n-1}$$

and the remaining values for X_i ($i = n - 2, n - 1, \ldots, 1, 0$) are solved by substituting backwards. That is

$$X_i = \delta_i - \Gamma_i X_{i+1}$$

Code for this technique is given in Listing 3.4.

Listing 3.4 tridiag.c

```
tridiag(a,b,c,d,x,n)
float  a[],b[],c[],d[],x[];
int  n;
{
           int  j;
           float  beta,*gamma,*delta;

           gamma = (float *)malloc(n*sizeof(float));
           delta = (float *)malloc(n*sizeof(float));

           /* forward elimination sweep */
           gamma[0] = c[0]/b[0];
           delta[0] = d[0]/b[0];
           for  (j=1;j<n;j++) {

                      beta = b[j]–a[j]*gamma[j–1];
                      gamma[j] = c[j]/beta;
                      delta[j] = (d[j]–a[j]*delta[j–1])/beta;
           }

           /* backward substitution sweep */
           x[n–1] = delta[n–1];
           for  (j=n–2;j>=0;j––) x[j] = delta[j]–gamma[j]*x[j+1];

           free(gamma);  free(delta);
}
```

3.6.2 A digression: periodic interpolation

The above scheme describes interpolation for a non-periodic knot vector. For interpolation of closed curves (such as that shown in Figure 3.34) a periodic knot vector, where all indices are computed modulus the period, is required and the resultant linear system is no longer tridiagonal and takes the form:

$$
\begin{bmatrix}
b_0 & c_0 & & & & a_0 \\
a_1 & b_1 & c_1 & & & \\
 & & & \ddots & & \\
 & & & a_{n-1} & b_{n-2} & c_{n-2} \\
c_{n-1} & & & & a_{n-1} & b_{n-1}
\end{bmatrix}
\begin{bmatrix}
X_0 \\ X_1 \\ \vdots \\ \vdots \\ X_{n-2} \\ X_{n-1}
\end{bmatrix}
=
\begin{bmatrix}
d_0 \\ d_1 \\ \vdots \\ \vdots \\ d_{n-2} \\ d_{n-1}
\end{bmatrix}
$$

Although the system is no longer tridiagonal, we can still exploit its structure to arrive at an efficient solution. We perform a forward substitution phase exactly as before, but additionally we compute and save values in the rightmost column. This gives:

$$
\begin{bmatrix}
1 & \Gamma_0 & & & & & \mu_0 \\
 & 1 & \Gamma_1 & & & & \mu_1 \\
 & & & \ddots & & & \\
 & & & 1 & \Gamma_{n-3} & \mu_{n-3} \\
 & & & & a_{n-2} & b_{n-2} & c_{n-2} \\
c_{n-1} & & & & & a_{n-1} & b_{n-1}
\end{bmatrix}
\begin{bmatrix}
X_0 \\ X_1 \\ \vdots \\ \vdots \\ X_{n-3} \\ X_{n-2} \\ X_{n-1}
\end{bmatrix}
=
\begin{bmatrix}
\delta_0 \\ \delta_1 \\ \vdots \\ \vdots \\ \delta_{n-3} \\ d_{n-2} \\ d_{n-1}
\end{bmatrix}
$$

Next we successively cancel, column by column, the leftmost value in the bottom row to arrive at:

$$
\begin{bmatrix}
1 & \Gamma_0 & & & & & \mu_0 \\
 & 1 & \Gamma_n & & & & \mu_1 \\
 & & & \ddots & & & \\
 & & & 1 & \Gamma_{n-3} & \mu_{n-3} \\
 & & & & a_{n-2} & b_{n-2} & c_{n-2} \\
 & & & & c_n & a_n & b_n
\end{bmatrix}
\begin{bmatrix}
X_0 \\ X_1 \\ \vdots \\ \vdots \\ X_{n-3} \\ X_{n-2} \\ X_{n-1}
\end{bmatrix}
=
\begin{bmatrix}
\delta_0 \\ \delta_1 \\ \vdots \\ \vdots \\ \delta_{n-3} \\ d_{n-2} \\ d_n
\end{bmatrix}
$$

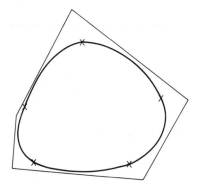

Figure 3.34 Interpolation through five data points (crosses) with a periodic knot vector.

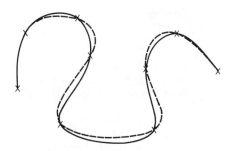

Figure 3.35 Interpolation using chord length parametrization (bold) compared with a uniform knot vector (dashed).

the bottom three rows are three independent equations in three unknowns and can easily be solved. The remaining values of X_i ($i = n - 4, n - 3, \ldots, 1,0$) are solved using backward substitution given

$$X_i = \delta_i - \mu_i X_{n-1} - \Gamma_i X_{i+1}$$

Listing 3.5 gives the necessary routines for this technique.

3.6.3 Chord length parametrization

Returning to the nonperiodic knot vector, we are now in a position to justify an earlier statement claiming that the introduction of a nonuniform B-spline offers us much better shape control than the uniform B-spline. The problem of assigning a knot vector to a curve is often stated as how to parametrize that curve. So far we have assumed a knot vector, or parametrization, for our interpolating curves. It turns out that certain methods of parametrization, the majority of them heuristic, produce significantly better results than others.

Figure 3.35 illustrates a case in point, showing two B-splines with different parametrizations interpolating the same set of points. The dashed line has a uniform knot vector whereas the unbroken line is parametrized using a heuristic known as chord length parametrization given by

$$\frac{t_{i+4} - t_{i+3}}{t_{i+5} - t_{i+4}} = \frac{|X_{i+1} - X_i|}{|X_{i+2} - X_{i+1}|}$$

that is, the knot spacing is proportional to the distance between the data points. Note how in comparison the uniform B-spline tends to oscillate and overshoot. The reason why uniform knot vectors are inferior is that they

do not take into account the geometry of the data points. The best intuitive explanation of this is by Farin [FARI90] where he compares the global parameter u to time and imagines a car travelling along a curve. For a uniform parametrization the car spends the same amount of time travelling between any two data points regardless of their distance apart. If the distance of a segment is large, the car will move at a high speed, compared to the speed at which it moves over a small segment. Since the car cannot abruptly change speed (continuous speed and acceleration being analogous to C^1 and C^2 parametric continuity) it will tend to overshoot. A car that adjusts the time spent between data points according to their distribution will offer a smoother ride and one way of achieving this is to have the knot spacing proportional to the distances between the data points. Figure 3.36 shows the differences between the curves is more pronounced as the distance between data points varies more widely.

Other heuristics for parametrizing interpolating B-splines exist (for example [FOLE89]). For our purpose,

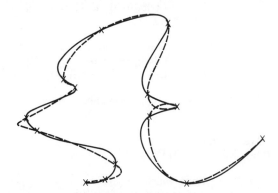

Figure 3.36 The same as Figure 3.35 but with data points unevenly spaced.

Listing 3.5   tridiag_circular.c

```
tridiag_circular(a,b,c,d,x,n)
float  a[],b[],c[],d[],x[];
int  n;
{
          int  i,j;
          float  beta,*gamma,*mu,*delta;
          float  bn,cn,dn,M[3][3],D[3],X[3];

          gamma = (float *)malloc(n*sizeof(float));
          delta = (float *)malloc(n*sizeof(float));
          mu    = (float *)malloc(n*sizeof(float));

          /* forward elimination sweep */
          gamma[0] = c[0]/b[0];
          mu[0]    = a[0]/b[0];
          delta[0] = d[0]/b[0];
          for  (j=1;j<n-2;j++) {

                    beta = b[j] - a[j]*gamma[j-1];
                    gamma[j] = c[j]/beta;
                    mu[j]    = -a[j]*mu[j-1]/beta;
                    delta[j] = (d[j]-a[j]*delta[j-1])/beta;
          }

          /* successive elimination of leftmost value in the bottom row */
          cn=c[n-1];bn=b[n-1];dn=d[n-1];
          for  (j=1;j<n-2;j++) {

                    bn = bn - mu[j-1]*cn;
                    dn = dn - delta[j-1]*cn;
                    cn = -gamma[j-1]*cn;
          }

          /* solve resultant three simultaneous eqns */
          M[0][0] = 1.; M[0][1] = gamma[n-3]; M[0][2] = mu[n-3];
          M[1][0] = a[n-2]; M[1][1] = b[n-2]; M[1][2] = c[n-2];
          M[2][0] = cn; M[2][1] = a[n-1]; M[2][2] = bn;
          D[0] = delta[n-3]; D[1] = d[n-2]; D[2] = dn;
          solve3(M,D,X);

          /* backward substitution sweep */
          for  (j=0;j<3;j++)  x[n-3+j] = X[j];
          for  (j=n-4;j>=0;j--)  x[j] = delta[j] -  gamma[j]*x[j+1] - mu[j]*x[n-1];

          free(gamma);  free(delta);  free(mu);
}

solve3(M,X,D)
float  M[3][3],X[3],D[3];
{
          float  m[2][2],d[2],piv;
          piv = -M[1][0]/M[0][0];
```

Listing 3.5   cont.

```
            m[0][0] = M[1][1] + piv*M[0][1];
            m[0][1] = M[1][2] + piv*M[0][2];
            d[0] = D[1] + piv*D[0];
            piv = −M[2][0]/M[0][0];
            m[1][0] = M[2][1] + piv*M[0][1];
            m[1][1] = M[2][2] + piv*M[0][2];
            d[1] = D[2] + piv*D[0];
            piv = −m[1][0]/m[0][0];
            X[2] = (d[1] + piv*d[0])/(m[1][1] + piv*m[0][1]);
            X[1] = (d[0] − m[0][1]*X[2])/m[0][0];
            X[0] = (D[0] − M[0][2]*X[2] − M[0][1]*X[1])/M[0][0];
}
```

however (see Section 3.7), the chord length parametrization proved sufficient.

3.7 Surface fitting

As we have pointed out, there are many applications where we wish to derive a composite patch representation from a three-dimensional field of data points. Fitting a parametric surface through an arbitrary set of data points is a difficult problem. Polygonal surface fitting is relatively trivial – it is just a case of joining the data points into polygonal facets. But parametric surface fitting requires us to construct an entire analytical description from a mere collection of points. Far more information has to be generated than actually exists so consequently a good deal of assumptions have to be made along the way.

Throughout most of this chapter we have stated that the properties of curves extend to surfaces in a manner that is natural and straightforward. Sadly this is not the case when moving from curve fitting to surface fitting. The transition introduces problems related to topology, interior control points and so on, that are unique to surfaces. Mathematically we can extend the above interpolation techniques from a curve domain to a surface domain. However, there are significant practical problems in fitting a composite net of patches through a field of data points. In the case of curves the only topology of the points is sequential – all that needs to be specified is the order in which the points are to be interpolated. This no longer holds when we move to surfaces – there is no such implicit connectivity in a field of data points through which a surface is to be fitted. We need to adopt a more ad hoc approach. Because of these difficulties the literature on surface fitting is notably sparse. Most texts, when discussing patches in a modelling context, consider the trivial problem of continuity across a few patches and leave it at that. Apart from a few notable exceptions [SCHM86, REEV90] surface fitting has been largely ignored.

In order to illuminate the issues involved, we shall take a specific approach based on a traditional approach known as 'lofting', and examine the various problems as they arise.

3.7.1 A B-spline surface fitter

Before computers were invented, designers of ships' hulls or aircraft fuselages would take a series of parallel cross-sections and construct a set of longitudinal curves across these sections, blending the two sets of curves together to form the final three-dimensional shape. Traditionally this was done full size and the only space available to carry out such a procedure tended to be a loft – hence the term 'lofting'.

We shall adopt a similar approach using the interpolation scheme of the nonuniform B-spline with chord length parametrization as described in Section 3.6.3. This interpolation scheme was chosen because of its known superiority over the uniform B-spline. The route we shall adopt will differ from the typical approach taken in computer graphics, which explicitly derives the net of control points by solving a set of simultaneous equations of u and v using tensor product interpolants. Instead, we take a route common in the automotive field where a network of interpolating curves is constructed – this curve network is then 'filled in' in order to generate surfaces.

The first thing to do is to construct a curve network that passes through the data points. We adopt the lofting paradigm insofar as we first construct a set of curves in one direction; let this be the direction of parameter u, that corresponds loosely to the cross-sectional curve sections above, followed by constructing a second set of curves that pass through this first set; let this be in the direction of parameter v, that corresponds loosely to the longitudinal curves above. These two sets of curves, connected at the data points, form our curve network. The interpolation procedure that constructs the curve network from the data points breaks down into the following steps (which are also represented schematically in Figure 3.37):

1. The data points are separated into groups – each group not necessarily containing the same number of data points. A curve is interpolated through each separate group. Each of these curves will have their own distinct knot vector. We shall call these curves the U-curves. Figure 3.37 shows three such U-curves interpolating through 2, 3 and 2 data points respectively.

2. Now because the tensor product representation of a B-spline surface has one knot vector for the u-direction and one for the v-direction, a single knot vector must be chosen for all the U-curves. This is done by taking the union of all the distinct knot vec-

tors to form one merged knot vector – which we shall call the U-knot vector. Each of the U-curves, in order to be described by the U-knot vector, has additional knots inserted where necessary. In our simplified figurative example, the central U-curve has three distinct knots including one interior knot whereas the other two U-curves have knot vectors with no interior knots. The U-knot vector will therefore be identical to the knot vector of the central U-curve and so the two end U-curves have to have this interior knot inserted. The inserted knots are shown by the circled crosses in Figure 3.37.

3. Data points for a given V-curve are obtained by moving along each of the U-curves for a given knot value of the U-knot vector. The V-curve is formed by interpolating through these data points, again by using chord length parametrization. This is shown in Figure 3.37. By their very construction, the V-curves intersect the U-curves at points of constant u.

4. Just as in step 2 the V-curves will have distinct knot vectors. The knot vectors are merged to form one knot vector, the V-knot vector, and knots are inserted along the V-curves where necessary. The inserted knots are shown by the squared crosses in Figure 3.37. Now, our original U-curves do not necessarily intersect the V-curves at points of constant v. A new set of U-curves that are constant in v is obtained by connecting points of constant v along the V-curves.

5. Figure 3.37 shows the final network of curves and its relationship to the original data points. Here the only curves drawn are either curves of constant u or cons-

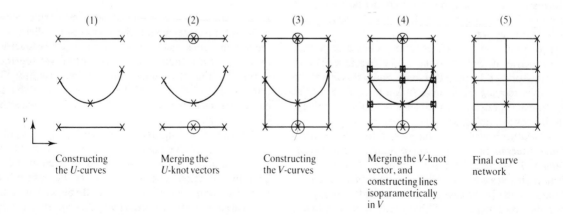

(1)	(2)	(3)	(4)	(5)
Constructing the U-curves	Merging the U-knot vectors	Constructing the V-curves	Merging the V-knot vector, and constructing lines isoparametrically in V	Final curve network

Figure 3.37   The five stages in constructing an isoparametric curve network from a set of data points.

tant v, and so the regions marked out by them are rectangular in u, v-space. This is a crucial point since they can now be represented as patches which also mark out rectangular domains in u, v-space. Note that in general one data point will have two isoparametric lines running through it.

Having obtained our network of curves, all that remains is to obtain from it a patch representation in order to arrive at a full surface description. This is done in two steps which are shown schematically in Figure 3.38.

6. We bypass the B-spline surface representation altogether by taking each curve in the curve network and converting it to Bézier form by multiple knot insertion (Section 3.5.7). The curve network thus has an alternative representation as a series of parametrically discontinuous single Bézier curve segments (Figure 3.38a and b).

7. Each rectangular region bounded by (u_i, v_j), (u_{i+1}, v_{j+1}) in parameter space is delineated from four Bézier curves from the previous step. We convert these four Bézier curves into a single Bézier patch (Figure 3.38c).

The details of step 6 are given in Section 3.5.7. Step 7 is a litle more involved and we now describe it in greater detail. Let our single Bézier patch be defined over the parametric domain s, $t \in [0, 1]$. We write:

$$Q(s, t) = \sum_{i=0}^{3} \sum_{j=0}^{3} p_{ij} B_i(s) B_j(t)$$

where $B_i(s)$ $(i = 0, \ldots, 3)$ are the Bernstein polynomials of degree 3. The values of $p_{ij}(i, j = 0, \ldots, 3)$ are obtained by expressing them in terms of the parametric derivatives of the surface at the corners of the patch. The values for these surface derivatives are obtained from the curve network. The relationship of the p_{ij} to the surface derivatives Q_s, Q_t and Q_{st} is found by differentiating the above expression and substituting for s, $t = 0, 1$. At the point $(s, t) = (0, 0)$, for example, it is easy to show:

$$p_{00} = Q(0, 0)$$

$$p_{01} = \frac{Q_t(0, 0)}{3} + Q(0, 0)$$

$$p_{10} = \frac{Q_s(0, 0)}{3} + Q(0, 0)$$

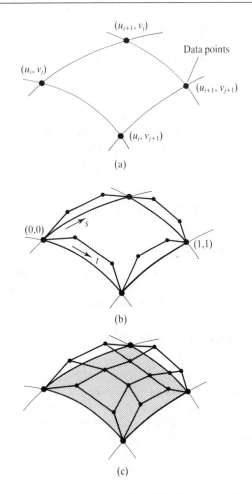

(a)

(b)

(c)

Figure 3.38 A B spline-surface fitter. (a) B-spline representation of curve network. (b) Individual Bézier segments between data points. (c) Bézier patches formed from Bézier segments.

$$p_{11} = \frac{Q_{st}(0, 0)}{9} + \frac{Q_s(0, 0) + Q_t(0, 0)}{3} + Q(0, 0)$$

Similar expressions at the remaining corners are easily derived. From these expressions it can be seen that the corner control points are just the corresponding points on the curve network. The remaining control points along the edges are related to the corresponding tangents along that edge and are readily obtained from the Bézier curve segment representation of the curve network. (Section 3.3.3 gives the simple relation between tangents at the end points and the control points of a Bézier curve segment.)

3.7.2 The twist vector

The inner control points are more problematic since they depend on the partial derivatives in both s and t, Q_{st}, and no immediate value for this can be obtained directly from the curve network. This quantity Q_{st} is called the 'twist vector' and has a neat geometrical interpretation. Rearranging the above expressions to get $Q_{st}(0,0)$ in terms of the control points p_{ij} yields:

$$Q_{st}(0,0) = 9\big((p_{11} - p_{10}) - (p_{01} - p_{00}) \big)$$

Let p be the point that makes the points $(p_{00}, p_{01}, p_{10}, p)$ a parallelogram, then by definition

$$p - p_{10} = p_{01} - p_{00}$$
$$p = p_{10} + p_{01} - p_{00}$$

The vector $p_{11} - p$ as shown in Figure 3.39 is a measure of the deviation of the quadrilateral $(p_{00}, p_{01}, p_{10}, p_{11})$ of the control net of the Bézier patch from a parallelogram. By above

$$p_{11} - p = (p_{11} - p_{10}) - (p_{01} - p_{00})$$
$$= 9 Q_{st}(0,0)$$

Early attempts at finding a surface representation from a curve network ignored the problems of finding a twist vector by simply setting it to zero. However, there is a problem with this. A surface that has zero twist everywhere is of the form:

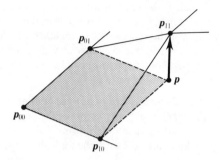

Figure 3.39   The twist coefficients are proportional to the deviations of the control polygon subquadrilateral from a parallelogram.

$$Q(s,t) = As + Bt + C$$

that is, a planar surface. If we set the twist to zero at the patch corners then, locally, the patch will be planar or flat. Setting the twist to zero produced flaws so standard in the CAD industry that they were given their own name, 'pseudo-flats'; these were places where it looked like a thumb had pushed the surface flat. Subsequent research [BARN78, FARI90] tackled the problem of estimating nonzero twist vectors which produced 'fuller' surfaces and we adopt one such method here. This is the so-called Adini's twist which considers the patch not as an isolated entity, but as part of a larger surface. The idea is to consider the point at which the twist is to be calculated as

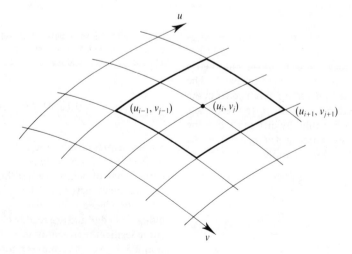

Figure 3.40   Adini's twist – four patches containing point (u_i, v_j) make up one large patch marked bold. From this larger patch the twist vector at the central point, $Q_{uv}(u_i, v_j)$, is obtained.

lying on the surface of a larger patch made up of the outer boundary curves of the four patches that share this point, as shown in Figure 3.40. This larger patch has a well-defined twist at the point in question given by:

$$Q_{uv}(u_i, v_j) = \frac{Q_v(u_{i+1}, v_j) - Q_v(u_{i-1}, v_j)}{u_{i+1} - u_{i-1}}$$

$$+ \frac{Q_u(u_i, v_{j+1}) - Q_u(u_i, v_{j-1})}{v_{j+1} - v_{j-1}}$$

$$- \frac{Q(u_{i+1}, v_{j+1}) - Q(u_{i-1}, v_{j+1}) - Q(u_{i+1}, v_{j-1}) + Q(u_{i-1}, v_{j-1})}{(u_{i+1} - u_{i-1})(v_{j+1} - v_{j-1})}$$

Figure 3.41 shows two patch surfaces illustrating the effect of nonzero twist. Both patch surfaces have identical underlying curve networks and differ only in the twists assigned to the patch. In one case the twist was set to zero, in the other Adini's method for calculating twist was used. The patch was lit so that a specular highlight

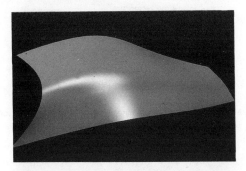

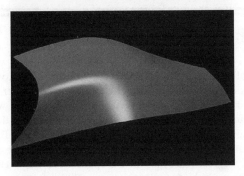

Figure 3.41 Illustrating the effect of nonzero twist. Both patch surfaces are the same except in the twist assigned to each. One has zero twist. One has a nonzero twist applied to it using Adini's method. The surface was lit so that a specular highlight follows a ridge along it. The zero twist patch contains a pseudoflat that breaks up the highlight.

followed a ridge along it. The zero twist patch contains a pseudo-flat that breaks up this highlight.

Finally, we draw the reader's attention to a rather subtle point that needs to be observed when implementing such a scheme. Care must be taken when transferring twist values obtained from the curve network to the single Bézier patch, as the parametrization of the surface in the two cases differs. For the patch in Figure 3.37 we have $Q(s, t), s, t \in [0, 1]$, whereas the curve network describes the same region of surface by $Q(u, v), u \in [u_i, u_{i+1}], v \in [v_i, v_{i+1}]$. Trivially, these are related by the expressions:

$$s = \frac{u - u_i}{u_{i+1} - u_i}$$

$$t = \frac{v - v_i}{v_{i+1} - v_i}$$

The expression connecting the twists in the two representations can be achieved by the chain rule for differentiation:

$$\frac{\partial^2 Q}{\partial s \partial t} = \frac{\partial^2 Q}{\partial u \partial v} \frac{\partial u}{\partial s} \frac{\partial v}{\partial t}$$

which by the above expression gives us:

$$Q_{st} = (u_{i+1} - u_i)(v_{i+1} - v_i) Q_{uv}$$

We now illustrate the results of this technique; the data points for all the models were collected using a 3D digitizer. Figure 3.42 shows the curve network obtained from a mask and Figure 3.43 the results of turning this network into a parametric surface. Figure 3.44 shows a training shoe, and Figure 3.45 a Boeing 747 aeroplane, the fuselage of which was obtained using surface fitting of data points obtained from a plastic kit model.

This scheme works well for curved objects with a relatively simple topology. Problems arise, however, when trying to apply it to objects with a more complicated topology. Connecting two curve networks together can only be done rigorously by merging the two knot vectors that lie along their common boundary. The merged knot vector can become very large making the surface expensive to store – each new inserted knot means the addition of many control points. This amplification of data can be countered to some extent by defining a tolerance when merging knot vectors, within which two knots are viewed to be sufficiently close together to be regarded as one.

The problems are due to the fact that we are defining

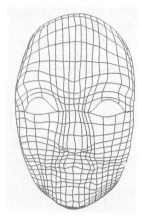

Figure 3.42 The curve network formed from data points output by a three-dimensional digitizer.

Figure 3.43 Transforming the curve network of Figure 3.41 into a parametric surface.

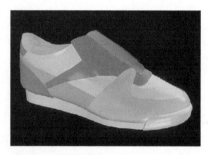

Figure 3.44 A shoe model obtained using the B-spline surface fitter on data points from a three-dimensional digitizer applied to a real shoe.

Figure 3.45 An aircraft model obtained using the B-spline surface fitter on data points from a three-dimensional digitizer applied to a plastic model.

a surface that is parametrically continuous across patch boundaries. A more flexible approach is to replace this condition with one that requires only geometric continuity to be observed across boundaries. This more relaxed condition allows an interpolation scheme to operate locally on the surface which in turn implies an ability to model more complex topologies. Sadly, however, the issue of geometric continuity with regard to surfaces is a complex one although [FARI90] gives a good description of the topic. Reeves [REEV90] gives a somewhat incomplete description of a surface fitter based on geometric continuity that was used to model the baby's face in *Tin-Toy*. The patches used were Catmull–Rom patches modified by a shape parameter heuristic developed for Catmull–Rom curves given in [DERO88].

3.8 B-spline curves: NURBS

B-spline curves divide into three categories: uniform, nonuniform and rational. The term 'uniform' refers to the knot spacing. In this section we will deal with nonuniform rational B-splines (NURBS). There are three reasons for using NURBS as opposed to B-splines: first, certain curves such as circles and cylinders cannot be correctly represented by uniform B-splines. This implies that surfaces such as spheres and cylinders cannot be represented by bicubic B-spline patches. Second, in the context of interpolating a curve through data points, NURBS are generally more useful than uniform B-splines. They will provide a smoother curve through unevenly spaced data points. Third, an 'extra' control facility (the weights) is available that allows more subtle shape control than that afforded by control point movement alone. These additional shape parameters affect the curve only locally and their behaviour can be precisely quantified. NURBS are a generalization of nonrational B-spline (and Bézier) forms.

A *rational* B-spline curve is defined by a set of four-dimensional control points:

$$p_i^w = \left(w_i x_i, w_i y_i, w_i z_i, w_i \right)$$

The perspective map of such a curve in three-dimensional space is called a rational B-spline curve:

$$p(u) = H \left\{ \sum_{i=0}^{n} p_i^w N_{i,k}(u) \right\}$$

$$= \frac{\sum_{i=0}^{n} p_i w_i N_{i,k}(u)}{\sum_{i=0}^{n} w_i N_{i,k}(u)}$$

$$= \sum_{i=0}^{n} p_i R_{i,k}(u)$$

where:

$$R_{i,k}(u) = \frac{N_{i,k}(u) w_i}{\sum_{j=0}^{n} N_{j,k}(u) w_j}$$

and it can be seen from this definition that a rational B-spline is defined in terms of the ratio of two polynomials. Rational B-splines have the same analytical and geometric properties as nonrational B-splines and if

$$w_i = 1 \qquad \text{for all i}$$

then

$$R_{i,k}(u) = N_{i,k}(u)$$

The w_i associated with each control point are called weights and can be viewed as extra shape parameters. It can be shown that w_i affect the curve only locally. If, for example, w_j are fixed for all $j \neq i$, a change in w_i only affects the curve over k knot spans (just as moving a control point only affects the curve over k spans). w_i can be interpreted geometrically as a coupling factor. The curve is pulled towards a control point p_i if w_i increase. If w_i are decreased the curve moves away from the control point.

3.9 β-splines

Another category of splines that offer more subtle control over the shape of a curve than that afforded by B-splines is β-splines [BARS83]. β-splines generally have the same properties as B-splines but, in addition, two extra control facilities are available. These are called tension (t) and skew (s) and they provide the manipulator with two fine-adjustment facilities in addition to the control vertices. When $t = 0$ (no tension) and $s = 1$ (no skew) the β-spline formulation reduces to a uniform cubic B-spline. Barsky categorized such a B-spline curve, in terms of his definition, as an unbiased, untensed β-spline.

A β-spline curve is defined by a sequence of $m - 2$ curve segments, the ith of which is:

$$p(u) = \sum_{r=-2}^{1} p_{i+r} b_r(s, t, u)$$

where:

p_i is a set of control points $\left[p_0, p_1, \ldots, p_m \right]$
$0 \leqslant u \leqslant 1$
$i = 2, \ldots, m - 1$

$b_r(s, t, u)$ is a cubic polynomial called the rth β-spline basis function. By relaxing the first and second derivative continuity requirement (C^2) for B-spline curves to unit tangent and curvature vector continuity (G^2), Barsky gives the following formulae for the value of the four basis functions for each curve segment as:

$$b_{-2}(s, t, u) = \left(2s^3/\delta \right) \left(1 - u \right)^3$$

$$\begin{aligned} b_{-1}(s, t, u) = (1/\delta) \; (&2s^3 u \left(u^2 - 3u + 3 \right) \\ &+ 2s^2 \left(u^3 - 3u^2 + 2 \right) \\ &+ 2s \left(u^3 - 3u + 2 \right) \\ &+ t \left(2u^3 - 3u^2 + 1 \right)) \end{aligned}$$

$$\begin{aligned} b_0(s, t, u) = (1/\delta) \; (&2s^2 u^2 \left(-u + 3 \right) + 2su \left(-u^2 + 3 \right) \\ &+ tu^2 \left(-2u + 3 \right) + 2 \left(-u^3 + 1 \right)) \end{aligned}$$

$$b_1(s, t, u) = (2u^3)/\delta$$

where

$$\delta = 2s^3 + 4s^3 + 4s + t + 2$$

When $s = 1$ the curve is said to be unbiased. The effect of increasing skew on the blending function is to introduce asymmetry (and incidentally discontinuous derivatives), pulling the peak of the blending function to the right. Increasing s causes the curve to skew to one side approaching the control polygon in an unsymmetric way. Replacing s by a reciprocal value causes the curve to be skewed in the opposite manner. The t parameter affects the curve symmetrically. Its effect on the symmetrical blending function is to make it 'peakier'. That is, the amplitude of the blending function increases and the centre section becomes thinner. The effect of this on the curve being modelled is to make it approach the control polygon, and for high values of t (for example, $t = 100$) the result is similar to linear interpolation. The effect of tension and skew is shown in Figures 15.14 to 15.18 for the Hermite basis. The practical importance of these 'tuning' parameters in the context of animation is discussed in Section 15.3.7.

3.10 Catmull–Rom splines

The Catmull–Rom splines [CATM74] can be used either as interpolating or as approximating splines. If used as interpolating splines, the piecewise cubic polynomial segments pass through all the control points except the first and the last (p_0 and p_m). This works by constructing a tangent direction L_i at p_i to be parallel to the chord through p_{i-1} and p_{i+1}. Once this tangent direction has been found, inner Bézier points are placed on L_i.

Using the same matrix formulation as we did for B-splines we have

$$Q(u) = UM_{CR}P$$

where:

$$M_{CR} = \frac{1}{2} \begin{bmatrix} -1 & 3 & -3 & 1 \\ 2 & -5 & 4 & -1 \\ -1 & 0 & 1 & 0 \\ 0 & 2 & 0 & 0 \end{bmatrix}$$

A Catmull–Rom spline is shown in Figure 15.14. Apart from the end point problem, another disadvantage of the Catmull–Rom spline is that it does not possess the convex hull property.

3.11 Converting between representations

One of the advantages of using the matrix formulation is that it facilitates an easy conversion of a curve from one basis to another. If it is required to obtain the control vertex set p_i in a representation M_i, given that we have the control points p_j in representation M_j, then we have, for the curves to be identical:

$$UM_i P_i = UM_j P_j$$

or

$$M_i P_i = M_j P_j$$

and

$$P_i = M_i^{-1} M_j P_j$$

For example, to convert a curve from a Bézier representation to a Catmull–Rom form, we have:

$$P_{CR} = M_{CR}^{-1} M_B P_B$$

$$= \begin{bmatrix} 6 & -6 & 0 & 1 \\ 1 & 0 & 0 & 0 \\ 0 & 0 & 0 & 1 \\ 1 & 0 & -6 & 6 \end{bmatrix} P_B$$

3.12 The history of Bézier representation

The motivation for the development of Computer Aided Geometric Design (CAGD) arose out of the development, in the late 1950s, of computer-controlled machines that were capable of producing three-dimensional shapes out of wood or steel. Such shapes could then be used as dies to stamp out products from sheet metal. Their main application at that time was in the car industry. Clearly a software description of the shape needed to be specified, and although the theory of parametric surfaces was being used in differential geometry, it had yet to be applied in engineering.

The breakthrough in the use of parametric representation, and the foundation of CAGD, came in the early 1960s. The two pioneers responsible were P. de Casteljau at Citroën and P. Bézier at Renault. Although de Casteljau's work was carried out slightly earlier than Bézier's, it remained unpublished (except as company reports) and the development of parametric representation, using the Bernstein basis, is normally attributed to P. Bézier [BEZI72]. The material that follows is a description of Bézier's reminiscences in 'How a Simple System was Born', published as an introduction to [FARI90].

Bézier described the problem in the early 1960s as an inconsistency between the final physical manifestation of a design, called the 'master model', and the specification of the design as traced out in the stylist's drawings. He states that this inconsistency results in '. . . discussion, argument, retouches, expenses and delay' and that '. . . no significant improvement could be expected as long as a method was not devised that provided an accurate, complete and indisputable definition of free form shape'. It was soon realized that a numerical description was necessary, with drawings relegated to a subsidiary role, their accuracy being of secondary import. The system that Bézier developed was called UNISURF.

An intriguing aspect in the development of UNISURF was the use of physical analogues along the way in the progressive development of the system. Examples of some of these are now described.

An early concept was a circular arc defined by the points formed from the intersection of two sets of strings stretched across a rectangular frame (Figure 3.46). If the frame is transformed (linearly) into a parallelogram, the circular arc becomes a segment of an ellipse. This early

development, that restricted curves to be arcs of ellipses was, of course, too restrictive, but it predicted the model of a curve definition in terms of a control polygon.

The next development was a curve defined by two corners of a cube; it could be defined by any two vertices of a cube. The cube could then be deformed into any parallelepiped. The basic curve that was used in this definition was the intersection of two cylinders.

This idea led directly to a curve being defined by the three sides of a quadrilateral. The first and third sides defined the end points and the tangent vector to the curve at the end points. At around the same time harmonic functions were discarded in favour of polynomials, and eventually it was found that the polynomials could be considered as sums of Bernstein functions.

Bézier describes a slight difficulty at this time:

> When it was suggested that these curves replace sweeps and French curves, most stylists objected that they had invented their own templates and would not change their methods. It was therefore solemnly promised that their secret curves would be translated into secret listings and buried in the most secret part of the computer's memory, and that nobody but them would keep the key of the vaulted cellar. In fact, the standard curves were flexible enough and secret curves were soon forgotten; designers and draughtsmen easily understood the polygons and their relation with the shape of the corresponding curves.

The extension to biparametric patches came about intriguingly by studying the 'sandbox' – a foundry process whereby sand is compacted in a specially shaped box. Figure 3.47 shows the idea. A surface is obtained by

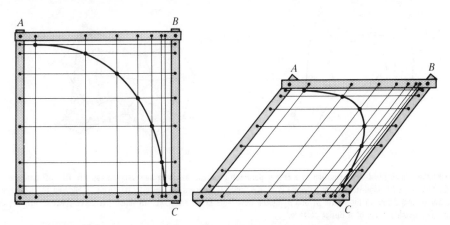

Figure 3.46 A circular arc defined by the intersection points of two sets of strings can be transformed into an ellipse (after [FARI90]).

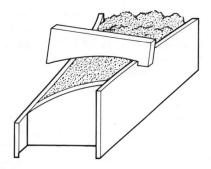

Figure 3.47   The concept of forming a surface in a sandbox (after [FARI90]).

scraping off the excess sand with a shaped template. Of course the shape of the template is fixed and the resulting surface is constrained in one parametric direction by this. However, this led to the concept of generating a surface

in the same way, but imagining the shape of the template to vary as it is moved over the sand – an old definition of a surface as the locus of a curve that is distorted as it moves.

This idea led directly to the definition of a surface patch in terms of a characteristic polygon. We now demonstrate this idea in Figure 3.48. Three boundary curves of a patch are defined as AB, BC and CD together with their polygons. We can define a patch by taking the curve BC and sweeping it towards its destination – the corner points AD. As the curve moves, its shape, and therefore the shape of its characteristic polygon p_0, p_1, p_2, p_3 changes. p_0 and p_3 follow the curves BA and CD, being analogous to the sides of the sandbox. p_1 and p_2 trace out two new curves as the moving curve changes shape. These have characteristic polygons EFGH and IJKL. Joining OF, JM, PG and KN gives us the nine polygons formed by the 16 control points of a Bézier bicubic parametric patch.

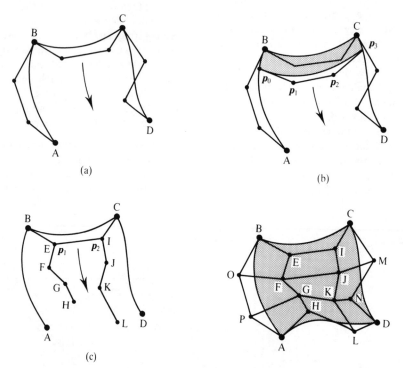

Figure 3.48   The sandbox analogy of the formation of a Bézier parametric patch. (a) Three boundary curves AB, BC, CD and their control polygons. (b) The curve BC (and its control polygon) is swept along the curves BA and CD. Its shape is allowed to change as it travels. (c) As the curve is swept and distorted the points p_1 and p_2 define new lines EFGH and IJKL. (d) When the curve reaches AD, OF, JM, PG and KN are joined giving the nine quadrilaterals of a Bézier surface.

4

The theory and practice of anti-aliasing techniques

Aliasing effects in radiosity are dealt with in Chapter 11. The effects of aliasing in the time domain are discussed at the end of this chapter and an implementation that uses stochastic sampling – distributed ray tracing – is discussed in Chapter 10. Aliasing in ad hoc shadow generation techniques is dealt with in Chapter 5.

Introduction

Traditionally anti-aliasing techniques in computer graphics have been viewed as a kind of voluntary add-on option, rather than as a vital or foundation technique in image synthesis. Aliases, after all, can be tolerated or not depending on the effort that we wish to devote to the creation of the image. In this text we take the view that anti-aliasing techniques are an integral and fundamental aspect of computer graphics and should be viewed in the same light as, say, interpolative shading or hidden surface removal algorithms. We thus present this material as a foundation technique.

Like many terms borrowed by computer graphics the word 'aliasing' is used rather loosely and generally means any unwanted artefact in the image. The most commonly discussed aliasing artefact is 'the jagged edge'; however,

this is not, strictly speaking, an aliasing artefact but is simply noise or detail introduced due to the nature of the sampling process – more about this later. Classical aliasing artefacts are caused by high-frequency information aliasing as low-frequency information. This occurs for example with coherent texture. High-frequency patterns appear as low-frequency patterns and interference effects are formed (see Figure 4.9). Aliasing also occurs in animation where frame undersampling can cause the well-known stationary (or going backwards) wagon wheel phenomenon (see Figure 4.36).

Most of the research into anti-aliasing in computer graphics is concerned with algorithms that perform anti-aliasing within the context of a practical rendering method such as ray tracing, radiosity or real-time scan line rendering. Considerable work has also been carried out in texture mapping, which is particularly prone to aliasing. Much effort has also gone into applying general methods that have come out of signal processing theory.

While these methods have their limitations in computer graphics, the underlying theory is important and useful.

In this chapter we will look firstly at the relevance of a theoretical model and then discuss the evolution of anti-aliasing techniques in computer graphics.

Considerable attention is given in the text to a practical method of implementing anti-aliasing for a polygonal renderer. This technique, the A-buffer, is becoming common in advanced rendering software and is a natural development of the basic Z-buffer renderer dealt with in Chapter 1.

4.1 A theoretical model: sampling and Fourier theory

Strict aliasing problems are caused by the inadequate sampling of continuous information. Although, as we shall see, this model is not always entirely appropriate in computer graphics, it is a useful starting point. While anti-aliasing algorithms are most easily understood in a mechanistic way, it is important to have a knowledge of the underlying theoretical base. This body of knowledge was mainly developed in the field of signal processing. We start by considering functions of a single variable – the application for which most of the theory was developed.

In this case we usually input to a processing system a continuous function of time. There are generally four stages in such systems. For example, in a digital telephone system (Figure 4.1), the first process converts speech into an electronic signal using an electromechanical transducer. This is then sampled by an analogue-to-digital converter and the signal is represented by a series of digital samples. In a telephone system the point of this is to enable the optimization of the bandwidth of the communications network. (Conversations can be more easily multiplexed if they are in digital form.) At the receiving end, analogue speech is reconstructed using a digital-to-analogue converter and a transducer is driven to give an audible version of the original speech. The reason for this diversion is that the same basic signal processing model is useful when considering the generation of an image in computer graphics. The differences between this model and the generation of images in computer graphics leads to the inherent difficulty of performing practical anti-aliasing operations.

Consider the first stage in this model – the sampling process. For functions of a single variable $I(x)$, sampling means collecting values of I at equally spaced intervals in x. For an image $I(x, y)$, sampling means collecting values of I at equally spaced intervals in x and y.

An important theorem – the sampling theorem – relates the resolution of the sampling grid to the nature of the image, or more specifically to the spatial frequencies in the image. (See [OPPE75] for a detailed treatment of digital signal processing.) It is intuitively obvious that the more we sample a function the better the sampled values approximate the function and that as the intervals between samples tend to zero the two will become indistinguishable. What is less obvious, and indeed quite surprising, is that for a certain class of functions – called bandlimited functions – there exists a well-defined critical sampling interval such that any sampling process whose interval falls within this critical value can recapture this function exactly. This critical value is related to the detail of the function to be sampled; obviously finer sampling grids are needed to recover images of greater detail. This is quantified in the sampling theorem, which for functions of a single variable can be stated as follows:

A continuous bandlimited function of a single variable can be completely represented by a set of samples made at equally spaced intervals. The intervals between such samples must be less than half the

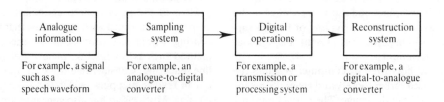

Figure 4.1 A conventional sampling and reconstruction system.

period (or greater than twice the frequency) of the highest frequency component in the function.

For example, if we consider a single sinusoidal function of x, it is easily seen that if the relationship between the sampling frequency and the function is as shown in Figure 4.2(a) then no information is lost. The sampling frequency in this case is greater than twice the frequency of the sinusoid. If the sampling frequency is equal to twice the sine wave frequency (Figure 4.2(b)) then the samples can coincide with the sine wave zero crossings as shown, and no information can be recovered from the samples concerning the sine wave. When the sampling frequency is less than twice that of the sine wave (Figure 4.2(c) and 4.2(d)) then the information contained in the samples implies sine waves (shown by the dotted lines) at lower frequencies than the function being sampled. These lower frequencies are known as 'aliases' and this explains the derivation of the term.

At this stage a brief excursion into Fourier theory is necessary as it will provide us with several important results that are necessary for a better understanding of aliasing. Readers unfamiliar with Fourier theory should consult a text such as [BRAC86]. Now information such as speech (or, more importantly for our purposes, imagery) of course is not a sine wave, but Fourier theory enables us to generalize the above situation by considering any signal $I(x)$ as a spectrum of sine waves using the Fourier integral

$$F(u) = \int_{-\infty}^{\infty} I(x) \exp(-i2\pi ux)\, dx \qquad \textbf{(4.1a)}$$

We state the reversibility of this transform by

$$I(x) = \int_{-\infty}^{\infty} F(u) \exp(i2\pi ux)\, du \qquad \textbf{(4.1b)}$$

$F(u)$ and $I(x)$ are said to form a Fourier transform pair. We define the operator $\supset$ to denote 'has a Fourier transform given by'. So the above reduces to

$$I(x) \supset F(u)$$

From school calculus we know that an integral can be regarded in the limit as the sum of an infinite number of

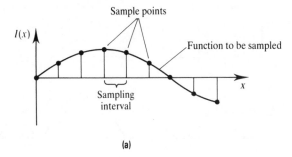

(a)

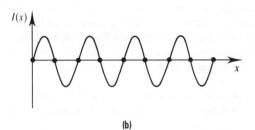

(b)

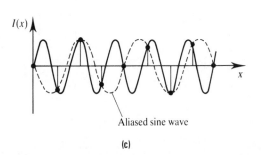

(c)

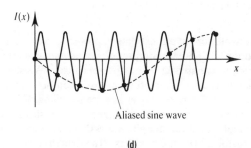

(d)

Figure 4.2 Representation of the sampling of a sine wave. (a) Sampling interval is less than one-half the period of the sine wave. (b) Sampling interval is equal to one-half the period of the sine wave. (c) Sampling interval is greater than one-half the period of the sine wave. (d) Sampling interval is much greater than one-half the period of the sine wave.

discrete terms. The integral (4.1a), then, can be regarded as being composed of an infinite number of sine waves where u determines the frequency of the waves. This follows from Euler's formula:

$$\exp\left(-i2\pi ux\right) = \cos\left(2\pi ux\right) - i\sin\left(2\pi ux\right)$$

Because of this, u is referred to as the frequency domain and, for our purposes, we shall hereafter refer to x as the space domain. Although $I(x)$ is typically a real function, $F(u)$ is generally complex and so is visualized via its amplitude and phase spectra which are defined as follows. If $F(u)$ has real and imaginary parts given by

$$F(u) = \text{Re}(u) + \text{Im}(u)$$

then the amplitude spectrum is

$$|F(u)| = \left(\text{Re}^2(u) + \text{Im}^2(u)\right)^{1/2}$$

and the phase spectrum is

$$\phi(u) = \tan^{-1}\left[\frac{\text{Im}(u)}{\text{Re}(u)}\right]$$

A single point in the amplitude spectrum, $|F(u)|$, specifies a single sine wave whose frequency is u Hz and whose amplitude is F (see Figure 4.6(a)). The corresponding point in the phase spectrum specifies the phase of the sine wave, or the point in the cycle that the sine wave has reached at $u = 0$. Adding together all the sinusoids in their appropriate amplitude and phase relationships synthesizes the function $I(x)$. Fourier synthesis, generating a function from a recipe of sine waves, is utilized in Chapters 7 and 18.

We now define another operator, $\star$, used to denote convolution. The convolution of two functions $I(x)$ and $g(x)$ is given by

$$I(x) \star g(x) = \int_{-\infty}^{\infty} I(\alpha)g(x-\alpha)\,d\alpha \qquad (4.2)$$

Convolution is an extremely powerful mathematical notion. Different interpretations of the convolution integral are used in many different fields. We shall see later that different interpretations in computer graphics lead to different strategies in supersampling.

The result we need to take from Fourier theory is the convolution theorem which states that if $I(x)$ has Fourier transform $F(u)$ and $g(x)$ has $G(u)$ then the convolution of the two has Fourier transform given by $F(u)G(u)$. The convolution theorem constitutes a basic link between the space and frequency domains. We write:

$$I(x) \star g(x) \supset F(u)G(u) \qquad (4.3a)$$

We say that convolution in the space domain corresponds to multiplication in the frequency domain. Because of the duality of the space and frequency domains an analogous result is that convolution in the frequency domain corresponds to multiplication in the space domain, that is:

$$I(x)g(x) \supset F(u) \star G(u) \qquad (4.3b)$$

Now, armed with these results, we can gain a better understanding of the sampling theorem. Consider a function $I(x)$, as shown in Figure 4.3(a), with Fourier transform $F(u)$. $I(x)$ is said to be bandlimited if its Fourier transform has no frequency components higher

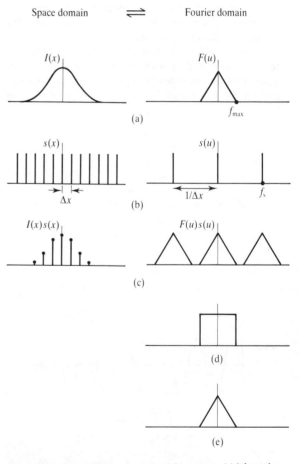

Figure 4.3 The sampling and reconstruction process. (a) Information function. (b) Sampling function. (c) Sampled information. (d) Reconstruction filter. (e) Reconstructed information.

than a finite value, f_{max}, say. Sampling $I(x)$ involves multiplying it by a sampling function $s(x)$. $s(x)$ is usually represented as an infinite train of impulse functions where the impulse function $\delta(x)$ is defined to be a pulse of extremely short duration and unit area, that is:

$$\delta(x) = 0 \qquad x \neq 0$$

$$\int_{-\infty}^{\infty} \delta(x) = 1$$

So that the convolution of an impulse function, located at $x = x_0$, with the information function is just the value of the information at that location:

$$I(x) \star \delta(x - x_0) = \int_{-\infty}^{\infty} I(\alpha)\delta(x - x_0 - \alpha)\,d\alpha = I(x - x_0)$$

$$(4.4)$$

If the impulses are separated by an interval Δx the sampling function, of frequency f_s, is given by:

$$s(x) = \sum_{n = -\infty}^{\infty} \delta(x - n\Delta x)$$

$$f_s = \frac{1}{\Delta x}$$

Now, the Fourier transform of a train of impulses is itself a train of impulses. Specifically it can be shown:

$$\sum \delta(x - n\Delta x) \supset \frac{1}{\Delta x} \sum \delta\left(\frac{u - n}{\Delta x}\right)$$

This is shown in Figure 4.3(b). Now from the convolution theorem we know that the Fourier transform of the sampled information $I(x)s(x)$ has a Fourier transform given by:

$$I(x)s(x) \supset F(u) \star \frac{1}{\Delta x} \sum \delta\left(\frac{u - n}{\Delta x}\right)$$

which by using (4.4) reduces to:

$$I(x)s(x) \supset \frac{1}{\Delta x} \sum F\left(\frac{u - n}{\Delta x}\right) \qquad (4.5)$$

showing that the transform of the sampled information is the transform of the information $F(u)$ plus copies of this transform that are separated at intervals of $1/\Delta x$. Now since $I(x)$ is bandlimited by f_{max} it is clear from Figure 4.3(c) that these repetitions of $F(u)$ will not overlap providing:

$$f_{max} < \frac{1}{2\Delta x}$$

that is:

$$f_s > 2f_{max}$$

Multiplying the spectrum with a reconstruction filter as shown in Figure 4.3(d) produces the spectrum of $I(x)$ uncorrupted as shown in Figure 4.3(e), that is, the original information has been completely recovered. f_{max} is known as the Nyquist limit – for complete recovery of the information the sampling frequency must be greater than twice this limit. Figure 4.4 shows the spectrum of the sampled information for sampling processes equal to and less than twice the Nyquist limit. In the latter case corruption from adjacent spectrum copies occurs – it is as if the spectrum has 'folded over' a line defined by the Nyquist limit. This folding is an information-destroying process – high frequencies (fine detail in images) are lost and reappear impersonating lower frequencies – hence the origins of the term 'aliasing', a term much used and, as we shall see later, abused in computer graphics.

Thus we conclude that aliasing occurs when:

1. The information is not bandlimited, that is, it contains frequencies extending to infinity. No matter how high, the sampling frequency corruption from adjacent spectrum copies is inevitable.

2. The sampling frequency is fixed. Frequencies in the information higher than $f_s/2$ will not be adequately represented but will appear as aliases.

In either case aliasing can be removed by filtering the image *prior* to sampling by using a lowpass filter whose cutoff frequency corresponds to half the sampling rate, that is, all components of $I(x)$ whose frequencies are

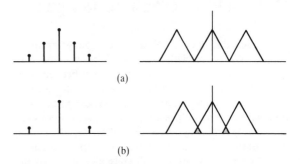

(a)

(b)

Figure 4.4 Varying the sampling frequency about the Nyquist limit.

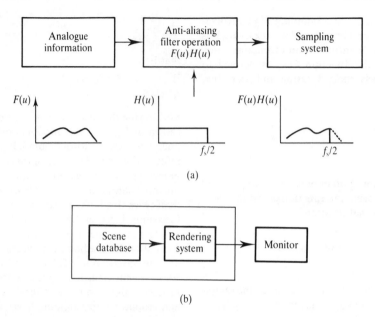

Figure 4.5 (a) A classical anti-aliasing filter. (b) A computer graphics generation system.

greater than $f_s/2$ are eliminated as shown in Figure 4.5(a). The prefiltering step thus forces the information to assume a Nyquist limit optimal to the sampling step. Although not all of the original information can be recovered, the prefiltering step ensures that what is recovered, and this is the maximum possible amount, is not misrepresented.

4.2 The model in the context of computer graphics images

How does this model relate to computer graphics images? We begin with a global look at rendering algorithms. Cook [COOK86] distinguishes between two types of rendering algorithms: analytic and discrete. Analytic algorithms can prefilter an image and take out its high frequencies before sampling the pixel values – an anti-aliasing filtering operation. Discrete algorithms only consider the image at regularly spaced sample points. Of the two types the discrete algorithms by far predominate since they are simpler, more elegant and

easier to implement than analytic methods.

We shall consider the discrete type in general (although we shall return to specific cases of analytic algorithms later in the chapter – see section 4.4) as shown by the representation in Figure 4.5(b). This diagram emphasizes that, unlike real data processes, there is no channel between analogue information (the scene database) and a sampler (the renderer) and no point at which a classical anti-aliasing filter can be inserted – in short, we cannot bandlimit the image. This is because for discrete algorithms the generation and sampling of the image are inextricably entwined. Just such an example of a discrete algorithm would be a Z-buffer based renderer (Chapter 1); polygons are fetched from the database, transformed into the image plane and pixels are assigned an intensity by interpolation along polygon edges. There is no continuous image function that is sampled – an image value is calculated at the sampled points. We can certainly increase the rate of sampling, a technique known as supersampling, but we cannot insert an anti-aliasing filter – a device that in a conventional real data environment operates in the continuous information domain. This model is important because it is the reason that supersampling, the easiest and most popular method of anti-aliasing, does not work in the degenerate case of high spatial frequencies that results from, say, coherent texture.

Another point we have to consider is that we now have images which are functions of two spatial variables over a two-dimensional sampling grid. The transform pair formulae for a two-dimensional transform follow naturally from their one-dimensional counterparts and are given by:

$$F(u, v) = \int_{-\infty}^{\infty} \int_{-\infty}^{\infty} I(x, y) \exp\left(-i2\pi\left(ux + vy\right)\right) dx dy$$

$$I(x, y) = \int_{-\infty}^{\infty} \int_{-\infty}^{\infty} F(u, v) \exp\left(i2\pi\left(ux + vy\right)\right) du dv$$

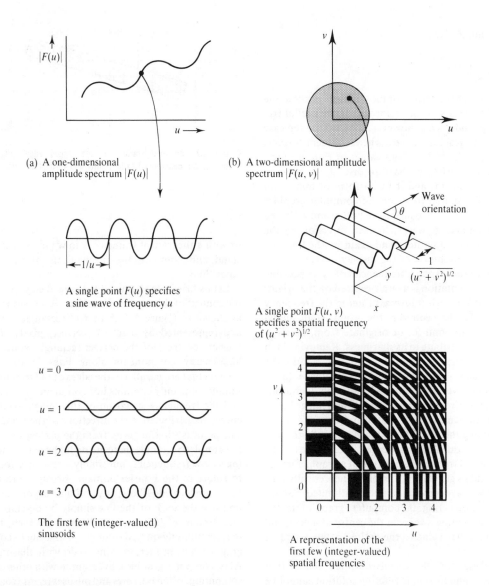

(a) A one-dimensional amplitude spectrum $|F(u)|$

A single point $F(u)$ specifies a sine wave of frequency u

$u = 0$

$u = 1$

$u = 2$

$u = 3$

The first few (integer-valued) sinusoids

(b) A two-dimensional amplitude spectrum $|F(u, v)|$

Wave orientation

θ

$\dfrac{1}{(u^2 + v^2)^{1/2}}$

A single point $F(u, v)$ specifies a spatial frequency of $(u^2 + v^2)^{1/2}$

A representation of the first few (integer-valued) spatial frequencies

Figure 4.6 1D and 2D amplitude spectra.

The information specified within a one-dimensional and a two dimensional transform is shown in Figure 4.6. In a transform of a one-dimensional function a single point $F(u)$ specifies a sine wave of frequency u. For a two-dimensional function the amplitude spectrum of $F(u, v)$ now specifies a set of spatial frequencies, sinusoidally corrugated surfaces with varying rates of undulation and varying orientations of the peaks and troughs. The frequency of a sinusoidal corrugation is given by:

$$f = \left(u^2 + v^2 \right)^{1/2}$$

Its orientation is given by:

$$\theta = \tan^{-1} \left(\frac{v}{u} \right)$$

The amplitude characteristic of most images peaks at the origin and decreases as the reciprocal of the spatial frequency magnitude. This, however, may not be the case with computer graphics images where coherent texture, for example, will result in high values of $F(u, v)$ away from the origin. Also, we have to distinguish between theoretical transforms and the transform of images on the screen. The spatial frequency of computer graphics abstractions can extend to infinity in both u and v. Screen images are limited, however, in each direction by the resolution of the frame store and again by the line rate and horizontal resolution of the display device.

The locus of equal spatial frequencies of every possible peak/trough orientation is a circle centred on the origin. This means that a perfect lowpass filter in the frequency domain is a cylinder centred at the origin. High spatial frequencies correspond to, or originate from, detail in the image and contribute to its sharpness. Removing high spatial frequencies to remove unwanted detail – the aliasing artefacts – also inevitably blurs the image. In the Fourier domain we can see that anti-aliasing operations are a tradeoff between artefact visibility and image blurring because we remove high spatial frequencies.

The sampling theorem also extends naturally to two-dimensional frequencies or spatial frequencies. The two-dimensional frequency spectrum of a graphics image in the continuous generation domain is theoretically infinite and, as we have seen, cannot be bandlimited. Sampling and reconstructing in computer graphics is the process of calculating a value at the centre of a pixel and then assigning that value to the entire spatial extent of that pixel.

We conclude, for the reasons outlined above, that Fourier theory and its simple filtering solution cannot be applied in computer graphics. However, it does supply

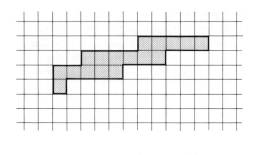

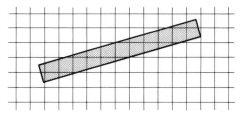

Figure 4.7 An exaggeration of 'the jagged edge'. High-contrast boundaries are constrained to horizontal and vertical directions.

us with a theoretical framework in which we can understand and compare the mechanisms of anti-aliasing algorithms.

Let us briefly look now at the jagged edge problem in the context of this model. Consider a discussion example as shown in Figure 4.7. A perfect rectangle is sampled and represented by a set of (perfect) pixels. The frequency spectrum of the perfect rectangle would exhibit high-energy components along lines in the Fourier domain that are parallel to the edges of the rectangle. The sampled line only contains horizontal and vertical edges and the frequency spectrum of this image would show energy redistributed in the directions of the u and v axes. The point is, that in going from the perfect rectangle to the sampled rectangle there are *no* high frequencies aliasing as low frequencies, but simply a tendency for energy to rotate in the Fourier domain. Because anti-aliasing filters are blurring filters, any anti-aliasing operation will improve the look of the line simply by de-emphasizing high-frequency information. We can see then, that the most commonly quoted example of aliasing in computer graphics has, in fact, nothing to do with aliasing at all. Alas, computer graphics, in common with other areas of computing, often borrows and misuses terms from older, more well-established disciplines.

4.3 Supersampling

Supersampling is the process by which aliasing artefacts in computer graphics are reduced simply by increasing the frequency of the sampling grid (that is, increasing the spatial resolution of the pixel array) and averaging the results down. Algorithmically this simple process means calculating a virtual image at a spatial resolution greater than the frame store resolution and averaging down to the final resolution. Intuitively we can see how this simple process deals with the artefacts described previously – we simply de-emphasize such artefacts by blurring them. It is sometimes called *post*filtering to emphasize the fact that we are filtering after sampling. It is the most widely used and misunderstood anti-aliasing method. There are two drawbacks to the approach:

1. The obvious technical drawback that there is both an economic and a technical limit to increasing the resolution of the virtual image, and

2. The theoretical drawback that since the frequency spectrum of computer graphics images can extend to infinity, increasing the sampling frequency does not necessarily solve the problem, it merely reduces aliasing by raising the Nyquist limit – we simply shift the effect up the frequency spectrum.

The latter objection is of more consequence and tells us that supersampling, though easy to perform, provides only an incomplete solution to the aliasing problem. To see why this is so it is necessary to look behind its apparent simplicity. In terms of our previously developed model and returning to Equation (4.5):

$$I(x)s(x) \supset \frac{1}{\Delta x} \sum F\left(\frac{u-n}{\Delta x}\right)$$

we see that the higher the sampling frequency f_s the smaller Δx and so the greater the distance $1/\Delta x$ in the frequency domain between the spectrum copies. So supersampling just pushes these copies further apart – any overlap is reduced but not necessarily eliminated. This is shown schematically in Figure 4.8 which shows, in the frequency domain, the difference between using an anti-aliasing filter and increasing the sampling frequency.

Consider a square image made up of $n \times n$ pixels of side Δx. The Nyquist limit of the pixel is $1/(2\Delta x)$, that is, frequencies higher than one cycle every two pixels will cause aliasing. Suppose we compute the image at twice

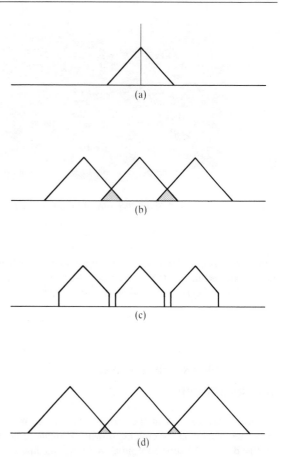

Figure 4.8 Increasing the sampling frequency does not necessarily eliminate aliasing. (a) Information spectrum. (b) Sampled spectrum. (c) Using an anti-aliasing filter before sampling. (d) Increasing the sampling frequency.

the resolution and average down. Effectively the image is made up of $2n \times 2n$ pixels of side $\Delta x/2$ giving a Nyquist limit of $1/\Delta x$ – twice the previous rate. Now only frequencies higher than one cycle per pixel will cause aliasing.

This effect is shown in Figure 4.9 which shows two images of a checkerboard extending to infinity towards the horizon. This image has become a de facto standard test picture for evaluating aliasing techniques since it is easy to produce and is degenerate in that it contains frequencies that increase to infinity – the closer the eye approaches the horizon, more and more checks fall underneath a pixel. One image is computed at four times the resolution of the other and averaged down but it still

(a)   (b)

Figure 4.9   The pattern in (b) is a supersampled version of that in (a). Aliases still occur but appear at a higher spatial frequency.

contains aliasing – the point at which aliasing starts has merely shifted upwards in the image. Aliasing remains but the onset occurs at a higher spatial frequency.

4.3.1 Supersampling and reconstruction

We now need to look at the process referred to in the previous section as 'averaging down'. Having looked at the defects of supersampling as far as its inability to deal with high-frequency aliases is concerned, we will now look at the options available within these limitations.

Supersampling is equivalent, theoretically, to a three-stage process. Algorithmically the second and third stages are combined. These stages are:

1. A continuous image $I(x, y)$ is sampled at n times the final resolution. In practice this means that we calculate $I(x, y)$ at n times the frame store resolution. This is a virtual image.
2. The virtual image is then lowpass filtered.
3. The filtered image is resampled at the final frame store resolution.

Stages 2 and 3 mean that when we generate the real (low resolution) image from the virtual (high resolution) image for each pixel value we take into account a *region* in the virtual image. The extent of that region determines the frequencies involved in the lowpass filter operation. The process is called (digital) convolution.

4.3.2 Convolution and filtering

We know already from Equation (4.3) that convolution in the space domain is equivalent to multiplication in the Fourier domain. Consider steps 2 and 3 in the previous section. The two-dimensional transform of the image is multiplied by a circularly symmetric filter function $H(u, v)$ that retains low spatial frequencies and deletes high ones. In the Fourier model a filtered image $I(x, y)$ is generated from the original image $I(x, y)$ as follows. $I(x, y)$ is transformed into the Fourier domain:

$$I(x, y) \supset F(u, v)$$

and the spectrum of $F(u, v)$ is multiplied by a filter function $H(u, v)$ that generally multiplies some frequencies and deletes others. The resulting spectrum is then transformed back to the space domain giving us the final frame store resolution image $I'(x, y)$. We write:

$$I'(x, y) \supset F(u, v) H(u, v)$$

but by the convolution theory, which states that multiplication in the frequency domain is equivalent to convolution in the space domain:

$$h(x, y) \star I(x, y) \supset F(u, v) H(u, v)$$

which gives:

$$I'(x, y) = I(x, y) \star h(x, y)$$

This is the most useful equation for filtering in computer graphics since in general we only have access to the space domain, $I(x, y)$, version of the image. Supersampling, then, is just digital convolution in the space domain. Using the two-dimensional discretized version of our definition of convolution (Equation 4.2) we write:

$$I'(x,y) = \sum_{i=x-k}^{x+k} \sum_{j=y-k}^{y+k} I(i,j)\, h(x-i,y-j) \qquad (4.6)$$

The values (x,y) and (i,j) are not continuous but represent values on a two-dimensional grid.

If we are supersampling a picture of constant intensity, I_0 say, we would expect a final image to be no different from its virtual image; that is, the filter must have zero effect on such an image. Substituting

$$I'(x,y) = I(x,y) = I_0$$

into Equation (4.6) gives:

$$\sum_{-k}^{k} \sum_{-k}^{k} h(x,y) = 1$$

that is, the filter weights must sum to unity.

It is instructive to examine the supersampling process more closely. Let S be the scaling factor between the virtual and final images. Consider the case where S is odd. (The case where S is even is a little trickier, since, unlike the odd case, the pixels of the final and virtual image are not aligned and implicit in Equation (4.6) is a grid common to both. This is best avoided.) Using Equation (4.6), we have

$$I'(i,j) = \sum_{p=Si-k}^{Si+k} \sum_{q=Sj-k}^{Sj+k} I(p,q)\, h(Si-p, Sj-q) \quad (4.7)$$

where:

$$S = 2k + 1$$

This is shown schematically in Figure 4.10 where pixels of the virtual image are referred to as 'superpixels'. From this we see that the pixels of the final image are located over superpixels (Si, Sj) of the virtual image. To calculate the value of the final image at (Si, Sj) we place the filter over this superpixel in the virtual image and compute the sum of the product of the filter weights and the surrounding superpixels. An adjacent pixel of the final image, at $(S(i+1), Sj)$ say, is calulated by moving the filter S superpixels to the right and repeating the operation. Thus the step length, in superpixels, of the filter is the same as the scale factor S between the real and virtual image.

The spatial extent of the filter determines its cutoff frequency. In this regard note that filtering is always a compromise. The wider the filter, the lower is its cutoff frequency but the more blurred is the final image. This tradeoff is shown in Figure 4.9.

We now consider the actual weights of the filter. The options available in supersampling are:

1. The value of S – the scaling factor between the virtual and real images (which we have decided should be odd in any practical context).

2. The choice of the extent and weights of the filter – that is, the values of k and $h\,(i,j)$.

As far as the first factor is concerned the answer is – the higher the value, the better the results will be. A high computational cost results, and if a Z-buffer algorithm is used this results in an S^2 storage requirement making it essentially a virtual memory technique. For, say, a medium-resolution image of 512×512 pixels it is usually considered adequate to supersample at $S = 3$ or $S = 5$.

Other disadvantages of the technique should be apparent. It is not a context-sensitive technique. The same computational effort is devoted to large areas of constant intensity as to, say, edges. This is inevitable. For example, a Z-buffer system would render regions of the screen covered by a single large polygon using incremental shading which uses constant delta values to calculate

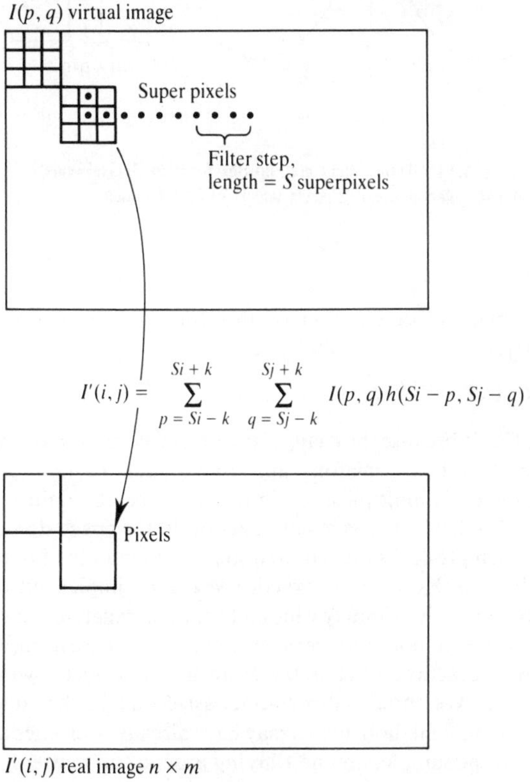

Figure 4.10 'Reducing' a virtual image by convolution.

the intensity of the next pixel from the previous pixel. This intensity is usually slowly varying. Supersampling in this case involves decreasing the size of delta thereby peforming more work but not necessarily generating more information. This is not the case, however, in ray tracing where no such exploitation of coherence is employed. Context-dependent supersampling is then possible and this is described in Section 4.6.

4.3.3 Filter options

Digital filter theory is a well-researched subject area and there are many books on the topic (for example [LUDE87]). The size of the filter in the space domain is inversely related to its cutoff frequency and the shape of the filter determines how well this cutoff is performed. An ideal lowpass filter is a step function in the frequency domain. In the pass band all frequencies are unaltered. Above the cutoff all frequency components are zeroized. In computer graphics, assuming one sample per pixel, a pixel grid of side Δx will have a Nyquist limit of $1/(2\Delta x)$. Frequencies higher than this 1/2 cycle per pixel (or one cycle every two pixels) must be eliminated or at least de-intensified. There are second-order considerations that arise out of the nature of the convolution operation, in particular the fact that the convolution is carried out over a small area – a window – causes certain problems.

We now discuss some filter shapes to illuminate these points. Again we will use a one-dimensional analogy and consider filters that are continuous functions of a single variable. We shall notate the filter as $h(x)$ with a Fourier domain representation $H(u)$. In computer graphics the filter will be a function of two spatial variables $h(x, y)$ and will, in most cases, be the surface of revolution formed from $h(x)$. An implementation of $h(x, y)$ is, of course, a discrete version of this surface of revolution.

Consider Figure 4.11 that shows three examples of possible filters. The first is a box function 1 pixel wide. From the Fourier representation it can be seen that this is a far from optimum filter. It does not cut off completely until twice the desired cutoff frequency, that is, it cuts off at one cycle per pixel, and it has large side lobes thus retaining unwanted components. The Fourier domain representation is called a 'sinc function':

$$H_1(u) = \frac{\sin(\pi u)}{\pi u}$$

The second filter is a triangle (a pyramid or a cone in two variables). This is better. (Incidentally the Fourier

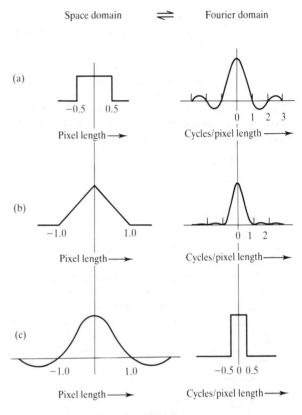

Space domain ⇌ Fourier domain

(a)

-0.5   0.5

Pixel length ⟶

0 1 2 3

Cycles/pixel length ⟶

(b)

-1.0   1.0

Pixel length ⟶

0 1 2

Cycles/pixel length ⟶

(c)

-1.0   1.0

Pixel length ⟶

-0.5 0 0.5

Cycles/pixel length ⟶

Figure 4.11   Three filters $h(x)$. (a) Box function (1 pixel wide). (b) Triangular function (2 pixels wide). (c) Sinc function.

domain representation of this filter is the square of H_1.)

$$H_2(u) = H_1^2(u)$$

(This is because the triangular function is the convolution of two box functions and convolution in the space domain is multiplication in the frequency domain.)

The best filter is a sinc function in the space domain which produces the required step function in the Fourier domain. However, in practice we cannot implement this because it is infinitely wide and contains negative weights and we cannot produce pixel intensities that are negative. Any practical filter is therefore not a perfect lowpass filter. We should also re-emphasize that in the supersampling method aliases may have already been encoded into the samples and no filtering process, no matter how perfect, can deal with this.

Another problem occurs when any practical implementation of a filter is concerned. Consider, for example, the sinc function and forget for a moment the problem of negative weights. If we simply implement this filter by truncating it abruptly then the characteristic in the frequency domain becomes 'ripply' and the sides slope. This can be seen by considering that the truncated sinc function in the space domain is the product of a sinc function and a box. The resulting Fourier domain representation is the convolution of the box transform (a sinc function) with the sine function transform (a box) which produces a box with sloping sides and ripples. What is the practical implication of this point? Just this: the wider the filter in the space domain, the better is the cutoff characteristic in the frequency domain, but for practical reasons we cannot increase the width of the filter without limit, and if we are going to use a truncated filter we must not truncate abruptly. The function that is used to decrease the filter weights towards zero is called a 'window function'. This can be categorized by specifying a practical filter as a product:

$$h'(x) = h(x)\, w(x)$$

where:

$h(x)$ is the ideal filter
$w(x)$ is the window function that enables a portion of the filter – a window – to be used

However, in practice unless the width of the filter is large, because a practical filter is a coarse discretization of an ideal filter, such subtle optimizations are not possible.

Finally, to return to the two-dimensional practical domain, Table 4.1 shows three filter kernels used by Crow [CROW81] to filter down a supersampled image. The cost implications of increasing the size of the filter are obvious. Using a 3×3 window requires $9n^2$ multiplications and additions to compute the final image, a 7×7 window requires $49n^2$ calculations, where n^2 is the number of pixels in the frame store. Also note that, in

practice, because both the filter and the virtual image are discretizations, the virtual image resolution must be taken into account when choosing a filter size. A 7×7 filter applied to a $3\times$ virtual image will produce more blurring than the same filter applied to a $7\times$ virtual image. The information on which a filter of a certain area operates decreases as the resolution of the virtual image increases.

4.3.4 Effect of postprogram hardware

You should be at least aware of the processes that a digital frame store image undergoes prior to finally appearing on the screen. The product of any programmed anti-aliasing operation is stored as an image in digital form in the frame store. This is then subject to two further processing operations. First it is passed on a scan line basis through a digital-to-analogue converter. This means that the electronics have to scan along horizontal lines in the frame store, deriving an analogue signal as a function of time. The converter samples each pixel intensity and 'holds' it for a duration equal to the time taken for the scanning beam to move across one pixel on the monitor screen – a sample-and-hold operation. This means that the horizontal operations are convolved with a box function one pixel wide. Also, the spot on the monitor itself exhibits an intensity distribution that is approximately a Gaussian function and the output of the digital-to-analogue converter is further convolved with a Gaussian function whose width depends on the physical size of the beam or spot. As far as the Gaussian blurring is concerned this is of little practical significance.

The digital-to-analogue conversion is more tricky. In supersampling for example, we have reconstructed from the supersamples using a filter in the discrete domain which is some approximation to the optimum reconstructing filter. This is a step function in the Fourier domain and a sinc function in the space or algorithm domain. However, the digital-to-analogue converter introduces a suboptimum filter – a box function in the space (or now the time) domain which is a sinc function in the Fourier domain with the consequent side lobes. Frequencies in the side lobe region that have been diminished by anti-aliasing operations may be restored by this filter. There would be no problem if these frequencies had been zeroized by the anti-aliasing operations, but as we have discussed, this is unlikely. Blinn [BLIN89] points out that there are two possible consequences of this. Either this is taken into account in the

Table 4.1 Bartlett windows used in postfiltering a supersampled image.

3×3			5×5					7×7						
1	2	1	1	2	3	2	1	1	2	3	4	3	2	1
2	4	2	2	4	6	4	2	2	4	6	8	6	4	2
1	2	1	3	6	9	6	3	3	6	9	12	9	6	3
			2	4	6	4	2	4	8	12	16	12	8	4
			1	2	3	2	1	3	6	9	12	9	6	3
								2	4	6	8	6	4	2
								1	2	3	4	3	2	1

conversion hardware – you have an expensive, high-quality frame buffer – or you have to take the effect of the conversion process into account.

4.3.5 Practical supersampling algorithms

Implemented naively, supersampling is usually a virtual memory technique. As far as a nonvirtual memory technique is concerned, two approaches suggest themselves. For an increase in resolution of S^2 we can simply project S^2 fragments of the virtual image onto the framestore by passing the scene through the renderer with different clipping parameters. There are extra processing overheads in that the scene has to be clipped S^2 times. Also, you cannot filter down the contents of a region independent of its neighbours. Depending on the filter size, bounding strips have to be carried over from one region to the next.

A more straightforward approach is simply to reorder the convolution. This method was first suggested by Fuchs *et al.* [FUCH85] and is taken up by Mammen in [MAMM89]. Here the idea is to tradeoff separate passes through a renderer against the S^2 memory requirements. In this method, irrespective of the supersampling resolution rates, the memory demands for a Z-buffer renderer are fixed at two frame stores.

The method is best explained by trivially changing the variables in Equation (4.7) to give us an alternative and equivalent definition of digital convolution. We rewrite:

$$I'(i,j) = \sum_{p=Si-k}^{Si+k} \sum_{q=Sj-k}^{Sj+k} I(p,q)\, h(Si-p, Sj-q)$$

as

$$I'(i,j) = \sum_{p=-k}^{k} \sum_{q=-k}^{k} h(p,q)\, I(Si-p, Sj-q) \qquad (4.8)$$

Consider the case where $S = 3$ and h is a box filter of unity weights, say:

$$h(p,q) = \frac{1}{9} \begin{pmatrix} 1 & 1 & 1 \\ 1 & 1 & 1 \\ 1 & 1 & 1 \end{pmatrix}$$

An implementation of Equation (4.8) can be achieved by computing nine images at the final resolution but sampling the virtual image at every three pixels. A 'normal' image is computed, together with eight others displaced by one pixel into the positions specified by the

filter kernel. These images are superimposed in turn by dividing by nine and summating. This process is exactly equivalent to computing nine images at the real resolution each displaced by one-third of a pixel, summating and then dividing. This is shown schematically in Figure 4.12. In practice we would implement this by using two frame stores. The current frame store computes the images, appropriately displaced, one after the other. When each displaced image is computed, it is blended into the destination frame store. In our simple example we would accumulate in the destination frame store each time one-ninth of the value from the current frame store. The image in the destination frame store becomes successively refined until eventually the final image is produced. Clearly the blending process will be a function of the filter coefficients and the order in which the subpixels are generated.

Previously the pixels (i, j) of the final image were located at intervals of S superpixels of the virtual image. In this case the virtual and final images are the same resolution so Equation (4.8) is rewritten as:

$$I'(i,j) = \sum_{p=-k}^{k} \sum_{q=-k}^{k} h(p,q)\, I\left(\frac{i-p}{S}, \frac{j-q}{S}\right)$$

where:

$$S = 2k + 1$$

Instead of sampling the screen at a higher resolution for the virtual image, we sample the screen at the same resolution as the final image but S^2 times. Each time the

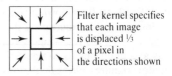

Filter kernel specifies that each image is displaced $\frac{1}{3}$ of a pixel in the directions shown

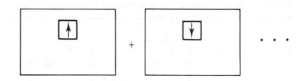

Images are computed and summated

Figure 4.12 Reordering the convolution is equivalent to summing nine images, eight of which are displaced as shown.

image is displaced over a series of subpixel positions given by:

$$\sum_{p=-k}^{k} \sum_{q=-k}^{k} \left(\frac{-p}{S}, \frac{-q}{S} \right)$$

Let the successive images be computed row by row. Pass n will thus correspond to subpixel position $(-p/S, -q/S)$ where:

$$n = p + k + S(q + k)$$

Associated with this pass will be the filter coefficient:

$$h_n = h(p, q)$$

and the subpixel image:

$$I_n(i, j) = I\left(\frac{i-p}{S}, \frac{j-q}{S} \right)$$

We can now write Equation (4.8) as a summation of over one variable:

$$I' = \sum_{n=0}^{S^2-1} h_n I_n$$

At the end of pass n the current frame store will contain I_n and the destination frame store will contain the successive refinement of the $n-1$ previous passes which we shall denote as I'_{n-1}. I_n is blended into the destination frame store using blending coefficients (α_n, β_n) to give I'_n (obviously $I' = I'_{S^2-1}$) where:

$$I'_n = \alpha_n I_n + \beta_n I'_{n-1}$$

The blending coefficients are given by:

$$\alpha_n = \frac{h_n}{\displaystyle\sum_{i=0}^{n} h_i} \qquad \text{and} \qquad \beta_n = 1 - \alpha_n$$

Details of the derivation are given in [MAMM89].

4.4 Approaches to filtering in the continuous domain

We recall that the disadvantage of the supersampling approach is that the filter operates on a sampled image. We stated that the easy classical solution was not avail-

able in computer graphics because unlike, say, image processing, a continuous image-to-sampler channel does not exist. The majority of rendering algorithms are discrete, where the generation and sampling process are inextricably entwined, such as in a ray tracer. Attempts have been made, however, to design algorithms that tackle the harder problem of filtering in the continuous domain by approximating the effect of convolution of a filter function, but these are extremely expensive. These are the analytic rendering algorithms referred to earlier, which are less common than the discrete type. Supersampling, you will recall, is just a process that can be appended to a standard renderer. This is convenient, because it means that anti-aliasing can be incorporated as an option in a standard system. Using the theoretically correct approach of filtering a continuous image means designing a special-purpose renderer.

We begin by looking at the general problem of filtering in the continuous image domain to see the ramifications this has for rendering design. Later we will look at practical systems.

Consider Figure 4.13 that shows a pixel grid superimposed on part of a set of overlapping polygons. Returning to our definition of convolution and restating (4.6) in its continuous form we have:

$$I'(x, y) = \int\int I(\alpha, \beta) h(x - \alpha, y - \beta) \, d\alpha \, d\beta$$

where h is a filter function and I the image. Just as we did in the discrete case, we can interpret this integral as

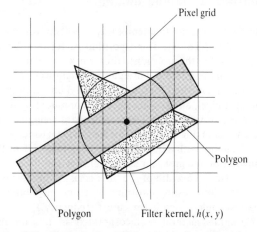

Figure 4.13 Filtering in the continuous domain. Every $I'(x, y)$ has to be evaluated by integrating the product of $I(x, y)$ and $h(x, y)$ over the extent of the filter kernel.

placing the filter at location (x, y) and convolving it with the image. Since the filter's kernel is usually finite in extent we need consider only those parts of the image that fall beneath it. In computer graphics we can denote that part of the image as a list of polygons and we can write:

$$I'(x, y) = \sum_{i=1}^{n} \iint I(\text{polygon}_i) h(x - \alpha, y - \beta) \, d\alpha \, d\beta$$

where:

$I(\text{polygon}_i)$ specifies the intensity across polygon i covered by the filter kernel

n is the number of polygons that lie underneath the filter kernel

Unfortunately it is practically impossible to evaluate this integral except by severe approximation or, alternatively, for the special case of flat shaded polygons. Although the polygon geometry can be dealt with in a continuous domain – precise coverage areas can be evaluated over pixel and filter extents – this is extremely expensive. However the intensity I has analytically too complex a variation over the polygon to enable it to be integrated and so one is forced to sample. This is why prefiltering or filtering any image function $I(x, y)$ in the continuous domain can only be approximated – we can perform area calculations in the continuous domain but intensity variations need to be discretized. We now look at some practical methods that attempt this approach.

4.4.1 Practical filtering in the continuous image domain

The first algorithm to attempt this approach was due to Catmull [CATM78]. This algorithm performs subpixel geometry for the polygons, thus working in the continuous image domain, but ignores variations in $I(x, y)$ in that it is a method for flat shaded polygons. It returns, for each pixel, an intensity which is computed by using the areas of visible subpixel fragments as weights in an intensity sum (Figure 4.14). This is equivalent to convolving the image with a box filter and using the value of the convolution integral at a single point as the final pixel value. (Note the width of the filter is less than ideal and a wider filter using information from neighbouring regions would give a lower cutoff frequency.)

Catmull's method is incorporated in a scan line renderer. It proceeds by dividing the continuous image generation domain into square pixel extents. An intensity for each square is computed by clipping polygons against

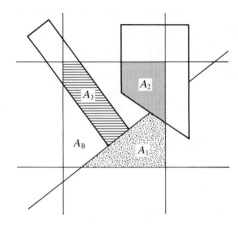

$$\text{Intensity} = I_1 A_1 + I_2 A_2 + I_3 A_3 + I_B A_B$$

Figure 4.14 Polygons are clipped against pixel edges and each other to yield a set of visible fragments.

the square pixel boundary. If polygon fragments overlap within a square they are sorted in z and clipped against each other to produce visible fragments. A final intensity is computed by multiplying the shade of a polygon by the area of its visible fragments and summing. For the example shown in Figure 4.14:

$$I(x, y) = I_1 A_1 + I_2 A_2 + I_3 A_3 + I_B A_B$$

where:

I_i is the (flat) intensity of polygon i
A_i is the (precise) area of polygon i
B is the background

Even ignoring intensity variations, the algorithm costs are severe. Using the algorithm with a wider filter kernel increases the costs even more. More polygons now have to be clipped, and the area of more clipped fragments computed for a filter kernel in each position of the filter specified by the convolution operation.

An efficient, but approximate, approach to continuous image domain filtering is suggested by Abram and Westover [ABRA85]. Again this method computes a weighted intensity for a pixel based on the area of subpixel fragments. Again it ignores intensity variations across the fragments which are too difficult and expensive to incorporate in the methods described in this section. Conveniently, intensity changes vary slowly over a subpixel fragment and any such changes are not as important as shape changes within a pixel. Thus all methods in this section are approximations to continuous filtering as far as shape, but not intensity, is concerned.

The efficiency of Abram's method resides in the precalculation of the convolution integral. This is done by a reordering of the convolution (similar to the rearrangement of the integral in the practical supersampling method described in Section 4.3.5 and [MAMM89]) and a recognition of the fact that polygons clipped by a square pixel boundary always tend to produce certain shaped fragments. Consider a fragment in a certain pixel. If a 3×3 filter kernel is employed then this fragment will effect the integral in the nine cases when the filter is centred on the neighbouring pixels (Figure 4.15). These nine contributions can be precalculated and stored in tables accessed by the fragment shape and the position of the fragment within the filter kernel.

The two main stages in the process are:

1. Find the visible fragments and identify or categorize their shapes.

2. Index a precomputed lookup table which gives the nine contributions for each shape. A single multiplication of the fragment's intensity by the precomputed contribution weighting gives the desired result.

Abram assumes that the shapes fall into one of seven categories:

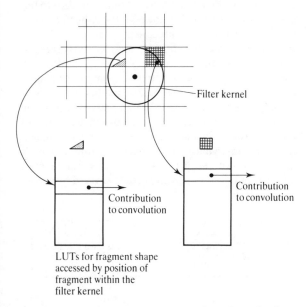

LUTs for fragment shape accessed by position of fragment within the filter kernel

Figure 4.15 A method for precalculating continuous image domain convolutions.

- There is no fragment in the pixel.

- The fragment completely covers the pixel.

- The fragment is trapezoidal and splits the pixel along opposite edges.

- The fragment is triangular and splits the pixel along adjacent edges.

- The complement of the previous (a pentagonal fragment).

- The fragment is an odd shape that can be described by the difference of two or more of the previous types.

- The fragment cannot be easily defined by these simple types.

Note that compared with Catmull's method which convolves with a box filter one pixel wide, the filter kernel is theoretically not constricted by shape or area.

The A-buffer

Another obvious practical approach to continuous filtering is to approximate the process by sampling the subpixel fragments. This tack is taken by Carpenter [CARP84], who uses bitmasks to area sample subpixel fragments (Figure 4.16), developing a technique known as the A-buffer. This method combines an approximation to continuous filtering with standard rendering methodology – essentially a Z-buffer approach. 'A-buffer' stands for anti-aliased, area-averaged accumulation buffer. (A simpler technique was developed by Fiume and Fournier [FIUM83].) The significant advantage of this approach is that at the subpixel level floating-point geometry calculations are avoided. Coverage and area weighting is accomplished by using bitwise logical operators between the bit patterns or masks representing polygon fragments. It is an efficient area sampling technique, where the processing per pixel square will depend only on the number of visible fragments.

In a sense, categorizing this technique as continuous image domain filtering is somewhat artificial. It approximates the shape of subpixel fragments but again assigns a single intensity to each pixel fragment. Thus, whether it is a valid example of continuous image domain filtering, or just an elegant and efficient approach to supersampling, is a matter of opinion. The power of the algorithm resides in its practical efficiency. If we compare the method with supersampling we see that supersampling is an approach that takes into account both

0	0	0	0	0	0	0	0
0	0	0	0	0	0	0	0
0	0	0	0	0	0	0	0
0	0	0	0	0	0	0	0

Figure 4.16   Pixel mask and grid.

shape and intensity at a subpixel level.

Because of its efficiency the A-buffer has proved to be one of the most popular filtering techniques for rendering. The vast majority of computer graphics animation on television is rendered using software that incorporates an A-buffer. In view of its importance we now describe its working in some detail.

The technique provides a discrete approximation to area sampling with a box filter which is usually a square with sides of length one pixel. Incoming polygons are clipped against scan lines and when a given scan line is processed, clipped against individual pixels. Prior to rendering a given pixel, there will be a list of polygon fragments ordered in z. The A-buffer technique represents each of these polygon fragments with a mask of bits – a bitmask.

Associated with the entire pixel will be a bitfield that covers it completely. Let us take a 32-bit integer (4 bytes) as an example. (This is the representation for an unsigned integer on standard workstations.) This arrangement is shown in Figure 4.16. (Of course in practice no one would use such an arrangement to represent a pixel since there is twice the resolution in the horizontal direction compared to the vertical; two such masks should be used in conjunction for the upper and the lower halves of the pixel.) The mask is 8×4 bits and it is associated with a grid of 9×5 which delineates the regions represented by each bit in the mask. Polygon fragments are 'snapped' onto the nearest point of this grid. Those bits that are deemed to lie within this snapped fragment constitute the bitmask of the fragment. This bitmask can be generated by traversing each edge of the fragment in turn. For each

edge a bitmask is obtained from a lookup table. As shown in Figure 4.17, the bitmask of an edge has 1s on the edge and to the right of it, and 0s elsewhere. The exclusive OR of all of the edge bitmasks of the fragment gives the complete bitmask of the fragment.

Listing 4.1 gives a code fragment for this procedure. The function *mask ()* returns a bitmask given the list of vertices (in screen space) of the pixel clipped fragment, and the screen space coordinates (x, y) of the bottom left-hand corner of the pixel. For each vertex the indices of the grid to which it gets snapped are calculated. For each edge the grid indices of the vertices that make up the edge are used to calculate an offset into a lookup table of edge bitmasks. Each grid location can form an edge with any of the others (including itself). The lookup table, which is ordered by grid locations, therefore contains 45 (9×5) bitmasks for each grid location and the mask table itself contains in total 45×45 bitmasks. The offset into the table for an edge with trailing vertex snapped to (iA, jA) and leading vertex snapped to (iB, jB) is given by:

$$45 \left(iA + 9jA \right) + iB + 9jB$$

Note that the bitmask in the lookup table for edge $((iA, jA), (iB, jB))$ is the same for edge $((iB, jB), (iA, jA))$.

So, now that we know how to allot each polygon fragment in the depth-sorted queue, all that remains is to find a colour for the pixel. The power of the A-buffer scheme lies in the fact that the subsequent subpixel hidden surface calculation is done largely using relatively inexpensive bitwise logical operations. For example, calculating subpixel areas is simply a matter of counting the number of bits in the bitmask that represents that area.

The process is driven by a search mask which, at any given z-depth, represents that part of the pixel that still remains visible. So starting at the head of the fragment queue the search mask, initialized to the full pixel mask, descends down the list until either the search mask becomes zero (the pixel is completely covered by preced-

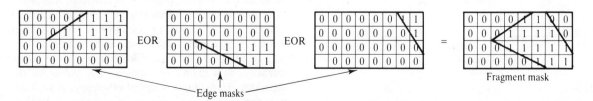

Figure 4.17   Construction of fragment mask from masks of its edges.

Listing 4.1   mask.c

```
#include  "masktable.h"

unsigned mask (vertex_list, vertex_no, x, y)
point *vertex_list;
int vertex_no,x,y;
{
            int i;
            point *vertex;
            unsigned int maskno = 0;
            int         p, q, r, s;

            vertex = vertex_list + vertex_no −1;
            x *= 8;
            y *= 4;
            r = vertex−>x * 8 +0.5;
            s = vertex−>y * 4 +0.5;
            q = 45*(r − x + 9 * (s − y));

            for (i=0; i < vertex_no ; i++) {

                    vertex = vertex_list+i;
                    r = vertex−>x * 8 +0.5;
                    s = vertex−>y * 4 +0.5;
                    p = r − x + 9 * (s − y);
                    maskno ^= masktable [p + q];
                    q = 45 * p;
            }
            return (maskno);
}
```

ing fragments) or the end of the list is reached. Figure 4.18 illustrates the principle, showing a list consisting of two fragments A and B, with A in front of B, in a pixel represented by a mask of 5×5 bits. The progression of the search mask as it descends the fragment list is shown.

When the search mask encounters a fragment, the area of the fragment visible is represented by a bitmask, M_{in}, obtained from ANDing together the search mask and bitmask of the fragment. We write:

$M_{in} = M_{search} \& M_{fragment}$

That part of the pixel that remains visible is given by:

$M_{out} = M_{search} \& {}^{\sim}M_{fragment}$

After passing by this fragment M_{out} becomes M_{search} for the remaining fragments and the process continues. All this can be neatly coded as a recursive routine (given in

[CARP84]), which returns a colour given a search mask and a list of fragments. Returning to our fragment, we obtain a colour C_{in} for its shaded value. The contribution the fragment makes to the final colour of the pixel is given by this colour weighted by the visible area. This area, A_{in}, is just the fractional bitcount of M_{in}. At a particular level of recursion, the colour C returned for M_{search} will be the contribution made by the fragment, plus the colour C_{out}, yet to be calculated, returned by calling the routine with the search mask set to M_{out} and the remaining fragments. We write:

$C = C_{in}A_{in} + C_{out}\left(1 - A_{in}\right)$

The bitmask approach also lends itself to handling transparent fragments. Where the approach falls down, however, is in the case of intersecting fragments – transparent intersecting fragments being most difficult of all. Carpenter [CARP84] provides a simple approx-

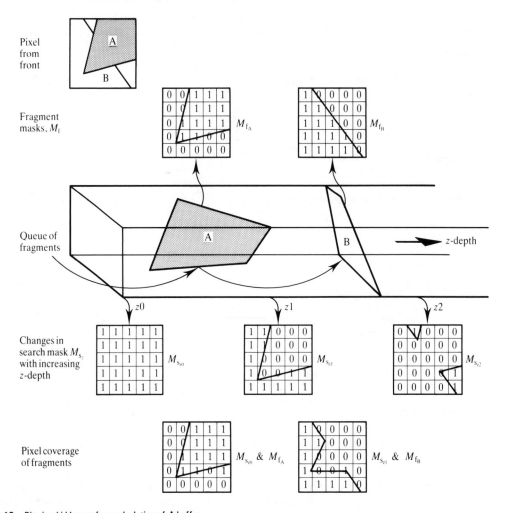

Pixel from front

Fragment masks, M_f

Queue of fragments

Changes in search mask M_s with increasing z-depth

Pixel coverage of fragments

Figure 4.18 Bitwise hidden surface calculation of A-buffer.

imation based on the minimum and maximum z-values of the intersecting fragments, claiming that for a typical image, the number of pixels that contain intersecting fragments is small enough to justify this approximation. Since one person's idea of a typical image is atypical for another, this approximation may not be accurate enough in which case two other solutions suggest themselves:

1. Clip the intersecting fragments against each other and process the bitmasks of the resulting nonintersecting fragments, or

2. Test explicitly for problematic pixels. If one is encountered, subdivide the pixel into four subpixels

and clip the fragment list of the pixels into these subpixels and process the resulting subpixel fragment lists. Repeat this process adaptively until the offending subpixels become negligibly small.

Finally, for those wishing to implement an A-buffer, the following points, based on the authors' experience, should be useful.

The quality of the rendering depends on the resolution of the pixel mask. Figure 4.19(a) shows a test pattern consisting of a set of thin radial lines, rendered black against a white background. Figures 4.19(b) and 4.19(c) each show the same enlarged section of the pattern. Both are rendered at the same pixel resolution as each other but (c) used a pixel mask twice the resolution of that used to produce (b). The greater number of bits in the pixel mask used in (c) gives a less coarse discretization of fragment area which manifests in the larger number of grey levels in the image. The choice of pixel mask resolution is a tradeoff between the improved rendering quality and the increased memory demands made by the larger lookup table for the edge masks. The size of the lookup table increases steeply with increasing pixel mask resolution.

Practical details concerning 'subpixel' renderers

Care must be taken to ensure that the polygon clippers in the renderer clip a given edge in the same direction. Referring to Figure 4.20: if an edge is clipped in the direction as defined by the polygon, then an edge that is shared by two neighbouring polygons will be clipped in opposite directions. This difference in clipping direction can cause the edges to stray numerically from each other, which in turn can lead to vertices that are supposedly coincident being snapped onto different points on the pixel grid. Holes then appear in the bitmask representation of the fragment. The longer the edge the greater the floating-point error introduced by the different directions. Shadow polygons that make up a shadow volume (see Section 5.13), which by definition have long edges, are particularly sensitive.

Significant speedups can be obtained by taking advantage of the spatial coherence of a scene. Spatial coherence means, in this context, that a considerable part of the image is taken up by single polygons that cover more than one pixel. We can exploit coherency at the scan line level by clipping a polygon (that has already been clipped to the scan line) into parts that partially obscure a pixel and parts that completely obscure one or more pixels as shown in Figure 4.21. Polygons of the latter type are called 'spans'. If a given pixel has a fragment list with a fragment from a span at the front of the queue, then spatial coherence tells us that there is a strong possibility that the same span will be at the head of the fragment list for the next pixel. The processing of the next pixel fragment list thus starts with this assumption and the minimum amount of processing is performed on the remaining fragments just to test this assumption. Spatial coherence thus translates to span coherence and for spatially coherent parts of the scene, the algorithm will 'run' along the spans, scan line by scan line. A related approach, based on so-called invisibility coherence is given in [CROW84].

Lastly, on a more general note concerning speedups for renderers, the implementor should be made aware that a lot of suggestions for improving efficiency fall into the category of ingenious, but complex, algorithms for very specific contexts that may save a few microseconds but which make your code unreadable. A more general computer science perspective that takes a 'global view' of

Figure 4.19 (a) A test pattern for the A-buffer. (b) A section of the pattern using a pixel bitmask of resolution 8 × 8. (c) A section of the pattern using a pixel bitmask of resolution 16 × 16.

(a)

(b)

(c)

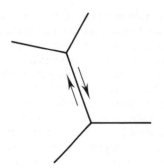

Figure 4.20   Opposite clipping directions of a shared edge.

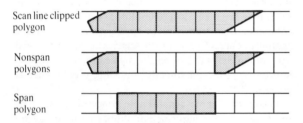

Figure 4.21   Formation of span polygon.

the renderer can be more fruitful. For example, the renderer devotes a lot of time to allocating and deallocating chunks of memory for storing data. A lot of these chunks are always the same size – such as those that are continually required to store the data structure for fragments lists. Using memory management techniques that recognize this fact can yield considerable dividends. One such scheme would be to hold a series of empty lists in memory for all the commonly used data structures. An empty list for fragments, say, would contain a list of previously allocated, but no longer needed, fragment structures. When the renderer needs memory for a new fragment, it looks first at this empty list. If there is nothing there it allocates space directly, otherwise it takes a fragment off the end of the list and uses that. Conversely, when the renderer no longer needs a fragment, instead of freeing it, it goes onto the end of the empty list. In the authors' experience, replacing the naive allocate/deallocate scheme with this way of managing memory can result in 100% speedup.

4.5   Stochastic sampling: introduction

As we have seen, sampling theory predicts that with a regular sampling grid, frequencies contained in the image that are greater than the Nyquist limit will alias. Although these higher frequencies can never be recovered, their appearances as aliases in the image are a direct consequence of the regularity of the sampling. The coherence of the samples interferes with the coherence of the image to produce the coherent errors called aliasing. If we make the samples irregular, in a controlled fashion, then these higher frequencies will appear in the image as noise rather than aliases. This perturbation of the sampling, and consequent tradeoff of aliasing against noise, is known as 'stochastic sampling'.

Intuitively it is easy to see how stochastic sampling is an improvement over uniform sampling. Small regions that fall between uniform sample points will tend to be detected by non-uniform sampling. In stochastic sampling every point in the image has a finite probability of being hit.

Stochastic sampling is an extremely powerful technique and its introduction to computer graphics has led to the development of distributed ray tracing where a whole new, previously unattainable class of phenomena, loosely called 'fuzzy', has become renderable (see Section 10.4). In terms of anti-aliasing, however, its power lies in the fact that the visual system finds the incoherency of noise much less noticeable than aliases which, by definition, have some coherence associated with them and so are more easily spotted. This fact is backed up by nothing less than the evolution of the human retina. Yellot [YELL82] points out that the human eye contains an array of nonuniformly distributed photoreceptors, and that this is the reason that the eye does not produce its own aliasing artefacts. Photoreceptor cells in the fovea are tightly packed and the lens acts as an anti-aliasing filter. However, in the region outside the fovea, the spatial density of the cells is much lower and in this region the cells are nonuniformly distributed. Analysis of the Fourier transform of this distribution shows that it is of the Poisson disc type (see Section 4.5.1).

We have seen that, with the exception of supersampling, different anti-aliasing techniques are applicable to different methods of rendering. This is especially true of stochastic sampling which is almost always associated with ray tracers. The ease with which a rendering algorithm can incorporate stochastic sampling depends on how easy it is to generalize the sampling process.

For a ray tracer this is trivial since there exists a natural division between the scene description – a collection of objects defined analytically – and the sampling – testing for the intersection of rays with these objects. No additional complexity is involved in firing a ray in one direction than any other so it is as trivial to fire a ray through any point on a pixel as through its centre.

The A-buffer, however, cannot employ stochastic sampling without significant modification. Here sampling involves clipping to scan lines then pixels in order to simulate a box filter. Highly customized techniques are used that exploit coherency and work on the scene's projection onto the screen. No obvious way of generalizing the sampling process without some kind of restructuring presents itself.

The simpler Z-buffer, the antecedent to the A-buffer, can be integrated with stochastic sampling without significant overhead. This was achieved most notably in the REYES system [COOK87]. Recall that the Z-buffer is a screen-sized array of pixels and z-values. Polygons are transformed into perspective space and their projections are checked against the screen sample points (x_s, y_s) to see which lie inside. An interior sample point has its value in the Z-buffer compared with the z-value at this point of the polygon (this is calculated by interpolation). Generalizing the sampling process follows from the fact that any point (x_s, y_s) on the screen can be a sample point.

The REYES system, of course, performs more than one sample per pixel by dividing the pixel into subpixels. All initial primitives (usually bicubic parametric patches) are 'diced' into 'micropolygons' no finer than approximately half a pixel wide (the Nyquist limit for an image) to ensure adequate representation of surface shading. A final pass filters the subpixel intensities to produce the final image (Figure 4.22).

Apart from the stochastic sampling of the pixel, the other aspect of the method is that it ignores the coherence approach of 'classical' rendering methods, by splitting up geometric primitives into micropolygons.

4.5.1 Theory of stochastic sampling

Given that stochastic sampling, by randomizing the sampling process, scatters high-frequency information into noise, the question arises: what type of random distribution to adopt? It may not be obvious that 'types' of randomness can be discussed at all since, by definition, they are unpredictable and have no analytical definition. But it turns out that the type of randomness used dictates the spectral character of the noise into which the higher frequencies are dispersed. We shall examine three classes of non-uniform patterns: Poisson, Poisson disc and jittered. These are shown in Figure 4.23,

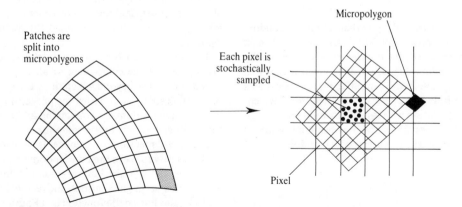

Figure 4.22 Patches are subdivided into micropolygons. These are shaded and visibility calculations are performed by stochastically sampling the micropolygons in screen space (after [COOK87]).

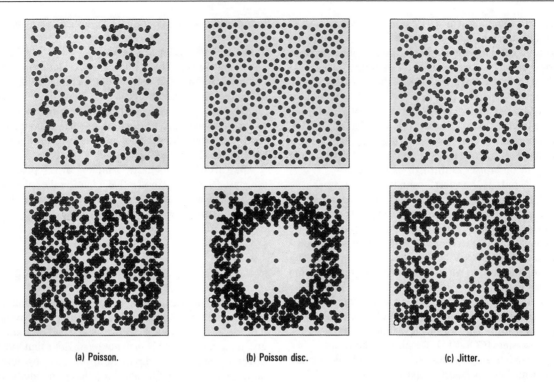

(a) Poisson.   (b) Poisson disc.   (c) Jitter.

Figure 4.23   Noise patterns (upper) and their Fourier transforms (lower).

each pattern containing 324 points, with their Fourier transforms beneath.

Poisson

This pattern is generated by adding points at random locations until the area is full. The distribution is uniform and, as to be expected, the Fourier transform is equally random, containing values distributed uniformly over all frequencies. Obviously this would be pretty useless as a filter because it does not discriminate between frequencies at all. Convolution with this filter would scatter high and low frequencies alike and the resultant sampled image would be masked in a veil of white noise.

Poisson disc

This is a generalization of Poisson sampling whereby each sample point satisfies a minimum-distance constraint, that is, no two points are closer than a cer-

tain distance. In practice this pattern is achieved by generating uniformly distributed points, as in Poisson sampling, but retaining only those that satisfy the minimum-distance constraint with respect to all previous sample points. This is extremely expensive; [MITC87] gives a more efficient method of generating an approximation to this distribution called the 'point-diffusion algorithm'.

The Fourier transform shows a delta function at the origin, the average component of all the samples, surrounded by a disc beyond which there exists white noise. As we shall see by considering the process in more detail in the frequency domain, convolving an image with this filter will give us stochastic sampling.

The one-dimensional analogue is shown in Figure 4.24. It is easy to see in the Fourier domain how frequencies above the Nyquist limit are mapped into noise. If we consider a single sinusoid above the limit (Figure 4.24(a)), this has a delta function as a Fourier transform. This is convolved with the Poisson disc (Figure 4.2(b)) to give Figure 4.24(c). Multiplication with an ideal reconstruction filter shows that the aliasing sine wave is

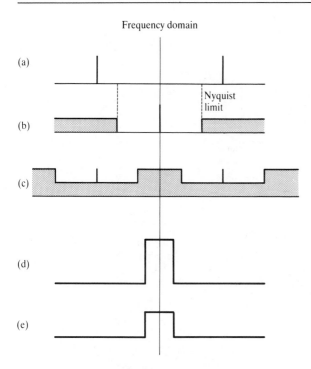

Frequency domain

(a)

Nyquist
limit

(b)

(c)

(d)

(e)

Figure 4.24 A one-dimensional frequency domain representation of the effect of Poisson disc sampling on an aliasing sine wave. (a) Delta function (transform of aliasing sine wave). (b) Transform of Poisson disc sampling function. (c) Convolution of Poisson disc with sine wave (sampled function). (d) Ideal reconstruction filter. (e) Aliasing sine wave maps into bandlimited noise.

mapped directly into white noise over the width of the filter in the Fourier domain. This property is also easily demonstrated in the space domain. Figure 4.25 shows a sinusoid above and below the Nyquist limit. The shaded band in each case represents a region in x in which a sample is likely to occur. The scale of Figure 4.25(a) is greater than that of Figure 4.25(b) and the width of the sample 'bucket' is the same in both cases. The corresponding amplitude range shows that in the first case the sine wave is sampled with a small perturbation. However, in the second case a sample will range over the complete peak-to-peak amplitude of the sine wave and the value sampled is effectively a random number in the peak-to-peak range. Thus the high-frequency sine wave is mapped into noise by the sampling process while the low-frequency wave has a small perturbation added to it. The lower the frequency with respect to the sampling frequency, the smaller the amplitude of the noise perturbation.

Jittered

Jittering is done by perturbing sample locations that are initially spaced regularly. In Figure 4.23(c) the samples were laid out on a square grid denoted by $(18i, 18j)$ and then jittered by an amount $(18(i + \Delta i), 18(j + \Delta j))$ where $\Delta i, \Delta j$ are random values $\in [0, 1]$. Comparing the jittered pattern with its Poisson disc counterpart we see that it is more clumpy, or granular, in appearance. Comparing their Fourier transforms is more instructive. We see that jittering in fact approximates a Poisson disc distribution but that the radius of the disc is appreciably smaller.

This increase in low-frequency noise would cause an image convolved with this filter to scatter the higher frequencies into noise of lower frequencies. This is important to note – since our visual system is more sensitive to low frequency noise than high frequency noise this makes jittering inferior to Poisson disc sampling. The same image rendered using jittering will appear noisier than when rendered using a Poisson disc distribution.

In practice, however, the relative ease with which jittering lends itself to computer graphics makes it the method that is used. As we have seen, sampling using jittering typically involves just randomly shifting the uniform sample points in the two spatial variables; the sample point usually at the centre of a pixel is perturbed to some location within it. Furthermore, sampling using a Poisson disc distribution is made more problematic in that it would require storing the values, once they have been generated, into a lookup table (don't forget also that the reconstruction filter, calculated by considering how each sample point affects neighbouring pixels, would also have to be stored in a lookup table). For a working example of jitter the reader is referred to Section 5.2.

This comparison between Poisson disc and jittered patterns is discussed extensively by Dippe and Wold [DIPP85] who, by expressing the patterns explicitly in terms of their probability distributions and using more sophisticated tools from Fourier theory, were able to set the comparison on a more rigorous, analytical footing. The following notational scheme is based on this work.

Continuing with our one-dimensional analogy, Poisson sampling, without the minimum-distance constraint, can be defined as:

$$s(x) = \sum_{k=0}^{K-1} \delta(x - x_k)$$

where:

x_k is a value chosen from a uniform distribution

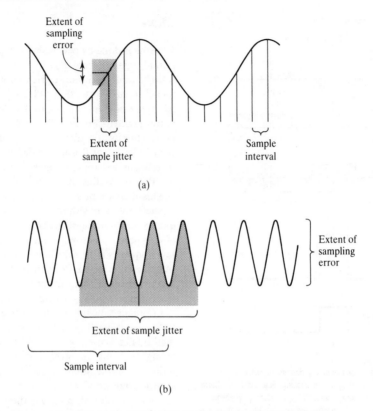

Extent of
sampling
error

Extent of
sample jitter

Sample
interval

(a)

Extent of
sampling
error

Extent of sample jitter

Sample interval

(b)

Figure 4.25   Sampling a sine wave whose frequency is (a) below and (b) above the Nyquist limit (after Cook).

$$p(x_k) = \begin{cases} 1/W & 0 < x_k < W \\ 0 & \text{elsewhere} \end{cases}$$

$K\,(= WR)$ is the number of delta functions

R is the sampling rate per unit distance

$[0, W]$ is the sampling window

If a minimum-distance constraint is introduced this can be specified by a sequential generation process:

$$x_{k+1} = x_k + l_k$$

where l_k is chosen from an exponential distribution:

$$p(l_k) = \begin{cases} R \exp\left(-R(l_k - l_{k0})\right) & l_k > l_{k0} \\ 0 & \text{elsewhere} \end{cases}$$

where:

l_{k0} is the minimum available distance between samples

The effective average rate is

$$R_e = \frac{R}{1 + Rl_{k0}}$$

and when

$$l_{k0} = 0$$

this becomes the Poisson pattern with

$$R_e = R$$

as $R \to \infty$ the sampling pattern tends to a regular pattern with

$$R = \frac{1}{l_{k0}}$$

Now from Fourier theory, we define the autocorrelation function $f(x) \odot f(x)$ of a function f(x) to be:

$$f(x) \odot f(x) = \int\limits_{-\infty}^{\infty} f(\alpha)f(\alpha + x)\,d\alpha$$

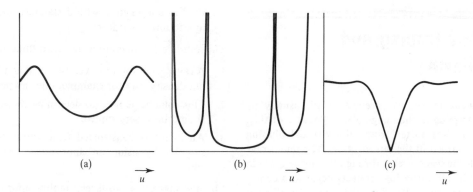

Figure 4.26 Sampling process power spectra (after [DIPP 85]).

Its counterpart in the frequency domain can be shown to represent how the power of the function is distributed over the frequencies, it being just the square $|F(u)|^2$ of the function's amplitude spectrum, and is called the power spectral density (PSD) of the function.

As usual, let $s(x)$ be the sampling function, then the sampled function $g(x)$ of the function $f(x)$ is just $g(x) = f(x)s(x)$. The autocorrelation of the sampled function is the product of the autocorrelation of $f(x)$ and $s(x)$. By the convolution theorem then, if the PSD of the sampled function is $\phi_g(u)$, we have:

$$\phi_g(u) = \phi_f(u) \star \phi_s(u)$$

where:

$\phi_f(u)$ is the PSD of the original function
$\phi_s(u)$ is the PSD of the sampling function

Now the autocorrelation of the above Poisson distribution is

$$\phi_s(u) = R + 2\pi R^2 \delta(u)$$

which gives us

$$\phi_g(u) = R \int_{-\infty}^{\infty} \phi_f(u)\,du + 2\pi R^2 \phi_f(u)$$

showing that the PSD of the sampled function is a broadband noise spectrum plus a scaled version of the original image. If the minimum-distance constraint is introduced, it can be shown [DIPP85] that:

$$\phi_s(u) = \begin{cases} \dfrac{R_e\{1 - 2Ru\,\sin\,(l_{k0}u) + 2R^2\cos\,(l_{k0}u) - 2R^2\}}{2Ru\,\sin\,(l_{k0}u) + 2R^2\cos\,(l_{k0}u) + u^2 + 2R^2} \\ \qquad\qquad\qquad\qquad\qquad\qquad\qquad u \neq 0 \\ 2\pi R_e^2 \delta(u) \qquad u = 0 \end{cases}$$

This function is shown in Figure 4.26(a) and 4.26(b) where $l_{k0}R$ has values 0.5 and 0.95 respectively. It is this function that the signal function is convolved with and this shows the effect of varying the minimum distance. Increasing the minimum distance implies less low-frequency noise and more high-frequency noise will be added to the spectrum of the sampled function $\phi_g(u)$. Once again, the importance of this is that the human visual system is more sensitive to low-frequency perturbations than it is to high-frequency noise.

Dippe then analyses jittering within this framework. Jittering in one dimension is given by:

$$x_k = y_k + j_k$$

where:

x_k is the jittered sample
y_k is the uniform sample
j_k is the jitter

If j_k is chosen from a distribution $P(j_k)$ uniform over the interval $[-1/2R, 1/2R]$ the Fourier transform $F(u)$ is given by:

$$F(u) = \frac{\sin\,(u/2R)}{u/2R}$$
$$= \mathrm{sinc}\,(u/2R)$$

and $\phi_s(u)$, the PSD of the sampling function, is given by:

$$\phi_s(u) = R\,[\,1 - \mathrm{sinc}^2\,(u/2R\,] + 2\pi R^2\,\delta(u)$$

This function is shown in Figure 4.26(c). The nature of the tradeoff between low-frequency and high-frequency noise is now different – in particular the high-frequency peak of the Poisson disc samples are now absent and, in accordance with our earlier discussion, there is more energy located in the lower frequencies.

4.6 Ray tracing and anti-aliasing

In ray tracing initial rays are generated, usually by uniform sampling in the image plane. Because of this, ray-traced images suffer from all the usual aliasing artefacts described in the introduction. The initial rays that sample the scene stream through the image plane in a coherent bundle. Aliasing artefacts occur as a consequence of, and are predicted by, the theory described in Section 4.1. Things are not so simple with the set of rays that shower the scene after being reflected or refracted by the first hit. Ray bundles are formed according to the geometry of the surface that spawned them. The coherence of the initial ray bundle is effectively destroyed and the relationship of rays, spawned by the first hit, to each other is unpredictable or scene dependent. After the first hit, rays will diverge and converge from the first and subsequent hits, spawning a set of rays that will generally sample the scene in an (unpredictable) uneven manner. However, set against this tendency is the fact that as the depth down the ray tree increases, the contribution of a ray becomes less and less important. The image of 'deeper' objects in a reflecting first-hit object generally becomes smaller and smaller as a function of the depth of the ray that hits it.

4.6.1 Nonuniform sampling and ray tracing

Like stochastic sampling, ray tracing specific solutions utilize the incoherent nature of the ray tracing algorithm. (Ray-traced images can, of course, be supersampled but given that ray tracing is an inherently expensive technique, supersampling is perhaps not the best approach.) Unlike most other rendering approaches ray tracing easily lends itself to nonuniform sampling.

An approach to nonuniform oversampling is given by [MITC87]. The method has two important attributes:

1. It is a context-dependent approach devoting most effort to areas of the image that require it, that is, it is adaptive.

2. The anti-aliasing module is algorithmically separate from the ray tracing module and it can therefore be used in conjunction with a standard ray tracer or indeed any ray tracer.

The anti-aliasing operations occur in three stages:

1. A ray tracing solution is constructed at a low sampling density, say for example, one ray per pixel.

2. This solution is used to determine those areas that should be supersampled.

3. An image is constructed from those nonuniform samples by using an appropriate reconstruction filter.

Mitchell suggests a two-level sampling approach, where the supersampling is carried out at either four or nine samples per pixel (making this approach cheaper than distributed ray tracing). Whether to supersample or not is a decision that must be taken by examining small areas of the low resolution samples (3×3 areas are used in [MITC87]). Mitchell points out that this approach is not infallible (nor theoretically correct). It will detect edges, where a 3×3 area straddles an edge, but it is likely to miss small isolated features. A contrast measure is used to make the decision. This is:

$$C = \frac{I_{max} - I_{min}}{I_{max} + I_{min}}$$

This yields three values of C in a conventional RGB ray tracer and different thresholds are used for the different wavelengths of $0.4, 0.3$ and 0.6 respectively. This enables a gross simulation of the fact that the eye's sensitivity to noise or aliasing artefacts is a function of colour. The method thus produces nonuniform samples in both the image and the RGB domain.

A problem that arises out of nonuniform sampling is reconstruction: how are the samples to be reconstructed into an (uniform) array of pixel intensities? We restate Equation (4.6) here; the convolution of a filter h with an image function where the sample points are uniformly spread:

$$I'(x,y) = \sum_{i=x-k}^{x+k} \sum_{j=y-k}^{y+k} I(i,j)\, h(x-i, y-j)$$

Here the summation, theoretically, is over the finite kernel of the filter which, for regular sampling, is a fixed number independent of the filter's position. Now, implicit in this equation is a normalizing factor (Section 4.3.2) that the filter weights sum to unity. If this factor is left constant and Equation (4.6) is used with nonuniform samples, the summation now, for a point (x,y), is over those sample points that fall within the kernel of the filter placed over that position – clearly a number that varies with position. So the intensity of the reconstructed value will fluctuate as a function of the spatial density of the samples. An approximate way to correct this is to renormalize (4.6) for each point (x, y), the normalizing factor varying as a function of local sampling density; this is known as a weighted average filter. Stated simply, the value of a pixel is the sum of the values of the sample points falling beneath the filter multiplied by their respective filter values, the total being normalized by dividing through by the total value of the filters. We write:

$$I'(x, y) = \frac{\sum\sum I(i, j) h(x - i, y - j)}{\sum\sum h(x - i, y - j)}$$

However, this breaks down when the variation in local sampling density is significant, that is, when a high-density and a low-density region are included in the same convolution area – the intensity of the high-density region will predominate. Mitchell [MITC87] instead suggested using a multistage filter. This means using weighted-average filters in cascade, that is, sequentially applying filters with lower and lower cutoff frequencies; an approach that tends to avoid the aforementioned difficulties. (With any set of practical filters the lower the cutoff frequency the greater the effective area over which the filter operates. The filter that is applied first will be the smallest.) In fact it can be shown [MITC87] that the effect of such an operation results in a filter transfer characteristic that approaches the ideal of a step function in the frequency domain.

In the case of jittering [COOK87] suggests that providing the random components of the sample points are small compared to the filter width, the effect of these random components during reconstruction can be ignored. The REYES system subdivides the pixel into 16 subpixels which are each individually jittered – a reconstruction filter being applied to the subsequent subpixel intensities.

Adaptive sampling is a name given to a technique reported by Dippe and Wold [DIPP85]. Like the previous technique it locally alters the sampling density until an image criterion is satisfied. This technique, however, uses stochastic sampling as a base sampling method and is therefore a variance reduction Monte Carlo method. If minimum-distance Poisson sampling is employed then the minimum-distance constraint needs to be reduced as the average sample density is increased. In jittered sampling a pixel region is subdivided into rectangular cells and a jittered sample is chosen within each cell. This process can be subject to further subdivision by taking a cell, using a line of constant x or y to randomly subdivide it into two subcells, placing the original sample in one subcell and calculating a new sample for the other. To reconstruct, Dippe uses a weighted-average filter whose width is calculated or optimized from the local sampling rate.

At this stage we should return to the technique called distributed ray tracing (described in Chapter 10). Here the initial rays are generated using stochastic sampling and subsequent rays are spawned from surface hits using a precalculated Monte Carlo technique. A decision is taken to subdivide each pixel region into 16 cells. No attempt is made to vary this subdivision according to image context and this is the difference between the techniques described in this section and the method known as distributed ray tracing.

A theoretical generalization of distributed ray tracing is given by Lee *et al*. [LEE85]. Lee considers distributed ray tracing to be a multidimensional sampling problem where at each hit the light source area, reflection direction and refraction direction all have to be sampled. Again in Cook's distributed ray tracing method precalculated importance sampling is used, given a priori knowledge of the nature of reflection/refraction functions, and the actual scene to be rendered and the image statistics have no influence on the sampling that is carried out during the generation of the image. Lee's approach is to make distributed ray tracing sensitive to the data being sampled using an adaptive variance reduction technique termed 'stratified sampling'.

4.7 Texture mapping and anti-aliasing

Anti-aliasing in the context of texture mapping can be treated as a special case because of certain attributes of the process. First, what is usually meant by anti-aliased texture mapping is a process that is confined *solely* to a texture mapping phase of a scene generation. The image may still require anti-aliasing by a general technique, even though anti-aliasing has been incorporated for the texture-mapped parts of the image. Secondly, the question may arise: why cannot general anti-aliasing techniques be applied to texture mapping? The answer is that they can, but texture mapping throws up unique problems (and pathological artefacts) and it also possesses an important attribute that can be exploited. This attribute is simply the fact that texture maps are known a priori and this opens up the possibility of precalculated convolutions. The unique problem thrown up by texture mapping is that correct filters need to vary in shape as a function of the actual texture mapping. These two aspects, precalculation of convolution integrals and approaches to space variant filtering techniques, have accounted for most of the research to date in anti-aliasing in texture mapping.

Let us consider first why texture mapping is so problematic in generating aliasing artefacts. By definition texture mapping usually contains a degree of coherence. The aliasing artefacts thrown up by such patterns are shown in Figure 4.9. In texture mapping we also have a problem that is sometimes referred to as compression. Consider a chequerboard pattern and a single object. If the object is a long way from the view point such that the entire chequerboard maps onto a single pixel, then if unfiltered mapping is employed the object would be completely black or white. Worse, if it was animated and remained the same size in the projection plane it would alternate between black and white as it moved. This is a simple manifestation of the general need for space variant filters.

Consider the problem in more detail. Figure 4.27 shows a pixel in the screen domain. If every point in the pixel outline were to be mapped into the texture domain,

then because of the nonlinear nature of the combination of the texture and perspective mapping process, this 'pre-image' or inverse pixel map of a pixel in the texture domain is a curvilinear quadrilateral, whose shape and area changes as a function of the mapping, requiring a space variant filter. Most algorithms deal with this requirement for space variant filtering by approximating the actual pre-image shape in some manner.

Texture mapping is described in detail in Chapter 6, here we confine ourselves solely to anti-aliasing considerations.

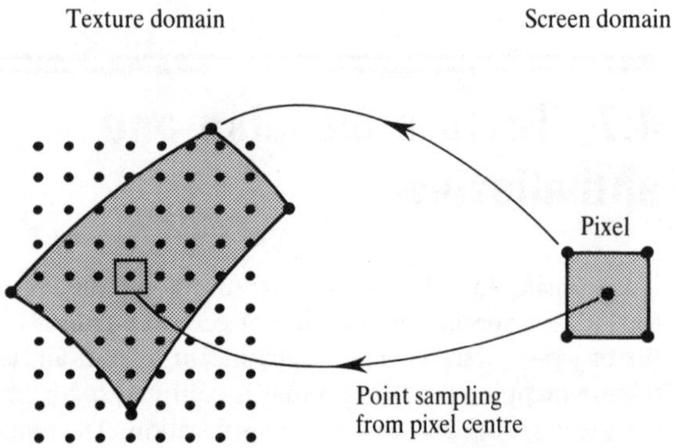

4.7.1 Precalculation techniques: mip-mapping

The most commonly used precalculation technique in texture mapping is mip-mapping [WILL83b]. This ignores the shape variations in the pixel inverse map, and uses a standard assumed shape of a square. The *area* of the filter, however, is allowed to vary. This is one of the easiest and most effective schemes to implement and we shall describe it therefore in some detail. Because of the precalculation the method is known as a constant cost filter – the cost is independent of the area in texture space into which a pixel maps. Instead of a texture domain comprising a single image, Williams uses many images, all derived by successively 'averaging down' the

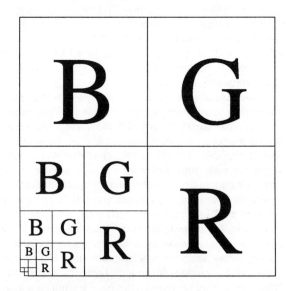

Figure 4.27 Pre-image of a pixel.

Texture domain   Screen domain

Pixel

Point sampling
from pixel centre

Figure 4.28 Memory format of a mip-map.

original image to lower resolutions. Each image in the sequence is at exactly half the resolution of the previous, that is, half the linear dimension and a quarter the number of samples of its parent.

Figure 4.28 shows the self-contained memory format of an RGB colour mip-map, say 512×512 pixels. The entire mip-map is contained within a 1024×1024 chunk of memory, with only one mip-map pixel at the bottom left-hand corner remaining unused. Plate 4 shows the actual maps used for Figure 6.3.

The mip-map in this example is a pyramid of 10 levels, each level being a representation of the original image filtered using a square box filter the sides of which are of length 2^k pixels, $0 \leqslant$ level $k \leqslant 9$. The base of the pyramid, defined to be level 0, is the original uncompressed image of 512×512 pixels convolved with a square box filter of length one pixel. The tip of the pyramid, defined to be level 9, is the entire original image convolved with a square box filter of length 512 pixels and compressed into one mip-map pixel.

The mip-map is accessed via three coordinates, u, v, d, as shown in Figure 4.29. (u, v) are the spatial coordinates of the map and represent the horizontal coordinates of the pyramid. d, the compression, is a measure of how much the texture is compressed beneath the screen pixel and can be thought of as the vertical coordinate of the pyramid.

In general, d will be calculated as a continuous value

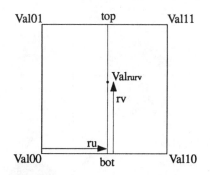

$$bot = Val00 + ru \, (\, Val10 - Val00)$$
$$top = Val01 + ru \, (\, Val11 - Val01)$$
$$Val_{rurv} = bot + rv \, (\, top - bot \,)$$

Figure 4.30 Bilinear interpolation.

and a blend is made between the two nearest mip-map levels using linear interpolation. u- and v-values are also, in general, continuous and bilinear interpolation is carried out to determine an intensity. Bilinear interpolation is shown in Figure 4.30 which illustrates the derivation of a single intensity Val_{rurv} by interpolating amongst the four nearest values. This 'interlevel' followed by 'intralevel' interpolation is an important part of the process; ensuring a continuous representation of the texture image as the surface moves with respect to the screen.

A reasonably accurate determination of d is crucial to the working of mip-mapping. If d is too large the image will appear blurred; too small and aliasing will not be reduced. Moreover the problems are compounded in that the further the ideal filter deviates from a square filter, the harder (and more ad hoc) it becomes to make a sensible choice for d.

In practice, for texture-mapped polygonal surfaces, the texture area subtended under the screen pixel is traced out by the u, v-coordinates associated with the vertices of the surface clipped to the screen pixel, as shown in Figure 4.31. This is an algorithmic approximation to the general inverse pixel map shown in Figure 4.27. In general this can be any arbitrarily shaped polygonal region which, under this scheme, will be approximated by a linear combination of square box filters. This is quite a crude approximation – particularly severe is the assumption that the texture is compressed equally in both the u- and v-directions.

None the less it is fair to say that, under all but the most pathological of conditions, mip-mapping provides one

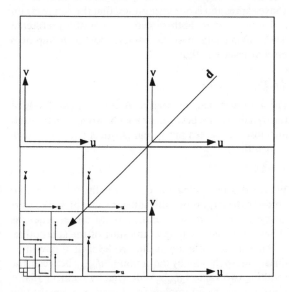

Figure 4.29 Coordinate system of a mip-map.

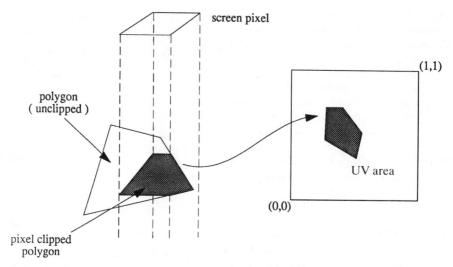

Figure 4.31 Pre-image of a pixel-clipped polygon.

of the most practical and efficient ways of filtering images that is visually acceptable. It has proved itself under the rigorous demands of the advertising industry and all instances of texture mapping in this book have been rendered using mip-mapping – as shown in Listing 4.2 where the subroutine *mip_map(map,u,v,d,colour)* returns a colour from the mip-map given *u*, *v* and *d*.

We now describe a particular derivation of *d* used to generate the texture-mapped images throughout this book. Let the *u*, *v*-coordinates of the entire mapped image cover the unit square [0,1]. Define the 'UVarea' of a closed region of the image to be the area of that region in (u, v) parameter space. The UVarea of one texture pixel is thus $1/512 \times 1/512 = 1/2^{18}$. Recall that at level *k* the image is filtered using a square box filter of side of length 2^k pixels, $0 \leqslant k \leqslant 9$. This is equivalent to saying that at level *k*, 2^{2k} texture pixels are compressed under a single mip-map pixel. The UVarea of a mip-map pixel at level *k* is thus given by:

$$\text{UVarea} = \frac{2^{2k}}{2^{18}} = 2^{2k-18}$$

We can therefore define the compression of an image under a screen pixel to be the square root of the UVarea that the pixel subtends:

$$d = (\text{UVarea})^{1/2}$$

This is the value for *d* that is passed to the routine *mip_map ( )* along with *u*, *v*-coordinates that are calculated by

taking the average of all the texture coordinates at the vertices of the clipped polygon. A working example of calculating *d* from the pre-image is given in Listing 6.1, Section 6.1.4. The approximation replaces the pre-image with a square of the same area whose axes are parallel to the texture axes and whose centre is at the centroid of the pre-image.

Note that implicit in taking the square root in the above expression is our assumption that the compression is symmetrical in both directions. For the prefiltered levels of the mip-map the compression of a mip-map pixel at level *k* is thus:

$$d = 2^{k-9} \qquad 0 \leqslant k \leqslant 9$$

For a given *d* then we need to find which two levels of the pyramid it lies between or which two mip-map pixels are closest to screen pixel, that is, for $d \in [0, 1]$ we seek *k* such that:

$$2^{k-9} < d < 2^{k-8}$$

We do this by testing for the inequality $2^{9-k}d > 1$ to hold for the largest possible integer value of *k*. We start at $k = 0$ and increase *k* until it is no longer true – as shown in the empty loop at the start of the subroutine.

Bilinear interpolation at the two levels is followed by linear interpolation by an amount d_{interp} between the resulting two values. d_{interp} is derived by realizing that it must also be the interpolate for *d* itself between the two values 2^{k-9} and 2^{k-8}, that is

Listing 4.2   mip_map.c

```
/*
            mip_map( ): Return colour from mip_map map given u,v and d.
*/

float floor();                          /* returns largest integer no greater than argument */
float clamp();                          /* clamps first argument in range of second and third */

void  mip_map(map,u,v,d,colour)
char  map[1024][1024];/* mip_map */
float u,v;/* texture coordinates in range [0,1] */
float d;/* compression in range [0,1] */
float colour[3];/* rgb value of colour */

{
        int id;
        float low_colour[3],high_colour[3];
        int singlelevel;/* boolean that holds if d is at top or bottom of pyramid */
        int mapsize;/* length in texture pixels of level */
        int iu,iv,ui,vi,iu_n,iv_n,ui_n,vi_n;/* offsets into mip_map */
        float bot,top,ru,rv,dinterp;/* interpolation parameters */

/*
        Find which two layers of the pyramid d lies between.
*/
        d  = clamp(d,0.,1.);
        id = floor(d*512.);
        singlelevel = ((id==0)||(id==512));
        for (mapsize = 512;id > 1 ;id >>= 1,mapsize >>= 1);

        iu = floor( u*mapsize );
        ru = u*mapsize − iu;
        iu_n = iu+1;
        iu = iu % mapsize;                  /* Wrap around the edge of the texture */
        iu_n = iu_n % mapsize;

        ui=iu+mapsize;
        ui_n=iu_n+mapsize;

        iv = floor( v*mapsize );
        rv = v*mapsize − iv;
        iv_n = iv+1;
        iv = iv % mapsize;
        iv_n = iv_n % mapsize;

        vi=iv+mapsize;
        vi_n=iv_n+mapsize;

/*
        Perform bilinear interpolation (as shown in Fig 4.30) at the lower level
        on the three colour components separately.
*/
```

Listing 4.2   cont.

```
        bot=map[ui][iv]+ru*(map[ui_n][iv]–map[ui][iv]);
        top=map[ui][iv_n]+ru*(map[ui_n][iv_n]–map[ui][iv_n]);
        low_colour[0]=bot+rv*(top–bot);

        bot=map[ui][vi]+ru*(map[ui_n][vi]–map[ui][vi]);
        top=map[ui][vi_n]+ru*(map[ui_n][vi_n]–map[ui][vi_n]);
        low_colour[1]=bot+rv*(top–bot);

        bot=map[iu][vi]+ru*(map[iu_n][vi]–map[iu][vi]);
        top=map[iu][vi_n]+ru*(map[iu_n][vi_n]–map[iu][vi_n]);
        low_colour[2]=bot+rv*(top–bot);

/*

        If singlelevel holds then we are either at the bottom or the top
        of the pyramid and  need only bilinearly interpolate at that
        one level. Otherwise must perform a bilinear interpolation at the
        next level up, which is half the linear dimension of the previous
        level.

*/

        if (singlelevel) {

                colour[0]  =  low_colour[0];
                colour[1]  =  low_colour[1];
                colour[2]  =  low_colour[2];
        }
        else {

                mapsize  >>=1;

                ru = (ru + (iu  %  2))/2;
                iu  >>=1;
                iu_n=iu+1;
                iu  = iu  %  mapsize;
                iu_n = iu_n  %  mapsize;

                ui=iu+mapsize;
                ui_n=iu_n+mapsize;

                rv = (rv + (iv  %  2))/2;
                iv  >>=1;
                iv_n=iv+1;
                iv  = iv  %  mapsize;
                iv_n = iv_n  %  mapsize;

                ui=iu+mapsize;
                ui_n=iu_n+mapsize;

                bot=map[ui][iv]+ru*(map[ui_n][iv]–map[ui][iv]);
                top=map[ui][iv_n]+ru*(map[ui_n][iv_n]–map[ui][iv_n]);
                high_colour[0]=bot+rv*(top–bot);
```

Listing 4.2   cont.

```
            bot=map[ui][vi]+ru*(map[ui_n][vi]−map[ui][vi]);
            top=map[ui][vi_n]+ru*(map[ui_n][vi_n]−map[ui][vi_n]);
            high_colour[1]=bot+rv*(top−bot);

            bot=map[iu][vi]+ru*(map[iu_n][vi]−map[iu][vi]);
            top=map[iu][vi_n]+ru*(map[iu_n][vi_n]−map[iu][vi_n]);
            high_colour[2]=bot+rv*(top−bot);

/*
        Linearly interpolate between the levels by an amount dinterp.
*/

            dinterp = mapsize*d−1.;
            colour[0]=low_colour[0]+dinterp*(high_colour[0]−low_colour[0]);
            colour[1]=low_colour[1]+dinterp*(high_colour[1]−low_colour[1]);
            colour[2]=low_colour[2]+dinterp*(high_colour[2]−low_colour[2]);
        }
}
```

$$d = 2^{k-9} + d_{interp}(2^{k-8} - 2^{k-9})$$

which gives:

$$d_{interp} = 2^{9-k}d - 1$$

For the purposes of clarity, Listing 4.2 presents the indexing of the mip-map for the separate colour components coded up in a straightforward manner. Advantage can be taken, however, of the memory organization – since everything is done in powers of 2, indexing can be done using relatively inexpensive binary scaling. This is left as an exercise for the reader.

As we stated earlier, there is no one correct way to calculate d and while the above derivation works well for texture mapping, we shall see later that for other mapping functions (see Section 6.3.1 on Chrome mapping) it falls down, and an alternative derivation must be sought.

Finally, the reader should be aware of the fact that although it is a useful technique, mip-mapping is limited in that it performs well only for a well-defined subset of shading practices. It is important to note that in order to calculate the compression, the notion of mip-mapping cannot be divorced from the notion of texture area. This fits in well with those shaders that are screen driven – as we have seen texture area is well defined, it being the area subtended in u, v-space of a pixel-clipped polygon. It also could work for a REYES-type system where the tex-

ture area would be the area subtended in u, v-space of a diced micropolygon. But for shaders that point sample, mip-mapping is irrelevant. Consider the case of ray tracing and consider a ray somewhere down a ray tracing tree that hits a texture-mapped surface. Given only one point of intersection it is impossible to calculate the compression of the surface at that point and alternative anti-aliasing schemes must be sought.

4.7.2 Precalculation techniques: summed area tables

An obvious disadvantage of mip-mapping is that the filter shape is always a square. Crow, in an elegant generalization of mip-mapping [CROW84], is able to incorporate rectangular filtering in a precalculation technique called 'summed area tables'. In this scheme a single table is precalculated wherein each value is effectively an encoding of the integral of the texture function over the area of interest. The table is indexed by a rectangular area, an approximation to the inverse pixel map. The rectangle's aspect ratio can of course vary and this is its advantage over the previous technique – it is a closer approximation to space variant filtering.

Each value in the table is the sum of the texture inten-

(a)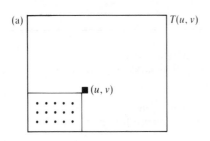

(b)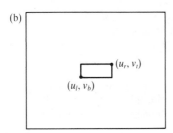

(c)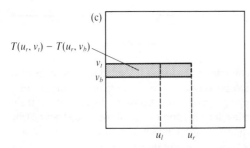

(d)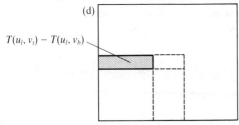

Figure 4.32 Crow's summed area table. (a) Summed area table: each pixel in the map is the sum of the pixel value plus the sum of all values in the lower left-hand corner. (b) The table is indexed by a rectangular approximation to the inverse pixel map.

sity at that location plus the sum of the intensities contained in the lower left-hand corner defined by that position (Figure 4.32(a)). Consider recovering a single value which is the sum over a rectangle defined by the values (u_r, v_t) and (u_l, v_b) as shown in Figure 4.32(b). The shaded strip of 4.32(c) is given by:

$$T(u_r, v_t) - T(u_r, v_b)$$

Subtracting the shaded strip of 4.32(d) given by:

$$T(u_l, v_t) - T(u_l, v_b)$$

gives the sum over the rectangle to be trivially

$$T(u_r, v_t) - T(u_r, v_b) - T(u_l, v_t) + T(x_l, y_b)$$

4.7.3 Space variant filters

The previous precalculation techniques worked by crudely approximating space variant filtering. Space variant filtering is not a well-researched topic and the general approach in computer graphics has been to approximate the inverse pixel image with a simpler mapping. In the precalculated techniques this was taken to be a square or a rectangle, the filter function itself being a box. In this section we examine nonbox-type filters that change shape as a function of the pixel mapping.

The first appearance of a space variant filter is given in a classic paper by Blinn and Newell [BLIN76]. (This paper also contains the first use of environment mapping.) In the work a 2×2 pixel region surrounding the current picture element is mapped into texture space, and is assumed to form a quadrilateral with straight edges. A pyramid is then distorted to fit this quadrilateral. This process is shown in Figure 4.33. Thus both the base shape and the weights of the filter change as a function of the inverse mapping.

We can define this process formally as follows. A point in texture space maps onto a pixel by the texture to screen mapping:

$$(x, y) = T(u, v)$$

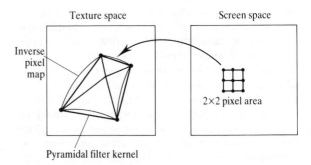

Figure 4.33 An early example of space variant filtering [BLIN76].

The inverse mapping that transforms a pixel into texture space is given by:

$$T^{-1}(x, y) = (u, v)$$

We define a filter kernel and note that this has a shape in texture domain given by:

$$h(u, v) = h(T^{-1}(x, y))$$

This defines a texture space filter that is space variant or a filter whose shape changes in texture space as a function of where it is positioned in screen space.

All approximate approaches to space variant filtering are elaborations of this basic approach and vary only in the nature and degree of approximation. For example, Feibush, Levoy and Cook [FEIB80] use a method where the convolution is carried out in screen space. Filter functions are placed in the required position in screen space and a bounding box found. This is inverse mapped into texture space and a bounding rectangle found for the resulting curvilinear quadrilateral. All the texture pixels in this rectangle are mapped into screen space and their

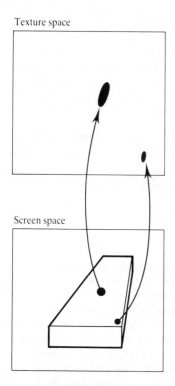

Texture space

Screen space

Figure 4.34 Circles in screen space always map into ellipses in texture space.

offset from the original reference position used to look up a table wherein is stored a weighting coefficient for the filter currently being used.

A number of schemes (for example [GANG82, GREE86]) use circular pixels in screen space as a device that facilitates approximation schemes to space variant filtering. These approaches rely on the fact that the inverse map of a circle is always an ellipse in texture space. Thus if the circle-for-square pixel approximation can be tolerated, we can exploit this fact. The circle-to-ellipse mapping is easy to visualize (Figure 4.34) and it is obvious that the major axis of the ellipse will align with the direction of the greatest compression.

Greene and Heckbert's approach is called elliptical weighted average (EWA) filter. In this method a pixel, approximated by a circle, is inverse mapped into an ellipse. A quadratic function $\phi(u, v)$ can be defined as:

$$\phi(u, v) = Au^2 + Buv + Cv^2$$

where:

$(u, v) = (0, 0)$ is the centre of the ellipse
$A = v_x^2 + v_y^2$
$B = -2(u_x v_x + u_y v_y)$
$C = u_x^2 + u_y^2$

where u_x denotes partial differentiation of u with respect to x and similarly for u_y, v_x and v_y.

The elliptical extent Q is enclosed in a bounding box. This space is then scanned and Q is evaluated using finite differences – texture pixels satisfying

$$Q(u, v) < F \qquad \text{for a threshold } F$$

where:

$$F = (u_x v_y - u_y v_x)^2$$

are mapped into screen space and used to index a lookup label that stores a filter function.

Currently the most accurate approach to space variant filters is a technique by Fournier and Fiume [FOUR88]. Here the filter kernel in texture space is modelled, rather than approximated, from a set of bicubic parametric patches. Precalculation of the convolution of the basis functions of these patches with the texture function T enables a constant time method. The method thus combines the attributes of precalculation and accurate space variant filtering.

The filter kernel in texture space is defined as:

$$h(u_c - u, v_c - v) = \bigcup_{\text{all patches}} \sum_{i=0}^{m} \sum_{j=0}^{m} p_{ij} B_i(u) B_j(v)$$

where:

p_{ij} is the set of coefficients determined from the values of $h(u, v)$ at the knots
B is a basis function

To evaluate the convolution contribution at a certain position in texture space we need to integrate over all the patches (the filter kernel) the product of $T(u, v)$ and the filter weights. This can be defined by:

$$I = \sum_{k,l} \int_{u=u_k}^{u_{k+1}} \int_{v=v_l}^{v_l+1} T(u, v) \sum_{i=0}^{m} \sum_{j=0}^{m} p_{ij} B_i(u) B_j(v) \,du dv \tag{4.9}$$

where:

k, l is the index of a patch in the array of patches that represents h

The coefficient matrix p_{ij} is independent of u and v over a patch and Equation (4.9) can be rewritten as:

$$I = \sum_{k,l} \sum_i \sum_j p_{ij} \int_{u=u_k}^{u_{k+1}} \int_{v=v_l}^{v_l+l} T(u, v) B_i(u) B_j(v) \,du dv$$

This form enables precalculation and the m^2 integrals:

$$C_{ij} = \int_{u=u_k}^{u_{k+1}} \int_{v=v_l}^{v_l+1} T(u, v) B_i(u) B_j(v) \,du dv$$

are evaluated for a particular $T(u, v)$ for every position of the filter on T. The required integral then reduces to:

$$I = \sum_{k,l} \sum_i \sum_j p_{ij} C_{ij}$$

Crucial to the efficient working of the scheme is the implementation of a method to select a number of patches to model the filter kernel that is appropriate for the degree of approximation required. As the accuracy required is increased more and more (smaller) patches are required. This implies that a *set* of C_{ij} is precomputed and stored in a pyramidal structure. Determining an accuracy for patch approximation is achieved by inverse mapping a test set of filter grid points and examining their spatial variance in texture space.

4.8 Anti-aliasing solid textures

In Chapter 8 we introduce the powerful and popular technique of solid textures. Here a three-dimensional texture field is defined and a surface is textured by 'placing' the object in the field, and obtaining a texture from the intersection of the surface of the object and the field. Aliasing artefacts can arise for exactly the same reasons as they do with standard texture mapping – a pixel may project into a region of texture that contains many variations over the projected area.

The advantage of solid texturing is that objects of arbitrary shape can be textured and an approach to anti-aliasing is to filter the three-dimensional field over a small *volume* of texture space that contains the surface element, just as we filtered over a small area of two-dimensional texture space.

Peachey [PEAC88] points out that the ideal solution is to convolve the texture field with a three-dimensional filter kernel representing a lowpass filter based on the pixel area, but because of the practicalities of the method this is rarely possible. He lists a number of possible approximate approaches as:

1. filtering by supersampling and convolving the three-dimensional texture values with a filter;

2. performing 1 by using precomputed three-dimensional lookup tables;

3. using a three-dimensional version of mip-mapping;

4. anti-aliasing measures built in to the texture definition.

The first three in the list are three-dimensional extensions of techniques described elsewhere in this chapter. Techniques that require storing a table of the texture definition seem highly impractical. Storage requirements are exorbitantly high for a three-dimensional field at reasonable resolution – one of the advantages of procedural texture is that the values do *not* have to be stored. We can conclude that the significant advantages of solid texture are countered with the difficulty of anti-aliasing. We now discuss the easiest option – built-in anti-aliasing.

4.8.1 Built-in filtering of three-dimensional textures

This is the most straightforward technique that can be employed; however, it does depend on the nature of the texture definition. The title refers to the fact that the equivalent of an anti-aliasing filter can be inserted into some three-dimensional texture procedures.

Consider the examples given in Chapter 7 (Fourier synthesis), and the simulation of turbulence. In the case of the definition given in Section 7.2.1, all we have to do is to ensure that we do not generate any frequency components greater than the Nyquist limit of 1/2 cycle per pixel. That is

$$2\pi p w_i \leqslant 1/2 \quad \text{where } p \text{ is the pixel size}$$

For similar reasons to those discussed in Section 7.2.1 we need to reduce the frequency components to zero gradually rather than abruptly. Peachey suggests reducing the frequency components from

$$2\pi p w_i = 1/4$$

The turbulence function described in Section 7.2.2 already contains an anti-aliasing measure. The number of 'noise' components and their frequency is actually controlled by the projected pixel size (see Listing 7.1).

4.9 Colour aliasing

Colour aliasing in computer graphics is an 'invisible' and relatively undiscussed phenomenon. It is a topic that in the past has been unimportant (most colours used in rendering are arbitrary or selected for effect). However if the computer graphics community is going to deal with *realistic* colour it has to be addressed. Realistic colour, where serious attempts are made to model the real variation in colour of an object as a function of lighting conditions, is likely to find applications in Computer Aided Architectural Design (CAAD), for example.

Let us first look at why we have a problem within colour variations. The answer is straightforward – we have a classic aliasing problem in colour space if we use the standard RGB or three intensity computer graphics model. As we discussed in Section 2.3.5, three samples in colour space cannot begin to capture the variations in

shaded intensity when a light source that possesses an energy distribution that is a function of wavelength illuminates an object that has a reflectivity characteristic which varies continuously with wavelength. A colour is a single point in a three-dimensional colour space that is computed eventually by integrating the results obtained by sampling reflectivity and illumination spectral functions, and inadequacies in sampling result in a shift away from the correct position of this point.

There is therefore no visual degradation of the image as far as spatial noise is concerned but simply a subtle shift in colour. (Note that banding, a highly *visible* defect in colour shading, is a separate phenomenon due either to underquantization or to using an insufficient number of levels to represent each of the coordinates in the reproduction device colour space.) This effect will occur to an exaggerated extent in ray-traced images where, depending on the trace depth, an intensity is evaluated in the recursion by multiplication with the 'deeper' intensity.

We will now briefly discuss the important aspects of correct colour computation in computer graphics. Colour science and its application in computer graphics needs a textbook in its own right; here we will attempt merely to give the reader an appreciation of the problem involved. For more information on this topic see [HALL89].

Consider first the difference between a correct approach and the standard approach. (This problem was also discussed in Section 2.3.5. We now look at it from an anti-aliasing view point.) In an accurate method we would wish to compute a triple representing a colour as follows:

$$R = \sum_\lambda F_\lambda \bar{r}_\lambda$$

$$G = \sum_\lambda F_\lambda \bar{g}_\lambda \qquad\qquad\qquad \textbf{(4.10)}$$

$$B = \sum_\lambda F_\lambda \bar{b}_\lambda$$

where:

R, G and B are known as tristimulus values

$\bar{r}_\lambda$ $\bar{g}_\lambda$ and $\bar{b}_\lambda$ are colour-matching functions, subjectively derived standard functions that blend with F_λ to enable a single R, G or B to be computed

F_λ is a function computed from the rendering method by evaluating equations on a wavelength by wavelength basis. We assume that F_λ has been evaluated at a sufficient number of wavelengths.

Now leaving aside the additional complications of monitor colour space we can compare this approach with the standard computer graphics methodology, which is:

$$R = F_R$$
$$G = F_G$$
$$B = F_B$$

where:

F_R, F_G and F_B are three values, calculated by three rendering equations, that use reflection coefficients and light source intensities at just three wavelengths (see Figure 2.12)

The only reported work into this problem is in [HALL83], [HALL89] and [MEYE88]. In these approaches a distinction is made between colour computation space wherein rendering is applied on a wavelength to wavelength basis and perceptual and display space. In colour computation space, spectral waves are sampled to determine coefficients for rendering equations. The question that arises is: how are the curves to be sampled? Using as a control an image made up of two overlapping filters rendered by evaluating intensities, at one nanometer increments between 360 mm and 830 mm, Hall [HALL83] compares a standard RGB approach with a spectral sample method. (Overlapping filters – semitransparent materials – were used because their transparency as a function of wavelength exhibits sharp changes.) Hall reported that the standard method yielded significant colour distortion whereas the nine sample method was a much better approximation to the control image.

Hall went on to address the problem of the sampling methodology, and suggested box sampling the spectral curves to provide coefficients for rendering. The rationale for this is, given that attempting to conform to the sampling theorem by taking sufficient samples of the spectral curves will result in an impossible number of rendering equations, is there a better approach than point sampling? Hall suggests box functions where equal area boxes of different widths are placed on the spectral curves and the height of each box is taken as the sample (Figure 4.35) – thus simultaneously sampling and low-pass filtering the spectral curve. The sampled coefficients are then used in rendering equations and box reconstruction functions used to provide the F_λ for Equation (4.10). The number and position of the samples was determined by a search that attempted to minimize perceptual error.

Meyer [MEYE88] also deals with this problem and evaluates a colour space for computation that is designed

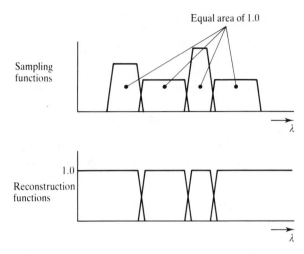

Figure 4.35 Box sampling and reconstruction functions for four spectral samples (after [HALL83]).

to minimize errors. He uses Gaussian quadrature with special weighting functions to select wavelengths for colour computation.

4.10 Aliasing in the time domain

In this chapter we have explored the causes of aliasing artefacts in computer images and emphasized that these arise from undersampling. Aliasing problems also exist in the time domain. Frames in an animation sequence can be seen as instantaneous samples, in the time domain, of a continuous motion sequence. Undersampling this continuous sequence produces certain problems. A temporal aliasing artefact that is analogous to the aliases that appear in coherent texture is the familiar wagon-wheel effect often seen in old westerns. This is illustrated in Figure 4.36 where in general fast speeds alias as slower speeds. The effect of these aliases is to produce weird visual effects in rotating objects, such as a stationary rotating wheel (the classic strobe effect) or a wheel rotating backwards.

Analogous to the jagged edge problem, which we decided was not strictly an aliasing artefact, is jerky

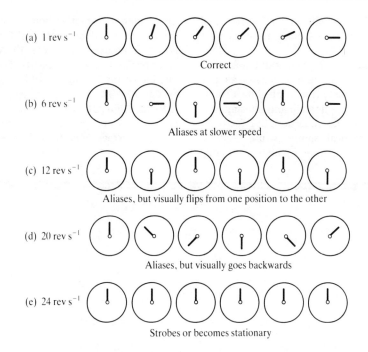

(a) 1 rev s^{-1}

Correct

(b) 6 rev s^{-1}

Aliases at slower speed

(c) 12 rev s^{-1}

Aliases, but visually flips from one position to the other

(d) 20 rev s^{-1}

Aliases, but visually goes backwards

(e) 24 rev s^{-1}

Strobes or becomes stationary

Figure 4.36 Undersampling a moving object means that a fast speed aliases as a slower one. This can produce bizarre visual effects. (a) Correctly sampled. (b) Undersampled, appears to rotate at 5 rev s^{-1}. (c) Undersampled, appears to rotate at 10 rev s^{-1}. (d) Undersampled, appears to rotate at 16.66 rev s^{-1}. (e) Undersampled, appears to rotate at 20 rev s^{-1}. All sampling rates are for (a), that is 20 frames per second.

motion. When the animation is viewed the motion may not appear smooth. This is despite all the care that we have taken with regard to interpolation techniques (see Chapter 15). It is just as if we have recorded motion using a film camera with an infinitely short exposure time. In computer graphics animation, a frame is rendered in an infinitely short time interval.

Anti-aliasing in the time domain can be performed by motion blurring. When a sequence is produced it is as if the virtual camera possessed a finite exposure and moving objects in a rendered frame appear blurred. This may appear to be a contradiction; motion in an animated sequence is better perceived if the moving detail is blurred, but the human visual system expects to see a loss of detail in the moving objects. (Incidentally, this fact is well known to traditional animators who use 'streak lines', or lines that trail from a moving object, to simulate this effect.)

As with anti-aliasing in the space domain, there are two possible approaches to the solution. Analogous to supersampling in the space domain, we can generate a series of frames in an interval centred on the precise sam-

ple time, and then use a filter to combine these images into a single frame. Alternatively we could try some algorithmic approximation to the continuous solution. Both techniques attempt to evaluate a three-dimensional convolution integral, rather than the two-dimensional one for static image functions. That is:

$$I'(x, y, T) = \iiint I(\alpha, \beta, t)\, h(x-\alpha, y-\beta, T-t)\, \mathrm{d}\alpha\, \mathrm{d}\beta\, \mathrm{d}t$$

Just as supersampling was not a theoretically correct method of spatial anti-aliasing, but a device that shifted artefacts up the frequency spectrum, so is supersampling in the time domain theoretically incorrect. The time domain analogy to Figure 4.9 is the effect produced by fast-moving objects whose screen space projection is thin. In such a case, instead of producing a blurred image, time domain supersampling may produce, in a single frame, a multiple image of the object. A series of separate objects may be apparent in the frame instead of a blur. Jerky motion still results; we have merely increased the object speed that we are able to deal with by producing blur. Just as our texture aliases still appeared, jerky motion still results, but at a higher object speed.

As you will realize, any motion blur solution is going to be very expensive. The processing penalty already invoked by spatial anti-aliasing is multiplied by a frame supersampling factor. In time domain anti-aliasing, this is further multiplied by a time supersampling factor.

Because of this, practical solutions use context-dependent anti-aliasing in the time domain, restricting the evaluation of motion blur to moving detail only. An early attempt at this is given in [POTM83] and this work is further discussed in Chapter 10. An elegant solution is given by Cook *et al.* [COOK84]. This simply extends his distributed ray tracing model into the time domain (see Section 10.4.4).

RenderMan [UPST89] provides a motion blur facility, but no implementation details are given. Plate 5 is a motion-blurred frame from Pixar's *Luxo Jnr*.

PART III

Advanced rendering techniques: approaches, applications and algorithms

5 Shadow generation techniques

This chapter deals with ad hoc algorithms for shadow production; shadows produced by radiosity and ray tracing algorithms are described in Chapters 8, 10 and 11 respectively. In particular the method of distributed ray tracing described in Section 10.4.3, that uses distributed ray tracing, should be compared with the method described in Section 5.2 of this chapter.

Introduction

Shadows play a subtle and vital role in our visual perception of an environment. The position and orientation provide information as to how objects relate to each other in space. Figure 5.1 is a simple example illustrating this point. It shows three spheres and a ground plane. In Figure 5.1(a) the sphere is rendered without a shadow and the eye has no way of telling how the two objects are positioned with respect to each other – the sphere could be floating anywhere above the plane. Introducing shadows provides the missing information and 'anchors' the sphere to the plane. Figure 5.1(b) shows the sphere to be resting on the plane and Figure 5.1(c) shows the sphere raised above it. Note that these two figures would be virtually identical (and the same as Figure 5.1a) if the shadows were not used. For this reason it is important to deal with shadows in computer graphics.

Two problems immediately present themselves. First, the shape of the shadow has to be computed. Although this is a trivial computation when shadows are cast onto a flat plane (see, for example, [BLIN88] for a method that simply forms a projection of the object on a flat plane), it becomes a difficult and time-consuming operation in the general case when shadows are cast onto other objects. Secondly, we need to compute the intensity of the light reflected from a shadow area. Now shadows are formed due to the local decrease in diffuse light because of the blocking of direct illumination. The intensity of this reflected light does not in general reduce to zero because of illumination arriving in the shadow area due to indirect reflection from other surfaces. The computation of this factor is strictly part of the global illumination problem. Although the standard algorithms attend to the first factor, computation of the second is only possible using a method such as distributed ray tracing (Chapter 10) or radiosity (Chapter 11). Both these models compute shadows as an integral part of a techni-

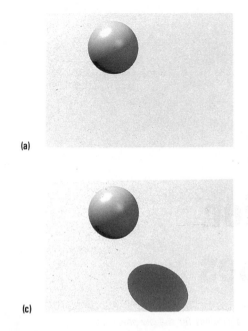

(a)

(b)

(c)

Figure 5.1 Spheres rendered above a plane of infinite extent. (a) No shadow – there is no way of telling how close the sphere is to the surface. (b) The sphere is resting on the surface. (c) The sphere is slightly above the surface.

que that attempts to deal with the global illumination problem.

In this chapter we shall be looking at empirical algorithms that deal with the geometrical problem (and the problem of distributed light sources). They were developed as part of a trend that saw many empirical embellishments to Phong-based rendering. They are still widely used because of the expense of the global techniques. Most empirical shadow algorithms generate an illusion of shadows by operating under the constraint of a point light source, and as we have already implied, the intensity within the shadow area is arbitrarily approximated. Typically, the light that casts the shadow is not considered when shading surfaces within this shadow. Standard Phong-based rendering considers direct illumination only – if a point on a surface can see a light then its contribution is calculated and simply added to the shaded value for that point. Conversely, if a point on the surface is in shadow, the light casting the shadow is completely ignored when the point is shaded.

The constraint of a point light source means that shadows will have hard edges, that is, there will be a sharp transition from a dark shadow area to a bright non-shadow area. This rarely occurs in practice because most light sources are not idealized point sources. A distributed light source will result in a shadow which is made up of an umbra and a penumbra region (Figure 5.2). The relative size of these regions is determined by the size of the distributed light source and its distance from the object. The umbra is that part of the shadow that is completely cut off from the light source and the penumbra is that part that receives some light from the source. By definition the penumbra always surrounds the umbra. Becaue of the visual importance of this, the effect of using the point light source approximation is much more deleterious in shadow generation than it is in Phong shading (where it is generally counteracted by causing the specular term to saturate – see Chapter 2).

The constraint of ignoring indirect reflection means that only direct illumination is considered. But light rays may reach the shadow area via an indirect route, after indirectly interacting with objects in the scene. Thus we have two factors that determine the intensity within a shadow area: the nature of the light source and the possible effect of indirect illumination. Interestingly, the earliest realization of the influence of indirect illumination on shadows, from the fifteenth century, comes from Leonardo da Vinci [KEMP89]. In a series of experiments, some of which were probably thought experiments or imaginary experiments, he used sources or lamps to illuminate simple objects such as spheres. He varied the size of the source and the size of the object and also varied the distance between the two. He introduced multiple sources and looked at how this resulted in a

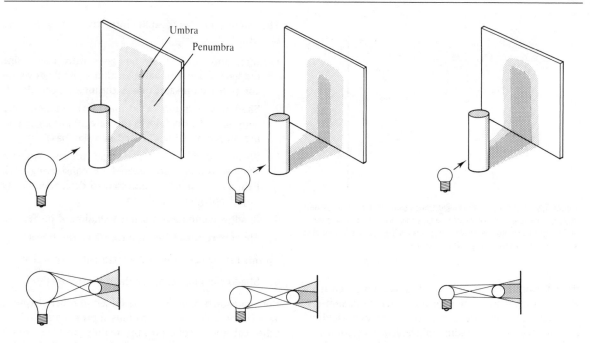

Figure 5.2 Intensity of reflected light in a shadow area: the umbra/penumbra effect due to the relative sizes of a light source and an object.

grading effect due to the multiple umbra/penumbra generated. He realized the dependence of shadows on global illumination and distinguished between primitive shadows (shadows that 'clothe the bodies to which they belong') and shadows cast by objects onto other objects, which he called derivative shadows (Figure 5.3). He described these as follows:

> Let the light on a flat surface be a, and the object which forms the primary shadow be bc. The wall de is the surface on which the derivative shadow is received at the place mn. The remainder, dn and me, continues to be illuminated by a, and the light from dn is reflected in the primitive shadow bc, and the light from me does the same. Thus the derivative shadow nm, which is not exposed to the light a, remains dark, while the primitive shadow is illuminated by the lit background which surrounds the derivative shadow. Therefore the derivative is darker than the primitive.

From the twentieth century we provide an example that demonstrates these points. Plate 6 was produced using the shadow volume technique described in this chapter.

This is a classic algorithm that computes shadow shape but not intensity. The shortcomings are obvious. Although the venetian blind pattern on the wall is reasonable, the extension of this onto the floor is manifestly wrong – the shadows are too strong or dark. It is as if the carpet were made up of stripes; the perception of the dark bands as shadows only comes from their geometrical association with other elements in the scene. We would expect the shadow/nonshadow contrast on the floor to be much weaker due to light reflecting from the wall onto the floor. The crudest of approximations to global illumination would be to increase the component of ambient light, thereby reducing the contrast, but this is far from satisfactory. Plate 7 was also produced using the shadow volume technique showing the effect of casting several shadow volumes from several lights. In this example the deficiencies are not so obvious because the presence of more than one light in the scene reduces the contrast of the individual shadows.

We conclude that empirical shadow algorithms are acceptable in the context of natural hard shadows (bright sunlight on a light wall, for example) but fall down where more subtle lighting interactions subsist. This is certainly

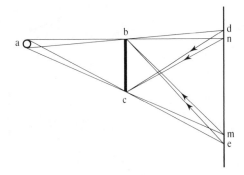

Figure 5.3 Leonardo da Vinci's illustration showing the influence of indirect illumination on the shadow area. Penumbra region dn and me reflect light back into the shadow area influencing the intensity of that area Leonardo termed the 'primitive' shadow.

the case with room interiors and, as we have seen from Plate 6, such models are manifestly lacking in subtlety.

Finally, consider three aspects or attributes of shadows that are exploited in traditional shadow algorithms:

1. If the illuminating source is a point source there is no penumbra to calculate and the shadow has a hard edge.

2. No shadows are seen if the view point and the light source are made coincident. This fact implies that shadows are areas which are hidden from the light source and therefore that hidden surface algorithms can be adapted to compute the shape of shadows.

3. If a scene is static then the shadows are fixed and do not change if only the view point is changed. If the relative position of the light source and the object are changed then the shadows have to be recalculated.

5.1 An overview of shadow algorithms

Shadow algorithms are categorized by Crow [CROW77], Bergeron [BERG86a], Max [MAX86a] and Woo *et al.* [WOO90]. Unlike hidden surface removal algorithms, where one method – the Z-buffer algorithm – now predominates, there does not appear to be any shadow algorithm that is more widely used than others.

The algorithms were split into five categories by Bergeron:

1. Integration of shadow polygons with a scan line hidden surface removal algorithm – the shadows are computed at the same time as the image is calculated.

2. Shadow generation based on transformations and clipping – the shadows in this category of algorithm are precomputed and stored in a database.

3. Shadow volumes – a two-stage process wherein shadow volumes are created by considering each light source and then accessed to determine if any object polygon is in shadow.

4. Shadow computation using a shadow Z-buffer.

5. Shadow computation in a recursive ray tracer.

To this list we can now add a sixth category which is:

6. Shadow computation by the radiosity method.

Both categories 5 and 6 are described in other chapters. We will now describe algorithms representative of the other categories concentrating mainly on categories 3 and 4, and we will introduce an original technique for soft shadow computation. This technique was influenced by the distributed ray tracing approach ([COOK84] and chapter 10). However it is intended as a stand-alone, add-on technique for shadow generation and we include it in this chapter.

The majority of the empirical algorithms break down the problem of generating shadows into two distinct stages. Shadow information is independent of view. The first stage is a view-independent preprocessing stage which generates information about the shadows followed by a second view-dependent stage which uses the information generated in the first stage to render the scene.

5.1.1 Integration of shadow computation with a scan line algorithm

This early algorithm ([APPE68, BOUK70]) depends on detecting, in a preprocessing step, all pairs of polygons that can interact to give shadows. For each polygon a secondary data structure is built up which points to all polygons that can possibly shadow it. These are known as shadow polygons. This is done by surrounding a point light source with a sphere and projecting polygons onto the surface of the sphere. Polygons that can interact will overlap on the surface of the sphere. The cost of this preprocessing step and the storage costs are the inherent drawbacks of the method.

In the rendering phase the secondary data structure is processed and information from the shadow polygons is integrated with a scan line hidden surface removal algorithm (Figure 5.4). For a polygon, if no shadow polygons exist then we proceed as normal. If a shadow polygon exists there are three possibilities:

1. The shadow polygon does not completely overlap the object polygon and the current visible scan line segment is not overlapped – proceed as normal.

2. The shadow polygon completely overlaps the current visible scan line segment and pixels within this segment are subject to a reduction in intensity.

3. The shadow polygon partially covers the current visible scan line segment. Here the segment is subdivided and the process is applied recursively until conditions 1 and 2 occur.

The algorithm can only deal with polygonal objects illuminated by point light sources and this generates hard shadows.

5.1.2 Derivation of shadow polygons from transformations

Developed in 1978 by Atherton, Weiler and Greenberg [ATHE78], this is a two-pass algorithm that first applies hidden surface removal to a view computed from the light source. As we implied in the introduction, this finds shadow polygons. Hidden surface removal is also computed from the view point and the results combined to produce a data structure of hard-edged shadows.

The algorithm is shown as a simple example in Figure 5.5. Only one shadow is shown for clarity. The object polygons are transformed into a coordinate system using the light source as a view point and hidden surfaces are removed using the Weiler–Atherton algorithm [WEIL77]. This produces a series of clipped (or complete) polygons that are visible from the light source. Clipped polygons are labelled with their parent polygon. This information is transformed back into the original modelling coordinate system and merged with the object database to produce a (view point independent) model that is enhanced with shadow polygons. The merged database can then be rendered from any view point. An important fact concerning this algorithm is that all the

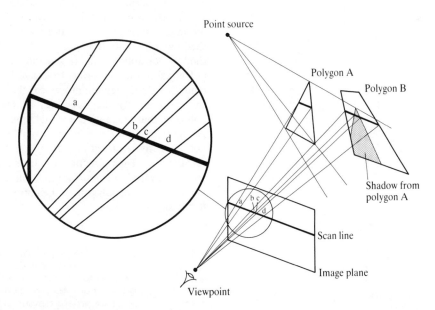

Figure 5.4 Integrating polygons in a scan line algorithm: at point a, polygon A is visible; at point b, polygon B is visible; at point c, polygon B is shadowed by polygon A; at point d, polygon B is visible.

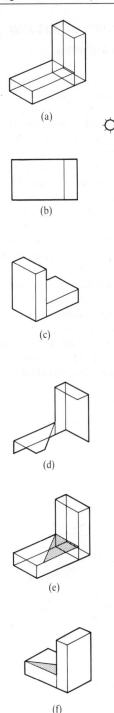

(a)

(b)

(c)

(d)

(e)

(f)

calculations are carried out in object space. This has two implications. First, it means that the calculations are carried out with object precision. The shadows, albeit hard edged, are computed exactly. Secondly, it is possible to extract quantitative information on shadow areas. This has implications for architectural CAD.

5.1.3 Shadow volumes

The first technique for rendering shadows that we shall look at in detail is Crow's shadow volume method [CROW77]. The algorithm, using point source lights, casts shadows off polygonal objects only, but since, historically, most practical rendering has been polygonal in origin this has not been unduly disadvantageous. Indeed, to date, it has been the commonest, most practical method of rendering shadows (examples of shadows created with this method are shown in Plates 6 and 7). The reader should bear in mind, however, that this method cannot naturally be extended to other classes of objects – most notable of which is the parametric surface (we shall return to this point later).

The basic idea is, given a light and a model, to generate a projected shadow volume – a region of space swept out by the silhouette edge of the model and the light – within which, by definition, objects are in shadow. The shadow volume for a single polygon is shown in Figure 5.6. It is a semi-infinite cone that is reduced to a finite volume by the intersection between it and the view frustum. The shadow volume itself is polygonal, being made up of shadow polygons which are generated and added to the polygonal database prior to rendering. During the rendering stage they are processed, that is, clipped and sorted in exactly the same way as real polygons or polygons that make up the actual models of the scene. However, shadow polygons are invisible, in that they are not explicitly rendered and do not affect the visibility calculations. Their function is, during the depth sort required by the hidden surface solution, to provide information to the real polygons of their positions with respect to the shadow volume.

Figure 5.5 Derivation of shadow polygons from transformations. (a) Simple polygonal object in modelling coordinate system. (b) Plan view showing the position of the light source. (c) Hidden surface removal from the light source as a view point. (d) Visible polygons from (c) transformed back into the modelling coordinate system. (e) (a) and (d) merged to produce a database that contains shadow polygons. (f) (e) can produce any view of the object with shadows.

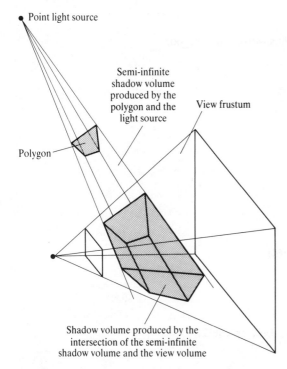

Figure 5.6 A shadow volume produced by a single polygon, a point light source and a view volume.

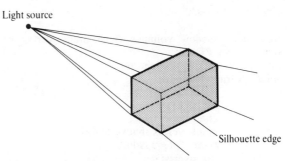

Figure 5.7 The silhouette edge of a simple object. The three visible polygons in the diagram cannot see the light. The three hidden polygons can see the light.

1. The polygon can see the light and the edge has no neighbours. In this case the edge lies along a topologically open edge of the model.

2. The polygon can see the light and the edge has neighbours which cannot. In this case the edge separates polygons on the surface where the surface curves behind itself with respect to the light (the silhouette).

Theoretically one could use the algorithm without neighbouring information. This would imply that every polygon making up the model is a surface to be considered in isolation. Each polygon that could see the light would therefore produce its own individual shadow volume as implied by Figure 5.6. However, the fact that the shadow data produced would be so large and the time taken to process it so long, means that this is not really a practical option. This is the reason why shadow volumes are unworkable for models that are not polygonal such as parametric surfaces. Even though a parametric surface when rendered is typically broken down to polygons (see Chapter 3), neighbouring information is not generally constructed and so an alternative method for casting shadows off parametric surfaces must be sought.

Once an edge $V_a V_b$ (Figure 5.8) has been identified as part of the silhouette edge, a shadow polygon is generated by casting edges $V_a S_a$ and $V_b S_b$ away from the light L. The construction of S_a, say, is done by making it collinear with V_a and L and placing it at a sufficiently large distance away from V_a to put S_a outside the viewing frustum of the image. The latter requirement ensures that when the shadow polygon is clipped to the viewing frustum the edge $S_a S_b$ will be clipped out and the resultant shadow volume will be well defined throughout the entire field of view.

We now describe in detail how these volumes are generated. Suppose, during the scene description, an object is tagged to cast a shadow from a given light. Before rendering then, this model is passed to the shadow volume generator, and the appropriate shadow volume is generated. Now in order for the algorithm to function correctly a polygon making up the model needs to know to which polygons, if any, it is adjacent. This we call 'neighbouring information' and it is encoded thus: each edge of a polygon has associated with it a pointer, or set of pointers, that points to polygons which share that edge. These polygons are defined to be the polygon's neighbours.

Each polygon making up the model is tested to see if one of its edges forms part of the silhouette edge of the model. A silhouette edge is the edge made up of one, or usually more than one, connected edges of the polygons of the model, that separates those polygons that can see the light from those that cannot. An edge of a polygon is deemed to be part of the silhouette edge if either of the following two conditions hold (Figure 5.7):

Listing 5.1   make_shadow_volumes.c

```c
#include "types.h"

void make_shadow_volumes (faces,nfaces,vertex_list,light,shadow_no,light_no)
struct facet *faces;
int nfaces,shadow_no,light_no;
point *vertex_list,light;
{
          int  i,j,k;
          char  *see_table;
          point  vertex,shadverts[4],L;
          float  *plequ,NdotL;
          int  nverts;

          see_table = malloc (nfaces+1);
          see_table[0] = 0;

          for (i = 0; i < nfaces; i++) {

                    vertex = vertex_list[faces[i].vptrs[0]];
                    L.x = light.x − vertex.x;
                    L.y = light.y − vertex.y;
                    L.z = light.z − vertex.z;

                    plequ = faces[i].plequ;
                    NdotL = L.x*plequ[0]+L.y*plequ[1]+L.z*plequ[2];
                    see_table[i+1] = (NdotL > 0.)? 1 : 0;
          }

          for (i = 0; i < nfaces; i++) {

                    if (see_table[i + 1]) {
                              nverts = faces[i].nverts;

                              for (j = 0; j < nverts; j++) {

                                        if (see_table[faces[i].nbrs[j]]) continue;

                                        shadverts[0] = vertex_list[faces[i].vptrs[j]];
                                        shadverts[1].x = shadverts[0].x + large*(shadverts[0].x − L.x);
                                        shadverts[1].y = shadverts[0].y + large*(shadverts[0].y − L.y);
                                        shadverts[1].z = shadverts[0].z + large*(shadverts[0].z − L.z);

                                        k = (k == nverts−1) ? 0 : j+1;
                                        shadverts[3] = vertex_list[faces[i].vptrs[k]];
                                        shadverts[2].x = shadverts[3].x + large*(shadverts[3].x − L.x);
                                        shadverts[2].y = shadverts[3].y + large*(shadverts[3].y − L.y);
                                        shadverts[2].z = shadverts[3].z + large*(shadverts[3].z − L.z);

                                        push_shadow_onto_scanlines(shadverts,4,shadow_no,light_no);

                              }
                    }
          }
          free(see_table);

}
```

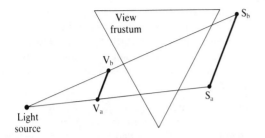

Figure 5.8 A single component of the silhouette – edge $V_a V_b$ produced a shadow edge $S_a S_b$ outside the view volume.

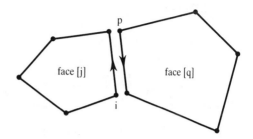

Figure 5.9 Convention for adjacent polygons sharing an edge.

The shadow polygon is then given a number identifying which shadow volume it is part of and another number indicating which light is responsible for its generation. It is tagged as to whether it is forward or backward facing with respect to the eye.

Listing 5.1 shows a pseudocode fragment, *make_ shadow_volumes( )*, of how a shadow volume might be generated. The model is represented as an array of polygons, *faces[ ]*, and a list of vertices, *vertex_list*. A polygon is given by the structure:

```
struct facet {
      float plequ [4];
      int nverts;
      int *vptrs;
      int *nbrs;
}
```

Where *plequ* holds the plane equation of the polygon, *nverts* the number of vertices and *vptrs* points to a list of offsets that locate the vertices in *vertex_list*. The jth vertex of the ith facet is thus given by *vertex_ list[faces[i].vptrs[j]]*. Encoding the neighbouring information is a little more involved. Any edge of a polygon is identified by its trailing vertex, that is, the jth edge of a polygon is that edge that starts at the jth vertex of the polygon. If two polygons share an edge, say edge i of *face[j]* is common to edge p of *face[q]* as shown in Figure 5.9, we write:

faces $[j]$.nbrs $[i]$ = q + 1
faces $[q]$.nbrs $[p]$ = j + 1

Any edge that has no neighbours will have zero in its *nbrs* location corresponding to condition 1 above.

The first thing the routine does is to construct a list of Booleans *see_table[ ]*, where *see_table[j + 1]* holds if *face[j]* can see the light. The first entry in the table is reserved for the empty condition, that is, no face cannot see the light and is needed in order to accommodate case

1 above. We can now say that an edge j of *face[i]* is part of the silhouette if it can see the light but one of its neighbours cannot, that is if *see_table[faces[i].nbrs[j]]* is zero. The faces are scanned in turn and, taking care to preserve the sense of the polygon, shadow polygons are built along the silhouette edge and put into the polygonal database via the routine *push_shadow_onto_scan- lines( )*.

Once part of the polygonal database, shadow polygons are processed in the same manner as all other polygons up to the depth sort at pixel level which we shall now discuss. In much the same way as one can tell whether a point on a scan line is inside or outside a closed polygon by counting the number of intersections the scan line makes with the polygon – if the count is even the point is outside; if odd, inside – at the depth sort a polygon from a model can determine whether it is outside or inside a given shadow volume by counting the shadow polygons that lie before it. A frontfacing shadow polygon puts anything behind it in shadow while a backfacing shadow polygon cancels the effect of a front-facing one. A polygon that lies between these two shadow polygons will be in shadow.

At each pixel a counter is assigned to each light casting a shadow volume. This counter is initialized to be 1 if the eye already lies inside the shadow volume, 0 otherwise. Descending down the depth-sorted list of polygons we increment the shadow count if we pass a frontfacing shadow polygon and decrement on passing a backfacing one. The value of the shadow counter when a 'real' polygon is encountered tells us whether the polygon is in shadow or not. An even value means it is outside; an odd value, inside. This is shown schematically in Figure 5.10. The polygon will use this value to switch on or off the appropriate light when it is passed to the shader.

In practice this algorithm is quite difficult to implement. The reasons for this are:

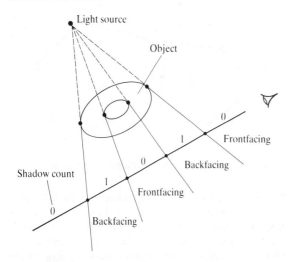

Figure 5.10 Showing frontfacing and backfacing polygons in the shadow volume.

1. The validity of the shadow volume depends directly on the validity of the neighbouring information. A correct shadow volume should contain a closed shadow sheet swept out by the light and a closed silhouette edge. However, if the model is complex, generating valid neighbouring information is not a trivial task. Errors in this neighbouring information could result in a silhouette edge that is not closed, or in the case of more than two edges at a vertex making up a silhouette edge, splitting in two. In either case the resultant shadow volume is ill defined.

2. Prior to rendering, in order to be completely general, the position of the eye with respect to the shadow volume needs to be determined. This can be done directly or, alternatively, the shadow sheet can be capped, at one end by the model that generates it, at the other end by the viewing frustum (this is not a trivial operation particularly if the shadow polygons are generated in any order). In the latter case the eye will always be outside such a capped shadow volume.

3. Polygonal renderers typically resort to some approximation when dealing with intersecting polygons. A shadow volume, by its very nature, will produce many intersections of shadow polygons with the scene thereby testing this approximation more rigorously than an identical picture without shadows. Thin shadow volumes grazing polygons at very small angles will be particularly problematic – consider the shadow cast by the arm of the angle-

poise lamp onto the wall in Plate 6 – clearly here the intersection approximation is breaking down. This problem is exacerbated further since the intersection delineates a hard edge separating a lit region from an unlit region, which as we have seen can be high in contrast.

Bergeron [BERG86a] generalized the algorithm of Crow making it more robust and enabling it to handle twisted nonplanar polygons and also tying up some loose ends concerning the shadow counter and different types of shadow volumes. This algorithm generated the shadows in the breakthrough animated sequence *Tony de Peltrie* (about a has-been piano player) of 1985.

5.1.4 Using shadow volumes to generate soft shadows

Another important extension to the shadow volume algorithm is due to Brotman and Badler [BROT84] who enabled soft shadows caused by distributed light sources to be computed. They combined the algorithm with an enhanced Z-buffer to enable umbra/penumbra effects to be generated by a superposition process. Soft shadows are computed by modelling distributed light sources as a series of points, stochastically chosen, each of which has its own shadow volume. Thus a point in the image can be enclosed by a number of shadow volumes and a 'darkness level' computed by linear superposition. An enhanced Z-buffer is used to store an entire record of information, rather than just the depth. In particular a counter is maintained that stores the number of shadow volumes which surround a pixel – the darkness level counter. As each shadow volume is processed, the value of the darkness level counter gives the current number of points in the array approximation to a distributed light source that does not illuminate the pixel. An attenuated intensity is calculated from:

$$I_{att} = \frac{I}{n}\left(n - dl\right)$$

where:

I_{att} is the intensity at a pixel due to a distributed light source
I is the total intensity of the light source
n is the number of points in the light source
dl is the darkness level at the pixel

Yet another extension for umbra/penumbra calculation is given by Nishita and Nakamae [NISH85]. This technique eschews the approximation of a distributed

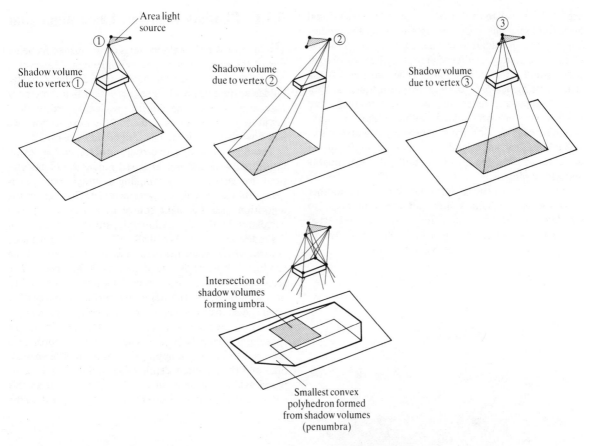

Figure 5.11 Penumbra/umbra derivations due to an area light source (from an illustration in [NISH85]).

light source as an array of points and treats it as an exact geometric entity (with a Lambertian distribution). Each vertex of the source is treated as a point light source that has an associated shadow volume (Figure 5.11). A penumbra and an umbra shadow volume is then computed. The penumbra shadow volume is the smallest convex polyhedron that can be found from the vertex shadow volumes and the umbra shadow volume is the intersection of these volumes.

5.1.5 Using shadow volumes as light volumes

If we invert the sense of the shadow volume, and say that a point on a surface inside the volume is in light and a point outside is in shadow, then the volume becomes a

light volume. Apart from this inversion, light volumes differ slightly from shadow volumes in that the light volume, unlike the shadow volume, can itself be rendered in order to simulate the scattering of light by a participating medium usually caused by minute impurities suspended within the medium itself, for example, dust particles in air. The rendering of the light volume is usually done in conjunction with a ray tracer. The section of the ray inside the light volume is calculated and a scattering function is integrated along the illuminated length of this ray. Typically the scattering function, involving inverse square laws and exponential attenuation, is computationally intensive making images of light volumes expensive to produce.

Max [MAX86a] used the shadow volume idea to model the effect of atmospheric illumination and shadows. In particular, he considered the complex case of beams of sunlight passing through the leaves of trees. In order to exploit coherency to its full, Max rejected the traditional horizontal scan line approach, restructuring the rendering to work on radial scan lines in polar coordinates. These radial lines were aligned along the direction of light propagation greatly simplifying the sorting of the shadow polygons. Nishita [NISH87] also took the light volume approach generating both light volumes and shadow volumes off objects falling within the light volumes. Nishita considered light sources with various variable angular intensity distributions of luminosity in order to simulate the effect of spotlights, searchlights and car headlights.

Finally, we refer the reader to a description of another variation of the light volume approach in order to simulate the effect of light, after having been refracted at the surface of water, then being scattered due to impurities in the water – see Section 10.1.

5.1.6 Shadow Z-buffer: basic algorithm

The shadow Z-buffer algorithm is distinguished by being one of the easiest algorithms to implement. However it suffers from the same disadvantages as the Z-buffer hidden surface removal algorithm – significant memory costs and aliasing. The aliasing problem is dealt with in detail in an extension described in the next section; we will now detail how the basic algorithm works.

The algorithm is a two-stage process and is easily integrated with a Z-buffer based renderer. Its calculations are carried out by sampling at image space precision – the cause of aliasing artefacts. The first pass of the algorithm uses the light source as a view point and calculates depth information only, storing the results in a shadow Z-buffer. We shall refer to this coordinate system, within which the shadow map (or contents of the shadow Z-buffer) is calculated, as light space. The second pass is the normal rendering phase modified to deal with shadows. If a point on a surface underneath a pixel is deemed to be visible then the screen space coordinates of the point (x,y,z) are transformed into light space coordinates (x',y',z'). The x'- and y'-coordinates are used to index the appropriate entry of the shadow map and the resultant depth value found there is compared against the value of z'. If z' is greater than this value there is an object nearer to the light source than the

(a)

(c)

(b)

Figure 5.12 The shadow Z-buffer technique. (a) A scene rendered with two light sources. (b) Depth map for the first light source. (c) Depth map for the second light source.

object currently being rendered and the current pixel is deemed to be in shadow and its intensity appropriately reduced.

Figure 5.12(a) shows a scene with two light sources where the shadows have been generated by using this technique. Figures 5.12(b) and 5.12(c) are the depth maps for the two light sources – the so-called shadow maps. Grey levels have been used to represent the range of floating-point z-values of the depth map; objects closer to the light are darker in the image.

The algorithm extends the inefficiency of the Z-buffer based renderer – calculations are performed on surfaces underneath pixels that are subsequently overwritten by values from surfaces that are closer to the eye. The amount of redundant calculation is increased further by the shadow calculation. Williams [WILL78] suggests a reordering of the algorithm as follows. The rendering phase proceeds without any shadow calculation at all, producing an image and a Z-buffer for that image. Shadows are added as a postprocess that is linear in the number of pixels in the image. For each pixel in the image the corresponding value in the Z-buffer is transformed into light space and compared against the corresponding value in the shadow Z-buffer as above, thus determining whether the pixel is in shadow or not. Efficiency is increased by performing the hidden surface calculation before the shadow calculation – thereby ensuring that we test for shadows only for those surfaces that we can see. Unfortunately, because we have already computed the image, the most that can be done on discovering that a pixel is in shadow, after the event of it being rendered, is to reduce its intensity by some arbitrary amount. This process may result in an image error. Precalculated specular highlights may appear in shadow regions – albeit with reduced intensity. This is clearly impossible.

Anti-aliasing and the shadow Z-buffer

Although the shadow Z-buffer is a simple and reasonably efficient algorithm it aliases badly. This is because the shadow Z-buffer is both created and accessed by point sampling. Analogous to the case of texture mapping from a two-dimensional texture domain, we see that the transformation of an image plane pixel in the shadow Z-buffer domain can be a region that encloses many shadow Z-buffer pixels. This situation is shown in Figure 5.13. Thus for a screen pixel a decision may have to be based on information from a number of shadow Z-

buffer pixels. Reeves, Salesin and Cook [REEV87] point out that this decision cannot be made by region filtering because the resultant filtered depth value would bear little relationship to the actual geometry of the scene and the result of the comparison would be binary (making soft anti-aliased edges impossible). Figure 5.14, based on an illustration by Reeves *et al.*, highlights the problem. Say a surface, enclosing a square region of 3×3 pixels in the shadow Z-buffer domain, has a z'-value of 49.8. Region filtering the projected area gives a value of 22.9, meaning that the surface is entirely in shadow. Reeves *et al.* solve this problem by first converting the shadow Z-buffer into a binary map that stores the comparison outcome. Region filtering this map then gives the result that only 55% of the surface is in shadow. The accurate percentage value is then used to reduce the image plane pixel intensity. This technique is called 'percentage closer filtering'.

There is still, however, a serious cost problem with the method. Prefiltering techniques, as described for texture

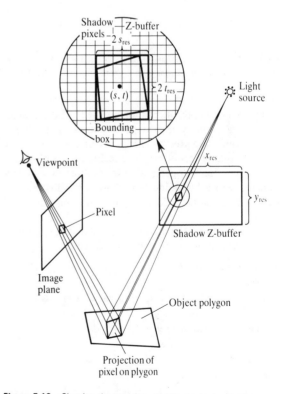

Figure 5.13 Showing the need for area filtering in the shadow Z-buffer algorithm.

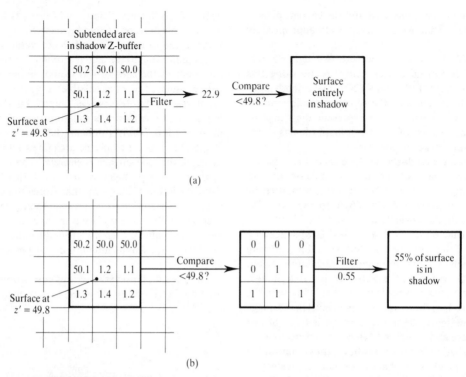

Figure 5.14 'Normal' and percentage closer filtering of the subtended area in a shadow Z-buffer (after an illustration in [REEV87]). (a) 'Normal' area filtering a shadow Z-buffer gives a binary result. (b) Percentage closer filtering.

mapping in Chapter 4, cannot be used. The transformation to a binary map depends on using unfiltered depth values and Reeves *et al.* suggest using a Monte Carlo sampling technique. The technique employed is to surround the mapped region in the shadow Z-buffer domain with a bounding box. This is subdivided and each subregion sampled by a jittered sample (Figure 5.15).

Code fragments for this method are given Listing 5.2. The shadow Z-buffer is given by structure

```
struct shadow_map   {
    float zmin;
    float Bias0, Bias1, dBias;   /* dBias = Bias1 − Bias0 */;
    int bl_map_x,bl_map_y;
    int tr_map_x,tr_map_y;
    int map_xres,map_yres;
    float *map;
}
```

Consider for a moment the usual coordinate spaces associated with the image plane. There is the coordinate

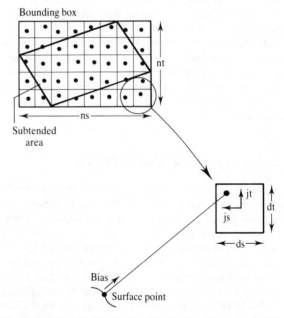

Figure 5.15 Sampling each pixel in the bounding box stochastically.

Listing 5.2   sample_shadow_map.c

```c
#include <math.h>
#include "shadow_map.h"
#include "message.h"

#define CLAMP(a, min, max)  ((a)<(min)?(min):((a)>(max)?(max):(a)))

static float ResFactor = 3.0;
static float MinSize = 2.0;

static int NumSamples = 16;
static int MinSamples = 3;

static float Bias0 = 0.03;
static float Bias1 = 0.04;

float SampleShadowMap(s_map, s, t, z, sres, tres)
struct shadow_map *s_map;
float s, t, z, sres, tres;
{
        int ns, nt, inshadow, i, j;
        float bias, ds, dt, js, jt, smin, tmin;
        int iu, iv;
        float Rand(), xresb2, yresb2;

        if (z < s_map->zmin)
                    return(0.0);

        xresb2 = (float)s_map->xres / 2.0;
        yresb2 = (float)s_map->yres / 2.0;

        s = s * xresb2 + xresb2;
        t = t * xresb2 + yresb2;

        sres = xresb2 * sres * ResFactor;
        tres = xresb2 * tres * ResFactor;

        if (sres < MinSize)
                    sres = MinSize;
        if (tres < MinSize)
                    tres = MinSize;

        if (s < (s_map->bl_map_x -  sres - 1) ||
                    s > (s_map->tr_map_x + sres + 1) ||
                    t < (s_map->bl_map_y -  tres - 1) ||
                    t > (s_map->tr_map_y + tres + 1))
                    return(0.0);

        if ((sres * tres * 4.0) < NumSamples)
                    {
                    ns = sres * 2.0 + 0.5;
                    ns = CLAMP(ns, MinSamples, NumSamples);
                    nt = tres * 2.0 + 0.5;
```

Listing 5.2 cont.

```
                    nt = CLAMP(nt, MinSamples, NumSamples);
                    }
        else
                    {
                    nt = sqrt(tres * NumSamples / sres) + 0.5;
                    nt = CLAMP(nt, MinSamples, NumSamples);
                    ns = ((float)NumSamples) / nt + 0.5;
                    ns = CLAMP(ns, MinSamples, NumSamples);
                    }

        ds = 2.0 * sres / ns;
        dt = 2.0 * tres / nt;
        js = ds * 0.5;

        jt = dt * 0.5;
        smin = s - sres + js;
        tmin = t - tres + jt;

        inshadow = 0;
        for (i = 0, s = smin; i < ns; i++, s += ds)
                    for (j = 0, t = tmin; j < nt; j++, t += dt)
                        {
                        iu = s + Rand() * js;
                        iv = t + Rand() * jt;
                        iu = s;
                        iv = t;
                        bias = Rand() * s_map->dBias + s_map->Bias0;

                        if (iu >= s_map->bl_map_x && iu <= s_map->tr_map_x
                                            && iv >= s_map->bl_map_y
                                            && iv <= s_map->tr_map_y)
                                    if (z > (s_map->map[s_map->map_xres *
                                            (iv - s_map->bl_map_y) +
                                            (iu - s_map->bl_map_x)] + bias))
                                        inshadow++;
                        }

        return((float)inshadow / (ns * nt)));
}
```

system based on the image plane after perspective projection – screen space; and there is the coordinate system of the rendered image where (x,y) refers to pixel (x,y) – raster space. There are direct parallels with the image plane of the shadow map and the pixels of the shadow map. The routine *SampleShadowMap( )* (Listing 5.2) converts incoming screen space coordinates of the shadow image plane (s,t), where s, $t \in [-1,1]$, given the bounds of the subtended area of the image *sres, tres* $\in$ [0,1], into the raster space coordinates of the shadow map.

We recall that a point cannot be in shadow if it lies in front of all points in the shadow map or if it projects onto the shadow image plane at a point outside the bounds of the shadow Z-buffer. After testing for these conditions and performing the coordinate transformation, the sampling parameters required to sample the shadow map are set up. *ns,nt* are the number of samples in the horizontal and vertical directions respectively (Figure 5.15) and are calculated given that:

ns*nt = NumSamples

and the sampling rate in both directions should be the same:

$$nt/tres = ns/sres$$

which gives, trivially:

$$nt = \left(tres*Numsamples/sres\right)^{1/2}$$
$$ns = NumSamples/nt$$

The sampling of the shadow Z-buffer is varied stochastically using jittering in two ways:

1. In the plane of the shadow Z-buffer by an amount (js, jt). This, as we have described, is to enable a cost reduction in filtering the area subtended in the shadow Z-buffer domain by the screen pixel.

2. An offset is given to the values of z'. Effectively this moves the current surface slightly closer to the light source. This prevents a surface from incorrectly shadowing itself if it so happens that it produces a z'-value that is slightly greater than the value stored in the shadow Z-buffer because this has been produced from a point nearby on the surface. This causes small grey spots to appear all over the surfaces that are not in shadow – so-called surface acne. The offset is a random number in the range $[Bias0, Bias1]$. All shadow rays are offset from the surface by a minimum amount given by $Bias0$.

Figures 5.16(a) and (b) show the importance of jittering these values. The scene description for these figures is the same (a blow-up of the spoon of Figure 5.12a) except Figure 5.16(a) is done without any jittering at all, that is, js, jt, $Bias0$ and $Bias1$ are all set to zero and $Numsamples$ is set to unity; whereas Figure 5.16(b) has these parameters set to sensible values. Problems of self-

intersection, by having no offset to the shadow ray, throw the rendering of the surface of the spoon into confusion. The effect of jittering (js, jt) within the shadow Z-buffer can be shown by examining the shadows of the spoon. Figure 5.16(a) was produced by point sampling the map without jitter, thereby simulating an ordinary Z-buffer algorithm, which produces unpleasant artefacts on the shadow edges. Figure 5.16(b) removes this by softening the edges with noise according to stochastic sampling theory. This has the visually agreeable effect of softening the hard shadow edges, although the claim that this algorithm can produce soft shadow effects is somewhat farfetched, since really it is just a product of the sampling and filtering process. For a more extensive treatment on the sampling parameters and their effects the reader is referred to [REEV87].

A criticism of this technique is that there is rather a lot of sampling parameters, some of which relate directly to the dimensions of the scene and which consequently have to be fine-tuned for a given scene. It would be better if the generation of optimal sampling parameters could be made more automatic.

The algorithm has a major advantage over those discussed previously in that the generation of shadows does not depend on the object's representation. This point is emphasized by creating a shadow Z-buffer picture of a parametrically defined object – the Utah teapot in Figure 5.12. Now both the shadow volume technique, as discussed, and a ray tracer (ray tracing parametric surfaces is very expensive) would have great difficulty making this image, whereas any picture that can be rendered, by definition, can produce a shadow Z-buffer and consequently shadows by this technique.

The algorithm works best for lights that are directional, thereby enabling the light space to be well defined

(a)

(b)

Figure 5.16   Jittering and bias and the shadow Z-buffer technique. (a) No jitter or bias – the surface shadows itself and aliasing effects are apparent on the shadow edge. (b) With jitter and a random bias value.

and have a finite region of influence, that is, spotlights. To be more precise, providing the light source's field of view subtends an angle less than π then it can be represented by a single shadow map. The algorithm becomes cumbersome to implement for lights that do not satisfy this constraint and cast shadows in all directions. In such cases a more complicated mapping scheme similar to environment mapping (see Chapter 6) would have to be employed.

5.2 An algorithm for anti-aliased soft shadows

This section describes a method for creating a soft shadow effect that concentrates on achieving the effect efficiently without paying too much attention to generality or theoretical niceties. Such practical ready-made solutions, which may be contemptuously referred to as hacks, are often sought in computer graphics, particularly in the entertainment industry, and should not be thought inferior to more academic and general algorithms which often prove to be so impractical that they are capable of producing only the simplest of images. All models of light–object interaction are simulations. The efficacy of the simulations needs to be judged from the quality of the image that is produced by it as well as the 'elegance' of the model. Recursive ray tracing is a good example of an elegant model producing deficient images. Nevertheless the technique that we describe in this section is an empirical or add-on method and is not part of a model that attempts to simulate global illumination (like ray tracing or radiosity). In addition, the method provides us with a good working example of stochastic sampling to which the reader is referred (Section 4.5.1).

As discussed earlier, hard-edged shadows are a somewhat unrealistic consequence of restricting lights to be point sources which hardly ever occur in real life. Removing this restriction and allowing lights to be of finite volume admits the possibility of soft shadows. A visible point on the surface which previously could see the light or not – one of two states – has now one of three states to choose from. It can either see the light, not see it or see part of it, when only part of the light is obscured by an intermediate object. This graduated

transition from seeing a partially obscured light, corresponding to the penumbra, to complete obscuration, corresponding to the umbra, causes the soft edge of the shadow (see Figure 5.2).

In this example we take our light source to be spherical and seek a measure of how much a visible point on a surface can see this light. This reduces to that fraction of the projected area of the light, as seen from the point, that is visible. The light arriving at this point will be proportional to this fraction and to the intensity of the light. As shown in Figure 5.17, the projected area of a sphere, of radius *light_radius*, seen from a point, a length *distance* from the centre of the sphere, is just a circle of radius *circle_radius*, where:

$$\text{circle\_radius} = \text{light\_radius} \cos\theta$$
$$\theta = \sin^{-1}\left(\text{light\_radius}/\text{distance}\right)$$

Consider the situation physically for a moment. Each point on the projected area of the light fires a light ray in the direction of the point. Some arrive at the point unimpeded and some get blocked by intermediate objects on the way. The count of those rays arriving over the total number fired is the fraction we seek. In reality the number of rays is not finite but we can approximate to

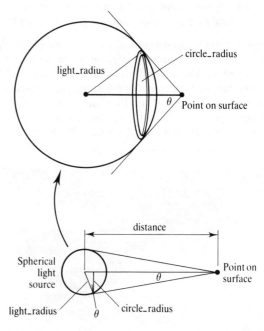

Figure 5.17 The area of a spherical light source that is seen by a point on a surface.

the situation by picking a finite number of locations on the light, jittering these locations, and shooting shadow rays from the point to these locations. (A theoretical justification for jittering is given in Chapter 4. It is also used in distributed ray tracing described in Chapter 10.)

How are we to choose those locations on the light? Clearly, in order not to prefer one part of the light to any other they should be regularly spaced. We could choose points spaced on a rectangular grid but a hexagonally packed grid seems intuitively more appropriate to the symmetry of a circle. This turns out to be a good choice for, as stated in [DIPP85], the optimal sampling pattern for 2D or spatial sampling is, in fact, the hexagonal lattice.

Figure 5.18 shows a hexagonal grid made up of 19 hexagons. This configuration was the sampling pattern used to create the soft shadows of Figure 5.19. This shows the effect of increasing the radius of the light source from zero, giving hard-edged shadows, to a certain value greater than zero and then twice that value. As expected, increasing the light radius increases the area of the penumbra – the shadow gets softer.

Listing 5.3 gives the relevant code fragments. *get_jittered_ray( )* returns a jittered ray direction, *jittered_dir*, given an index, *ray_no*, into the sampling pattern represented as an array, *circle[ ][ ]*, of unjittered hexagonal centres. The ray is shot from the point in a direction that is randomly jittered about the centre of the hexagon by an amount controlled by *jitter_offset*. *L* is the vector from the point to the centre of the spherical

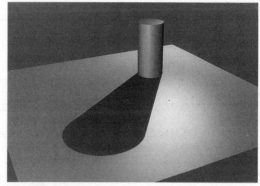

(a) *r* = 0. Point light source.

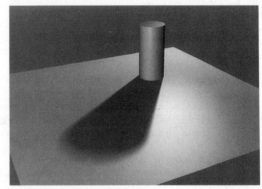

(b) *r* = *R*. Finite radius light source.

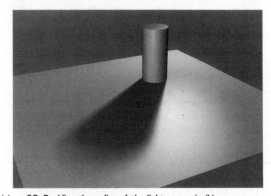

(c) *r* = 2*R*. Doubling the radius of the light source in (b).

Figure 5.19 The soft shadow algorithm and light sources of different radii.

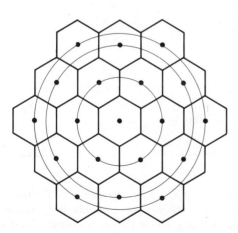

Figure 5.18 Hexagonal grid used as a basis for jitter sampling a spherical light source.

Listing 5.3   get_jittered_ray.c

```c
#include "types.h"

double random(); /* returns a random number in the range [0,1] */

float circle[19][2] = {
0.750,0.433,0.000,0.866,-0.750,0.433,-0.750,-0.433,0.000,-0.866,0.750,-0.433,
0.000,0.000,
0.750,0.000,0.375,0.650,-0.375,0.650,-0.750,0.000,-0.375,-0.650,0.375,-0.650,
0.375,0.216,0.000,0.433,-0.375,0.217,-0.375,-0.216,0.000,-0.433,0.375,-0.217};

float jitter_offset = 0.075;

void get_jittered_ray(rayno,L,distance,light_radius,jittered_dir)
int rayno;
point L,*jittered_dir;
float distance,light_radius;
{
        double theta;
        float circle_radius,circle_distance;
        point ray;
        float deltax,deltay,a,b,c,mu;

        theta = asin((double)(light_radius/distance));
        circle_radius = light_radius*cos(theta);
        circle_distance = distance-light_radius*sin(theta);

        /* jitter a ray initially along z axis within circle of circle_radius
            a distance circle_distance from origin */

        deltax = jitter_offset*random();
        deltay = jitter_offset*random();
        ray.x = circle_radius*(circle[rayno][0]+deltax);
        ray.y = circle_radius*(circle[rayno][1]+deltay);
        ray.z = circle_distance;

        /* rotate ray so that the z axis aligns along L */

        a=L.x;b=L.y;c=L.z;
        mu = sqrt((double)(b*b+c*c));
        jittered_dir->x = mu*ray.x + a*ray.z;
        jittered_dir->y = -a*b*ray.x/mu + c*ray.y/mu + b*ray.z;
        jittered_dir->z = -a*c*ray.x/mu - b*ray.y/mu + c*ray.z;
}
```

light. Initially the light is made to lie on the z-axis and the relevant direction is constructed by jittering in the *xy*-plane. The relevant rotation required to rotate the light into its correct position is then applied to the jittered ray.

The routine *get_jittered_ray( )* is called by *soft_* *shadow( )* (Listing 5.4) which returns that fraction of the light visible at the point position. *ray_hit( )* returns true if a ray hits anything in the ray tracing database. *soft_ shadow( )* is optimized to exploit the spatial coherence of the scene by a careful ordering of the hexagonal centres

Listing 5.4   soft_shadow.c

```c
#include "types.h"

int ray_hit();

void soft_shadow(position,light,light_radius,visible_fraction)
point position,light;
float light_radius,*visible_fraction;
{
        int ray_no,no_unblocked_rays;
        struct ray_type ray;
        point L;
        float distance;

        L.x = light.x - position.x;
        L.y = light.y - position.y;
        L.z = light.z - position.z;
        distance = sqrt(L.x*L.x+L.y*L.y+L.z*L.z);
        L.x /= distance;
        L.y /= distance;
        L.z /= distance;
        ray.pos = position;

        for (ray_no=0,no_unblocked_rays=19;ray_no<19;ray_no++) {

                get_jittered_ray(ray_no,L,distance,light_radius,&ray.dir);

                if (ray_hit(&ray)) no_unblocked_rays--;
                if (ray_no == 6 ) {
                        if (no_unblocked_rays == 12) {

                                no_unblocked_rays = 0;
                                break;
                        }
                        else if (no_unblocked_rays == 19) break;
                }
        }
        *visible_fraction = (float)no_unblocked_rays / 19.0;

}
```

in the array *circle [ ][ ]*. Typically only a small area of the image will be part of a penumbra – most positions lie completely in, or out of, shadow. The first seven locations of *circle [ ][ ]* are the six outermost ones and the central one. We know that if we fire rays towards the outer edge of the light and fire one at the centre and, taken together, they all hit an object before reaching the light, then probably the light is completely obscured. Conversely, we know if they can all see the light then probably the light is completely visible. These assumptions significantly increase efficiency and only fall down for occluding objects that are very small compared to the light.

Another useful speedup, and a standard technique employed by many ray tracers, is to exploit the coherence inherent in the scene by storing the most recent face to be hit by a shadow ray. This face is then tested against the next shadow ray for the possibility of a hit. The rationale behind this is that the shadow rays will probably be shot from points that are on the same surface

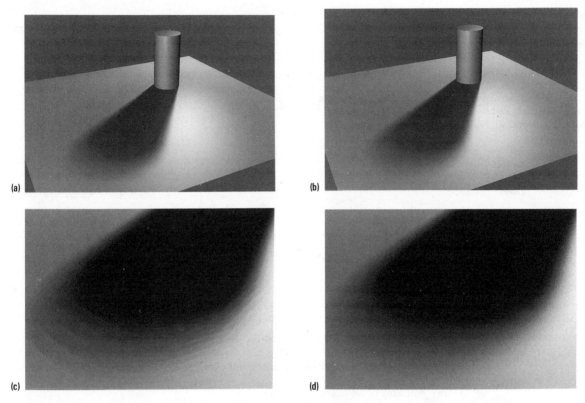

Figure 5.20   (a) The effect obtained by setting the jitter to zero. (b) Nonzero jitter anti-aliases the soft shadows. (c) Closeup of (a). (d) Closeup of (b).

and quite close together. The second shadow ray therefore stands a good chance of hitting the same face as the first. In the event that it does not the whole of the ray tracing database has to be traversed.

Figures 5.20(a) and (b) and the corresponding closeups demonstrate the idea. Figures 5.20(c) and (d) show the theory of stochastic sampling in practice. Figures 5.20(a) and (c) are generated without perturbing the ray directions by making *jitter_offset* zero. The sampling is therefore regular and we see aliasing – coherent errors produced by a coherent sampling pattern interfering with a coherent scene. The pattern is, in effect, caused by 19 separate shadows from 19 separate, regularly spaced point lights. Figures 5.20(b) and (d) show the effect of jittering the shadow rays by making *jitter_offset* nonzero. Substituting noise for aliasing gives a visually more acceptable result. There is a tradeoff between noise and aliasing and the number *jitter_offset* has to be fine-

tuned to achieve this balance – too small and aliases start to appear, too large and the penumbra becomes too noisy.

5.3 Shadows from transparent objects

The case where shadows are cast from transparent objects is far more complex than casting shadows from opaque objects, and it is questionable as to whether it is correct to consider this as a shadowing effect or not. The effect is a combination of two separate phenomena:

1. *Absorption*   As the light passes through the object some of its energy may be absorbed. Usually this absorption occurs at preferred wavelengths causing the light to change colour on exiting the object.
2. *Dispersion*   Unless the object/medium interface has a refractive index of unity, light rays will change direction by refraction on entering or leaving the object. The light becomes dispersed – different regions of space will contain greater concentrations of light energy than others. Any object placed in this region of 'bent' light will reflect this variation of intensity producing so-called caustics on its surface.

Case 2 has serious ramifications. Because of the light rays changing direction it is no longer appropriate, when testing whether a point is in shadow or not, to sit at that point and look only in the direction of light, since rays from the light may be arriving by an indirect route involving any number of refractions. These complications put a correct treatment of light passing through transparent objects outside the scope of the basic 'can we see the light or can't we see the light?' type shadowing algorithms enumerated above.

Although some authors [WOO90] have tried to extend the definition of shadows to include the occlusion of transparent objects, we shall confine the definition of shadows to be the effect of occluding opaque objects only. In your authors' opinion the phenomenon of light passing though transparent objects is part of the global illumination problem as an instance of the specular to diffuse transfer of light. Within this context, readers are thus referred to Chapter 10, where the subject is discussed extensively.

6 | Mapping techniques: texture and environment mapping

The mandatory topic of anti-aliasing texture-mapped objects is covered in Chapter 4. The efficacy of the techniques described in this chapter depend on effective anti-aliasing and are meant to be used in conjunction with the specific technique of mip-mapping. Procedural texture mapping, where a procedure definition generates a textured pattern, is dealt with in Chapter 7. Chapter 14 contains material on organizing texture mapping by using 'shade trees'. View-dependent techniques such as environment mapping are usually classified as texture mapping techniques and we have included them in this chapter. However, they can also be viewed as 'first hit' ray tracing techniques. This point is dealt with in Chapter 9. A special case of chrome mapping involving water waves is given in Chapter 18.

Introduction

Ad hoc shadows (Chapter 5) and texture mapping are the two main 'add-on' techniques that are used to embellish visually the 'plastic object floating in free space' effect of Phong-shaded objects.

In this chapter we will look at a variety of mapping techniques that can all be described mathematically as:

$$R_3 \rightarrow R_2$$

mappings, where the texture or detail is essentially a two-dimensional image or pattern and the goal of the technique is to map such texture or detail onto the object in three dimensions. In general this involves finding two

u, v - values from three values from one of the three-dimensional coordinate spaces. Apart from the critical consideration of anti-aliasing (Chapter 4) we are generally concerned with two considerations in this type of texture mapping:

1. What attribute or parameter of the model or object is to be modulated to produce the desired textural effect?

2. How is the texture mapping to be carried out? Given that a texture is defined in a two-dimensional domain and an object exists in three dimensions, we need to define a mapping between these domains.

In a review paper Heckbert [HECK86] categorizes the parameters that can be modulated to provide a textural impression. A modified version of this categorization is as follows:

1. *Surface colour (diffuse reflection coefficient(s))* This is the most commonly used parameter for texture mapping and involves, for example in a simple reflection model, modulating the diffuse coefficient. The first example of this was [CATM74].

2. *Specular and diffuse reflection (environment mapping)* This method is now known as environment mapping and has come to be regarded as a separate technique rather than as a category of texture mapping. It is described in a separate section below and was first developed by Blinn [BLIN76].

3. *Normal vector perturbation* This is an elegant device, again developed by Blinn [BLIN78a], that 'tricks' a simple reflection model into producing what appears to be a perturbed surface. This is done by perturbing the geometry of the model, specifically the surface normal. An extension to this technique is given in [KAJI85] which Kajiya calls 'frame mapping'. In this method a 'frame bundle' rather than just a normal vector is perturbed. A frame bundle for a surface is a local coordinate system given by the tangent, binormal and normal to the surface. Kajiya points out that this approach allows a mapping of the directionality of surface features such as hair, cloth or brushed metal. Such surfaces that exhibit preferred directions when reflecting or refracting light are said to be anisotropic.

4. *Specularity* Although this effect was reported by Blinn (yet again) in [BLIN78b] it does not seem to have been used to any great extent. The attribute modulated is the surface roughness function in the Cook–Torrance reflection model (Chapter 2). An

example of a surface with variable shininess is an object painted with textured paint.

5. *Transparency* An example of the modulation of transparency is given in [GARD85]. This particular example is interesting in that it is not strictly a method of applying texture to an object, but a method of generating a complete object – a cloud – using a mathematical texture function to modulate the transparency of an ellipsoid. A real-life example of this case is chemically etched glass.

In this chapter we will describe three general approaches or categories:

1. General texture mapping where a pattern in a two-dimensional texture domain is 'pasted' onto the object, as if it were a piece of wallpaper, and in effect becomes part of the object database. That is, when the object is moved the texture pattern moves with it.

2. View-dependent mapping techniques, such as chrome, environment, reflection and refraction mapping. These are devices whereby an associated environment is reflected in the object. The pattern seen by the viewer depends on the viewing direction. The difference between 1 and 2 is exemplified by a rotating reflecting sphere. If an environment-mapped sphere rotates about its own axis nothing changes. If a texture-mapped sphere rotates the texture pattern will also rotate.

3. Bump mapping techniques: in a sense the term texture mapping is somewhat misleading. What we usually mean by texture is the macroscopic perturbation of the surface geometry. In computer graphics, texture mapping usually results in the modulation of the diffuse reflection coefficients of the surface. The surface is still flat but its colour changes. Bump mapping is a technique that *apparently* alters the geometry of the surface.

6.1 Texture mapping and object representation

Most of the work in this chapter is concerned with mapping a two-dimensional texture pattern onto a polygonal object. As we keep emphasizing, polygonal representation is almost a de facto standard and embellishing such objects with two-dimensional texture obtained, for example, by frame grabbing, is a popular technique. Unfortunately using a polygonal object results in certain problems. Unlike analytically defined objects (see Section 6.2) the mapping or projection function has to be obtained in some ad hoc manner. We can see this by returning to our pasting analogy. We cannot paste a two-dimensional pattern onto a polygonal object of arbitrary shape without cutting the pattern. What we do in practice, and in line with the nature of polygonal representation, is to take the vertices of the polygon and associate a texture map coordinate (u, v) with each vertex. This throws up two problems:

1. Deriving a mapping or projection function $F(\ )$ such that:

    $$(u, v) = F(x, y, z)$$

    where (x, y, z) are usually the coordinates of the object to be mapped (these coordinates are usually specified in object space). This 'sowing' of u, v-values onto the object can be regarded, as we shall see, as a modelling function.

2. Deriving a method whereby the renderer can associate texture values internal to the polygon, as the polygon gets clipped and rendered. As the object gets passed to the renderer the texture is only defined at the vertices of each polygon.

We can solve the first problem by using standard mapping or projecting functions. Two commonly used projection functions are the cylindrical and spherical mapping functions. We then adopt various strategies to deal with the fact that, in general, the objects onto which we are texture mapping are not spheres or cylinders.

Consider first cylindrical mapping: given a parametric definition of the curved surface of a cylinder (θ, z), the projection function to get the texture coordinates is trivial (Figure 6.1). Any point on the curved surface of a cylinder of radius r and height h is represented as:

$$(r\cos\theta, r\sin\theta, hz)$$

where $0 < \theta < 2\pi$ and $0 < z < 1$

We can associate texture values (u, v) with a point on the cylinder by

$$(u, v) = (\theta/2\pi, z) \qquad u, v \in [0, 1]$$

For a spherical mapping things are more problematic. Mapping a plane onto a sphere produces unbounded distortion at the poles, and the many considerations involved would fill an entire textbook (for example, [KELL46]). Consider as an example mapping texture onto a part of a sphere (Figure 6.2). We have the parametrization:

$$(r\cos\theta\sin\phi, r\sin\theta\sin\phi, r\cos\phi)$$

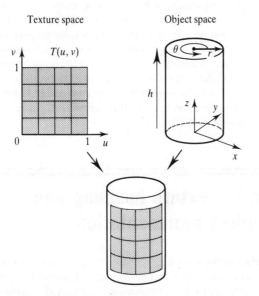

Figure 6.1   The cylindrical mapping.

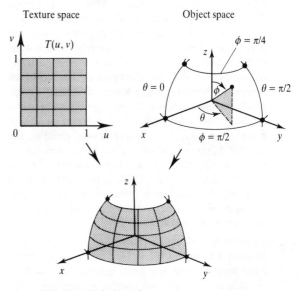

Figure 6.2   The spherical mapping.

Figure 6.3 Texture mapping: cylindrical, spherical and planar mapping.

where $0 \leqslant \theta \leqslant \pi/2$ and $\pi/4 \leqslant \phi \leqslant \pi/2$

We can then define a mapping function as before:

$$(u, v) = \left(\frac{\theta}{\pi/2}, \frac{(\pi/2) - \phi}{(\pi/4)} \right) \qquad u, v \in [0, 1]$$

Note that both these definitions are canonical transformations, mapping the unit texture domain into object space. All the standard two-dimensional transformations – scale, translation, rotation, shear and so on – can be applied to these texture coordinates. A simple example of three mappings – cylindrical, spherical and planar – is shown in Figure 6.3. These were rendered in conjunction with mip-mapping. The mip-maps for the texture map are shown in Plate 4.

6.1.1 Practical mapping techniques: mapping during modelling

As we have remarked, the objects onto which we wish to paste a texture are not, in general, cylindrical or spherical. In this section we will look at two strategies that enable us to use a cylindrical or spherical mapping, first in the case where the object is approximately cylindrical or spherical and second, the case where no such shape constraints are placed on the object.

We will illustrate this strategy by a simple example – the bananas in Plate 8. (Incidentally this is a frame from an animation sequence and the fruits are meant to be floating.) Plate 8(a) shows the texture map that was

used to texture the bananas. In this case a cylindrical mapping was employed, and the banana was originally modelled as a polygonized cylinder. This basic model is then shaped into the final banana by pinching the ends and applying a nonlinear bending transformation (see Section 17.4.1) to the cylindrical model. The u, v-values associated with each vertex effectively become part of the object database and are carried unchanged through the subsequent modelling stages. Texture maps for the apple and pear, in which cases spherical mappings were used, are shown in Plates 8(b) and (c).

6.1.2 Practical mapping techniques: two-stage mapping

A strategy that does not impose any constraints on the shape of the object was introduced by Bier and Sloan [BIER86]. This technique is not dissimilar to the technique outlined in the previous section. The basis of the method is as follows:

1. The first stage is a mapping from two-dimensional texture space to a *simple* three-dimensional intermediate surface such as a cylinder:

   $$T(u, v) \to T'(x_i, y_i, z_i)$$

   This is known as the S-mapping.

2. A second stage maps the three-dimensional texture pattern onto the object surface:

   $$T'(x_i, y_i, z_i) \to O(x, y, z)$$

   This is referred to as the O-mapping.

These combined operations can distort the texture pattern onto the object in a 'natural' way, for example, one variation of the method is a 'shrinkwrap' mapping, where the planar texture pattern shrinks onto the object in the manner suggested by the eponym.

For the S-mapping Bier describes four intermediate surfaces: a plane at any orientation, the curved surface of a cylinder, the faces of a cube and the surface of a sphere. Clearly the choice of the intermediate surface is context dependent. In particular it depends on the geometric form of the object surface that is receiving the texture. For example, a cylindrical surface could not be

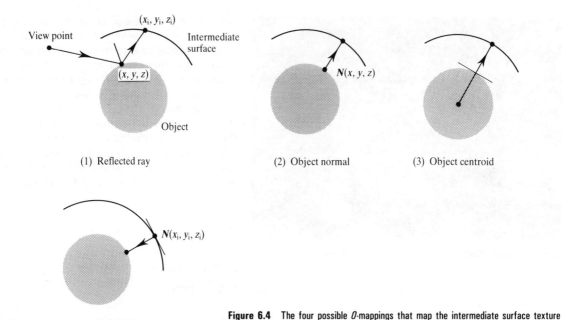

(1) Reflected ray   (2) Object normal   (3) Object centroid

(4) Intermediate surface normal

Figure 6.4   The four possible O-mappings that map the intermediate surface texture T' onto the object.

used if the O-mapping ended up on the top or bottom of the cylinder.

Various possibilities occur for the O-mapping where the texture values for $O(x, y, z)$ are obtained from $T'(x_i, y_i, z_i)$, and these are best considered from a ray tracing point of view. The four O-mappings are shown in Figure 6.4:

1. The intersection of the reflected view ray with the intermediate surface, T' (this is in fact environment mapping).

2. The intersection of the surface normal at (x, y, z) with T'.

3. The intersection of a line through (x, y, z) and the object centroid with T'.

4. The intersection of the line from (x, y, z) to T' whose orientation is given by the surface normal at (x_i, y_i, z_i).

Excluding the first, which is concerned with environment mapping (rather than mapping texture onto a surface) we have three O-mappings and four S-mappings giving a total of twelve possible combinations. Bier and Sloan state that only five of these combinations are useful. And, for example, they give the name 'shrinkwrap' to the combination of cylinder S-mapping with intermediate surface normal O-mapping.

6.1.3 Practical mapping techniques: reverse projection

Another useful method that imposes no constraints on the shape of the textured object is one that we have categorized as a 'reverse projection' technique. This practical technique is best used in conjunction with objects that have a plane of symmetry. Consider the ducks in Plate 9. These were texture mapped in the following way. The bounding box of the duck was obtained. Two coordinates of the normalized bounding box were associated with the texture coordinates. Mathematically we orthographically project the (u, v)s using one of the coordinate planes. Suppose we choose the y, z-plane (Figure 6.5). The bounding box is the rectangle described by the 'minimax' coordinates (x_1, y_1, z_1) and (x_r, y_r, z_r). The projection function (u, v), $(u, v \in [0, 1])$ is simply

$$(u, v) = \left(\frac{y - y_1}{y_r - y_1}, \frac{z - z_1}{z_r - z_1} \right)$$

Now from this we can see that the texture gets pasted onto the object without any regard for the x-coordinate of the duck. Thus distortion of the texture domain is unavoidable. The strategy is to paint the texture map *after* the texture coordinates have been sown onto the

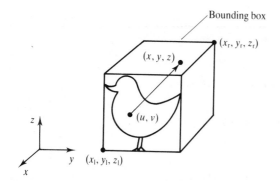

Figure 6.5 Reverse projection method used to texture map the ducks in Plate 9.

object thereby accommodating the distortion within the painting process. A cycle of painting and rendering loops is performed and the texture map is manually altered to account for the distortion of the projection. The frog (Plate 9) was also textured in a similar way.

6.1.4 Mapping polygon interior points

So far we have described how to associate u, v-values with polygon vertices during the modelling stage. The obvious problem that arises out of this is how does the renderer deal with interior polygon points. (This problem is intimately connected with anti-aliasing and this section should be read in conjunction with Section 4.7.)

An obvious solution would be to include the u, v-coordinates along with the screen coordinates and normals of the polygons as they are loaded into the renderer from the object's description. As the picture is rendered the polygons get clipped. We could then interpolate the u, v-coordinates along the clipped edges of the polygon just as the normals are interpolated for Phong shading. This would be an approximation, however, and prone to the usual problems associated with edge interpolation in perspective space – particularly the fact that for polygons of more than four vertices the interior interpolation is inherently ill-defined.

We shall describe two superior solutions to this problem. One covers the ideal case when the projection function is known and well defined for every point on the object; another deals with the more general case where the projection function is neither known nor well defined, in which case the only information available to us is the texture coordinates at the vertices.

When the projection function is known it can be taken along with the polygon as it gets clipped within the renderer. The vertices of the pixel-clipped polygon are transformed back to object space, then the projection function is applied to these transformed vertices to yield the u, v-coordinates of the clipped polygon.

Listing 6.1 shows this process in action, *texture_map (map, vertex_no, vertex_list, uvproject, colour)* passes a list, *vertex_list*, of *vertex_no* vertices making up the pixel-clipped polygon and the projection function *uvproject( )* that originally sowed the u, v-coordinates onto the surface. *transform(fromspace, tospace, ptfrom, ptto)* transforms a point *ptfrom* in space *fromspace* to point *ptto* in space *tospace*. *uvproject(point, u, v)* returns the u, v-coordinates from given point *point*. The vertex is transformed from screen space to the space in which the projection function was invoked – this is usually the object space. The average value of the u, v-coordinates and the compression (see Section 4.7.1) are calculated and passed onto *mip_map( )*.

Knowledge of a projection function at the time of rendering is a somewhat special case. More common are cases when the projection function is either not known, or the texture coordinates are 'sown' onto object vertices using some ad hoc technique which cannot be represented by a single, simple analytical function. We now describe a tried and tested method to handle this more general situation.

To first order, the simplest way in which texture coordinates can vary across a polygon is linearly in the plane of the polygon. We make the assumption that the texture coordinates will vary linearly independent of the method that has sown texture coordinates onto the vertices. Of course, if the texture mapping operation produces wildly varying texture coordinates this assumption will not hold. The only solution then is to subdivide the polygons and redo the texture mapping – as the polygons get smaller and smaller the approximation to linearity will become more and more accurate, just as in calculus, when moving towards a point on a curve, the closer you get to the point the more you will tend to move along the tangent at that point.

We shall consider the variation of texture coordinate u only – the treatment of v being exactly the same. Given linearity then, the variation of u with $\boldsymbol{x}$ across the plane of the polygon, shown schematically in Figure 6.6, is given by:

$$u = T \cdot \left(x - x_0 \right) + u_0$$

where:

Listing 6.1   texture_map.c

```c
#include "types.h"

/*
        texture_map() : return colour from texture_mapped polygon
*/

void texture_map (map, vertex_no, vertex_list, uvproject,colour)
char map[1024][1024];/* mip_map */
int vertex_no;/* no of vertices making up polygon */
point *vertex_list;/* list of vertices */
void (*uvproject)();/* projection function sowing (u,v)'s onto object */
float colour[3];

{
        point       *screen_vertex,object_vertex;
        float       last_u,last_v,u,v,uav,vav,d,texture_area=0.;
        int  i;

        /* get (u,v) coordinates of last vertex in list */
        screen_vertex = vertex_list + vertex_no − 1;
        transform("screen,"object",screen_vertex,&object_vertex);
        uvproject(object_vertex,&last_u,&last_v);

        for (i=0; i < vertex_no; i++) {

                /*
                Calculate the area in texture space by summing the areas of
                the trapezia under each side.
                */

                screen_vertex = vertex_list + i;
                transform("screen,"object",screen_vertex,&object_vertex);
                uvproject(object_vertex,&u,&v);
                texture_area += (u + last_u) * (v − last_v);
                uav += u;
                vav += v;
                last_u = u;
                last_v = v;

        }
        texture_area *= 0.5;
        uav /= vertex_no;
        vav /= vertex_no;
        d = sqrt(fabs(texture_area)); /* Our approximation for the compression */
        mip_map(map,uav,vav,d,colour);

}
```

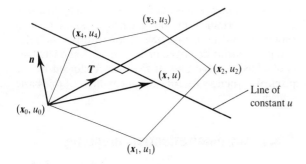

Figure 6.6 Linear variation of texture in plane.

u_0 is the value of u at x_0

T is the direction along which u varies most rapidly

If we represent the projection function as

$$u = f(x, y, z)$$

then T represents the gradient operator applied to this function. Because we are assuming linearity we can write:

$$T = \nabla f = \left(\frac{\partial f}{\partial x}, \frac{\partial f}{\partial y}, \frac{\partial f}{\partial z} \right)$$

Lines lying in the plane of the polygon that are perpendicular to this vector are thus lines of constant u. We call this vector T, the texture vector. The problem thus reduces to the following: given the vertices of a polygon and the associated texture values represented by a sequence of quadruples, (x_0, u_0), (x_1, u_1), (x_2, u_2), . . ., find T. It is solved by constructing and solving for the three simultaneous equations:

$$u_a = T \cdot (x_a - x_0) + u_0$$
$$u_b = T \cdot (x_b - x_0) + u_0 \qquad \qquad \text{(6.1)}$$
$$T \cdot n = 0$$

where:

n is the normal to the plane of the polygon

The values for (x_a, u_a) and (x_b, u_b) are obtained from the sequence of quadruples above. We now consider a detail of implementation. Care must be taken when choosing these values and attention must be paid to numerical precision. The renderer has no prior knowledge as to the order in which these numbers arrive or their values. The following conditions must be obeyed: x_a must be chosen to be sufficiently far from x_0, x_b must be chosen such that it is sufficiently far away from them

both, and the three values, x_0, x_a and x_b, taken together must not be collinear or nearly so. Once the texture vector has been calculated, T, x_0 and u_0 (and the corresponding values for the texture coordinate v) are taken along with the polygon as it gets clipped within the renderer. As the polygon gets clipped the function (6.1) is used on the world coordinates of the vertices of the clipped polygon to yield the u, v-values. Function (6.1) is thus used in exactly the same way as one would use a projection function (if it existed) and so can be thought of as a locally derived projection function applicable only over the polygon in question.

6.2 Mapping onto bicubic parametric patches

If the object is represented parametrically, texture mapping is straightforward, since a parametric patch, by definition, already possesses u, v-values over its surface.

The first use of texture in computer graphics was a method developed by Catmull [CATM74]. This technique was applied to bicubic parametric patch models; the algorithm subdivides a surface patch in object space, and at the same time executes a corresponding subdivision in texture space. The idea is that the patch subdivision proceeds until it covers a single pixel (a standard patch-splitting algorithm is described in detail in Chapter 3). When the patch subdivision process terminates the required texture value(s) for the pixel is obtained from the area enclosed by the current level of subdivision in the texture domain. This is a straightforward technique that is easily implemented as an extension to a bicubic patch renderer. A variation of this method has been used recently by Cook et al. [COOK87] where object surfaces are subdivided into 'micropolygons' and flat shaded with values from a corresponding subdivision in texture space.

An example of this technique is shown in Plate 10. Here *each* patch on the teapot causes subdivision of a single texture map, which is itself a rendered version of the teapot. For each patch, the u, v-values from the parameter space subdivision are used to index the texture map whose u, v-values also vary between 0 and 1. This scheme is easily altered to, say, map four patches into the entire texture domain by using a scale factor of two in the u, v-mapping.

6.3 View-dependent mapping techniques

These techniques can be regarded as approximations to ray tracing, as we shall discuss in Chapter 9. A texture is mapped onto the object by reflecting or refracting 'beams' from the eye point. The aim of the technique is to approximate the reflection of an environment, or pseudo-environment, in the case of reflection or chrome mapping, in the object.

The general approach common to these techniques is: for each pixel-clipped polygon, we construct a beam (Figure 6.7) formed by the clipped polygon and the reflection vectors at the vertices of the clipped polygon. For each vertex a normal has been interpolated as part of Phong shading and the reflection/refraction vector is calculated from this normal and the eye point (see Chapter 8). This beam is then reflected or refracted from

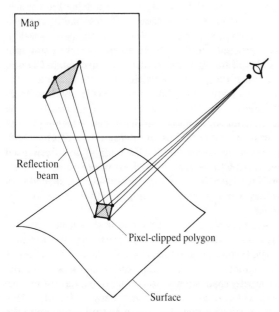

Figure 6.7 The general approach used in view-dependent mapping techniques.

the surface and projects onto an area on a map in a way that is determined by the method used. The area subtended on the map is then used to drive the mip-mapping scheme described in Section 4.7.1 and a colour is obtained for that part of the surface clipped by the pixel. We will now describe the possibilities of this basic scheme.

6.3.1 Chrome/reflection mapping

In this technique beams are traced from the eye to the object and reflected beams terminate in a two-dimensional map at their second hit. A popular example of this is known colloquially as 'chrome' mapping. This is a technique that is a cheap form of environment mapping and is so called because it enables any arbitrary pattern in the two-dimensional chrome map space to be reflected onto a surface such as chrome, approximating the effect of an environment reflected into the surface of a highly reflecting object. The efficacy of the technique depends on the fact that most shiny objects do not have perfect surfaces – the surfaces usually exhibit some degree of roughness and reflections from the environment are consequently blurred. Rather than go to the expense of full environment mapping (which is itself a cheap approximation of ray tracing) why not store an arbitrary two-dimensional map, which, used with reflection mapping, will give an impression of environment mapping?

Two examples are shown. First, the saxophone (Plate 11). This has two maps associated with it. One map is used to colour the keys and one is used for the main body of the instrument. This illustration demonstrates the power of the technique in that it produces an effect that seems to be somewhere between reality and an artist's stylization. The second example (Plate 12) shows an excerpt from an animation sequence. The fleur de lys rotates in three-dimensional space and is rendered according to values obtained from a reflection map that is stationary. This technique is extremely useful in animation because it gives an effect of an object moving in an environment (that the object reflects) at little expense.

Chrome-mapped title sequences currently abound on TV. Most have disturbing animation discontinuities at edges or boundaries between polygon faces. This is due to objects that are crudely built containing neighbouring polygons over which the surface normal, and consequently the reflected vector, is discontinuous (such a discontinuity of $\pi/2$ occurs when moving across the edge of a cube). The reflected vectors map onto completely different regions of the chrome map and hence the resulting colours picked up exhibit visual discontinuities in the animation. This is because maps usually contain coherent detail and this 'runs' independently across different faces in the object or character as it is moved. This ubiquitous error looks banal. In the case of the block letters beloved 'creatives' in the advertising world, putting a bevel along the edges would remove the problem. The fleur de lys escapes this effect because it is a carefully defined, well-built object over which the surface normals vary smoothly.

Note that this technique differs from 'standard' texture mapping in that the texture imposed on the object varies as the view point changes. In the case of texture mapping the u, v-coordinates are a function of the object only. They are pasted onto it as part of the object's description and carried through the rendering process undisturbed. In the case of chrome mapping the u, v-coordinates are a function of the object's position, surface normal and its orientation with respect to the eye – a relationship that clearly changes as the object moves around the scene. The difference is easily illustrated by considering a simple example. A texture-mapped rotating sphere would exhibit a rotating pattern that moved with the sphere, but a chrome-mapped rotating sphere would exhibit a stationary pattern, because the object is effectively stationary with respect to the eye. On the other hand, the pattern on a sphere translating through the environment would remain stationary, with respect to the object, whereas a chrome-mapped sphere would change its appearance as it moved. Thus chrome mapping is no different to standard texture mapping unless it is animated.

Chrome mapping can be implemented by employing a sphere as an intermediate surface in the scheme described in Section 6.1.2. Mapping the two-dimensional chrome map into the sphere, as is well known, is difficult to perform without distortion. A commonly used mapping is the 'latitude–longitude' projection (Figure 6.8):

$$u = \tfrac{1}{2}\left(1 + 1/\pi \tan^{-1}\left(R_y/R_x\right)\right) \quad -\pi < \tan^{-1}(\ ) < \pi$$

$$v = \frac{R_z + 1}{2}$$

$$\left.\right\} \ (6.2)$$

This caters for all possible directions of the reflected vector. In special cases where the reflected vector may be restricted to a particular set of directions 'customized' mapping functions can be written. One such customized

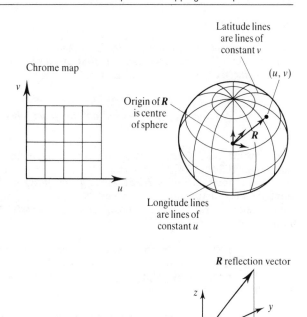

Figure 6.8 The mapping function is equivalent to surrounding the object with a sphere.

chrome mapping function appears in Section 18.3.2 for the rendering of water waves.

Now the function above is one of a family of spherical projections which contain singularities at poles. At these singularities small changes in the reflection vector produce large changes in the texture coordinates. In this case as $R_z \rightarrow \pm 1$, both R_x and $R_y \rightarrow 0$ and so R_y/R_x becomes ill-defined. Translated into texture coordinates, as $v \rightarrow 1$ or 0 the behaviour of u starts to break down. Visually, this corresponds to 'spikes' on the surface where the singularity picks up wildly varying regions of the map. This can be overcome by blurring the map at the poles as a preprocess and explains why chrome maps (Plate 11) are usually soft.

chrome_map ( ) in Listing 6.2 shows our implementation of chrome mapping. We use mip-mapping (Chapter 4) as the anti-aliasing technique. Recall that this requires a closed region – the texture area – to be traced out in texture or u, v-space. This is done pixel by pixel via the mapping (6.2) which is applied to the reflected vectors of the polygon to be chrome mapped (once this polygon has been clipped to the pixel). The reflected vectors taken together form a reflected beam whose interior projects

Listing 6.2   chrome_map.c

```
#include "types.h"

void normalize();/* normalizes its argument */
void reflect();/* third argument is first argument reflected about second */
void chrome();√* our version of Eqn 6.2*/

/*
           chrome_map() : return colour from chrome mapped polygon
*/

void chrome_map (map, vertex_no, vertex_list,normal_list, colour)
char map[1024][1024];/* mip_map */
int vertex_no;/* no of vertices making up polygon */
point *vertex_list;/* list of vertices */
point *normal_list;/* corresponding list of normals */
float colour[3];
{
        point       *screen_vertex,eye_vector,*normal,R;
        float       last_u,last_v,u,v,uav,vav,d;
        float       uv_edge_length,edge_compression = -1.;
        int  i;

        screen_vertex = vertex_list + vertex_no - 1;
        normal = normal_list + vertex_no -1;
        transform("screen,"camera",screen_vertex,&eye_vector);
        eye_vector.x *= -1.; eye_vector.y *= -1.; eye_vector *= -1.;
        normalize(&eye_vector);
        reflect(eye_vector,normal,&R);
        chrome(R,&last_u,last_v);


        for (i=0; i < vertex_no; i++) {

                screen_vertex = vertex_list + i;
                normal = normal_list + i;
                transform("screen,"camera",screen_vertex,&eye_vector);
                eye_vector.x *= -1.; eye_vector.y *= -1.; eye_vector.z *= -1.;
                normalize(&eye_vector);
                reflect(&eye_vector,normal,&R);
                chrome(R,&u,&v);

                uv_edge_length = (u-last_u)*(u-last_u) + (v-last_v)*(v-last_v);
                if (uv_edge_length>edge_compression) edge_compression=uv_edge_length;

                uav += u;
                vav += v;
                last_u = u;
                last_v = v;

        }
        uav /= vertex_no;
        vav /= vertex_no;
        edge_compression = sqrt(edge_compression);
        mip_map(map,uav,vav,edge_compression,colour);

}
```

onto the enclosing surface (see Figure 6.7). The clipped polygon is passed to the routine as a list *vertex_list* of *vert_no* vertices and the corresponding list of normals *normal_list*. The vertices are in screen space and are transformed to eye space. Finding the vector to the eye is consequently trivial and *chrome( )*, the routine's version of (6.2), maps this reflected vector into u, v-space.

We now consider the calculation of the compression value required for the mip-map. In the case of mip-mapping (Chapter 4) the compression was defined as the square root of the texture area. Chrome mapping can produce reflection beams that subtend wide texture areas that are generally more irregular than those found in normal two-dimensional texture mapping. For this reason, the approximation for compression constructed for texture mapping does not work well for chrome mapping. We need a more severe method for extracting a value for the compression. This is done by calculating the compression the texture suffers along an edge of the polygon (*edge_compression* in Listing 6.2) as opposed to calculating the compression by considering the texture area over the polygon. This is simply the length of the edge in u, v-space. The maximum length over all edges is taken as the compression. Effectively, the texture region is approximated by a square centred at the centroid of the region whose sides, parallel to the texture axis, are as long as the longest edge of the region. This procedure guarantees that the approximating square encloses the texture region – thereby ensuring correct, if somewhat soft, anti-aliasing.

Note that this approximates to a suggestion made in [WILL83b] for calculating the compression d, given by:

$$d = \text{max of} \left[\left(\left(\frac{\partial u}{\partial x} \right)^2 + \left(\frac{\partial v}{\partial x} \right)^2 \right)^{1/2}, \left(\left(\frac{\partial u}{\partial y} \right)^2 + \left(\frac{\partial v}{\partial y} \right)^2 \right)^{1/2} \right]$$

our practical implementation of this function being:

$$d = \left(\Delta u^2 + \Delta v^2 \right)^{1/2}$$

where Δu and Δv are the lengths in u and v of the edge in u, v-space, Δx and Δy being set to unity since the pixel is of unit length.

Finally we note the similarity between this technique and cone tracing (see Section 10.3).

6.3.2 Refraction mapping

Refraction mapping, as we have implemented it, uses the same algorithmic framework as chrome/reflection map-ping with two differences. First, we calculate refraction beams, rather than reflected beams. Secondly, we project the refracted beam directly onto a planar (two-dimensional) map. With refraction mapping we want to see the *effect* of the refraction and it is more convenient to use a coherently patterned planar map. Note that because we are no longer using a spherical mapping, we have to guarantee that the reflected vectors hit the map. Two examples are given in Plates 13 and 14. In the first example, eye beams hit a perturbed water surface (see Chapter 18 for further details on modelling a perturbed water surface) then refract through the water onto an underlying pattern – the refraction map (Figure 6.9). In this case the map consists of a set of colour bars. In the water examples one surface is a set of long-crested waves and the other is a set of circular waves.

The second example shows a solid hemisphere resting on a chequerboard. It is instructive in that the hemi-sphere with the flat side up is far more convincing, or at least makes sense, whereas the inverted example is unsuccessful. The reason for this lies in the geometric constraints of the method. The hemisphere is resting on a flat chequerboard and there are no other objects in the scene. Both objects are surrounded by black space. Rays that emerge from the hemisphere which do not hit the chequerboard return a contribution of black. These examples were generated by refracting from one surface only. If we were doing this correctly, or using a conven-

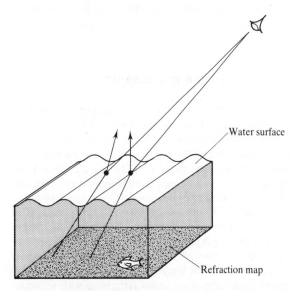

Figure 6.9 Refraction mapping onto a planar map to simulate distortion seen through a perturbed water surface (Plate 13).

tional ray tracing technique, we would trace rays or beams through two refractions, one for the front and one for the back surface.

Finally, the two techniques of reflection and refraction mapping are easily combined. Ts'o and Barsky [TSO87] do precisely this to render water waves. They linearly combine the values from reflection and refraction maps. In this application the reflection and refraction planes are both parallel to the water surface and the problems encountered in chrome mapping, due to the R_3 to R_2 nature of the mapping function, do not occur.

The reflectivity is calculated using Fresnel's equation which, for efficiency, is approximated by a piecewise function. For angles of incidence approaching the grazing angle, this is given by (see Section 2.5.1):

$$\mu = \frac{(n-1)^2}{(n+1)^2} \approx 0.02 \qquad \left(\text{for water} \right)$$

and this comprises the first segment in the piecewise function. The second segment is approximated by a parabolic function with its minimum at 45°, and we have:

$$\mu = \begin{cases} 0.02 & \phi < \pi/4 \\ \dfrac{392}{25\pi^2}\left(\phi - \pi/4\right)^2 + 0.02 & \phi \geqslant \pi/4 \end{cases}$$

Ts'o and Barsky also find it useful to dither or randomly perturb the reflection and refraction vectors so that slight blurring occurs. This technique is, of course, an ad hoc approximation to distributed ray tracing on the one hand and using prefiltered texture on the other.

6.3.3 Environment mapping

The equivalent of environment mapping in films became a common technique in the 1960s and its use as a cinematic device made it part of popular culture, which is no doubt one of the reasons for its ubiquity in computer graphics. One of the first films to use it was *Cool Hand Luke*, a film about life on the chain gang. In this movie the character of Boss Godfrey was made convincingly sinister by the use of mirrored sun glasses. The camera frequently zoomed to his face, revealing images of convicts at work in brown earth against a bright blue sky. Another example that has become part of modern visual culture are the images of lunar explorers with their tinted spherical helmet visors reflecting, with stunning clarity, the surrounding lunar landscape.

Environment mapping is a scheme that improves on the mapping techniques of the previous two sections. Its usefulness lies in the fact that, for a reflective object embedded in a complex environment, ray tracing the reflections would be prohibitively expensive. Environment mapping gives us these reflections more cheaply, though with loss of accuracy. Its computation, aside from the task of initially constructing the maps themselves, is independent of the level of detail of the surroundings.

In environment mapping, the object is surrounded by a closed three-dimensional surface onto which the environment is projected. Reflected rays are traced from the object, hit the surface and then index into the map. It is essentially the same as chrome mapping except that the map consists of an image of the environment as seen from the centre of the space that contains the object to be environment-mapped. With environment mapping we are generally interested in seeing recognizable detail in the reflected information.

In all environment mapping methods the accuracy depends on the object being positioned at the centre of this surface, usually a cube or a sphere, and it is assumed that the objects in the environment are distant from the object receiving the environment map. As the object becomes large with respect to those contained in the map, or the object is positioned a long way from the map's centre, the geometric distortion increases. This is because the environment map is created as a projection from a single point at the centre of the surface.

Geometric distortion can be reduced by ray tracing those objects in the environment that are too close to the reflective object. If the reflecting object itself is sufficiently complex then this may also have to be ray traced to account for self reflections which, of course, environment mapping cannot handle. Hall [HALL86] separates objects (other than the reflecting object) into an immediate secondary environment, which is ray traced, and a remote secondary environment, which is turned into the environment map. The criterion of separation is based on the magnitude of the solid angle an object subtends on the reflecting object.

The first use of environment mapping was by Blinn and Newell [BLIN76]. Here the object is deemed to be positioned at the centre of a large sphere, onto the interior of which the environment is projected. The mapping used a latitude–longtitude map indexed by the reflected ray. This is identical to the mapping suggested in Section 6.3.1 for chrome mapping.

Note that this index function uses only the direction of

R, leading to significant errors in planar surfaces on large objects that will tend to index into the same point on the map. Furthermore, the mapping is essentially a spherical projection and contains a singularity at $(0, 0, R_z)$, that is, as R_x and R_y both tend to zero *u* becomes ill defined varying more and more rapidly. Recall that in chrome mapping this can lead to 'spikes', but in this case it is precisely compensated for when building the environment map leading to a corresponding distortion in the map around the singularities. This is a disadvantage since unfortunately this can only contribute to the degradation of the final effect. In fact, the only difference between latitude–longitude environment mapping and chrome mapping is that the former stores the environment in its map whereas the latter is any arbitrary image. In terms of implementation the two methods are identical. So, just as with chrome mapping, anti-aliasing is mandatory.

A much superior environment mapping technique is presented by [GREE86c], where the environment is projected onto the six sides of a cube. The mapping function, though still $R^3 \to R^2$, is no longer spherical and contains no singularities and much less distortion. Also, a more detailed and sharper effect is produced since an environment map that consists of six mip-maps contains six times the information of a single latitude–longitude map. Environment maps are constructed by taking six images, from a fixed point, in six mutually orthogonal directions; either with a camera whose field of view is $\pi/2$ or by using a renderer to construct the maps from a modelled scene. These six images are then converted into six mip-maps. The main problem with a real camera is that it is difficult

to construct the six component map without encountering both geometric and illumination dicontinuities at the seams or boundaries of the six component pieces. None the less, this technique is popular as it provides a neat way of blending computer-generated objects and live action sets. A computer graphics object environment mapped in this way 'sits' more naturally in the scene when it is seen to reflect objects that it appears to be surrounded by.

An elaborate use of environment mapping in an animated sequence appears in the film *The Abyss* [ILM90]. This involved reflecting an environment in a transparent animated object – the so-called pseudopod – and both reflection and refraction were used. The environment maps were constructed by photographing the sets. The result was composited into live action with human actors appearing in the same environment as that mapped onto the pseudopod.

Plate 15 shows a map created in this way. The environment is the interior of a room. Careful examination of the illustration reveals discontinuities that occur at the seams due to camera geometry problems and lighting irregularities. Plate 16 shows an object rendered using this map. As can be seen the kettle appears genuinely to be part of the scene.

Six views of a synthetic scene can, of course, be computed with a seamless fit across the boundaries as shown in Plate 17, which shows two environment maps taken at the centre of the room and at the centre of the teapot respectively. Note that objects close to the camera, such as the chair, suffer appreciable distortion. Plate 18 shows

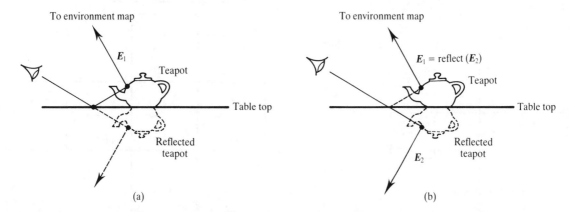

Figure 6.10 (a) Reflecting the environment in the reflection of the teapot requires three hits using the standard ray tracing paradigm. (b) Using a reflected object to generate E_2 and then reflecting E_2 gives E_1.

the teapot reflecting the environment map of Plate 17.

The alert reader will notice that the reflection of the teapot in the table top is also environment mapped correctly. This would not come out of the standard scheme. The ad hoc approach we used was to consider the reflected object itself to be an object that is environment mapped. (This is easy to do as the table top is planar). Then, to index into the same map, the reflected vector itself has to be reflected about the table top; in terms of Figure 6.10, E_2 then becomes identical with E_1. The reflection is computed as a separate pass and composited into the final image afterwards.

This example provides a glimpse into the underworld of making computer images where any convenient short-cut is taken to make an image look correct. This practice is ubiquitous though understated.

We now consider some implementation details. The mapping consists simply of projecting the reflection beam onto the sides of the cube. A typical texture area that now runs over a number of maps is shown in Figure 6.11.

Listing 6.3 shows *environment_map( )* which takes the same arguments as *chrome_map( )*, apart from the map *envmap* which is now six mip-maps. The faces of the cube, numbered as shown in Figure 6.12, are each allotted a bit in an integer code, enabling us to define the edge of the cube to be the sum of the two faces that make up that edge. The reflection beam is traversed and the projection onto the unit cube is stored in the array *cube[ ]*. For each face over which the projection occurs, the colour is calculated for that mip-map and added to the final colour once it has been weighted by the texture area on that face. The environment map unfolded in Figure 6.12 shows how, for each separate face, the u, v-coordinates relate to the coordinates of the projected point. These transformations are carried out in the routine *project( )*. Face 4, for example, in the direction of negative y, has u increasing along positive x and v increasing along negative z. The transformation of a

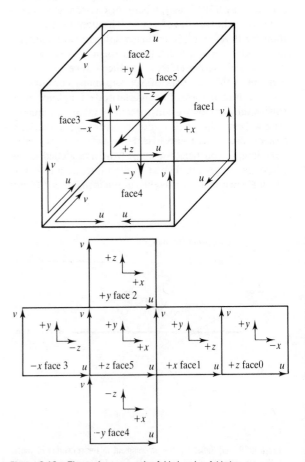

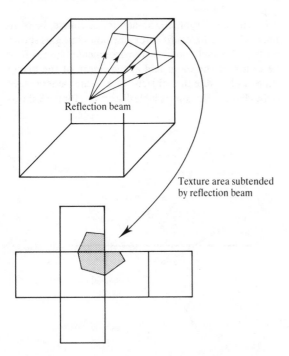

Figure 6.11 Texture area subtended by reflection beam for environment mapping.

Figure 6.12 The environment cube folded and unfolded.

Listing 6.3   environment__map.c

```
#include  "types.h"

#define  max_no 30

/* face and edge numberings - see Fig 6.12 */
#define  face0  1
#define  face1  2
#define  face3  8
#define  face4  16
#define  face5  32

#define  edge01  3
#define  edge02  5
#define  edge03  9
#define  edge04  17
#define  edge12  6
#define  edge23  12
#define  edge34  24
#define  edge41  18
#define  edge51  34
#define  edge52  36
#define  edge53  40
#define  edge54  48

void        normalize();
void        reflect();
void        get_reflected_normal();
void        get_face_intersection ();
void        get_edge_intersection()
void        project ();

point       cube[max_no];/* stores the projection of the reflected beam onto the cube */
int               cube_no;/* stores the no of points making up the projection */
float       uv[max_no][2];/* stores uv values of this projection for a given face */

/*
            environment_map() : return colour from environment mapped polygon
*/
void environment_map (envmap, vertex_no, vertex_list,normal_list, colour)
char envmap[6][1024][1024];/* environment map consisting of six mip_maps */
int vertex_no;/* no of vertices making up polygon */
point *vertex_list;/* list of vertices */
point *normal_list;/* corresponding list of normals */
float colour[3];
{
            point       last_R,R,pt;
            float       last_u,last_v,u,v,uav,vav,d,texture_area,total_area;
            int         i,j;
            int         projection_bit;/* stores all the faces the reflected beam projects onto */
            int         edge,last_face,current_face,project_face;
            float       run_colour[3];
```

Listing 6.3   cont.

```
        cube_no = 0;
        projection bit = 0;
        total_area = 0;

        /* find intersection the reflected vector from the last vertex in the list makes with the cube */
        i = vertex no-1;
        get_reflected_normal(vertex_list+i,normal_list+i,&lastR);
        get_face_intersection (&lastR, &cube[cube_no], &last_face);
        cube_no++;
        projection_bit |= last_face;
        for (i=0; i < vertex_no; i++) {

                get_reflected_normal(vertex_list+i,normal_list+i,&R);
                get_face_intersection (&R, &pt, &current_face);

                /* if the last reflected ray intersected a face different from the current
                ray, we must find the intersection the reflected beam makes  with the
                corresponding edge */
                if (current_face != last_face) {
                        edge = current_face | last_face;
                        get_edge_intersection (&lastR, &R, edge, &cube[cube_no]);
                        cube_no++;
                        projection_bit |= current_face;
                }

                cube[cube_no] = pt;
                cube_no++;
                last_face = current_face;
                last_R = R;
        }

        colour[0] = colour[1] = colour[2] = 0;
        for (i=0,project_face=1; i<6; i++,project_face+=project_face) {

                if (project_face & projection_bit) {

                        /* get the projection in UVspace on project_face */
                        project (project_face);
                        last_u = uv[0][0];
                        last_v = uv[0][1];
                        uav = 0.;
                        vav = 0.;
                        texture_area = 0.;

                        for (j = 1; j < cube_no; j++) {

                                u = uv[j][0];
                                v = uv[j][1];
                                texture_area += (u + last_u) * (last_v - v) / 2;
```

Listing 6.3 cont.

```
                                      last_u = u;
                                      last_v = v;
                                      uav += u;
                                      vav += v;
                            }
                            uav /= (cube_no–1);
                            vav /= (cube_no–1);
                            d = sqrt(fabs(texture_area));
                            mip_map(envmap[i], uav, vav, d, run_colour);

                            /* add the colour contribution weighted by the area */
                            colour[0] += run_colour[0] * texture_area;
                            colour[1] += run_colour[1] * texture_area;
                            colour[2] += run_colour[2] * texture_area;
                            total_area += texture_area;
                  }
         }

         /* normalize the weightings */
         colour[0] /= total_area;
         colour[1] /= total_area;
         colour[2] /= total_area;
}
/*
         Given a screen_vertex and its normal get_reflected_normal() returns
         the reflected vector in world space – this is assumed, and is usually
         the case, to have axes parallel to the axes of the environment map.
*/
void get_reflected_normal(screen_vertex,normal,worldR)
point *screen_vertex,*normal,*worldR;
{
         point eye_vector,cameraR;

         transform("screen,"camera",screen_vertex,&eye_vector);
         eye_vector.x *= –1.; eye_vector.y *= –1.; eye_vector *= –1.;
         normalize(&eye_vector);
         reflect(eye_vector,normal,&cameraR);
         transform_vector("camera","world",&cameraR,worldR);
         normalize(worldR);
}
/*
         get_face_intersection() returns the face of the cube the normal intersects
         and the point of intersection.
*/
void get_face_intersection (normal, pt, face)
point *normal, *pt;
int *face;
{
         point      n = *normal;
         float t;
```

Listing 6.3   cont.

```
                /* test nz direction */
                if (n.z. < 0) { /* test intersection with face5 */
                        t= -0.5 / n.z;
                        pt->x = n.x * t; pt->y = n.y * t; pt->z = n.z * t;
                        if (fabs (pt->x) < 0.5 && fabs (pt->y) < 0.5) {
                                *face = face5;
                                return;
                        }
                }
                else if (n.z > 0) { /* test intersection with face0 */
                        t = 0.5 / n.z;
                        pt->x = n.x * t; pt->y = n.y * t; pt->z = n.z * t;
                        if (fabs (pt->x) < 0.5&& fabs (pt->y) < 0.5) {
                                *face = face0;
                                return;
                        }
                }

                /* test ny direction */
                if (n.y < 0) { /* test intersection with face4 */
                        t= -0.5 / n.y;
                        pt->x = n.x * t; pt->y = n.y * t; pt->z = n.z * t;
                        if (fabs (pt->x) < 0.5 && fabs (pt->z) < 0.5) {
                                *face = face4;
                                return;
                        }
                }
                else if (n.y > 0) { /* test intersection with face2 */
                        t = 0.5 / n.y;
                        pt->x = n.x * t; pt->y = n.y * t; pt->z = n.z * t;
                        if (fabs (pt->x) < 0.5 && fabs (pt->z) < 0.5) {
                                *face = face2;
                                return;
                        }
                }

                /* test nx direction */
        if (n.x < 0) { /* test intersection with face3 */
                t= -0.5/n.x;
                pt->x = n.x * t; pt->y = n.y * t; pt->z = n.z * t;
                if (fabs (pt->y) < 0.5 && fabs (pt->z) < 0.5) {
                        *face = face3;
                        return;
                }
        }
        else if (n.x > 0) { /* test intersection with face1 */
                t = 0.5 / n.x;
                pt->x = n.x * t; pt->y = n.y * t; pt->z = n.z * t;
                if (fabs (pt->y) < 0.5 && fabs (pt->z) < 0.5) {
                        *face = face1;
                        return;
```

Listing 6.3   cont.

```
                    }
              }
}
/*
          get_edge_intersection( ) returns the intersection of the cube edge
          with the reflected beam
*/
void get_edge_intersection (n1, n2, edge, pt)
point *n1, *n2, *pt;
int edge;
{
          float a, b, c;
          float x0, y0, z0, f, g, h;
          float denom, t;

          /* Get plane eqn: ax + by + cz = 0 from two normals n1 and n2. */
          a = n1->y*n2->z - n1->z*n2->y;
          b = n1->z*n2->x - n1->x*n2->z;
          c = n1->x*n2->y - n1->y*n2->x;

          /* Set up line eqn of edge. */
          x0 = y0 = z0 = 0.; f = g = h = 0.;
          switch (edge) {

                    case edge01: x0 = z0 = 0.5; g = 1; break;
                    case edge02: y0 = z0 = 0.5; f = 1; break;
                    case edge03: x0 = -0.5; z0 = 0.5; g = 1; break;
                    case edge04: y0 = -0.5; z0 = 0.5; f = 1; break;
                    case edge12: x0 = y0 = 0.5; h = 1; break;
                    case edge23: x0 = -0.5; y0 = 0.5; h = 1; break;
                    case edge34: x0 = y0 = -0.5; h = 1; break;
                    case edge41: x0 = 0.5; y0 = -0.5; h = 1; break;
                    case edge51: x0 = 0.5; z0 = -0.5; g = 1; break;
                    case edge52: y0 = 0.5; z0 = -0.5; f = 1; break;
                    case edge53: x0 = z0 = -0.5; g = 1; break;
                    case edge54: y0 = z0 = -0.5; f = 1; break;

          }

          /* return intersection of plane and edge */
          denom = a*f+b*g+c*h;
          t = -(a*x0 + b*y0 + c*z0)/denom;
          pt->x = x0 + f*t;
          pt->y = y0 + g*t;
          pt->z = z0 + h*t;
}
/*

          project( ) projects the polygon described in the array cube [] onto
          a given face of the cube and converts into UVspace storing the
          results into the array uv[]

*/
```

Listing 6.3 cont.

```
void project (face)
int face;
{
     int i;

     switch (face) {

             case face0:
                     for (i = 0; i < cube_no; i++) {
                             uv[i][0] = -cube[i].x + 0.5;
                             uv[i][1] = cube[i].y + 0.5;
                     }
             break;

             case face1:
                     for (i = 0; i < cube_no; i++) {
                             uv[i][0] = cube[i].z + 0.5;
                             uv[i][1] = cube[i].y + 0.5;
                     }
             break;

             case face2:
                     for (i = 0; i < cube_no; i++) {
                             uv[i][0] = cube[i].x + 0.5;
                             uv[i][1] = cube[i].z + 0.5;
                     }
             break;

             case face3:
                     for (i = 0; i < cube_no; i++) {
                             uv[i][0] = -cube[i].z + 0.5;
                             uv[i][1] = cube[i].y + 0.5;
                     }
             break;

             case face4:
                     for (i = 0; i < cube_no; i++) {
                             uv[i][0] = cube[i].x + 0.5;
                             uv[i][1] = -cube[i].z + 0.5;
                     }
             break;

             case face5:
                     for (i = 0; i < cube_no; i++) {
                             uv[i][0] = cube[i].x + 0.5;
                             uv[i][1] = cube[i].y + 0.5;
                     }
             break;
     }
}
```

point $(x, -0.5, z)$ on this face into u, v-coordinates is thus given by:

$$u = x + 0.5$$
$$v = -z + 0.5$$

Unlike chrome mapping, the reflected vector must be in a coordinate frame whose axes are parallel to the axes of the environment map. Since the environment map is usually built by pointing the camera along the coordinate axes (in both directions) in world space, the reflected vector must also be in world space. Hence the need for *transform_vector( )* which works in the same way as *transform( )* except that it takes vectors from space to space instead of points from one space to another.

A word of caution: six mip-maps can make serious demands on memory. Plate 19 took a surprisingly long time to compute. Closer inspection revealed that whenever an environment-mapped spoon was small in screen space then, under such a pixel, the computer spent most of its time thrashing, as the six mip-maps being accessed in an effectively random order, were being constantly paged.

6.4 Bump mapping

Bump mapping, a technique developed by Blinn [BLIN78], is an elegant device that enables a surface to appear as if were wrinkled or dimpled without the need to model these depressions geometrically. Instead, the surface normal is angularly perturbed according to information given in a two-dimensional bump map and this 'tricks' a local reflection model, wherein intensity is a function mainly of the surface normal, into producing local variations on a smooth surface. The only problem with bump mapping is that because the pits or depressions do not exist in the model, a silhouette edge that appears to pass through a depression will not produce the expected cross-section. In other words the silhouette edge will follow the line of the model.

It is an important technique because it appears to texture a surface in the normal sense of the word rather than modulating the colour of a flat surface. Bump mapping has been used to emulate the bark on the branches of a tree [OPPE86]. Plate 20 shows another example, the bump map providing wavy lines of perturbations that simulate wrinkles in leather.

Texturing the surface in the rendering phase, without perturbing the geometry, bypasses serious modelling problems that would otherwise occur. If the object is polygonal the mesh would have to be fine enough to emulate the perturbations of the texture map – a serious imposition on the original modelling phase.

In implementing bump mapping, a scheme is required that perturbs the normal vector in a way that is independent of the orientation and position of the surface. For a particular point on the surface, the normal at that point must always receive the same perturbation. If this is not the case, then in an animation sequence the bump-mapped detail will animate as the object moves. This is achieved by basing the perturbation on a coordinate system based on local surface derivatives.

If $O(u, v)$ is a parametrized function representing the position vectors of points O on the surface of an object, then the normal to the surface at a point is given by:

$$N = O_u \times O_v$$

where O_u and O_v are the partial derivatives of the surface at point O lying in the tangent plane (Figure 6.14).

We define two other vectors that lie in the tangent plane. These are

$$A = N \times O_v$$

and

$$B = N \times O_u$$

D is the perturbation vector derived from components of these two vectors and summing D and N gives N', the perturbed vector:

$$N' = N + D$$

The vectors A, B and N form a coordinate system in which D is defined that is independent of the global orientation and position of the surface.

We now address the problem of the value of D. The components of D are given by:

$$D = B_u A - B_v B$$

where B_u and B_v are the partial derivatives of the bump map $B(u, v)$. Thus we define a bump map as a displacement function or height field but use its derivatives at the point (u, v) to calculate D. This can be shown as follows. Consider Figure 6.13 that shows a one-dimensional analogy or cross-section of the process. We first add a small increment, derived from the bump map $B(u, v)$ to $O(u, v)$ to define $O'(u, v)$:

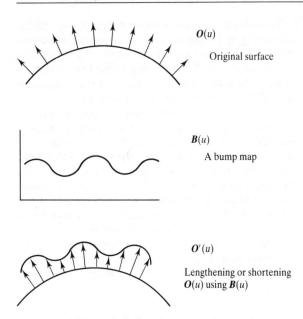

$O(u)$

Original surface

$B(u)$

A bump map

$O'(u)$

Lengthening or shortening $O(u)$ using $B(u)$

$N'(u)$

The vectors to the 'new' surface

Figure 6.13 A one-dimensional example of the stages involved in bump mapping (after [BLIN78b]).

$$O'(u, v) = O(u, v) + B(u, v)\frac{N}{|N|}$$

Now differentiating this equation gives:

$$O'_u = O_u + B_u\frac{N}{|N|} + B\left(\frac{N}{|N|}\right)u$$

$$O'_v = O_v + B_v\frac{N}{|N|} + B\left(\frac{N}{|N|}\right)v'$$

If B is small (that is, the bump map displacement function is small compared with its spatial extent) the last term in each equation can be ignored and

$$N'(u, v) = O_u \times O_v + B_u\left(\frac{N}{|N|} \times O_v\right) + B_v\left(O_u \times \frac{N}{|N|}\right)$$

$$+ B_u B_v\left(\frac{N \times N}{|N|^2}\right)$$

The first term is the normal to the surface and the last term is zero, giving:

$$D = B_u(N \times O_v) - B_v(N \times O_u) \qquad \text{where } N/|N| \text{ is written as } N$$

or

$$D = B_u A - B_v B$$

A geometric interpretation of this is given in Figure 6.14. D is a vector in the plane of A and B whose components are given by B_u and $-B_v$. N' is then given by:

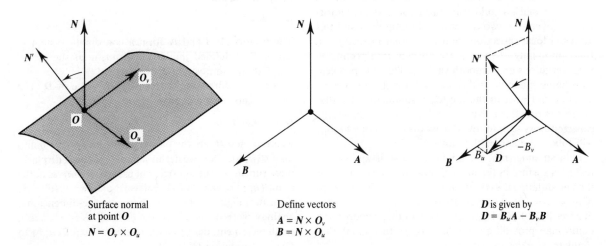

Surface normal at point O

$N = O_v \times O_u$

Define vectors

$A = N \times O_v$
$B = N \times O_u$

D is given by
$D = B_u A - B_v B$

Figure 6.14 Geometric interpretation of bump mapping.

$$N' = N + D$$

which is the required result.

One of the problems of bump mapping examined by Blinn is its dependence on the scale of the object. If the surface definition function is scaled by a factor of two then the length of the normal vector is scaled by four, but the length of D is only scaled by two. This is because the object is scaled but the displacement function B is not. The effect of this is to smooth out the wrinkles as the surface is stretched – clearly undesirable. Blinn suggests deriving a D which is scale invariant:

$$D' = a D \frac{|N|}{|D|}$$

A choice for the value of a is given as

$$a = \left(B_u^2 + B_v^2 \right)^{1/2}$$

Blinn also discusses the anti-aliasing problem, pointing out that the normal techniques for anti-aliasing texture mapping, described in Chapter 4, are not relevant because the bump map displacement values are not linearly related to the final intensity values. Filtering the bump map will simply smooth out the bumps and the only alternative is to map at subpixel resolution and average. However, this is clearly a very expensive operation and Blinn does claim that some improvement can be obtained by area filtering the bump map.

Another approach to wrinkling a surface is to use displacement maps where a two-dimensional height field is used to perturb a surface point along the direction of its surface normal. The major practical difference between this method and bump mapping is the difficulty in incorporating it in a standard polygon mesh renderer. Bump mapping can be merged into a normal interpolation scheme and the same polygonal model can be used to produce both a smooth object and a bump-mapped object. For polygonal objects, displacement mapping is most easily incorporated into the modelling phase. Displacement mapping need only be considered when the detail must be made visible on silhouette edges otherwise bump mapping is preferable.

7 Procedural texture mapping and modelling

This chapter deals with procedural modelling and procedural texture generation. An important procedural modelling technique, and one that has a claim to generality, is Fourier synthesis. Fourier theory is dealt with in some detail in Chapter 4. Fourier techniques are also used in Chapter 18 (Procedural animation). They are particularly amenable to animation. Anti-aliasing of solid textures is covered in Chapter 4.

Introduction

Procedural modelling techniques are now well established in computer graphics. Possibly the most common and most successful is the use of fractal techniques to generate terrain. We can identify two motivations for using procedural modelling in computer graphics. First, if we can model an object or a phenomenon from a procedure and a parameter set then we can use time-varying parameters to generate an animation sequence. (Examples of procedural modelling used in animation are given in the related material in Chapter 18. In this chapter we shall concentrate on static models except for the example in Section 7.2.3.) The second motivation for this type of modelling is low-cost visual complexity. A model consisting of highly detailed mountain terrain generated by fractal subdivision is a good example here. The terrain may consist of thousands of polygons resulting in a three-dimensional object that would be virtually impossible to build in any other way. In addition, of course, we would

expect to generate many different geometric instances of a terrain model by appropriate variations of parameter sets or initial values. This production of 'cheap' complexity was called 'database amplification' by Smith [SMIT84].

Despite the many impressive images produced by such techniques, an obvious drawback of them is their inevitable specificity. The techniques, which are theoretically disparate to a large extent, have evolved to satisfy narrow application areas. Fractal subdivision is good for mountain terrain and little else. Even different terrain demands a different model. (Gardener, for example, uses Fourier techniques for gentler landscapes [GARD84].) Particle techniques are superb for such phenomena as waterfalls and fireworks. For certain botanical models generative grammars are useful. To a great extent this model specificity is inevitable. The geometric forms and complexities of entities in nature are gloriously diverse and we would expect mathematical models to reflect this fact. At the moment, the most powerful approach, in terms of the potential diversity of models that it can handle, is one that preceded computer graphics by a century or so. This is the use of the Fourier domain (see Section 7.3).

Closely related to procedural modelling techniques is the use of a procedure to define texture. This approach has proved to be a powerful method for generating textures of different dimensionality. Again the method suffers from the constraints of the specificity of the definition.

Reflecting the specificity of current models, this chapter will concentrate on detailing a number of different procedural approaches to the generation of imagery. Rather than attempt to categorize or unify these techniques theoretically, we will categorize them by application area. This chapter then consists of a list of the most popular approaches to procedural modelling.

7.1 Fractal-based terrain generation

Now one of the most ubiquitous techniques in computer graphics, this is a subdivision technique that generates a three-dimensional terrain model as a polygon-based object. The number of polygons can be very large and is controlled by the depth of the subdivision. The resulting model does not require any specialized rendering techniques and can be injected into a standard polygon mesh renderer.

The term 'fractal' was originally coined by Benoit Mandelbrot [MAND77, MAND82]. It was used to describe a particular attribute of certain natural phenomena. For example, an aerial view of a coastline will tend to exhibit a so-called statistical self-similarity that is independent of the scale of the image. A characteristic jaggedness will be seen whether the view is from 5 miles up or 5 metres up and this will continue down to a microscopic level. Fractal geometry provides an analytical framework for certain aspects of this ubiquitous phenomenon in nature.

In computer graphics the term 'fractal' is used somewhat loosely and has been extended beyond Mandelbrot's original definition but this technicality need not concern us here.

To create a three-dimensional terrain model we start with some coarse approximation to the final landscape – say, for example, a pyramid to simulate a moun-

tain – and then recursively subdivide each facet in the original model to the required depth or level of detail. Clearly subdivision in this context means both splitting the polygon into smaller and smaller parts and, at the same time, spatially perturbing these parts. The initial gross shape of the object is retained to an extent that depends on the perturbation applied at each subdivision level.

The amount of detail created by the perturbation has to be in proportion to the scale over which the perturbation is carried out. Thus, central to the working of fractal subdivision is the modification of the scale of the perturbation at a given level as a function of that level. The higher the level, the smaller is the perturbation. If this were not the case mountains would get higher and higher. Mathematically, the recursion can be thought of as a geometric progression which has to converge to a finite limit.

The subdivision algorithm most commonly used was developed by Fournier *et al.* [FOUR82] and this is most easily explained by looking at the subdivision of a line rather than a polygon. This algorithm was developed as a cheap alternative to the more rigorous procedures suggested by Mandelbrot. It uses self-similarity and conditional expectation properties of fractional Brownian motion to give an estimate of the increment that is used in the line subdivision.

Consider the line (t_i, f_i), (t_{i+1}, f_{i+1}) shown in Figure 7.1. We wish to subdivide this line by perturbing its midpoint in a direction normal to the line. This pro-

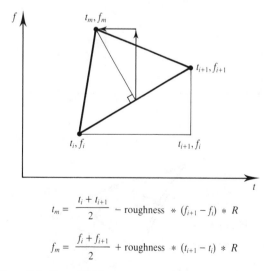

$$t_m = \frac{t_i + t_{i+1}}{2} - \text{roughness} * (f_{i+1} - f_i) * R$$

$$f_m = \frac{f_i + f_{i+1}}{2} + \text{roughness} * (t_{i+1} - t_i) * R$$

Figure 7.1 Line subdivision.

duces two new lines which, with the original line, form an isosceles triangle. This procedure is adopted so that the displacement depends on the orientation of the line segment, and is not tied to the coordinate system in which the line is embedded. The recursive formula that subdivides such a line segment is:

$$t_m = \frac{t_i + t_{i+1}}{2} - \text{roughness} * \left(f_{i+1} - f_i\right) * R$$

$$f_m = \frac{f_i + f_{i+1}}{2} + \text{roughness} * \left(t_{i+1} - t_i\right) * R$$

where:

R is a random number in the range -1 to $+1$

'roughness' determines the extent of the perturbation – a parameter of the procedure in which the recursive formula is embedded

Note that here the perturbation automatically decreases as the recursion level increases, since it is scaled by the length of the line – the smaller the line, the smaller the perturbation. To see how to extend this technique to polygon objects that consist of, say, triangles, we consider a single triangle in world space. This represents a single facet in the object. We form four subdivision products by connecting the edge midpoints together and, at the same time, displacing each midpoint along a line normal to the plane of the original triangle (Figure 7.2).

There are two difficulties that emerge from this

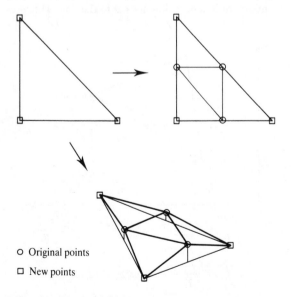

○ Original points

□ New points

Figure 7.2 Triangle subdivision.

method. These are categorized by Fournier as internal and external consistency problems. Internal consistency requires that the shape generated should be the same irrespective of the orientation of the object that is subject to the subdivision. Also, coarser details should remain the same if the object is rendered at a higher resolution. To satisfy internal consistency, the random numbers generated must not be a function of the position of the points, but should be unique to the point itself. We need to associate an invariant point identifier with each point. In terrain generation this problem can be solved by giving each point a key value that is used to index a Gaussian random number generator. A hash function can be used to map the two keys of the end points of a line to a key value for the midpoint. Scale requirements of internal consistency mean that the same random numbers must always be generated in the same order at a given level of subdivision.

External consistency is harder to maintain. Within the mesh of triangles every triangle shares each of its sides with another and the same random displacements must be generated for corresponding points of different connecting triangles. This is already solved by using the key value of each point and the hash function, but another problem still exists – that of the direction of the displacement.

To prevent gaps opening up, we have to arrange that the direction of displacement out of a shared edge is along a normal that is the average of the normals of the polygons that contribute to the edge – exactly the strategy that is adopted in Gouraud shading. This problem arises at each level of subdivision and extending the averaging strategy down through all subdivision levels is expensive. An easier and cheaper solution is to use a displacement that is always normal to the plane of the original polygon.

So far nothing has been said about the termination criteria used for fractal subdivision. Let us return, for a moment, to the coastline example mentioned at the start of this section. Whether 5 miles away or 5 metres away, the self-similarity property means that the coastline will look more or less the same. But at 5 miles distant the eye will not be able to pick out the detail visible at 5 metres – this detail is simply too small to see. This suggests that the termination criteria should be based on the distance between the terrain and the eye or, in other words, screen driven.

Fractal polygons are input to a renderer at their coarsest level of detail and the subdivision proceeds within the renderer. Termination occurs when subdivision of a given element results in a shaded value which is the same as that obtained from shading the element without subdivision. Many texts state (incorrectly) that this is equivalent to stopping the subdivision when the element projected onto the screen subtends an area less than one pixel. Great care must be taken to employ a correct set of termination criteria when rendering fractals.

Whatever the criteria used, subdivision invariably proceeds *within* the renderer which reads in the raw model only. Were this not the case, that is, if the fractal was subdivided down to its final form outside the renderer and then read in, memory and file I/O demands would be excessive. The renderer generates detail only when it is needed for a given pixel, thereby mimimizing memory overheads. Now the renderer needs to calculate, for all objects that fall within the viewing frustum, their projection on the screen.

Finding this projection for fractal elements is not as straightforward as finding the projection of a normal polygon, since, unlike a polygon, the final physical representation of the fractal is not fully determined until after the final subdivision has occurred. So the renderer, when shading a given pixel, has to process all fractal elements that *might* affect the value of that pixel. Recall that the sum of the perturbations, applied at every level of subdivision, can be thought of as making up a geometric progression that must converge, hence at any given level the fractal can be bounded in space. It is the projection of the bounding box on the screen that marks out what pixels it may affect. Figure 7.3 shows this working in conjunction with a scan line based renderer. Here the bound for the element in question is given by R and the projection of this box onto the screen enables us to 'hang' the fractal element off the correct scan line. A similar technique of projecting bounding volumes for rendering objects can be found in Chapter 18, where the

element to be rendered is a section of water that is offset by travelling sine waves.

7.1.1 Visual defects in fractal terrains

One of the visual defects that exist in fractal landscapes is 'creases'. Because of the nature of the method, original polygons, prior to subdivision, tend to be large; the purpose of the method is to create a detailed model from a gross original shape. Now any vertex in the model is displaced once only and subdivision edges will align themselves along the original polygon edges resulting in creases; despite the detail in the subdivision this alignment of edges is noticeable, particularly from a high view point. The original (unsubdivided) model survives in the detail. A crude practical remedy to this is to hide the landscape with fog. This diminishes the creasing problem and also allows the subdivision to stop at a lower level.

A problem arises in animation if the subdivision criterion is screen driven – for example, subdivide until the area of the polygon is less than one pixel. In this case, when the polygon moves, a situation easily occurs where polygons are subdivided to a different level in different frames. This results in a characteristic bubbling effect in the sequence.

The problem of creasing, in common with most artefacts in computer graphics, becomes glaringly noticeable when the terrains are used in an animated sequence. Although creasing may be tolerable in a static image, it is certainly a problem in animated sequences. A solution to the creasing problem is given in [MILL86].

Plate 21 shows fractal terrains generated using the subdivision method and are two frames from an animated sequence – a flight over a model of Korea. This pair shows the effect of different viewing distances. The original model for this sequence was built from large-scale geographical data by using data from maps.

Plate 22 shows a view up a valley with fog used to diminish the visibility of the creases, as we discussed.

7.2 Three-dimensional texture domain techniques

In Chapter 6 we introduced ad hoc texture mapping techniques that forced a degree of generality on specific

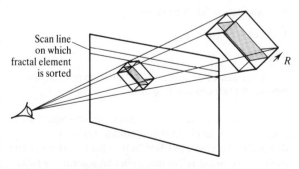

Figure 7.3 Screen projection of fractal element.

mapping functions such as the cylindrical projection function. We stated that although mapping a two-dimensional texture pattern onto an object was a popular technique, it suffered from the constraint that it was difficult to map such a pattern onto an object of arbitrary shape. The reasons for this are twofold:

1. Two-dimensional texture mapping based on a surface coordinate system can produce large variations in the compression of the texture that reflect a corresponding variation in the curvature of the surface.

2. Attempting to texture map continuously the surface of an object possessing a nontrivial topology can quickly become very awkward. Textural continuity across surface elements that can be of a different type and can connect together in any ad hoc manner is problematic to maintain.

Three-dimensional texture mapping neatly circumvents these problems since the only information required to assign a point a texture value is its *position* in space. Assigning an object a texture just involves evaluating a three-dimensional texture function at the surface points of the object.

The method is to define procedurally a texture field in object space. Given a point (x, y, z) on the surface of an object, the colour is defined as $T(x, y, z)$, where T is the value of texture field. That is, we simply use the identity mapping (possibly in conjunction with a scaling):

$$u = x \quad v = y \quad w = z$$

where

(u, v, w) is a coordinate in the texture field

This can be considered analogous actually to sculpting or carving an object out of a block of material. The colour of the object is determined by the intersection of its surface with the texture field. The method was reported simultaneously by Perlin [PERL85] and Peachey [PEAC85] wherein the term 'solid texture' was coined.

The procedural nature of the texture definition is a mandatory aspect of the method. The memory costs involved in storing a high-resolution three-dimensional texture field would be prohibitive. The disadvantage of the technique is that although it eliminates mapping problems, the texture patterns themselves are limited to whatever definition you can analytically construct. This contrasts with a two-dimensional texture map; here *any* texture can be set up by using, say, a frame-grabbed image from a television camera.

We begin by illustrating the technique using two examples of simple procedural definitions. First, consider Plate 23. In this trivial example, 125 cubes were rendered and the single colour of each cube was obtained by the identity mapping between the coordinate of a reference vertex on each cube and the corresponding RGB value in an RGB cube defined exactly over the domain of the scene.

The second example (Plate 24) uses a more complicated geometry for the texture definition. The idea here is to simulate wood grain by using a set of concentric cylinders. These are defined such that if (x, y, z) is in the space of any cylinder, the colour is dark, otherwise it is light. Interest can be added to the effect by three simple extensions: tilting the long axis of the cylinders with respect to the long dimension of the wood block, and perturbing and twisting the cylinders. The example demonstrates how you can build up a three-dimensional texture definition in stages, each step further elaborating the definition. First, we make the field a modular function of r, the radius of the cylinder. For a particular cylinder we have:

$$r_1 = \left(u^2 + w^2\right)^{1/2}$$

Second, we can perturb r with a sinusoidal function, or with any function that simulates the deviation of wood growth away from a perfect cylinder:

$$r_2 = r_1 + 2\sin\left(a\theta\right)$$

then we can apply a small twist along the axis of the cylinders:

$$r_2 = r_1 + 2\sin\left(a\theta + v/b\right)$$

where:

a, b are constants
$\theta = \tan^{-1}\left(u/w\right)$

We can then index the texture by

$$(x, y, z) = \text{tilt}\left(u, v, w\right)$$

where:

'tilt' is any desired tilt function implementing any rotation between the two coordinate systems

In this example we have used a three-dimensional texture field to model an effect that would in reality be a three-dimensional texture. In Plate 24 the visible texture on the ends of the wood is circular – the end grain – whereas the grain tends to run along the side faces of the block.

This effect would be tedious to model using two-dimensional texture mapping.

In 1989 Perlin [PERL89] extended the solid texture technique and developed a method that he called 'hypertexture'. The distinction between the two approaches is in the nature of the object definition and the rendering method. In the solid texture approach a three-dimensional texture field is used to evaluate the texture of a solid object at its (well-defined) surface. With hypertexture the object has no surface. Instead it is defined as a density function and the texture is evaluated throughout the entire space of the object and rendered using a volume rendering algorithm (Chapter 13). Perlin uses this approach to produce such effects as hair, fur, fire, glass, fluid flow and erosion effects, and states in [PERL89]:

> Many objects, such as fur or woven materials, have a complex definition which is at best awkward, and at worst impossible to describe by a surface model. For other objects, such as eroded materials or fluids, a highly complex boundary is actually an artefact of a process that is often more readily described volumetrically. Still other objects such as flame, clouds or smoke, do not have a well defined boundary at all.

The method is both a modelling and a texture technique. The object is modelled using an 'object density function' $D(X)$ which describes the density of a three-dimensional shape for all points X in the object. This function defines a 'soft' region of the object and may surround a solid (opaque) core. Within the soft region a 'density modulation function' is applied to model the form of the texture. A $D(X)$ may be defined in terms of the three-dimensional noise function described in the next section.

To create a particular effect, density modulation functions are nested (compare with the nested development of the wood grain example in this section) and the hypertexture is defined by:

$$H(D(X), X) = f_n(\ldots, f_2(f_1(f_0(D(X)))))$$

where f_i are the density modulation functions.

7.2.1 Three-dimensional noise

A popular class of procedural texturing techniques all have in common the fact that they use a three-dimensional or spatial noise function as a basic model-ling primitive. These techniques, the most notable of which is the simulation of turbulence (discussed in the next section), can produce a surprising variety of realistic, natural-looking texture effects. In this section we will concern ourselves with the issues involved in the algorithmic generation of the basic primitive – solid noise.

Perlin [PERL85] was the first to suggest this application of noise, defining a function noise( ) that takes a three-dimensional position as its input and returns a single scalar value. Ideally, the function should possess the following three properties:

1. statistical invariance under rotation;

2. statistical invariance under translation;

3. a narrow bandpass limit in frequency.

The first two conditions ensure that the noise function is controllable, that is, no matter how we move or orientate the noise function in space, its general appearance is guaranteed to stay the same. The third condition enables us to sample the noise function without aliasing. While an insufficiently sampled noise function may not produce noticeable defects in static images, if used in animation applications, incorrectly sampled noise will produce a shimmering or bubbling effect. (This is similar to the bubbling of moving fractals discussed in Section 7.1.1. They also generate detail through the use of random numbers.)

Perlin's method of generating noise is to define an integer lattice, or a set of points in space, situated at locations (i, j, k) where i, j and k are all integers. Each point of the lattice has a random number associated with it. This can be done either by using a simple lookup table or, as Perlin suggests, via a hashing function to save space. The value of the noise function, at a point in space coincident with a lattice point, is just this random number. For points in space not on the lattice the noise value is obtained by interpolation from the nearby lattice points.

Figure 7.4(a) shows a piece of two-dimensional noise produced using the code given in Listing 7.1. For simplicity the implementation is in two dimensions – the extension to three dimensions being trivial. The function *linear_noise( )* returns a value obtained by bilinear interpolation, first in the direction of u and then in the direction of v, of a two-dimensional integer lattice represented by the array of random numbers *noise[i][j]*, $0 \leqslant i, j <$ *Size*. Modulus arithmetic modulo *Size* is used to wrap around the lattice enabling us to define noise, albeit somewhat repetitively, over the entire plane. The direc-

Listing 7.1 turbulence.c

```c
#define SIZE 575

        extern float noise[SIZE][SIZE];
        extern float scale,pixel_size ;


float turbulence(u,v)
float u,v;
{
        float t = 0.;
        float linear_noise();

        while (scale > pixel_size) {

                t += linear_noise(u/scale,v/scale)*scale;
                scale /= 2.;
        }
        return(t);
}


float linear_noise(u,v)
float u,v;
{
        int iu,iv,ip,iq;
        float du,dv,bot,top;

        iu = u;
        iv = v;
        du = u-iu;
        dv = v-iv;

        iu = iu % SIZE;
        iv = iv % SIZE;
        ip = (iu+1) % SIZE;
        iq = (iv+1) % SIZE;

        bot = noise[iu][iv] + du*(noise[ip][iv]-noise[iu][iv]);
        top = noise[iu][iq] + du*(noise[ip][iq]-noise[iu][iq]);

        return(bot+dv*(top-bot));

}
```

tional artefacts in Figure 7.4(a) are apparent and these result from the discontinuity in gradient of bilinear interpolation as it crosses different regions delineated by the lattice points. (Note that, once again, there are parallels with fractals, *vis-à-vis* the creasing effect discussed in Section 7.1.1.) Replacing linear interpolation by cubic interpolation improves the situation to a degree,

although the directional artefacts are still apparent. Figure 7.4(b) shows the noise pattern produced by the same noise lattice as was used for Figure 7.4(a), but this time the lattice values are used as control points for a B-spline interpolation scheme along the two axes.

These directional artefacts, to which the human visual system is particularly sensitive, show up a flaw in the

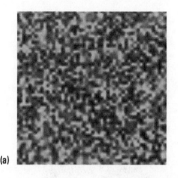
(a)

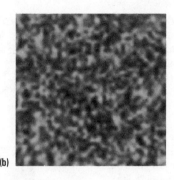
(b)

Figure 7.4   The three-dimensional noise function. (a) A section through the three-dimensional function obtained by linear interpolation. (b) A section through the three-dimensional noise function using B-spline interpolation.

sense that the above property (statistical invariance under rotation) is no longer satisfied. Lewis [LEWI89] states that whatever the interpolation scheme (Perlin employs Hermite interpolation), if it is carried out in several dimensions, using a separable tensor product of a one-dimensional interpolation that acts along the preferred direction of the coordinate axes, then directional artefacts are unavoidable. Lewis offers two alternative algorithms for synthesizing solid noise, based on signal processing techniques, that are artefact free. However, for practical purposes, it is worthwhile bearing in mind that providing you are not rendering noise directly, the procedural transformation it undergoes in most texturing applications can disguise these directional trends. This includes the application to turbulence that we now discuss.

7.2.2 Simulating turbulence

A single piece of noise can be put to use to simulate a remarkable number of effects. By far the most versatile of its applications is the use of the so-called turbulence function, as defined by Perlin, which takes a position x and returns a turbulent scalar value. It is written in terms of the progression (a two-dimensional version of which is coded in Listing 7.1):

$$\text{turbulence}\left(x\right) = \sum_{i=0}^{k} \text{abs} \left(\frac{\text{noise}\left(2^{i}x\right)}{2^{i}} \right)$$

The summation is truncated at k which is the smallest integer satisfying

$$\frac{1}{2^{k+1}} < \text{the size of a pixel}$$

The truncation band limits the function ensuring proper anti-aliasing. Consider the difference between the first

two terms in the progression, noise (x) and noise $(2\,x)/2$. The noise function in the latter term will vary twice as fast as the first – it has twice the frequency – and will contain features that are half the size of the first. Moreover, its contribution to the final value for the turbulence is also scaled by one half. This should sound familiar – at each scale of detail the amount of noise added to the series is proportional to the scale of detail of the noise and inversely proportional to the frequency of the noise. It is just self-similarity again and is analogous to the self-similarity obtained through fractal subdivision, except that this time the subdivision does not drive displacement, but octaves of noise, producing a function that exhibits the same noisy behaviour over a range of scales. That this function should prove so useful is best seen from the point of view of signal analysis, which tells us that the power spectrum of *turbulence ( )* obeys a $1/f$ power law, thereby loosely approximating the $1/f^{2}$ power law of Brownian motion.

The turbulence function in isolation represents only half the story, however. Rendering the turbulence function directly results in a homogeneous pattern that could not be described as naturalistic. This is because most textures which occur naturally contain some nonhomogeneous structural features and so cannot be simulated by turbulence alone. Take marble, for example, which has easily distinguished veins of colour running through it that were made turbulent before the marble solidified during an earlier geological era. In the light of this fact we can identify two distinct stages in the process of simulating turbulence – they are:

1. Representation of the basic, first-order, structural features of a texture through some basic functional form. Typically the function is continuous and contains significant variations in its first derivatives.

2. Addition of second and higher order detail by using turbulence to perturb the parameters of the function.

The classic example, as first described by Perlin, is the turbulation of a sine wave to give the appearance of marble. Unperturbed, the colour veins running through the marble are given by a sine wave passing through a colour map. For a sine wave running along the x-axis we write:

$$\text{marble}(x) = \text{marble\_colour}\left(\sin(x)\right)$$

The colour map *marble_colour( )* is a spline, mapping a scalar input to an intensity. Visualizing this expression, Figure 7.5(a) is a two-dimensional slice of marble rendered with the colour spline given in Figure 7.5(b). Next we add turbulence:

$$\text{marble}(x) = \text{marble\_colour}\left(\sin(x + \text{turbulence}(x))\right)$$

to give us Figure 7.5(c), a most convincing simulation of marble texture. Figure 7.6 is rather inferior and grainier and was obtained by replacing the spline in *marble_colour( )* with a straight line, thus making the intensity values proportional to input. We can conclude from this that the variation of the derivative of the colour map plays a vital role in the synthesis of the pattern – regions where the intensity varies sharply delineate between the basic marble colour and the veins running through it. Plate 25 shows the effect in three dimensions: *marble _colour( )* is now made up of three separate splines, one for each of the R, G, B components.

Of course, use of the turbulence function need not be restricted to modulate just the colour of an object. Any

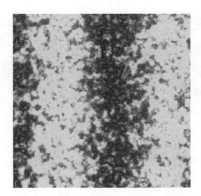

Figure 7.6 The effect obtained by using a straight line, instead of a spline, to modulate intensity (compare with Figure 7.5).

parameter that affects the appearance of an object can be turbulated. Oppenheimer [OPPE86] turbulates a sawtooth function to bump map the ridges of bark on a tree. An example of turbulence driving the transparency of an object is given in Plate 26. The clouds are modelled by texturing an opacity map onto a sphere that is concentric with the Earth. The opacity map was created on a paint program; clouds are represented as white blobs with soft edges that fade into complete transparency. These edges become turbulent after perturbation of the texture coordinates.

(a)

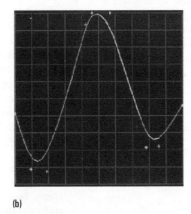

(b)

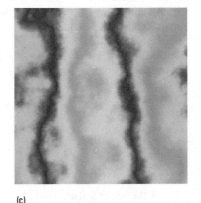

(c)

Figure 7.5 Simulating marble – see also Plate 25. (a) Unturbulated slice obtained by using the spline shown in Figure 7.5(b). (b) Colour spline used to produce Figure 7.5(a). (c) Marble section obtained by turbulating the slice shown in Figure 7.5(a).

7.2.3 Animating turbulence

We conclude our discussion on turbulence with an example of how to animate it. The turbulence function can be defined over time as well as space simply by adding an extra dimension representing time to the noise integer lattice. So the lattice points will now be specified by the indices (i, j, k, l) enabling us to extend the parameter list to noise (x, t) and similarly for turbulence (x, t). Internal to these procedures the time axis is not treated any differently than the three spatial axes.

We want to simulate fire, so the first thing that we do is to try to represent its basic form functionally, that is a 'flame shape'. The completely ad hoc nature of this functional sculpting is apparent here. The final form decided on was simply that which, after experimentation, gave the best results. We shall work in two-space owing to the expense of the three-dimensional volumetric approach referred to at the end of the last section.

A flame region is defined in the x,y-plane by the rectangle with minimax coordinates $(-b, 0)$, (b, h). Within this region the flame's colour is given by:

$$\text{flame}(x) = (1 - y/h)\,\text{flame\_colour}(\text{abs}(x/b))$$

This is shown schematically in Figure 7.7. *flame_colour (x)* consists of three separate colour splines that map a scalar value x to a colour vector. Each of the R, G, B splines has a maximum intensity at $x = 0$ which corresponds to the centre of the flame and a fade off to zero intensity at $x = 1$. The green and blue splines go to zero faster than the red. The colour returned by *flame_colour( )* is weighted according to its height from the base of the flame to get an appropriate variation along y. The flame is rendered by applying *flame( )* to colour a rectangular polygon that covers the region of the flame's definition. The opacity of the polygon is also textured by

using a similar functional construction. The result is shown in Plate 27 (top); below, the turbulated counterpart is obtained by introducing the turbulence function thus:

$$\text{flame}(x, t) = (1 - y/h)\,\text{flame\_colour}(\text{abs}(x/b) + \text{turbulence}(x, t))$$

Plate 28 shows an animated sequence of a flame positioned in a scene. The supposed flickering reflection of it on the walls is simulated by a separate, wobbling light source. Since we are rendering only two dimensions, the process can be visualized with a piece of three-dimensional noise, replacing the z-axis with time. We are simply rendering successive slices of noise which are perpendicular to the time axis and equispaced by an amount corresponding to the frame interval. It is as if we are translating the polygon along the time axis. We discovered, however, that mere translation in time is not enough; recognizable detail in the flame, though changing shape with time, remained curiously static in space. This is because there is a general sense of direction associated with a flame; convection sends detail upwards. This was simulated, and immediately gave better results, by moving the polygon down in y as well as through time, as shown in Figure 7.8. The final construction is thus:

$$\text{flame}(x, t) = (1 - y/h)\,\text{flame\_colour}(\text{abs}(x/b) + \text{turbulence}(x + (0, t\Delta y, 0), t))$$

where Δy is the distance moved in y by the polygon relative to the noise per unit time.

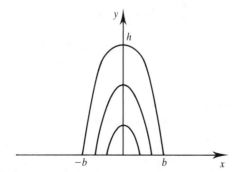

Figure 7.7 Flame function.

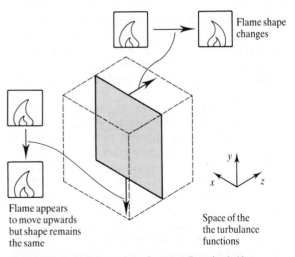

Figure 7.8 Animating turbulence for a two-dimensional object.

7.3 Fourier synthesis

Fourier synthesis is one of the most general and powerful techniques that can be applied to both modelling and the generation of texture patterns. In Chapter 18 (Procedural animation) we look at the special case of Fourier synthesis used to generate wind-perturbed water waves, and this context is described in some detail. In this section we will describe the general approach of Fourier synthesis.

Fourier synthesis in computer graphics appears to have been first used by Schachter [SCHA80] to generate a two-dimensional texture pattern for use in flight simulators. In this application, the amplitude of spatial frequencies $F(u, v)$, sometimes called long-crested waves, are used to provide a two-dimensional procedural texture which is then pasted onto a flat plane to simulate the texture of terrain. A pattern is produced by a summation of a number of component waves of varying frequency and phase. In Chapter 18 we use the amplitude of $F(u, v)$ as a height field to model the geometry of water waves. These then are two examples of Fourier synthesis in the two-dimensional Fourier domain used both for modelling and to provide a texture pattern.

More generally we can use summations of three-dimensional frequency components to model three-dimensional objects and provide three-dimensional texture field definitions. Gardener in particular has specialized in this field [GARD84, GARD85 and GARD88], simulating clouds by using a Fourier-synthesized three-dimensional texture field to modulate the shading and transparency of clouds and to model landscapes and trees. This gives some idea of the generality of Fourier synthesis against which the specificity of fractal terrain generation seems rather restricting.

Fourier synthesis can be approached either by manipulations in the space domain or by manipulations in the Fourier domain followed by a reverse Fourier transform (see Chapter 4 for further details on Fourier theory). The difference is shown schematically in Figure 7.9 (see also Figure 4.6). This shows the possible approaches that we might adopt to define a $T(x, y)$ – a two-dimensional texture definition – by combining spatial frequency components. If we are working in the space domain the user has the notion of a sum of a set of sinusoidal corrugations. In the upper illustration, these are represented as a set of parallel lines (to indicate

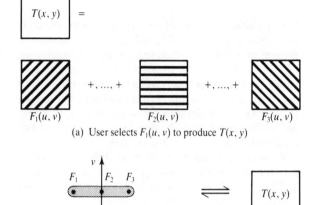

(a) User selects $F_i(u, v)$ to produce $T(x, y)$

(b) User selects an *area* in $F(u, v)$ space to produce $T(x, y)$

Figure 7.9   Fourier synthesis can be 'driven' from the space domain or the Fourier domain.

the peaks and troughs). The coefficients of the summation are varied by altering the relative amplitude of the individual components, the orientation (of their peaks and troughs) and their phase. Alternatively we can work directly in the Fourier domain, selecting certain areas which we know, a priori, will result in a pattern of a certain textural nature.

Gardener adopts the first approach using the following expression for three-dimensional Fourier synthesis:

$$T(x, y, z) = \sum_{i=1}^{n} C_i \left[\cos\left(\omega_{xi} x + \phi_{xi} \right) + A_0 \right]$$
$$\sum_{i=1}^{n} C_i \left[\cos\left(\omega_{yi} y + \phi_{yi} \right) + A_0 \right]$$
$$\sum_{i=1}^{n} C_i \left[\cos\left(\omega_{zi} z + \phi_{zi} \right) + A_0 \right] \quad \textbf{(7.1)}$$

where:

$C_{i+1} \approx 0.707 C_i$

$\omega_{xi+1} \approx 2\omega_i$ (similarly for ω_{yi+1} and ω_{zi+1})

$\phi_{xi+1} \approx \pi/2 \cos\left(\phi_{zi} z \right)$

$\phi_{yi+1} \approx \pi/2 \cos\left(\phi_{xi} x \right)$

$\phi_{zi+1} \approx \pi/2 \cos\left(\phi_{yi} y \right)$

$A_0 \quad \approx 1$

Gardener calls this a 'spectral function' and it is one of an infinity of particular combinations of harmonic functions. In other words, a particular set of $F_i(u, v)$ are selected and are specified in such a way as to allow for parametric variation. It is important to realise that this is not a general Fourier synthesis technique, but the fine-tuning of one particular spectral function. We can easily see the nature of the function in two-space. If we leave out all the fine-tuning parameters and set $i = 1$ we have:

$$T(x, y) = \cos(\omega_1 x)\cos(\omega_1 y)$$

That is a regular array of sinusoidal bumps or, in terms of Figure 7.9, the product of two long-crested waves $F(0, v)$ and $F(v, 0)$. Fine-tuning the parameters in Equation (7.1) transforms this basic pattern into a surprising number of variations.

This function was used to model the amorphous shapes of trees and clouds. A basic geometric primitive of an ellipsoid had both its surface shading and its transparency modulated by this function. The shaggy boundary of the trees and clouds is captured by the transparency modulation.

A further generalization afforded by Fourier synthesis is suggested by Gardener [GARD88]. He distinguishes between two modelling requirements: 'micromodelling needed to represent the intricate detail of natural features such as the leaves on trees and wrinkles in the terrain, and macromodelling needed to represent large scale structure in nature, such as the major topography of hills and the clustering of trees'. In addition he suggests how Fourier synthesis can be used, not only to model the trees themselves, but also to control their placement in the terrain.

7.4 Grammar-based modelling

The next technique that we shall examine in this chapter is that of grammar-based modelling. Like all techniques described in this chapter, grammar-based modelling possesses a specificity, and up to now these techniques have mainly been used to model trees and plants.

First described from the computer graphics view point by Smith [SMIT84], most work in this field is based on a parallel graph grammar, developed by Lindenmayer [LIND68], called an L-system. Basically this is a system that specifies a construction such as a plant or a tree, as a sentence (a series of words or some other notation) in the language that the grammar defines. The grammar is specified as a set of pictorial rewrite rules, and a parser based on these rules converts the sentence into the image.

Although most systems that have been developed could be said to be based on an L-system, the precise or rigid nature of formal grammar systems makes them unwieldy as generators of complex plant models. Algorithms that model plants and trees are best described as procedures, implementing rewrite rules, but allowing complex visual attributes and the probabilistic rather than the deterministic application of the production rules. We will now look at two examples that illustrate these points.

First, consider a simple *n*-ary tree made up of straight lines (Figure 7.10). The basic rewrite rule is:

Tree :: = branch + tree

or in words: 'a tree is a branch with a tree on the end of it'. Thus we see that a production rule contains graphics primitives together with spatial operators that specify a spatial relationship between the primitives.

Figure 7.10 was generated by a simple recursive procedure that implements the above rule together with the following enhancements. The figures in the left-hand column were generated from the basic production, but the number of branches and the angles between them were allowed to vary amongst the figures. The figures in the right-hand column were generated by injecting a random perturbation into the branch length and angle.

This trivial two-dimensional illustration shows how a grammar controls the underlying structure. To turn this into a tree modeller we need to specify productions in three-space and give the primitives complex attributes, such as: the branches are cylinders with bending; diameter reduction as a function of length; bark texture.

An impressive and instructive example of tree modelling is given in [BLOO85]. Here we see an ad hoc approach to modelling a maple tree. There is no explicit attempt at generalization, and ad hoc solutions were sought for each aspect of the modelling. For example, branches were modelled by sweeping circles along a spline, the bark texture was bump mapped, the leaves were texture mapped from photographs, and so on.

In contrast, in de Reffye's work [DERE88] the modelling is more formalized and growth/age is simulated. This approach enables the author to generate a wide variety of different tree species. Plate 29 shows examples created using this approach.

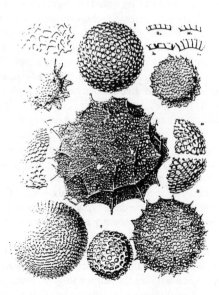

Figure 7.10   *n*-ary trees.

A method that maintains the rigour of an L-system to produce three-dimensional models is given in [PRUS88]. Here the L-system is maintained to generate the topology of the branching system in trees and plants. Geometric and other attributes are then directly imposed on the skeleton in the following way. A production from the L-system is scanned from left to right and symbols are interpreted as commands which control a three-dimensional 'turtle'. The turtle possesses state attributes such as position, orientation, current colour and line-width. This simple system extends the *n*-ary trees of Figure 7.10 into the third dimension. Phyllotaxis and developmental leaf models are also used in this work.

Although much of this work in computer graphics has been developed to model trees and plants, there is no reason why this approach cannot be extended to nontree-like structures as the final example, taken from [LOPE90], will illustrate. Again this is a two-dimen-

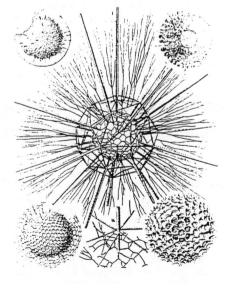

Figure 7.11   Radiolaria.

sional kernel of a modeller that could be extended to handle three-dimensional primitives and their relationship to each other. Consider Figure 7.11 that shows a selection of Radiolaria. We could approach the modelling of such a species in two-space by using the following primitives:

pentagon
circle
triangle
box (rectangle or square)

We combine such primitives, generating a more complex form from the previous by using 'distributions'. These are concerned with distributing primitives around each other in a radially symmetric manner imitating the symmetry exhibited by the specimens in Figure 7.11. The following distributions were used:

edge
corner
centre

For example, the sentence:

square, corner, triangle, centre, circle, nil

would produce Figure 7.12.

Geometric attributes need to be associated with the primitives. In this simple demonstration these involve, for example, allowing triangles of different sizes. Figure 7.13 shows different productions of the same sentence:

circle,edge,triangle1,edge,triangle2,edge,triangle3,nil

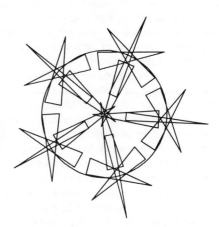

Figure 7.13 Three productions from the sentence 'circle, edge, triangle1, edge, triangle2, edge, triangle3, nil'.

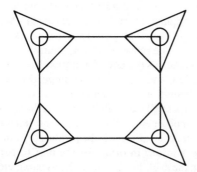

Figure 7.12 The production from the sentence 'square, corner, triangle, centre, circle, nil'.

Currently it is an open question as to whether these techniques will prove to be a useful modelling method when extended to three-space. Although it is theoretically simple to extend a grammar to three-space the associated attribute problems and the specification of spatial relationships may prove too unwieldy to incorporate in a grammar form.

7.5 Evolutionary procedural modelling

We conclude this chapter with a description of two systems that take a different and innovative approach to modelling through procedures than those that we have previously encountered. All the techniques discussed so far are more or less deterministic in nature, in that the users must conceive and understand the procedure that is used to generate the model. Using an evolutionary approach, however, the users remove themselves from a complete analytical understanding of the processes involved. A biological analogy is appropriate here. An evolutionary algorithm is designed to cycle through the reproduction and mutation of form to produce a potentially infinite variety of structures. The users' role is to select which structures to mate within each reproduction cycle, thereby driving the evolution in a preferred direction. Although the users effectively lose complete control over every detail of the resulting structure, they do not have to understand the underlying process involved and can produce forms that would have been impossible to create analytically and impossible to visualize beforehand. The computer becomes, in effect, a creative partner in the design process, provoking the users into making decisions and selections. Clearly such schemes are particularly suited to areas of artistic design as the applications that we shall discuss below demonstrate.

The concepts of genotype and phenotype, found in biological evolution, are equally applicable to simulated evolution. A genotype is a piece of coded information which, through developmental rules, finds its expression in the resultant generated phenotype. In biology the genotype is the DNA double helix and the phenotype is the biological organism that results from this genotype. In simulated evolution the genotype is defined by the evolutionary algorithm and is usually a set of procedure

parameters or a set of symbolic expressions. The process of reproduction takes two or more genotypes and combines them to produce new genotypes. For evolution to occur there must be variation, that is, reproduction must produce child genotypes that differ in some way from the parents. In biology this variation is assured through the way the genotypes combine and through random mutation. In nature, at least according to Darwin's theory, the survival of a given genotype is determined by how well its phenotype performs within its environment. In artificial evolution, selection is driven by the aesthetic whim of the users – they simply choose which one survives. Survival of the fittest is replaced with survival of the most visually interesting.

The work of Todd and Latham [TODD91] is a good example of an evolutionary algorithm. Called 'Mutator' the genotype is a set of procedure parameters, called a parameter vector, that drives a variety of routines within a constructive solid modeller, producing a phenotype that is the resultant assembled structure. The components of the parameter vector control the number of entities that make up the structure, the transformations that are applied to each of these entities, and so on. For example, a horn form phenotype is produced from a genotype that specifies a sequence of spheres of variable radius, the shrinkage or expansion of these spheres, and the bend and twist that is applied to this sequence.

The n-component parameter vector can be thought of as specifying an n-dimensional genetic space of form, and with the Mutator program provides a way of subjectively exploring this space. Given a genotype V_{state} representing the state of the form, mutated versions V_{mut} are generated by:

$$V_{mut} = V_{state} + \text{mutrate} * \text{rand} * V_{diff}$$

where 'rand' is a random number in the range $[-1, 1]$ and V_{diff} is a vector that scales separately the amount of perturbation applied to each component of the vector, reflecting the fact that different parameters have different scales. The remaining term, 'mutrate', is a global scalar that controls the rate of mutation from generation to generation and facilitates an important aspect of simulated evolution. If the mutation rate is too high, then the phenotypes will lack stability, that is, the children will bear little or no resemblance to the parent. If it is too low, then insufficient variety will be produced from generation to generation. In order for the user to participate usefully in the evolutionary process this parameter has to be carefully tuned. Initially the mutation rate is high, permitting a fast exploration of a large section of the genetic space of the model, and when the user wishes to converge on some desired form, the mutation rate is decreased with increasing generations – the lower mutation rate giving more sensitive control. In the absence of a workable formula for mutation rate against generation, Mutator achieves this tuning by allowing the rate to be controlled manually.

Additional control over the evolution process is provided by establishing a general direction V_{dir} in which the user moves through the genetic space of forms. Instead of choosing a single mutation from a set of several, the user can assign relative weights A and B to each of the mutations presented, according to whether it is agreeable or not:

$$V_{dir} = BV_{dir} + A \left(V_{mut} - V_{state} \right)$$

where

$B > 0$ and $A \leqslant 0$ according to whether the mutation is desirable or not

If the mutation is desirable then the direction moved from parent to child is added into the general direction in which the user is moving. If disagreeable then the direction is subtracted thereby moving away from the undesirable region of genetic space. The starting point for the next set of mutations is given by taking the most favoured mutation, represented by V_{best} and moving in this direction. Thus:

$$V_{state} = V_{best} + V_{dir}$$

This refinement, which in the conventional wisdom cannot be said to exist in biology, enables the user to make an overall decision about the best general direction in which to move in genetic space, rather than taking a path consisting of a series of steps of unconnected directions. The effect of such directed steering, analogous to steepest ascent optimization, enables the user to focus more efficiently on forms of interest.

Forms are mated by generating a parameter vector from two or more parent vectors in a variety of ways. Random selection takes for each component of the child vector the corresponding component of a randomly chosen parent vector. Weighted averaging generates a component as a weighted average of the corresponding components of the parent vectors. It is reported that averaging produces rather more bland offspring than the random selection method – a result to please 'dyed in the wool' Darwinists. If a form consists of many subforms the parameters of each subform can be grouped together and the mating operations can be applied to these groups

as a whole. In this way the children can inherit recognizable features from their parents.

Plate 30(a), (b) and (c) show some results from the Mutator program. (a) and (b) show how forms are evolved from one another for each generation. Mutator presents the user with nine forms: an original and eight mutations. (c) shows more complex fruits obtained further down one of Mutator's evolutionary trees. Artistically this program has been very useful. Latham enjoys a worldwide reputation as a computer graphics artist and exhibits his work in many countries.

Our final example of evolutionary procedural modelling is taken from the work of Karl Sims [SIMS91], which describes two kinds of evolutionary techniques: one for evolving plant structures, similar in approach to the previous example, and the other for evolving images. We focus on the latter where the genotype is an arbitrary symbolic LISP expression with an arbitrary collection of arguments somewhere amongst which is included an image or images. The phenotype is the image resulting from the straightforward evaluation of this expression. The symbolic expression can consist of any number of basic functions which are taken from a function set of standard LISP functions, such as:

$+, -, *, /,$ mod, round, min, max, bw-noise, sin, cos, $\ldots$

A full list is given in the work. Each of these functions takes a predefined number of arguments and returns a colour value – either scalar for black and white images or vector for colour. The expressions can thus be viewed as image processing operations. The random arguments that can be generated for these expressions include random scalars, vectors or any of the LISP expressions from the function set or the variables x, y corresponding to the pixel coordinates of an image. In contrast to the method of Todd and Latham we can see that this technique contains procedural information as well as just parametric data within its genotype. Consequently the notion of a finite dimensional genetic space no longer applies since the evolutionary process itself may generate new procedures or new parameters.

Under this scheme, at a given point in the genetic space, we have an image which is the evaluation of the symbolic expression and its arguments. For evolution to occur the symbolic expression is mutated and the resulting expression is evaluated to generate the new image. The symbolic expression is represented as a tree structure with either arguments or expressions situated at each node. A recursive mutation scheme is employed, the tree is traversed node by node and each node is subject to a possible mutation depending on the type of the node. Each type of mutation has a mutation frequency associated with it according to the type of the node. The variety of possible mutations allowed is wider than the previous example. Just as in the previous example, if the node is an argument then it can be mutated by applying a random perturbation to this argument. In addition, any node can mutate by suddenly changing to a new random expression. Functions can mutate to new functions. An expression consisting of an argument and a function can be replaced by an argument, or can itself become the argument for a new function.

Not surprisingly, those mutations that represent a sudden leap to another point in genetic space can result in a significant alteration of the phenotype. In order that the system will not 'run wild', the mutation frequency of each type of mutation is adjusted such that a decrease in complexity is slightly more probable than an increase. Once again the rate of mutation against successive generations is a critical factor. This is controlled by making the overall mutation frequency inversely proportional to the length of the parent expression. As the expressions get longer the phenotype images become more complex and start to stabilize from generation to generation. Images start to converge to a certain form. Since the expressions can become prohibitively expensive to compute, the system performs some internal selection aside from that of the user. For each expression an estimate of the compute speed is calculated and slow expressions are eliminated before ever being displayed to the user.

Mating symbolic expressions depends on a comparison of their tree structures. If the structures are similar, then the nodes of the parents are traversed in tandem and the nodes of one or the other are copied into the child. If the structures are significantly different, then crossing over is performed. The tree of one parent is traversed and a node, chosen at random, is replaced by a random node from the other parent. The variation produced by the second mating technique is much larger than that of the first.

Plate 31(a), (b) and (c) show three evolved phenotypes taken from this system and demonstrate the considerable variation it is capable of producing. Sims quotes at least 10 to 40 generations required to generate interesting images. Typically, the symbolic expressions are so long that they defy the user's understanding, which is tantamount to saying that they would be impossible to generate analytically. The genotype for Plate 31(a) illustrates this point:

$$(\text{round}(\log(+y(\text{color-grad}(\text{round}(+(\text{abs}(\text{round}$$
$$(\log(+y(\text{color-grad}(\text{round}(+y(\log(\text{invert y})15.5)))$$
$$x)3.1\ 1.86\ \#(0.95\ 0.7\ 0.59)1.35))0.19)x))(\log(\text{invert}$$
$$y)15.5))x)3.1\ 1.9\ \#(0.95\ 0.7\ 0.35)1.35))0.19)x)$$

Plate 31(b) was created before the genotype-saving facility was written and is thus an example of an extinct, artificially evolved form.

8 Ray tracing I: basic recursive ray tracing

Recursive ray tracing uses a local reflection model for the calculation of the direct or local term. Local reflection models are discussed in Chapter 2. Ray-traced imagery produces aliasing artefacts and anti-aliasing approaches for standard ray tracing are given in Chapter 4. Ray tracing is used in volume rendering algorithms (Chapter 13). The view-dependent mapping techniques discussed in Chapter 6 are a form of (first-hit) ray tracing. An attempt to evaluate specular reflections in the radiosity method has been made by using ray tracing (Chapter 11).

The next four chapters deal with the ray tracing and radiosity methods, both of which are ad hoc methods for different aspects of the global illumination problem. Global illumination is dealt with more generally in Chapter 12.

Introduction

As any reader of an elementary physics textbook will verify, ray tracing was not invented by the computer graphics community. An early use in geometric optics is contained in René Descartes' treatise, published in 1637, that explained the shape of the rainbow. From experimental observations involving a spherical glass filled with water, Descartes used ray tracing as a theoretical framework to explain the phenomenon. Applying the already known laws of reflection and refraction, he showed that rainbows occur when the sun is able to reflect and refract light through 42° with respect to an observer. This is explained in further detail at the end of this chapter.

This traditional application of ray tracing to the modelling of the propagation of electromagnetic energy through various environments is not ignored by all ray tracing software writers, and systems are available that perform the dual function of abstract image synthesis and the simulation of the behaviour of electromagnetic waves.

Ray tracing in computer graphics began around 1980 and was extensively researched in the subsequent decade. It produced, for the time, startlingly clear 'super real' images but at a high cost. Early research concerned itself with efficiency schemes and research was also devoted to overcoming the disadvantage of tracing infinitesimally thin rays.

Ray tracing is a versatile technique that uses the same model to integrate aspects of light/object interaction that were previously handled by separate ad hoc algorithms – reflections, hidden surface removal and shadows. Its versatility is also demonstrated in the diversity of the contexts in which it serves as the basic tool for light/object interaction. In Chapter 13 a version of ray tracing is used as a foundation technique in volume rendering and in Chapter 10 we develop the relatively unexplored area of light/water interaction using ray tracing. Limited ray tracing is also used to enhance the basic radiosity solution (Chapter 11).

This chapter looks at the basic theory necessary to implement a recursive ray tracer. Chapter 9 deals with the practical problems involved in building a ray tracer that works in reasonable time and Chapter 10 looks at how the image quality of a ray tracer can be improved.

8.1   Recursive ray tracing

Although some use of ray tracing appears in [APPE68] for hidden surface removal and in [GOLD71], ray tracing is generally deemed to have begun a decade ago [KAY79, WHIT80] as a rendering technique for computer graphics. Kay and Greenberg [KAY79] considered refraction, but it was Whitted [WHIT80] who suggested the first general ray tracing paradigm, integrating reflection, refraction, hidden surface removal and shadows into a single model.

Recursive ray tracing in its simplest form traces the path of specularly reflected and transmitted (or refracted) rays through an environment. A ray is traced, for each pixel, from an eye or view point through the pixel and into the scene. The rays are usually considered to be infinitely thin, and reflection and refraction occur without any spreading, that is, the reflecting or refracting interface is considered to be perfectly smooth. This fact gives recursive ray-traced images their unique signature – they usually consist of shiny objects exhibiting sharp multiple reflections.

Such images are super-real – they are never experienced in everyday life. Multiple reflections do not occur in reality with undiminished sharpness, because interfaces are never smooth, and rays are reflected/refracted and spread at the same time. The only real situation in which sharp multiple reflections are likely to occur is in

a room where the walls consist of mirrors. In fact one of the immediate subjective aspects of recursive ray-traced images is their unfamiliarity – a common reaction of naive implementors, such as students, faced with sharp multiple reflections is to express doubt about their geometric correctness.

Despite the expense of the technique and its questionable utility in the context of synthesizing real images, much work has been devoted to recursive ray tracing approaches. This is no doubt because the images produced are undoubtedly impressive. Considerable effort has gone into investigating ways of overcoming the high computational demands of recursive ray tracing, and ray tracing speedup techniques have become a major research area.

In your authors' opinion the utility of ray tracing lies in methods that are simplifications, or limited implementations, of recursive ray tracing and include, for example:

- soft shadows
- refraction and reflection mapping
- 'chrome' mapping
- environment mapping
- caustics
- standard renderer add-on

These can be used where required to enhance standard techniques. Here the idea is that if a scene can be adequately rendered for the most part by using say, Phong shading, why not do just this and use ray tracing in the scene only where absolutely necessary. Of course this is a completely nonrigorous approach but ray tracing is an approximate hybrid model anyway, as we shall see, and in practice there is no good reason for not mixing ray tracing with cheaper methods.

We will concentrate initially on a comprehensive overview of recursive ray tracing.

8.2   Recursive ray tracing: illumination model

One of the attractions of a recursive ray tracer is that it can incorporate in a single framework:

- hidden surface removal
- shadow computation
- reflection of light
- refraction of light
- global specular interaction

Consider Figure 8.1. This attempts to show how a ray traced through a scene will enable the computation of the intensity of the pixel associated with the ray. Assuming the sphere and the cylinder are completely opaque, and that the cube is partially transparent, we can trace three rays in the direction of light propagation:

1. A ray from the light source that will reflect off the cylinder and refract through the cube to the pixel of interest.

2. A ray from the light source that will reflect directly from the cube to the pixel of interest.

3. A ray from the light source that reflects off the sphere and then off the cube to the pixel of interest.

The first ray is 'indirect' – the light propagates along four separate paths in its journey from the light source to the pixel. The second ray is 'direct'. Although both these rays

are technically indirect, we distinguish between rays that reach the eye due to a single reflection and rays that are the result of multiple reflections. The distinction between these two ray types introduces an inconsistency into the model that is the origin of the ray-traced signature of images. This is an important point that we will return to later.

Ray tracing is often perceived as a tree creation process and this is a useful paradigm because it is a direct analogy of the method used when it is implemented in a language that supports recursive procedure calls (there is no point in attempting to implement recursive ray tracing in a language that does not support recursion). A tree for one pixel for the scene shown in Figure 8.1 is given in Figure 8.2(a). In this figure, each node represents a recursive call of a general ray tracing procedure. Such ray trees are subsets of a general binary tree that will have a refracted and a reflected branch emanating from each node. If a ray intersects an object then, in general, it spawns two rays – a reflected ray and a transmitted or refracted ray. Each of these rays produces two rays at the next interface and a recursive trace continues until either a predetermined recursive depth is exceeded, or a ray hits nothing and is allotted a background colour. Herein lies the high computational cost of recursive ray tracing.

To return to Figure 8.1, in practice if the cube is in front of the cylinder and the sphere is outside the view volume, an observer will see a refracted image of the cylinder through the cube and a reflection of the sphere in the cube. We would also expect to see, within the sphere reflection, an image of the cylinder, and so on.

In any implementation we trace rays *backwards* from the view point through each pixel and into the scene. That is, we trace in the reverse direction of light propagation. This is because we are only interested eventually in a fixed number of rays – those that pass through the view plane – say, one per pixel. An infinity of rays emanate from a light source and it is difficult, therefore, to trace rays in the direction of light propagation. (There is current confusion on the use of the adjective 'backwards' when applied to the direction of a ray trace. In Chapter 10 we use the term 'backwards ray tracing' to mean a method that traces rays in the opposite direction to conventional ray tracing, that is, from the light source in the direction of light propagation. This is perhaps illogical but it appears to be the most common semantic.)

The initial rays from the pixel into the scene effectively perform hidden surface removal. In a naive ray tracer a ray is tested against every object in the scene for intersection. If more than one object intersects the ray then the

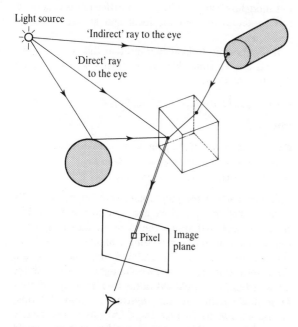

Figure 8.1 Direct and indirect rays that travel from the light source to a pixel.

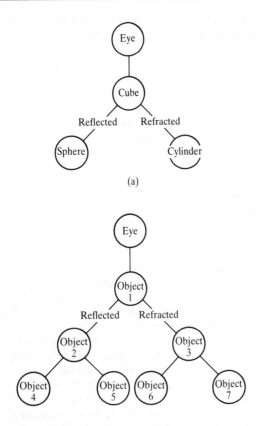

(a)

(b)

Figure 8.2   Ray tracing as a tree. (a) Tree for ray shown in Figure 8.1. (b) Ray trees are subsets of a general tree.

one that is nearest to the ray origin is the selected intersection. Moving in the direction reverse to that of light propagation the last direction to be traced is from the surface to the light corresponding to direct illumination. This direction is not calculated using the reflection/refraction laws that govern ray/surface interaction. At this point the ray tree terminates in one of two ways:

1. A local reflection model is brought into play (the theoretical inconsistency is discussed below).

2. A shadow feeler (Section 8.4.1) is fired directly from the surface to the light – the result dictating whether or not to involve the local reflection model.

The reflection and refraction vectors evaluated at every ray surface intersection are described fully in Chapter 2 and are restated here for convenience:

$$R = 2(N \cdot L)N - L$$

$$T = \frac{n_1}{n_2}L - \left[\cos \theta_t + \frac{n_1}{n_2}(L \cdot N) \right] N$$

At each intersection point, we have:

$$I = I_{\text{local}} + k_{\text{rg}}I_{\text{reflected}} + k_{\text{tg}}I_{\text{transmitted}}$$

the light reflected from a point on a surface is the linear combination of three terms. First, a local term due to direct illumination, or light travelling from the light source directly to the intersection point on the surface. We can use any of the direct reflection model descriptions in Chapter 2 to implement this term. For example, using a version of the Phong model (enhanced to include refraction – see Chapter 2):

$$I_{\text{local}} = I_a k_a + I_{\text{source}} \left[k_d (N \cdot L) + k_{\text{rl}}(N \cdot H)^{ns} + k_{\text{tl}}(N \cdot H')^{nt} \right] \qquad (8.1)$$

where for a given light source only one of the last two terms is active. (A single light source cannot be in a position to both reflect and refract light to a viewer.) To the local component we add two global terms representing light that arrives at a point due to reflection from another object or transmission through the object if it is partially transparent. Hall and Greenberg [HALL83] elaborate this model by using the Fresnel coefficient (as described in Chapter 2) in both the local and global reflection coefficients.

It is important to bear in mind that this is a recursive process and to state this fact explicitly we can rewrite Equation (8.1) as:

$$I(P) = I_{\text{local}}(P) + k_{\text{rg}}I(P_r) + k_{\text{tg}}(P_t)$$

where:

P is the intersection of the point under consideration
P_r is the first hit of the reflected ray from P
P_t is the first hit of the transmitted ray from P

This approach is the commonest implementation of a recursive ray tracer and we can note that in fact it is a hybrid model that treats the same surface differently depending on which term is being evaluated. In the direct specular term, spread is calculated empirically, using a direct reflection model, and a point light source produces a blurred specular highlight rather than an image of itself as a single point. In the ray-traced nonlocal terms, spreading due to surface imperfections is completely ignored because this would mean that each ray would spawn a large number of reflected and refracted rays making the computational problem completely impossible. Thus rays from direct illumination are spread (empirically) but rays from the eye (traced rays) are not. The nonlocal terms are evaluated by considering the interaction of infinitesimally thin reflected and transmitted rays. This is, of course, an inherent contradiction in the model and underlines the fact that models in computer graphics are a combination of theoretical and empirical 'fixes' that are tuned to produce acceptable images. Whitted discusses a scheme [WHIT80] for dealing with specular reflections consistently by using a perturbation scheme, not unlike bump mapping (Chapter 6) that spawns a set of perturbed rays at each intersection point, but even this is prohibitively expensive and no practical implementations are reported.

We now list a number of practical points that are not explicitly contained in the above formulae:

1. k_a and k_d are wavelength-dependent functions as before and the local contribution would be evaluated for each colour band of interest; k_{rg} and k_{tg} are also wavelength dependent.

Listing 8.1   TraceRay.c

```
#include  "types.h"

void  TraceRay(start,direction,depth,colour)
point   start,direction;
int  depth;
colours *colour;
{
        int  ray_hit();
        point hit_point, reflected_direction, transmitted_direction;
        colours local_colour, reflected_colour, transmitted_colour;
        object hit_object;

        if (depth > MAXDEPTH) *colour = BLACK;
        else {

                /* Intersect ray with all objects and find intersection point
                ( if any ) that is closest to start of ray */

                if (ray_hit( start, direction, &hit_object, &hit_point )) {

                        /* contribution of local colour at intersection point */
                        shade( hit_object, hit_point , &local_colour );

                        /* calculate direction of reflected and refracted rays */
                        calculate_reflection( hit_object, hit_point, &reflected_direction );
                        calculate_transmission( hit_object, hit_point, &transmitted_direction );

                        TraceRay( hit_point, reflected_direction, depth+1, &reflected_colour);
                        TraceRay( hit_point, transmitted_direction, depth+1, &transmitted_colour);

                        /* combine colours according to surface properties of hit_object */
                        Combine( hit_object, local_colour, reflected_colour, transmitted_colour, colour);

                }
                else *colour = BACKGROUND_COLOUR;

        }

}
```

2. Theoretically the global reflection coefficient k_{rg} should be identical to k_{rl} (and k_{tg} to k_{tl}). However, we are using a hybrid model as we have discussed and in practice it is convenient to use k_{rl} to control the intensity of the (local) highlight separately from the intensity of the global mirror reflections.

3. $I_{reflected}$ and $I_{transmitted}$ are RGB vectors since they are returning intensities that will, in general, contain a local component (because of the recursive nature of the process).

4. It may be necessary to include a distance attenuation coefficient with k_{rg} and, more importantly, k_{rl}.

Code to control a simple recursive ray tracer is given in Listing 8.1.

8.3 Recursive ray tracing: intersections

A naive ray tracer follows rays from the eye and an intersection test is carried out by checking the ray against every object in the scene. If more than one object is intersected by the ray then the coordinates of the nearest hit (along the ray) are used by the model. A direct intensity is calculated at that point, reflected and transmitted rays are spawned and the process is called recursively. If no strategy, other than brute force, is adopted for the intersection checks, then a recursive ray tracer will spend most of its time testing for intersections. Whitted [WHIT80] estimates that, for scenes of moderate complexity, a recursive ray tracer will spend up to 95% of its time locked into intersection tests. Two problems need to be dealt with:

*   performing the intersection checks;

*   adopting a strategy, other than brute force, that guides the order in which the checks are performed.

The computational expense of a single intersection test depends on the object representation. Quadric surfaces such as spheres abound in ray-traced images because it is easy to check a line against a sphere for intersection. Also spheres are used frequently as bounding volumes. Here complex objects are enclosed in bounding spheres and intersections with the object are only considered if

the ray intersects the bounding sphere. Two advantages of the sphere as a bounding volume are:

*   It is easy to enclose the object in a sphere.

*   Intersection checks are quick.

Spheres also possess disadvantages as discussed in Section 9.6.2.

Checking a ray against a complex polygon mesh object is easy but expensive, unless the object definition is structured in a way that facilitates quick checking, say, for example, a hierarchical definition of polygons of increasing resolution. Intersecting a ray with bicubic patches is expensive if solved analytically.

One of the important advantages of the ray tracing approach is that the intersection calculations are separate from that part of the process that traces the ray and calculates the pixel intensity. This means that different types of object definition can easily be added to a ray tracer if new intersection modules are written. This is not the case with standard rendering techniques, where the complete process is designed for, say, polygons or bicubic patches and where the reflection model is inextricably coupled to the process of scan conversion.

8.3.1 Intersections: ray/sphere

As a simple initial example of an intersection calculation we now deal with the case of the sphere. The intersection between a ray and a sphere is easily calculated. If the end points of the ray are (x_1, y_1, z_1) and (x_2, y_2, z_2) then the first step is to parametrize the ray (Figure 8.3):

$$x = x_1 + (x_2 - x_1)t = x_1 + it$$
$$y = y_1 + (y_2 - y_1)t = y_1 + jt$$
$$z = z_1 + (z_2 - z_1)t = z_1 + kt$$

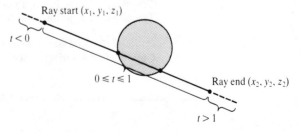

Figure 8.3 Intersecting a ray with a sphere using a parametrized line. Values of the parameter t along the ray.

or, more succinctly:

$$R(t) = O + D * t$$

where:

R is a set of points on the line

O is the origin of the ray

D is the direction vector of the ray

A sphere at centre (l, m, n) of radius r is given by:

$$(x - l)^2 + (y - m)^2 + (z - n)^2 = r^2$$

Substituting for x, y and z gives a quadratic equation in t of the form:

$$at^2 + bt + c = 0$$

where:

$$a = i^2 + j^2 + k^2$$
$$b = 2i(x_1 - l) + 2j(y_1 - m) + 2k(z_1 - n)$$
$$c = l^2 + m^2 + n^2 + x_1^2 + y_1^2 + z_1^2 - 2(lx_1 + my_1 + nz_1 + r^2)$$

If the determinant of this quadratic is less than 0 then the line does not intersect the sphere. If the determinant equals 0 then the line grazes or is tangential to the sphere. The real roots of the quadratic give the front and back intersections. Substituting the values for t into the original parametric equations yields these points. Figure 8.3 shows that the value of t also gives the position of the points of intersection relative to (x_1, y_1, z_1) and (x_2, y_2, z_2). Only positive values of t are relevant and the smallest value of t corresponds to the intersection nearest to the start of the ray.

Other information that is usually required from an intersection is the surface normal (so that the reflected and refracted rays may be calculated) although, if the sphere is being used as a bounding volume, only the fact that an intersection has ocurred, or not, is required.

If the intersection point is (x_i, y_i, z_i) then the normal at the intersection point is:

$$N = \left(\frac{x_i - l}{r}, \frac{y_i - m}{r}, \frac{z_i - n}{r} \right)$$

Haines [HAIN89] points out that the special case of a sphere is worth further study from an efficiency point of view, and rather than just evaluating the quadratic, suggests the following strategy, summarized here without mathematical detail:

1. Find if the ray's origin is outside the sphere.

2. Find the closest approach of the ray to the sphere's centre.

3. If the ray is outside and points away from the sphere, the ray must miss the sphere.

4. Else, find the squared distance from the closest approach to the sphere surface.

5. If the value is negative, the ray misses the sphere.

6. Else, from above, find the ray/surface distance.

7. Calculate the intersection coordinates.

8. Calculate the normal at the intersection point.

8.3.2 Intersections: ray/polygon

If an object is represented by a set of polygons then the straightforward approach for each polygon is to:

1. Obtain an equation for the plane containing the polygon.

2. Check for an intersection between this plane and the ray.

3. Check that this intersection is contained by the polygon.

For example, if the plane containing the polygon is:

$$ax + by + cz + d = 0$$

and the line is defined parametrically as before, then the intersection is given by:

$$t = -\frac{ax_1 + by_1 + cz_1 + d}{ai + bj + ck}$$

(If the denominator is equal to zero the line and plane are parallel.) The straightforward method that tests a point for containment by a polygon is simple but expensive. The sum of the angles between lines drawn from the point to each vertex is 360° if the point is inside the polygon, but not if the point lies outside. A fast direct containment test for polygons that are convex is given in [BADO90].

8.3.3 Intersections: ray/box

Ray/box intersections are important because boxes may be more useful bounding volumes than spheres, particularly in hierarchical schemes. Also, generalized boxes can be used as an efficient bounding volume (see [KAY86] and Section 9.2).

Generalized boxes are formed from pairs of parallel planes, but the pairs of planes can be at any angle with respect to each other. In this section we consider the special case of boxes forming rectangular solids, with the normals to each pair of planes aligned in the same direction as the ray tracing axes or the object space axes.

To check if a ray intersects such a box is straightforward. We treat each pair of parallel planes in turn, calculating the distance along the ray to the first plane (t_{near}) and the distance to the second plane (t_{far}). The larger value of t_{near} and the smaller value of t_{far} are retained between comparisons. If the larger value of t_{near} is greater than the smaller value of t_{far}, the ray cannot intersect the box. This is shown, for an example in the x, y-plane, in Figure 8.4. If a hit occurs then the intersection is given by the larger value of t_{near}.

A more succinct statement of the algorithm comes from considering the distance between the intersection points of a pair of parallel planes as intervals. Then if the intervals intersect, the ray hits the volume. If they do not intersect the ray misses.

Distances along the ray are given for the x-plane pairs as follows. If the box extent is (x_{b1}, y_{b1}, z_{b1}) and (x_{b2}, y_{b2}, z_{b2}) then:

$$t_{1x} = \frac{x_{b1} - x_1}{x_2 - x_1}$$

is the distance along the ray from its origin to the intersection with the first plane, and:

$$t_{2x} = \frac{x_{b2} - x_1}{x_2 - x_1}$$

is the distance to the second plane. The calculations for t_{1y}, t_{2y} and t_{1z}, t_{2z} are similar. The largest value out of the t_1 set gives the required t_{near} and the smallest value of the t_2 set gives the required t_{far}. The algorithm can exit at the y-plane calculations.

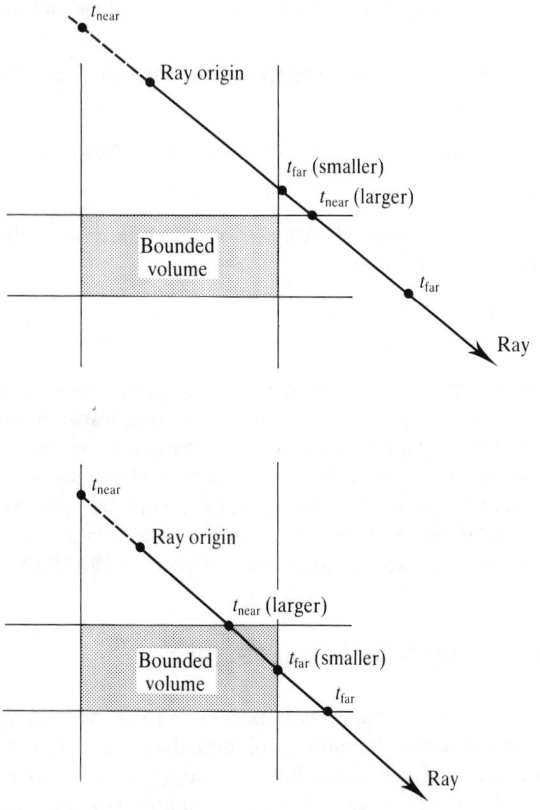

8.3.4 Intersections: ray/quadrics

The sphere example given in Section 8.3.1 is a special case of rays intersecting with a general quadric. Ray/quadric intersections can either be dealt with by considering the general case or 'special' objects, such as cylinders, can be treated individually for reasons of efficiency.

The general implicit equation for a quadric is:

$$Ax^2 + Ey^2 + Hz^2 + 2Bxy + 2Fyz + 2Cxz + 2Dx + 2Gy + 2Iz + J = 0 \tag{8.2}$$

which is equivalent to:

$$[x, y, z, 1] \begin{bmatrix} A & B & C & D \\ B & E & F & G \\ C & F & H & I \\ D & G & I & J \end{bmatrix} \begin{bmatrix} x \\ y \\ z \\ 1 \end{bmatrix} = 0$$

Following the same approach as we adopted for the case of the sphere, we substitute Equation (8.2) into a quadratic in t and obtain the coefficients a, b and c for the quadratic as follows:

$$a = Ax_d^2 + Ey_d^2 + Hz_d^2 + 2Bx_dy_d + 2Cx_dz_d + 2Fy_dz_d$$
$$b = 2\big(Ax_1x_d + B(x_1y_d + x_dy_1) + C(x_1z_d + x_dz_1)$$
$$\quad + Dx_d + Ey_1y_d + F(y_1z_d + y_dz_1) + Gy_d + Hz_1z_d + Iz_d\big)$$
$$c = Ax_1^2 + Ey_1^2 + Hz_1^2 + 2Bx_1y_1 + 2Cx_1z_1 + 2Dx_1 + 2Fy_1z_1$$
$$\quad + 2Gy_1 + 2Iz_1 + J$$

Figure 8.4 Ray/box intersection.

where:

(x_d, y_d, z_d) is the normalized ray direction

The equations for the quadrics are:

1. Sphere:

    $$(x - l)^2 + (y - m)^2 + (z - n)^2 = r^2$$

    where (l, m, n) is, as before, the centre of the sphere.

2. Infinite cylinder:

    $$(x - l)^2 + (y - m)^2 = r^2$$

3. Ellipsoid:

    $$\frac{(x - l)^2}{\alpha^2} + \frac{(y - m)^2}{\beta^2} + \frac{(z - n)^2}{\Gamma^2} - 1 = 0$$

    where α, β and Γ are the semi-axes.

4. Paraboloid:

    $$\frac{(x - l)^2}{\alpha^2} + \frac{(y - m)^2}{\beta^2} - z + n = 0$$

5. Hyperboloid:

    $$\frac{(x - l)^2}{\alpha^2} + \frac{(y - m)^2}{\beta^2} - \frac{(z - n)^2}{\Gamma^2} - 1 = 0$$

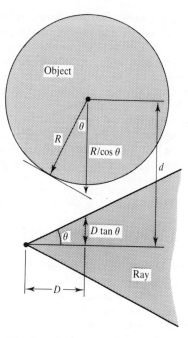

Figure 8.5 Ray/object intersection in cone tracing (a ray is a cone).

8.3.5 Intersections in beam tracing

Beam tracing is the general term applied when a bundle of rays, rather than a single ray, is traced. The idea is that a ray is now a geometrical entity, such as a cone, rather than the abstraction of a single line. This approach confers both efficiency advantages and benefits concerning realism. These are discussed more fully in Section 9.5. One of the simplest beam tracing schemes (discussed in Section 10.3) traces a cone formed by the bundle of rays diverging from a point.

Although beam tracing solves some of the problems associated with tracing infinitesimally thin rays, there is generally a price to be paid – the increase in the complexity of the geometric calculations. For example, Heckbert and Hanrahan ([HECK84] and Section 10.3) constrain the objects in the scene to be polygonal and introduce simplifications in the refraction calculations.

In cone tracing, (see [AMAN84] and Section 10.3) the objects are constrained to be spheres and polygons. A cone intersects a sphere if (Figure 8.5):

$$D \tan \theta + \frac{R}{\cos \theta} > d$$

where:

θ is the spread angle of the cone

R is the radius of the sphere

d is the distance between the point on the cone axis that is nearest to the centre of the sphere

D is the distance between this point on the cone axis and the cone origin

In cone tracing not only is it necessary to calculate an intersection, but the ratio between the cross-section of the beam and the area of intersection of the object needs to be established. This integration and the need for it is discussed in Section 10.3. Here we will consider the geometry.

Consider, for example, the cone/sphere intersection. The fractional overlap between the ray cone and the sphere is given by the area of intersection of the outline of the sphere (a circle), and the outline of the cone (also a circle) at the point where the cone is closest to the sphere.

Calculating the intersection between a cone and a

plane is straightforward. If the plane is not behind the ray origin and the axis is not parallel to the plane, the intersection of the axis and the plane can be calculated. This method can be extended to the cone/polygon intersection by using a point-in-polygon containment test, but because fractional coverage needs to be evaluated, it is more efficient to project the polygon vertices onto a plane perpendicular to the cone centre line. The cross-section of the cone onto the projected polygon is now a circle, and the problem reduces to finding the area of overlap between the circle and the projected polygon.

8.3.6 Intersections: other objects

If the objects are procedurally defined then the method used depends on the type of the definition. Kajiya [KAJI83] gives efficient methods for three procedurally defined types: fractal surfaces, prisms and surfaces of revolution. A prism is a surface defined by translating a plane curve orthogonally and Kajiya points out that many objects used in computer graphics can be defined as (collections of) prisms, for example, block letters, machine parts formed by extrusion and simple models of urban architecture.

Details on intersecting a ray with bicubic patches are to be found in [JOY86, BARR86, STEI84, HANR83, KAJI82, POTM81 and WHIT80]. Whitted [WHIT80] uses an expensive approach which extends the bounding sphere approach to bicubic patches. Each patch on a surface is enclosed in a bounding sphere. If the sphere is intersected by a ray the patch is subdivided using a standard patch subdivision algorithm, and each patch subdivision product is enclosed in a bounding sphere. This process is continued until either a bounding sphere, of preset minimum radius, is reached or the ray does not intersect the sphere. This recursive process of subdivision, enclosure in a bounding sphere and checking for intersection between the ray and the sphere will eventually produce a point of intersection whose accuracy is determined to within the radius of the minimum bounding sphere. In contrast, Kajiya [KAJI82] uses a direct numerical approach to ray/patch intersection. The obvious question here is: given the extra coding complexity and computational cost incurred in intersection calculations with 'difficult' objects, is the benefit obtained from ray tracing worth it?

8.4 Simple shadows in ray tracing

8.4.1 Opaque objects

Shadows are the local decrease in the diffuse light reflected from a surface due to the blocking of direct illumination. There are two considerations involved in shadow calculations – the shape or extent of the shadow and its intensity. In a ray tracing model they would be correctly handled by a scheme that incorporated diffuse interaction. The intensity of light from a shadow area is a function of the diffuse emission from nearby surfaces. We simulate this effect in ray tracing (as in standard shadow algorithms) by deciding whether a point is in shadow or not. If it is, I_{local} at this point is decreased by some (arbitrary) amount. Whether a point is in shadow or not is determined by casting a ray from each intersection point to the light source (or to each light source if there is more than one). If this so-called 'shadow feeler' intersects any object then the point of interest is deemed to be in shadow, provided that the intersected object lies between the light source and the current point that is being tested. The simplest model would assume a point light source and this gives hard-edged shadows. (Soft shadows in the context of ray tracing are discussed in Sections 10.4.3 and 5.2.) Note that, in general, shadow feeler/object intersections should be somewhat easier than general ray/object intersections because we do not have to find the nearest object to the ray origin. Only the fact that an intersection has occurred interests us. This will generally simplify intersection calculations.

Shadow calculations impose a computational overhead in ray tracing that increases rapidly as the number of light sources increases. In a naive ray tracer the shadow feeler intersection tests rapidly predominate as the number of light sources multiplies. In a standard ray tracer each intersection would now spawn $n + 2$ rays – a reflected and refracted ray and n shadow feelers, where n is the number of light sources.

Haines and Greenberg [HAIN86] use a 'light buffer' as a shadow testing accelerator. Shadow testing times were reduced using this procedure by a factor of between 4 and 30. Here the idea is to construct lists of potential light blockers.

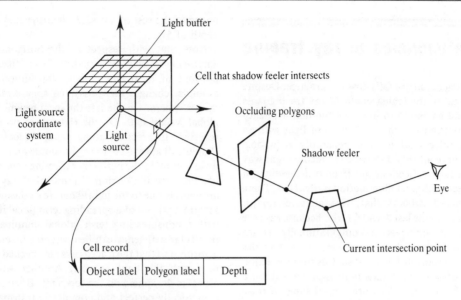

Figure 8.6 Shadow testing accelerator of [HAIN 86].

The method precalculates, for each point light source, a light buffer which is a set of pointers, geometrically disposed as two-dimensional arrays on the six faces of a cube surrounding a point light source (Figure 8.6). To set up this data structure all polygons in the scene are cast or projected onto faces of the cube, using as a projection centre the position of the light source. Each cell in the light buffer then contains a list of polygons that can be seen from the light source. The depth of each polygon is calculated in a local coordinate system based on the light source position, and the records are sorted in ascending order of depth. This means that, for a particular ray, there is immediately available a list of those object faces that *may* occlude the intersection point under consideration.

Shadow testing reduces to finding the cell through which the shadow feeler ray passes, accessing the list of sorted polygons and testing the polygons in the list until occlusion is found, or the depth of the potentially occluding polygon is greater than that of the intersection point (which means that there is no occlusion because the polygons are sorted in depth order). Note the similarity between this method and the hemicube form factor determination procedure described in Chapter 11. This is an application in shadow testing of the 'standard' philosophy of reducing the context-dependent costs by performing as much of the context-free computation as a preprocessing phase.

Finally, storage requirements are prodigious and depend on the number of light sources and the resolution of the light buffers. The resolution of the buffers in turn determines the accuracy of the shadows.

8.4.2 Partially transparent objects

Semitransparent objects are different from opaque objects in that both a shadowing due to absorption and caustics occur (see Chapter 10 for a description of the phenomenon of 'caustics'). Caustics can only be dealt with by backwards ray tracing (see Section 10.1.3). Shadows and semitransparent objects are discussed in Section 5.3.

Another problem that arises with semitransparent objects is that they act, in general, as colour filters, and the colour of the shadow may not necessarily be simply a diminution of the colour of the surface on which the object falls. This means that, compared with the solution for opaque objects, we need to use shadow feelers for each colour band of interest, together with a distance attenuation function. A method of dealing with partially transparent objects is discussed extensively in Chapter 10.

8.5 Deficiencies in ray tracing

The ray tracing paradigm falls down in practice. Despite claims of realism, the real strength of ray tracing is its generality and its ability to integrate the major phenomena that contribute to the interaction of light with an object. The price paid for this generality is 'wrong' images. We have already discussed the inconsistent way in which specular reflections are treated depending on whether direct or indirect illumination is involved. There are two other drawbacks that have attracted major research efforts in the last decade. First, because rays are infinitely thin, it is only possible computationally to trace specular reflection and transmission. This excludes major light transport mechanisms such as the interaction of diffuse surfaces, and results in images that exhibit a distinctive ray-traced signature. Modelling diffuse interaction by extending the simple ray tracing method would mean that at each intersection a large number of rays would be spawned and the method would quickly become computationally impossible. Second, even with this restriction, a naive ray tracer is hopelessly impractical because of the time spent in intersection testing. This resulted in a number of efficiency schemes that are described in the next chapter.

Finally, we refer to two demonstrations of simple recursive ray tracing. These demonstrations were contrived to illuminate both the inadequacies or contradictions in a ray-traced image, as well as their strength. Plate 32(top) shows a ray-traced image of a rather contrived scene containing a mix of reflective and refractive spheres against a striped background. The background colour in all other directions is blue. Each sphere displays a different mix of local colour and reflection and refraction properties. The sphere at the bottom left is red. The spheres in the bottom row become increasingly reflective from left to right. The sphere at the bottom right is wholly reflective. Moving upwards, the spheres become more transparent. The sphere at the top left is partially (50%) transparent and completely nonreflective. The sphere at the top right is completely transparent and looks rather strange. Completely transparent objects are only encountered in ray-traced images. The other spheres illustrate intermediate cases.

The trace depth used to produce Plate 32(bottom left) was 6. The full effect of this can best be seen in the reflective sphere at the bottom right. This sphere contains an image of the rest of the scene (constructed with a trace depth of 5).

Note that with respect to the horizontal variation 'increasing reflectivity' actually refers to the relative proportions of local and global contributions. This, for example, changes the glossy red sphere into a perfect mirror sphere. On the left the local weight is 1 and the global weight is 0. On the right these proportions are reversed. In practice, going along the bottom row we should still always see the light source and it should end up as a point in the perfectly reflecting sphere. Problems like this arise in this simple approach to ray tracing and are entirely due to the hybrid nature of the model and the incorrect mixing of a spreading term (local illumination) with a nonspreading term (global illumination). (This particular deficiency can be overcome by enhancing the algorithm so that the traced rays are checked for intersection with the light source.) Another wrong-looking aspect is the sphere on the top right. Because the sphere is physically perfect and completely transparent it does not really give any sense of 'being looked through' onto a striped background. Rather the refracted background appears to be a surface texture.

Plate 32(bottom right) shows a simple scene comprising three spheres, one completely opaque and the other two perfectly reflective. The image is traced to a recursive depth of 6. The four subimages shown alongside were generated by tracing to depths of 1, 2, 3 and 4. We have set the local specular coefficient in the reflective spheres to 0, and this has the effect of rendering the sphere as black in the depth 1 image. As the depth increases you can see what happens with respect to the black sphere effect: it recedes further and further into indirect reflections.

8.6 A historical digression: the rainbow

As we mentioned in the introduction, an early use of ray tracing was employed by Descartes in 1637 that explained the shape of the rainbow as a segment of the circumference of a circle. He applied the already discovered laws of reflection and refraction to spherical water drops in an elegant demonstration of the rainbow formation.

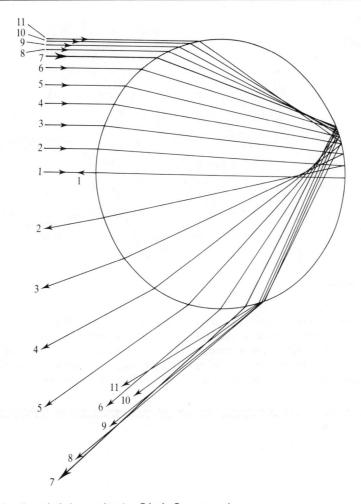

Figure 8.7 Tracing rays through a spherical water drop (ray 7 is the Descartes ray).

Rays entering a spherical water drop are refracted at the first air/water interface, internally reflected at the water/air interface and finally refracted as they emerge from the drop. As shown in Figure 8.7, horizontal rays entering the drop above the horizontal diameter emerge at an increasing angle with respect to the incident ray. Up to a certain maximum the angle of the exit ray is a function of the height of the incident ray above the horizontal diameter. This trend continues up to a certain ray, when the behaviour reverses and the angle between the incident and exit ray decreases. This ray is known as the Descartes ray, and at this point the angle between the incident and exit ray is 42°. Incident rays close to the Descartes ray

emerge close to it and Figure 8.7 shows a concentration of rays around the exiting Descartes ray. It is this concentration of rays that makes the rainbow visible.

Figure 8.8 demonstrates the formation of the rainbow. An observer looking away from the sun sees a rainbow formed by '42°' rays from the sun. The paths of such rays form a 42° 'hemicone' centred at the observer's eye. (An interesting consequence of this model is that each observer has his own personal rainbow.)

This early, elegant use of ray tracing did not, however, explain that magical attribute of the rainbow – colour. Thirty years would elapse before Newton discovered that white light contained light at all wavelengths. Along with

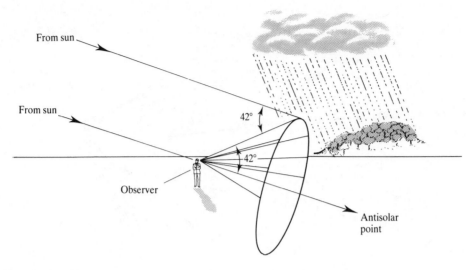

Figure 8.8 Formation of a rainbow.

the fact that the refractive index of any material varies for light of different wavelength, Descartes' original model is easily extended. About 42° is the maximum angle for red light, while violet rays emerge after being reflected and refracted through 40°. The model can then be seen as a set of concentric hemicones, one for each wavelength, centred on the observer's eye.

This simple model is also used to account for the fainter secondary rainbow. This occurs at 51° and is due to two internal reflections inside the water drops.

9 | Ray tracing II: practical ray tracing

Introduction

This chapter looks at how we can implement ray tracers that work in a reasonable time either by speeding up the basic process or by exploiting a limited version of ray tracing to produce certain effects without paying a high cost penalty.

All efficiency schemes are alternatives to the brute-force approach of testing every ray spawned against all objects in the scene. They work either by trying to optimize this search by enclosing the objects in bounding volumes or by preprocessing the scene to yield a secondary data structure that guides the ray trace. Efficiency schemes are also concerned with the intersection problem because a naive ray tracer is mostly bound in intersection calculations.

One of the difficulties of surveying ray tracing speedup schemes is that no quantitive comparisons are available; the treatment here attempts to describe and categorize the algorithms and to point out the similarities and distinctions amongst them. No consideration is given to hardware-oriented techniques. These are considered to be outside the scope of this text.

Thus the major developments in ray tracing have addressed the inherent deficiencies in the model, or have developed efficiency schemes that attempt to reduce the computational cost. We start by looking at efficiency schemes and then at the ways in which ray tracing can be used selectively – limited implementation schemes.

9.1 Adaptive depth control

This first elaboration is not an efficiency scheme that utilizes a geometric device, but simply results from the fact that it is not necessary, with most scenes, to trace rays to any great depth. In a naive ray tracer, a trace is terminated when either a ray hits nothing and is allotted a background intensity or when a preset maximum trace depth is reached. The idea discussed in this section is to vary the trace depth according to the nature of the region through which a set of connected rays travels. Thus a speedup is achieved by pruning different branches of the tree to different depths and the overall number of rays traced should be reduced. We should note that if we do not apply some kind of pruning technique we would end up tracing more and more rays that contribute a decreasing amount to the final pixel value – most of the effort would go into calculating effects of rays deep down the tree that may have an imperceptible effect on the final image.

Hall and Greenberg [HALL83] point out that the percentage of the scene that consists of highly transparent and reflective surfaces is, in general, small and it is thus inefficient to trace every ray to a maximum depth. (In a sense this is something of a contradiction. Ray tracing is often used with scenes that *do* contain transparent and reflective surfaces in abundance, so that the strength of the method is made apparent.) Hall suggests using an adaptive depth control that depends on the properties of the materials with which the rays are interacting. The properties of the region through which the ray is being traced now determines the termination depth, which can be any value between unity and the preset maximum depth.

Rays are attenuated in various ways as they pass through a scene. When a ray is reflected at a surface, it is attenuated by the global specular reflection coefficient for the surface. When it is refracted at a surface, it is attenuated by the global transmission coefficient for the surface. For the moment, we consider only this attenuation at surface intersections. A ray that is being examined as a result of tracing through several intersections will make a contribution to the top-level ray that is attenuated by several of these coefficients.

Any contribution of a ray low down in a trace hierarchy will be attenuated by the product of all the global transmission and reflection coefficients 'above' it. If this product is below a certain threshold, there is no point in continuing with the trace process. So adaptive depth control is implemented by accumulating the product of the global transmission and reflection coefficients as a ray is traced.

Another way in which a ray can be attenuated is by passing for some distance through an opaque material. This can be dealt with by associating a transmittance coefficient with the material composing an object. Colour values would then be attenuated by an amount determined by this coefficient and the distance a ray travels through the material. A simple addition to the

intersection calculation in the ray tracing procedure would allow this feature to be incorporated.

The use of adaptive depth control will prevent, for example, a ray that initially hits an almost opaque object, from spawning a transmitted ray that is then traced through the object and into the scene. The intensity returned from the scene may then be so attenuated by the initial object that this computation is obviated. Thus, depending on the value to which the threshold is preset, the ray will, in this case, be terminated at the first hit.

For a highly reflective scene with a maximum tree depth of 15, Hall and Greenberg [HALL83] report that this method results in an average depth of 1.71, giving a large potential saving in image generation time. The actual saving achieved will also depend on the nature and distribution of the objects in the scene.

9.2 Bounding volumes

The previous section looked at how we can prune the ray tree; this section deals with efficiency within each branch of the ray tree. Bounding volumes are a scheme that was developed to speed up intersection testing. First suggested by Clark [CLAR76], they were used by Whitted in ray tracing [WHIT80]. Each object in the scene is encased in a bounding volume. The rationale is that an

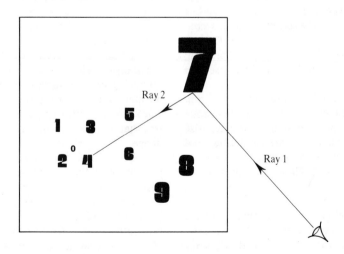

Figure 9.1 A simple scene consisting of 10 objects.

object of arbitrary complexity can be enclosed in a simple bounding volume, such as a sphere. Ray tracing then proceeds by testing for intersection against bounding volumes. If a ray does not intersect a bounding volume sphere, for example, it cannot intersect the object. For an object that contains a large number of polygons, this test can improve efficiency considerably, because it saves unnecessary testing of the ray against every polygon in the object. Spheres have commonly been used as bounding volumes because, as outlined in the previous chapter, intersecting a ray with a sphere is computationally simple. However, their suitability is critically dependent on the shape of the object they are enclosing. For example, long thin objects will result in a bounding volume where most of the volume is empty and a ray intersecting such a bounding volume will unnecessarily test the object. Figures 9.1 and 9.2 demonstrate the idea. A contrived two-dimensional environment is made up of 10 objects – the characters 0 to 9. We consider the adventures of two rays – an initial eye ray and the first reflected ray (ray 1 and ray 2 respectively). In a naive ray tracer ray 1 would be tested against all the objects in the scene. A hit against object 7 would be established and the reflected ray would be similarly tested against all objects in the scene, making a total of 20 intersections tests for these 2 rays. Figure 9.2 is a representation of a process that is identical except that the exhaustive testing is now dealing with simple objects – the spherical bounding volumes – to test for intersection. A full intersection test is only carried out on object 7 and object 4.

Weghorst *et al*. [WEGH84] point out that the simplicity of the intersection test should not be the sole criterion in the selection of a bounding volume. They define a 'void' area of a bounding volume to be the difference in area between the orthogonal projections of the object and bounding volume onto a plane perpendicular to the ray and passing through the origin of the ray (see Figure 9.3). They show that the void area is a function of object, bounding volume and ray direction and define a cost function for an intersection test:

$$T = b * B + i * I$$

where:

T is the total cost function

b is the number of times that the bounding volume is tested for intersection

B is the cost of testing the bounding volume for intersection

i is the number of times that the item is tested for intersection $\left(\text{where } i \leqslant b\right)$

I is the cost of testing the item for intersection

It is pointed out by the authors that the two products are generally interdependent. For example, reducing B by reducing the complexity of the bounding volume will almost certainly increase i. A quantitive approach to selecting the optimum of a sphere, a rectangular parallelepiped and a cylinder, as bounding volumes, is given. Using bounding volumes in this way does not cut down

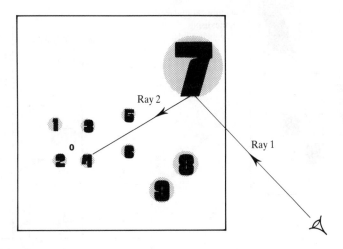

Figure 9.2   Unstructured bounding volumes (spheres).

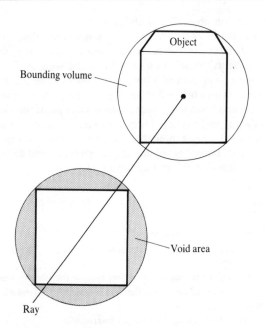

Figure 9.3 The 'efficiency' of a bounding volume is a function of the void area.

on the number of intersection checks, but it reduces their average complexity (rays that actually pierce an object have their intersection test overheads increased).

A common extension to bounding volumes, first suggested by Rubin and Whitted [RUBI80] and discussed in [WEGH84], is to attempt to impose a hierarchical structure of such volumes on the scene. If it is possible, objects in close spatial proximity are allowed to form clusters and the clusters are themselves enclosed in bounding volumes. This is demonstrated in Figure 9.4. The ray tracer initially 'sees' a hierarchy of bounding volumes and a descent through this hierarchy continues only from those nodes where intersections occur. The implication here is that we can further exploit the bounding volume approach and cut down on the intersection testing and calculation time by attempting to structure the bounding volumes in a way that reduces the number of intersection tests. This method makes the time spent on intersection tests logarithmic rather than linear in n – the number of objects in the scene.

Ray 1 now tests against 3 bounding volumes and 1 object (rather than 10 objects). Ray 2 tests against 3 bounding volumes, enters the cluster and tests against 3 more bounding volumes and finally 3 objects. This results in a total of 4 object intersection tests and 9 bounding volume tests compared with 20 object intersection tests for the unstructured environment.

This time boxes have been used as bounding volumes. A box has a more difficult intersection test than a sphere (see Section 8.3.3). However, it is easier to set up a hierarchy with boxes than it is with spheres. Boxes can be

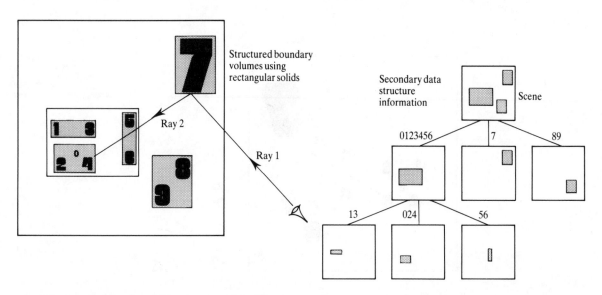

Figure 9.4 Structured bounding volumes using rectangular solids.

nested inside each other using simple comparisons on each face.

Thus a scene is grouped, where possible, into object clusters and each of those clusters may contain other groups of objects that are spatially clustered. Ideally, high-level clusters are enclosed in bounding volumes that contain lower level clusters and bounding volumes. Clusters can only be created if objects are sufficiently close to each other. Creating clusters of widely separated objects obviates the process. The potential clustering and the depth of the hierarchy will depend on the nature of the scene; the deeper the hierarchy the greater the potential savings.

Although this technique removes the linear dependence of intersection calculation overheads on scene complexity, it still has a high cost. This is because every ray descends through a tree hierarchy from the root and the bounding volumes may themselves be inefficient. Also, considerable user investment is required to set up a suitable hierarchy. Kay and Kajiya [KAY86] give a list of desirable properties for any hierarchical scheme. These are:

1. Any given subtree should contain objects that are near each other. 'Nearness' is relative, but the lower the subtree is with respect to the entire hierarchy, the nearer the objects should be to each other.

2. The volume of each node should be minimal.

3. The sum of the volume of all bounding volumes should be minimal.

4. The construction of the tree should concentrate on the nodes nearer the root of the tree. Pruning a branch of the tree there allows a large subtree to be removed from further consideration, whereas pruning one lower down removes just a few bounding volumes and objects from further consideration.

5. The time spent on constructing the hierarchy tree should more than pay for itself in time saved rendering the image.

Kay and Kajiya [KAY86] introduce a new type of bounding volume which can be made to fit the convex hulls of objects tightly. The authors also claim that the ray intersection test requires little computation. Their method thus overcomes the void area problem while retaining the advantages of a hierarchical bounding volume scheme. Objects are enclosed by bounding volumes made from polyhedra consisting of pairs of parallel planes. The method is a generalization of the bounding boxes in Section 8.3.3. The volume is formed

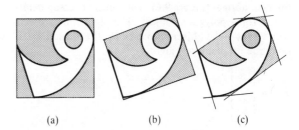

(a)   (b)   (c)

Figure 9.5 Comparing the efficiency of bounding volumes. (a) Box. (b) Oriented box. (c) 'Slabs'.

from the intersection of the slabs contained by each pair of parallel planes. In three-dimensional space we need a minimum of three independent plane sets to form a closed volume. However, more than three may be used depending on the tightness of the fit required. In the bounding box the slabs defined by a pair of planes were constrained to be parallel to an axis of the object coordinate system. In this case the slabs can have any orientation. The difference this generalization can make to the efficiency of a bounding volume is suggested in Figure 9.5.

A pair of planes needs now to be categorized by a vector P representing the coefficients of the plane:

$$Ax + By + Cz - d = 0$$

$$P = (A, B, C)$$

is the normal to the plane which is d units from the origin. Computation costs and storage are constrained by restricting the orientation of the plane sets to preset directions, that is, a set of normals is chosen in advance. For objects that are unknown in advance, the tightness of the bounding volume is, in general, going to depend on the size of the normal set.

For any object a bounding volume is thus defined as a subset of these normals together with a d_{near}, d_{far}

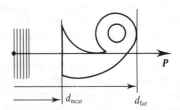

Figure 9.6 A slab is defined by a normal vector P and two scalars d_{near} and d_{far}.

for each normal (Figure 9.6). This subset is easily determined for a polygonal object. The algorithm projects each vertex in the object onto each P_i, the normal specifying the ith plane set, giving:

$$d_{ij} = P_i \begin{bmatrix} x_j \\ y_j \\ z_j \end{bmatrix}$$

where:

(x_j, y_j, z_j) is the jth vertex in the object vertex list

The d_{near} and d_{far} values for the ith plane set are then given by the minimum and maximum of d_{ij} over all the vertices in the object. Intersection testing involves a simple generalization of the intersection box testing given in Section 8.3.3.

9.3   First-hit speedup

Earlier it was pointed out that even for highly reflective scenes, the average depth to which rays were traced was between 1 and 2. This fact led Weghorst [WEGH84] to suggest a hybrid ray tracer where the intersection of the initial ray is evaluated during a preprocessing phase using a hidden surface algorithm. The implication here is that the hidden surface algorithm will be more efficient than the general ray tracer for the first hit. Weghorst suggests executing a modified Z-buffer algorithm, using the same viewing parameters. Simple modifications to the Z-buffer algorithm will make it produce, for each pixel in the image plane, a pointer to the object visible at that pixel. Ray tracing, incorporating adaptive depth control, then proceeds from that point. Thus the expensive intersection tests associated with the first hit are eliminated.

Results in [WEG84] show that incorporating adaptive depth control, hierarchical bounding volumes and first-hit speedup shows improvements that appear to be inversely dependent on scene complexity. For a scene of reasonable complexity the computation time is approximately half that of a naive ray tracer using spherical bounding volumes.

9.4   Limited implementation techniques

9.4.1   Standard renderer add-on

An obvious way to reduce the cost of ray tracing is to use it only in a restricted way, rather than employing it as a general rendering technique. As mentioned in the introduction, the real utility of ray tracing lies in using it in some limited way to enhance images created by other methods. Unless a scene is highly contrived, recursive ray tracing is generally not warranted. The approach is to exploit the benefits of ray tracing, where the context warrants it, without having to pay the price of a full recursive ray tracer.

Plate 74 is an example. Here a selected object is ray traced and the remainder of the scene is rendered by a standard renderer. In this case it is the water surface that is ray traced. The scene was rendered using a standard renderer with a 'ray tracing back end' attached to it. In this scheme the hidden surface is solved for a pixel using an A-buffer scan line algorithm, thereby enjoying the advantages of first-hit speedup (see [WEGH84] and the previous section). An object that projects onto the current pixel is shaded according to a tag which is part of the object description. If the tag is not set the object is shaded normally using a default shader. (This could be a local reflection model. In the case of the water in Plate 74 the default or nonray-traced shade is given by a chrome map.) If it is tagged to be ray traced, and it is visible, then a ray is constructed from the eye to the surface, the reflected/refracted ray computed and sent to the ray tracer. The ray tracer then tests this ray with other objects in its database.

Finally, note that the scheme is theoretically nonsensical – any surface that is reflective enough to possess specular highlights is glossy enough to have objects reflected in it. Recall that a specular highlight is just the reflection of the light source blurred to some degree. It is, therefore, not formally justifiable to select some objects to be ray traced, leaving others to be shaded by a local model that incorporates specular highlights.

9.4.2   Mapping techniques

A simple and effective ray tracing technique is to calculate the first (and possibly second) reflected and refracted ray, when an eye ray or initial ray hits an object, and to terminate this ray on a surface on which a two-dimensional map has been projected. This is an R_3 to R_2 mapping where the direction of the reflected or refracted ray (R_x, R_y, R_z) is mapped onto the u, v-coordinates of the texture map. We write:

$$f:R^3 \rightarrow R^2$$

where

$$(u, v) = f(R_x, R_y, R_z)$$

Such techniques are used extensively as simple low-cost methods that diminish the homogeneous and plastic effect of standard Phong shading. The significant benefit gained from using maps in conjunction with ray tracing is that effective filtering techniques, developed for texture mapping, can be used to give some of the effects only otherwise possible by using distributed ray tracing.

We have decided to classify these schemes as texture mapping techniques and have included them in Chapter 6. However, they can equally be regarded as limited implementation ray tracing. They are normally integrated with a standard renderer that deals with polygonal models.

The significant difference between these schemes and standard ray tracing is that the algorithm is 'driven' from the object surface. A reflection or refraction ray is spawned from the current pixel projection and this ray is *guaranteed* to hit a map. There is *no* intersection testing.

9.5 Ray coherence: beam tracing

The foundation of this approach is a recognition of the fact that tracing infinitesimally thin rays through an environment is basically a bad idea that can be improved by broadening the width of the ray. Heckbert and Hanrahan [HECK84] exploit the coherence that is available from the observation that, for any scene, a particular ray has many neighbours each of which tends to follow the same path. Rather than tracing single rays, then, why not trace groups of parallel rays, sharing the intersection calculations over a bundle of rays? This is accomplished by recursively applying a version of the Weiler–Atherton hidden surface removal algorithm

[WEIL77]. The Weiler–Atherton algorithm is a projection space subdivision algorithm involving a preliminary depth sort of polygons followed by a sort of the fragments generated by clipping the sorted polygons against each other. Finally, recursive subdivision is used to sort out any remaining ambiguities. This approach restricts the objects to be polygonal, thus destroying one of the important advantages of a ray tracer which is that different object definitions are easily incorporated due to the separation of the intersection test from the ray tracer.

The initial beam is the viewing frustum. This beam or bundle of rays is traced through the environment and is used to build an intersection tree, different to a single ray tree in that a beam may intersect many surfaces rather than just one. Each node in the tree now contains a list of surfaces intersected by the beam.

The procedure is carried out in a transformed coordinate system called the beam coordinate system. Initially this is the view or eye coordinate system. Beams are volumes swept out as a two-dimensional polygon in the x, y-plane is translated along the z-axis.

Reflection (and refraction) are modelled by calling the beam tracer recursively. A new beam is generated for each beam/object intersection. The cross-section of any reflected beam is defined by the area of the polygon clipped by the incident beam and a virtual eye point (Figure 9.7).

Apart from the restriction to polygonal objects, the approach has other disadvantages. Beams that partially intersect objects change into beams with complex cross-sections. A cross-section can become disconnected or may contain a hole (Figure 9.8). Another disadvantage is that refraction is a nonlinear phenomenon and the

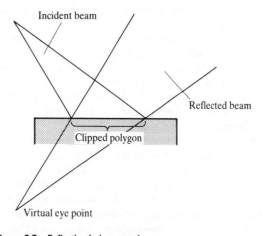

Figure 9.7 Reflection in beam tracing.

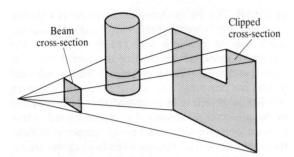

Figure 9.8 A beam that partially intersects an object produces a fragmented cross-section.

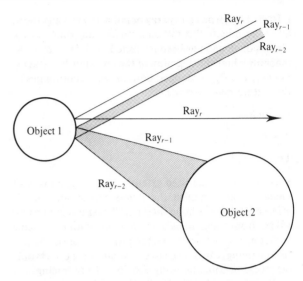

Figure 9.9 Ray coherence: the path of the previous ray can be used to predict the intersections of the current ray.

geometry of a refracted beam will not be preserved. Refraction therefore has to be approximated using a linear transformation.

The motivation of Heckbert and Hanrahan's method was mainly efficiency. Beam tracing is also used to increase the realism of ray-traced imagery. We return to the topic of beam tracing to discuss this aspect in Chapter 10.

Another approach to beam tracing is the pencil technique of Shinya *et al.* [SHIN87]. In this method a pencil is formed from rays called 'paraxial rays'. These are rays that are near to a reference ray called an 'axial ray'. A paraxial ray is represented by a four-dimensional vector in a coordinate system associated with the axial ray. Paraxial approximation theory, well known in optical design and electromagnetic analysis, is then used to trace the paraxial rays through the environment. This means that for any rays that are near the axial ray, the pencil transformations are linear and can be represented by 4×4 matrices. Error analysis in paraxial theory supplies functions that estimate errors and provides a constraint for the spread angle of the pencil.

The 4×4 system matrices are determined by tracing the axial ray. All the paraxial rays in the pencil can then be traced using these matrices. The paraxial approximation theory depends on surfaces being smooth so that a paraxial ray does not suddenly diverge because a surface discontinuity has been encountered. This is the main disadvantage of the method.

An approach to ray coherence that exploits the similarity between the intersection trees generated by successive rays is suggested by Speer *et al.* [SPEE86]. This is a direct approach to beam tracing and its advantage is that it exploits ray coherence without introducing a new geometrical entity to replace the ray. The idea here is to try to use the path (or intersection tree) generated by the

previous ray to construct the tree for the current ray (Figure 9.9). As the construction of the current tree proceeds, information from the corresponding branch of the previous tree can be used to predict the next object hit by the current ray. This means that any 'new' intervening object must be detected as shown in Figure 9.10. To deal with this, cylindrical safety zones are constructed around each ray in a ray set. A safety zone for ray$_{r-2}$ is shown in Figure 9.11. Now if the current ray does not pierce the

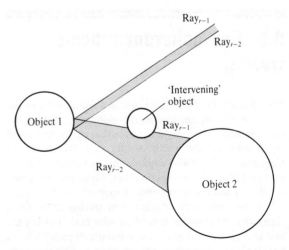

Figure 9.10 'Intervening' object in the path of ray *r*.

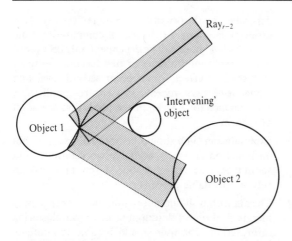

Figure 9.11 Cylindrical safety zones.

cylinder of the corresponding previous ray, and this ray intersects the same object, then it cannot intersect any new intervening objects. If a ray does pierce a cylinder, then new intersection tests are required as in standard ray tracing, and a new tree that is different to the previous tree is constructed.

In fact, Speer *et al.* report that this method suffers from the usual computational cost paradox – the increase in complexity necessary to exploit the ray coherence properties costs more than the standard ray tracing as a function of scene complexity. This is despite the fact that two-thirds of the rays behave coherently. The reasons given for this are the cost of maintaining and pierce-checking the safety cylinders, whose average radius and length decrease as a function of scene complexity.

9.6 Spatial coherence

9.6.1 Three-dimensional subdivision and spatial coherence

One way to address the problem of unrealistic computation time is to exploit the spatial coherence of objects. Until recently object coherence in ray tracing has generally been ignored. The reason is obvious. By its nature a ray tracing algorithm spawns rays of arbitrary direction anywhere in the scene. It is difficult to use such 'random' rays to access the object data structure and efficiently to extract those objects in the path of a ray. Unlike an image space scan conversion algorithm where, for example, active polygons can be listed, there is no a priori information on the sequence of rays that will be spawned recursively by an initial or view ray. Naive ray tracing algorithms execute an exhaustive search of all objects, perhaps modified by a scheme such as bounding volumes, to constrain the search. Bounding volume schemes work by associating a volume with an object; in contrast, spatial subdivision schemes work by *representing* objects as volumes by labelling three-space – the object becomes the volume.

The idea behind spatial coherence schemes is simple. The space occupied by the scene is subdivided into regions. Now, rather than check a ray against all objects or sets of bounded objects, we attempt to answer the question: is the region, through which the ray is currently travelling, occupied by any objects? Either there is nothing in this region, or the region contains a subset of the objects. This group of objects is then tested for intersection with the ray. The size of the subset and the accuracy to which the spatial occupancy of the objects is determined varies, depending on the nature and number of the objects and the method used for subdividing the space. It is worth considering the other major distinguishing feature of the approach. Three-dimensional subdivision schemes divide the space into labelled regions that are nonoverlapping. If the regions are processed in order along the ray from its origin then the first object encountered is the first hit. Thus the two major contributions to overheads in naive ray tracing are completely eliminated. These drawbacks of conventional ray tracing are: first, rays are generally checked against all objects; and secondly, rays are checked against objects even although the ray may be distant from the object. Thus the sort process of a conventional ray tracer is replaced by a preprocessing subdivision.

This approach, variously termed 'spatial coherence', 'spatial subdivision' or 'space tracing' has been independently developed by several workers, notably [GLAS84, KAPL85 and FUJI86]. All of these approaches involve preprocessing the space to set up an auxiliary or secondary data structure that contains information about the object occupancy of the space. Rays are then traced using this auxiliary data structure to enter the object data structure at the relevant place. Note that this philosophy (of preprocessing the object environment to reduce the computational work required to compute a view) was first employed by Schumaker *et al.* [SCHU69] in a hidden surface removal algorithm developed for flight simulators. In this algorithm, objects in the scene are clustered into groups by subdividing the space with planes. The spatial subdivision is represented by a binary tree. Any view point is located in a region represented by a leaf in the tree. An online tree traversal for a particular view point quickly yields a depth priority order for the group clusters. The important point about this algorithm is that the spatial subdivision is computed offline and an auxiliary structure, the binary tree representing the subdivision, is used to determine an initial priority ordering for the object clusters. The motivation for this work was to speed up the online hidden surface removal processing and enable image generation to work in real time.

Dissatisfaction with the bounding volume or extent approach in reducing the number of ray/object intersection tests appears, in part, to have motivated the development of spatial coherence methods [KAPL85]. One of the major objections to bounding volumes has already been pointed out. Their 'efficiency' is dependent on how well the object fills the space of the bounding volume. A more fundamental objection is that such a scheme may increase the efficiency of the ray/object intersection search, but it does nothing to reduce the dependence on the number of objects in the scene. Each ray must still be tested against the bounding extent of every object and the search time becomes a function of scene complexity. Also, although major savings can be achieved by using a hierarchical structure of bounding volumes, considerable investment is required to set up an appropriate hierarchy, and, depending on the nature and disposition of objects in the scene, a hierarchical description may be difficult or impossible. The major innovation of the methods described in this section is to make the rendering time constant (for a particular image space resolution) and eliminate its dependency on scene complexity.

The various schemes that use the spatial coherence approach differ mainly in the type of auxiliary data structure used. [KAPL85] lists six properties that a practical ray tracing algorithm should exhibit if the technique is to be used in routine rendering applications. Kaplan's requirements are:

1. Computation time should be relatively independent of scene complexity (number of objects in the environment, or complexity of individual objects), so that scenes having realistic levels of complexity can be rendered.

2. Time per ray should be relatively constant, and not dependent on the origin or direction of the ray. This property guarantees that overall computation time for a shaded image will be dependent only on overall image resolution (number of first level rays traced) and shading effects (number of second level and higher level rays traced). This ensures predictable performance for a given image resolution and level of realism.

3. Computation time should be 'rational' (say, within an hour) on currently available workstations, and should be 'interactive' (within a few minutes) on future affordable processor systems.

4. The algorithm should not require the user to supply hierarchical object descriptions or object clustering information. The user should be able to combine data generated at different times, and by different means, into a single scene.

5. The algorithm should deal with a wide variety of primitive geometric types, and should be easily extensible to new types.

6. The algorithm's use of coherence should not reduce its applicability to parallel processing or other advanced architectures. Instead, it should be amenable to implementation on such architectures.

Kaplan summarizes these requirements by saying, '. . . in order to be really usable, it must be possible to trace a large number of rays in a complex environment in a rational, predictable time, for a reasonable cost.' Spatial coherence approaches are now described in some detail.

9.6.2 Octrees

An octree is an established hierarchical data structure that specifies the occupancy of cubic regions of object space. The cubic regions are often called 'voxels' and generally vary in size. The variation in size means that large empty regions, or large regions that contain a single object, are not subdivided to the same extent as regions that contain a larger object. This feature, however, does have a drawback in that it can lead to trees which are extremely unbalanced and which incur high search costs. Octrees have been used extensively in image processing and computer graphics (see, for example, [DOCT81, JACK80, MEAG82 and YAMA84]).

An octree is a data structure that describes how the objects in a scene are distributed throughout the three-dimensional space occupied by the scene. The ideas involved in an octree representation can be more easily demonstrated by using a 'quadtree' to represent the occupancy of a two-dimensional region. Figure 9.12 shows a two-dimensional scene that contains three objects. The topmost node of the tree that represents this structure is the entire region. We then divide this region into four subregions, represented by four child nodes in the tree. Any subregion that contains an object or part of an object is further subdivided. This process continues until the subdivision reaches some predetermined limit. Terminal nodes are either empty or contain a labelled object. Subdivision in the case of an octree means that we start with a cube.

An octree is a representation of the objects in a scene that allows us to exploit spatial coherence because objects that are close to each other in space are represented by nodes that are close to each other in the octree.

When tracing a ray, instead of doing intersection calculations between the ray and every object in the scene, we can now trace the ray from subregion to subregion in the subdivision of occupied space. For each subregion that the ray passes through, there will only be a small number of objects (typically one or two) with which it could intersect. Provided that we can rapidly find the node in the octree that corresponds to a subregion that a ray is passing through, we have immediate access to the objects that are on, or close to, the path of the ray. Intersection calculations need only be done for these objects. If space has been subdivided to a level where each subregion contains only one or two

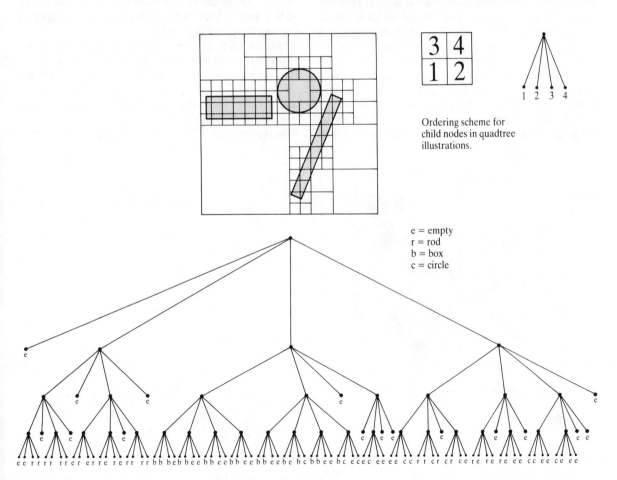

Ordering scheme for child nodes in quadtree illustrations.

e = empty
r = rod
b = box
c = circle

Figure 9.12 Quadtree representation of a two-dimensional scene at the pixel level. A similar method is used to represent a three-dimensional scene by an octree.

objects, then the number of intersection tests required for a region is small and does not tend to increase with the complexity of the scene.

In order to use the space subdivision to determine which objects are close to a ray, we must determine which subregion of space the ray passes through. This involves tracking the ray into and out of each subregion in its path. The main operation required during this process is that of finding the node in the octree, and hence the region in space, that corresponds to a point (x, y, z).

The overall tracking process starts by detecting the region that corresponds to the start point of the ray. The ray is tested for intersection with any objects that lie in this region and if there are any intersections, then the first one encountered is the one required for the ray. If there are no intersections in the initial region, then the ray must be tracked into the next region through which it passes. This is done by calculating the intersection of the ray with the boundaries of the region and thus calculating the point at which the ray leaves the region. A point on the ray a short distance into the next region is then used to find the node in the octree that corresponds to the next region. Any objects in this region are then tested for intersections with the ray. The process is repeated as the ray tracks from region to region until an intersection with

an object is found or until the ray leaves occupied space.

The simplest approach to finding the node in the octree that corresponds to a point (x, y, z) is to use the octree to guide the search for the node. Starting at the top of the tree, a simple comparison of coordinates will determine which child node represents the subregion that contains the point (x, y, z). The subregion corresponding to the child node may itself have been subdivided and another coordinate comparison will determine which of its children represents the smaller subregion that contains (x, y, z). The search proceeds down the tree until a terminal node is reached. The maximum number of nodes traversed during this search will be equal to the maximum depth of the tree. Even for a fairly fine subdivision of occupied space, the search length will be short. For example, if the space is subdivided at a resolution of $1024 \times 1024 \times 1024$, then the octree will have depth 10 ($= \log_8(1024 \times 1024 \times 1024)$).

We can summarize by explicitly stating the two fundamental operations required when tracking a ray through an octree structure. First, we have to find the voxel associated with a point in three-dimensional space, and secondly, we have to find a point, on the track of the ray, that is just inside the next region.

In the example in Figure 9.13 the space has been sub-

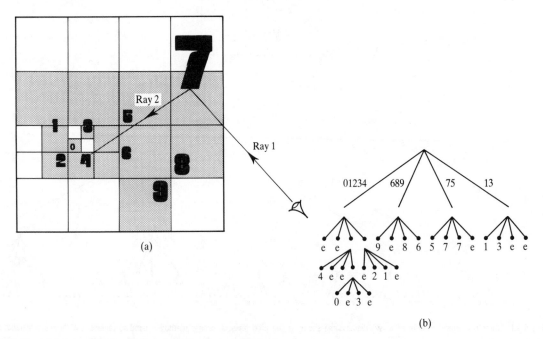

(a)

(b)

Figure 9.13   (a) Octree subdivision. (b) Secondary data structure information.

divided until each subregion contains only a single object. Ray 1 will test object 7. Ray 2 will test object 5, object 6 and object 4. The process terminates when the first intersection is found.

The tradeoffs available in an octree scheme should be fairly obvious. We can limit the depth of any branch of the tree but this increases the number of intersection candidates for the smallest voxel. Alternatively, if we subdivide until a voxel contains a single object, the maximum length of any branch may become long.

The disadvantage of using octrees, with implied cubic subdivision, can be seen from examining Figure 9.13. Depending on the nature of the scene, it is possible to have large volumes that contain only a single small object. Many rays may enter this region that do not intersect the object. This situation is similar to using a bounding volume that contains a large void area because its shape is less than optimum for the shape of the object it encloses.

Further variations of the spatial subdivision approach are described by Glassner [GLAS84] and Fujimoto *et al.* [FUJI86]. Glassner describes an alternative method for finding the node in the octree corresponding to a point (x, y, z). In fact, he does not store the structure of the octree explicitly, but accesses information about the voxels via a hash table that contains an entry for each voxel. The hash table is accessed using a code number calculated from the x, y, z-coordinates of a point. The overall ray tracking process proceeds as described in our basic method.

9.6.3 SEADS

In [FUJI86] an alternative approach to tracking the ray through the voxels in the octree is described. Now the subdivision is independent of the nature of the scene and this potential disadvantage is balanced against the faster tracking available from a uniform system. In particular, floating-point multiplication and division can be eliminated.

To understand the method it is convenient to start by ignoring the octree representation. We first describe a simple data structure representation of a space subdivision called SEADS (Spatially Enumerated Auxiliary Data Structure). This involves dividing all of occupied space into equally sized voxels regardless of occupancy by objects. The three-dimensional grid obtained in this way is analogous to that obtained by the subdivision of a two-dimensional graphics screen into pixels. Because

regions are subdivided regardless of occupancy by objects, a SEADS subdivision generates many more voxels than the octree subdivision described earlier. It thus involves 'unnecessary' demands for storage space. However, the use of a SEADS enables very fast tracking of rays from region to region. The tracking algorithm used is an extension of the DDA (Digital Differential Analyser) algorithm used in two-dimensional graphics for selecting the sequence of pixels that represents a straight line between two given end points. The DDA algorithm used in two-dimensional graphics selects a subset of the pixels passed through by a line, but the algorithm can easily be modified to find all the pixels touching the line. [FUJI86] describes how this algorithm can be extended into three-dimensional space and used to track a ray through a SEADS three-dimensional grid. The advantage of the '3D-DDA' is that it does not involve floating-point multiplication and division. The only operations involved are addition, subtraction and comparison, the main operation being integer addition on voxel coordinates.

In the example shown in Figure 9.14, ray 1 tests object 7, ray 2 tests object 5, object 6 then objects 3,4 and 0, the process terminating with a hit on object 4. You can see from this example that there will be a tradeoff between the resolution of the grid boxes, with respect to the resolution of the scene, and the size of the secondary data structure. The higher the resolution of the grid, the fewer objects within each box and the less intersection testing per ray. Set against this is the increase in the volume of information in the secondary data structure.

The heavy space overheads of the complete SEADS can be avoided by returning to an octree representation of the space subdivision. The 3D-DDA algorithm can be modified so that a ray is tracked through the voxels by traversing the octree. In the octree, a set of eight nodes with a common parent node represents a block of eight adjacent cubic regions forming a $2 \times 2 \times 2$ grid. When a ray is tracked from one region to another within this set, the 3D-DDA algorithm can be used without alteration. If a ray enters a region that is not represented by a terminal node in the tree, but is further subdivided, then the subregion that is entered is found by moving down the tree. The child node required at each level of descent can be discovered by adjusting the control variables of the DDA from the level above. If the 3D-DDA algorithm tracks a ray out of the $2 \times 2 \times 2$ region currently being traversed, then the octree must be traversed upwards to the parent node representing the complete region. The 3D-DDA algorithm then continues at this level, tracking

Uniform subdivision

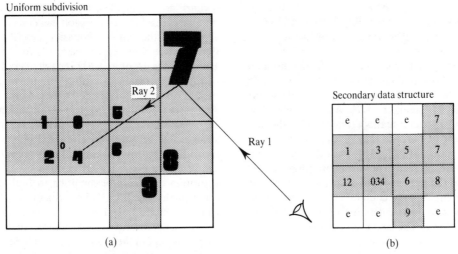

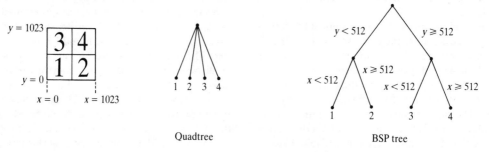

Figure 9.14   (a) Uniform subdivision (SEADS). (b) Secondary data structure information.

the ray within the set of eight regions making up the parent region. The upwards and downwards traversals of the tree involve multiplication and division of the DDA control variables by 2, but this is a cheap operation. We can see that 3D-DDA works on the uniform subdivision at a given level and the octree is traversed vertically to different levels of subdivision. Another possibility is to subdivide using a noncubic shape. This is binary space partitioning.

9.6.4 Binary space partitioning

In this scheme the auxiliary structure used to represent the subdivision is essentially an octree, but the precise data structure representation used to index the octree differs from those described previously. It is termed a 'binary space partitioning tree' or BSP tree.

Figure 9.15 demonstrates the idea in two dimensions. It contains a one-level subdivision of a square region

together with the one-level quadtree representation and the corresponding BSP tree. A simple extension to three dimensions enables an octree to be coded as a BSP tree. Each nonterminal node in the BSP tree represents a single partitioning plane that divides occupied space into two. A terminal node represents a region that is not further subdivided and would contain pointers to data structure representations of the objects intersecting that region (again typically one or two).

A BSP tree would be used in ray tracing in just the same way as in the basic octree technique described earlier. To track a ray into a new region, a point (x, y, z) in that region is generated. The node in the tree corresponding to this point is found by checking the point (x, y, z) against the plane equation at each node and following the appropriate branch at each node. The ray is then checked for intersection with any objects in the region represented by the terminal node of the BSP tree that is found by this search.

Figure 9.15   Quadtree and BSP tree representations of a one-level subdivision of a two-dimensional region.

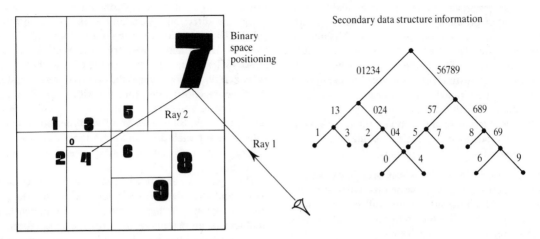

Figure 9.16

When a BSP tree is used to represent a subdivision of space into cubic cells, it shows no significant advantage over a direct data structure encoding of the octree. However, nothing said above requires that the subdivision should be into cubic cells. In fact, the idea of a BSP tree was originally introduced in [FUCH80] where the planes used to subdivide space could be at any orientation. In [FUCH80], the BSP structure was used as an aid to sorting the planes in a scene into a back-to-front ordering consistent with a given view point. The planes used to subdivide space were the planes defined by the polygons constituting the scene. These planes could lie at any orientation.

In ray tracing, it is convenient if the partitioning planes lie at right angles to the object space axes as this simplifies the test to see on which side of a plane a point lies. However, a scheme where the position of the partitioning planes depends on the distribution of the objects within occupied space has certain advantages.

Objects will often be unevenly distributed throughout occupied space. This is particularly the case when the 'objects' are actually patches used to approximate the surfaces of real objects. A single real object will be represented by a large cluster of patches in space and there will be relatively large regions of empty space between objects.

Figure 9.16 shows an example. Ray 1 traverses the BSP tree and tests objects 5 and 7, spawning ray 2. Ray 2 tests object 5, object 6, 0 and 4, finding a hit on object 4.

At this stage we examine two potential problems that can occur with both uniform and nonuniform subdivision schemes. First, we need to guard against repetitive intersection calculations in subdivision schemes where an object can appear in a number of adjacent voxels. Figure 9.17(a) shows an example where an object may be tested twice for intersection. This can be prevented by storing a unique tag for each ray and associating this tag with the object when the first intersection test is performed. Instead of testing the object again for intersection, the

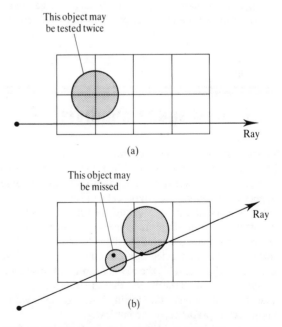

Figure 9.17 Potential problems in space subdivision schemes. (a) An object that appears in more than one voxel may be retested. (b) An object may be missed because the first intersection occurs with a further object.

results of the previous test are made available. The second potential problem is shown in Figure 9.17(b). Here a further object records a hit – the first hit encountered along the ray. However, another object is actually nearer the ray origin. The condition to prevent objects being erroneously missed is that the voxel tracking process can only be terminated when the nearest intersection point is contained within the current voxel.

Finally, we summarize and compare the three spatial coherence methods by listing their most important efficiency attributes:

- *Octrees* Good for scenes whose occupancy density varies widely – regions of low density will be sparsely subdivided, high-density regions will be finely subdivided. However, it is possible to have small objects in large regions. Stepping from region to region is slower than with the other two methods because the trees tend to be unbalanced.

- *SEADS* Stepping is faster than an octree but massive memory costs are incurred by the secondary data structure.

- *BSP* The depth of the tree is smaller than an octree for most scenes because the tree is balanced. Octree branches can be short or very long for regions of high spatial occupancy. The memory costs are generally lower than those of an octree. Void areas will tend to be smaller.

9.7 Ray space subdivision

In this unique scheme, suggested by Avro and Kirk [AVRO87], instead of subdividing space according to occupancy, ray space is subdivided into five-dimensional hypercubic regions. Each hypercube in five-dimensional space is associated with a candidate list of objects for intersection. That stage in space subdivision schemes where three-space calculations have to be invoked to track a ray through object space is now eliminated. The hypercube that contains the ray is found and this yields a *complete* list of all the objects that can intersect the ray. The cost of the intersection testing is now traded against higher scene preprocessing complexity.

A ray can be considered as a single point in five-dimensional space. It is a line with a three-dimensional origin together with a direction that can be specified by two angles in a unit sphere. Instead of using a sphere to categorize direction, Avro and Kirk use a 'direction cube'. (This is exactly the same tool as the light buffer used by Haine and Greenberg – see Section 8.4 and [HAIN86].) A ray is thus specified by the 5-tuple (x, y, z, u, v), where x, y, z is the origin of the ray and u, v the direction coordinates, together with a cube face label that indicates which face of the direction cube the ray passes through. Six copies of a five-dimensional hypercube (one for each direction cube face) thus specify a collection of rays having similar origins and similar directions.

This space is subdivided according to object occupancy and candidate lists are constructed for the subdivided regions. A 'hyper-octree' – a five-dimensional analogue of an octree – is used for the subdivision.

To construct candidate lists as five-dimensional space is subdivided, the three-dimensional equivalent of the hypercube must be used in three-space. This is a 'beam' or an unbounded three-dimensional volume that can be considered as the union of the volume of ray origins and the direction pyramid formed by a ray origin and its associated direction cell (Figure 9.18). Note that the beams in three-space will everywhere intersect each other, whereas their hypercube equivalents in five-space do not intersect. This is the crux of the method – the five-space can be subdivided and that subdivision can be achieved using binary partitioning. However, the construction of the candidate lists is now more difficult than with object space subdivision schemes. The beams must be intersected with the bounding volumes of objects. Avro and Kirk report that detecting polyhedral intersections is too costly and suggest the approximation where beams are represented or bound by cones interacting with spheres as object bounding volumes.

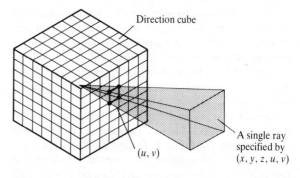

Figure 9.18 A ray (or beam) as a single point in (x, y, z, u, v) space.

10 Ray tracing III: advanced ray tracing models

Distributed ray tracing, described in this chapter, incorporates stochastic anti-aliasing, the theory of which is further discussed in Chapter 4. One of the main topics that we discuss in this chapter is backwards ray tracing. This is closely related to the radiosity method discussed in Chapter 11 and comparisons are made at the appropriate points.

Another approach to ray tracing, based on the rendering equation, is given in Chapter 12.

Introduction

In the decade that has seen ray tracing develop into (almost) a standard rendering technique, most research has concentrated on speedup techniques as we have outlined in preceding chapters. This is simply because ray tracing cannot be used routinely without significant speedup and the development of efficiency schemes enabled the commercial use of ray tracing.

With the possible exception of anti-aliasing, much less research has been devoted to improving the quality and correctness of ray-traced images and to overcoming the deficiencies that we have discussed. These are much more difficult problems than efficiency schemes. The elegant distributed ray tracing scheme of Cook [COOK84b] is a notable exception, and perhaps it was the very success of this approach that discouraged further research into image quality in ray tracing.

This chapter, then, is concerned with alternatives to the normal ray tracing geometry which samples the scene by tracing infinitesimally thin rays through it. We also look at approaches to diffuse interaction which generally requires both a change in the geometry and a reversal in the direction of ray tracing. This technique is known as 'backwards ray tracing'. In terms of the light transfer mechanisms discussed in Chapter 12, we examine in this chapter alternative ray tracing approaches that:

1. implement specular to diffuse transfer;

2. implement global diffuse interaction;

3. improve the realism of global specular interaction.

Backwards ray tracing, or ray tracing from the light source, is an approach that was first suggested in 1986 [AVRO86]. It has been taken up more recently in [CHAT87] and [ZHU88]. This technique has the potential to cope with certain aspects of diffuse interaction, and can be used in certain contexts as a cheap alternative to radiosity. We also discuss techniques that concentrate on increasing the reality in ray-traced imagery and which will diminish the immediately recognizable signature of an image that has been produced by a conventional naive ray tracer.

10.1 Backwards ray tracing

Standard ray tracers omit all consideration of indirect illumination except pure specular interaction given by the ray tracing paradigm. In general these higher order effects are responsible for much of what we see. Consider, for example, diffuse interaction. A single light source, such as a window, will only tend to directly illuminate surfaces opposite it. Other surfaces are lit by diffuse interaction. Diffuse interaction between surfaces is ignored by both standard reflection models and the simple ray tracing model described in Chapter 8. In each case, diffuse interaction is approximated by a constant. We have discussed that ray tracing from the eye cannot be used to evaluate diffuse interaction because of the computational cost; this section introduces feasible methods to the solution of the problem. Another important topic is correct shadow modelling – the intensity of the diffuse light within a shadow and the fact that most shadows have soft edges may depend as much on diffuse interaction as the obscuring effect of the object. Colour bleeding is discussed in Chapter 11 as a subtle second-order effect that also depends on diffuse interaction. Finally, caustics – observed for example, when light interacts with water – can be regarded as local variations of diffuse light. Refractive effects concentrate the light in certain regions and dilute it in others.

Even the correct modelling of a light source is difficult with normal ray tracing. In Figure 10.1 none of the eye rays traced through the object hit the light sources modelled as points. This issue is 'glossed over' in a conventional ray tracer by using a hybrid model, where effects due to direct illumination are modelled using a local Phong reflection and transmission term (see Section

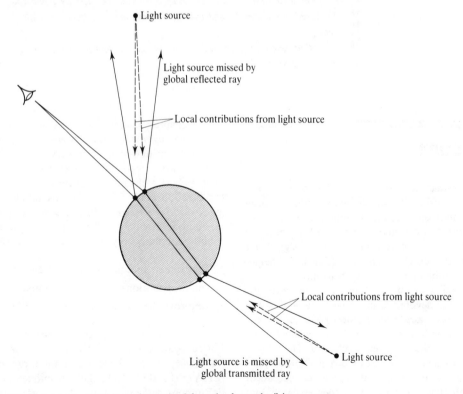

Light source

Light source missed by global reflected ray

Local contributions from light source

Local contributions from light source

Light source is missed by global transmitted ray

Light source

Figure 10.1 Eye rays cannot in general be used to gather information from point light sources.

8.2). Thus we 'mix' empirically blurred local terms with precisely traced global terms. Figure 10.1 demonstrates the necessity for this hybrid model in a conventional ray tracer – it would otherwise be nearly impossible to gain information from the light sources, as we shortly discuss.

Diffuse interaction can be handled by the radiosity method, but normally this does not calculate specular interaction. Some of the more important effects of diffuse interaction, such as colour bleeding and caustics, can be incorporated into the ray tracing paradigm by using backwards ray tracing. In the case of radiosity we have a straight implementation of a rigorous theory, while backwards ray tracing is an algorithmic variation of general ray tracing that in some way prevents the otherwise intractable computational effort of evaluating diffuse interaction by conventional ray tracing. (Here we have a problem of terminology. We are using the term 'reverse' or 'backwards' ray tracing because ray tracing from the light source is the reverse of conventional ray tracing. Some authors (notably Glassner [GLAS89]) prefer to label conventional ray tracing as backwards ray tracing and ray tracing from the light source as forwards ray tracing because this describes the actual direction of propagation of the light. This confusion is unfortunate.)

To understand the need for backwards ray tracing we show why forward ray tracing falls down in certain contexts by considering the following example. Figure 10.2 shows a table lamp illuminating a table directly along LT and indirectly by light reflecting off the mirror along LMT. The latter direction, because of the specular bounce off the mirror, is an example of the specular to diffuse transfer mechanism (see Chapter 12), and it is this mechanism to which backwards ray tracing is eminently suited. A standard ray tracer fires rays from the eye through the image plane and into the scene. Suppose one such ray, ET, hits the table at T. Further rays are then spawned at T to determine its illumination. The ray tracer knows that if T can see the light it will contribute to its illumination so a shadow ray TL is sent to the light. Unfortunately, it is completely ignorant of light arriving by the second, indirect route. The only way it can find this is by accident, that is, by firing enough rays in enough directions such that one coincides with the direction TM.

Clearly if we extend forward ray tracers to cope with indirect light then they would have to work very hard by sampling the whole environment and pumping out an enormous number of rays in order to ensure a high enough probability of arriving at the light indirectly. In fact, only the most sophisticated of forward ray tracers

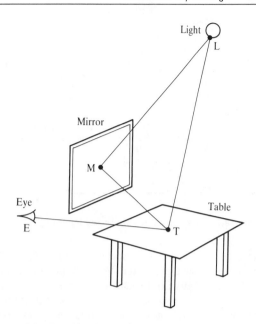

Figure 10.2 Illustrating the need for backwards ray tracing.

([KAJI86] and Chapter 12) has managed to do this. In his work Kajiya produced caustics caused by light passing through glass balls by using an intelligently optimized generalization of ray tracing – path tracing. Even so, in order to ensure that the rays, after being refracted through the glass balls, had a high enough probability of hitting the light source, the light source had to be specified as an area source roughly the same size as the glass balls and had to be positioned near to the balls.

The problem is fundamental and is due to the fact that we are tracing in precisely the reverse direction to that in which light is propagated. Only the light energy that happens to coincide with the path of forward rays is taken into account. A far more intuitive approach for specular-to-diffuse transfer is to shoot rays from the light thereby following the direction of the illumination and removing our ignorance of indirect illumination. Basically, it boils down to the fact that in this context, it is far more natural to ask the question: where does the light go to? rather than: where is the light coming from?

Backwards ray tracing usually implies two passes. Rays are traced first from the light source and then from the eye. Figure 10.3 shows the idea. Rays are cast from the light source onto the surface of interest, in this case the plane supporting the sphere. Diffuse illumination can be approximated from the ray hits on this surface and the

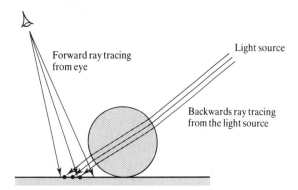

Figure 10.3 Illustrating the idea of two-pass ray tracing.

surface can be considered to possess illumination over its extent due to the light source. For example, the spatial density of ray hits can be used to approximate diffuse illumination on the surface. The second pass traces rays from the eye and picks up the diffuse illumination showered on the scene in the first pass as if it was a surface property.

10.1.1 Two-pass ray tracing

In this section, by way of a practical introduction to backwards ray tracing, we deal with the complex effect of caustics – beautiful phenomena that occur whenever light interacts with a refracting material, in particular, water. Later, in Section 10.2, we go on to look at how backwards ray tracing can be used in the more general application of diffuse interaction.

Backwards ray tracing is a method that enables caustics to be modelled. Caustics are the patterns of light that appear on a surface due to light reflecting from a curved specular surface or refracting through an inhomogeneous medium. Common examples are light passing through a wineglass onto a table top and the patterns formed on the base and sides of a swimming pool due to light refracting through the water from a wind-perturbed surface. Caustics form because rays from a light source converge and diverge when interacting with objects in an environment.

We can consider caustics to be a form of diffuse reflection, where the spatial density of reflected rays leaving the surface changes, resulting in patterns of light and dark areas. Caustics formed on second-hit surfaces, such as the base of a swimming pool, are an example of

specular-to-diffuse transport (see Chapter 12 for a discussion of light transport models). Any light propagation from a second to a third and subsequent hits is pure diffuse interaction. In this section we model caustics generally as second-hit phenomena, although the method can theoretically be extended to include transport of the nature:

specular → specular → specular → . . . → specular → diffuse

Arvo [ARVO86] suggests tracing rays from the light onto the caustic surface. Note that this is a view-independent process. Such rays converge on certain areas on the target surface to form caustics. The intensity of the caustic on a flat surface can be determined from the spatial density of the ray hits. A second pass uses conventional ray tracing from the eye to compute a final view-dependent image.

Central to the working of such a strategy will be how information derived during the first pass is communicated to the second or, to borrow a phrase from Arvo, how the rays 'meet in the middle'. Arvo suggests achieving this via an illumination map, consisting of a grid of data points, which is pasted onto each object in the scene in much the same way that a texture map would be. A given illumination ray, originating from the light, strikes an object at a point and deposits a certain amount of energy in the surrounding data points and continues on its course, reflecting and refracting through the scene. The first pass consists of 'showering' the scene with these illumination rays. By ignoring first generation hits which directly illuminate an object, upon completion of this 'showering' the illumination map will provide a measure of the indirect illumination received by the object. During the second pass a ray striking the object will pick up a value for this indirect illumination using bilinear interpolation between nearby data points.

The first phase, by using infinitely thin illumination rays to deposit quanta of energy, is point sampling the specular-to-diffuse energy distribution of the scene. Again, since there is no reason to assume this distribution to be slowly varying, this approach will be highly prone to aliasing problems. This aliasing is compounded further as the discretization of the illumination maps into data points may introduce yet more artefacts. Indeed, a faithful representation of a specular-to-diffuse effect of a given frequency will require construction of an illumination map of greater frequency of data points and, in turn, showering sufficient illumination rays to ensure that hits on the map are many times as dense as these data points. Clearly this approach is extremely expensive. Plate 33 shows a scene computed using this method.

10.1.2 Light beam tracing

We now present a two-pass algorithm, the first pass based on a variation of backwards ray tracing called 'backwards beam tracing', that provides a solution of specular-to-diffuse transfer in polygonal environments including shadowing effects (which, as we shall see, are different from conventional computer graphic shadows). The algorithm is closest in spirit to a suggestion made by Heckbert and Hanrahan ([HECK84] and Section 9.5), and it is from here that it takes its name.

In the algorithm, objects in the environment are separated into specular and diffuse objects. Specular objects retransmit the light incident upon them, by reflection or refraction, onto the diffuse objects.

First pass: backward beam tracing

For each polygon of each specular object we construct a light beam by casting rays from each vertex to the light. Next we construct the transmitted light beam, by reflection or refraction with the vertex normals, and sweep this beam throughout the entire scene testing for intersections with diffuse polygons. If an intersection occurs we project the transmitted light beam onto the plane of the diffuse polygon. Shown in Figure 10.4 are two such light beams, the first of which becomes divergent after refraction, spreading the light over a larger area than that of the specular polygon, the second, convergent, focusing light onto the plane of the diffuse polygon.

This projection forms the caustic polygon which is allotted an intensity and a tag signifying which diffuse polygon is responsible for its generation. The caustic polygon is added to the polygonal database as a surface detail polygon, that is, a polygon which does not affect the shape of an object – only its shading. This step has the usual advantages of view independence, namely, it need only be computed once providing the spatial relationships between the objects and lights remain unchanged.

Since, under this scheme, the resolution of the specular polygons dictates the resolution of the transmitted light beam, the size of the specular polygon is critical. A given specular object may be faithfully represented by polygons of a given size. But the resolution required to repre-

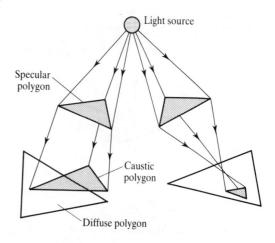

Figure 10.4 Generation of caustic polygons in light beam tracing.

sent the object may well be inadequate when representing the light this object transmits. This is not surprising since there is no guarantee that their respective Nyquist frequencies are the same. In general, it was found that the specular polygons had to be much smaller when modelling the light than when modelling the object itself.

Second pass: rendering

The rendering phase proceeds largely as it would normally, with only one exception. If a diffuse polygon is visible under a pixel we check to see if it has any caustic polygons associated with it. In general, a diffuse polygon may intersect more than one light beam and so can have more than one attendant caustic polygon. The intensity of the caustic polygon is simply added to the diffuse component of the final shaded value of the diffuse polygon.

What intensity are we to assign to the caustic polygon? Let us assume that distances between the light and objects are large compared to distances between the objects themselves. (If this is not the case an extension to include $1/r^2$ falloff is straightforward.) The specular polygon, then, has an intensity, I, incident upon it. The fraction of energy, E, arriving on the specular polygon is the product of I and the area of the polygon 'seen' by the light, that is, its area projected in the direction of the light L. Referring to Figure 10.5 then, we have:

$$E = I \left(N \cdot L \right) \text{AreaSpec}$$

where N, the normal associated with the plane of the specular polygon, is usually different from the normals

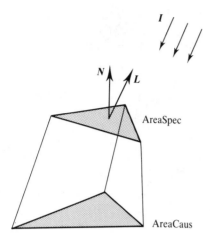

Figure 10.5 Generation of $I_{caustic}$.

at the individual vertices. Assuming that the specular polygon absorbs no energy, E will thus be the energy incident on the caustic polygon. We can easily include an absorption coefficient into the calculation should this assumption not hold. Providing the specular polygon is small enough such that the variation of distances between points on the specular polygon and points on the caustic polygon is negligible, we can say that this energy will be distributed uniformly over the caustic polygon. The intensity of the caustic polygon $I_{caustic}$, is thus:

$$I_{caustic} = \frac{E}{AreaCaus}$$
$$= I \left(N \cdot L \right) \frac{AreaSpec}{AreaCaus} \qquad (10.1)$$

This term resembles the form factor of the radiosity method (Chapter 11). This is not surprising since its derivation starts from similar considerations of energy transfer, projected areas, and so on. Indeed, removing the assumptions made about distances in the derivation would take us even closer to a form factor definition. This suggests that the step of constructing caustic polygons from specular polygons could be construed as constructing special, simplified, adaptive form factors that take full advantage of an a priori knowledge of light propagation in the environment. Compare this to the traditional method of building form factors which entails a somewhat arbitrary dicing up of surfaces completely independently of the light distribution. (Many radiosity algorithms quote this independence/ignorance of lights as an advantage – while it may be a plus in terms of

generality it is certainly not a good advertisement for the rendering of complex images efficiently.)

The algorithm has the following advantages:

1. *Ease of implementation* Since the caustic polygons translate into surface detail polygons during the second pass, standard depth buffer or ray tracing renderers need only minor modification to implement the algorithm.

2. *Efficiency* Above all the algorithm is efficient; as we shall see later, frame times are sufficiently small to enable animated caustic sequences to be produced. Reasons for this efficiency include the following:

    (a) The reduction of caustic polygons to surface detail polygons in the second pass removes the need to clip the caustic polygon to its diffuse polygon in the first pass. During the rendering a caustic polygon is only rendered if its diffuse polygon is behind it. In the case of depth buffer renderers, regions where the caustic polygon exists and the diffuse polygon does not are masked out by the pixel mask of the diffuse polygon. In the case of ray tracers these regions are not even considered since ray/caustic polygon intersections are only tested for after a ray/diffuse polygon intersection occurs.

    (b) Optimization techniques developed for ray/object intersections in forward ray tracers, such as space partitioning or bounding volumes, can be adopted when testing for transmitted beam/diffuse polygon intersections during the first pass.

3. By replacing rays which point sample the environment with beams, we avoid aliasing problems associated with the former. By using light beams we are effectively tracing a bundle of rays with an intensity varying as the density of rays in the bundle changes through the optical system. As shown in Equation (10.1) this density is inversely proportional to the bundle's cross-section, or, in our terminology, the area of the caustic polygon.

4. The intricacy of the light pattern produced on the diffuse surface is directly related to the geometric complexity of the specular surface. The greater the variation in curvature of the specular surface the greater the directions over which incident light is dispersed. By driving the method from the specular surface, regions over which the curvature varies rapidly can be sampled more intensively (such an example appears later). Such adaptive sampling

enables sharply varying specular-to-diffuse pheno-mena to be represented, thereby extending the range over existing techniques which hitherto have con-fined themselves to rendering only the vaguest of effects.

We now look at caustics in more detail and see how the algorithm can be applied to these phenomena. The name 'caustics', derived from the fact that a lens can focus sunlight to burn a hole in a surface, is a term taken from classical optics and is completely synonymous and inter-changeable with our term 'specular-to-diffuse transfer' from computer graphics. We include a discussion of the treatment of caustics within classical optics here [BORN64], since it provides us with valuable insights into the precise nature of specular-to-diffuse transfer.

10.1.3 Backwards ray tracing and caustics

We start with some definitions. If a curve exists such that it is tangent to a family of curves but is not itself a member of that family, then it is the envelope of that family. Let the family of curves be those rays transmitted from a specular surface, then the caustic surface is the envelope of the transmitted rays. Also, since the evolute of a surface is the locus of its centre of curvature, an alternative and equivalent definition of a caustic surface would be the evolute of the transmitted wavefront.

Figure 10.6 shows clearly an example of a caustic surface formed after reflection, called a 'catacaustic', created when light travelling parallel to the axis of revolu-tion of a spherical mirror is reflected by it. The caustic can be shown to be an epicycloid, the cusp of which is at the principal focus of the mirror. An everyday example is the bright line on the surface of a cup filled with liquid – caused by intersections between rays of light reflected from the cylindrical wall of the cup and the liquid.

Figure 10.7 shows another caustic formed by refrac-tion in water. Caustics formed by refraction are called 'diacaustics'. In this case the water's surface is deformed by a vortex shed from an object, say a paddle, moving through the water. The vortex causes a caustic whose sec-tion, such as would be seen at the bottom of a tank, con-sists of two concentric circles bounding a bright ring as shown in Figure 10.7. A radial slice of this section in rela-tion to the caustic surface is shown diagrammatically at the foot of the figure. The circles on the edges of the ring,

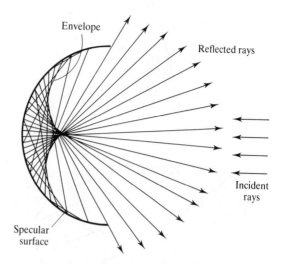

Figure 10.6   Reflected caustic in spherical mirror.

caused by intersection with the caustic surface, are brightest; the interior of the ring where light is refracted away from the axis of the vortex is darkest. Studies of such patterns have enabled Berry and Hajnal in 'The Shadows of Floating Objects and Dissipating Vortices' [BERR83] to predict analytically the shape of the vortex to be a blend of a parabolic core surrounded by a hyper-bolic surface.

Let us look at the caustic surface more closely. Con-sider the specular surface described by curvilinear coor-dinates (u, v) as shown in Figure 10.8. Each point

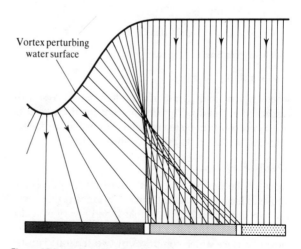

Figure 10.7   Refracted caustic through water vortex.

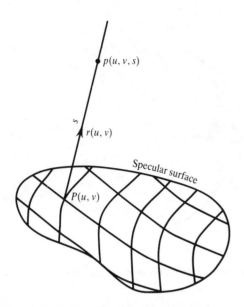

Figure 10.8   A specular surface with curvilinear coordinates.

$P(u, v)$ on the surface has a transmitted ray in the direction of $r(u, v)$ associated with it. Any point p on this ray is given by:

$$p(u, v, s) = P(u, v) + sr(u, v)$$

where s is the length along Pp. Foci occur where rays emanating from the surface intersect, or to translate into terms of differential geometry, where points on these rays are separated by a distance that is of second or higher order, that is:

$$p(u, v, s) = p(u + du, v + dv, s + ds)$$

which, expanding out, gives:

$$p_u du + p_v dv + p_s ds = 0$$

where p_u, p_v and p_s are the partial derivatives with respect to u, v and s. This implies that the three vectors p_u, p_v and p_s are coplanar which is equivalent to saying that their scalar triple product vanishes, that is:

$$[p_u, p_v, p_s] = 0$$

Now p is linear in s, and p_s is independent of s, so the above reduces to a quadratic in s. This means that there are two foci on each light ray. As u and v vary over the specular surface the foci will trace out the corresponding caustic surface which comprises of two separate caustic sheets. This is a remarkable result; although the transmitted light may create structures rivalling a pinnacled cathedral in complexity, each light ray will be tangent to the two sheets.

These caustic sheets meet at cusps or folds, which are actually sections of three-dimensional catastrophes, and are the proper study of catastrophe optics [BERR80]. Returning to Figure 10.6, one of these sheets is a trumpet-shaped surface of revolution, whose cross-section is an epicycloid; the other degenerates to a line segment lying on the axis of revolution. In the case of Figure 10.7 the caustic sheets consist of two roughly cylindrical sheets joined at a cusp-edged ring.

Returning to our algorithm, the diffuse polygon can be interpreted as sampling slices of this partially concealed structure. The intersection of the plane of the diffuse polygon with this structure provides us with a cross-sectional view of it – a picture made up of caustic polygons. This picture will depend largely on the orientation and distance between the diffuse polygon and the caustic surface.

If the diffuse polygon is close to one of the caustic sheets and more or less tangential to it, it will appear approximately uniformly lit – the intensity increasing the closer the diffuse polygon gets to the sheet. If the diffuse polygon is more or less normal to a caustic sheet, the variation of light intensities across it will increase the closer it gets to the sheet – until it actually intersects the sheet whereupon it will have a bright line running through it. The farther the diffuse polygon gets from the caustic surface, the more negligible and uniform the effect becomes as the light rays become more dispersed, that is, as the specular-to-diffuse effect tends to diffuse. The latter consideration provides us with a bound beyond which specular-to-diffuse effects can be ignored. The caustic surface is bounded by that focus which is farthest from the specular surface. Diffuse objects whose distance from the specular surface is significantly greater than this bound need not be scanned against the transmitted light beams.

10.1.4 Shadows and caustics

The algorithm also solves for shadowing effects on the diffuse surface within the context of first generation specular-to-diffuse transfer (conventional shadows are cast on the specular surface and can be ignored here). There are two distinct cases depending on whether the shadowing object is:

1. between the light and the specular surface, or

2. between the specular surface and the diffuse surface.

These cases have to be treated separately, but both produce shadowing effects on the diffuse surface that differ from 'traditional' computer graphics shadows. In case 1 a straight silhouette edge may produce a shadow on the diffuse surface whose edge is not, in general, straight, as the light gets 'bent' at the specular surface. In case 2 the shadowing object, embedded in this region of 'bent' light, occludes light rays that are travelling in directions other than the traditional direction, that is, directly from the light.

Case 1 has to be dealt with in the view-independent phase. Each ray of the light beam is tested for hits with objects between the specular polygon and the light. If a specular polygon is completely occluded it is passed over. If it is partially obscured we recursively subdivide the specular polygon – processing the smaller ones that can see the light as normal. The subdivision stops when the area of the specular polygon falls below a predefined level. An alternative approach here would be to clip out the silhouette of the obstruction from the beam cross-section and to continue to process the remainder similar to [HECK84]. We adopted the recursive subdivision strategy – wary of fragmented, nonconvex polygons that can be produced by recursively clipping.

Case 2 can be handled in either the view-independent or the view-dependent phase. If it is solved in the former we proceed largely as in case 1 except each ray of the transmitted light beam is tested for hits with objects between the specular surface and the diffuse surface. To solve in the view-dependent phase we carry over the rays of the transmitted light beam from the view-independent phase as the normals of a caustic polygon. A caustic polygon underneath a pixel can only make a contribution to that pixel then, if the rays fired in the direction of its normals hit the specular surface before they hit anything else.

10.1.5 Light/water interaction

As stated previously, we confined our application to model a specific subset of first generation specular-to-diffuse transfer, namely the simulation of light/water interaction where the water surface acts as the specular surface. Our principal justification lies in the fact that no computer graphics model of these phenomena has previously been presented and the results achieved are realistic in terms of rendering, animation and demands made upon the computer thus extending the class of natural phenomena capable of being effectively simulated.

Strong sunlight incident on water that is gently perturbed, by wind say, will produce familiar sinuous shifting patterns of light on objects beneath the water's surface as they intersect the diacaustic. Such patterns were studied and painted by Hockney [HOCK71]. Plate 34 is taken from an animated sequence showing these effects as viewed underwater when a shaft of light, coming through a window say, is incident on the surface of an indoor pool. These images were generated using an enhanced depth buffer renderer. Note, as predicted in Section 10.1.3, the sides of the pool, which are roughly tangential to the diacaustic, are more uniformly lit than the floor, which is roughly normal to the diacaustic and contains the greatest variation of light intensities.

As the pattern is driven directly by the water surface, animating the pattern entails animating the water surface. The water surface consists of a polygonal mesh made up of triangles displaced by a height field. The height field is a superposition of a distribution of sine waves of varying frequency and amplitude (as used in [MAX81] to which the reader is referred); since the details of the surface modelling are not essential to the application, more sophisticated water models may easily be substituted. Since, under this model, the wave speed is a function of its frequency and gravity – animating the water surface consists of deciding upon an appropriate frequency/amplitude distribution and fine-tuning the time interval over consecutive frames to achieve the desired effect.

Figure 10.9 shows three frames taken from a sequence that vizualizes the working of this algorithm. Several water triangles are selected and the light beams constructed from them by backwards ray tracing are shown rendered transparently. The sequence shows how the refracted part of the beams varies in time as the water is animated. In the first slide the specular polygons from these beams are rendered on the base of the pool. The relationship between the cross-section of beam as it cuts the base of the pool and the intensity of the resultant specular polygon is clearly seen. The next slide shows the addition of a few more specular polygons from 'unseen' beams, and the final slide shows how all the specular polygons together make up the caustic pattern.

Under certain conditions, particles or impurities in the water that are within the transmitted beams may become visible by scattering the light – enabling us in effect to see

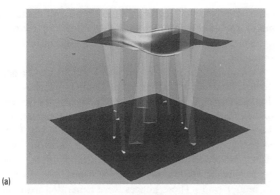

(a)

(b)

(c)

Figure 10.9 Three frames taken from a sequence that visualizes the working of this algorithm. Several water triangles are selected and the light beams constructed from them by backwards ray tracing are shown rendered transparently. The sequence shows how the refracted part of the beams varies in time as the water is animated. In (a) the specular polygons from these beams are rendered on the base of the pool. The relationship between the cross-section of beam as it cuts the base of the pool and the intensity of the resultant specular polygon is clearly seen. (b) shows the addition of a few more specular polygons from 'unseen' beams and (c) shows how all the specular polygons together make up the caustic pattern.

the transmitted light beam as opposed to cross-sections of it. As the water surface changes shape regions that previously dispersed the light may now focus it and vice versa – causing the beams themselves to change shape accordingly.

If the triangles in the polygonal mesh are sufficiently small, the variation of the refracted rays along an edge of a triangle can be ignored. This approximation enables us to represent the beams as polygonal illumination volumes. These beams are shown in Plate 34, and are rendered using a modified version of the light volume rendering technique as proposed in [NISH87]. As in that paper, assuming uniform particle density, we integrate intensities of the scattered light along segments of rays that lie within the illumination volumes. But we also include an additional term in the integration to account for the concentration, or dispersion, of light within the beam.

Plate 35 is taken from an animated sequence of an outdoor swimming pool seen from above. These images were generated using a standard ray tracer. Strictly speaking, the additional refraction of rays from the diffuse surface, through the water, to the eye means this is an example of specular-to-diffuse-to-specular transport. The animation is particularly effective since it is really the combined effect of two separate animations – one imposed on the other. The underwater animating pattern is seen through an animating water surface. These figures also show the shadow cast by the diving board on the pool – an example of case 1 in Section 10.1.4. Plate 35 (bottom) shows the shadow with the water surface taken away, clearly illustrating the point that straight silhouette edges can produce shadows with curved edges.

Since the water surface changes frame for frame, the view-independent phase consisting of generating the caustic polygons must be calculated likewise. By taking advantage of the fact that we are considering first generation effects only, a transmitted beam can only contribute to an image if it is itself within the image; significant improvements in efficiency were obtained by first testing for intersections between the transmitted beam and the viewing frustrum of the image, rejecting those that fell outside.

We now consider a rather subtle example of light/water interaction caused by a meniscus. A pencil partially immersed in water under an overhead light will produce a bifurcated shadow separated by a whitened gap which has been termed the 'shadow-sausage effect' [ADLE67]. Both the dry and submerged parts of the pencil cast normal shadows (cases 1 and 2 of Section 10.1.4, respectively) but the meniscus generates caustics which concentrate light in the gap area thereby washing out the shadow one would expect to find. Plate 36 shows a good approximation of this phenomenon with the front section of the bowl removed for clarity. The meniscus is represented as an elliptical annular region over which the normals are varied from the unperturbed vertical state on the exterior boundary to the contact angle with the shaft at the interior. This contact angle changes round the shaft, being greatest where the pencil forms an acute angle with the water and least where the angle is most obtuse. Both the shadows and caustics were calculated at the view-independent phase by adaptively subdividing the water surface – performing more work around shadow edges and the meniscus.

Finally, we give an example of caustic patterns formed from reflection, rather than refraction. This is shown in Plate 37 where the caustics on the hull are formed from reflection of light from the perturbed water surface. This also differs from the swimming pool example in that the surface receiving the caustics is curved rather than planar.

10.2 Backwards ray tracing: diffuse interaction

Compared with the radiosity method of determining diffuse interaction, backwards ray tracing has not received much attention. It was first suggested by Heckbert and Hanrahan [HECK84] and then by Arvo [ARVO86]. The first full implementation appears to be by Chattopadhyay and Fujimoto [CHAT87].

Heckbert's method is, in principle, a recursive ray tracer that starts from the light source and uses an efficiency scheme (beam tracing) to determine diffuse interaction. The main thrust of Heckbert's paper is the application of the beam tracing method to speed up conventional or eye ray tracing (Section 9.6.5) and he suggests applying exactly the same method to backwards tracing from the light source. Note that this scheme can be imagined as tracking the propagation of light as it leaves a light source, hits the first surfaces, reflects off them and illuminates the second hit surfaces that are not seen by the light source. These rays hit third surfaces and so on.

Chattopadhyay's method [CHAT87] can be viewed in the same light, as you might say, and the computation in this case is made possible by the combination of an iterative method and the use of a three-dimensional grid system. These methods are similar both theoretically and in effect to the radiosity method, but contain differences that will be dealt with later.

The computational explosion is avoided in Chattopadhyay's method by first locating, using backwards ray tracing, all those surfaces that can see the light source. These initial surfaces are then themselves treated as light sources and an iterative process is started in which the diffuse interaction between all surfaces is considered.

Comparing this with the conventional ray tracing paradigm, rays are traced from the light source to each 'seen' surface, that is, surfaces that can see the light source. This identifies those surfaces that receive direct illumination and act as 'initial' diffuse reflectors or secondary sources in the iterative process.

The method is again a two-pass approach: the first pass – ray tracing from the light source(s) and evaluating diffuse interreflection – is view independent; the second pass – conventional ray tracing from the eye – is view dependent. The local diffuse term in Equation (8.1) is replaced by two terms:

$$I_{diffuse} = I_{direct\ diffuse} + I_{indirect\ diffuse}$$

The first pass, initially by ray tracing from the light source, finds all the surfaces that receive direct illumination. This depends not only on whether they can be seen by the light source, but also on their k_d value and their orientation with respect to light sources. Surfaces that reflect direct illumination of an intensity lower than some threshold can be ignored. The iteration that evaluates diffuse interreflection only considers such surfaces, and the iteration proceeds by treating each surface that emits diffuse light reflected from a light source as a light source itself.

The iteration proceeds, effectively tracking the propagation of light from the nth hit surface to the $(n + 1)$th hit surface. The process terminates when the maximum intensity difference, for all surfaces, over two iterations falls below a threshold. The intensity of the secondary surfaces is initially set to zero and it is assumed that secondary surfaces can only affect the intensity of other secondary surfaces. The process will gradually converge because at any point in the iteration the intensity is reduced by the product of all the diffuse reflection coefficients of surfaces that contribute to the light at the current point of interest.

Note that the evaluation of this term should obviate the need for a constant ambient term, since, as we have discussed, this is just an approximation to diffuse inter-reflection. However, a small ambient component may be necessary if the iteration is stopped early, leaving some surfaces dark. There is an obvious parallel to the use of a (decreasing) ambient component in the progressive refinement manifestation of the radiosity method (Chapter 11) where an ambient term is used to illuminate a partially complete solution.

Geometrically, the scene is contained in a regular three-dimensional grid and ray tracing uses a three-dimensional DDA (see Section 9.6.3). The intensities associated with a secondary surface are held at the vertices of the voxels that contain the secondary surface and these intensities are then used as light sources with respect to all other secondary surfaces as the iteration proceeds.

We have mentioned that the method is similar in effect and execution to the progressive refinement method used in radiosity. There are, however, major differences. The radiosity method is a rigorous, theoretically correct technique that evaluates, to within the patch subdivision accuracy, a precise value for diffuse illumination on surfaces in a closed environment. The above iterative method is an approximate technique that works for either a closed or an open environment. Another significant difference is that the relative orientation of two interacting surfaces and the effect of this on the intensity of the diffuse interaction are not accounted for in the above method. In the radiosity method the form factors are a function of the relative orientation of pairs of surfaces.

An obvious theoretical solution is to spawn a set of reflected rays in directions perturbed according to the perturbations in the surface at the intersection point; but this is subject to the same computational explosion that we discussed in the context of tracing diffuse rays. The methods in this section are ways in which more information is extracted from the environment, such that blurred reflections and soft shadows can be modelled. The methods in this section and the next are inextricably bound up with anti-aliasing and the material should be read in conjunction with the relevant material in Chapter 4. Generally in these two sections we will describe how the algorithms work, giving a more theoretical justification in Chapter 4.

In 1984 two papers were published that addressed the deficiencies that arise from tracing infinitesimally thin beams. Amantides [AMAN84] suggested ray tracing with conical beams and Cook [COOK84b] introduced the elegant and more general technique of distributed ray tracing that unified problems in both the space and time domain and proposed a multidimensional probabilistic sampling technique. Both solutions still only deal with specular-to-specular interaction but increase the realism of the mechanism.

In cone tracing we consider how blurred reflection (and refraction) and soft shadows can be modelled using the device of considering a ray as a cone. (Replacing a single ray with a geometric entity was discussed in Section 9.5. There the motivation was efficiency.) The cone

10.3 Cone tracing

We have discussed the fact that because conventional ray tracing uses infinitesimally thin rays, the images produced exhibit a distinct ray-traced signature. The most obvious of these are perfectly sharp multiple reflections, which do not tend to occur in reality because surfaces are never perfectly smooth. This effect is further exacerbated by the use of a hybrid model which will impose, on the same object, a blurred reflection of the direct light sources, together with perfect reflections of nearby objects. Similarly, shadow rays and point light sources produce perfect or hard-edged shadows.

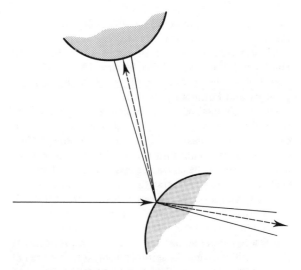

Figure 10.10 Reflection and refraction using cones to simulate spread due to surface roughness.

model used is a right circular cone, represented by an apex, a centre line and a spread angle. Standard reflection/refraction formulae can be applied to the centre line to track the cone through object space. This is equivalent to considering bundles of rays rather than a single ray. In Figure 10.10 a single ray hits a surface, the resultant reflected and refracted rays spread about the mirror direction over a solid angle that will be a function of the nature of the surface roughness. If we assume that the ray bundles form, say, a regular cone, then those points that the cone base intersects on the second-hit surface are merged or integrated into a single point at the first hit, and the first-hit object will reflect a blurred image of the second object. (The simple case of intersection of a cone and a sphere was discussed in Section 8.3.5). Note that the degree of blurring will be a function of the distance of the reflected object from the surface in which it is reflecting (Figure 10.11). The reason for this is that the longer the cone gets, the larger is its base area.

Figure 10.12 shows that soft-edged shadows are formed by having a light source that possesses a spatial extent (that is, it is not a point source). In the illustration the shadow will graduate from its darkest value, through a continuous decrease in intensity, to the no shadow area. The intensity of points within this graduation can be determined by casting bundles of shadow feelers, forming cones rather than a single ray. This approach cannot correctly account for shadows cast by transparent objects.

Amantides [AMAN84] points out that a cone is a mathematically convenient approximation to defining ray beams more correctly as pyramids. These would be set up initially using the eye as the apex of the pyramid together with four planes that are formed by the pixel sides. Although a variation of this approach is implemented by Hanrahan (see Section 9.5) as an efficiency scheme, Amantides points out that it is lacking in many respects as a general scheme, because intersection

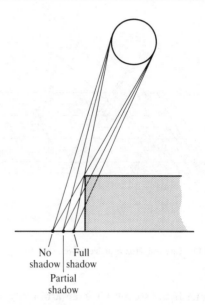

Figure 10.12 Casting cones from an area in shadow to a distributed light source.

calculations become too involved when curved surfaces are considered. Thus a simple cone is proposed to approximate the pyramid, where the initial cone has its apex at the eye and has a radius at the image plane of one pixel width. Intersection calculations now involve not only hit determination, but also the calculation of the area of the object intersected by the cone and the integration of this information to give a single value at the cone apex.

Soft shadows and blurred reflection can be evaluated by controlling the radius of the cone to simulate the effect of surface roughness. In the case of soft shadows, the cone can be made to fit the light source, and an intensity can be evaluated according to the fraction of the cone intersecting the light source, compared with the fraction intersecting the object. Blurred reflections can be simulated to any degree by varying the angle of the cone, and the method correctly simulates the dependence of the degree of blurriness on distance. The examples given in [AMAN84] are somewhat limited in that they are textures based in a planar map reflecting from an object. Here the integration of the cone intersection area is relatively straightforward (Figure 10.13). (In fact if cone tracing terminates at the second hit on a planar map, then reflection/refraction mapping (Section 6.3.1) used along with a filtering technique (Chapter 4) is exactly

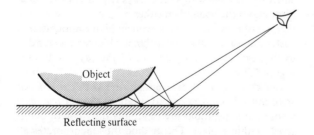

Figure 10.11 The degree of blurring of an object reflected in a surface is a function of the distance of the object from the surface.

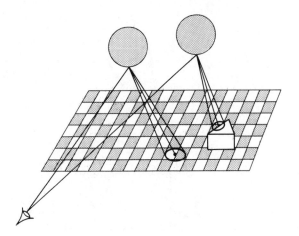

Figure 10.13 Easy and difficult problems with cone tracing.

equivalent.) If the second hit is an arbitrarily shaped object, the evaluation of the integral over the area of intersection is clearly much more difficult. In the general case where the cone partially intersects a number of objects, a sorted list must be obtained and the fractional coverage of each object calculated and included in the integration. This problem is addressed by the next technique.

10.4 Distributed ray tracing

The previous technique overcame the problem of generating a set or bundle of rays by making a ray a single geometric entity. Distributed ray tracing [COOK84b] overcomes the problem by using a ray bundle of infinitesimally thin rays but limiting, in a probabilistic manner, the number of rays in the bundle. Again this technique is bound up with aliasing considerations, fully discussed in Chapter 4. The process of distributing rays means that as well as embracing the phenomena described below, stochastic anti-aliasing becomes an integral part of the method.

Here we describe the algorithm heuristically and discuss how it deals with conventional ray tracing deficiencies, leaving the theoretical base for discussion in Chapter 4. Distributed ray tracing is in fact a Monte Carlo technique that eliminates the infinitesimally thin

beam disadvantage of standard ray tracing and replaces it with an integral over the reflection/transmission characteristics. The value of this integral is estimated by a Monte Carlo solution.

Distributed ray tracing is an elegant technique that unifies the problems of:

- blurred reflections,
- blurred refractions,
- soft shadows,
- depth of field (focusing), and
- blur due to relative motion of the virtual camera and the scene

and it is currently the most general image synthesis technique, as far as the breadth of the phenomena that it simulates is concerned.

Depth of field, where objects are in focus or blurred as a function of their distances from the camera, simulates a camera view, rather than a human eye view, and can be used for artistic effect. (Although the human eye lens has a finite depth of field, we appear not to perceive the effect of this, presumably because of our ability to concentrate on objects of interest.) Motion blur simulates the effect of relative motion between a camera and a scene and it is one of the few practicable methods of temporal anti-aliasing.

Another way of looking at distributed ray tracing is to consider sharp reflections and sharp shadows as aliasing artefacts and to propose that a theoretically correct anti-aliasing approach will produce the blurred phenomena. In this model, conventional ray tracing is seen as a sampling process in three-dimensional space and distributed ray tracing as an elegant method of overcoming the artefacts produced by the inadequacies of regular sampling.

The problems of simply increasing the number of rays in a bundle are obvious. If we try to replace the geometric entity of the cone with a set of rays regularly distributed throughout the cone, then either we have to cast a large number of rays, with the consequent high computational cost, or aliasing will occur within the blurred regions due to the regular sampling pattern of the ray bundle (see Figure 5.20).

Cook's method of distributing rays within a cone or solid angle is constrained to produce 16 rays per pixel whose initial positions are randomly distributed, or jittered, within a pixel. The method thus incorporates all the aforementioned phenomena at a cost that is no greater than the cost of 4×4 supersampling. This technique of estimation by sampling is a variance reduction technique. It can be theoretically described in terms of anti-aliasing theory (Chapter 4) or it can be viewed as a sampling method in Monte Carlo theory. The domain of interest, in this case the pixel, is uniformly subdivided and a random position is chosen within each subdivided cell.

10.4.1 Reflection/transmission

As well as generating an estimate for the integral over a pixel by spawning 16 initial rays, we have to sample the reflection/transmission characteristic at each hit. Consider first how the method deals with reflected rays. Figure 10.14 shows a single ray from a pixel hitting two objects. At the first hit the direction of the reflected ray is not necessarily the 'true' reflected direction, R, (it is precisely this deviation that gives blurred reflections). Instead, jitter is used to implement 'importance' sampl-

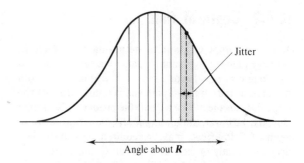

Figure 10.15 Importance sampling a reflection function.

ing. Here an emerging reflected direction is chosen on the basis of a precalculated importance-sampled reflection function. Given the angle between the reflected ray and the surface normal a lookup table stores a range of reflection angles and a jitter magnitude. Figure 10.15 shows how importance sampling works. Sampling intervals are distributed over the reflection function on an equal area basis, so that more samples occur around the largest values of the function. Each region corresponds to a single emerging reflection angle and each sample point is positioned at the centre of the region and jittered within this region.

The fact that rays emerge at some direction other than the previous reflected direction means that the second hit will occur at a different position to that given by the hit of the precise reflected direction (dashed lines in Figure 10.14). Each object may exhibit a different specular reflection function and so the second object may index into a different table.

So far we have said nothing about how each lookup table index is chosen. Each ray derives an index as a function of its position in the pixel. The primary ray and all its descendants have the same index. This means that a ray emerging from a first hit along a direction relative to R will emerge from all other hits in the same relative R direction for each object. This ensures that each pixel intensity, which is finally determined from 16 samples, is based on samples that are distributed, according to the importance sampling criterion, across the complete range of the specular reflection functions associated with each object. Note that there is nothing to prevent a lookup table being two-dimensional and indexed also by the incoming angle. This enables specular reflection functions that depend on angle of incidence to be implemented. Finally, note that transmission is implemented in exactly the same way using specular transmission functions about the refraction direction.

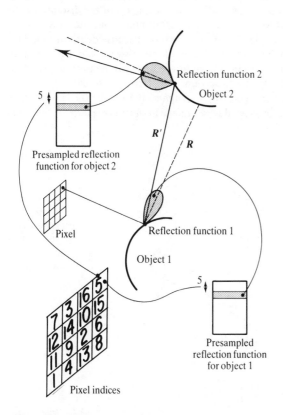

Figure 10.14 Distributed ray tracing and reflected rays.

10.4.2 Depth of field

Objects in computer graphics are normally rendered in an image plane using a pinhole camera model. That is to say, no matter how far or how near the objects are from the camera, they are always in sharp focus. Most of the time this is deemed to be a desirable property. In certain contexts, however, simulating a real camera to achieve depth of field effects may be required. Depth of field means that only objects at a certain distance from the camera lens are in sharp focus. Further and nearer objects produce a blurred image on the film plane. Depth of field causes the blurring of all objects that are not near to, or in the focal plane of, the lens. Compare this with the blurring due to transmission and reflection from a rough surface as described in the previous section. This causes blurring of reflections in objects but does not blur first-hit objects. Depth of field effects do blur first-hit objects.

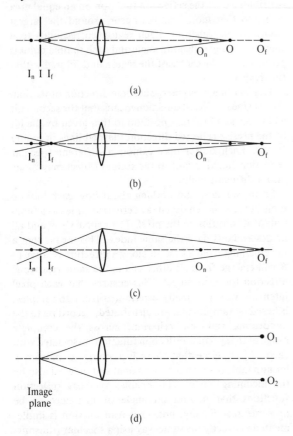

Figure 10.16 Depth of field effects.

Figure 10.16 demonstrates the principle of depth of field. Figure 10.16(a) shows three points and the position of the images formed of these points by a convex lens. O_f, the further object, is focused in the front of the image plane and O_n is focused behind the image plane. Figures 10.16(b) and (c) show that O_f will image as a circle at I, the image plane, and that the radius of this circle depends on the aperture or effective diameter of the lens.

Like the transmission/reflection blurring phenomena, blurring due to finite depth of field requires that a number of rays must be cast. This is easily seen by considering Figure 10.16(d) that shows two distant objects O_1 and O_2 which converge onto the same pixel. If a single ray is cast from the pixel then information will only be gathered from one object.

More subtle ramifications of depth of field considerations are evident. We will first consider an earlier approach and look at its shortcomings. The first attempt to simulate depth of field was by Potmesil [POTM81]. Potmesil rendered scenes in sharp focus (that is, without a lens) then convolved each image object with a blurring filter whose radius was a function of the distance of the object from the lens. Cook points out that this is not a completely correct approach because depth of field also affects the visibility of an object, and the visibility calculations for an image that is to be postprocessed do not take into account this effect of the virtual lens. Consider Figure 10.16(a) again. Because of the lens all three objects produce an image in the image plane. If the scene

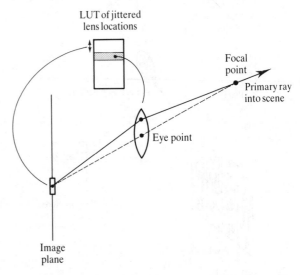

Figure 10.17 Distributed ray tracing and depth of field.

is computed without the lens and postprocessed, only O_n would be visible. Thus depth of field calculations should be integrated with the ray tracing and the lens should be effectively treated as another object in the scene.

Cook implements depth of field into his method by placing a lens in front of the image plane. For one of the 16 pixel rays a line is drawn from the pixel to the eye point, which in this model is at the centre of the lens (Figure 10.17). The focal point on this ray is calculated. Next a point on the lens is obtained by indexing into a jittered lens location table as a function of the position of the ray in the pixel. The primary ray corresponding to the initial pixel ray is then given by the line from the point to the focal point. This ray is then traced to the first hit spawning a reflected or transmitted ray.

The effect of depth of field is controlled by the diameter of the lens, F/n, where F is the focal length of the lens and n is the f-stop number.

10.4.3 Shadows

Soft shadows occur wherever a distributed light source interacts with an opaque object producing a grading from an umbra to a penumbra to a nonshadow area. The distributed ray tracing philosophy extends the normal ray tracing shadow feeler approach by distributing shadow feelers. Again, importance sampling is used and the targets on a distributed light source are selected on the basis of the brightness of different parts of the light source – its distribution function – and the projected area of the light source as seen from the surface under consideration.

The advantage of this approach over cone tracing is that banding should not occur. Banding in graded shadows is a manifestation of aliasing and in this context distributed ray tracing is inherently an anti-aliasing operation. This is further discussed in Chapter 5.

10.4.4 Motion blur

Motion blur is temporal anti-aliasing. We have discussed how the 'perfect' camera model of computer graphics eliminates depth of field. In animated sequences, the normal rendering process functions like a camera that possesses an infinitely short exposure time and this

eliminates the blurring of the image due to relative motion between an object and the film plane. When a series of images, generated without motion blur, is displayed as an animated sequence, the illusion of smooth motion is diminished by strobing effects. As human beings we expect to see loss of detail in moving images. This fact was recognized early by traditional animators who used 'speed lines' or 'streak lines' to enhance the illusion of motion. These were simply horizontal lines that trailed out from behind a running character. (See Chapter 4 for a further discussion on temporal anti-aliasing.)

The supersampling approach to motion blur is expensive and Cook deals with the problem by extending the distributed ray tracing philosophy into the time domain. An earlier attempt at computationally viable motion blur is described by Potmesil [POTM83] wherein a frame is calculated and blurred by convolving with the spread function of the camera motion. This, like Potmesil's approach to depth of field, is a postprocessing operation and Cook points out that again this is not a correct solution. Within the time interval that comprises the virtual camera's exposure or shutter time the visibility calculation may change. A single object moving against a background will reveal information in the background that may not be hidden if a frame is rendered at a particular instant. There can also be problems due to changes in shading. Cook gives the example of a textured spinning top, where the texture blurs but the highlight and shadow both remain stationary and unblurred. In other contexts both the highlight and the shadows of a moving object are blurred.

Motion blur is accounted for in distributed ray tracing by extending the distributed sampling and jittering into the time domain and computing a solution that extracts information from the scene over the duration of the shutter exposure time. Objects are moved as required in the time period and visibility consequently changes over this time interval. This method ensures that highlights and shadows are blurred or not, depending on the nature of the motion.

Cook distributes rays in time by using the position of the initial ray to index into a lookup table that contains prejittered importance samples from a temporal filter. The information out of this table is a set of times at which to sample over the shutter time. An example of a motion-blurred image generated using this approach is shown in Plate 5.

11 || Radiosity methods

Chapter 12 describes how the radiosity method can be extended to provide a general global illumination model. Also, theoretical consideration of the radiosity method as a global illumination model is given in Chapter 12.

Introduction

Along with ray tracing, the radiosity method forms one of the two major 'post-Phong' approaches to rendering objects. The revolution in image quality created by such approaches was underpinned by their ability to model interaction between objects and other objects or between objects and their environment.

Pre-ray tracing models approximated directly reflected light, or light from a source reflected once from a surface towards the eye. Diffuse interaction was crudely approximated by using an 'ambient light' term which, despite the implied ambition of the name, was usually deemed to be a constant. (We use the past tense to indicate the state of affairs prior to ray tracing and radiosity, but of course Phong models are still the de facto rendering technique in current computer graphics.) The only interaction that is usually modelled with Phong-like approaches is shadows. These are treated by ad hoc algorithms entirely separately, resulting in geometrically correct hard-edged shadows with arbitrary light intensities within the shadow. (An exception to this statement is the early environment mapping of Blinn [BLIN76].)

Ray tracing and radiosity approaches are completely diverse, both algorithmically and in the nature of the images that they produce. The radiosity method is a theoretically rigorous method that provides a solution to diffuse interaction within a closed environment. The solution is view independent and is based on subdividing the environment into discrete patches, or elements, over which the light intensity is constant. Because of this it is difficult to include specular reflection as part of the solution. Although the view-independent nature of the radiosity solution is always claimed to be a major advantage without qualitification, we should note that we pay a high processing cost for it and view independence is not always required. View-independent solutions come into their own in such contexts as architectural design, where we may compute a solution that is then used to render arbitrary 'walks-through' or animated sequences of different views.

Ray tracing solves the problem of specular interaction between objects by casting infinitesimally thin eye rays into the environment. In ray tracing, rays are cast into the environment by discretizing the image plane. Thus we can cast rays at the rate of 1 per pixel, n per pixel or we can cast rays adaptively (as in [MITC87]) and trace their reflection and transmission at each interface they encounter. Although ray tracing deals effectively with specular interaction, diffuse interaction, as we have discussed, is not easily incorporated into a standard ray tracing scheme. Standard ray tracing, even with its limitations, is not a theoretically correct approach and ray-traced images carry a distinct signature that was originally claimed as increased realism. However, ray-traced images are imitations of scenes that are not normally encountered in real life.

Reality is much more evident in the radiosity approach, despite the inability of the method to account for specular interaction. Radiosity is most successful in dealing with manmade environments, interiors of offices, factories and the like, and has certainly produced the most impressive computer graphics images to date.

Both approaches carry a heavy cost penalty over standard rendering methods. A kind of futuristic Parkinson's law seems to operate in computer graphics research. It's not so much a case of the rendering costs expanding to meet the processing facilities available; more that the practical feasibility of methods are based on the assumption that appropriate hardware will emerge in five years' time, or whenever. The validity of this approach is a matter of opinion. Although it is impossible to compare like with like, there is generally one order of magnitude difference in processing time between ray tracing and radiosity. Plate 73 is an example created at Cornell University, where most of the development work in radiosity has taken place. It is a steel mill constructed from 30 000 patches that took 190 hours to compute on a VAX 8700.

Because it is a method where a solution 'emerges' from a set of linear equations describing the geometrical basis of patch interaction, radiosity is not as amenable to efficiency research as ray tracing, and the major developments have consisted of mechanisms that allow an approximate solution to be viewed at an early stage. This is in direct contrast to ray tracing, where a large number of diverse speedup techniques have been suggested.

Diffuse interaction is extremely important in interior environments. Both the variation in the intensity of light and the colour across, say, a diffusely reflecting wall surface are a function of the light sources *and* the interactions between surfaces. Many surfaces in an interior gather no direct illumination and receive diffuse reflections from other surfaces. An object that is lit only by light reaching the object indirectly from a source reflecting from a wall, say, may have a colour that is different from the colour of the object when it is viewed in direct illumination. A brightly coloured object positioned next to, say, a white surface may 'spill' or 'bleed' colour into the surface.

We should qualify all remarks on colour bleeding with a consideration of colour constancy, that remarkable attribute of human colour vision where colour is perceived as a permanent unchanging attribute of the object (except under degenerate viewing conditions), rather than as a wavelength-dependent phenomenon that changes as a function of the spectrum of the illuminating source. This raises the question: do we actually perceive colour bleeding to any great extent, and, if not, is there any point in modelling it? (The example given by Greenberg *et al.* [GREE86a] is a startling, but highly contrived context, in which colour bleeding is noticeable). In most practical cases we submit that colour bleeding is almost imperceptible. Colour bleeding has to fight against colour constancy. Where we produce colour bleeding in a solution on a computer graphics monitor, we are already, like the photographic process, transforming reality into a two-dimensional version, where our colour constancy may break down. In other words, it may be that in explicitly rendering colour bleeding we tend towards higher artificiality rather than higher reality. Perhaps we should respect the colour constancy ability of human beings and *not* render it. This aspect is an open question and is an example of how we must be careful not to assume that advances in the ability to render colour effects accurately on a wavelength-by-wavelength basis is necessarily the best thing to do. Another aspect related to the modelling of colour bleeding is colour aliasing (dealt with in Chapter 4). There is little or no point in modelling subtle colour phenomena, such as colour bleeding, without taking this into account.

In this respect, however, it is important to observe that Cornell, the major developers of the method, have rigorously tested the main aspects of their algorithm by placing a computer-generated model side by side with a 'real' view of a simple environment. Both the computer graphics monitor and the real scene were viewed through optical cameras in an arrangement that concealed the structure of the experiment from the participants. The participants could only look into the viewing system of two cameras and were asked to judge the displays simultaneously [MEYE86]. Also, physical comparisons were made using measuring instruments. Results showed that, in comparing the physical scene against the computer graphics abstraction, subjects did no better in distinguishing between the real and the unreal than they would have by simple guessing.

Shadows have always been problematic in computer graphics and all shadow approaches, until very recently, were ad hoc measures, completely divorced from the reflection model calculations. In such methods, the shape of a shadow is calculated from a geometrically based algorithm and the intensity within the shadow is estimated on some arbitrary basis. Both the variation of intensity and the soft edge of shadows can be considered to be a part of the diffuse interaction phenomenon. Shadows are the local decrease in diffuse illumination due to the blocking of direct illumination. The intensity of the light emitted from a shadow area is a function of the diffuse reflection from surfaces near to the shadow area. Shadows are simply part of the diffuse interaction problems and are incorporated, by definition, within the radiosity method. Although, we should observe that hard shadow edges are illumination boundaries or high-contrast intensity transitions, and such areas have to be treated specially in the radiosity method, say by sub-dividing the solution, so that the nature of the edge is revealed.

The radiosity method was first introduced to the computer graphics community in 1984 at Cornell University [GORA84] and until very recently most of the development work has taken place in this institution. This pioneering work was followed by an efficient method for evaluating the form factors – the mechanism whereby the radiation relationship between patches is related to the geometry [COHE85]. Various reports emerged from Cornell, culminating in 1988 [COHE88] in a method that enabled a solution to be viewed at an early stage. This approach was designed to mitigate the severe time costs of the radiosity method.

11.1 Formulation of the radiosity matrix

The radiosity approach to rendering has its basis in the theory of heat transfer or interchange between surfaces [SIEG84]. This theory was applied to computer graphics in 1984 by Goral *et al.* [GORA84] and a system of equations that describes the interreflections between surfaces in a closed environment was set up. Surfaces in the environment are assumed to be perfect (or Lambertian) diffusers, reflectors or emitters. Such surfaces are assumed to reflect incident light in all directions with equal intensity. A formulation for the system of equations is facilitated by dividing the environment into a set of rectangular areas. In the Cornell literature these areas are called 'patches'. The radiosity over a patch is constant and the accuracy of the solution depends on the initial

discretization of the environment. Initially this discretization will be set up as part of the scene database.

The radiosity, B, of a patch is the total rate of energy leaving a surface and is equal to the sum of the emitted and reflected energies. An equation can be formulated for the radiosity of a single patch by using a geometric entity called a 'form factor'.

If we consider two patches, P_i and P_j, then the energy interchange between these patches is a function of the geometrical relationships, such as distance, between the patches and their relative orientation. High energy interchange will occur, for example, between two patches that are close together and parallel to each other. We can set up an equation that relates the energy reflected from a patch to any self-emitted energy plus the energy incoming from all other patches as follows:

$$B_i \, dA_i = E_i \, dA_i + \rho_i \int_j B_j \, dA_j \, F_{dA_j \, dA_i} \qquad (11.1)$$

that is:

Radiosity × area = emitted energy + reflected energy

where:

Reflected energy = reflection coefficient × energy incident on the patch from all other patches

and where:

E_i is the light emitted from a patch (units identical to B_i: energy unit time^{-1} unit area^{-1})

ρ_i is the reflectivity of the patch or the fraction of the light incident on a patch that is reflected back into the environment

$F_{dA_j \, dA_i}$ is the form factor between the elements dA_j and dA_i or the fraction of energy leaving dA_j that arrives at dA_i

For a closed environment an energy equilibrium must establish itself and a set of linear equations is formulated by repeating Equation (11.1) for each patch in the environment. For an environment that has been discretized into n patches over which the radiosity is constant, Equation (11.1) becomes:

$$B_i A_i = E_i A_i + \rho_i \sum_{j=1}^{n} B_j F_{A_j A_i} A_j$$

or simplifying the notation:

$$B_i A_i = E_i A_i + \rho_i \sum_{j=1}^{n} B_j F_{ji} A_j \qquad (11.2)$$

where we now assume that B and E do not vary across the extent of a patch. A reciprocity relationship exists between form factors [SIEG84] – the energy interchange depends only on the relative geometry of the patches:

$$F_{ij} A_i = F_{ji} A_j$$

$$F_{ij} = F_{ji} \frac{A_j}{A_i}$$

Using this relationship in Equation (11.2) yields the basic radiosity relationship:

$$B_i = E_i + \rho_i \sum_{j=1}^{n} B_j F_{ij}$$

Such an equation exists for each patch, and in a closed environment a set of n simultaneous equations in n unknown B_i values is obtained:

$$\begin{bmatrix} 1-\rho_1 F_{11} & -\rho_1 F_{12} & \cdots & -\rho_1 F_{1n} \\ -\rho_2 F_{21} & 1-\rho_2 F_{22} & \cdots & -\rho_2 F_{2n} \\ \cdot & & \cdots & \cdot \\ \cdot & & \cdots & \cdot \\ \cdot & & \cdots & \cdot \\ -\rho_n F_{n1} & -\rho_n F_{n2} & \cdots & 1-\rho_n F_{nn} \end{bmatrix} \begin{bmatrix} B_1 \\ B_2 \\ \cdot \\ \cdot \\ \cdot \\ B_n \end{bmatrix} = \begin{bmatrix} E_1 \\ E_2 \\ \cdot \\ \cdot \\ \cdot \\ E_n \end{bmatrix}$$

$$(11.3)$$

The E_i values are nonzero only at surfaces that provide illumination and these terms represent the input illumination to the system. In a practical environment most of these will be zero. Note that we assume that the emitters are Lambertian, a clear simplification of the real intensity distribution of light sources. The equation set is an expression of energy equilibrium for a particular wavelength. In practice, E_i and ρ_i are both functions of wavelength. (F_{ij} will also be wavelength dependent, but this is ignored.) Thus a set of equations needs to be solved for each colour band of interest. This can be the normal computer graphics RGB paradigm, or because, as we have already remarked, the radiosity method deals with subtle colour phenomena such as colour bleeding, colour aliasing considerations (Chapter 3) can be taken into account and solutions evaluated at more than three wavelengths.

We can note that $F_{ii} = 0$ for a plane or convex surface – none of the radiation leaving a surface will strike itself. Also, from the definition of form factors the sum of any row of form factors equals unity. Because ρ_i is always less than unity the matrix is 'diagonally dominant' and a solution by the Gauss–Seidel method (see [WATT89]) is guaranteed to converge.

A solution yields a single radiosity value B_i for each patch in the environment – a view-independent solution.

(It is as if we started a standard rendering process with a database that already possessed vertex intensities.) The B_i values can then be used in a standard Gouraud renderer and a particular view of the environment constructed from the radiosity solution. In fact, as we have already mentioned, any number of arbitrary views can be constructed by postprocessing the radiosity solution. This scheme is particularly apt when animated 'walks-through' are required for a scene; the animation is now easily handled interactively in real time (with the migration of standard rendering techniques onto silicon). This state of affairs is summarized in Figure 11.1, where it is important to note the different start points for the modification loops.

If we assume that only the reflectivities of the patches and the properties of the emitting patches are wavelength dependent then the colour of the surfaces in the scene, and the light sources, can be changed without recalculating the form factors. The cost of the method is bound in form factor calculations and n^2 form factors must be determined for an environment. Cohen and Greenberg [COHE85] show that the form factor computation is approximately an order of magnitude greater than both stages of solving the set of equations and

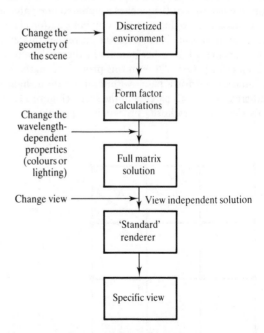

Figure 11.1 Stages in a complete radiosity solution. Also shown are the points in the process where various modifications can be made to the image.

rendering a view. The more important modification loop is the one that changes the view point. Here there is no need to recompute a solution and the same (view-independent) radiosity data is used to calculate any view.

At this point we mention some considerations that concern the use of radiosity data with a standard renderer. First, radiosity values are constant over the extent of a patch. A standard renderer requires vertex radiosities or intensities. These can be obtained for a vertex by computing the average of the radiosities of patches that contribute to the vertex under consideration. Vertices on the edge of a surface can be allocated values by extrapolation through interior vertex values, as shown in Figure 11.2.

Note that the solution of the matrix (see [WATT89]) progresses one row at a time, where a current estimate B_i is used to multiply all the reflectivity/form factor products in the row. The first iteration starts with most B_is set to zero and those in a row with nonzero E_i set to that value. If we were to display the solution as it proceeded, the resulting image would at first display only the emitting surfaces – the rest of the environment would be dark. As the solution progresses, the estimates for each patch are gradually updated and those patches with high form factors emerge first from the gloom. For each iteration, the intensity of the patches is updated one patch at a time according to their row position in Equation (11.3). Each patch intensity is based on the current estimates of the radiosities of all other patches in the environment. Cohen *et al.* [COHE88] term this process as 'gathering' to indicate that for a patch within an iteration, light is gathered in from all patches in the scene (Figure 11.3a). This view of the radiosity process is important because

it is a recognition both of the visual abstraction of a solution in progress, and of the fact that it can be reordered. This leads to the method described in Section 11.1.2, where early images that approximate a complete solution are produced.

Up to now we have said nothing about the evaluation of form factors. In [GORA84] form factors are calculated by numerical integration for a simple convex environment where every patch can see every other patch. In general, for more complex environments a patch will only partially 'see' another patch because an intervening patch may be positioned between them. This problem needs to be considered in form factor evaluations. A full discussion on form factors is postponed until Section 11.2 because the precise nature of form factor evaluation depends on the particular form of the solution used.

11.1.1 Increasing the accuracy of the solution

Most of the computation in the radiosity method is taken up by the calculation of the form factors and the size of the problem is a function of the number of patches squared. The quality of the image is a function of the size of the patches and it is pointed out in [COHE86] that in regions of the environment, such as shadow boundaries, that exhibit a high radiosity gradient, the patches should be subdivided.

Cohen *et al.* [COHE86] develop a technique called 'substructuring' and the idea is to generate an accurate solution for the radiosity of a point from the 'global' radiosities obtained from the initial 'coarse' patch computation. Patches are subdivided into areas called 'elements'. Element-to-patch form factors are calculated where the relationship between element-to-patch and patch-to-patch form factors is given by:

$$F_{ij} = \frac{1}{A_i} \sum_{q=1}^{R} F_{(iq)j} A_{(iq)}$$

where:

F_{ij} is the form factor from patch i to patch j
$F_{(iq)j}$ is the form factor from element q of patch i to patch j
$A_{(iq)}$ is the subdivided area of element q of patch i
R is the number of elements in the patch

Patch form factors obtained in this way are then used in a standard radiosity solution.

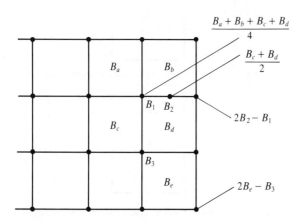

Figure 11.2 Computing vertex radiosities.

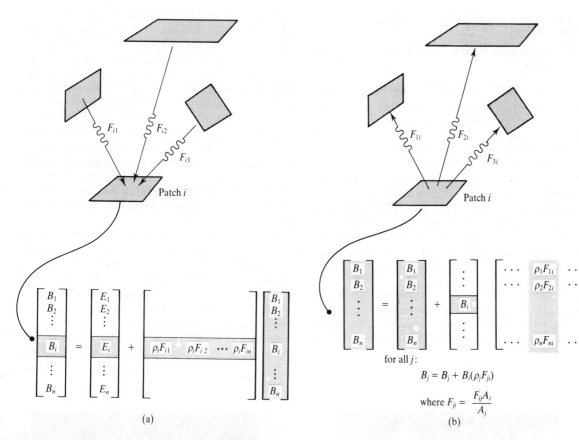

(a)

(b)

$$B_j = B_j + B_i(\rho_j F_{ji})$$

$$\text{where } F_{ji} = \frac{F_{ij} A_i}{A_j}$$

Figure 11.3 (a) 'Gathering': standard Gauss–Seidel solution of the radiosity matrix. The radiosity of a single patch i is updated for each iteration by gathering radiosities from all other patches. (b) 'Shooting': the radiosity of all patches is updated for each iteration (Section 11.1.2). A diagrammatic representation of the difference between the standard radiosity solution and the progressive refinement method (after [COHE88]).

This increases the number of form factors from $N \times N$ to $M \times N$, where M is the total number of elements created, and naturally increases the time spent in form factor calculation. Patches that need to be divided into elements are revealed by examining the graduation of the coarse patch solution. The previously calculated (coarse) patch solution is retained and the fine element radiosities are then obtained from this solution using:

$$B_{iq} = E_{iq} + \rho_{iq} \sum_{j=1}^{n} B_j F_{(iq)j} \qquad (11.4)$$

where:

B_{iq} is the radiosity of element q
B_j is the radiosity of patch j
$F_{(iq)j}$ is the element q to patch j form factor

In other words, as far as the radiosity solution is concerned, the cumulative effect of elements of a subdivided patch is identical to that of the undivided patch; or, subdividing a patch into elements does not affect the amount of light that is reflected by the patch. So, after determining a solution for patches, the radiosity within a patch is solved independently among patches. In doing this, Equation (11.4) assumes that only the patch in question has been subdivided into elements – all other patches are undivided. The process is applied iteratively until the desired accuracy is obtained. At any step in the iteration we can identify three stages:

1. Subdividing selected patches into elements and calculating element-to-patch form factors.

2. Evaluating a radiosity solution using patch-to-patch form factors.

3. Determining the element radiosities from the patch radiosities.

where stage 2 just occurs for the first iteration – the coarse patch radiosities are calculated once only. The method is distinguished from simply subdividing the environment into smaller patches. This strategy would result in $M \times M$ new form factors (rather than $M \times N$) and an $M \times M$ system of equations.

Subdivision of patches into elements is carried out adaptively. The areas that require subdivision are not known prior to a solution being obtained. These areas are obtained from an initial solution and are then subject to a form factor subdivision. The previous form factor matrix is still valid and the radiosity solution is not recomputed. Only part of the form factor determination is further discretized and this is then used in the third phase (determination of the element radiosities from the coarse patch solution). This process is repeated until it converges to the desired degree of accuracy. Thus image quality is improved in areas that require more accurate treatment.

An example of this approach is shown in Figure 11.4 and Plate 38. The three illustrations show a typical scene constructed to demonstrate the efficacy of the method – a room interior with largish flat surfaces, strip lights and windows. The scene is shown divided into patches and after substructuring. Plates 38 and 39 show the result of the method with the scene lit by the windows and by the strip lights respectively. Careful examination of these reveals banding artefacts on the ceiling. Plate 40 attempts to demonstrate the effect of colour bleeding by exaggeration. Here the ceiling is coloured bright red and the remaining surfaces are coloured as before. The ceiling colour is distributed throughout the environment as shown. High reflectivities were used to exaggerate the effect.

What information to use in the coarse patch solution is one of the problems with this method. A better solution is obtainable if the element-to-patch form factors are summed and used to calculate patch-to-patch form factors, but without an initial solution no automatic subdivision criterion is available. Thus the coarse patch radiosities must be based on patch-to-patch form factors, or an initial subdivision has to be specified manually. Another practical problem with the technique

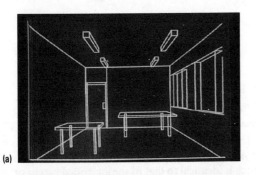
(a)

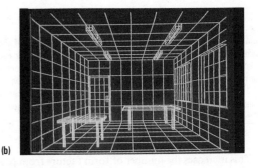
(b)

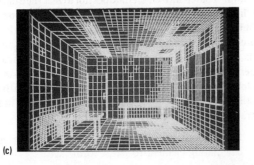
(c)

Figure 11.4 A simple scene used in the radiosity method. (a) Original surfaces. (b) Surfaces divided up into patches. (c) Patches subdivided into elements using the substructuring method.

is that the extrapolation process, to calculate vertex radiosities from patch radiosities, is now far more cumbersome than it is for a surface that has been regularly subdivided into patches.

In the same paper [COHE86], details are given on merging texture mapping with the radiosity solution. This involves retaining the idea of a patch having constant radiosity over its extent, calculating the radiosity solution and then texture mapping during the rendering phase.

For a pixel in the image plane the texture mapping is computed by:

$$B_{\text{pixel}} = B_{\text{average}} \times \frac{R_{\text{pixel}}}{R_{\text{average}}}$$

where

B_{pixel} is the final radiosity of a pixel

B_{average} is the radiosity derived from the element radiosity solution

R_{pixel} is the reflectivity given by the texture map for the pixel

R_{average} is the average reflectivity of the texture map

Cohen points out that this technique enables the contribution from, say, a painting, to the illumination of the environment to be the same as if it were one average colour.

11.1.2 Reordering the solution for progressive refinement

Unlike other major image synthesis techniques, the radiosity method has not, to date, been taken up by the computer graphics community, presumably because of the extremely large computational overheads of the method. In a paper published in 1988 [COHE88], Cohen *et al.* address this problem and develop an important technique called 'progressive refinement'.

The general goal of progressive or adaptive refinement can be taken up by any slow image synthesis technique, and it attempts to find a compromise between the competing demands of interactivity and image quality. A synthesis method that provides adaptive refinement would present an initial, quickly rendered image to the user. This image is then progressively refined in a 'graceful' way. Cohen defines this as a progression towards higher quality, greater realism, and so on, in a way that is automatic, continuous and not distracting to the user. Early availability of an approximation can greatly assist

in the development of techniques and images, and reducing the feedback loop by approximation is a necessary adjunct to the radiosity method.

The radiosity method is particularly suited to this approach – the spatial resolution of the image remaining constant, while the illumination calculations are refined. This contrasts with the options in ray tracing where the only simple refinement process, which does not involve losing previously calculated information, is to increase the two-dimensional spatial resolution progressively.

The two major practical problems in the radiosity method are the storage costs and the calculation of the form factors. Cohen points out that for an environment of 50×10^3 patches, even although the resulting square matrix of form factors may be 90% sparse (many patches cannot see each other) this still requires 10^9 bytes of storage (at four bytes per form factor).

Both the requirements of progressive refinement and the elimination of precalculation and storage of the form factors are met by an ingenious restructuring of the basic radiosity algorithm. The stages in the progressive refinement are obtained by displaying the results as the iterative solution progresses. The solution is restructured and the form factor evaluation order is optimized so that the convergence is 'visually graceful'. This restructuring enables the radiosity of all patches to be updated at each step in the solution, rather than a step providing the solution for a single patch. Maximum visual difference between steps in the solution can be achieved by processing patches according to their energy contribution to the environment. The radiosity method is particularly suited to a progressive refinement approach because it computes a view-independent solution. Viewing this solution (by rendering from a particular view point) can proceed independently as the radiosity solution progresses.

In the conventional evaluation of the radiosity matrix a solution for one row provides the radiosity for a single patch i:

$$B_i = E_i + \rho_i \sum_{j=1}^{n} B_j F_{ij}$$

This is an estimate of the radiosity of patch i based on the current estimate of all other patches. This is the 'gathering' process alluded to in Section 11.1. If viewed dynamically, each patch intensity is updated according to its row position in the radiosity matrix.

The idea of the progressive refinement method is that the entire image is updated at every iteration, rather than a single patch. Cohen *et al.* [COHE88] term this as 'shooting', where the contribution from each patch *i* is distributed to all other patches. The difference between these two processes is illustrated diagramatically in Figures 11.3(a) and (b). This reordering of the algorithm is accomplished in the following way.

A single term determines the contribution to the radiosity of patch *j* due to that from patch *i*:

B_i due to $B_j = \rho_i B_i F_{ji}$

This relationship can be reversed by using the reciprocity relationship:

$$B_j \text{ due to } B_i = \rho_j B_i F_{ij} \frac{A_i}{A_j}$$

and this is true for all patches *j*. This relationship can be used to determine the contribution to *each* patch *j* in the environment *from* the single patch *i*. A single radiosity (patch *i*) shoots light into the environment and the radiosities of all patches *j* are updated simultaneously. The first complete update (of all the radiosities in the environment) is obtained from 'on the fly' form factor computations. Thus an initial approximation to the complete scene can appear when only the first row of form factors has been calculated. This eliminates high startup or precalculation costs.

Steps in the process can be displayed in a progressive refinement sequence if we add ΔB_j to each patch *j* in the iteration sequence. This is accomplished as follows:

repeat
  for {*each patch i*} **do**
  {*position a hemicube on
  patch i and calculate form
  factors F_{ij} (for the first iteration)*}
  for {*each patch j ($j \neq i$)*}**do**
    $\Delta \text{Rad} := \rho_j \Delta B_i F_{ij} A_i / A_j$
    $\Delta B_j := \Delta B_j + \Delta \text{Rad}$
    $B_j := B_j + \Delta \text{Rad}$
  $\Delta B_i = 0$
until convergence

where ΔB_j is the difference between the previous and current estimates of B_j. Thus as the iteration progresses ΔB_j reduces as B_j becomes more and more accurate and the ambient term decreases.

This process is repeated until convergence is achieved. This is carried out by subdividing patches and examining the radiosity gradient between neighbouring elements. All radiosities B_i and ΔB_i are initially set either to zero or to their emission values. As this process is repeated for each patch *i* the solution is displayed and at each step the radiosities for each patch *j* are updated.

If the output from the algorithm is displayed without further elaboration then a scene, initially dark, gradually gets lighter as the incremental radiosities are added to each patch. Cohen optimizes the 'visual convergence' of this process by sorting the order in which the patches are processed according to the amount of energy that they are likely to radiate. This means, for example, that emitting patches, or light sources, should be treated first. This gives an early well-lit solution. The next patches to be processed are those that received most light from the light sources and so on. It is pointed out by Cohen that, by using this ordering scheme, the solution proceeds in a way that approximates the propagation of light through an environment. In reality, for a light source such as sunlight streaming through a window, most of the ambient light comes from the *first* bounce of the light from the surfaces in the room. Although this produces a better visual sequence than an unsorted process, the solution still progresses from a dark scene to a fully illuminated scene. To overcome this effect an arbitrary ambient light term is added to the intermediate radiosities. This term is used only to enhance the display and is not part of the solution. The value of the ambient term is based on the current estimate of the radiosities of all patches in the environment, and as the solution proceeds and becomes 'better lit' the ambient contribution is decreased.

The idea is that as the solution progresses the quality or 'correctness' of the image increases and the role of the estimated ambient contribution decreases. The ambient contribution at any stage is determined as follows. First, an approximate form factor definition is introduced. This ignores the geometric relationship between a pair of patches and defines an approximate form factor that depends only on the patch *j*. This estimated form factor is given by:

$$F_{ij \text{(estimated)}} = \frac{A_j}{\sum\limits_{j=1}^{n} A_j}$$

which is the fraction of the environment taken up by the area A_j. Secondly, an average reflectivity for all patches in the environment is given by:

$$\rho_{\text{average}} = \frac{\sum\limits_{i=1}^{n} \rho_i A_i}{\sum\limits_{i=1}^{n} A_i}$$

Consider now light incident on the environment. This will be reflected once, twice, and so on, and an overall reflection factor, μ, can be defined as:

$$\mu = 1 + \rho_{\text{average}} + \rho_{\text{average}}^2 + \rho_{\text{average}}^3 \cdots = \frac{1}{1 - \rho_{\text{average}}}$$

These definitions can be used in an estimated ambient term:

$$I_a = \mu \sum_{j=1}^{N} \Delta B_j F_{ij\,(\text{estimated})}$$

The complete progressive refinement algorithm can now be summarized. Four main stages are completed for each iteration. These are:

1. Find the patch with the greatest radiosity or emitted energy.

2. Evaluate a 'column' of form factors, that is, the form factors from this patch to every other patch in the environment.

3. Update the radiosity of each of the receiving patches.

4. Reduce the temporary ambient term as a function of the sum of the differences between the current values calculated in 3 and the previous values.

(Note that if adaptive subdivision is incorporated into the method it is the 'receiving patches' that are subdivided and the progressive refinement algorithm computes form factors from a patch to elements or subdivision products.) For example, in a room an area light source may be the first shooting patch chosen. The form factors from the light source to every other surface are evaluated and radiosity is distributed to every other receiving surface. A desk top directly opposite the light may be the next 'source' chosen and the process continues.

Finally, we should note the similarity between this approach and backwards or two-pass ray tracing. In backwards ray tracing, light propagation is traced from the light source and in, for example, Chattopadhyay's scheme [CHAT 87], an iterative process calculates a solution for diffuse interreflection. This solution is view independent and a particular view is constructed by conventional or forward ray tracing. The process is algorithmically similar to the progressive refinement radiosity solution. The differences are that the radiosity method is an equilibrium technique for closed environments and the diffuse interaction between patches is modelled accurately by using form factors (at least to within the accuracy of the form factor determination). In particular

this accounts for the relative orientation of patches. Interaction between surfaces in backwards ray tracing is based on distance.

Cohen *et al.* categorize the basic algorithmic options in the radiosity method as follows:

1. *Gathering* A term used to represent the basic approach described in Section 11.1. A matrix of form factors is precomputed, stored and used in a traditional Gauss–Seidel solution. If the solution is viewed as it progresses, estimated patch radiosities are updated in their order in the matrix formulation.

2. *Shooting* A reversal of this solution process. Light from each patch is shot into the environment and the entire scene is updated for each iteration. This approach is visually optimized by treating patches in an order that takes into account the amount of energy they are likely to radiate.

3. *Shooting and ambient* An ambient term is now included so that early approximations are visible. At each iteration the quality and accuracy of the solution increases and the ambient fraction is diminished.

11.2 Concerning form factors

There are a number of problems associated with form factors in the radiosity method. These are:

1. The calculation of the form factor values. Except for cases where both the shape and the relationships of patches are highly constrained, and where the values can be calculated by formula, the computation of the form factors is a distinctly nontrivial high-cost operation.

2. The form factor calculation between two patches has to take into account any intervening patch, except in convex environments where there are no occluding patches. The Cornell method integrates the first two factors into one elegant algorithm – the hemicube method.

3. Using the standard full matrix formulation implies that the form factors have to be calculated and stored in advance. This imposes complexity constraints on the scene. Even though the form factor matrix may

be, for example, 90% sparse (most patches cannot see each other), scenes of between 10^4 and 10^5 patches require 3.6×10^8 to 3.6×10^{10} bytes to store the form factors (at an accuracy of four bytes per form factor).

11.2.1 Form factor definition

To recap: the form factor between two patches is an expression of the radiative exchange between them, or the fraction of energy leaving one patch that arrives at the other. We start by considering the form factors between two infinitesimal surfaces with differential areas dA_i and dA_j. The solid angle subtended by dA_j at dA_i is given by (see Chapter 2):

$$d\omega_{ij} = \cos\phi_j \frac{dA_j}{r^2}$$

This is the solid angle for an observer at dA_i (Figure 11.5). The energy leaving the differential area dA_i that reaches dA_j is given by:

$$dE_i\, dA_i = I_i \cos\phi_i\, d\omega_{ij}\, dA_i$$
$$= I_i \cos\phi_i \cos\phi_j\, dA_i \frac{dA_j}{r^2}$$

The total energy leaving the elemental area dA_i in all directions into the hemisphere centred on that area is

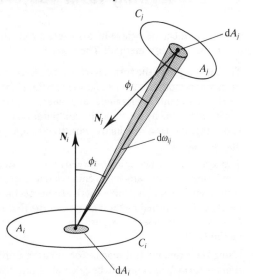

Figure 11.5   Form factor geometry for two patches A_i and A_j.

$E_i dA_i$. Form factor is defined between the two elemental areas dA_i and dA_j as:

$$F_{dAidAj} = \frac{\text{Radiative energy reaching } dA_j \text{ from } dA_i}{\text{Total energy leaving } dA_i \text{ in all directions}}$$

The total energy leaving dA_i is given by integrating over the hemisphere centred on dA_i. For an ideal Lambertian surface:

$$E_i = I_i\pi$$

that is, the intensity is independent of direction for a diffusely emitting or reflecting surface and:

$$F_{dAidAj} = \frac{I_i \cos\phi_i \cos\phi_j\, dA_i\, dA_j}{I_i\, dA_i\, \pi r^2}$$
$$= \frac{\cos\phi_i \cos\phi_j\, dA_j}{\pi r^2}$$

The next step is to compute the form factor from the differential area dA_i to the patch A_j. This is obtained by integrating the differential-to-differential-area form factor over A_j:

$$F_{dAiAj} = \int_{Aj} \frac{\cos\phi_i \cos\phi_j\, dA_j}{\pi r^2}$$

and is the fraction of the radiative energy leaving dA_i in all directions in the hemispherical space centred on dA_i that reaches the patch A_j. We can now define the patch-to-patch form factor:

$$F_{AiAj} = F_{ij} = \frac{\text{Radiative energy reaching } A_j \text{ from } A_i}{\text{Total radiative energy leaving } A_i \text{ in all directions}}$$

This is given by integrating over A_i and taking the area average, again because the intensity I_i is independent of direction and position over A_i:

$$F_{ij} = \frac{1}{A_i} \int_{Ai} \int_{Aj} \frac{\cos\phi_i \cos\phi_j}{\pi r^2}\, dA_j\, dA_i \qquad (11.5)$$

and herein lies a calculation problem. Calculating the form factors between two elemental surfaces is straightforward. Evaluation of the form factor between an elemental surface and a finite surface – a patch – requires one area integral, and calculating F_{ij} requires two area integrals. Such integrals are difficult to perform analytically except for highly constrained geometries. The next section concentrates on methods for determining the form factors.

Finally, we bring together attributes of form factors

briefly mentioned in the previous section. The reciprocity relationship gives:

$$A_i F_{ij} = A_j F_{ji}$$

For a closed environment, from the definition of form factors we have the summation relationship:

$$\sum_{k=1}^{n} F_{ik} = 1 \qquad \text{for } i = 1 \text{ to } n$$

Form factors F_{ik} are the fractions of total energy leaving A_i and they must summate to unity in an enclosure because all the energy leaving A_i must end up in other patches.

If a surface is flat (or convex) none of the radiation leaving the surface will strike itself *directly*. Thus:

$$F_{ii} = 0$$

for a plane or convex surface. For a concave surface, of course:

$$F_{ii} \neq 0$$

11.2.2 Form factor determination: numerical

The earliest radiosity paper [GORA84] used direct numerical integration, converting the double area integral into a double contour integral (Stoke's theorem):

$$F_{ij} = \frac{1}{2\pi A_i} \oint_{C_j} \oint_{C_i} \ln(r)\,dx_i dy_j + \ln(r)\,dy_i dy_j + \ln(r)\,dz_i dz_j$$

where dx, dy and dz are the projections of the contour increment onto the coordinate axes.

This is computationally expensive and is only appropriate for simple environments. An occluding or intervening patch between patches i and j changes the shape of the contours and the determination of such a shape would be extremely difficult for, say, the case of a number of intervening patches.

A similar numerical integration approach was also taken by Nishita and Nakamae [NISH85]. In this case the occluding patch problem was solved by performing visibility between pairs of vertices. The method, however, that has become prominent integrates form factor determination with a solution to the intervening patch problem and this is now described.

11.2.3 Form factor determination: hemicube

In 1985 the Cornell team introduced the hemicube method which simultaneously offered an efficient (but approximate) method of form factor determination and a solution to the intervening patch problem. This method was then used in all the subsequent radiosity developments of Cornell. (A similar method was used by Haines and Greenberg ([HAIN86] and Chapter 8) to accelerate shadow testing in ray tracing).

There are two underlying justifications for the use of the hemicube for determining F_{ij}. We first consider Equation (11.5). If the distance r between the two patches is large compared to the area of the patch then the value of the inner integral does not change much over the range of the outer integral (providing there are no intervening patches). In this case the effect of the outer integral is, approximately, a multiplication by unity and we have:

$$F_{ij} \approx F_{dAiAj} = \int_{Aj} \frac{\cos\phi_i \cos\phi_j}{\pi r^2}\,dA_j$$

or the area-to-area form factor is approximated by the differential-to-finite-area form factor. The second justification is based on the Nusselt analogue [SIEG84]. Figure 11.6 shows this diagrammatically where the form factor of the patch is equivalent to the fraction of the unit circle that is formed by taking the projection of the patch

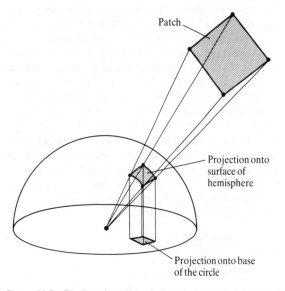

Figure 11.6 The Nusselt analogue.

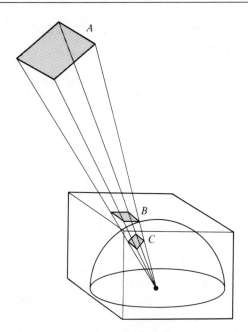

Figure 11.7   The justification for using a hemicube. Patches *A*, *B* and *C* have the same form factor.

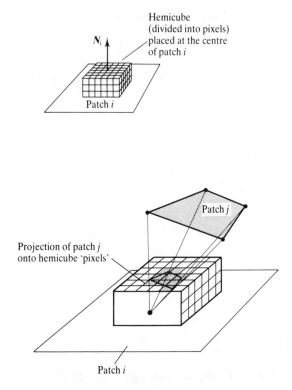

Figure 11.8   Evaluating the form factor F_{ij} by projecting patch *j* onto the faces of a hemicube centred on patch *i*.

onto the hemisphere surface and projecting it down onto the circle. It follows from this that any patch that has the same projection on the surface of the hemisphere has the same form factor. This means that we can project onto the face of a cube rather than a hemisphere, an algorithmically more convenient solution (Figure 11.7).

A hemicube is constructed around the centre of each patch A_i with the hemicube *z*-axis and the patch normal coincident (Figure 11.8). The faces of the hemicube are divided into elements which Cohen terms 'pixels', a somewhat confusing use of the term since we are operating in object space, and every other patch A_j is projected onto the hemicube. Each pixel on the hemicube can be considered as a small patch and a differential-to-finite-area form factor, known as a 'delta form factor', defined for each pixel. The form factor of a pixel is a fraction of the differential-to-finite-area form factor for the patch and can be defined as:

$$\Delta F_{dAiAj} = \frac{\cos \phi_i \cos \phi_j}{\pi r^2} \Delta A$$

$$= \Delta F_q$$

where ΔA is the area of the pixel.

These form factors can be precalculated and stored in a lookup table. This is the foundation of the efficiency of the method. Again using the fact that areas of equal projection onto the receiving surface surrounding the centre of patch A_i have equal form factors, we can conclude that F_{ij}, for any patch, is obtained by summing the pixel form factor onto which patch A_j projects (Figure 11.9). A three-dimensional version of a Cohen–Sutherland clipper [SUTH74a] is used to clip the projections against the hemicube edges to obtain the set of pixels onto which a patch projects.

The occluding or intervening patch problem is easily solved using the hemicube method. For each hemicube placement on patch A_i every patch A_j is projected. If a hemicube pixel contains the projection from two patches then their distances can be compared and the nearer patch deemed to be the one that is 'seen' through that particular pixel. A patch label buffer needs to be maintained for each hemicube pixel that at any stage in the

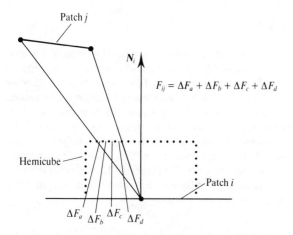

$$F_{ij} = \Delta F_a + \Delta F_b + \Delta F_c + \Delta F_d$$

Figure 11.9 F_{ij} is obtained by summing the form factors of the pixels onto which patch *j* projects.

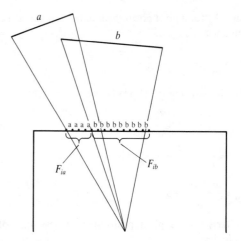

Figure 11.10 Pixels are labelled with the identity of the nearest patch. When a projection sequence for patch *i* is complete F_{ij} can be evaluated.

sequence contains the label of the nearest patch encountered so far in that direction. At the end of the projection sequence we will then have connected sets of pixels that are the projections of the nearest patch, and the summations for each F_{ij} can then proceed (Figure 11.10). Note the similarity to the Z-buffer algorithm. Here we are maintaining identity information rather than intensity information. Thus we have

$$F_{ij} = \sum_q \Delta F_q$$

where *q* is that set of pixels onto which a patch A_j projects. Thus form factor evaluation now reduces to projection onto mutually orthogonal planes and a summation operation.

The precalculation of ΔF_q is straightforward. For

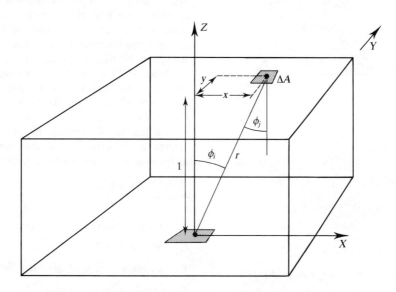

Figure 11.11 Geometry of delta form factors for a pixel ΔA on top of the hemicube (after [COHE85]).

example, for a pixel positioned on the top surface of the hemicube:

$$\Delta F_q = \frac{1}{\pi \left(x^2 + y^2 + 1\right)^2} \Delta A$$

This derives (Figure 11.11) from:

$$r = \left(x^2 + y^2 + 1\right)^{1/2}$$
$$\cos\phi_i = \cos\phi_j$$
$$= \frac{1}{\left(x^2 + y^2 + 1\right)^{1/2}}$$
$$\Delta F_q = \frac{\cos\phi_i \cos\phi_j}{\pi r^2} \Delta A$$

Similarly, for a pixel positioned on the side of the hemicube:

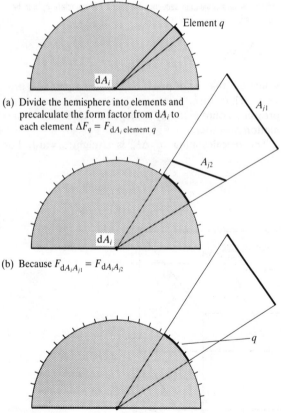

(a) Divide the hemisphere into elements and precalculate the form factor from dA_i to each element $\Delta F_q = F_{dA_i, \text{element } q}$

(b) Because $F_{dA_iA_{j1}} = F_{dA_iA_{j2}}$

(c) We have for any patch projection $F_{dA_iA_j} = \sum_q \Delta F_q$

where q is the set of elements onto which the patch projects

Figure 11.12 A representation of the hemicube method of form factor determination.

$$\Delta F_q = \frac{z}{\pi \left(y^2 + z^2 + 1\right)^2} \Delta A$$

The projection of patches onto the hemicube is also straightforward. The projection centre is the part at which the cube is placed and each face defines a viewing frustrum – in the z-direction a full face of the hemicube produces a square 90° frustrum. Each of the four half-faces produces a rectangular frustrum. The edges of the hemicube define clipping planes and patches are projected onto each face of the hemicube. The complete process is summarized in Figure 11.12, where for the sake of clarity, a hemisphere has been used instead of a hemicube.

11.2.4 Form factor determination: ray tracing

A related method to the hemicube approach retains the advantages of precalculation of delta form factors, together with a solution to the occluding patch problem that does not require the maintenance of an item buffer. This is accomplished by ray tracing [BU89]. A hemisphere, with its surface divided into area elements that each has an associated precalculated delta form factor, is placed over the centre of each patch i. Rays are traced through each element into the environment and the nearest patch hit, patch k, means that the delta form factor of the element through which the ray has been traced contributes to F_{ik}. The order of processing is now changed and the inner loop of this algorithm evaluates the nearest hit from all patches in the environment for a single hemisphere 'pixel'. Thus an item buffer does not need to be maintained. Also the process is immediately implementable in parallel hardware since all ray calculations are identical.

Calculations of the hemisphere pixels are accomplished as follows. Recall that we define a delta-differential-to-finite-area form factor as:

$$\Delta F_{dAiAj} = \frac{\cos \phi_i \cos \phi_j}{\pi r^2} \Delta A$$

For the hemisphere pixels (Figure 11.13):

$$\Delta A = r^2 \Delta \theta \Delta \Omega \sin \Omega$$

We can use an index (l, m) for a hemisphere pixel:

$$\theta = i(\Delta \theta) \quad i = 0, 1, \ldots, k-1$$
$$\Omega = j(\Delta \Omega) \quad j = 0, 1, \ldots, k/4$$

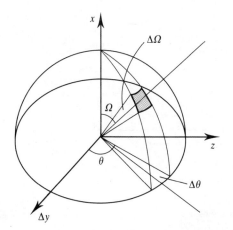

Figure 11.13 Hemisphere subdivision for form factor determination by ray tracing.

and

$$\Delta \theta = \Delta \Omega = \frac{2\pi}{k}$$

Note that in this context:

$\cos \phi_i = \cos \Omega$

and

$\cos \phi_j = 1$

Thus:

$$\Delta F_{i,j} = \frac{\cos \Omega}{\pi r^2} r^2 \Delta \theta \Delta \Omega \sin \Omega$$

$$= \frac{2\pi}{k^2} \sin 2 \Omega$$

For $j = 0$ a unique pixel exists:

$$\Delta A = \pi r^2 \sin^2 (\Delta \Omega)$$

and

$$\Delta F = \sin^2 (\Delta \Omega)$$

Finally, we should note that this approach exchanges the coding complexity of the hemicube-based algorithm for that of a ray tracing algorithm. It is doubtful that a naive ray tracer will compete with the speed of the hemicube approach and some kind of efficient ray tracer must be employed. This factor, however, depends upon the complexity of the scene.

11.2.5 Form factor determination: problems with the hemicube or hemisphere pixel schemes

The hemicube and hemisphere methods are essentially the same, only the way in which they deal with the intervening patch problem is different. Both methods solve a difficult integral by dividing the differential-area-to-finite-area form factor calculations into units that possess an analytical solution. F_{dAiAj} is approximated by the sum of a set of delta differential-area-to-finite-area form factors, ΔF_{dAiAj} or ΔF. Both methods suffer from certain disadvantages inherent in the nature of their geometry.

One of the most serious problems is aliasing caused by the regular division of the hemicube into uniform pixels. Errors clearly occur as a function of the size of the hemicube pixels due to the assumption that patches will project exactly onto an integer number of pixels. This is similar to aliasing in ray tracing. We attempt to gather information from a three-dimensional environment by looking in a fixed number of directions. In ray tracing these directions are given by evenly spaced eye-to-pixel rays. In the radiosity method, by projecting the patches onto hemicubes we are effectively sampling with projection rays from the hemicube origin. Figure 11.14 shows a two-dimensional analogue of the problem where a number of identical polygons project onto either one or two pixels depending on the interference between the projection rays and the polygon grid. The polygons are of equal size and equal orientation with respect to patch i. Their form factors will be different (because ϕ_i is different for each polygon) but not in the ratio 2:1 as suggested by the figure. Recall, with reference to the figure, that polygons project onto a hemicube pixel as shown, because when two polygons land on the same pixel the nearest is selected.

The geometry of any practical scene can cause problems with the hemicube method. The accuracy of the hemicube method depends on the distance between the patches involved in the calculation. When distances reduce to zero the method falls down. This situation occurs in practice, for example when an object is placed on a supporting surface. The errors in form factors occur precisely in those regions from which we expect the radiosity technique to excel and produce subtle phenomena such as colour bleeding and soft shadows. Baum *et al.* [BAUM89] quantify the error involved in form factor determination for proximal surfaces, and

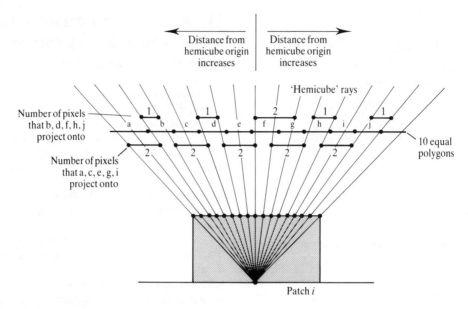

Figure 11.14   Interference between hemicube sampling and a set of equal polygons (after [WALL89]).

demonstrate that the hemicube method is only accurate in contexts where the interpatch distance is at least five patch diameters.

A problem occurs with light sources. In scenes that the radiosity method is used to render, we are usually concerned with large area sources such as fluorescent lights. As with any other surface in the environment we divide the light sources into patches and herein lies the problem. For a standard solution, an environment will be discretized into patches where the subdivision resolution depends on the area of surface (and the accuracy of the solution required). However, in the case of light sources, the number of hemicubes required or the number of patches required depends on the distance from the closest surface it illuminates. A hemicube operation effectively reduces an emitting patch to a point source. Errors will appear on a close surface as isolated areas of light if the light source is insufficiently subdivided.

With strip lights, where the length-to-breadth ratio is great, insufficient subdivision gives rise to banding or aliasing artefacts that run parallel with the long axis of the light source. These are clearly shown in Plate 41. This is identical to Plate 39 except that the intensity of the light is turned up to exaggerate the problem.

Problems are embedded in the approximation:

$$F_{AiAj} = F_{ij} \approx F_{dAiAj}$$

The hemicube evaluates a form factor from a differential area to a finite area. The final solution is a set of radiosity values for each patch where vertex radiosities are extrapolated from these. The radiosity values used in the view-dependent computation are not determined directly. This can cause visible discontinuities when rendering curved surfaces approximated by polygons because 'independent' extrapolated values are obtained for each polygon and the normal Gouraud technique of calculating vertex intensities based on average or vertex normals is not available.

The other context in which the differential-area-to-finite-area form factor approximation falls down is the intervening patch problem. Figure 11.15 illustrates the idea. Here the form factor from patch i to patch j is calculated as if the intervening patch did not exist, because patch j can be seen in its entirety from the hemicube origin.

A subtle point that needs to be considered is the importance of the errors implicit in the hemicube algorithm with respect to the standard solution versus the progressive refinement solution. The validity of the differential area to finite area approximation to form factors holds up well in the standard solution. If it is substructured, then placing the hemicube over the substructured elements is equivalent to evaluating the outer integral. However, in the progressive refinement method we have:

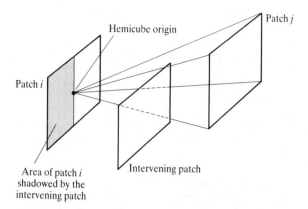

Patch j

Hemicube origin

Patch i

Intervening patch

Area of patch i
shadowed by the
intervening patch

Figure 11.15 All of patch *j* can be seen from the hemicube origin and the $F_{dA_iA_j}$ approximation falls down.

$$\Delta B_j = B_i \begin{bmatrix} \rho_1 F_{1i} \\ \rho_2 F_{2i} \\ \cdot \\ \cdot \\ \cdot \\ \rho_n F_{ni} \end{bmatrix}$$

Substructuring employed in the progressive refinement method implies that the receiving patches are subdivided and that form factors are calculated from the large shooting patch *i* to the subdivided receiving patch *j*. In this case, the distance approximations become much more of a problem. Generally, we can say for an environment that the standard method and the progressive refinement method do not converge to the same solution.

11.2.6 Source-to-vertex form factors

A progressive refinement algorithm that uses source-to-vertex form factors is the basis of work by Wallace *et al.* [WALL89] and this is incorporated in a commercially available radiosity facility (Starbase from Hewlett-Packard company). This approach is designed to overcome two of the major disadvantages of the hemicube method explained in the previous section; aliasing due to interference between the regular hemicube projection rays and the polygon mesh, and aliasing due to inadequate hemicube sampling of a source. Note the distinction between hemicube projection ray sampling – the number of pixels on the hemicube – and hemicube sampling – the number of hemicubes that are used on a source.

These problems are eliminated by using source-to-vertex form factors in the solution. This is a recognition of the fact that the renderer finally requires vertex radiosities. (In the hemicube method these are obtained by extrapolation from the patch radiosities.) Refer again to Figure 11.14. Here the form factors from the patch *i* to the polygons depend on the position of the intersection of the hemicube projection rays with respect to the polygon vertices. Ideally we would like to make the projection rays coincide with the polygon vertices, and Wallace *et al.* effectively accomplish this by defining source-to-vertex form factors. At each stage in a progressive refinement solution a form factor is computed from every vertex to the current source (that is, the source that currently possesses the greatest amount of energy). In this way the radiosity is guaranteed to be computed at each vertex. A ray tracing paradigm is used both to provide a numerical integration for the form factor and to solve the intervening patch problem. The accuracy of the computed form factors and hence the solution depends on the number of rays cast from the vertex to the source. A result can be obtained by using a single ray from the vertex to the source centre. More accurate form factors can be computed by increasing the number of rays used. Wallace *et al.* suggest various ways of increasing the number of rays. The easiest approach is simply to increase the number of sample points and calculate the form factors, repeating the process until two consecutive calculations converge to within a tolerance. It is important not to have a uniform distribution of rays or sampling points, otherwise aliasing will return and Wallace *et al.* suggest jittering the sample points on the source.

To determine the source-to-vertex form factor we start with the same formula used for a hemicube pixel contribution:

$$\Delta F_{dA_vA_s} = \frac{\cos \phi_{vi} \cos \phi_{si}}{\pi r^2} \Delta A_s$$

where dA_v is the vertex and ΔA_s is a delta area on the source (rather than a pixel on the hemicube). The next step is to approximate the delta area with a simple finite geometry that possesses an analytical solution for its form factor and $F_{dA_vA_s}$ is evaluated by summing as many ΔFs that are sampled by the ray tracing process (Figure 11.16):

$$F_{dA_vA_s} = \sum_i \frac{\cos \phi_{vi} \cos \phi_{si}}{\pi r_i^2} \Delta A_s$$

The next step is to approximate each delta area with a geometry that possesses an analytical solution. The

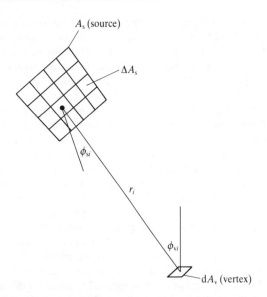

Figure 11.16 Dividing a source into delta areas with known form factors to calculate $F_{dA_v A_s}$.

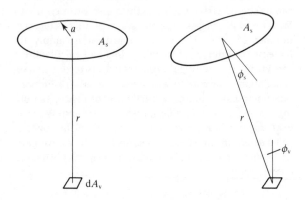

Figure 11.17 A geometry with an analytical solution.

particular finite geometry chosen by Wallace *et al.* is differential area (vertex) to a parallel opposing disk ΔA_s (Figure 11.17). The form factor for this set up is [SEIG84]:

$$\Delta F_{dA_v A_s} = \frac{a^2}{r^2 + a^2}$$

where:

a is the radius of the disk

Using reciprocity we have:

$$\Delta F_{A_s dA_v} = \frac{dA_v}{\pi r^2 + A_s}$$

For a disk at any orientation (Figure 11.17):

$$\Delta F_{A_s dA_v} = \frac{dA_v \cos\phi_v \cos\phi_s}{\pi r^2 + A_s}$$

If the source is divided into *n* delta areas, and if sample points are distributed uniformly on the scene, the total form factor is given by

$$F_{A_s dA_v} = dA_v \frac{1}{n} \sum_{i=1}^{n} H_i \frac{\cos\phi_{vi} \cos\phi_{si}}{\pi r_i^2 + A_s/n}$$

Now given that

$$B_v A_v = \rho_v B_s A_s F_{sv}$$

the radiosity at a vertex due to illumination by a source is:

$$B_v = \rho_v B_s A_s \frac{1}{n} \sum_{i=1}^{n} H_i \frac{\cos \phi_{vi} \cos \phi_{si}}{\pi r_i^2 + A_s/n}$$

and this gives the value required for every vertex at each step in the progressive refinement method. H_i is a binary-valued function that is set to zero if the *i*th ray from the vertex cannot reach the *i*th sample point because of an intervening patch.

11.2.7 Hybridized form factors

The philosophy of this approach, introduced by Baum *et al.* [BAUM89], is simple. It is to retain the major benefit of the hemicube algorithm – computational efficiency – and to use this method to calculate most form factors, using an analytical technique when the form factor method falls down. As discussed in Section 11.2.5, the hemicube method is inappropriate for light sources and when patches are close together. In Baum's method these are calculated analytically and the hemicube is retained for visibility determination only.

Recall that in the hemicube method a receiving patch is projected onto the hemicube pixels. Each pixel is a delta form factor ΔF and the patch-to-patch form factor is calculated by summing the ΔFs for these pixels onto which the receiving patch projects. The ΔFs are precalculated and, as pointed out in Section 11.2.5, this method falls down when surfaces are adjacent. Other problems arise from the efficiency of the approximation

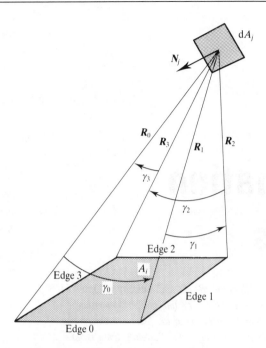

dA_j

N_j

R_0 R_3 R_1 R_2

γ_3

γ_2

Edge 2 γ_1

Edge 3 A_i

γ_0

Edge 1

Edge 0

Figure 11.18 Geometry for analytical form factor determination (after [BAUM89]).

that equates the form factor to a differential area to a finite area formulation.

When accurate form factor determination is required, Baum's method evaluates the inner integral of

$$F_{ij} = \frac{1}{A_j} \int_{Ai} \int_{Aj} \frac{\cos\Theta_i \cos\phi_j}{\pi r^2} \, dA_j \, dA_i$$

analytically and the outer integral numerically using summation across projected pixels in the hemicube. As before, a hemicube is placed at the centre of the shooting patch. Form factors are now calculated individually from receiving elements to *each* pixel on the hemicube onto which the elements project using Stoke's theorem. Using a derivation given in [HOTT67] he calculates the inner integral, a differential area to finite area form factor as

$$F dA_j A_i = \frac{1}{2\pi} \sum_{k \in k_i} N_j \cdot E_k \qquad (11.6)$$

where:

N_j is the surface normal of the differential surface dA_j

E_k is a vector of magnitude equal to the angle γ_k and direction given by the cross product of the two vectors R_k and R_{k+1} (Figure 11.18)

k_i is the set of edges of the patch A_i

The formula is used to evaluate an element-to-patch form factor $F_{(iq)j}$ or F_{ej}. This is integrated into the normal hemicube summation (or inner integral) as follows. Each element in the patch will project onto a number of pixels. For each pixel onto which an element projects, Equation (11.6) is used to evaluate a form factor. This is weighted by the area of the pixel projected onto the element, divided by the total visible element area. A summation of these element form factors, analytically calculated, is performed using the normal hemicube approach and this accounts for the outer integral. F_{ej} is a weighted average of samples, where each element is subdivided into small areas. Baum *et al.* point out that the magnitude of F_{ej} no longer depends on the number of hemicube pixels onto which the elements project and, as well as solving the proximating problem, the method deals with aliasing due to an element projecting onto a small number of hemicube pixels.

The use of the accurate analytical method or the standard hemicube method can be determined from the distance between the element and the shooting patch.

To deal with intervening patch problems – another source of error – Baum *et al.* suggest first detecting that the problem has occurred and then subdividing the shooting patch until the subdivision components are either fully visible or fully invisible from each element in the scene. The need for subdivision can be detected by evaluating the following summation after finding all the element-to-patch form factors for a patch:

$$\sum_e \frac{A_e}{A_j} F_{ej}$$

Baum *et al.* state that if this total exceeds unity by a significant amount then visibility errors exist for more than one surface in the environment. In this event the shooting patch needs to be subdivided and the procedure applied recursively to each subpatch.

12 Global illumination models

We introduced ray tracing (Chapters 8–10) and radiosity (Chapter 11) prior to this chapter as successful, but partial, global illumination techniques. This chapter order reflects both the historical emergence of the techniques and usage of the methods. Currently there is no fully accepted complete global illumination model, and this chapter takes the form of a review of the more important work.

Introduction

In this chapter we will examine global illumination models. We will also introduce a model – the rendering equation – that can be used formally to categorize the inadequacies of the various incomplete global models.

First of all, we start with an empirical model or visualization introduced by Wallace *et al*. [WALL87]. This is a much simpler concept than the rendering equation and was used by Wallace in an extension of the radiosity method to include specular surfaces.

The concept is the classification of the nature of the light transport mechanism between two surfaces. This is demonstrated in Figure 12.1 that shows, for pairs of surfaces, the different transfer mechanisms possible. These are:

(a) diffuse to diffuse;

(b) specular to diffuse;

(c) diffuse to specular;

(d) specular to specular.

Global illumination cannot be evaluated using a single transport mechanism and it is the interaction of different transport mechanisms along a light propagation path that causes the difficulty. Light can arrive at a surface after several interactions with several surfaces where any of the above transport mechanisms may be involved. Figure 12.2 demonstrates this problem and shows that postprocessing a radiosity solution with ray tracing, and extending the method to cover specular surfaces, can never be correct because specular-to-specular interaction may arise from diffuse-to-diffuse interaction that is nearer the light source in the propagation path. It also shows that the radiosity method cannot be correct for scenes that contain specularly reflecting objects, because specular-to-diffuse transport is not modelled by the basic radiosity method. The energy contributed to the diffuse reflection of surface 3 by specular light from surface 2 will not be taken into account.

Radiosity has thus emerged as being the most suitable method for solving the diffuse-to-diffuse interaction component. It deals correctly with global interaction for a diffuse environment where the relationship between any pair of surfaces is always diffuse to diffuse. Ray

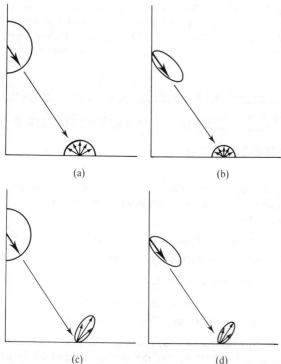

(a)   (b)

(c)   (d)

Figure 12.1 The four 'mechanisms' of light transport: (a) diffuse to diffuse; (b) specular to diffuse; (c) diffuse to specular; (d) specular to specular (after [WALL87]).

tracing correctly handles perfect specular-to-specular transport and deals with diffuse-to-specular transport empirically. Illumination at a surface point hit by an nth-generation ray is calculated by applying a local reflection model and any resultant diffuse component is passed up the ray tree over a specular path.

We remarked in Chapter 10 that in order for ray tracing to handle the diffuse-to-diffuse component many rays would have to be fired from a ray/object intersection in many directions to many layers of recursion – a practically impossible approach. (We should also note that even if it were possible to adopt such a strategy, much unnecessary repetitive work would be carried out because diffuse contributions typically change slowly over pixels.)

We will see in this chapter that attempting to include specular-to-specular transport in the radiosity method is problematic and that the general approach to incorporating specular interaction and retaining the view-independent nature of the radiosity solution very soon becomes impossible practically.

Radiosity and ray-traced images have their own unique signatures. Radiosity images tend to be used to simulate

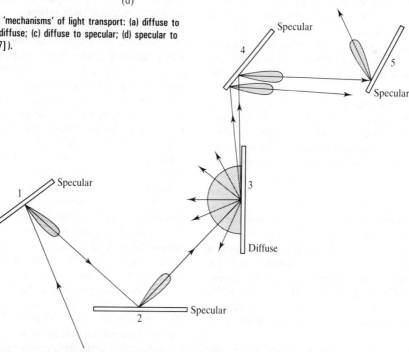

Figure 12.2 The effect of a single diffuse reflector in a 'chain' of specular reflectors.

softly lit interiors while ray tracing images have as their hallmark shiny objects exhibiting sharp multiple reflections. This aesthetic separation between image types can now be seen as a function of the underlying transport mechanisms that each method uses.

Finally, consider the second mechanism – specular-to-diffuse transport. This occurs when light reflecting from the specular surface, or refracting through one surface hits a diffuse surface. This mechanism is responsible for a variety of important effects – light interacting with water or glass, for example – and it can be incorporated into ray tracing by involving a two-pass method wherein the specular-to-diffuse transport is implemented by tracing light from the source – backwards ray tracing (see Chapter 11). In radiosity, the incorporation of this mechanism was also achieved by a two-pass mechanism described in Section 12.1 [WALL87]. Wallace *et al.* treat the specular surface as an additional route by which light leaving one diffuse patch may reach another. The method restricts the specular surface to be a perfect mirror. Practical contexts appropriate to this method are such things as the effect of light from a desk lamp bouncing off a mirror and hitting a table top.

Thus at the moment radiosity is firmly based on the diffuse-to-diffuse mechanism. The extension to incorporate specular to diffuse is restrictive. Ray tracing handles specular to specular and diffuse to specular; but the latter mechanism is not handled correctly. Backwards ray tracing provides a more flexible extension for the specular-to-diffuse mechanism than the two-pass radiosity approach.

It is impossible to separate this discussion from the goals of computer graphics. Is it necessary to calculate global illumination accurately? This question is part of a more general point that should concern the computer graphics community: is photorealism a desirable goal and to what limits should we chase it? Undoubtedly, the current state of affairs is unsatisfactory – the two major post-Phong or second generation rendering methods produce recognizably different versions of reality. On the other hand, there are other aspects of photorealism that are blithely ignored. Radiosity claims an accurate solution for diffuse environments, but correct colour (or colour aliasing) is an ignored topic because of the expense of evaluating a solution at more than three wavelengths. It may be that there are considerations that should take precedence over the pursuit of a global illumination solution.

Currently, the most practical approach to a complete global illumination method is the merging of radiosity and ray tracing. We describe two approaches to extending radiosity. The first one is a development of Wallace's work [WALL87]. The second is derived from the rendering equation which we will also describe.

12.1 Combining radiosity and ray tracing

This, like backwards ray tracing, is a two-pass approach. The first pass uses an enhanced radiosity method and accounts for:

- diffuse-to-diffuse mechanisms, and
- specular-to-diffuse mechanisms.

The second pass accounts for:

- diffuse-to-specular mechanisms, and
- specular-to-specular mechanisms.

Merging ray tracing and radiosity is not straightforward. It is not correct to use ray tracing independently to calculate specular interreflection and radiosity to evaluate diffuse interreflection because there is no way of separating the phenomena. Specular interreflection may arise from diffuse interreflection and vice versa as shown in Figure 12.2. In this illustration specular interaction leads to a diffuse interaction. Then, because of the geometry of the surfaces, the interaction becomes specular again. Ray tracing would miss the final two surfaces in the sequence. In other words, ray tracing would stop at the diffuse patch and would not consider specular interaction between the subsequent patches, and radiosity would not consider the specular energy transport onto the diffuse patch.

Early in the development of the radiosity method it was realized that specular interaction would have to be incorporated into the technique if the approach was to become a general rendering tool with any ambition towards being a global illumination model. This has proved extremely difficult and, at the time of writing (1992), no single practical solution has been accepted by the computer graphics community. First, let us examine the practical reasons for this difficulty. The basic radiosity method assumes diffuse reflectivity and emissivity and the bidirectional reflectivity reduces to a constant, allowing the radiosity of a patch or element to be represented by a single number. Radiosity, as a view-independent process, must, by necessity, discretize the whole environment and then sample it to provide a solution. The ability to produce a solution in an acceptable time depends on the discretization being coarse. In contrast, the view-dependent specular contributions to an image can vary rapidly over adjacent image pixels and this cannot be recovered by interpolating across relatively wide patch vertices. Subdividing the patches to a level such that when projected onto the image plane they are roughly the same size as a pixel would take the method into the realm of impossibly expensive computation.

The first attempt at incorporating specular interreflections suffered from precisely this problem because the view independence of the radiosity solution was extended into the specular domain. This was work carried out by Immel *et al.* [IMME86] that extends the basic radiosity approach to include directional reflectivity. This was done by replacing the single relationship between two patches (expressed as a form factor) by a relationship between a single outgoing reflection direction for a patch and all outgoing directions for all other patches. This was accomplished using an extension of the hemicube, a full cube, where each cube pixel corresponds to a single outgoing direction. These cubes, known as 'global cubes', are oriented in the world coordinate system, rather than taking their orientation from the patch. A massive set of equations results and, when solved, produces a specular and diffuse view-independent solution. A view-dependent image is created by interpolating from the resulting radiosity intensities that also now incorporate directional information. The method will converge to an accurate specular solution as the discretization of the environment is increased, but this just makes the method more and more intractable. The images produced by Immel *et al.* at an affordable discretization contain artefacts. The realization that a view-independent solution, incorporating specular interaction, at an acceptable quality was computationally impossible led to the development of the two-pass method that computes both a view-independent (diffuse) and a view-dependent (specular) solution by merging radiosity and ray tracing.

12.1.1 The two-pass approach

The two-pass approach is a view-independent/view-dependent sequence and is enhanced radiosity followed by enhanced ray tracing. The idea [WALL87] is built on the recognition that calculation of view-dependent specular contributions and view-independent diffuse contributions are computationally tractable; whereas view-independent specular solutions (and view-dependent diffuse components) are, with current resources, impossible. This then is the background to the two-pass approach. We should also comment that although much is made of the phrase 'view independence', a view-independent solution is a consequence of basic radiosity and is not, except in the special application of animated walks-through, an advantage.

The preprocess in the enhanced radiosity method

In the preprocess, or view-independent solution, specular transport is accounted for, but only to the extent necessary to calculate the diffuse component accurately. This, of course, is the third transport mechanism described at the beginning of this chapter – diffuse to specular.

The first pass of the two-pass approach has been formalized by Rushmeier and Torrance [RUSH90] and we will adopt their notation here. The method fully accounts for ideal specular and ideal diffuse reflection and ideal specular and ideal diffuse transmission. The practical limitation of the method is that the number of specular surfaces that are involved in the interaction of diffuse surfaces should be small.

Rushmeier and Torrance develop a general equation for the radiant intensity of a surface in a closed environment. They then derive the basic radiosity equation using intensities rather than radiosities:

$$I_i = I_{\mathrm{e},\,i} + \rho_{\mathrm{d},\,i} \sum_{j=1}^{N} I_j F_{ij}$$

where, for an ideal diffuse surface, intensity and radiosity are related by:

$$I_i = \frac{B_i}{\pi}$$

This basic equation is then elaborated, under certain constraints, to account for extensions that are due to the diffuse-to-specular transfer mechanism. The basic radiosity method is also enhanced to include transmission effects. These are now described.

Diffuse transmission

Diffuse transmission occurs, for example, through a light shade. If we assume that there is no specular interaction the basic equation becomes:

$$I_i = I_{e,i} + \rho_{d,i} \sum_{j=1}^{N} I_j F_{ij} + \tau_{d,i} \sum_{j=1}^{N} I_j T_{ij} \qquad (12.1)$$

where $\tau_{d,i}$ is the diffuse transmittance for patch i. We introduce a new form factor that accounts for interaction between ideal diffuse surfaces due to transmission and this is called a 'backwards diffuse form factor'. It expresses that fraction of diffuse energy that has been transmitted through patch i that reaches patch j. The form factor T_{ij} can be calculated in the same way as F_{ij}, except that the integration is performed over a hemisphere placed on the reverse side of the surface. Thus if the hemicube algorithm is being used for form factor determination it would be placed on the front side to calculate F_{ij} and on the back side for T_{ij}. Geometrically, then, the form factors T and F are similar.

The question of what is the front side and what the back side of a patch is context dependent. A shade surrounding a lamp has an obvious back and front side. On the other hand, an isolated sheet of glass has no back and front sides, and would have to be defined as two patches, at the same position in space. For example, if we have two such patches labelled m and n, then we have:

$$T_{nj} = F_{mj} \quad \text{and} \quad T_{mj} = F_{nj}$$

Specular transmission
The next extension, to incorporate specular transmission, is made possible by the constraint that no two specular surfaces can see each other (but nevertheless contribute to diffuse interaction through the specular-to-diffuse mechanism). If we consider two interacting diffuse patches then their interaction will clearly change if a specular transmitting surface is placed between them. Also, if we express intensity as a sum of a diffuse and a specular component, we have:

$$I_i = I_{d,i} + I_{s,i}$$

and the specular component can be written as:

$$I_{s,i} = \tau_{s,i} I_{d,i}$$

where:

$\tau_{s,i}$ is the specular transmittance for patch i

Using this we can extend Equation (12.1) as follows:

$$I_i = I_{e,i} + \rho_{d,i} \sum_{j=1}^{N} \left\{ I_j F_{ij} + \tau_{s,j} \sum_{p=1}^{N} I_p T_{f,\,ijp} \right\}$$

$$+ \tau_{d,i} \sum_{j=1}^{N} \left\{ I_j T_{ij} + \tau_{s,j} \sum_{p=1}^{N} I_p T_{b,\,ijp} \right\} \qquad (12.2)$$

The first terms in the braces within the outer summation accounts for Equation (12.1) and you can see that this equation has been extended by two innermost summations. The first innermost summation (multiplied by the reflectivity $\rho_{d,i}$) is saying that when we consider the incoming energy from all other patches in the scene, onto the patch i, there may be a contribution due to specular transmission. Consider a particular value of j in the outer summation. We consider the energy arriving at patch i leaving patch j and this is expressed as the form factor F_{ij}. If patch j is a specular transmitter it will transmit light to patch i from surfaces that patch i can *see* through it. To evaluate this contribution an integration of light intensity over patch j has to be performed. This is equal to the sum of the integrals of light intensity over patches p that are visible through patch j (Figure 12.3). This is denoted by a geometric factor, known as a 'window' form factor and designated $T_{f,\,ijp}$. This can be evaluated again by a hemicube approach. Figure 12.4 shows a hemicube placed on patch i. This patch can see a certain area of patch p through the specularly transmitting surface patch j. This overlap area projects onto the hemicube and delta contributions are used as normal to evaluate the required form factor.

We have to extend the contribution due to transmission through the patch i in a similar way. In the subex-

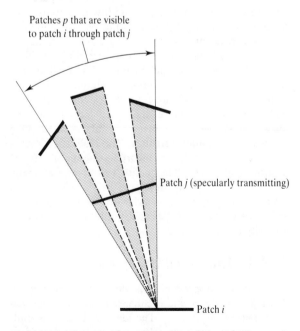

Figure 12.3 Illustrating the extension for a single specularly transmitting patch j.

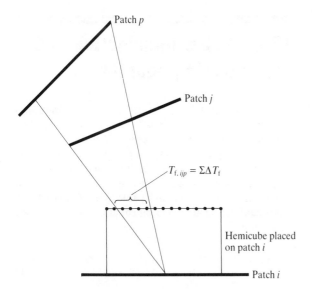

Figure 12.4 Window form factor is calculated by summing over the area on the hemicube projected from that area seen on patch p from patch i through patch j.

pression multiplied by the transmissivity $\tau_{d,i}$, we have an inner summation that includes the window form factor $T_{b,ijp}$ evaluated in the same way as $T_{f,ijp}$ except that the hemicube is placed on the back of the patch i.

Specular reflection

Incorporation of specular-to-diffuse interaction completes the generalization of the view-independent phase. Just like the previous extension, the view independence is made possible by the constraint that no two specular surfaces can see each other, but nevertheless contribute to interaction between patches. Wallace *et al.* [WALL87] originally coined the term 'mirror' form factors and considered the case of specular patches consisting of perfect mirrors, that provided an additional path over which the two diffuse patches could see each other (Figure 12.5). This extra interaction is taken into account by a mirror form factor, the form factor between a patch and a virtual patch in a virtual environment. Mirror form factors can then be calculated in exactly the same way as conventional form factors once the geometry of the virtual world is computed.

Rushmeier and Torrance deal with this mechanism by simply extending the case of specular transmission. This results in an extension of Equation (12.2) with two more inner summations to give:

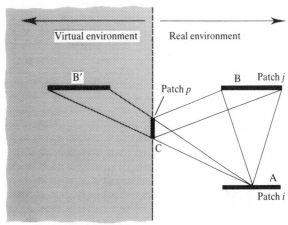

Figure 12.5 The concept of a mirror form factor.

$$I_i = I_{e,i} + \rho_{d,i} \sum_{j=1}^{N} \left\{ I_j F_{ij} + \tau_{s,j} \sum_{p=1}^{N} I_p T_{f,ijp} + \rho_{s,j} \sum_{p=1}^{N} I_p F_{f,ijp} \right\}$$

$$+ \tau_{d,i} \sum_{j=1}^{N} \left\{ I_j T_{ij} + \tau_{s,j} \sum_{p=1}^{N} I_p T_{b,ijp} + \rho_{s,j} \sum_{p=1}^{N} I_p F_{b,ijp} \right\}$$

where:

$F_{f,ijp}$ is the forward mirror form factor
$F_{b,ijp}$ is the backward mirror form factor

This device incorporates specular reflection by considering it as specular transmission from a virtual environment. The specular patch is considered as a specular transmitter that receives light from the virtual patch. The mirror image form factors are found in the same way as the window form factors, except that the surfaces that transmit light through the patch in question are virtual surfaces.

The postprocess in the enhanced radiosity method

The view-dependent or postprocess deals with the specular-to-specular and diffuse-to-specular mechanisms using a ray tracing approach. Normal ray tracing, of course, deals with specular-to-specular transfer. To calculate the diffuse-to-specular mechanism properly, an integration of incoming intensities should be performed over the entire hemisphere at the point of interest, weighted by the bidirectional specular reflectivity.

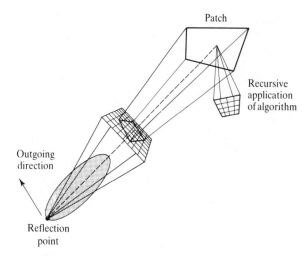

Patch

Recursive
application
of algorithm

Outgoing
direction

Reflection
point

Figure 12.6 Sampling intensities using a square pyramid to approximate the reflection lobe (after [WALL87]).

However, Wallace *et al.* [WALL87] make the assumption that only a small fraction of the incoming rays over the hemisphere contribute to the outgoing specular bump. They use a rectangular reflection frustum to simulate the specular bump and this method also incorporates the specular-to-specular mechanism (Figure 12.6). Incoming diffuse intensities that contribute to each reflection frustum are calculated by linear interpolation from the view-independent/preprocess patch vertex intensities.

The reflection frustum is implemented geometrically as a square pyramid, whose end face is divided into $n \times n$ 'pixels'. Visible surfaces are determined by using a conventional Z-buffer algorithm with a very low resolution of the order of 10×10 pixels. The incoming intensity 'seen' through a reflection frustum pixel is simply the intensity of the surface seen by that pixel, that is, the intensity calculated in the preprocess or view-independent phase. If a visible surface is specular then the process is applied recursively as in normal ray tracing.

The incoming intensities that stream through each pixel are summed to simulate the specular spread and can also be subjected to a weighting function that simulates the shape of the specular spread. Wallace *et al.* limit the amount of work that has to be done at this stage by limiting the recursive depth over which the process operates and also by reducing the pixel resolution of the end face of the reflection frustum as a function of trace depth.

12.2 Global illumination and the rendering equation

In 1986 Kajiya [KAJI86] introduced the rendering equation, the purpose of which is '. . . to provide a unified context for viewing them [rendering algorithms] as more or less accurate approximations to the solution of a single equation.' The idea is that since local and global reflection/illumination models describe the same physical phenomena, they should all be able to be compared to a single equation. The rendering equation, using Kajiya's notation is:

$$I(x, x') = g(x, x') \left[\epsilon(x, x') + \int_s \rho(x, x', x'') I(x', x'') \, dx'' \right]$$

where:

$I(x, x')$ is the transport intensity or the intensity of light passing from point x' to point x

$g(x, x')$ is the visibility function between x and x'. If x and x' cannot see each other this is zero. If they are visible then g varies as the inverse square of the distance between them.

$\epsilon(x, x')$ is the transfer emittance from point x' to x

$\rho(x, x', x'')$ is the scattering term or bidirectional reflectivity with respect to directions x' and x''. It is the intensity of the energy scattered towards x by a surface point located at x' arriving from point or direction x''

The integral is over s, all points on all surfaces in the scene. The equation simply states that the transport intensity from point x' to point x is equal to the sum of the light emitted from x' in the direction x and the *total* light scattered from x' towards x from *all* other surfaces in the scene. The radiosity equation immediately follows from this if the reflectivity is reduced to a constant (see below).

Kajiya states that the equation is formulated as a base against which computer graphics models can be compared; it is not intended to model all optical phenomena. In particular, the effects of phase, diffraction and transmission through participatory media are not taken into account. Wavelength dependence is not stated explicitly and is to be understood.

The important point to realize is that I appears in both sides of the equation and this recursive relationship reflects the global illumination problem. The equation can be rewritten as:

$$I = g\epsilon + gR(I)$$

where R is a linear integral operator. In this form the equation can be inverted as follows:

$$(1 - gR)I = g\epsilon$$

which gives

$$
\begin{aligned}
I &= (1 - gR)^{-1}g\epsilon \\
&= g\epsilon + g(Rg)\epsilon + g(Rg)^2\epsilon + g(Rg)^3\epsilon + \dots \\
&= \sum_{i=0}^{\infty} g(Rg)^i\epsilon
\end{aligned}
\tag{12.3}
$$

This series expresses the intensity transfer between two points as the sum of successively scattered terms. The first term is a direct term. The second term describes the illumination from light sources impinging on x' and reflected along the direction x – a once-scattered term. The third term accounts for the illumination that arrives at x' via an intermediate surface – a twice-scattered term – and so on.

In local reflection models only the first two terms are considered and x is the eye. The emitters are usually point light sources and the series reduces to:

$$I = g\epsilon + gR_1\epsilon$$

The ϵ term, implicit in R_1, can be directional or bidirectional depending on the model used. R_1 can sum over a number of light sources. The first term is nonzero only for those points x' that correspond to the light source. Note that R_1 operates directly on ϵ (rather than $g\epsilon$) implying that visibility between a light source and the point x' is not considered – shadows are not computed.

In the basic ray tracing model [WHIT80], we have:

$$I = \sum_{i=0}^{\infty} g(R_{rt}g)^i\epsilon$$

This was the first computer graphics model to deal (partially) with global illumination. Here R_{rt} operates on $g\epsilon$ because shadows are normally incorporated into a basic ray tracing implementation. R_{rt} is the sum of two delta terms – the reflected and refracted rays together with a local or direct model. The series is restricted to small values of i (typically around 3).

To see the relevance of the rendering equation to the radiosity equation we first consider that the radiosity solution is based on energy equilibrium in a closed environment that is made up entirely of perfect diffuse surfaces. This means that the bidirectional reflectivity function reduces to a constant:

$$\rho(x, x', x'') = \rho_0$$

The radiosity $dB(x')$ of a surface element dx' is the hemispherical integral of the energy leaving the surface. Attaching a coordinate frame to the points x and x' to define a normal, largest and binormal vector, it can be shown [KAJI86]:

$$
\begin{aligned}
dB(x') &= dx' \int_s I(x, x')\,dx \\
&= dx' \int \left\{ g(x, x')[\epsilon(x, x') + \rho_0 \int_s I(x', x'')\,dx''] \right\} dx
\end{aligned}
$$

The emittance term for the surface element is either zero, or

$$dB_e(x') = dx'\pi\epsilon$$

ϵ is now the energy emitting into the hemisphere associated with dx'. Similarly, it can be shown the reflectance term is either zero, or

$$dB_r(x') = dx'\rho_0\pi H(x')$$

where H is the energy incident on the surface element dx', giving

$$dB(x') = \pi \left[\epsilon + \rho_0 H(x') \right] dx'$$

and this should be compared with the 'standard' radiosity equation. In the light of the rendering equation, radiosity can be seen as a discretization of the variable space. x, x' and x'' become the patches of the radiosity approach rather than single points and this reduces the rendering equation into a set of linear equations.

12.2.1 The path tracing solution to the rendering equation

Kajiya's rendering equation fulfils two functions. First, as explained in the previous section, it provides a unifying framework into which such apparently diverse methods as ray tracing and radiosity can be incorporated and compared. Secondly, by application of a Monte Carlo method, the equation can be directly solved giving a robust, but expensive, solution to the global illumination problem.

The rendering equation is a Fredholm integral of the second kind. This is a type of integral where the unknown function appears both inside and outside the integral. Its major application is in particle dynamics in quantum physics. To solve this equation Kajiya uses an algorithm based on a Monte Carlo method. This is simply an extension of a Monte Carlo method that is used to solve sets

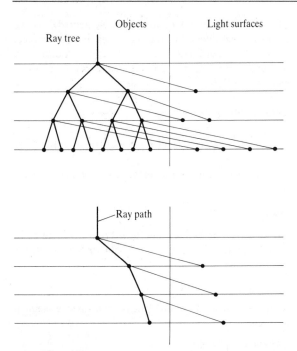

Figure 12.7 Kajiya's conceptual illustration of ray tracing and path tracing (after [KAJI86]).

of linear simultaneous equations described in [RUBE81].

Kajiya's algorithm is basically a forward ray tracer that captures the desired global phenomena by intelligently sampling the theoretically infinite ray space. Variance reduction techniques are used to control the sampling. Kajiya calls his solution 'path tracing' and this describes one of the major differences between the method and standard ray tracing. The integral is estimated over 40 pixel samples or paths. Instead of branching at each intersection with a reflected and refracted ray, Kajiya follows a single path, in effect sampling the tree that results from conventional ray tracing. At each intersection a single path is followed and a ray is shot towards the light source. This idea is illustrated in Figure 12.7 where it can be seen that a path is a sample of a single ray extracted from a standard ray tree. We could look on the method as a forward ray tracer that captures the desired global phenomena by retrieving a sampled version of the complete ray space. Instead of trying to generate an impossibly large number of rays, the ray space is sampled using an appropriate variance reduction technique. Kajiya points out that this diagram reflects an important fact – that because surfaces are mostly non-emitters or passive, the first generation or initial rays are

the most important in terms of the variance of the final integral. Despite this, conventional ray tracing results in an increasing workload as the ray generation number increases. More and more work is carried out for less and less contribution to the final pixel value. A path is effectively a ray tree with a branching ratio of one and there are as many first generation rays as there are higher generation rays.

At this stage it is useful to compare this method with the distributed ray tracing technique described in Chapter 10. Essentially, they are both different manifestations of the same approach in that they are both ray tracing methods that use Monte Carlo sampling techniques to provide an accurate estimate of an 'impossible' integral. However, the distributed ray tracing approach is not a complete solution to the global illumination problem. It uses the Monte Carlo method to estimate the integral operator R for realistic (blurred) specular interaction and the other phenomena described in Chapter 10, but does not deal with diffuse interaction. Using an estimate of 16 rays per pixel, the underlying ray tree is a conventional branching structure with three rays spawned for every hit. At each hit the direction of the outgoing rays are perturbed according to the reflection/transmission characteristics and importance sampling criteria.

We can also note that path tracing is a forward ray tracing approach that overcomes, for example, the problem that is addressed in Chapter 10 by backwards ray tracing, or tracing rays from the light source. It therefore captures, for example, the phenomena of caustics described in Chapter 10.

To return to the algorithm. A valid view of the process is that it is a simple forward ray tracer that is controlled by a framework that intelligently samples the ray tree to provide a Monte Carlo estimate for each pixel. The method that selects or distributes initial rays over the pixel is called 'hierarchical integration'. This is one of a family of variance reduction techniques that shoots rays from a pixel in a way that tends to reduce the variance of the pixel estimates. Five such techniques are discussed by Kajiya in the context of ray tracing. The other part of the algorithm that requires a selection decision is in the path to follow at each ray/object intersection or hit. Kajiya points out that it is important to maintain the correct proportion of reflection, transmission and shadows rays that contribute to each pixel and to ensure that the sample distribution of ray types matches the actual distribution (given by object information).

Because the path tracing method is based on a standard

ray tracing approach, there is still a difficulty with diffuse interaction, which requires a large number of estimates by definition to compute an accurate solution. This problem is addressed by Ward [WARD88]. Ward's method exploits two characteristics of illuminance over a scene. First, the samples required to evaluate diffuse interaction at a point of interest are a function of the illuminance gradient at that point. Secondly, diffuse interaction computations can be speeded up by allowing an element of view independence. In Ward's method a separate data structure is used to cache illumination values and the ray tracing proceeds, either by using previously calculated values (the 'secondary' method) or by calculating new values (the 'primary' method).

12.3 The extended two-pass method for global illumination

Although Kajiya's work on the rendering equation and methods of solving it was published in 1986, the approach does not seem to have been taken up by the computer graphics community. Instead, as we have seen, work has developed to generalize both the radiosity and ray tracing methods to overcome their mutual exclusivity.

Currently, the most general work on global illumination is due to Sillion [SILL89] and this extends Wallace's two-pass approach [WALL87]. Similar to the method in Section 12.1.1, Sillion uses the rendering equation as a starting point. Recall that in Wallace's method the first pass used the radiosity method to calculate global diffuse intensity and included the interaction of diffuse patches via an intermediate patch. The specular path was constrained to be a perfect planar mirror because this enabled a virtual environment of patches to be conducted and the hemicube algorithm was retained to solve the radiosity pass.

Silicon overcomes this restriction, and in the first pass form factors are found by ray tracing conferring the following extensions:

1. Specular surfaces can be of any shape.

2. Any number of specular reflection paths can be included.

3. Refractions can be incorporated.

Theoretically the method is developed from the rendering equation and this, together with its generality, makes it appropriate for inclusion in this chapter. To simplify discussion of linear integral operations Sillion rewrites Equation (12.3) as:

$$I = \sum_{i=0}^{\infty} R^i g\epsilon$$

where the visibility function g is now incorporated into the reflection operator R. The bidirectional reflectivity function is expressed as the sum:

$$\rho(x, x', x'') = \rho_d(x') + \rho_s(x, x', x'')$$

where we assume that reflectivity can be expressed as the sum of a diffuse component and a specular component. The rendering equation, if all emitters are diffuse, becomes:

$$I(x, x') = g(x, x') \left\{ \epsilon(x') + \rho_d(x') \int_s I(x', x'') dx'' \right\}$$
$$+ g(x, x') \int_s \rho_s(x, x', x'') I(x', x'') dx''$$
$$= g(x, x') \beta(x') + TI(x, x')$$

where T is a linear integral operator that transforms I into *one* specular reflection and/or refraction over all the scene. Thus we can write:

$$I = \sum_{k=0}^{\infty} T^k g\beta$$
$$= Sg\beta$$

where S is now a global specular operator specifying the effect of all global specular reflections on I. Also we can write:

$$\beta = \epsilon + DI$$

where D is the diffuse reflection integral operator giving:

$$\beta = \epsilon + DSg\beta$$

The importance of this result is that it is a formal specification of the first pass of a general two-pass radiosity/ray tracing approach to global illumination. It says that the isotropic distribution, the component of I that depends only on x', is given by the sum of the emitted energy and a global evaluation of the diffuse illumination, taking into account diffuse-to-diffuse transfer that travels over specular paths. The diffuse reflection operator in the standard radiosity equation is replaced by the product DS. The equation can be solved using the radiosity method if 'extended' form factors are used in the radiosity matrix. An extended form factor F_{ij} is defined as the proportion of energy leaving patch i that strikes patch j after any number of specular reflections or refractions. This suggests that extended form factors need to be calculated by ray tracing and this is precisely the approach that is adopted by Sillion. Recall that in the standard radiosity approach, for a patch i, many other patches, perhaps partially obscured by intervening patches, will project onto the hemicube cen-

tred on i. In the case of extended form factors, just as in ray tracing, any patch j that can 'see' patch i through a set of specular paths of arbitrary complexity is included in the definition. It is the calculation of these extended form factors that gives the method its generality.

Once the extended form factors are calculated, the standard radiosity method is used to calculate the diffuse illumination distribution β. This then is the first pass of the method.

The second pass calculates the effect of global operator S, and uses, just as Wallace's technique does, standard ray tracing.

13 | Volume rendering techniques

Introduction

Volume rendering along with animation are the major tools used in 'Visualization in Scientific Computing' (ViSC) and we will preface this chapter with a short discussion on ViSC. Although many techniques in computer graphics are used in ViSC, this text is concerned with rendering techniques and we will look in this chapter at volume rendering and its applications in ViSC. Undoubtedly, volume rendering is the most important technique in ViSC, and the development of this rendering technique was the main factor in the growth of ViSC as a subject in its own right.

The basis for a new application area in computer graphics is motivated by two factors. First, the sheer bulk of data, usually multivariate, produced by scientific computing models now tends to be so large that conventional visualization methods are no longer adequate. For example, the bulk of data that is transmitted from Earth resources satellites has now grown to such proportions that most of it can only be stored rather than analysed. The second factor is the existence of workstations with performance characteristics that were not available a few years ago, when scientific computing was bound to such devices as incremental plotters. These attributes are:

1. High resolution colour, enabling subtle changes in complex data sets to be visualized. An early example of this is the colour composites produced from remote sensing satellite data. Monochromatic data collected in different spectral bands can be selected, combined and displayed using pseudocolour.

2. The ability to render three-dimensional objects and data sets. A good example of this is the visualization of ancient archaeological sites [REIL87]. Here the computer graphics abstraction – rendering three-dimensional data collected from the site – reveals form and detail not visible in reality because of ground cover by trees and scrub.

3. The ability to represent four-dimensional data, either by using colour facilities in three-space or by animating three-space.

4. The ability to interact at a high level with any or all of these facilities. Feedback in a visualization process can make apparent structure and anomalies not visible in 'lower level' manifestations of the data.

In a recent panel [MCOR87], ViSC was defined as follows:

> Visualization transforms the symbolic into the geometric, enabling researchers to observe their simulations and computations. Visualization offers a method for seeing the unseen. It enriches the process of scientific discovery and fosters profound and unexpected insights. In many fields it is already revolutionizing the way scientists do science.
>
> Visualization embraces both image understanding and image synthesis. That is, visualization is a tool both for interpreting image data fed into a computer, and for generating images from complex multidimensional data sets. It studies those mechanisms in humans and computers which allow them in concert to perceive, use and communicate visual information. Visualization unifies the largely independent but convergent fields of:

Computer graphics
Image processing
Computer vision
CAD
Signal processing
User interface studies

Richard Hamming observed many years ago that 'the purpose of (scientific) computing is insight, not numbers'. The goal of visualization is to leverage existing scientific methods by providing new scientific insight through visual methods. An estimated 50% of the brain's neurons are associated with vision. ViSC should aim to put that neurological machinery to work.

Finally, visualization will certainly become one of the stable major application areas of computer graphics long after the ephemeral needs of the advertising and entertainments industry have waned. In the Steven Coons Award Lecture in 1987, D. Greenberg [GREE87] made the following points:

> It is important to apply computer graphics to science and not to spend so much of our effort on film or video. During the past two decades, too great a proportion of our energies have been directed towards the creation of images and the ability to make a flashy presentation. . . . If computer graphics is to have a role in improving the future of our civilization, the real value will be in its application to science, engineering and design.

13.1 Volume rendering: an overview

A recently accepted term, 'volume rendering' is perhaps not the best phrase to describe techniques that enable the visualization of sampled scalar functions of three spatial dimensions. Currently, the major application area in this field is medical imaging, where volume data is available from X-ray Computer Tomography (CT) scanners, and more recently from other imaging technologies such as Positron Emission Tomography (PET) scanners. CT scanners produce three-dimensional stacks of parallel plane images that each consists of an array of X-ray absorption coefficients. Typically, X-ray CT images will possess a resolution of $512 \times 512 \times 12$ bits and there will be up to 50 slices in a stack. The slices are 1–5 mm thick at an interslice distance of 1–5 mm. Image resolution is

a function of radiation strength and dosage. In this respect it is useful to bear in mind that the most impressive or highest resolution images currently seen in the computer graphics literature are of data that has been obtained from cadavers.

In the two-dimensional domain, clinicians can view these images one plane at a time. The significant advantage of CT images is that they contain information from one transverse plane only. A conventional X-ray image contains information from all planes normal to the beam, and the result is an accumulation of shadows that are a function of the density of the tissue, bone, organs and so on, that absorb the X-rays.

The availability of stacks of parallel plane images motivated the development of techniques for viewing such volume data sets as a three-dimensional field rather than as individual planes. This gives the immediate advantage that the information can be viewed from any view point.

In this chapter we look at techniques that have been developed to display such volume data sets on a computer graphics monitor as some projection of the data rather than a cross-section of it.

As far as volume data sets are concerned, these can be generally categorized into two sources:

1. Empirical data sets constructed from a mathematical model such as Computational Fluid Dynamics (CFD).

2. Data sets derived from an object, such as by tomographic scanning in the medical field.

(A third categorization is where the data set is some kind of computer graphics model. The only example of this at the moment is in [KAJI89].) Both categories can be handled by volume rendering techniques.

In the latter case any visualization techniques have to deal with fixed data which generally involves resampling and consequent generation of artefacts.

When data is being generated out of a mathematical model then some interaction between visualization and data generation may be possible. For example, regions of interest may be visualized and then defined in greater detail by re-entering the generation phase.

At this stage we should note that the data acquisition technology or methodology will impose usually one of a number of data element volume geometries on the data set. Nonuniform data geometries are common in computational fluid dynamics, meteorology, geology and so on, and produce data with various imposed geometries. Perhaps the most common data geometry is a regular volume set of equally sized voxels. The second most

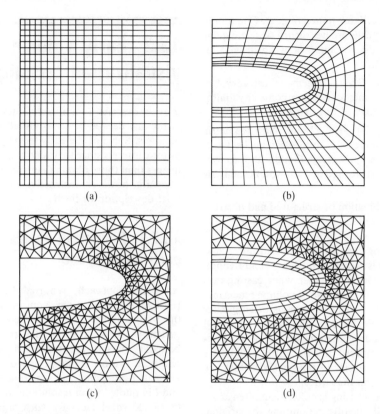

Figure 13.1 A two-dimensional illustration of common data volume geometries (based on an illustration by Speray and Kennon [SPER90]). (a) Rectilinear. (b) Structured. (c) Unstructured. (d) Hybrid.

common is a data set that consists of rectangular-shaped voxels, where the size of the voxels may increase, for example, in regions of high variation, and decrease in regions of low variation. In frequency terms the three-dimensional sampling frequency varies according to the frequency of the data. This occurs with CFD data. Medical images usually consist of uniformly sized rectangular voxels with the long dimension between the tomographic planes. The third possibility is data cells of arbitrary shape. This may happen again in CFD where cells surrounding, for example, an airfoil section, may take their shape from the geometry of the section. In CFD data from a gas turbine the cells may be wedge shaped, having two sides that are planar, two sides that are concentric cylindrical surfaces and two parallel sides. Forcing values at the vertices of such a cell into a regular volume grid, for input to a rendering algorithm, is effectively a resampling process that may introduce artefacts. This is somewhat equivalent to the 'snapping' problem, mentioned in Chapter 1, where real-world coordinates are mapped to integer screen coordinates.

Speray and Kennon [SPER90] suggest the following taxonomy of data volume geometries. They list seven types and categorize the indexing required to access an element's world coordinates. These are:

1. *Cartesian* (i, j, k) Typically known as a voxel grid, the data elements are cubic and axis aligned. This is the protocol 'preferred' by most volume rendering algorithms.

2. *Regular* $(i*dx, j*dy, k*dz)$ As the first category, except that the cells are rectangular. In CT data the spatial resolution within a plane is usually much greater than the interplane resolution (as we discussed at the beginning of this section). A common approach is to force the data into category 1 (cubic voxels) by using linear interpolation.

3. *Rectilinear* $(x[i], y[j], z[k])$ As the second category except that the distance between cells can vary (Figure 13.1a).

4. *Structured* or *curvilinear* $(x[i, j, k], y[i, j, k]$

$z[i,j,k]$) The cells are nonrectilinear. Commonly used in CFD, the cells are hexahedra or rectangular cells warped to fill a volume or wrap around an object (Figure 13.1b).

5. *Block structured* Several systems of category 4 in the same data volume; used to overcome any limitations in the topology of this category.

6. *Unstructured* $(x[i],y[j],z[k])$ No geometric constraints are imposed. The cells may be tetrahedra, hexahedra, prisms, pyramids and so on. Unstructured grids are used in finite volume analysis (Figure 13.1c).

7. *Hybrid* A combination of structured and unstructured grids (Figure 13.1d).

A technique for cutting these geometries to display cross-sections interactively is presented by Speray and Kennon and a similar approach can be taken when casting rays through such data for the purpose of volume rendering.

The dimensionality of data volumes is often greater than three. For example, Hibbard and Santek [HIBB89] describe a weather model containing 10^9 points in a five-dimensional array composed of a $100 \times 100 \times 30$ lattice at 100 time intervals where 30 physical variables are defined at each point on the lattice.

In volume rendering aliasing problems can often arise. All methods esentially involve resampling the original data. This is a different situation to that normally encountered in computer graphics where the programmer generates the data. If the data has been obtained from a physical experiment, or is medical data, then the computer graphics practitioner has little or no control over the original sampling frequency. Undersampling may have already occurred due to deficiencies in the data collection technology with respect to small detail in the object under investigation. In ultrasonic scanning, for example, the sampling frequency is limited by the wavelength of the sound used in the transducer. However, with most data collection technologies, it is usual for the original data to be processed by an anti-aliasing or lowpass filter, and a volume renderer can assume that no aliases are present in the original data. Given this we note that the most common volume rendering technique – additive reprojection – is a resampling method. The original data volume may be subject to a rotational transformation to align it with a desired view direction, prior to resampling by a parallel ray set. We may conclude that although it may be there are no aliases in the original data set (by design), we may introduce aliases in the resampling process.

13.2 Early volume visualization techniques

We now describe a set of techniques that have been used in the last decade or so to visualize three-dimensional data sets. Some of the early techniques are now only of historic interest since they tend to produce lower quality images than those obtainable from the later techniques. They are, however, instructive and we have included a brief description of them.

13.2.1 Rendering voxels in binary partitioned space

An early approach, reported by Herman and Liu [HERM79], applies an appropriate threshold to a three-dimensional data set to detect organs and other structures. This partitions the space and the resulting boundary voxels are treated as opaque cubes and rendered. A more elaborate approach (described below) extracts a polygonal surface from the voxels. Herman and Liu quote 'organ resolutions' in the order of 10 000 to 15 000 voxel faces for such organs as the heart or lungs. This gives a 'blocky' type solid whose appearance can be improved by lowpass filtering.

A shade is assigned to each face using a variant of Warnock's reflection model, which uses a standard cosine term, together with a distance attenuation effect (see Section 2.3.2). A Z-buffer algorithm is used for hidden surface removal. Herman and Liu make the point that after the data space is partitioned, they could go on to approximate the surface by larger polygons or bicubic patches, but they state that this may lead to quantitive inaccuracy that may be undesirable for measurement purposes. This statement accurately predicts the disadvantages of later methods that extract a geometric representation of an organ surface.

We can sum up the important features of this approach, with respect to visualization, as:

- A binary decision is made on partitioning, using a three-dimensional boundary tracking algorithm.

- After this decision is made there is no further 'interference' with the data.

The point concerning 'interference' is of critical importance in most visualizations of volume data. In medical

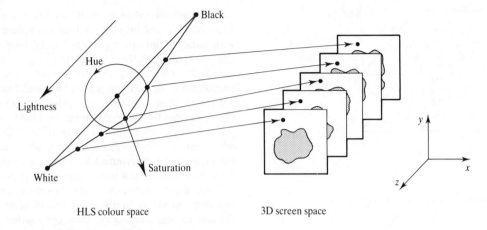

Figure 13.2 $2\frac{1}{2}$D pseudocolour mapping for volume data.

imaging, for example, the image is an abstraction created from the data – it is a creation that can never be viewed in reality – and has been described by the oxymoron 'noninvasive vivisection'. The clinician must therefore be protected from artefacts unwittingly introduced by the visualization method.

This basic technique of visualizing individual voxels can be improved by using the value of the local gradient to determine the normal N used in shading calculations. If the volume data set V is a differentiable scalar field:

$$V(x, y, z) = V(X)$$

where ∇ is the gradient vector field operator, that is:

$$\nabla V(X) = (\partial V/\partial x, \partial V/\partial y, \partial V/\partial z)$$

For V defined on a regular grid this can be approximated by central differences:

$$\left(\tfrac{1}{2}\left(V(x_{i+1}, y_j, z_k) - V(x_{i-1}, y_j, z_k)\right)\right),$$
$$\tfrac{1}{2}\left(V(x_i, y_{j+1}, z_k) - V(x_i, y_{j-1}, z_k)\right),$$
$$\tfrac{1}{2}\left(V(x_i, y_j, z_{k+1}) - V(x_i, y_j, z_{k-1})\right)$$

Note that it may be that this approximation can only be used if the data is smoothed – it is clearly sensitive to noise perturbations. We can either compute the gradient from the 6 central neighbours (as above) or from all the 26 neighbours in the $3 \times 3 \times 3$ neighbourhood of the voxel under consideration.

Depending on the algorithm used, savings can be made by calculating the surface normal in screen space. Here we have:

$$V = Z(x, y)$$

and

$$\nabla V = (\partial Z/\partial x, \partial Z/\partial y, 1)$$

This technique suffers from lack of dynamic range in the orientation of the computed normals and consequently gives images whose shading dynamic range is low.

13.2.2 A colour-only $2^1/_2$D technique

This technique, reported by Farrell [FARR83], involves no interference with the original data other than pseudocolour enhancement and is a precursor of the most recent methods described below. Farrell simply overlays successive two-dimensional frames, displacing each image in x and y. Intensity within a particular frame is mapped into a hue according to a normal pseudocolour enhancement mapping. However, the colour selected in the three-dimensional space is a function of the z-depth of the image and decreasing lightness is used in planes of decreasing z. An HLS colour model is used and the functioning of the complete three-dimensional colour mapping is easily considered by imagining a single point of equal value in each plane. This will be coloured according to its value and z-depth and the path of the colour in HLS space will be a straight line towards the black point (Figure 13.2).

Farrell implements an indexing facility that allows an interactive view point change amongst eight options and also considers other facilities that have now become standard in volume rendering. These include using a cut plane to display detail in a plane parallel to the y, z-plane.

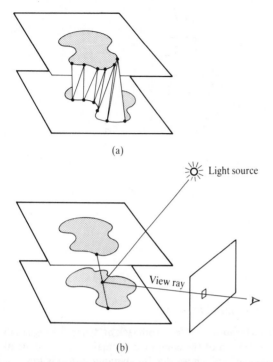

(a)

(b)

Figure 13.3 Projecting/shading from contour data. (a) Skimming algorithm used to produce an interslice polygon set. (b) Direct ray tracing.

13.3 Intermediate geometric representation techniques

The next major stage in the evolution of visualization techniques from three-dimensional medical images is methods that extract an intermediate geometric representation of the surface and then use conventional techniques to render the surface. Within this category there are two subdivisions: first, techniques that operate on the slices by applying two-dimensional tracking algorithms and then extracting a surface between consecutive contours (for example [PIZE86, RHOD88]); and a technique that applies an isovalue surface detector to each set of eight voxel vertices in the data set, to produce a large set of voxel-sized polygons which are then rendered ([WYVI86a, LORE87]).

In [PIZE86] an edge tracking algorithm defines regions of interest in each slice in the form of contours. A polygon mesh connecting contours in adjacent slices can then be formed using a 'skimming' algorithm – see, for example [GANA82] (Figure 13.3a).

The approach taken in [RHOD88] is just as simple. View rays are cast into the contour stack, and intersect with notional lines between 'equivalent' voxels in each contour (Figure 13.3b). The notion of equivalent voxels comes by considering the first voxels that the ray encounters both from the plane above and below which are greater than some threshold value. The geometry of these lines yields a normal that can be used to shade the pixel through which the view ray is cast. One of the advantages of this technique is that shadows are easily, but expensively, determined by casting a shadow feeler from each intersection point to the light source.

Both these approaches are essentially two-stage methods, operating firstly in the two-dimensional slice domain to track contours, then considering adjacent slices, or contours, in three-dimensional stack space. One of the major disadvantages of this approach is that ambiguities arise when attempts are made to connect equivalent points on contours. There is no guarantee that the tracking will detect only single contours in each slice. Particular deficiencies arise in branching structures, such as blood vessels, where a single contour in one plane relates to two contours in an adjacent plane, implying a branch has occurred between planes. This problem becomes even more difficult if the distance between slices becomes large with respect to the size of the cell in the contour plane.

Generally the limitations of such methods arise from their nonisotropic nature in three-space. One algorithm is used to track contours in the contour plane and a completely different heuristic is used to join contours between planes. Both the contour boundary and the surface that joins contours between planes are, however, part of the same surface and it undesirable to treat them in different ways.

The next approach – the marching cubes algorithm – is more general in the sense that it extracts a surface directly from the acquired data and is isotropic in three-space. The algorithm is somewhat more complicated than the aforementioned approaches and we shall devote more attention to it.

13.3.1 The marching cubes algorithm

The marching cubes algorithm was independently reported by Wyvill and McPheeters in 1986 [WYVI86a] and by Lorenson and Cline in 1987 [LORE87]. The only significant difference in the two approaches is in the respective application areas. Wyvill uses the algorithm to extract an isosurface from an analytical field defined by a set of key points. Lorenson uses the approach to process three-dimensional medical data. A full implementation of the marching cubes algorithm, together with a comprehensive listing, is given at the end of this chapter. Here we will confine ourselves to a brief overview.

Both algorithms essentially operate in two phases. In the first pass a surface value is defined by the user and all those cubes or voxels that are intersected by the surface are found. Wyvill does this by using a recursive procedure (not unlike 'flood fill' algorithms which fill closed regions in two-dimensional space) that starts with a seed cube and examines each cube's neighbour to see if that cube is intersected by the surface. If it is added to a queue its neighbours are examined and so on until all cubes forming the boundary set have been found. In this stage is embedded the disadvantage of the algorithm, which is that, like the first algorithm described, a binary decision is taken on the existence and/or position of the surface.

In the second phase of the algorithm those cubes in the boundary set are examined and a set of connected polygons are produced for rendering. This is done as follows. For each cube in the boundary set, its vertex is either inside, outside or equal to the value of the desired surface. This fact determines the topological relationship of the surface to the cube. The fact that each cube possesses eight vertices and that there are two states of inside and outside means that there are 2^8 or 256 different ways in which a surface can intersect a cube. Consideration of symmetry reduces the problem to 14 possible relationships between that part of the desired surface that intersects the cube and the cube edges. These cases are shown in Figure 13.4. Here vertices are marked with spheres or left empty depending on whether they exhibit an inside or an outside value (and by symmetry, an outside or inside value). From this it can be seen that the simplest case occurs when all vertices are outside the desired value. The next case, in order of complexity, is when a single triangle will separate one vertex from all others. The third case requires a rectangle, and so on, until all possible relationships are accounted for. The exact position of the intersections of each surface with its cube edges is found by linear interpolation. Lorenson reports that higher degree interpolation yields little or no improvement over the linear approach. Thus we can see that this scheme enables (simultaneously) the extraction of a surface and the extraction of a polygon mesh model of that surface from a three-dimensional dataset.

Vertex normals at each triangle vertex are found by interpolating from the normals at the associated cube which are themselves found from the gradient as described in Section 13.2.1. It is not clear that there is any advantage in deriving shading normals from the gradient of voxel values, rather than from the polygons themselves. Having used the marching cubes algorithm to derive a surface, on the basis of an underlying assumption that a spatially continuous surface or shell exists, it is quicker to use the geometry of the resulting triangle mesh and derive vertex normals in the standard way (if fast rendering hardware is available). This is certainly the case in the context that the implementation in Section 13.6 is applied to. Here we know a priori that a single surface exists. The data set in this context is binary. On the other hand, we can say that the extracted surface is one step removed from the original data. It may be more accurate to use normals abstracted by the gradient method. After all, the context is visualization and the vertex normal averaging abstraction is, to some extent, an arbitrary operation. The methods certainly give different results and a pictorial comparison is to be found in [TIED90]. Hohn et al. [HOHN90] conclude that in the context of medical imaging 'surface rendering is decisively improved by using gray level gradients for the determination of the surface normals'.

Note, however, that a shading normal has to be extracted from the gradient in the technique described in Section 13.4 which does not make a decision on the existence of a surface.

Finally, note that the marching cubes algorithm must produce a triangle mesh at a 'reasonable' resolution in three-space if the normal polygon mesh aliasing artefacts are to be avoided. This depends on regular voxel data at a high resolution. Gallager and Nagtegaal [GALL89] address the problem of fitting a 'good' surface through coarsely spaced points. Here bicubic patches, rather than triangles, are the surface unit. In this extension to the marching cubes algorithm, vertex positions and shading normals are computed from the cube corner points and from these a bicubic patch can be derived if some assumptions are made concerning the shape of a patch that fits the calculated parameters. Adjacent surface patches are slope continuous at the vertices, but not necessarily along the edge of the patch. The technique has particular application in finite element models, where the resolution of the computed data is constrained by the calculation overheads.

13.3.2 The use of pseudocolour in surface extraction algorithms

When the data to be visualized is generated from a mathematical model or simulation, it may be multi-valued in the sense that several variables – such as velocity, temperature or pressure – are recorded at each sample location. We may wish to extract an isosurface in

Figure 13.4 Marching cubes algorithm: the polygons emerge from the 14 possible relationships between an isosurface and the cube that it passes through. The spheres are cube vertices that are inside the isosurface. The precise position of each polygon is found by interpolation.

one variable, defined by a geometric transfer function and sampled with a marching cubes approach, and then to texture this isosurface using a pseudocolour transfer function defined for another variable. However, when attempting to visualize two scalar fields simultaneously in this way, confusion can arise owing to the use of colour for two conflicting purposes: namely to convey both the three-dimensional nature of the isosurface, via the application of shading, and the variation of the additional variable superimposed on the surface, via pseudocolouring.

Plate 42 depicts isosurfaces of zero u-velocity (long axis direction) extracted from a Navier–Stokes CFD simulation of a reverse flow pipe combustor, the chamber of which is indicated by the wireframe cylinder. The primary flow direction is from left to right. Air is forced in under compression at the left, and dispersed by two fans. Eight fuel jets, situated radially approximately halfway along the combustor, are directed in such a way as to send the fuel mixture in a spiralling path towards the front of the chamber. Combustible mixing takes place in the central region and thrust is created at the exhaust outlet on the right. The isosurfaces shown connect all points where the net flow in the long axis is zero. This image shows flange-like hoops attached to the air intake fans, a central portion with eight lobes extend-

ing toward the fuel jets, a tubular core surrounded by a crenellated ring and eight smaller surfaces associated with secondary air inlets further down the chamber.

Plate 43 illustrates the same isosurface conventionally shaded with pseudocolouring superimposed according to field temperature. A spectral colour path, from blue to magenta, around the circumference of the HSV cone is used. Plate 44 shows a cutaway view of the same scene, rotated to display the internal detail of the isosurface near the front of the chamber. In Plate 45, the same variables are depicted but now the colour scale comprises six equally spaced vertical slices through the HSV cone. Note the false contouring on the lobes near the fuel jets, indicating high temperature gradients in these areas. Whether using a discontinuous pseudocolour mapping that produces false contours is useful or not depends on the application and personal preference.

In these examples we have sought to isolate hue as the pseudocolour, from the level of saturation and brightness as determined by the shading model. The vertical dimension in HSV space is used for shading information and a circumferential path or hue selected as a pseudocolour scale. Perceptual ambiguities result from the fact that ordinarily we experience the phenomenon of colour as a *single* complex sensation. Thus it may be difficult to

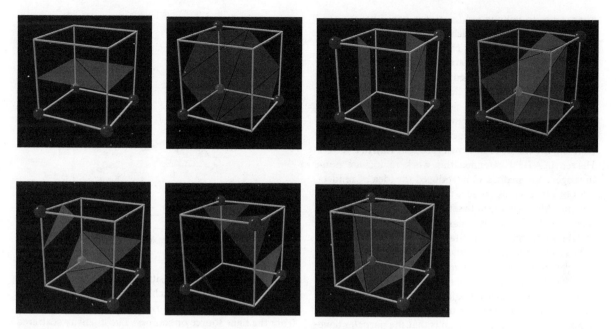

Figure 13.4 (*cont.*)

interpret the geometry of the isosurface in areas of rapidly shifting hue, or to relate with accuracy the final surface colour back to the colour scale. Simultaneous contrast effects make it difficult to perceive subtle variations of intensity within relatively uniform regions of colour, while highly convoluted surfaces are often awkward to comprehend from still frames. Fortunately, many of these ambiguities can be resolved by interactive techniques – giving the user the facility to reposition the view point or light sources, or to manipulate the colour map.

13.4 Volume rendering by ray casting

It has already been stated that the major disadvantage of the previous technique is that a binary decision has to be made on the position of the intermediate surface that is extracted and rendered (although in many cases a precise surface location is exactly what is required). The philosophy of the algorithms described in this section is to make best use of the three-dimensional information and not to attempt to impose any geometric structure upon it. Extracting an intermediate structure can lead to

the introduction of so-called false positives – that is, artefacts that do not exist – and discarding small or poorly defined features – so-called false negatives.

Another problem with medical images is that the acquisition resolution may be so low that extracting a surface is extremely inappropriate. The important limitation, however, of surface extraction techniques is not the fact that they may suffer from inaccuracies, but that they display a projection of an (infinitely) thin shell suspended somewhere in the acquisition space. This is certainly inadequate with medical images which may originate from material such as fluid that may be partially transparent and should therefore be modelled as such. It may also be important to see structures within structures in computed data sets such as molecular models. The use of transparency means that we can avoid making a decision on a surface and 'wisps' of material that may be discarded by a surface extraction technique can be retained in the visualization. In effect both the interface between materials and the interior of the material can be visualized.

13.4.1 Theory

To overcome these limitations, ray casting through the volume that is considered to be made up of transparent or partially transparent structures is employed. Current approaches to volume rendering are based on approx-imations to Blinn's approach [BLIN82a] that rendered objects made up of a large collection of small spherical particles, enabling the appearance of clouds and the rings of Saturn to be synthesized. Assuming homogeneous material, Blinn analytically derived a lighting model that was a function of 'optical depth' and the angle of the illuminating source. In this model clouds can be lit from any direction and the viewer can be positioned anywhere enabling the clouds to be flown through. Kajiya and von Herzen [KAJI84] extended this work to include non-homogeneous media and introduced the idea of render-ing objects, such as clouds, by ray tracing through the volume. Although the data sets that are volume rendered do not tend to be clouds or gases, liberal extensions from this theory are made to facilitate visualizations of volume data sets such as medical imagery.

A volume is made up of a number of spherical particles that both scatter and attenuate light passing through the volume. Both attenuation and scattering depend on the density of the particles. The underlying assumption that supports practical computation is that the particles have low albedo. The albedo of a particle is its reflectivity, that is, the proportion of incident light reflected from the particle. When light strikes a particle it is scattered and impinges on other particles, where it is scattered towards other particles and so on. (An observable effect of this is the way in which the Earth's surface can alter the appearance of clouds. When the sun shines through a cloud layer, some light is scattered towards the viewer. Light is also scattered to the Earth's surface, where it is rescattered and impinges again on the cloud layer. The nature and extent of this ground scattered light affects the appearance of the clouds and is particularly marked in the difference between clouds viewed in a snow-covered landscape (high albedo) compared with their appearance when seen from a low albedo terrain.) If the particles all have low albedo, a single scattering approx-imation is reasonably valid, and for any particle we only consider the light scattered once from the light source to the eye.

A ray casting algorithm casts parallel rays from the viewer into the volume. At each point along the ray the progressive attenuation due to the particle field is com-puted. At the same time the light scattered in the eye direction from the light source is computed at each point. These values are integrated along a ray and a single brightness value is computed for each ray.

Currently, most volume rendering that uses ray casting is based on the Blinn/Kajiya model. Here we have a

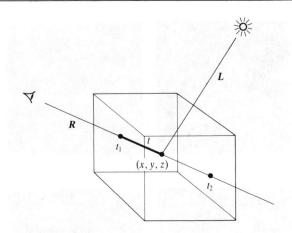

Figure 13.5 A ray *R* cast into a scalar function of three spatial variables.

volume that exhibits a density $D(x, y, z)$, penetrated by a ray *R* (Figure 13.5). At each point along the ray we have an illumination $I(x, y, z)$ reaching the point (x, y, z) from the light source or sources. The intensity scattered along the ray to the eye depends on this value, a reflection function or phase function *P*, and the local density $D(x, y, z)$. The dependence on density expresses the fact that a few bright particles will scatter less light in the eye direction than a number of dimmer particles. The density function is parametrized along the ray as:

$$D(x(t), y(t), z(t)) = D(t)$$

and the illumination from the source as:

$$I(x(t), y(t), z(t)) = I(t)$$

and the illumination scattered along *R* from a point distance *t* along the ray is:

$$I(t)D(t)P(\cos\theta)$$

where:

θ is the angle between *R* and *L*, the light vector, from the point of interest

If there is more than one light source then we have:

$$\sum_n I_n(t)D(t)P(\cos\theta_n)$$

Note that the determination of $I(t)$ is not trivial and means computing how the radiation from the light source is attenuated and/or shadowed in its journey through the volume to the point of interest. This is identical to the computation of how the light scattered at point (x, y, z)

is affected in its journey along R to the eye. In most algorithms this calculation is ignored and $I(x, y, z)$ is deemed to be the same throughout the volume. This emphasizes that in most practical applications we are interested in visualization, and including the line integral from a point (x, y, z) to the light source may actually be disadvantageous. For example, in the visualization of medical data it would be impossible to see into regions surrounded by bone, if the bone was considered dense enough to shadow light. However, in applications where internal shadows are appropriate, this integral has to be evaluated.

We can calculate the attenuation due to the density function along a ray as:

$$\exp\left(-\tau \int_{t_1}^{t_2} D(s)\,\mathrm{d}s\right)$$

where:

τ is a constant that converts density to attenuation

and the intensity of light arriving at the eye along direction R due to all the elements along the ray is given by:

$$B = \int_{t_1}^{t_2} \left(\exp\left(-\tau \int_{t_1}^{t} D(s)\,\mathrm{d}s\right)\right) \left(I(t)D(t)P(\cos\Theta)\right)\mathrm{d}t \tag{13.1}$$

13.4.2 Typical algorithms

Algorithms that are based on this general technique involve a simplification of integral (13.1). Two approaches that have been used in medical imagery are now described. The technique that Drebin [DREB88] refers to as 'additive reprojection' has been explored by several authors. The method, in effect, 'collapses' or projects voxels along a certain viewing direction. Intensities of voxels along parallel viewing rays are projected to provide an intensity for a pixel in the viewing plane. A viewer can elect for voxels of a particular depth to be given a maximum opacity so that the 'depth' to which the volume field is visualized, and thus the number of planes that overlap in the view plane, can be controlled. The important degrees of freedom that computer graphics brings to the data are: first, the volume can be visualized from any direction; and secondly, hidden surface removal can be implemented so that, for example, front ribs can be made to obscure back ribs. Finally, colour can be used to enhance interpretation. Basically, options are available

concerning the way in which information is integrated along a view ray.

Additive reprojection methods all make use of a voxel lighting model that involves a simple combination of reflected and transmitted light from the voxel. All such approaches are a subset of the model shown in Figure 13.6. This shows a single voxel illuminated by two light sources. One light source is a directional source to which the voxel reacts as a function of its reflecting properties, the other is light incoming from the neighbouring voxel along the view ray. The outgoing light can be made up of the following contributions:

1. Light may be reflected along the view ray direction due to reflection from a directional light source interacting with a surface fragment contained by the voxel.

2. Incoming light may be attenuated by the existence of a partially opaque surface.

3. If the voxel is homogeneous then it will act as a partially opaque gel and filter incoming light.

4. The voxel may be self-luminous.

5. A combination of the above factors.

The incoming light may result from background illumination or from light that has been transmitted or reflected along the view ray direction from voxels further along the line of the view ray.

A typical implementation of this approach is described by Levoy [LEVO88]. In this paper, results are produced

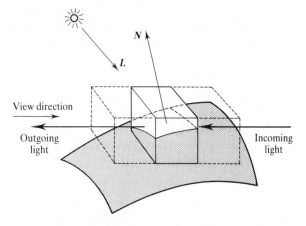

Figure 13.6 The outgoing light is made up of: (1) light reflected in the view direction from the light source; (2) incoming light filtered by the voxel; (3) any light emitted by the voxel.

from a stack of 113 transverse slices, each of resolution 256×256 (acquired from a cadaver), showing an air/skin interface and a tissue/bone interface. Levoy calls his technique 'direct volume visualization' and states that the process is more to do with enhancing the original data than with rendering. In this respect it bears some relationship to the earlier technique [FARR83] described in Section 13.2.2 that uses no data transformation but colour.

Levoy describes his technique as consisting of two pipelines – a visualization pipeline and a classification pipeline. The output from these two pipelines is then combined by volumetric compositing to produce the final image.

In the visualization pipeline the acquisition data, in the form of voxels, is shaded. That is, *every* voxel in the data is allocated a shade using a local gradient approximation to obtain a 'voxel normal' as described in Section 13.2.1. This normal is then substituted into a standard Phong reflection model to obtain an intensity. The output from this pipeline is a three colour component intensity for each voxel in the data set, $C(X)$. The fact that every voxel in the volume is rendered explains the use of the term 'volume rendering'.

In completely homogeneous regions the gradient is of course zero. The shade or colour returned from such regions is therefore unreliable. In Levoy's method this is dealt with by basing an opacity for each voxel on the gradient. The gradient is simply multiplied by the opacity. Homogeneous regions produce a zero opacity and the unreliable colours do not affect the final image.

The purpose of the classification pipeline is to associate an opacity with each voxel. The colour parameters that are used in the shading model must also be assigned by the classification pipeline. The classification of opacity is, of course, context dependent and the application of Levoy's technique is in X-ray CT images where each voxel value in the original data is an X-ray absorption coefficient. In this pipeline, Levoy employs a technique that is designed to retain 'wisps' or isolated regions of tissue of a particular density, that may be discarded by cruder classification methods. If, for example, simple thresholding is used, as in:

$$X \in V_a \quad \text{if } V(X) < T$$
$$X \in V_b \quad \text{if } V(X) > T$$

where:

V_a and V_b are volumes of different tissue types a and b

then it is possible for thin regions of type a to be represented by voxels:

$$V(X) > T$$

Using the following restrictions on the nature of the data, Levoy invokes a classification scheme, where values of $V(X)$ between two tissue types of values n and $n + 1$ are assigned an opacity between values α_n and α_{n+1}. The restrictions are that the original data contains CT numbers that fall within a small neighbourhood of some known value, that tissue of each type touches, at most, two other types, and that if the types are ordered by CT number, each type only touches types adjacent to it. That is, given N tissue types:

$$f_{Vn} \quad n = 1, \ldots, N$$

such that:

$$f_{Vm} < f_{Vm+1} \quad m = 1, \ldots N - 1$$

then no tissue of CT number f_{Vn1} touches any tissue of CT number

$$f_{Vn2} \quad |n_1 - n_2| > 1$$

We can then write:

$$\alpha(X) = \begin{cases} \alpha_{Vn+1} \left\{ \dfrac{V(X) - f_{Vn}}{f_{Vn+1} - f_{Vn}} \right\} \\ \quad + \alpha_{Vn} \left\{ \dfrac{f_{Vn+1} - V(X)}{f_{Vn+1} - f_{Vn}} \right\} \\ \quad\quad \text{if } f_{Vn} \leqslant V(X) \leqslant f_{Vn+1} \\ 0 \quad\quad \text{otherwise} \end{cases}$$

This opacity classification is further enhanced by considering that the final visualization is improved if the opacity of tissue interiors is de-emphasized and the opacity of the boundaries enhanced. This can be done by multiplying the opacity value by the local gradient:

$$\alpha'(X) = |\nabla V(X)| \alpha(X)$$

We now have two values associated with each voxel:

$C(X)$ a shade calculated from a reflection model using the local gradient

$\alpha(X)$ an opacity derived from tissue type of known CT values, with intermediate opacities retained

The next stage, called 'volumetric compositing', is to produce a two-dimensional projection of these values in the view plane. Rays are cast from the eye into the voxel array and the $C(X)$ and $\alpha(X)$ are 'combined' or projected into single values to provide a final pixel intensity (Figure 13.7). For a single voxel along a ray, the standard transparency formula is:

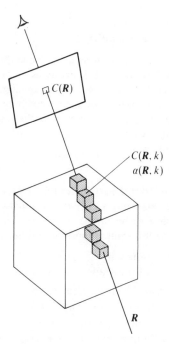

Figure 13.7   Casting rays through an array of voxels.

$$C_{out} = C_{in}\left(1 - \alpha(X)\right) + C(X)\alpha(X))$$

where:

C_{out} is the outgoing intensity/colour for voxel X along the ray
C_{in} is the incoming intensity for the voxel

This can be considered, as mentioned earlier, to be a resampling process and various options are available. We could simply interpolate from the vertex values of the voxel that the ray passes through, but it is more correct to consider neighbouring voxels (8 or 26) and trilinearly interpolate, to yield values that lie exactly along a ray.

The intensity due to the set of voxels that intercept the ray is given by:

$$C(R) = \sum_{k=0}^{K} \left\{ C(R, k)\alpha(R, k) \prod_{i=k+1}^{K} \left(1 - \alpha(R, i)\right) \right\}$$
(13.2)

where:

(R, k) is the kth voxel along the ray R
$C(R, 0) = C_{background}$
$\alpha(R, 0) = 1$

It is easily seen from this that all voxels along the ray, that are in front of any voxel with opacity = 1, contribute to the visualization. Note that the intensity equation must be evaluated at three colour bands for a standard colour image.

At this stage it is useful to compare Equation (13.2) with the general integral for ray tracing volume densities (Equation 13.1). First, the attenuation. Here opacity has replaced attenuation, where:

Opacity = 1 − attenuation

and a value along the ray is multiplicatively accumulated along the ray. Consider the remaining factors in Equation (13.2). A number of theoretical extrapolations are implied. First, the light source is assumed to be uniformly visible from each voxel, and each voxel sees an external light source through a perfectly transparent gel. In other words, we consider attenuation when light is travelling through the volume from the voxel to the eye, but not when it is going from the light source to the voxel. The product of the volume density and the phase function in Equation (13.1) is replaced by the gradient-calculated shading values for the single voxel. Here we are replacing a volume density weighting and an isotropic phase function with a surface shaded with an nonisotropic reflection model (in this case the Phong model). Essentially we are distributing a light model within the volume instead of spherical particles.

A similar approach is adopted by Drebin [DREB88]. Here the voxels are classified with a specific anatomical label – fat, tissue, bone and so on – using a *probabilistic* classifier. The distributions of each type are known a priori and, together with the fact that not more than two tissue type distributions overlap (for example, the air distribution overlaps with the fat distribution but not with bone), each voxel is assigned a material percentage. This reflects the fact that a voxel may straddle the boundaries of regions that contain different materials. The histogram of the voxel intensities, that is, the original data, forms the basis for this decision. The difference between this approach and the previous is that more than one label may be associated with each voxel. The colour opacity label associated with a voxel is:

$$C = \sum_{i=1}^{n} p_i C_i$$

where:

n is the number of materials in the voxel
p_i is the percentage of material in the voxel
C_i is the colour of the material multiplied by its opacity, that is $C_i = \left(\alpha_i R_i, \alpha_i G_i, \alpha_i B_i, \alpha_i\right)$ where for simplicity α_i is assumed to be independent of wavelength

The surface normal computation is based on the gradient of the density field D of the voxel where:

$$D = \sum_{i=1}^{n} p_i \mu_i$$

where:

μ_i is the density assigned to material i

Drebin defines the composition process in terms of a composition operator, **over**. The standard transparency equation for a single voxel:

$$C_{\text{out}} = C_{\text{in}}\left(1 - \alpha_z\right) + C_z \alpha_z$$

becomes:

$$C_{\text{out}} = C \,\textbf{over}\, C_{\text{in}}$$

where:

$$C = C_z \alpha_z$$

Drebin also generalizes the process to distinguish among the different contributions to outgoing light from a voxel along a view ray that were mentioned above. In this method a voxel is, in general, deemed to consist of three 'colour regions' (Figure 13.8), namely C_f, the parameters associated with the volume region in front of an assumed surface, C_s the parameters associated with the surface and C_b the parameters of the region behind the surface. C_{out} now becomes:

$$C_{\text{out}} = \left(C_f \,\textbf{over}\, \left(C_s \,\textbf{over}\, \left(C_b \,\textbf{over}\, C_{\text{in}} \right) \right) \right)$$

A surface strength volume:

$$S = |N|$$

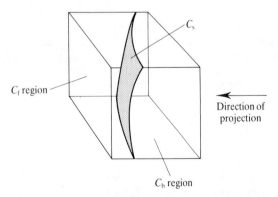

Figure 13.8   The two voxel regions have colour parameters associated with them.

where

$|N|$ is the magnitude of the gradient

is defined and is used to weight C_s. Thus if, for example, S is low then the voxel is acting as a homogeneous semi-opaque gel that does not reflect any light from the light source, but only modulates incoming light. No direct reflected light emanates from the interior of a homogeneous voxel. In contrast, Levoy's technique, above, simply uses:

$$C = C_s$$

We can summarize the attributes of such techniques as they involve visualizing a three-dimensional scalar field, using the well-worn technique of pseudocolour enhancement with the following important additions:

1. Interaction with a light source is possible so that the perception of the shape of isosurfaces is enhanced.

2. Transparency is incorporated so that structures within structures can be visualized.

3. The 'depth' to which the volume is penetrated is infinitely adjustable by assigning appropriate opacity values to the field.

4. Because of 3 no decision need be made on the existence of an isosurface.

5. Viewing the data set from an arbitrary view point is possible.

Further elaborations of this basic approach are to be found in [SABE88] and [UPSO88].

Sabella elaborates/generalizes the reflection or shading algorithm, which in the above implementations is a single scattering model – light is directly reflected from the light source to the eye via the virtual surface. In Sabella's method the complete volume field is considered to be a 'varying density emitter' and the light reflected in the viewing direction, from a point, is calculated using a scattering model in conjunction with Kajiya's model. The volume is considered to be equivalent to a system of particle light sources and the spatial density of the particles is used in a version of Kajiya and von Herzen's brightness equation to calculate the intensity along a view ray.

In Upson and Keeler's implementation, the problem of interpolation within a voxel is examined. Given that in most practical or simulated volume data sets discontinuities are unlikely to occur, this method addresses the fact that the values at the corners of each voxel are samples from a well-behaved function of three spatial variables, and that values within a voxel can be obtained by trilinear interpolation.

Finally, note that although this section is concerned with volume rendering by using transparency, there is nothing to prevent the marching cubes algorithm being used in conjunction with transparency. Isosurfaces with different values can be rendered with opacity. Also, the ray cast approach can be used to render surfaces by the appropriate setting of the opacity coefficients. Plate 46 shows two skulls rendered from the same data set. The first was produced by the marching cubes algorithm and the second uses ray casting. In the ray cast image the individual slices are apparent.

13.4.3 Resampling problems in ray cast volume rendering

Volume rendering is unique in computer graphics in that we normally wish to render from real data, rather than from a mathematical definition or description. The nature of the data is usually, but not always, point samples, and we can either assume that the data field is constant within a voxel or that we have a 'cubic' cell with samples defined at each corner. Treating the data as homogeneous voxels makes few assumptions about its nature, but leads to images with a distinct blocky signature. Most approaches view the data as cells with corner samples.

Volume rendering algorithms generally work by first transforming the data set so that the desired view angle is achieved by a set of rays that is parallel and perpendicular to the image plane. This is necessary otherwise random access would be required to the data set. The best way to do this is by a multipass transformation, full details of which can be found in [HANR90a] where the required transformation is decomposed into three passes.

A problem results when a perspective projection is required. A divergent ray set is used and as the distance along the ray increases, then two adjacent rays will miss more and more of the data. Small objects will be missed and aliasing artefacts will be generated. In most contexts a parallel projection will suffice and this problem is avoided.

When the data volume is rotated resampling has to be performed by the ray casting algorithm. This is not unlike the problem of mapping texture from a two-dimensional texture domain. You will remember that the

correct approach to this problem is to integrate over the area of the inverse pixel projection in the texture domain, or to perform some algorithmic approximation to this process. In the case of volume rendering we generally want to gather information from a number of voxels when we resample. Technically, we need to extend our two-space filtering techniques into three-space and filter information from a number of voxels using a three-dimensional filter kernel. Not much work has been carried out in this area. An exception is [WEST90].

The actual structure of the rendering algorithm has ramifications for the resampling process and we can classify the algorithms according to whether they are object space driven or image space driven. (Some authors use the categorization of front mapping or back mapping.)

Image space algorithms cast a set of parallel rays, say one from each pixel, into a data volume that, in general, will have been rotated to provide the desired view. (If a perspective image is required then the rays will diverge rather than be parallel.)

The structure of an image space algorithm is:

For each ray
  While accumulated opacity < a threshold
    Compute the surface normals
    Classify the voxel, assigning three colour parameters and an opacity
    Accumulate colour and opacity
  Render the pixel from which the ray emanates

This algorithm is illustrated in Figure 13.9.

The order of the mapping can be reversed by object-based algorithms. Such algorithms have the structure:

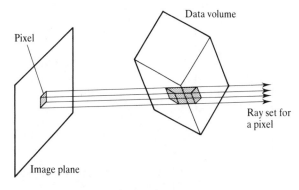

Figure 13.9 Image space algorithm: the data volume is transformed to give the required view. The ray set is then always perpendicular to the view plane (unless a perspective image is computed).

For each cell in the data set

Compute the gradient

Compute the projection of the cell on the image plane (this will generally enclose a number of pixels)

For each pixel within the projection

Integrate from the nearest edge of the cell to the farthest edge. This integration will involve trilinear interpolation of the scalar field from the vertex values of the cell (Figure 13.10)

Accumulate the colour and opacity values into the pixel

The outermost loop of the algorithm ensures that all the data is resampled irrespective of viewing variables. The data volume is resampled at the cell resolution. The disadvantage of this method is the much higher cost. It is, however, easily parallelized – cells can be processed independently of each other.

The difference between the two methods can be summarized by the following two questions:

1. In backwards mapping or image space based algorithms: which voxels or data cells contribute to this pixel?

2. In forward mapping, or object space based algorithms: which pixels does a voxel contribute to?

Finally, we return to the point of anti-aliasing. The only way to anti-alias in the image space algorithm is to fire more rays (stochastically or otherwise). With the object space approach it is clearly possible to approximate convolution over a three-dimensional filter kernel.

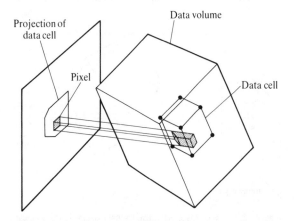

Figure 13.10 *Object space algorithm: a data cell distributes values over pixels contained within its projection.*

13.5 Segmentation techniques

Although the additive reprojection technique solves some of the problems of the intermediate surface approach, its drawback is precisely due to its claimed advantage. Because no binary decision is made, too much information may be presented to the user in certain contexts, leading to difficulties in viewer interpretation. Also, it is not clear that additive reprojection is universally superior to intermediate surface detection. For example, Höhne *et al.* [HÖHN89] state: 'Our experience with three-dimensional visualization of tomographic volumes shows that if exact surfaces can be determined, non-transparent rendering yields the best results'.

There are two ways in which the additive reprojection technique can be adapted. First, interaction can be employed as a powerful aid to interpretation allowing the user to alter, say, the depth of the visualization. Currently, the only bar to effective interaction is lack of computing power to facilitate a real-time, or near real-time, response. The second possibility is to retain the advantages of additive reprojection, but to cut down on the sheer bulk of data that bombards the viewer. This data reduction can be effected by segmentation techniques. Regions of little interest or that are poorly defined can be 'eroded' to highlight data that is important.

Höhne addresses the problem of visualization of small detail, such as blood vessels, where the diameter of the vessel may not exceed one voxel. Here the region containing the volume of interest is not large enough for the marching cubes algorithm to work and standard volume rendering will tend to swamp the detail of the structures to be viewed. Two approaches are described in [HOHN89]. In the first extremely simple technique, the volume is segmented by displaying only the maximum intensity along any ray (which in this case belongs to blood vessels). This is a simple thresholding approach that isolates or segments any structure that exhibits a voxel intensity greater than the threshold. The ray tracing serves only to create a projection of the structure from the desired view point.

A more general approach to segmentation, where a three-dimensional region around a voxel of interest is considered, is implemented by extending edge detection techniques, originally developed for image processing, into the three-dimensional domain. Höhne uses a three-dimensional extension to the Marr–Hildreth operator

[MARR80]. The Marr–Hildreth operator is a combination of two standard image processing operations, and can be defined as:

$$V'(X) = \triangledown^2(V(X) \star G(X, \sigma))$$

where:

$V(X)$ is the volume data set
$V'(X)$ is the processed or filtered data set
$G(X, \sigma)$ is a three-dimensional Gaussian function
$\star$ is the convolution operator
$\triangledown^2$ is the Laplacian operator

This can be interpreted as follows. First, the original voxel intensities are convolved with the Gaussian function:

$$G(X, \sigma) = G(r) = \frac{1}{\sigma^2(2\pi)^{3/2}} \exp\left(\frac{-r^2}{2\sigma^2}\right)$$

where:

$$r^2 = x^2 + y^2 + z^2$$

In the frequency domain this is equivalent to multiplying the Fourier transform of V with that of G. Because the Fourier transform of a Gaussian function is also a Gaussian, this is a bandpass operation centred on zero spatial frequency. This effectively limits the rate at which voxel intensities can change as a function of σ. The result of this process is then subject to the Laplacian operator – an orientation-independent second-order differential operator:

$$\triangledown^2 V(X) = \left\{ \frac{\partial^2 V}{\partial x^2} + \frac{\partial^2 V}{\partial y^2} + \frac{\partial^2 V}{\partial z^2} \right\}$$

This can be digitally approximated by:

for any element $V(X) = V(x, y, z)$

$$\triangledown^2 V(x, y, z) \approx \left| (27V(x, y, z) - \sum_{i=-1}^{1} \sum_{j=-1}^{1} \sum_{k=-1}^{1} V(x+i, y+j, z+k))/26 \right|$$

that is:

$$\triangledown^2 V(x, y, z) \approx | V(x, y, z) - (\text{the sum of the 26 neighbours of } V(x, y, z)/26) |$$

In other words, the Laplacian is proportional to the difference between the voxel intensity at a point and the average voxel intensities over a three-dimensional annular region surrounding the point. V' can now be thresholded and used for region labelling and segmentation. Overall the Gaussian, by smoothing, determines the spatial resolution and the Laplacian locates the gradient extrema.

Drebin [DREB88] generalizes the concept of segmentation to include common operations such as cross-sectioning or cut planes, using the term 'matte volumes'. A matte value is defined as a scalar fraction, which is the percentage of the voxel contained by the matte. Matte volumes can be any geometric shape or computed region. For example, an air matte volume is the region not contained in any material percentage volumes.

13.6 Marching cubes implementation

The code for the marching cubes algorithm (Listing 13.1) is not amenable to presentation as a fragment or a skeleton and we have decided to present a complete program, together with a description. The suite of programs implements the marching cubes algorithm by outputting a faceted model given input data of a series of equi-spaced, planar, closed contours (Figure 13.11). Of course, in this context a model could have been built using a skinning algorithm to join the contours with triangular facets (Figure 13.3) but the application was chosen deliberately to test the marching cubes algorithm.

Figure 13.12 shows an athlete's head that was built using this implementation. The input data, laser scanned from a statue, consisted of 222 contours of over 120 000

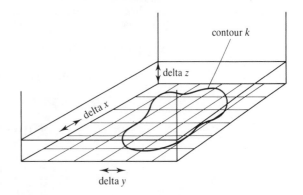

Figure 13.11 Contour data defined in separate planes.

Listing 13.1   march.c

```
#include "contour.h"

            int  bit0  =  1;
            int  bit1  =  2;
            int  bit2  =  4;
            int  bit3  =  8;
            int  bit4  =  16;
            int  bit5  =  32;
            int  bit6  =  64;
            int  bit7  =  128;

void  march(start_contour,end_contour,filename)
int  start_contour,end_contour,filename;
{
            int  i,j,k;
            int  cube_index;
            void  load_facet();
            void  initialize_model_data(),write_model_file(),loadslice();
            char  *alloc();
            int  *lowslice,*highslice,offset;

            initialize_data();
            outsidesliceA  =  (int *)alloc(NI*NJ*sizeof(int));
            outsidesliceB  =  (int *)alloc(NI*NJ*sizeof(int));
            xedge  =  (int *)alloc(NI*NJ*sizeof(int));
            yedge  =  (int *)alloc(NI*NJ*sizeof(int));
            topyedge  =  (int *)alloc(NJ*sizeof(int));
            zedge  =  (int *)alloc(NJ*sizeof(int));

            for  (k  =  0;k  <  NK;k++){

                        if  (k  ==  start_contour)  {
                                    loadslice(start_contour);
                                    loadxedgeandyedge(start_contour);
                        }
                        loadslice(k+1);
                        lowslice  =  (k  &  1)  ?  outsidesliceA  :  outsidesliceB;
                        highslice  =  (k  &  1)  ?  outsidesliceB  :  outsidesliceA;

                        for  (i=0;i<NI-1;i++)  {

                                    if  (i==0)  loadzedgeandtopyedge(k);

                                    for  (j=0;j<NJ-1;j++)  {

                                                if  (j==0)  loadold10ptandold6pt(k,i);

                                                offset  =  NJ*i+j;
                                                cube_index  =  0;
                                                if  (*(lowslice+offset))  cube_index  |=  bit0;
                                                if  (*(highslice+offset))  cube_index  |=  bit4;
                                                offset++;
```

Listing 13.1 *(cont.)*

```
                                    if (*(lowslice+offset)) cube_index |= bit3;
                                    if (*(highslice+offset)) cube_index |= bit7;
                                    offset = NJ*(i+1)+j;
                                    if (*(lowslice+offset)) cube_index |= bit1;
                                    if (*(highslice+offset)) cube_index |= bit5;
                                    offset++;
                                    if (*(lowslice+offset)) cube_index |= bit2;
                                    if (*(highslice+offset)) cube_index |= bit6;


                                    if ((cube_index != 0) && (cube_index != 255))
                                            load_facet(cube_index,i,j,k);


                        }
                }
        }

        write_model_file(filename);
}
```

data points. The output data set consisted of over 400 000 facets.

Throughout the description, in an attempt at generality, unnecessary details of the programming are kept hidden from the reader; where assumptions are made, however, they are stated. In particular, no details of the library of low-level routines that manipulate and process the contour data are given – we only include a description of their functionality. This is because the library is application dependent – any readers using this description as a basis for their implementations will almost certainly want to insert their own routines here.

Any nontrivial application of this algorithm must be capable of handling large amounts of data, so its design must observe both efficiency and machine limitations. To this end we have constructed an implementation that takes its shape from attempting to:

- make full use of coherency, no intersection of a contour with an edge is calculated more than once;
- minimize the amount of memory that needs to be allocated.

march( ) – the top-level routine produces a model, of name *filename*, from the contours called *start_contour*

Figure 13.12 Three views of an athlete's head built using the marching cubes algorithm applied to the contour data obtained from a laser scanner. The input consisted of 222 contours of over 120 000 data points. The output from the algorithms consisted of 400 000 polygons.

to *end_contour*. We assume that the contours have already been read in, are ordered in increasing z and can be indexed by integer k identifying the contour lying in the plane:

z = start_z + delta_z * k

initialize_data( ) initializes the data structures necessary in order to write the final model out using *write_model_data( )*. We also set up parameters defining the region of space over which we wish to march as a rectangular lattice, thus:

$\big($start_x,start_y,start_z$\big)$ is the origin

$\big($NI * delta_x,NJ * delta_y,NK * delta_z$\big)$ are the sides

The input data is:

NK – the number of contours that we are sampling

delta_z – the spacing of the contours

$\big($start_x,start_y,start_z$\big)$ – the minimum point of data to be sampled

$\big($end_x,end_y,end_z$\big)$ – the maximum point of data to be sampled

NI, NJ $\big($to be varied according to the resolution of the model$\big)$ – the number of sample points taken along directions x and y, with spacing of delta_x and delta_y respectively

So we define element (i,j,k) to be at position (x,y,z) in march space, where:

x = start_x + i * delta_x

y = start_y + j * delta_y

z = start_z + k * delta_z

As far as memory allocation is concerned, in order to minimize this, only two slices, *outsidesliceA* and *outsidesliceB*, of the space over which we are marching, are held in memory at any one time. Each slice represents a contour as an array[*NI*][*NJ*] of booleans defined thus:

for a given k, element $\big($i,j$\big)$ of the slice holds if and only if the point $\big($i,j,k$\big)$ is outside contour k

The edge allocations exploit coherency by storing the intersections that the cube edges make with the contours and are global to Listing 13.2 (explained shortly).

The march step takes us from element (i,j,k) in march space to element (i,j + 1,k). We march (as shown in Figure 13.15(b)), pixel by pixel (incrementing j), then row by row (incrementing i), then slice by slice (incrementing k). At each element we consider the cube associated with it. We find which of the cubes in Figure 13.4 corresponds to the cube at (i, j, k). This is done by interrogating the relevant locations of the slices to construct an index

cube_index which will be used to access the appropriate data in *load_facet( )* (Listing 13.2).

Recall that any vertex of the cube can either be in or out of the model (Section 13.3.1). With eight vertices in a cube there are a possible 256 ways in which the cube can be aligned to the model. By assigning a bit to each vertex we can construct an index to that cube that defines uniquely the space partitioned within it. If the cube is entirely inside (*cube_index*==0) or entirely outside the model (*cube_index*==255) there is no contribution to be made.

load_facet( ) – the heart of the algorithm (Listing 13.2) – produces facets given a cube positioned in march space at (*imarch,jmarch,kmarch*) of index *cube_index*. *cube_index* gives us the topology of the surface within the cube. *load_facet( )* finds the locations of the intersections, orders them into triangular facets and adds them to the model.

At this stage a brief digression on how facet information is encoded within the model is necessary (see also Section 1.1). A model contains both vertex data and facet data. The vertex data consists of a chunk of contiguous

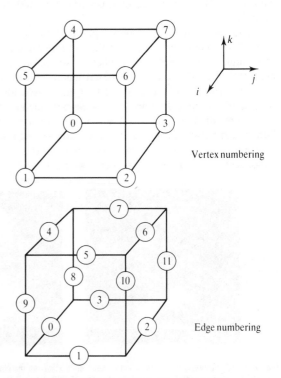

Vertex numbering

Edge numbering

Figure 13.13 Vertex and edge conventions for a cube.

Listing 13.2   load_facet.c

```
#include  "facet_data.h"
#include  "edge_data.h"
#include  "contour.h"

        int  old6pt,old10pt;

void  load_facet(cube_index,imarch,jmarch,kmarch)
int  cube_index,imarch,jmarch,kmarch;
{
        int  edge_table[12],edge,vertex_list[3];
        int  vert_offset;
        int  i,j;
        int  offset;

        i=0;
        while(edge_data[cube_index][i] != −1) {

                edge = edge_data[cube_index][i];

                switch (edge) {

                        case 0 :

                                offset = NJ*imarch+jmarch;
                                vert_offset = *(xedge+offset);
                                break;

                        case 1 :

                                offset = NJ*(imarch+1)+jmarch;
                                vert_offset = *(yedge+offset);
                                break;

                        case 2 :

                                offset = NJ*imarch+jmarch+1;
                                vert_offset = *(xedge+offset);
                                break;

                        case 3 :

                                offset = NJ*imarch+jmarch;
                                vert_offset = *(yedge+offset);
                                break;

                        case 4 :

                                vert_offset = old6pt;
                                offset = NJ*imarch+jmarch;
                                *(xedge+offset) = vert_offset;
                                break;
```

Listing 13.2 *(cont.)*

```
        case 5 :

                contour_intersect(5,imarch,jmarch,kmarch,pt);
                vert_index++;
                add_vertex(vert_index,pt);
                *(topyedge+jmarch) = vert_index;
                vert_offset = vert_index;

                if (imarch == (NI-2)) {
                        offset = NJ*(NI-1)+jmarch;
                        *(yedge+offset) = vert_index;
                }
                break;

        case 6 :

                contour_intersect(6,imarch,jmarch,kmarch,pt);
                vert_index++;
                add_vertex(vert_index,pt);
                old6pt = vert_index;
                vert_offset = vert_index;
                if (jmarch == (NJ-2)) {
                        offset = NJ*imarch+NJ-1;
                        *(xedge+offset) = vert_index;
                }
                break;

        case 7 :

                vert_offset = *(topyedge+jmarch);
                offset = NJ*imarch+jmarch;
                *(yedge+offset) = vert_offset;
                break;

        case 8 :

                vert_offset = *(zedge+jmarch);
                break;

        case 9 :

                vert_offset = old10pt;
                *(zedge+jmarch) = vert_offset;
                break;

        case 10 :

                contour_intersect(10,imarch,jmarch,kmarch,pt);
                vert_index++;
                add_vertex(vert_index,pt);
                old10pt = vert_index;
                vert_offset = vert_index;
```

Listing 13.2 *(cont.)*

```
                            if (jmarch == NJ-2) {
                                *(zedge+NJ-1) = vert_offset;
                            }
                            break;

                case  11 :

                            vert_offset  =  *(zedge+jmarch+1);
                            break;
                }
                edge_table[edge]=vert_offset;
                i++;
        }
        i=0;
        while((facet_data[cube_index][i] != -1)&&(i != 12)) {

                for  (j=0;j<3;j++) {
                        vertex_list[j]=edge_table[facet_data[cube_index][i+j]];
                }
                add_facet(3,vertex_list);
                i+=3;

        }
}
```

memory, with vertices arranged sequentially, called *vertex_table*. The facet data points to a vertex via an index which forms an offset from the bottom of *vertex_table* to its location. The reason why the data is ordered in this way is that in general, one vertex may be pointed to by more than one facet – indeed for smooth shading this is, of course, essential.

A single facet, then, consists of a list of vertex indices of vertices constituting the facet. The order in which these vertices are traversed defines the sense of the facet. Here we adopt the convention that the outward side of a facet is that side where the vertices trace out anticlockwise.

We number the edges and vertices of the cube as shown in Figure 13.13. The arrays *facet_data[256][12]* and *edge_data[256][12]* hold the facet information for all 256 permutations of the cube. The cube can be intersected on a maximum of all 12 of its edges (where the number of intersections is less, redundant data locations are filled with −1). An example will show best how the facet information is encoded.

Consider Figure 13.14, which shows a particular con-

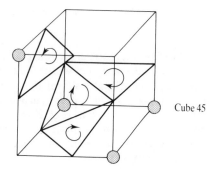

Cube 45

Figure 13.14 A particular cube topology.

figuration of the cube and its partition using triangles. The marked vertices, numbered 0, 2, 3, and 5 are outside the model – the sum of their bits, that is the *cube_index*, is 45. The array elements are:

facet_data $[45]$ = 11,10,8,8,10,0,10,1,0,5,4,9
edge_data $[45]$ = 11,1,0,4,5,8,9,10,−1,−1,−1,−1

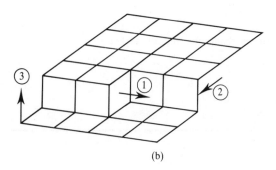

Figure 13.15 Showing the buffers used by the program.

By drawing a line from the centre of each edge in the facet data to the centre of the next, and so on, for all edges, you will trace out the triangles shown in the figure. Clearly a vertex may be referred to more than once within the same element of facet data. The *edge_data* is derived from *facet_data* by removing multiple occurrences of vertices and then ordering the edges in a specific way (more about this later).

When a new intersection of an edge with the model is calculated, it is loaded into *vertex_table* and referred to by its index. Depending on the value of (*imarch, jmarch,kmarch*) and the edge, this index is loaded into one of the vertex buffers ensuring that should a subsequent step in the march contain this vertex also, it is not recalculated. This also ensures that adjacent facets from adjacent marching cubes will share the same vertices along the common edge. Once again these buffers have been constructed in an attempt to minimize memory allocation and to maximize coherence. Figure 13.15(a)

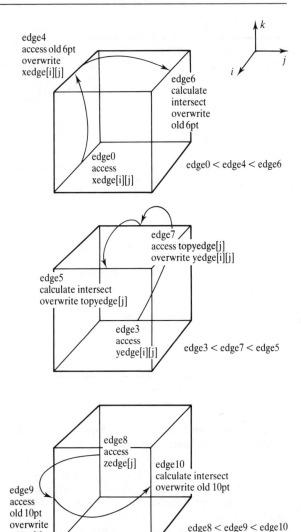

Figure 13.16 Ordering of the edge data.

shows the buffers associated with one position in march space, the buffers *xedge* and *yedge* span the whole slice (*kmarch* = constant) and the buffers *topyedge* and *zedge* span the row (*imarch* = constant) along which we march. As this point gets 'marched over' it becomes redundant in the sense that the vertex stored by the location will not be accessed again. Buffers *xedge* and *yedge* take advantage of slice-to-slice coherence just before leaving point (i,j,k), element (i,j) of *xedge* and *yedge* store indices for the next slice up, that is, the point (i,j,k + 1). Similarly, buffers *zedge* and *topyedge* take advantage of row-to-row coherence; element j of the buffers store indices ready for the next row (i + 1,j,k). *old10pt* and *old6pt* store the intersections of edges 10 and 6 of the previous pixel and so take advantage of pixel-to-pixel coherence. At a given march point the vertices on any of the edges drawn in Figure 13.15(b) will be stored by the various buffers.

Clearly the order in which the buffers are accessed and then updated is crucial. For example, we must be sure to access the index for the vertex along *edge3* stored in the buffer *yedge[i][j]* before we overwrite it with the index for that calculated along *edge7* in preparation for the next slice up. Figure 13.16 shows the ordering of the edge numbers in *edge_data* that is required to avoid this.

Consider Figure 13.17 which assumes the cube to be in the interior of march space. By taking advantage of coherency, new intersections will have to be calculated only if the model intersects edges 5,6 or 10 – intersections along any other edge will have been previously calculated in the march, that is, they can be found from a previous slice, line or pixel by accessing one of the vertex buffers. The call to *contour_intersect( )* in the case of edge 5,6 or 10 then calculates this intersection point,

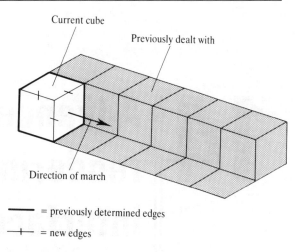

Figure 13.17 A marching cube showing new edges and previously determined edges.

and pushes it on the top of the vertex table using *add_vertex( )*.

The first **while** loop takes the vertex pointers of the intersection points, for each edge in *edge_data*, and loads them into an array called *edge_table*. The second **while** loop adds triangular facets to the model using the facet data and *edge_table* via *add_facet*.

14

Advanced rendering interfaces: shading languages and RenderMan

In this chapter we introduce the elegant technique of texture trees, which organize the selection and mixing of texture maps. Basic texture mapping techniques are dealt with in Chapter 6.

Introduction

In the foregoing material we have described rendering as a pipeline process, passing a model through various processing stages until the shaded object appears on the screen. The initial stages are well-defined geometric operations and transformations, and are basically the same for all renderers. The final stages deal with shading and it is in this part of the renderer that there is a need for a user interface that enables a person to utilize the facilities embedded in the renderer by the designer. Of course, for a renderer with very basic facilities, this is a simple matter involving no more than a selection of options – Gouraud or Phong shading, shadows or no shadows, and so on. For a renderer that offers a number of different reflection models, texture maps and transparency, things are more complex and there is a need for a 'shading language'.

This need for a 'shading language' was born from the recognition that a remarkable variety of visually rich images can be created with objects having a simple shape and complex shading. The idea was first floated by Cook [COOK84a] and was eventually developed into the design of RenderMan [PIXA88, UPST89]. We can do no better here than reproduce quotes from [UPST89]. On the importance of the shading phase of a modern renderer Upstill states:

Once an image synthesis program exists, the shader also becomes the focus of user expectations. As visually oriented animals, people are very sensitive to subtleties of shading, and that sensitivity expresses itself as a nearly limitless demand for subtle, flexible control over shading. At the same time the more successful a program is, the wider the range of physical reality it is expected to duplicate. Both of these facts place extraordinary demands on the shading portion of any renderer.

He justifies the need for a shading language by saying:

There is an alternative, based on giving the user more access to the shading system itself, rather than its external interface. The critical thing is to give users access to the useful parts of the system without burdening them with irrelevant details. . . . By writing an appropriate shader in the shading language, a programmer can extend old shading models or implement entirely new ones, light sources can be defined with any radiant distribution, and new and novel surface properties can be introduced easily. Any parameter to these processes can be set up with a constant value, a value that varies smoothly over a surface, or one modulated arbitrarily by a surface map.

This is an important development in image synthesis. Most commercially available systems implement a single parametrized system with a plethora of add-on features. This is usually some variation on the strategy whereby variable effects are achieved by altering the coefficients and parameters of a preprogrammed shading equation which is hardwired into the renderer.

We start our look at shading languages by considering relatively high-level approaches – shade trees and block shaders. We will then look at the progression of this idea to a more powerful, low-level approach where the user has access to, and can manipulate, variables in the environment that previously were unavailable having been buried deep in the code of the renderer.

14.1 Shade trees and block shaders

Cook's approach to a shading language involves eliminating 'fixed' reflection equations, such as the

Phong model with its linear combination of terms involving dot products, and allowing a user to specify the components in a shading operation and the way in which these components combine. This approach allows for both the specification of existing shading methodologies and an experimental testbed where new combinations can be experimented with. Cook separated the shading process into the conceptually independent tasks of light source specification, surface reflectance and atmospheric effects.

Specification of the surface reflectance proved to be the most flexible and powerful. This is done using a shade tree which organizes the shading operations into a tree structure. The idea of using a tree is to facilitate the combination of several effects at a given surface point into the overall process. Let us assume that the root node of the tree is at the top and the leaves are at the bottom. Values pertinent to the shading process (Cook terms them 'appearance parameters'), are generated at the leaves of the tree. These values are then passed upwards and are manipulated at nodes. A node takes one or more of these values and combines them together to produce a single value which in turn is passed upwards. Finally, arriving at the top of the tree, the output is the value passed by the root node which is the final shaded colour value for that surface.

For example, breaking down the operation of Phong shading into a shade tree gives us a specular node and a diffuse node, where the inputs to the diffuse node are the surface normal and a light vector producing an intensity value. A specular node takes three values, the surface normal, the eye position and the surface roughness and outputs a specular component. A standard Phong reflection model can then be represented as a tree (Figure 14.1).

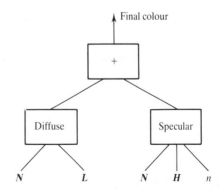

Figure 14.1 The Phong reflection model represented as a shade tree.

A high-level, interactive, graphical implementation of Cook's shade trees is given by Abram and Whitted [ABRA90]. The underlying design philosophy of the system is, as Abrahams states:

> The major design challenges of building block shaders are first, to provide a comprehensive set of primitive functions at an appropriate level, and second, to build an efficient apparatus that supports the construction and the execution of a shading network.

A user builds a shade tree or shading network as a set of connected blocks, like those shown in Figure 14.2. Associated with each block is a 'tab' or point of connection and the shade trees are defined by linking these tabs together. Unlike Cook's shade trees where the calculations proceeded in a fixed order (bottom to top), the user has explicit control over the order of execution of the shading modules, and networks such as Figure 14.2 cannot be interpreted as dataflow diagrams. The tabs have an associated type – 'before', 'during' or 'after' – that determines the time of execution of the module with respect to the execution of the parent process. Before and after processes proceed independently of the parent module, a during process is called by the parent module. Such a system masks the user from the inner workings of the shader function. Because of the rapid feedback the user quickly gains experience through experimentation.

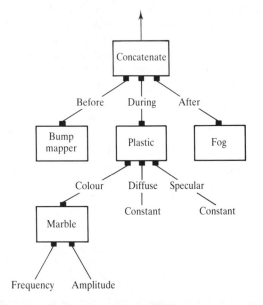

Figure 14.2 Shading network (after [ABRA90]).

The shading network in Figure 14.2 renders a model with marble texture controlling the colour coefficients in the plastic shader. The model is also bump mapped and atmospheric haze is added.

Cook's idea was extended by Perlin [PERL85] who constructed a shading language embedded in an environment called a Pixel Stream Editor (PSE). The PSE allows for a more general flow of control structures than those provided by the original shade tree. The language supports conditional and looping control structures, function definitions and logical operators. One of the consequences of the use of such a system is that it enables the rendering process to be broken down into intermediate images or stages, where each stage is a single pass through the PSE.

The PSE is a program that operates on every pixel in an array producing an output array of pixels; in this sense it functions in the same way as a powerful filter. In a sense, the use of the term 'pixel' in this context is slightly misleading. An intermediate image can consist of an array of records where each record may contain such entities as a surface normal. Perlin gives the following example for diffuse shading. An input image contains the variables 'surface', a surface identifier, 'point', the coordinates of the point on the surface visible at this pixel and 'normal', the surface normal at that point. The image that produced this information would typically be the output of a hidden surface removal algorithm. If the output image is to consist of the variable 'color', then:

if surface == 1
  color = [1 0 0] ∗ max(0.1, dot(normal, [1 0 0]))
else
  color = [0 0 0.1]

will produce a diffusely shaded red object lit from the positive x-direction against a blue background.

Finally, Hanrahan [HANR90a] points out that in Perlin's model shading is viewed essentially as a postprocess that occurs after visibility calculations. The visibility calculation is relegated to a single pass through the PSE. This makes it very difficult to use the language to implement global illumination models such as radiosity or ray tracing, where much more information is required by the shader than mere surface visibility. Another drawback to the approach is that the distinctions made by Cook during the shading process between light source specification and surface reflectance is no longer observed.

In a culmination of ideas, the strength of Cook's approach (which was conceptually to separate and modularize the geometric, material and environmental factors that determine shading) was combined with the strength of Perlin's approach (which was to provide a full and flexible language definition) into one shading language called RenderMan, which we shall cover in some detail at the end of this chapter.

14.1.1 Texture trees

By way of illustration of the power and flexibility afforded by the shading language approach, we describe in detail a specific implementation of a subset of Cook's shade trees. These are called 'texture trees' as the emphasis here is on the use of texture mapping to specify and manipulate the shading properties of a surface. This implementation has proven itself to be invaluable within the commercial production environment as a way of quickly and easily increasing the visual richness of image. In support of this claim, examples of texture trees taken from production are described in detail at the end of this section.

We now describe the implementation details. The trees are restricted to having a maximum of two branches, the left and the right branch. The only values that are passed along the branches are colour values. The nodes and leaves of the tree contain data, that is, parameters specified by the user, and pointers to functions, again user specified, that process the data. The power behind shade trees comes from the fact that the user can specify which functions to load into the tree as well as just the parameters. At a node or a leaf any number of texture mapping operations or basic mathematical manipulation can be applied in any order to the surface, altering its shading parameters. The difference between leaves and nodes is shown schematically in Figure 14.3. The evaluation of a leaf will, among other things, always return a colour value. Each node contains a function pointer, the evaluation of which produces a number, *mask_no*, which linearly interpolates between the colours arriving from the left and right branches, coll and colr respectively, and passes the interpolated colour back up the tree. Trivially:

$$col = coll + mask\_no \left(colr - coll \right)$$

Shading can occur anywhere within the tree denoted by • phong. If shading occurs at a node then it occurs after the left and right branches have been evaluated.

This simple scheme can be implemented using a single recursive routine *evaluate_tree( )* as shown in Listing 14.1. *evaluate_tree( )* takes a polygon *poly*, a texture tree

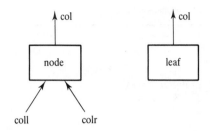

Figure 14.3 Operation of a node and leaf in our texture tree implementation.

tree and produces a colour *col*. If the routine is passed a node it evaluates the function pointer assigned to that node and then recursively evaluates the left and right branches, waiting for the results and then passing back the interpolated colour. The downward recursion stops when it reaches a leaf, whereupon the function *evaluate_leaf( )* generates a colour value and the recursion starts to retrace its steps back to the root node. The pointer *∗tree* points to a linked hierarchy of structures. Each individual structure is either a node or a leaf structure. The structure TREE is defined to be the union of these two structures. Both leaf and node structures contain the member:

int type

so that they can identify themselves to the routine. The function pointer in the node structure that returns the interpolant for the left-hand and the right-hand branches is the member:

float $\left(∗\text{func} \right) \left(\right)$

Now for some examples of texture trees, starting with relatively simple trees and graduating through to more complex examples that have been used in production. These latter examples, through their ingenuity of construction, make evident the fact that shading involves a lot of trickery that has no basis whatsoever in the physical process that is being emulated. If it looks correct it is correct.

Consider the texture maps *stars* and *polka* as shown in Figure 14.4. The cube shows the effect of applying the texture tree to its surface. At the root node the texture map *polka* is used as a mask, its evaluation at the surface of the cube returns a monochrome colour value which is used to specify the $mask\_no \in [0,1]$. Completely black areas of the map will take the evaluation of the tree down the left branch only, whereas conversely, completely white areas of the tree will correspond to going down

Listing 14.1 evaluate_tree.c

```c
#include "types.h"

void evaluate_tree (poly, tree, col)
struct polygon *poly
union TREE *tree;
float col[3];
{
            float mask_no;
            float coll[3],colr[3]

            if (tree->node.type == NODE) {

                    mask_no = (*(tree->node.func)) (poly, tree);

                    if (mask_no == 0)
                            evaluate_tree (poly, tree->node.left, col);
                    else if (mask_no >= 1)
                            evaluate_tree (poly, tree->node.right, col);
                    else {
                            evaluate_tree (poly, tree->node.left, coll);
                            evaluate_tree (poly, tree->node.right, colr);
                            col[0] = coll[0] + mask_no * (colr[0] − coll[0]);
                            col[1] = coll[0] + mask_no * (colr[1] − coll[1]);
                            col[2] = coll[0] + mask_no * (colr[2] − coll[2]);
                    }
            }
            else evaluate_leaf (poly, tree, col);
}
```

only the right branch. The uvscale at that node is used to denote a *local* scaling operation applied to the uv texture coordinates on the surface of the cube. The scaling operation is only active at this node – other parts of the tree will still pick up the original texture coordinates. In this case, the uvscale magnifies the texture map *polka*. Down the right branch the map *stars* is used directly to texture map the colour of the surface; down the left branch the map *stars* is used as a mask, effectively inverting the colours assigned by the right branch. The second example (Figure 14.5) shows the effect of using a texture tree to drive the opacity of the surface. (An opacity of 0 is completely transparent and an opacity of 1 completely opaque.)

Plate 47 shows frames taken from an architectural job for the visualization of the new Hong Kong airport. Texture trees were used for the sea, the mountains and the concrete surface of the airport itself. The maps *height*, *forest* and *sea* are shown alongside and were created by

rendering the mountains orthographically from above. In the case of map *sea*, the mountains were simply set to black and rendered against a white background. Map *forest* was created similarly with the additional use of a paint program. Map *height* is a standard height field for the mountain. The mountain was rendered from above using the grey scale as a texture map – black at $v = 0$ varying linearly to full white at $v = 1$. Lines of constant colour in the map height therefore correspond to contours of the mountain.

Consider the texture tree for the mountain. At the root, the map forest is used as a mask to separate regions of the mountain that have forest on them from those that don't. Forest regions have their colour specified by a texture map *forest colours*. Regions not in forest have a colour assigned to them according to the height of the surface. This is done by using the map *height* as a mask and assigning green to the lowlands and brown to the highlands.

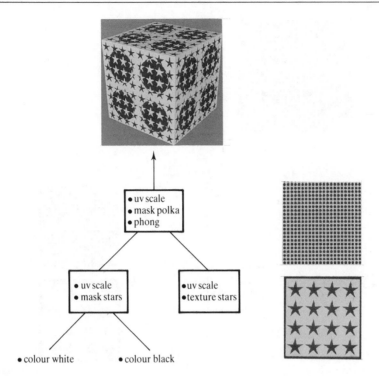

Figure 14.4 Texture tree example 1.

The sea was modelled as a flat polygonal surface. The idea was to have the colour of the sea vary from a sandy colour at the shoreline to create the effect of beaches, to a light-blue colour near the shore through to a darker blue as the sea got deeper. This was done by taking the map sea as a starting point and blurring it by softening the edges to various degrees. Three maps were created – sand, shallow water and deep water – each map being more blurred, or softer, than the previous. The illustration shows an enlargement of the same region from each of the three maps. These maps were used as masks in the texture tree shown to create the desired effect.

The problems with the concrete were that a single texture map applied across the whole of the airport would not have produced the required level of detail, and that a single texture map pasted over smaller sections of the concrete would have produced the detail required but also a regular pattern. What was needed was a way of increasing the detail more or less randomly without incurring too many overheads. A typical map used in the texture tree for the concrete is shown. Maps similar to these were used as masks at the nodes of the texture tree which was about three levels deep. More or less random

uvscales were applied at each of the nodes – they were applied such that more and more texture was compressed within a given region the lower down the tree was the node. At the leaves of the tree a variety of differing colours appropriate to concrete were assigned to the surface. The texture tree worked in such a way as to provide the required level of detail and, at the same time, because of the random scalings of the texture coordinates at the nodes, to break up any regular patterns that might otherwise have been discernible to the eye.

Our final example of texture trees is also one of the subtlest. A sequence involving a cola bottle was requested by a client who, wanting to suggest that the cola was deliciously cold, specified that drops of water should appear on the label. It was felt that too much effort would be involved modelling the drops polygonally and so a solution was sought using texture trees. Two maps were used and are shown alongside the finished product (Plate 48). These are: map *drops*, which was created by rendering a random assortment of spheres, and map *label*. They were arranged into a texture tree as shown. The map drops separates regions of the label that have drops on them from those that don't.

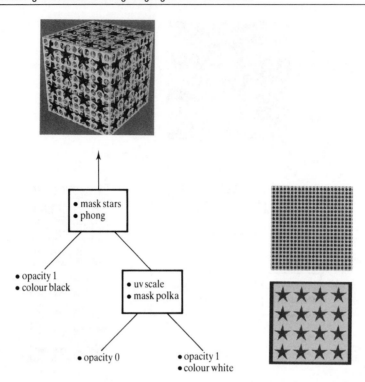

Figure 14.5   Texture tree example 2.

Going down the right branch we simulate the effect of drops. First, the map drops is used again – this time as a bump map to simulate the curvature of the water drops. Second, a slight uvscale is applied prior to texture mapping the label. This produces a slight shift in the label underneath the drops thereby simulating the refraction of the light through the water. Finally, in order to simulate the different reflectivity properties of the drops and the label, the right-hand branch was given a larger specular coefficient than the left branch. Because of this difference, Phong shading has to take place at both leaves. The final result is shown together with a closeup.

14.2 RenderMan shading language

14.2.1 Introduction

The ideas discussed in the previous section have been generalized into a complete shading language in Render-

Man [PIXA88, UPST89, HANR90]. The RenderMan shading language is part of the RenderMan interface – an attempt to standardize the way in which computer graphics image specifications are passed to different rendering programs. Part 1 of the specification is a collection of procedures that describe the scene to the rendering program; Part 2 is the shading language that programs the shading facilities of the renderer in detail. Among the motivations for RenderMan, Hanrahan discusses the following points. The language should allow 'tricks' to be incorporated, providing a testbed for experimentation with different effects. For example, many effects in shading are achieved by various combinations of texture with local reflection models. This fact should be recognized and facilities for developing such tricks incorporated in the language. Shading models are currently an active area of research and are being changed and modified all the time. This supports the notion of shaders as procedures.

The goals of the language are quoted in [HANR90] as:

1. To develop an abstract shading model based on ray optics that is suitable for both global and local

illumination models. It should also be abstract in the sense of being independent of a specific algorithm or implementation in either hardware or software.

2. To define the interface between the rendering program and the shading modules. All the information that might logically be available to a built-in shading module should be made available to the user of the shading language.

3. To provide a high-level language that is easy to use. It should have features – point and colour types and operators, integration statements, built-in functions – that allow shading calculations to be expressed naturally and succinctly.

A possible criticism of the shading language can be levelled at its ease of use with regard to the nature of the high-level facilities that it provides. On the one hand, the language is strongly typed and facilities are supplied to allow users to write shaders and experiment with shader combinations. However, this is low-level access in terms of computer graphics theory, and to use the full power of the language a user needs to be extremely well-versed in the general areas that the language deals with (such as shading models, texture mapping and filtering methods). The subtle possibilities that flow from the language are not really accessible to nonexpert users. Perhaps this is unavoidable – but it is likely to be a brake on the popularization of the language.

The language enables procedures called 'shaders' to be written. These simulate local processes and can be used either singly or together – several types of shaders being used to contribute to the final image. Shader types are distinguished by the inputs they use and the kind of output they produce. The three major types of shaders are:

1. *Light source shaders* Calculate the colour of light emitted from a light source. They take as input the position of a light source and the direction of a surface point from the light. They output the colour of the light striking that surface point. Typically, light sources may possess a frequency spectrum, an intensity, a directional dependency and a distance related falloff.

2. *Surface reflectance shaders* Implement a local reflection model and compute the light reflected in a particular direction by summing over the incoming light and considering the reflective properties of the surface. They make no assumption about the source of the incoming light distribution which can either come direct from a light source or be secondary reflected light from another object.

3. *Volume shaders* Implement the effect of light passing through a volume of space. This can be a volume exterior to the object, in which case the shader is an atmospheric shader, or it may be a volume interior to the object.

Hanrahan defines these shaders as components or terms in the rendering equation (see Chapter 12 for a full treatment of this equation):

$$I(x, x') = g(x, x') \left[\epsilon(x, x') + \int_s \rho(x, x', x'') I(x, x'') dx'' \right]$$

The light source shader calculates the term $\epsilon(x, x')$, the surface shader the term $\rho(x, x', x'') I(x', x'')$ and the volume shader calculates $g(x, x')$. Upstill [UPST89] uses a simpler nonrecursive definition to show the relationship among shaders based on the transport of light from a single direct source to a viewer. He calls this definition a 'dataflow model'. Figure 14.6 shows a set of five shaders operating in a sequence based on the direction of light propagation from the source to the viewer. Each shader module accepts a particular input depending on its type, and produces an output. Of the five shaders, one is a light source shader, two are surface shaders and three are volume shaders associated with the space between the light source and the object, the space interior to the object and the space between the object and the viewer. As the figure implies, shading in RenderMan can be seen as a ray tracing model. When a ray travels through space it is modulated by the volume shader associated with that space. A ray striking a surface invokes the surface shader associated with the object to spawn new rays. Communication between shaders is accomplished via the global variables shown in Figure 14.6.

The shaders are functionally independent and a surface shader may be chosen without regard to the nature of a volume shader, for example. Shaders are embedded in a predefined rendering system that is wholly transparent to the user and a sequence of shaders makes up a model. Shaders can be added to or taken away from the model and the passage of light from a source to a viewer can be as complex or as simple as is necessary.

One of the more ambitious aspects of RenderMan is giving the writer of a shader the ability to implement a global illumination model. The implication is that a user can produce a global illumination model without having to implement specific models such as radiosity or ray tracing which, as we have seen, carry high complexity overheads and constraints.

We will now describe the language in some detail.

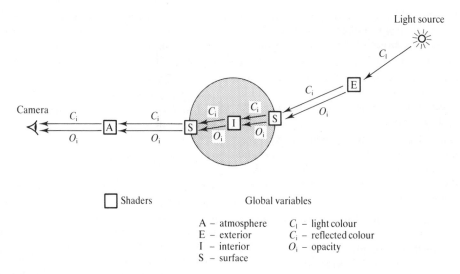

Figure 14.6 RenderMan dataflow model of shaders.

Although the language contains control structures and facilities to be found in C-like high-level languages, we will restrict the following discussion to those unique facilities that are concerned with shading. The idea is not to give sufficient detail to enable the reader to become adept at using RenderMan, but to discuss those aspects that are of general importance in supplying a user with shading facilities. (For a comprehensive treatment on how to use the language the reader should refer to [UPST89].)

To date it is the only attempt to formalize access to the facilities embedded in an advanced renderer and it is thus worthy of some study.

14.2.2 Data types in RenderMan

Two special data types are used in RenderMan – **color** and **point**. As with any special data type in a high-level language they enable a user to refer to and manipulate an entity by referring to it by a single name. The data type **color** is used to represent the colour of light emanating from a source and the reflectivity or opacity coefficients used in reflection model equations.

Color has an undefined structure and RenderMan will support a colour representation in a number of colour spaces apart from the pseudostandard triaxial RGB space. The operators '+' and '*' are used in conjunction with this data type and they are independent of the number of samples used in the colour representation.

Constants can be assigned to a **color** data type by combining a declaration and initialization statement. For example:

color c = **color** "rgb" $(1, 0, 0)$

and

color c = **color** "hsv" $(0, 1, 1)$

both declare a **color** variable 'c' and assign saturated red to it.

The expression:

$$c = refl * max(0, L \cdot N)$$

implements simple diffuse shading. c and refl are variables of type **color**, L and N are variables of type **point**. L and N are, of course, vectors (the light direction vector and the surface normal – just the vectors that we have used elsewhere in the text) and the operator '·' implements a dot product. '*' is a multiplication operator that multiplies corresponding components of the multicomponent types together.

The expression:

$$\underline{Ci} = refl * (Ka * ambient() + Kd * diffuse(Nf))$$

may be found as part of a matte surface shader. $\underline{Ci}$ is the global variable that takes information out of the shader and must be assigned to. refl is a local variable. Both are of type **color**. Ka and Kd are scalar instance variables.

(Note that this is slightly different to the convention that we used in Chapter 2 where Kd was a triple.) 'ambient' and 'diffuse' are standard functions. 'Diffuse' calculates the dot product, as we would expect, using the argument Nf, a variable of type **point**.

As we have already implied, predefined global variables are used to communicate information or results from one shader module to another. Ci represents the output from a shader and Cs its current surface colour, or reflectivity coefficient, that is bound to the object. The reflected light from a point is Ci and this will normally be an expression involving the incoming light and Cs. In its simplest form this will be:

Ci = Os ∗ Cs ∗ (an implementation of a reflection model)

Os is the opacity of the surface where a completely opaque surface will have its opacity set to one. An opacity Oi is associated with the light ray and normal surface shaders will contain the assignment:

Oi = Os

Associating an opacity with a light ray is a confusing concept but it generalizes transparency (note that in this respect Oi is of the same type as Ci).

14.2.3 RenderMan surface shaders

Although shaders are similar, from a user view point, to procedures in a high-level language, a necessary distinction is made between the output information that the

shader calculates and the formal argument list. The shader arguments define the properties of the shader and are set up by using instance variables. A shader is called or executed by the rendering system and information is passed to the shader by the renderer via global variables. Instance variables customize a shader and shaders with identical functionality can appear more than once with different instance variables. It is impossible for a shader to transfer control to another shader.

Listing 14.2 is an example taken from [UPST89]. This is the code for one of RenderMan's standard or predefined shaders and it implements standard Phong shading. Further examples of more elaborate shaders are given in [UPST89]. From this it can be seen that the language is superficially similar to C. A shader is defined by preceding its definition with one of the shading language keywords: **light, displacement, surface** or **volume**.

A shader is attached to an object using a procedure call when the object is declared and a RenderMan procedure exists for each type of shader. RenderMan supports a set of five standard shaders.

Surfaces are shaded by associating a shader instance with each point in the parameter space of a surface. A point in parameter space is categorized by the predefined global variables u and v. For bicubic patches u and v are in the range 0 to 1 as you would expect (Chapter 3). For polygons they are defined to be the x- and y- coordinates of the polygon in object or world space.

As well as attaching a shader to a surface, RenderMan uses the concept of a shading rate. This is useful when

Listing 14.2 RenderMan standard shader – surface shades implementing Phong shading

```
/*
 * plastic(): give the appearance of a plastic surface
 */
surface
plastic(
    float Ks        = .5,
          Kd        = .5,
          Ka        = 1,
          roughness = .1;
    color specularcolor = 1)
{
    point Nf = faceforward(N, l);

    Oi = Os;
    Ci = Os*(Cs*(Ka*ambient() + Kd*diffuse(Nf)) +
             specularcolor*Ks*specular(Nf,-l,roughness)));
}
```

scenes are being developed and enables a user to exploit the tradeoff between image quality and rendering time – a point that we have often raised in the text. The shading rate is the frequency, with respect to pixels, at which the surface shader is applied. A surface can be shaded at the rate of 1 evaluation per pixel or cruder, but faster shading can be specified (see Section 1.6.2 for a non-RenderMan implementation of this technique). The shading rate is given as an area (a value of 1, for example, will cause the surface to be shaded about once per pixel) and it can vary from surface to surface. The other attribute used in the application of a shader is shading interpolation. This can either be constant – points on the surface between calculated values take the shade of the nearest calculated value – or it can be smooth and an interpolation scheme is applied. If the shading rate is set to a value that is larger than a polygon, and the shading interpolation is smooth, then Gouraud shading results.

One of the more advanced constructs available in the RenderMan shading language is the **illuminance** construct. This facility integrates the incoming light over a cone centred on the point that the surface shader is currently applied to. The nature and accuracy of the integration is transparent to the user. The syntax of the construct is:

illuminance(position[, axis, angle]) statement

and for each source of illumination within the cone the statement is executed once with global variables $\underline{\text{Cl}}$ and $\underline{\text{L}}$ set to the arriving light colour and the direction towards the source. (These variables are redefined for

each light source.) 'Position', the mandatory argument, is of type **point** and specifies the position of the cone apex. 'Axis' and 'angle' give the necessary information to define a particular integrating cone (Figure 14.7).

The following example implements diffuse shading:

illuminance$(\text{P}, \text{N}, \text{PI}/2)$
   $\underline{\text{Ci}} +{=} \text{refl} * \underline{\text{Cl}} * \underline{\text{L}} \cdot \text{N};$

In this case the cone is widened to a hemisphere. The effect of this construct is different to the statement at the beginning of Section 14.2.2 in two ways. First, it deals with all light sources that are contained wholly or partially within the cone (the previous statement would have to be embedded in a loop to do this). Second, because of the integration over the cone, it makes no assumptions about the nature of the light source, which may be an area or distributed source. (If the previous statement is used without further elaboration, the implication is that the light source is a point source).

14.2.4 RenderMan and global illumination models

The issue of global illumination models and RenderMan is currently an area of development. Hanrahan [HANR90] states:

> The language presented does pose some difficult and challenging problems for graphics algorithms developers. The specification of area and procedural light sources was designed for full generality, but as a result is beyond the capability of current lighting and shading algorithms, since they assume that the renderer can correctly integrate over directional or positional distributions. However it seems likely that distributed stochastic sampling [COOK86] would yield good approximations to these integrals, although this is certainly an area that needs more research. Also global illumination models such as radiosity work only with simple diffuse shading formulae. Implementing a global illumination algorithm for the procedural shaders described in this language is also an area for future research.

Classical ray tracing can be implemented directly using the **illuminance** construct with 'angle' set to 0. The shading language ignores the difference between light coming from light sources and that coming from other surfaces. Alternatively, a built-in function, **trace**, can be employed.

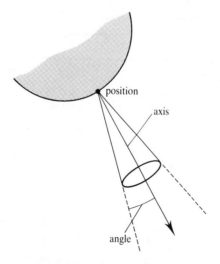

Figure 14.7 The variables used in the **illuminance** construct.

In theory, the **illuminance** construct could also be used to implement radiosity. However, one of the main development threads in the radiosity method has been efficiency (or the production of results in any reasonable time). This has led to the development of such specific evaluation methods as the hemicube algorithm for form factor determination. It is difficult to see how a radiosity method could be built on a general implementation of the **illuminance** construct without very heavy processing costs being incurred.

14.2.5 RenderMan light source shaders

Light source shaders accord a user the same freedom in specifying a light distribution as is available for a surface shader. A completely general specification for a light source would enable a user to define the colour of emitted light as a function of position and direction. In Render-Man two constructs are available to facilitate light source specification. They are **illuminate** and **solar**. These can be viewed as inverses of the **illuminance** statement. The two constructs, **illuminate** and **illuminance**, are declared in a similar manner and the **illuminate** construct has the syntax:

illuminate $\left(\text{position}\left[,\text{axis, angle}\right]\right)$ statement

Within statement the global variables $\underline{Cl}$ and $\underline{L}$ are set to the colour of the emitted light and the direction towards a surface point. Generally a light source shader will contain an **illuminate** construct. A shader that does not contain an **illuminate** statement will be an ambient source.

A point light source that implements an inverse square law falloff would be set up by:

illuminate $\left(\underline{P}\right)$
$\quad\underline{Cl} = \left(\text{intensity}*\text{lightcolour}\right)/\underline{L}\cdot\underline{L};$

The absence of 'axis' and 'angle' implies that light is emitted in all directions from the reference position $\underline{P}$. The code for the standard light shader is given in Listing 14.3.

An area light source is easily defined for an arbitrary geometry. We simply associate a light source shader with a surface (analogous to attaching a surface shader to an object). The **illuminate** construct within the shader is associated with each point on the light surface and an area light is simulated as a set of single light sources, each of which has an **illuminate** construct. For example:

illuminate $\left(\underline{P}, N, PI/2\right)$
$\quad\underline{Cl} = \left(\text{intensity}*\text{lightcolour}\right)/\underline{L}\cdot\underline{L};$

defines a light source with a hemispherical distribution centred on $\underline{P}$. Attaching this shader to a particular surface, such as a rectangle for a fluorescent light, will produce an area source with a uniform distribution.

The **illuminate** and **illuminance** statements are associated by the renderer and Upstill suggests that these illumination constructs are perceived as coroutines. The renderer calculates the intersection of both cones provided that the apex of each cone is contained within the other.

The **solar** construct is used to model distant light sources that may cast light in a certain direction from an unspecified or distant point. The **solar** construct has a similar syntax to the **illuminate** statement except that the position parameter is omitted. The syntax is:

solar $\left(\left[\text{axis,angle}\right]\right)$ statement;

The most common distant light source is the Sun and this can be modelled by:

Listing 14.3 RenderMan standard shader – point light source shader

```
/*
 * pointlight(): provide a light with position but no orientation
 */
light
pointlight(
    float intensity  = 1;
    color lightcolor = 1;
    point from       = point (0,0,0));/*light position*/
{
    illuminate(from)
        Cl = intensity*lightcolor/L · L;
}
```

solar (direction, 0) ;

   Cl = intensity ∗ suncolour;

$\overline{\text{Cl}}$ is only nonzero in directions that match 'direction', that is, the source is acting as if it were positioned at infinity and the light rays were parallel. If 'angle' is nonzero then the statement is executed for directions within the direction given by 'axis'. An example that uses this attribute is given by:

solar (−y, PI/2)

   Cl = intensity ∗ atmoscolour;

which simulates skylight on an overcast day. It assumes that the scene is set up with positive y as the up direction. The direction that axis is set to is the opposite of this and angle is set to $\pi/2$. This means that for any surface point distant light will be summed over a hemisphere – a good approximation to reality.

RenderMan supports four standard light source shaders. These are: ambient, distant, point and spotlight. The distant light source uses the **solar** construct, the point and spotlight use the **illuminate** statement and the ambient source uses neither.

14.2.6 RenderMan volume shaders

At the time RenderMan was developed, volume rendering was in its infancy and there are few language facilities provided to support volume rendering. RenderMan distinguishes between an exterior volume shader, such as one that implements depth cueing or fog effects, and an interior volume shader in which will be implemented the volume rendering algorithms discussed in Chapter 13. Figure 14.6 distinguishes conceptually between these two types of volume shader.

14.2.7 Mapping functions

In RenderMan all images that can be mapped onto a surface are called texture maps and mapping functions are provided for basic texture maps (**texture**), bump mapping (**bump**), environment maps (**environment**) and shadow maps (**shadow**). All these maps are made in advance by texture creation procedures. The values returned from the maps are filtered.

Texture mapping in RenderMan

Basic texture mapping from a two-dimensional texture domain, as described in Chapter 6, is supported by RenderMan. A texture map is created by calling a procedure that reads from an image file. Predefined global variables s and t (both specified over the range 0 to 1) define the texture map space.

The texture map is accessed, usually from within a shader, by first defining a mapping between parameter space and texture space. Four coordinates define a rectangle in texture space that is to be associated with the unit square in parameter space. This facility can be used either to project part of a texture map onto an entire parametrized surface or to project multiple copies of the map onto the surface.

Once the mapping is defined, access to the texture image is via a texture map index function. This has the syntax:

color texture (string name [channel] , texture coordinates, parameter list)

This returns a type **color**. (A basic texture map can also return a type **float**.) The texture coordinates consist either of a single two-dimensional coordinate or four two-dimensional coordinates specifying a single sample or a quadrilateral area over which filtering is performed to return a value. The parameter list controls the quality of the filtering performed, using such parameters as sampling rate.

Within a shader **texture** would be used to return a value for the global variable Ci and shading would then subsequently proceed as normal. Thus we could write

$\underline{\text{Ci}}$ = **color texture** (texturemap)

$\underline{\text{Ci}}$ = refl ∗ (Ka ∗ ambient ( ) + Kd ∗ diffuse (Nf))

An interesting use of **texture** described in [UPST89] is to access a texture map from within an **illuminate** statement thus turning the light source into a slide projector.

Bump mapping in RenderMan

Bump maps, as we saw in Chapter 6, perturb the surface normal and trick the eye into seeing depressions or pits in the surface when points are shaded using this surface normal. Also, you will recall that the normal has to be perturbed in a way that is independent of the position and the orientation of the surface. The input information to the access function thus has to contain a local set of mutually orthogonal axes to enable a normal perturbation. The syntax of the access function is:

point bump (string name [channel] , normal, dPds, dPdt, texture coordinates, parameter list)

The first three arguments after the map name define the aforementioned coordinate system. The other parameters are the same as for basic texture mapping. An example access is:

$\underline{N}$ += bump (mapname, $\underline{N}$, dPdu, dPdv)

that uses the three predefined global variables. The globals dPdu and dPdv are the derivatives of the surface position in the appropriate directions in parameter space.

14.2.8 Displacement shaders

A shader that can be used as an alternative to a surface shader employing **bump** is a displacement shader. You will recall that a visual flaw in classic bump mapping is that no perturbation or displacement is ever visible along a silhouette edge. A displacement shader actually perturbs the surface on a point-by-point basis, using some kind of displacement calculated procedurally or accessed from a map, that provides surface geometry variations in an easier and more convenient facility than specifications in the modelling phase. For example, a cylinder could be displaced to turn it into a bolt with a helical thread. (In this respect the use of the word shader is somewhat confusing – a displacement shader alters the surface geometry, it does *not* affect the global variable $\underline{Cl}$.) Clearly a displacement shader can be used as an alternative to bump mapping to avoid its disadvantage. An example of an approach that may be taken within a displacement shader is:

$\underline{P}$ += −1 * **texture** (pits);
$\underline{N}$ = **calculatenormal** ($\underline{P}$)

This would inserts pits in the surface, according to a height field in a texture map, by displacing $\underline{P}$ in a direction opposite to that of $\underline{N}$. $\underline{N}$ then needs to be recalculated because the relationship between $\underline{P}$ and its neighbouring points is now changed.

When a displacement shader is declared, any associated surface will not be shaded until the displacement is made.

14.2.9 Environment mapping in RenderMan

For environment mapping, RenderMan supplies an access function whose syntax is given by:

environment (name [channel] , direction, parameter list)

The indexing parameter in this function is 'direction' which is of type **point**. This will normally be the mirror direction associated with the view vector as we described in Chapter 6. Alternatively, if this direction is specified by four **points** then the return value is given by filtering over the region subtended by these vectors as suggested by Figure 6.11. Facilities are available for making an environment map and either the sphere or cube paradigm can be used.

An environment map access could be included in a surface shader by using, for example, the following code:

$\underline{M}$ = **reflect** ($\underline{In}$, Nf);
$\underline{M}$ = **transform** ("world", **point** "world" $(0, 0, 0) + \underline{M}$);
env = **color environment** (mapname, $\underline{M}$);
$\underline{Ci}$ = (Ka * ambient ( ) + Ks * (env + **specular** ($\underline{Nf}$, $-\underline{In}$, rough)))

The two lines before the environment map access calculate a reflection vector $\underline{M}$ (in the mirror direction to the camera or view direction given by $\underline{In}$) and transform this into the environment map coordinate system (the vector $\underline{M}$ is translated from a position on the surface of the object to the point from which the environment map was rendered).

14.2.10 Shadows in RenderMan

Shadows appear to be evaluated in RenderMan using the anti-aliased shadow Z-buffer technique described in Section 5.1.6. You will recall that this technique returns a float giving the percentage of points in shadow in the projected area of the pixel due to a point light source. This appears to create a difficulty, since RenderMan allows a distributed light source to be defined, and to create a shadow Z-buffer for each point on an area light is obviously impractical.

Shadow maps can be accessed directly to determine whether a point is in shadow or not. Also, a shadow map can be used within a light source shader. Used within a shader the access to the shadow map will attenuate the global variable $\underline{Cl}$ when the shader is instanced. For example:

$$\text{attenuation} \mathrel{*=} \textbf{shadow}\left(\text{shadowname}, \underline{Ps}\right)$$
$$\underline{Cl} = \text{attenuation} * \text{intensity} * \text{lightcolour}$$

could appear within the scope of an **illuminate** statement in a light source shader. 'shadowname' is the name of a shadow map created by a shadow making procedure and $\underline{Ps}$ is a global variable of type **point** in the light coordinate system, that is, the coordinate system in which the depth map was created.

PART IV

Advanced animation

15 | Overview and low-level motion specification

This chapter deals in depth with the specification of motion characteristics using splines. An exhaustive theoretical treatment of parametric representation is given in Chapter 3.

Introduction

In its simplest form, computer animation simply means using a standard renderer to produce consecutive frames, wherein the animation consists of relative movement between rigid bodies and possibly movement of the view point or virtual camera. This form of computer animation is exactly analogous to model animation – beloved by makers of space films – where scale models are photographed by special cameras using devices such as periscope lenses. The obvious advantage of computer animation is that the model does not have to be physically built (although building a database of a complex model for computer graphics is in many instances just as time consuming). Another advantage is that the camera is virtual, which means that there is absolutely no restriction on its movement.

To get away from the inherent limitations of this approach researchers have developed a number of tools that are intended to allow the animator to move closer to the possibilities that exist in traditional or manual animation and these techniques are the basis of the remaining chapters in this text.

Three-dimensional computer animation has unique advantages not available in traditional animation. For example, animation can be produced directly from models or sets of equations specifying the dynamic behaviour of structures or machines and this has major implications in the field of scientific visualization. This kind of animation is sometimes qualified by the term 'simulation' and it is dealt with in Chapter 18. It is, by definition, capable of producing extremely realistic animation. At the same time it is difficult to set up, apart from simple cases, and current research (for example, [PLAT88, MOOR88, HAHN88]) is concerned with such issues as how rigid bodies of arbitrary shape behave after a collision, how nonrigid bodies deform during a collision, and so on. Computational fluid dynamics is another example of the current simulation approach. The term refers to the numerical solution of the partial differential equations that determine certain aspects of fluid flow. Animated film of such phenomena as shock waves and vortices have been produced from such data.

Although most three-dimensional computer animation is produced for the ephemeral world of television advertising and the film industry, it is likely in the future that three-dimensional animation will develop into a scientific tool.

A well-developed application of three-dimensional computer animation is flight and military simulation. Here, standard three-dimensional animation techniques are used with environments based on real places such as international airports. A sequence is produced in real time that is controlled from electromechanical devices 'driven' by the pilot. The real-time requirement usually constrains the animation to consist of flat or Gouraud-shaded polygons with texture mapping.

A recent, and somewhat bizarre, application of three-dimensional animation is the production of sequences by litigants in court cases involving, for example, car accidents. A plaintiff hires a production company to provide a sequence that is a computer re-enactment of an accident. The scope for misrepresentation in presenting to a jury a video sequence that purports to be reality makes this application a manifest absurdity. Its adherents claim that it is no more than a presentation of the evidence in a way that jury members can easily comprehend.

Historical development

Historically, the earliest types of motion control system to be developed were scripting systems. Scripting systems involve the user in writing a script in an animation language. The advantages and limitations of this methodology are apparent. It presupposes a skill or facility in the language that has to be learnt. Animators tend to be artists rather than computer scientists and it is debatable whether this approach is desirable. The quality of the animation produced by such systems depends on the ability of the animator–programmer to bridge the gap between programming constructs and their visual effect. However, considerable effort has gone into the development of such systems and these are described in Section 15.2. The advantages of this approach are also obvious. The script is analogous to a program in a high-level language and thus offers the same advantages to an animator as a programming language does to a general-purpose programmer. These are: the ability to edit a sequence – progressive refinement facility; the ability to accumulate expertise by building up library facilities; the ability to approach more and more complex problems by using accumulated expertise.

A significant development that came out of the scripted approach to computer animation was the introduction of the concept of an 'actor' – an object that

possesses its own animation and interaction rules. An animator can set up or define such objects and subsequently refer to them as single entities. This is analogous to the ability to define complex types in standard high-level languages.

Such a philosophy was developed because systems were developed by computer scientists already well versed in this approach. Also, at the time such developments were taking place, workstations were not powerful enough to support real-time animation development. The ability to preview an animation sequence, make alterations to, say, an object path, and immediately view the result of the alteration in the form of a new sequence has only recently become possible on medium-price workstations. A simple interactive motion control system is scriptless (although more ambitious interactive systems may produce a script that can be subsequently edited). It allows an animator to set up a sequence by, say, interactively specifying a path and kinetic characteristic, using standard two-dimensional interactive graphics devices, and then to specify that an object be controlled by such information and preview the resulting animation sequence – usually in wireframe. Most animations today are done on an interactive system.

Crossover with traditional animation

In traditional animation characterization is usually achieved by using flat-shaded two-dimensional characters and the precise shading of three-dimensional objects is absent. In Disney's productions the characters are flat shaded and the illusion of movement through three-dimensional space is carried by the fluidity of the characters, the imaginative use of perspective in the background and the choreography of the virtual camera. The first traditional animation to feature shaded characters and objects to any extent is *Who Framed Roger Rabbit?* animated by Richard Williams. This film makes a feature of integrating live action with animated characters, and the complexity of the interaction is assisted by employing shading in the animated overlays.

In his film, *Luxo Jr.*, that has become something of a landmark in three-dimensional computer animation, John Lasseter used an articulated real object – an anglepoise or Luxo lamp – and successfully imparted a degree of 'Disney' type characterization with this unlikely object. The characterization was achieved by involving the well-known principles of traditional animation [LASS87]. Lasseter defines these and describes how they have been used in developing animation as a major art form by Disney animators. For example:

- *Squash and stretch* (also described in Chapter 17) which emphasizes the rigidity and the mass of an object by distorting it as a function of certain actions.

- *Secondary action* the action of an object resulting from another action.

- *Appeal* creating a design or action that the audience enjoys watching.

The film *Luxo Jr.* evokes the coy, sentimental hallmark of the many Disney productions.

The most important source for traditional animation principles is the book *Disney Animation: The Illusion of Life* by Thomas and Johnston [THOM84] which contains a distillation of Disney's experience, including that gained during the formative period between the late 1920s and the late 1930s where animation was elevated from a novelty to an art form. This work is significant since importing principles of animation established over many years of traditional animation can only speed the evolution of computer animation into an art form also.

15.1 Animation as control hierarchy

When we talk about computer animation techniques we are usually referring to motion control systems. There are many complexities and subtleties involved in the specification of the motion of objects in three-space, and many different ways in which the problem is approached. Compare this state of affairs to the different rendering techniques which have an underlying theory that knits them all together into one single unit – the renderer. Animation techniques have no such commonality and are far more disparate and isolated. This lack of unity is the most serious problem facing computer animation today. Although rendering has mastered enough of the visual complexity of the world to achieve near photo-realism, the field of animation has yet far to go in order to master a comparable degree of complexity of the world in motion. In spite of this, in this section we will

attempt a broad categorization of mainstream animation techniques.

The most useful way of classifying the multitude of computer animation techniques or motion control systems used in computer graphics is according to the level of abstraction that specifies the motion [WILH87]. A high-level animation system allows the animator to specify the motion in abstract general terms, whereas a low-level system requires the animator to specify individual moving parameters manually. High-level commands describe behaviour implicitly in terms of events and relationships, whereas lower level commands are far more explicit.

To animate just one rigid object with 6 degrees of freedom over 5 seconds, at 30 frames per second, requires 9000 numbers. Animating a fully defined human figure with over 200 degrees of freedom is another order of magnitude altogether. The purpose of a control hierarchy is to reduce the amount of numbers that the animator has to specify. The high-level system leaves it to the computer to generate the typically voluminous amounts of low-level data. Just as in high-level programming languages, the high-level constructs get compiled down to lower levels. Any one level will map parametric input into more verbose lower level parametric output. This process stops at the lowest level which corresponds to the specification of the entire data for all the degrees of freedom of all the moving parts for all the frames of the motion.

Clearly then, it is essential for the animator to impose some kind of control hierarchy on the task of motion specification; otherwise the animator would have to specify every moving parameter by individually assigning a value for each frame. Naturally, early research into motion control systems started at the lowest of levels producing frames by 'inbetweening' keyframes using splines (Section 15.3.1). This ground has been well covered and it is now a relatively easy task to move an object along a path in space. Now consider how to go about animating something as elaborate as, say, the charge of the Light Brigade. Only a fool would use a basic inbetweening system to achieve this. The sheer amount of data to be specified, to spline through every hoof of every horse, every blade of every sword would quickly overwhelm the animator.

The desire to achieve more and more complex animation has shifted the focus of research into constructing higher level systems where the aim is to orchestrate such complexity in a manageable way. This has led to a corresponding shift away from solving purely mathematical problems to the problems of building architectures of organizational software that can accomplish at least the following: compile the high-level commands down to the lower levels; ensure that all the lower level animation tools interact with each other correctly; have the upper levels respond to feedback from the lower levels, and so on. This task is made even more difficult in that the end product has to be easy to use and flexible. The work of Zeltzer [ZELT82], one of the relatively few researchers to have considered animation within this context, is particularly relevant here.

Currently at the top end of the spectrum of computer animation productions lies Pixar's *Tin Toy*, produced in 1988. This is a good example of a relatively high-level motion control system involving the combination of several animation techniques. Pixar describe the production in the following way:

> *Tin Toy*, produced by Pixar's Animation Production Group, is the first computer animated film ever to win an Oscar. The film blends a number of computer animation techniques while telling the humorous story of a wind-up toy's first encounter with a boisterous baby. Consistent with previous films by Pixar, *Tin Toy* emphasizes the narrative aspects of film making in addition to the technical demands of computer animation . . .
>
> The film is Pixar's first work to feature the animation of a human character. To accomplish this, a three-dimensional model of the baby's body was digitized from clay figures merged with a skeletal description of the character. Special software fits the body model to animation of the skeleton, so that the body model moves and flexes according to the animator's directions.
>
> The animation of the facial expression . . . required the definition of more than 40 facial muscles which were grouped by function to allow the animator better control of facial expression. Animation of the wind-up toy was augmented through the use of procedural animation and dynamics techniques.

At the other end of the spectrum lies the much more common animation sequence, best typified by the infamous term 'flying logo'. Here the logo, usually made up of monolithic letters, moves gracefully into view and gently tumbles into the final position. Variations on this basic theme, including the many guises which the flying logo assumes, is doggedly pursued by 'creatives' within the advertising industry and it is best left in their hands.

Although distinctly hackneyed, this type of animation is important since it invariably uses splines to specify motion control. These spline techniques are part of the first level of control, or abstraction, to be imposed on the task of motion specification. Spline-driven animation along with various other low-level techniques are discussed in this chapter.

Between the two levels of animation control falls a large body of animation techniques. Numerous disparate medium-level animation techniques have established themselves by marking out a domain of animation applications to which they are particularly suited. They are generally disqualified from being high-level techniques, however, precisely because of this specialization. We include a brief overview of them here; they will be covered in more detail in subsequent sections. These categories are not necessarily exhaustive nor mutually exclusive.

15.1.1 Procedural animation

In this category, control over motion specification is achieved through the use of procedures that explicitly define the movement as a function of time. Naturally, such a vague definition encompasses a very large range of work. At one end of the spectrum we can generate animation sequences that are simply the visualization of laws of physics, for example the scientific visualization of fluid flow.

Dynamic simulation has proved an invaluable tool for animating so-called secondary action. The term 'secondary action' comes from traditional two-dimensional animation, meaning action that is subsidiary to the main action of the scene – its function being to embellish and enhance this primary action. Since, in the majority of cases, this secondary action is just a Newtonian-type reaction to the primary action, the laws of dynamics are particularly applicable. For example, *Tin Toy* shakes his head producing the secondary action of the plume on his helmet wobbling.

However, there is no reason why the animator should be forced to obey these laws as Gomez [GOME87] points out: 'A brief review of classical animation shows this point: although Wily Coyote falls in a fashion that may be related to $d = at^2/2$, it usually does not happen until he has been walking on air for a few seconds (the *Cartoon Laws of Motion*)'. Consequently, the spectrum shifts through to purely empirical procedures that are designed specifically with the artistic expression of the animator in mind, where analytical functions are set up arbitrarily to achieve the desired result. A good example of this is the functional sculpting of facial muscles that control facial expression (see Section 17.7).

Because historically, the field of physics has been around a lot longer than computer animation, the physically based techniques far outweigh those developed for the 'animator as artist'. This imbalance needs to be addressed. Procedural animation forms the subject of Chapter 18.

15.1.2 Representational animation

This category extends the field of animation beyond that of specifying how a rigid object is to move in space by allowing the object itself to change shape and by animating the shape change. The data that represents the object thus becomes animated. We separate this category into two subsections:

1. *The animation of articulated objects* An articulated object is made up of connected segments or links whose motion relative to each other is somewhat restricted. This subject, along with the related topics of forward and inverse kinematics, is discussed the Chapter 16.

2. *Soft object animation* This includes the more general techniques for deforming and animating the deformation of objects. Chapter 17 is devoted to the techniques of arbitrary shape change. These techniques are extremely important in that they allow some basic principles of traditional two-dimensional character animation to be carried over into three-dimensional computer animation (it being well-nigh impossible to bring characterization into an environment of solid rigid bodies).

Note that as a consequence of allowing for this type of animation, the traditional distinction between modelling and animation breaks down since the problems of how an object is represented and how this representation is animated are intimately linked. This section, perhaps more than any other topic, cries out for higher levels of control where the hierarchy controls the specification of modelling as well as motion. Problems, such as how to put the skin on an articulated figure automatically, or

how to control the muscles that control facial expression manageably, are only beginning to be addressed [CHAD89, REEV90].

15.1.3 Stochastic animation

This controls the general features of the animation by invoking stochastic processes that generate large amounts of low-level detail. This approach is particularly suited to particle systems, discussed in detail in Chapter 18. Phenomena such as waterfalls [SIMS90], fireworks and fields of wind-perturbed grass [REEV83] have been modelled using this approach.

15.1.4 Behavioural animation

In this class the animator exerts control by defining how objects behave or interact with their environment. The animator does this by endowing actors, or character entities in the animation, with a local perception of the environment and a set of rules telling them how to react.

For example, Reynolds [REYN87] refers to this as 'what would happen if . . .' animation or behaviour simulation. In this intriguing study he simulates flocking behaviour in birds and fishes. Each simulated member of the flock is an independent actor that navigates 'according to its local perception of the dynamic environment, the laws of simulated physics that rule its motion, and a set of behaviours programmed into it by the animator'.

15.1.5 Low-level control

Starting with first principles, the remainder of this chapter is devoted to the techniques that, under our paradigm of animation as hierarchy of control, correspond to the different ways of imposing the first level of abstraction on the task of motion specification. Fundamental to this level is the problem of how best to parametrize the basic ways of moving about in space. Taken in order the subjects covered are: scripting systems, keyframing, spline-driven animation and the parametrization of orientation.

15.2 Scripting systems

With the advent of interaction in production animation, scripting systems have decreased somewhat in popularity. We shall therefore deal briefly with them by introducing a few examples.

Many animation scripting systems have been developed. These are extremely diverse. Possibly the best known and most quoted are ASAS (Actor Script Animation System) [REYN82] and MIRA [MAGN85].

ASAS was the first system to introduce the concept of an actor. This addresses the problem of objects that possess their own animation. For example, if a car moves along a specified path with a certain velocity, its wheels have to be moved at an appropriate angular velocity. An animator controlling the animation of a number of cars is concerned with the relationships between the cars, not with the 'internal' animation of each car. This can be embedded in the definition of the actor. An actor in ASAS is also able to communicate with other actors by sending messages. Thus actors can operate independently or, by communicating with each other, operate in synchronization.

ASAS is an environment that allows geometric objects, operations on these objects and animate blocks that allow *actors* to be 'directed'. Reynolds uses the term 'actor' which he describes as a chunk of code that will be executed once each frame. An actor is responsible for a visible element in an animation sequence and the code chunk will contain all values and computations which relate to that object. Scenes in a production sequence are analogized by **animate** blocks which comprise the coarse structure of the action.

The following example from [REYN82] is a script that contains one **animate** block. This block starts two similar actors, a green spinning cube and a blue spinning cube at different times. Both actors then run until the end of the block.

```
(script spinning-cubes
    (local: (runtime 96)
            (midpoint (half runtime)))
    (animate (cue (at 0)
                  (start(spin-cube-actor green)))
             (cue (at midpoint)
             (start (spin-cube-actor blue)))
             (cue (at runtime)
                  (cut))))
```

An actor is 'awakened' by the operator **start** once per frame; its local variables are restored, its definition invoked. Variables are then saved and the actor deactivated.

In the above script the operator spin-cube-actor is defined as follows:

```
(defop spin-cube-actor
    (param: color)
    (actor (local: (angle 0)
                   (d-angle (quo 3 runtime))
                   (my-cube (recolor color cube)))
           (see(rotate angle y-axis my-cube))
           (define angle
                   (plus angle d-angle))))
```

This definition operates on a single parameter – color – and returns an actor. Three local variables are associated with the actor; a start angle, an incremental angle and a colour.

ASAS can be considered as an extension to LISP and, although Reynold states that the language has been used commercially, it presupposes that the animator posseses a familiarity with LISP-type programming. Reynolds implies that a production is undertaken by a collaboration between 'several people, some responsible for artistic issues and others responsible for technical issues'.

Another scripting system development is due to Thalmann and Thalmann [THAL87] and is somewhat confusingly known under a variety of guises. MIRA uses a scripting language called CINEMIRA – an extension of Pascal – in a way that is convenient for the specification of an animation script. The particular aspects of the Pascal philosophy that are used to support animation are extended data types and structured programming concepts. Further development of this system involved the design of an artist-oriented interface called MIRANIM. The idea here is to retain the advantages of a detailed scripting language and at the same time provide a higher level facility for artists.

MIRANIM contains a modelling system for building objects and an artist-oriented editor called ANIMEDIT that eventually produces a script in CINEMIRA. The modelling system is fairly standard, allowing, for example, construction of volumes of revolution from arbitrarily shaped curves. The purpose of ANIMEDIT is 'to allow the animator to specify a complete script without programming'.

The ANIMEDIT system contains eight operational modes:

1. *Variable mode*   This mode allows the animator to create extended variables, with motion laws and so on. It is not made clear in [THAL85] exactly how a (computer-unskilled) animator can set these up.

2. *Object mode*   This mode sets up the system's modelling capabilities and allows the animator to create objects and operate on their attributes.

3. *Decor mode*   Similar to the previous mode, it facilitates the building of backgrounds and so on.

4. *Actor mode*   In this mode the animator defines actors (animated objects) together with the transformations to which they have to be subjected.

5. *Camera mode*   This is similar to the actor mode as far as movement is concerned. (Clearly the camera cannot take attributes such as colour.)

6. *Light mode*   Position and colour of light sources can be defined together with their motion.

7. *Animation mode*   This mode directs the action, starting and stopping actors, cameras and so on.

8. *Control mode*   Controls entry to other modes.

Finally, a script is produced in CINEMIRA. Thalmann points out that the concept of an actor is readily incorporated in such a system.

In MIRA much of this philosophy is enabled by extending Pascal-type declarations. For example, consider declaring a vector type:

```
type TVEC = animated VECTOR;
        val ⟪0, 10, 4⟫ . . UNLIMITED;
        time 10. .13;
        law ⟪0, 10, 4⟫ + ⟪3, 0, 0⟫ ∗ (CLOCK-10);
        end;
var VEC : TVEC;
```

Here a vector is defined that starts at time 10 and moves with constant velocity ⟪3, 0, 0⟫ from the point ⟪0, 10, 4⟫ stopping at time 13. Actors can take on such information from a single assignment statement.

15.3 Motion control

15.3.1 Keyframing

Keyframe systems take their name from the traditional hierarchical production system first developed by Walt Disney. In these systems, skilled animators would design or choreograph a particular sequence by drawing frames that established the animation – the so-called keyframes. Their particular skills lay in being able to animate convincingly a character that they had designed. The production of the complete sequence was then passed on to less skilled artists who used the keyframes to produce 'in between' frames.

The process is best implemented as a real-time system, the animator interactively respecifying or adjusting keyframes as a sequence loops.

The emulation of this technique by the computer, whereby interpolation replaces the inbetween artist, producing the inbetweens automatically, was one of the first computer animation tools to be developed. This technique was quickly generalized to allow for the interpolation of any parameter affecting the motion, thereby providing a higher level of control than traditional keyframing. For this reason we shall use the term 'key parameter' rather than keyframe, since the latter implies that keyframes exist, whereas the former does not necessarily. Care must be taken when parametrizing the system since interpolating naive, semantically inappropriate parametrizations can yield inferior motion. Figure 15.1 illustrates a case in point. The animation is simply the rotation of a line through $\pi/2$. The left-hand diagram generates inbetweens by interpolating the angle of rotation, whereas the right-hand diagram, mimicking traditional two-dimensional keyframing, interpolates the end points of the rotation. Obviously in this case the angle of rotation should be interpolated. A far more subtle example that indicates the importance of choosing how to parametrize the animation occurs when considering animating three-dimensional orientations as we shall see in Section 15.3.8.

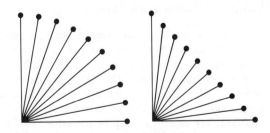

Figure 15.1   Interpolating rotation: angle (left) produces a different motion compared with interpolating end points (right).

The keyframing approach carries certain disadvantages. First, it is only really suitable for simple motion of rigid bodies. Second, care must be taken to ensure that no unwanted motion excursions are unwittingly introduced by the interpolant. None the less, interpolation of keyframes remains fundamental to most animation systems. Moreover, the demand made on motion specification by motion blur techniques, that is, requiring it to be specified for a noninstantaneous time interval within a frame corresponding to that time the shutter in a film camera remains open, can only reinforce the role of interpolation within animation.

The mathematical techniques of interpolating a spline through key parameters will not be covered here as it is dealt with in detail in Section 3.6.

15.3.2 Spline-driven animation

By spline-driven animation we mean the explicit specification of the motion characteristics of an object by using cubic splines. The manner in which these splines are constructed is left open-ended but the most useful practical system is to have an animator interactively shape the curves, and then to view the resulting animation in real time. Spline-driven animation by definition includes keyframing as a subset.

The first application of splines to drive animation that we shall look at is the most basic one – that of moving an object along a path in space. We specify, in ways to be described, a path of the object $Q(u)$ in three-space and a velocity curve $V(u)$, in two-space, of the object along the path. To generate an animation sequence we need to find the position of the object along the path at equal intervals in time corresponding to the frame interval. If we are using parametric representation to represent the characteristics, then this process is distinctly nontrivial.

15.3.3 Splining translation

Suppose we have an object that is required to move along a given path specified by a spline $Q(u)$ from start to end, that is, from $u = 0$ to $u = 1$ over a given number of frames with a uniform speed. The computer's task is to find a set of points along this spline such that the distance travelled along the curve between consecutive frames is a constant. The object can then be positioned at these points frame for frame. Naively, one might compute these points by evaluating $Q(u)$ at equal values of u. This will only work, however, if the parameter u is proportional to the distance travelled along the curve, called the

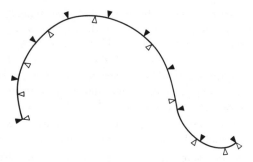

Figure 15.2   Intervals of equal parametric length (outlined arrowheads) do not correspond to equal intervals of arclength (black arrowheads).

arclength, which in general will not be the case. Just such a parameter exists, however, and this is called the arclength parameter. In the special case of the parameter being proportional to arclength, the spline is said to be parametrized by arclength. We shall see that for splines the relationship between the parametrizing variable and the arclength is very nonlinear.

Figure 15.2 shows a spline with 10 points at equal intervals of u marked by the outlined arrowheads and 10 points spaced out at equal intervals of arclength marked out by the black arrowheads – clearly the latter are positioned at equal distances along the curve whereas the former are not. Without the arclength parameter it is not possible to have an object move with uniform speed along a spline, or indeed with any sensible control.

15.3.4 Arclength parametrization

In general, driving an object positioned on a curve $Q(u)$ by a velocity curve

$$V(u) = (t(u), s(u))$$

that plots the arclength s, or distance travelled, against time, requires the curve to be reparametrized in terms of s. Since s is a strictly increasing function of u the reparametrization can always be effected without ambiguity as there is a one-to-one correspondence between s and u. Now since the arclength is a function of u, we write:

$$s = A(u)$$

The reparametrization is from:

$$Q(u) \text{ to } Q(A^{-1}(s))$$

and we need to find the function A^{-1}. One could suggest parametrizing the curve in terms of its arclength initially, thereby bypassing the need for this reparametrization altogether, but this will not work since we cannot establish arclength until we have established the curve and we cannot establish the curve without the arclength. The reparametrization is therefore unavoidable.

In practice, the parametrization is not straightforward. The function $A(\ )$ cannot be represented analytically and so cannot be inverted to give $A^{-1}(\ )$. Because of this the functional evaluation of $A^{-1}(\ )$ has to be done numerically. This breaks down into two stages:

1. The inversion of $s = A(u)$ to $u = A^{-1}(s)$ is replaced by a search for a value of u that has a corresponding arclength close to the given s value. So to evaluate $u_\alpha = A^{-1}(s_\alpha)$ say, we find a value of u such that the corresponding arclength $s = A(u)$ lies within a certain tolerance of s_α.

2. Step 1 requires the evaluation of $s = A(u)$. As already stated this is not an analytical function and is an integral that requires the use of a numerical integration routine for its solution.

Step 1 is done by taking advantage of the fact that the arclength is strictly monotonically increasing. That is, if u_1, u_2 are two values of u such that $A(u_1) < A(u_2)$ then $u_1 < u_2$. We can thus base our search on the simple bisection method which converges to a solution by successively bisecting the interval within which the solution must lie. It works as follows. In our example suppose the interval $[u_1, u_2]$ contains the solution u_α. $[u_1, u_2]$ is bisected into the two subintervals $[u_1, u_3]$ and $[u_3, u_2]$ where $u_3 = (u_1 + u_2)/2$ and the value of

$$s_3 = A(u_3)$$

is found. Now we know that by definition, given s_α, the value of u_α that we seek is given by:

$$s_\alpha = A(u_\alpha)$$

so by the monotonicity of $A(\ )$ if $s_3 < s_\alpha$ then $u_3 < u_\alpha$ and the solution must lie in the upper subinterval. Similarly if $s_3 > s_\alpha$ the solution lies in the lower subinterval (Figure 15.3). Starting with the interval $[0, 1]$ this process is repeated until the variation of the arclength over the interval within which s_α lies is sufficiently small.

Step 2 requires the definition of arclength $s = A(u)$. The geometrical interpretation of arclength in cartesian coordinates is now given. Let

$$Q(u) = (x(u), y(u), z(u))$$

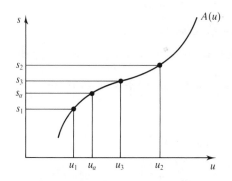

Figure 15.3 Interval bisection.

then the element of arclength ds between points $Q(u)$ and $Q(u + du)$ is given by (Figure 15.4):

$$ds = \left(dx^2 + dy^2 + dz^2\right)^{1/2}$$

$$= \left(\left(\frac{dx}{du}\right)^2 + \left(\frac{dy}{du}\right)^2 + \left(\frac{dz}{du}\right)^2\right)^{1/2} du$$

Integrating this equation from an initial fixed point on $Q(u)$, say u_0, gives us the arclength:

$$s(u) = \int_{u_0}^{u} \left(\left(\frac{dx}{du}\right)^2 + \left(\frac{dy}{du}\right)^2 + \left(\frac{dz}{du}\right)^2\right)^{1/2} du \qquad (15.1)$$

which is the distance along the curve from the point $Q(u_0)$ to the point $Q(u)$. Since we are considering cubics we can write:

$$Q(u) = \mathbf{a}u^3 + \mathbf{b}u^2 + \mathbf{c}u + \mathbf{d}$$

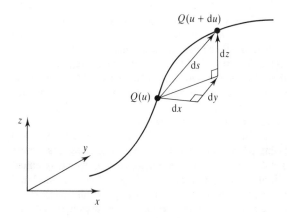

Figure 15.4 Geometric definition of arclength ds.

and

$$x(u) = a_x u^3 + b_x u^2 + c_x u + d_x$$

similarly for $y(u)$ and $z(u)$. Equation (15.1) reduces to:

$$s(u) = \int_{u_0}^{u} \left(Au^4 + Bu^3 + Cu^2 + Du + E \right)^{1/2} du \qquad (15.2)$$

where:

$$A = 9\left(a_x^2 + a_y^2 + a_z^2\right)$$
$$B = 12\left(a_x b_x + a_y b_y + a_z b_z\right)$$
$$C = 6\left(a_x c_x + a_y c_y + a_z c_z\right) + 4\left(b_x^2 + b_y^2 + b_z^2\right)$$
$$D = 4\left(b_x c_x + b_y c_y + b_z c_z\right)$$
$$E = c_x^2 + c_y^2 + c_z^2$$

Now this function will not integrate so we need to choose a numerical routine. For simplicity we choose the extended Simpson's rule, where the interval $[a, b]$ over which we integrate is subdivided into an even number of n subintervals of width h. The integrand is evaluated at these points and the result is given by:

$$\int_a^b f(u)\,du = h/3 \; (f_0 + 4f_1 + 2f_2 + 4f_3 + \ldots + 2f_{n-2}$$
$$+ 4f_{n-1} + f_n) + 0(h^4)$$

where:

$$f_i = f(u_i) \qquad u_i = a + \frac{i}{n}(b-a) \qquad \text{and } h = \frac{1}{n}$$

So far we have only considered arclength over a single curve segment. For a composite curve $Q(u)$ consisting of several curve segments, there is a minor complication in that we need to precompute a table of u against accumulated arclength $Q(u)$ at the segment boundaries in order to find the relevant segment to begin our search. Let u_i denote the start of segment i then the entry of the table at i will contain u_i and $Q(u_i)$, the sum of the arclengths of the preceding segments. Given a value s_α the table is searched to find the relevant segment i such that $Q(u_i) < s_\alpha < Q(u_{i+1})$. The solution thus lies in the segment i between u_i and u_{i+1} and we therefore start our search here, after converting to the local arclength parameter given by $s_\alpha - Q(u_i)$.

In Listing 15.1 *ArclengthPoint(spline,s,pt)* returns a point *pt* on the spline which has arclength s where $s \in [0, 1]$. The routine *SetLengths( )*, which is called initially, sets up the table *seg_lengths [ ]* of accumulated arclengths referred to in the previous paragraph. *Arclength(ustart,uend)* returns the arclength of the current curve segment across the interval [*ustart,uend*]. *SegCoef(spline,i)* sets up the relevant coefficients for the current segment, indexed by i, to be used by *ArcIntegrand( )* which is the integrand of Equation (15.2).

Numerically, a more sophisticated technique for computing arclength can be found in [GUEN90] which addresses the question of accuracy more rigorously. The evaluation of $s = A(u)$ in step 2 is done using a numerical integration technique based on Gaussian quadrature that recursively subdivides the curve. A table of subdivision points is created, each entry containing a pair of values (u_i, s_i). (Here u_i is not restricted to segment boundaries but can be any value along the curve.) Adaptive integration is employed to build the table – the interval of integration is divided in half. The sum of the two integrations over the subhalves is compared to the integration over the whole interval. If the difference is less than the desired accuracy the subdivision is repeated; if not, an entry into the table is made. This ensures that the arclength is represented to the same degree of accuracy across the entire length of the curve. After building this table subsequent arclength calculations are greatly decreased. For a given u the relevant interval $[u_i, u_{i+1}]$ such that $u_i < u < u_{i+1}$, is located and the remaining integration over $[u_i, u]$ can be done using the more efficient nonadaptive Gaussian quadrature. The inversion of

$$s = A(u)$$

in step 1 is replaced by the Newton–Raphson iteration of $f(u)$, where:

$$f(u) = s - A(u)$$

It converges rapidly and requires little calculation of each iteration, although it is unstable when the space curve's derivatives approach zero.

Finally, the reader should note that in certain circumstances both of the above methods may prove unsatisfactory. An animator editing an animation sequence by continually refining the curves and viewing the results may find that the time taken by the above routines between these iterative cycles is frustratingly long. A cheaper method must therefore be sought. One such method found to be useful in the authors' experience is based on forward differencing. Forward differencing provides a computationally economic way of generating a sequence of points, $Q(i\Delta u)$ for $i = 0,1,2\ldots$ on a curve spaced at equal intervals Δu of u. Using forward differences a table can be built up of accumulated chordlength against u, entry i corresponding to $u_i = i\Delta u$ contains

Listing 15.1   ArcLengthPoint.c

```
        float  total_length;
        float  seg_lengths[MAX_NO];

void  ArcLengthPoint(spline,s,pt)
float  spline[][3];
float  s;
float  pt[3];
{
        float  ArcLength();
        float  uL=0.,uR=1.,usearch;
        float  segment_dist,ssearch;
        int  segment_no=0;

        /* Find curve segment within which s lies */
        do segment_no++;
        while  (seg_lengths[segment_no] < s);
        segment_no--;
        segment_dist = total_length*(s-seg_lengths[segment_no]);

        /* Set up necessary coefficients relvant to that segment */
        SegCoef(spline,segment_no);

        /* Search segment for local parameter tsearch that globally gives
        us an arc length within SEARCH_TOL of s */
        do {

                usearch = (uL+uR)/2.;
                ssearch = ArcLength(uL,usearch);

                if (segment_dist < ssearch+SEARCH_TOL) uR = usearch;
                else {
                        uL = usearch;
                        segment_dist -= ssearch;
                }
        } while ((segment_dist>ssearch+SEARCH_TOL)||(segment_dist<ssearch-SEARCH_TOL));
        GetPointOnSpline(usearch,pt);

}

float  ArcLength(ustart,uend)
float  ustart,uend;
{
        float  ArcIntegrand();
        float  h,sum,u;
        int  i;

        /* Compute arc length using the extended Simpson's rule */
        h=(uend-ustart)/(float)ITERATION_COUNT;
        sum=0.;
        u=ustart+h;

        for (i=2;i<=ITERATION_COUNT;i++) {
```

Listing 15.1   *(cont.)*

```
                    if  (!(i&1))  sum  +=  4.0*ArcIntegrand(u);
                    else  sum  +=  2.0*ArcIntegrand(u);
                    u  +=  h;
          }
          return(h*(ArcIntegrand(ustart)+sum+ArcIntegrand(uend))/3.0);
}

void  SetLengths(spline,npoints)
float  spline[3];
int  npoints;
{
          int  i,no_segments;
          float  arclength,ArcLength();

          no_segments  =  npoints  −  3;
          arclength  =  0.;

          seg_lengths[0]  =  0;
          for  (i=0;i<no_segments;i++)  {

                    SegCoef(spline,i);
                    arclength  +=  ArcLength(0.,1.);
                    seg_lengths[i+1]  =  arclength;
          }
          total_length  =  arclength;
          for  (i=0;i<=no_segments;i++)  seg_lengths[i]  /=  total_length;
}
```

$$\sum_{j=1}^{i} d_j \qquad d_j = |\varrho(u_j) - \varrho(u_{j-1})|$$

This is shown schematically in Figure 15.5. Finding u given s reduces to finding the relevant chord within which s must lie and linearly interpolating along it. (Note that in the limit $\Delta u \to 0$ this procedure approaches arclength parametrization.)

In practice this method is considerably faster than the other two approaches, particularly if the forward dif-

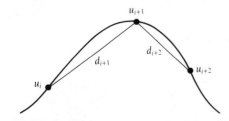

Figure 15.5   Forward differencing and accumulated chord length.

ference scheme is hardcoded into matrix form as part of a dedicated graphics engine. The coarse nature of the approximation, which becomes apparent when moving slowly along relatively long space curves, requires one of the more accurate methods to be employed when the animator, satisfied with his adjustments, wishes to render the final sequence.

Having achieved our reparametrization of a curve in terms of arclength, the motion of an object moving with a specified velocity along the curve becomes meaningful and so we can now turn our attention to the velocity curve.

15.3.5 Velocity curves

The velocity curve is a two-dimensional spline of distance travelled, or arclength, against time. We write:

$V(u) = (t, s)$ $t = T(u)$ and $s = S(u)$

Now finding the value of s given a value of t is not straightforward since the curve is parametrized in terms of u. Just as in the preceding section, a reparametrization is required that reparametrizes the velocity curve as a function of time. Again, as in the preceding section we avoid the inversion

$$u = T^{-1}(t)$$

replacing it with a search for a value of u that has a time close to the required value. Thus:

$$u_\alpha = T^{-1}(t_\alpha)$$

becomes a search for a value of u such that

$$t = T(u)$$

lies within a certain tolerance of t_α, and so the corresponding value for the arclength $s(u)$ will be sufficiently close to the required $s(u_\alpha)$.

Listing 15.2 gives the routine *Along2Arc(t)* that returns a value of s given the value of t on the curve (t, s), where:

$$t = a_0 u^3 + b_0 u^2 + c_0 u + d_0$$

and

$$s = a_1 u^3 + b_1 u^2 + c_1 u + d_0$$

Once again a simple bisection method is an appropriate search strategy. Referring back to the previous section and comparing Figure 15.6 with Figure 15.3 we can see that this requires that the function

$$t = T(u)$$

is strictly monotonically increasing. That is:

if $u_1 < u_2$ then $T(u_1) < T(u_2)$

Fortunately this requirement is not restrictive since, should monotonicity not hold, that is, should $T(u)$ decrease with respect to u, then the velocity curve will double back on itself as shown in Figure 15.7. This implies that an object being driven by this velocity curve is at more than one position at a given time – a physically meaningless state of affairs. Note that this restriction is not the same as requiring the velocity curve to be monotonic with respect to u. Under this scheme, velocity curves such as that shown in Figure 15.8 are perfectly 'legal'. An object being driven by a velocity curve of this

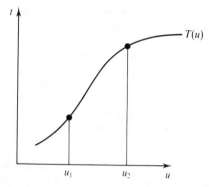

Figure 15.6 Bisection can be applied to $T(u)$ in the same manner as Figure 15.3.

Listing 15.2 Along2Arc.c

```
float  Along2Arc(t)
float  t;
{
           float  uL=0.,uR=1.;
           float  s,usearch,tsearch;

           do {
                    usearch  =  (uL+uR)/2.;
                    tsearch  =  usearch*(c[0]+usearch*(b[0]+usearch*a[0]))+d[0];
                    if  (t < tsearch+SEARCHTOL)  uR  =  usearch;
                    else  uL  =  usearch;
           } while ((t > tsearch+SEARCHTOL) || (t < tsearch−SEARCHTOL));
           s  =  usearch*(c[1]+usearch*(b[1]+usearch*a[1]))+d[1];
           return(s);
}
```

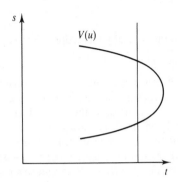

Figure 15.7 A double-valued velocity curve: a physically meaningless state of affairs.

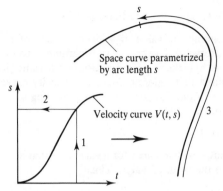

Figure 15.9 The sequence of operations required to find a point on the space curve at a given point t in time.

form along a space curve would start at the beginning of the path with a nonzero speed, gradually slow down and come to rest at the maximum of $V(u)$, and then start to move back to the beginning again increasing its speed as it did so.

To summarize, given a space curve and a velocity curve, the sequence of operations required to find the position along the space curve at a given time is shown schematically in Figure 15.9. Starting at t we find s from the velocity curve and then move s along the space curve. The strengths of such a scheme are as follows:

1. It may or may not be used as a key parameter interpolation system. A great deal of attention has been given to such systems – in your authors' opinion too much, since for many animations the specification of the exact state of the motion at a given frame is not always critical. Looser methods of spline construction that avoid interpolation also avoid the problems

with interpolating through a nonuniformly spaced set of key parameters (Section 3.6).

2. The space curve and velocity curve, whether interpolated or not, are specified independently. Different velocity curves can be tried on the same space curve and vice versa. Modification of the motion can be made without affecting the space curve.

3. Working with velocity curves is intuitive. Useful curves can be stored by the animator and used across a wide variety of applications. Figure 15.10 shows the working of one such 'library' velocity curve – the ease-in, ease-out curve and its effect on the space curve. Equal intervals along the time axis generate, frame for frame, corresponding positions along the space curve. You can see how the arclength intervals decrease as we approach either end of the curve. This corresponds to starting from zero velocity and gently accelerating to a maximum speed at the centre of the curve, then gently decelerating back down to rest.

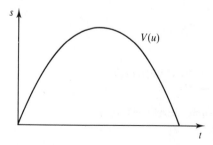

Figure 15.8 Monotonicity of $T(u)$ with respect to u does not imply monotonicity of $V(u)$ with respect to u.

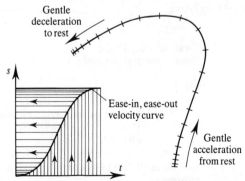

Figure 15.10 The working of the ease-in, ease-out velocity curve. Equal intervals in time map onto the intervals shown on the space curve.

15.3.6 General kinetic control

The velocity curve of the preceding section can be generalized to drive any motion parameter; there is no reason why it should be restricted to arclength alone. The term 'motion parameter' then encompasses anything that moves in the animation sequence apart from the usual kinetic variables such as position and orientation. Movement could also include colour and transparency, for example, in short anything that is representable by numbers the animator may animate. Moreover, if the parameter the velocity curve drives is fed into a spline of motion parameters, just as we fed arclength into a spline of key positions, then all the advantages enumerated above are automatically inherited.

Steketee and Badler [STEK85] were among the first to recognize the power of specifying a velocity curve, which they call a 'kinetic spline', to drive an independently splined motion parameter. Termed the 'double interpolant' method, they created the following two interpolations:

1. *The 'position' spline* Let the motion parameter to be interpolated be ϕ. ϕ is specified at n key values, $\phi_0, \ldots, \phi_{n-1}$. The position spline is constructed by assigning a keyframe number to each key value and interpolating through the resulting tuples $(\phi_0, 0)$, $\ldots, (\phi_{n-1}, n-1)$.

2. *The kinetic spline* Each keyframe number is assigned a time. The kinetic spline interpolates through the resulting pairs $(0, t_0)$, $\ldots$, $(n-1, t_{n-1})$.

Calculating a value for the motion parameter proceeds in a manner identical to the above. The kinetic spline provides a keyframe number given a time. The keyframe number is then fed into the position spline to give a value for the motion parameter. Steketee also includes a discussion of a slightly higher level of control than just interpolation, concerned with the transition between one motion of an object ending and another beginning. Our arclength parametrization/velocity method above can be thought of as falling into the double interpolant class – where the intermediate interpolant is arclength along a space curve instead of keyframe number.

15.3.7 Basis considerations

So far we have made no mention of what type of spline, or what basis we should use. The above techniques are sufficiently general to allow for any basis. The B-spline is, however, most commonly used since smooth motion implies second-derivative continuity which, as we saw in Section 3.5, the B-spline guarantees. Furthermore, the local control property of the B-spline enables the animator to make small adjustments to the animation without the adjustments affecting the entire sequence. Work has been done, however, on developing a class of splines whose properties are particularly relevant to a keyframing animation system and it is to these that we now turn our attention.

Following the development of Kochanek [KOCH84] we start by considering the Hermite basis. (For a wider ranging treatment of interpolating splines the reader is referred to [DUFF86].) A Hermite cubic spline segment interpolates two of its control points. The remaining two specifications are not positions but vectors that determine the tangent of the curve at the interpolated points. If the segment consists of control points at (p_0, p_1, p_2, p_3) then the tangent at p_0 is given by p_2 and the tangent at p_1 is given by p_3. (*Caveat lector*: there is a confusion in the literature concerning the order in which the points and tangents that make up the basis functions appear. Different sources [FARI90] and [UPST89] quote different orders.) Figure 15.11 shows the effect of varying the magnitude of the tangents on the shape of the curve. This dependency gives the basis the rather unpleasant property of not being affine invariant. The basis functions are:

$$b_0(u) = 2u^3 - 3u^2 + 1$$
$$b_1(u) = -2u^3 + 3u^2$$
$$b_2(u) = u^3 - 2u^2 + u$$
$$b_3(u) = u^3 - u^2$$

A keyframing system supplies n key positions $P_0, \ldots, P_{n-1}$ but Hermite interpolation requires the tangents

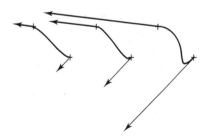

Figure 15.11 The effect of varying tangent magnitude on a Hermite curve segment.

$T_0, \ldots, T_{n-1}$ to be specified in order to make up the curve consisting of $n - 1$ segments $(P_0, P_1, T_0, T_1), \ldots,$ $(P_{n-2}, P_{n-1}, T_{n-2}, T_{n-1})$ (Figure 15.12). Kochanek suggests making the tangent T_i at P_i a weighted sum of the source chord $P_i - P_{i-1}$ and the destination chord $P_{i+1} - P_i$ (Figure 15.13). The parametrization of this weighting into tension, bias and continuity is done to allow the animator to fine-tune the animation, either globally or locally, without changing the key positions. Figure 15.14 shows a series of splines, each derived from the same set of key positions. The differences in shape is due entirely to altering the tension and bias parameters, the working of which we shall now describe.

The tension parameter, t, controls how sharply the curve bends at a key position by controlling the magnitude of the tangent at that position:

$$T_i = \left[\frac{1-t}{2}\right]\left(\left(P_{i+1} - P_i\right) + \left(P_i - P_{i-1}\right)\right)$$

The default, $t = 0$, is the Catmull–Rom spline (Figure 15.14(a)). Increasing the tension reduces the magnitude of the tangent vector down to zero at $t = 1$ (Figure 15.14(b)), where the curve is at its tightest. For $t > 1$ the curve will loop at the key position. Decreasing the tension

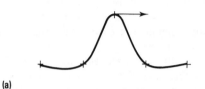

(a)

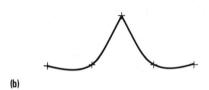

(b)

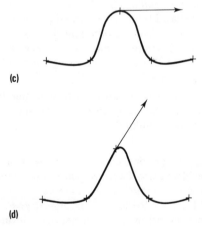

(c)

(d)

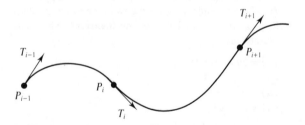

Figure 15.12   Tangent vectors over two segments of a curve.

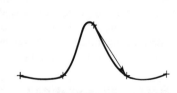

(e)

Figure 15.14   The effect of the tension and bias parameters on the interpolating spline. (a) Default tension and bias; (b) Increasing tension; (c) Decreasing tension; (d) Increasing bias; (e) Decreasing bias.

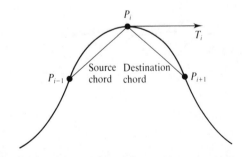

Figure 15.13   Source and destination chords for P_i.

causes the curve to slacken, or balloon out, at the key position. Figure 15.14(c) is at $t = -1$.

The bias parameter b controls the relative weighting of the source and destination chord, which dictates the direction of the tangent at a key position. Assuming $t = 0$, we have:

$$T_i = \left(\frac{1+b}{2}\right)(P_i - P_{i-1}) + \left(\frac{1-b}{2}\right)(P_{i+1} - P_i)$$

When $b = 1$ (Figure 15.14(d)) the tangent vector's direction coincides with the source chord; $b = 0$ is the default again (Figure 15.14(a)) and $b = -1$ aligns the tangent vector to the destination chord (Figure 15.14(e)).

The bias parameter simulates the traditional animation effect of following through an action as 'overshooting' the key position ($b = 1$) or exaggerating a movement by 'undershooting' a key ($b = -1$).

Implicit so far in our description of Hermite interpolation is parametric continuity between adjacent segments. The curve, however, can be broken at its key positions in which case separate tangents have to be specified for the end of one segment and the start of the next. Specifying a different tangent either side of a key position will reduce the continuity at that point. If the tangents have the same direction but different magnitudes the continuity is reduced to G^1; different directions reduce it further to C^0. Kochanek [KOCH84] introduces a continuity parameter that controls the difference between the two tangents either side of a key position of a broken curve.

The tension, bias and continuity parameters are all very well for specifying the shape of the curve, but what about controlling the speed of the motion? A major weakness of this scheme is that motion specification is secondary to shape specification. Assuming parametric continuity between segments, the time t is made to vary as the parameter u of the curve $Q(u)$. Position P_i is specified at frame t_i, where $P_i = Q(t_i)$ and the intervals between frames t_i and t_{i+1} are generated by stepping along the segment i at equal parametric intervals of width

$$\Delta u = \frac{1}{t_{i+1} - t_i}$$

Now since the Hermite is uniformly parametrized, that is, the parametric lengths of each segment are the same, it follows that the keyframes must also be equally spaced – a severe restriction to place on any animator.

In order to allow for a nonuniform spacing of keyframes, if time varies as the curve parameter, we must allow for a nonuniformly parametrized curve, that is, let the curve segments have parametric intervals of different length. Let us consider just such a curve with global parameter U and key positions at $t_0, \ldots, t_{n-1}$. The local parameter of segment i is given by:

$$u = \frac{U - t_i}{t_{i+1} - t_i}$$

Parametric continuity of the curve at $U = t_i$ implies that dQ/dU is the same if we approach it from either side of P_i. That is:

$$\left.\frac{dQ}{dU}\right|_{u \to t_i} = \left.\frac{dQ}{dU}\right|_{t_i \leftarrow u} \tag{15.3}$$

but by the chain rule of differentiation:

$$\frac{dQ}{dU} = \frac{dQ}{du} \cdot \frac{du}{dU} = \frac{1}{t_{i+1} - t_i}\frac{dQ}{du}$$

where i is the segment within which U falls. Substituting this into (15.3) gives:

$$\left.\frac{1}{t_i - t_{i-1}}\frac{dQ}{du}\right|_{u \to t_i} = \left.\frac{1}{t_{i+1} - t_i}\frac{dQ}{du}\right|_{t_i \leftarrow u}$$

that is, there is a discontinuity in the local derivatives across the key position by an amount given by:

$$\frac{dQ/du\,|_{t_i \leftarrow u}}{dQ/du\,|_{u \to t_i}} = \frac{t_{i+1} - t_i}{t_i - t_{i-1}} \tag{15.4}$$

The procedure for accommodating nonuniformly spaced keyframes is to construct the animation as if the keyframes were uniformly spaced and then to break the curve at each key position by weighting the tangents at the start and end of each segment i by amounts

$$\frac{2(t_{i+1} - t_i)}{t_{i+1} - t_{i-1}} \quad \text{and} \quad \frac{2(t_{i+1} - t_i)}{t_{i+2} - t_i}$$

This result is quoted in [KOCH84] and also in [DUFF86] where the above spline formulation is put into a more general class of interpolating splines. These weights satisfy Equation (15.4) showing that if the geometrically continuous broken curve were reparametrized to become parametrically continuous (as, by definition, it must) then this new parametrization would coincide with the nonuniformly spaced keyframe parametrization of the above.

These complications arise because the motion specification is not properly divorced from the path specification. Moreover, as we have seen, driving the motion via u directly has a disadvantage in that it is impossible to get an object moving with constant speed along the path. Only the rigorous approach of arclength reparametrization, which treats the specification of path and motion completely separately, can provide this.

15.3.8 Parametrization of orientation

This section deals with the problems that are encountered when parametrizing the space of all possible orientations of an object, where all orientations, or rotations, take place about a point fixed in space with respect to that object. We begin by looking at a common, but as we shall see somewhat inadequate, method for animating rotation – Euler angles.

Euler angles

Historically, the most popular parametrization of orientation space, well established through appearing in standard maths and physics textbooks, has been in terms of Euler angles, where a general rotation is described as a sequence of rotations about three mutually orthogonal coordinate axes fixed in space. (Note that the rotations are applied to the space and not to the axes.) This has led to animators setting up general orientation as a composite of these axis rotations which we will call 'rolls': x-roll for rotation about the x-axis, y-roll for rotation about the y-axis and z-roll for rotation about the z-axis. These rolls, in homogeneous matrix notation, give rise to the principal rotation matrices shown in Figure 15.15.

The precise order in which these rolls are applied lead to different definitions of the parametrization of orientation in terms of Euler angles. These considerations do not concern us here. In general, an angular displacement has three degrees of freedom, and since each principle rotation matrix has but one degree of freedom, a minimum of three principle rotations must be combined to represent a general angular displacement. Let us choose an x-roll, followed by a y-roll, followed by a z-roll. Our parametrization of orientation space is thus a general rotation matrix $R(\theta_1, \theta_2, \theta_3)$ in terms of the Euler angles $\theta_1, \theta_2, \theta_3$ given by:

$$
\begin{bmatrix}
c_2 c_3 & c_2 s_3 & -s_2 & 0 \\
s_1 s_2 c_3 - c_1 s_3 & s_1 s_2 s_3 + c_1 c_3 & s_1 c_2 & 0 \\
c_1 s_2 c_3 + s_1 s_3 & c_1 s_2 s_3 - s_1 c_3 & c_1 c_2 & 0 \\
0 & 0 & 0 & 1
\end{bmatrix}
$$

where:

$$s_i = \sin \theta_i \quad \text{and} \quad c_i = \cos \theta_i$$

In general there are 12 possible ways in which to define a rotation in terms of Euler angles, each one resulting in a different form for the above rotation matrix.

Because of its historical popularity, computer animation systems were quick to use Euler angles as parameters for animating orientation. There are two major drawbacks to this approach, however. The first is a practical

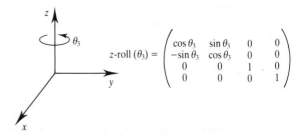

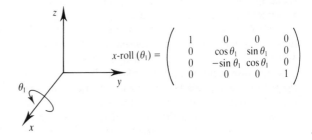

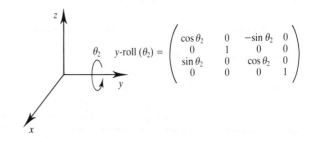

Figure 15.15 The principal rotation matrices.

problem often encountered by animators trying to set up an arbitrary orientation using Euler angles, and the second is a mathematically deep objection to their use when interpolating orientation. Both of these problems occur because Euler angles ignore the interaction of the rolls about the separate axes. As we shall see these rolls are not independent of each other.

Euler angles and Gimbal lock

'Gimbal lock' is a term derived from a mechanical problem that arises in the gimbal mechanism used to support a compass or gyroscope. These generally consist of three concentric frames or rings and under certain rotations a degree of freedom is lost – the mechanism exhibits gimbal lock.

Suppose an animator uses the above parametrization to set up an arbitrary orientation. First, the animator applies an x-roll, then a y-roll and finally a z-roll in order to move an object into a required orientation. Suppose further that during this process the animator innocently specifies a y-roll of $\pi/2$. In dismay he will discover that the subsequent rotation about the z-axis has an effect that is no different to rotating about the x-axis initially. In order to understand this consider the effect a y-roll has on the x-axis, about which we have already performed a rotation of amount θ_1. Although, as you will remember, the rolls act on points in the space – we are not rotating the coordinate axes which remain fixed – we can still talk about the *effect* on the x-axis. This is because the rolls are applied in a fixed order and subsequent rolls have the *effect* of rotating in space the axes about which the preceding rolls have been applied. We track the effect a y-roll of $\pi/2$ has on the preceding x-roll by rotating the x-axis as if it were embedded in the object. Thus the effect of a y-roll of $\pi/2$ is to rotate the x-axis to x' (Figure 15.16), which is in alignment with the z-axis. Consequently any z-roll of θ_3 could have been achieved by an x-roll of $-\theta_3$. Effectively, now that we are in this configuration with the x- and z-axes aligned, it is impossible to rotate the object about the x-axis.

This sudden loss of a degree of freedom is extremely irritating to the animator. Mathematically, the animator has unwittingly stumbled upon a singularity in the parametrization, where θ_1 and θ_3 become associated with the same degree of freedom. To see the reason for this mathematically, we set $s_2 = 1$ and $c_2 = 0$ into the rotation matrix, reducing it to $R(\theta_1, \pi/2, \theta_3)$ given by:

$$\begin{bmatrix} 0 & 0 & -1 & 0 \\ \sin(\theta_1 - \theta_3) & \cos(\theta_1 - \theta_3) & 0 & 0 \\ \cos(\theta_1 - \theta_3) & -\sin(\theta_1 - \theta_3) & 0 & 0 \\ 0 & 0 & 0 & 1 \end{bmatrix}$$

Using different formulations of Euler angles in the general rotation matrix does not remove this singularity.

Euler angles and interpolation

We now consider the problem of interpolation when Euler angles are used. Suppose the three Euler angles are

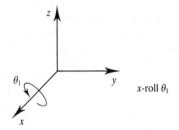

x-roll θ_1

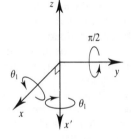

x-roll θ_1 followed by y-roll $\pi/2$

x axis effectively gets rotated to x' axis

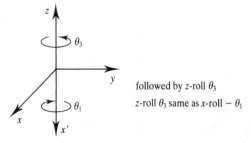

followed by z-roll θ_3

z-roll θ_3 same as x-roll $-\theta_1$

Figure 15.16 Illustrating the loss of one degree of freedom – gimbal lock.

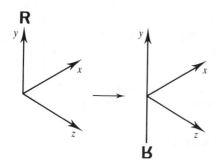

Figure 15.17 The start and finish positions for the animation of the block letter 'R'.

used as key parameters in an interpolating system. Suppose also that key orientation i is described by the triple $(\Theta_{1i}, \Theta_{2i}, \Theta_{3i})$ and interpolation is carried out by interpolating through the three Euler angles separately in a manner identical to interpolating translation, that is, by separately interpolating through the x, y and z components of key positions (x_i, y_i, z_i). This means that at a certain frame t, the interpolated values $(\Theta_1(t), \Theta_2(t), \Theta_3(t))$ are combined to produce the rotation matrix $R(\Theta_1(t), \Theta_2(t), \Theta_3(t))$ which is applied to the object. There is a problem with this approach, however. The hidden assumption behind such a scheme is that rotations act just like translations – but they do not. That this is so should be apparent from the fact that rotation involves multiplication, whereas translations only involve addition. Moreover, as is well known, rotation matrices do not commute in multiplication, whereas translation matrices do under addition.

Consideration of a specific example will reveal the inadequacy of the Euler angle parametrization more clearly. Let our object be a block letter 'R' and let it be initially offset from the origin along the y-axis by a

nonzero amount. The final orientation is the reflection of the object in the x, z-plane as shown in Figure 15.17. The animator's task is to set up an animation that rotates the letter from the start to the final orientation. There is more than one way to achieve this movement. One way would be a single rotation of π about the x-axis (Figure 15.18(a)). An alternative is to first perform a y-roll of π followed by a z-roll of π (Figure 15.18(b)). Both routes reach the end position but get there in different ways. Generating inbetweens via linear interpolation to give rotation matrices for the intermediate frames gives us the sequence of rotation matrices:

$$R(0, 0, 0), \ldots, R(\pi t, 0, 0), \ldots, R(\pi, 0, 0) \quad t \in [0, 1]$$

for the first route, and:

$$R(0, 0, 0), \ldots, R(0, \pi t, \pi t), \ldots, R(0, \pi, \pi)$$

for the second route. The effect of these two sequences for our example is shown in Figures 15.19(a) and (b). Clearly, the two moves are very different; the first produces a simple steady rotation, whereas the second both rotates about the y-axis and simultaneously twists about the z-axis. In general, specifying orientation moves in this manner can easily produce such contorted movements, as the object is only allowed to twist about separate coordinate axes.

Although this example is somewhat contrived, it should be clear that it represents a dilemma for the animator. Depending on the choice of principal rotations there is more than one way to get from one key orientation to another. Compare this to interpolating translation between successive key positions in cartesian coordinates. The movement is always the same. If linear interpolation is employed, for example, the move is always along a straight line from one key position to the other. Using Euler angles for interpolation to get from

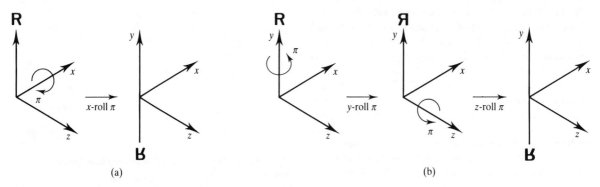

(a)   (b)

Figure 15.18 The two routes for the animation of the block letter 'R'.

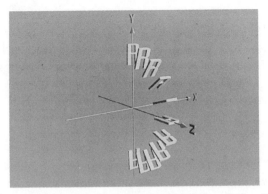 

Figure 15.19 Euler angle parametrization. (a) A single x-roll of π. (b) A y-roll of π followed by a z-roll of π.

one orientation to another is not unique. Why is there this difference? The answer lies in the fact that the components of cartesian coordinates are truly independent of each other, whereas Euler angles are not. Interpolating Euler angles treats them as if they were independent of each other and completely ignores the effect they have on each other. The animator is forced into specifying orientation as a composition of rotations about three separate axes, the order of which must be strictly observed. Moreover, different coordinate systems will produce different moves through identical key orientations. We conclude that Euler angle interpolation produces a motion as inappropriate as that obtained by interpolating position through key positions specified in spherical polar coordinates as opposed to cartesian coordinates.

Euler's theorem tells us that it is possible to get from one orientation to any other by a simple steady rotation about a single axis. Interpolation between two key orientations should produce precisely this simple rotation. Euler rotation is inadequate because, as we have seen, given two successive rotations the notation does not provide close expressions to determine the angle and the axis of the resultant rotation. What we seek is a parametrization of orientation that can accommodate the interaction of rotations within its working, thereby enabling us to:

1. guarantee a simple steady rotation between any two key orientations, which we know must exist, and

2. define moves that are independent of the choice of the coordinate system.

Luckily such a parametrization exists, but in order to discuss it we need to introduce a notation implied by Euler's theorem – angular displacement.

Angular displacement

We define orientation as an angular displacement given by (θ, n) of an amount about an axis n. Just as we did for Euler angle notation, we shall derive the rotational matrix in terms of this new notation, so instead of $R(\theta_1, \theta_2, \theta_3)$ we write $R(\theta, n)$. Consider the angular displacement acting on a vector r taking it to position Rr as shown in Figure 15.20.

The problem can be decomposed by resolving r into components parallel to n, $r_{\parallel}$, which by definition remains unchanged after rotation, and perpendicular to n, $r_{\perp}$ in the plane passing through r and Rr.

$$r_{\parallel} = (n \cdot r)n$$
$$r_{\perp} = r - (n \cdot r)n$$

$r_{\perp}$ is rotated into position $Rr_{\perp}$. We construct a vector perpendicular to $r_{\perp}$ and lying in the plane. In order to evaluate this rotation, we write:

$$V = n \times r_{\perp} = n \times r$$

So

$$Rr_{\perp} = (\cos \theta)r_{\perp} + (\sin \theta)V$$

hence

$$\begin{aligned} Rr &= Rr_{\parallel} + Rr_{\perp} \\ &= Rr_{\parallel} + (\cos \theta)r_{\perp} + (\sin \theta)V \\ &= (n \cdot r)n + \cos \theta (r - (n \cdot r)n) + (\sin \theta)n \times r \\ &= (\cos \theta)r + (1 - \cos \theta)n(n \cdot r) + (\sin \theta)n \times r \quad \textbf{(15.5)} \end{aligned}$$

And now, we beg the reader's indulgence for an apparent *non sequitur*, the relevance of which will be revealed at the end of the digression.

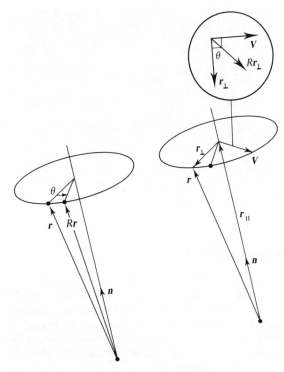

Figure 15.20 Angular displacement (θ, n) of r.

Quaternions

The great mathematician Sir William Hamilton had been interested in complex numbers since the early 1830s. Complex numbers have the form:

$$a + ib$$

where a and b are real and the multiplication rules are:

$$1^2 = 1 \quad \text{and} \quad i^2 = -1$$

These complex numbers define a plane – the complex plane – where one axis is real and the other imaginary. For over 10 years Hamilton tried to extend this concept in order to define a complex volume by searching for a second imaginary axis. Just such a number would have three components: one real and two imaginary. This, however, he could not do. Then, on 16 October 1843, when walking past Broome Bridge in Dublin towards the Royal Irish Academy, where he was to preside over a meeting, Hamilton, in a flash of inspiration, realized that three rather than two imaginary units were needed, with the following properties:

$$i^2 = j^2 = k^2 = -1$$
$$ij = k \quad \text{and} \quad ji = -k$$

with the cyclic permutation $i \rightarrow j \rightarrow k \rightarrow i$. Such was his elation, Hamilton carved these formulae on the side of the bridge and called the number:

$$q = a + bi + cj + dk$$

a 'quaternion'.

For our purposes we shall use the condensed notation:

$$q = (s, v)$$

where:

$$(s, v) = s + v_x i + v_y j + v_z k$$

s is thought of as the scalar part of the quaternion and v the vector part with axes i, j and k. Using the above rules it is easy to derive the following properties. The multiplication of two quaternions:

$$q_1 = (s_1, v_1) \quad \text{and} \quad q_2 = (s_2, v_2)$$

is given by:

$$q_1 q_2 = (s_1 s_2 - v_1 \cdot v_2, \; s_1 v_2 + s_2 v_1 + v_1 \times v_2)$$

The multiplication of two quaternions is thus a quaternion. Mathematically, we have defined a group. Stated somewhat simplistically, a group is just a set of elements with a rule defining their multiplication such that the result of this multiplication is itself an element of that group. Groups can be constructed completely arbitrarily, though a surprising number of groups are relevant to the physical world. We shall see that a subgroup of the quaternion group is closely related to the group of rotations or, more precisely, the group of rotation matrices.

Note that except for the cross product term at the end of the previous equation, it bears a strong similarity to the law of complex multiplication:

$$(a_1 + ib_1)(a_2 + ib_2) = (a_1 a_2 - b_1 b_2) + i(a_1 b_2 + a_2 b_1)$$

The cross product term has the effect of making quaternion multiplication noncommutative.

We define the conjugate of the quaternion:

$$q = (s, v) \text{ to be } \bar{q} = (s, -v)$$

The product of the quaternion with its conjugate defines its magnitude:

$$q\bar{q} = s^2 + |v|^2 = |q|^2$$

Finally, as promised, we come to the point of all this, which is contained in the following properties. Take a pure quaternion (one that has no scalar part):

$p = (0, r)$

and a unit quaternion

$q = (s, v)$ where $q\bar{q} = 1$

and define

$R_q(p) = qpq^{-1}$

Using our multiplication rule, and the fact that $q^{-1} = \bar{q}$ for q of unit magnitude, this expands to:

$R_q(p) = (0, (s^2 - v \cdot v)r + 2v(v \cdot r) + 2\,sv \times r)$ **(15.6)**

This can be simplified further since q is of unit magnitude and we can write:

$q = (\cos\theta, \sin\theta n)$ $|n| = 1$

Substituting into Equation (15.6) gives:

$$R_q(p) = (0, (\cos^2\theta - \sin^2\theta)r + 2\sin^2\theta\, n(n \cdot r) \\ + 2\cos\theta \sin\theta\, n \times r) \\ = (0, \cos2\theta\, r + (1 - \cos2\theta)\, n(n \cdot r) \\ + \sin2\theta\, n \times r)$$ **(15.7)**

Now compare this with Equation (15.5). You will notice that aside from a factor of 2 appearing in the angle they are identical in form. What can we conclude from this? The act of rotating a vector *r* by an angular displacement (θ, n) is the same as taking this angular displacement, 'lifting' it into quaternion space, by representing it as the unit quaternion $(\cos(\theta/2), \sin(\theta/2)\, n)$ and performing the operation $q(\ )\bar{q}$ on the quaternion $(0, r)$. We could therefore parametrize orientation in terms of the four parameters:

$\cos(\theta/2), \sin(\theta/2)\, n_x, \sin(\theta/2)\, n_y, \sin(\theta/2)\, n_z$

using quaternion algebra to manipulate the components.

In practice this would seem an extremely perverse way of going about things were it not for one very important advantage afforded by the quaternion parametrization. Two quaternions multiplied together, each of unit magnitude, will result in a single quaternion of unit magnitude. If we use unit quaternions to represent rotations then this translates to two successive rotations producing a single rotation. Now a variation of Euler's theorem states that two successive rotations is equivalent to one rotation. So we can see that inherent in the algebra of the quaternion group is Euler's theorem. The single steady rotation between successive keyframes that we seek is provided for us automatically by the rules particular to the parametrization and contained in the statement:

$R_{q''} = R_q R_{q'}$ where $q'' = qq'$

Let us now return to our example of Figure 15.17 to see how this works in practice. The first single *x*-roll of π is represented by the quaternion:

$(\cos(\pi/2), \sin(\pi/2)\,(1,0,0)) = (0,(1,0,0))$

Similarly, a *y*-roll of π and a *z*-roll of π are given by $(0,(0,1,0))$ and $(0,(0,0,1))$ respectively. Now the effect of a *y*-roll of π followed by a *z*-roll of π can be represented by the single quaternion formed by multiplying these two quaternions together:

$$(0,(0,1,0))\,(0,(0,0,1)) = (0,(0,1,0) \times (0,0,1)) \\ = (0,(1,0,0))$$

which is the single *x*-roll of π. From this we can see that the cross product term in (15.7) can be thought of as correcting for the interdependence of the separate axes that is ignored by Euler's angle notation.

An additional advantage afforded by using quaternions is that the gimbal lock singularity, which is a consequence of using three parameters to parametrize orientation, disappears.

Much of what now follows is based on the work of the researcher who brought quaternions to the attention of the computer graphics community. The interested reader is referred to [SHOE85] and [SHOE87] for further detail. The latter reference concerns itself more with the practical details of an implementation.

Interpolating using quaternions

Given the superiority of quaternion parametrization over Euler angle parametrization, this section covers the issue of interpolating rotation in quaternion space. Consider an animator sitting at a workstation and interactively setting up a sequence of key orientations by whatever method is appropriate. This is usually done with the principal rotation operations, but now the restrictions that were placed on the animator when using Euler angles, namely using a fixed number of principal rotations in a fixed order for each key, can be removed. In general, each key will be represented as a single rotation matrix. This sequence of matrices will then be converted into a sequence of quaternions. Interpolation between key quaternions is performed and this produces a sequence of inbetween quaternions, which are then converted back into rotation matrices. The matrices are then applied to the object. The fact that a quaternion interpolation is being used is transparent to the animator.

Moving into and out of quaternion space

The implementation of such a scheme requires us to move into and out of quaternion space, that is, to go from a general rotation matrix to a quaternion and vice versa. It can be shown that the effect of taking a unit quaternion:

$$q = \left(\cos(\Theta/2), \sin(\Theta/2)\ n\right)$$

and performing the operation $q(\ )q^{-1}$ on a vector is the same as applying the following rotation matrix to that vector:

$$\begin{bmatrix} 1 - 2Y^2 - 2Z^2 & 2XY - 2WZ & 2XZ + 2WY & 0 \\ 2XY + 2WZ & 1 - 2X^2 - 2Z^2 & 2YZ - 2WX & 0 \\ 2XZ - 2WY & 2YZ + 2WX & 1 - 2X^2 - 2Y^2 & 0 \\ 0 & 0 & 0 & 1 \end{bmatrix}$$

where the quaternion $(\cos(\Theta/2), \sin(\Theta/2)\ n)$ is written as $(W, (X,Y,Z))$, the notation used in Listing 15.3. By these means then, we can move from quaternion space to rotation matrices. Listing 15.3 gives the conversion from quaternion space to rotation matrix in the routine *quattomat(q, mat)*.

The inverse mapping from a rotation matrix to a quaternion is only slightly more involved. All that is required is to convert a general rotation matrix:

$$\begin{bmatrix} M_{00} & M_{01} & M_{02} & 0 \\ M_{10} & M_{11} & M_{12} & 0 \\ M_{20} & M_{21} & M_{22} & 0 \\ 0 & 0 & 0 & 1 \end{bmatrix}$$

into the matrix format directly above. The resulting quaternion is trivially $(W, (X, Y, Z))$. Given a general rotation matrix the first thing to do is to examine the sum of its diagonal components M_{ii} where $0 \leqslant i \leqslant 3$. This is called the trace of the matrix. From the above format we know:

$$\text{trace} = 1 - 2Y^2 - 2Z^2 + 1 - 2X^2 - 2Z^2 + 1 - 2X^2 - 2Y^2 + 1$$
$$= 4 - 4\left(X^2 + Y^2 + Z^2\right)$$

Since the matrix represents a rotation we know that the corresponding quaternion must be of unit magnitude, that is:

$$X^2 + Y^2 + Z^2 + W^2 = 1$$

and so the trace reduces to $4W^2$. Thus for a 4×4 homogeneous matrix we have:

$$W = \left(\text{trace}\right)^{\frac{1}{2}}$$

The remaining components of the quaternion (X, Y, Z) which, as you will recall, is the axis of rotation scaled by half the sine of the angle of rotation, are obtained by combining diagonally opposite elements of the matrix M_{ij} and M_{ji} where $0 \leqslant i,j \leqslant 2$. We have:

$$X = \frac{M_{21} - M_{12}}{4W} \qquad Y = \frac{M_{02} - M_{20}}{4W} \qquad Z = \frac{M_{10} - M_{01}}{4W}$$

For zero W these equations are undefined and so other combinations of the matrix components, along with the fact that the quaternion is of unit magnitude, are used to determine the axis of rotation. Listing 15.3 gives the code in full for moving from rotation matrices to quaternions in the routine *mattoquat(mat,q)*.

Having outlined our scheme we now discuss how to interpolate in quaternion space. Since a rotation maps onto a quaternion of unit magnitude, the entire group of rotations maps onto the surface of the four-dimensional unit hypersphere in quaternion space. Curves interpolating through key orientations should therefore lie on the surface of this sphere. Consider the simplest case of interpolating between just two key quaternions. A naive, straightforward, linear interpolation between the two keys results in a motion that speeds up in the middle. This is because we are not moving along the surface of the hypersphere but cutting across it. In order to ensure a steady rotation we must employ spherical linear interpolation, where we move along an arc of the geodesic that passes through the two keys. (Figure 15.1 showing the differences between interpolating position and interpolating rotation angle is entirely analogous to this situation.) Technically, the metric of the hypersphere's surface is said to be the same as the angular metric of the rotation group.

The formula for spherical linear interpolation is easy to derive geometrically. Consider the two-dimensional case of two vectors A and B separated by angle Ω and vector P which makes an angle Θ with A as shown in Figure 15.21. P is derived from spherical interpolation between A and B and we write:

$$P = \alpha A + \beta B$$

Trivially, we can solve for α and β given:

$$|P| = 1$$
$$A \cdot B = \cos \Omega$$
$$A \cdot P = \cos \Theta$$

to give:

$$P = A\frac{\sin\left(\Omega - \Theta\right)}{\sin \Omega} + B\frac{\sin \Theta}{\sin \Omega}$$

Listing 15.3 quatlib.c

```
#define  X  0
#define  Y  1
#define  Z  2
#define  W  3
#define  EPSILON  0.00001
#define  HALFPI  1.570796326794895

            int  nxt[3]  =  {Y,Z,X};

void  quattomat(q,mat)
float  q[4];
float  mat[4][4];
{
          double  s,xs,ys,zs,wx,wy,wz,xx,xy,xz,yy,yz,zz;

          s  =  2.0/(q[X]*q[X]  +  q[Y]*q[Y]  +  q[Z]*q[Z]  +  q[W]*q[W]);

          xs  =  q[X]*s;  ys  =  q[Y]*s;  zs  =  q[Z]*s;
          wx  =  q[W]*xs;  wy  =  q[W]*ys;  wz  =  q[W]*zs;
          xx  =  q[X]*xs;  xy  =  q[X]*ys;  xz  =  q[X]*zs;
          yy  =  q[Y]*ys;  yz  =  q[Y]*zs;  zz  =  q[Z]*zs;

          mat[0][0]  =  1.0  -  (yy  +  zz);
          mat[0][1]  =  xy  +  wz;
          mat[0][2]  =  xz  -  wy;

          mat[1][0]  =  xy  -  wz;
          mat[1][1]  =  1.0  -  (xx  +  zz);
          mat[1][2]  =  yz  +  wx;

          mat[2][0]  =  xz  +  wy;
          mat[2][1]  =  yz  -  wx;
          mat[2][2]  =  1.0  -  (xx  +  yy);

          mat[0][3]  =  0.;  mat[1][3]  =  0.;  mat[2][3]  =  0.;  mat[3][3]  =  1.;
          mat[3][0]  =  0.;  mat[3][1]  =  0.;  mat[3][2]  =  0.;

}
void  mattoquat(mat,q)
float  mat[4][4];
float  q[4];
{

          double  tr,s;
          int  i,j,k;

          tr  =  mat[0][0]  +  mat[1][1]  +  mat[2][2];
          if  (tr  >  0.0)  {

                    s  =  sqrt(tr  +  1.0);
                    q[W]  =  s*0.5;
                    s  =  0.5/s;

                    q[X]  =  (mat[1][2]  -  mat[2][1])*s;
                    q[Y]  =  (mat[2][0]  -  mat[0][2])*s;
                    q[Z]  =  (mat[0][1]  -  mat[1][0])*s;
          }
```

Listing 15.3   *(cont.)*

```
            else {

                        i = X;
                        if (mat[Y][Y] > mat[X][X]) i = Y;
                        if ·(mat[Z][Z] > mat[i][i]) i = Z;
                        j = nxt[i] ; k = nxt[j];

                        s = sqrt( (mat[i][i] − (mat[j][j]+mat[k][k])) + 1.0);

                        q[i] = s*0.5;
                        s = 0.5/s;
                        q[W] = (mat[j][k] − mat[k][j])*s;
                        q[j] = (mat[i][j] + mat[j][i])*s;
                        q[k] = (mat[i][k] + mat[k][i])*s;

            }

}
void  slerp(p,q,t,qt)
float  p[4],q[4];
float  t;
float  qt[4];
{
            double  omega,cosom,sinom,sclp,sclq;
            int  i;

            cosom = p[X]*q[X] + p[Y]*q[Y] + p[Z]*q[Z] + p[W]*q[W];

            if ( (1.0 + cosom) > EPSILON ) {

                    if ( (1.0 − cosom) > EPSILON ) {

                                omega = acos(cosom);
                                sinom = sin(omega);
                                sclp = sin( (1.0 − t)*omega )/sinom;
                                sclq = sin( t*omega )/sinom;
                    }
                    else {

                                sclp = 1.0 − t;
                                sclq = t;
                    }
                    for (i=0;i<4;i++) qt[i] = sclp*p[i] + sclq*q[i];

            }
            else {

                    qt[X] = −p[Y]; qt[Y] = p[X];
                    qt[Z] = −p[W]; qt[W] = p[Z];
                    sclp = sin((1.0 − t)*HALFPI);
                    sclq = sin(t*HALFPI);
                    for (i = 0; i< 3; i++) qt[i] = sclp*p[i] + sclq*qt[i];


            }

}
```

Spherical linear interpolation between two unit quaternions q_1 and q_2, where:

$$q_1 \cdot q_2 = \cos \Omega$$

is obtained by generalizing the above to four dimensions and replacing Θ by Ωu where $u \in [0,1]$. We write:

$$\text{slerp}\,(q_1, q_2, u) = q_1 \frac{\sin(1-u)\,\Omega}{\sin \Omega} + q_2 \frac{\sin \Omega u}{\sin \Omega}$$

Listing 15.3 gives a code fragment for this. *slerp (p,q,t,qt)* returns the interpolated quaternion *qt*, for *t* between *p* and *q*. The routine caters for the special cases where the keys are very close together, in which case we approximate using the more economical linear interpolation and avoid divisions by very small numbers since

$$\sin \Omega \to 0 \quad \text{as } \Omega \to 0$$

The case where *p* and *q* are diametrically opposite, or nearly so, also requires special attention.

Now, given any two key quaternions, *p* and *q*, there exist two possible arcs along which one can move, corresponding to alternative starting directions on the geodesic that connects them. One of them goes around the long way and this is the one that we wish to avoid. Naively, one might assume that this reduces to either spherically interpolating between *p* and *q* by the angle Ω, where:

$$p \cdot q = \cos \Omega$$

or interpolating in the opposite direction by the angle $2\pi - \Omega$. This, however, will not produce the desired effect. The reason is that the topology of the hypersphere of orientation is not just a straightforward extension of the three-dimensional Euclidean sphere. To appreciate this, it is sufficient to consider the fact that every rotation has two representations in quaternion space, namely *q* and $-q$, that is, the effect of *q* and $-q$ is the same. That this is so is because algebraically the operator $q(\ )q^{-1}$ has exactly the same effect as $(-q)\,(\ )\,(-q)^{-1}$. Thus, points diametrically opposed represent the same rotation. Because of this topological oddity care must be taken when determining the shorter arc. A strategy that works is to choose interpolating between either the quaternion pairs *p* and *q* or *p* and $-q$. Given two key orientations *p* and *q* find the magnitude of their difference, that is $(p-q) \cdot (p-q)$, and compare this to the magnitude of the difference when the second key is negated, that is $(p+q) \cdot (p+q)$. If the former is smaller then we are already moving along the smaller arc and

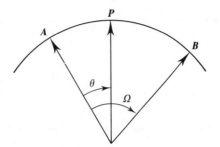

Figure 15.21 Spherical linear interpolation.

nothing needs to be done. If, however, the second is smaller, then we replace *q* by $-q$ and proceed. These considerations are shown schematically in Figure 15.22.

So far we have described the spherical equivalent of linear interpolation between two key orientations, and, just as was the case for linear interpolation, spherical linear interpolation between more than two key orientations will produce jerky, sharply changing motion across the keys. What is required for higher order continuity is the spherical equivalent of the cubic spline. Unfortunately, because we are now working on the surface of a four-dimensional hypersphere, the problem is far more complex than constructing splines in three-dimensional Euclidean space. [DUFF86] and [SHOE87] have tackled this problem. We shall describe the approach made in [SHOE87] since it pays greatest lip service to implementation points.

The following construction enables us to think of a cubic spline as a series of three linear interpolations. By extension [SHOE87] takes three spherical linear interpolations and defines a cubic spline on the surface of a sphere. Consider four points (S_0, S_1, S_2, S_3) at the corners of the rectangle shown in Figure 15.23. We linearly interpolate by an amount $u \in [0,1]$, along the horizontal edges to get the intermediate points S_α, S_β, where:

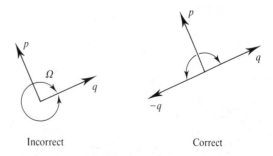

Incorrect   Correct

Figure 15.22 Shortest arc determination on quaternion hypersphere.

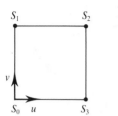
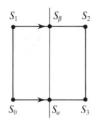
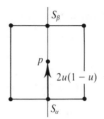
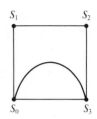

Figure 15.23 The quadrangle construction for a parabola.

$$S_\alpha = S_0(1-u) + S_3 u$$
$$S_\beta = S_1(1-u) + S_2 u$$

Now we perform a vertical linear interpolation by an amount

$$v = 2u(1-u)$$

to get the point

$$p = S_\alpha(1-v) + S_\beta v$$

As u varies from 0 to 1, the locus of p will trace out a parabola. This process of bilinear interpolation, where the second interpolation is thus restricted, is called 'parabolic blending'. Böhm [BÖHM82] shows how, given a Bézier curve segment (b_0, b_1, b_2, b_3) one can derive the quadrangle points (b_0, S_1, S_2, b_3) of the above construction. This has the geometric significance of enabling us to visualize the cubic as a parabola whose quadrangle points are not necessarily parallel or coplanar. The cubic can be thought of as a warped parabola as shown in Figure 15.24.

The mathematical significance of this construction is that it shows how to construct a cubic as a series of three linear interpolations of the quadrangle points. [SHOE87] takes this construction onto the surface of the four-dimensional hypersphere by constructing a spherical curve, using three spherical linear interpola-

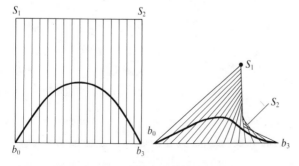

Figure 15.24 A warped parabola is a cubic.

tions of a quadrangle of unit quaternions. This he defines as squad( ), where:

$$\mathrm{squad}(b_0, S_1, S_2, b_3, ut) = \mathrm{slerp}(\mathrm{slerp}(b_0, b_3, ut),$$
$$\mathrm{slerp}(S_1, S_2, ut), 2u(1-u))$$

Given a series of quaternion keys one can construct a cubic segment across keys q_i and q_{i+1} by constructing a quadrangle of quaternions $(q_i, a_i, b_{i+1}, q_{i+1})$ where a_i, b_{i+1} have to be determined. These inner quadrangle points are chosen in such a way to ensure that continuity of tangents across adjacent cubic segments is guaranteed. The derivation for the inner quadrangle points is difficult, involving as it does the calculus and exponentiation of quaternions and we will just quote the results, referring the interested reader to [SHOE87]:

$$a_i = b_i = q_i \exp\left(-\frac{\ln(q_i^{-1}q_{i+1}) + \ln(q_i^{-1}q_{i-1})}{4}\right)$$

where, for the unit quaternion:

$$q = (\cos\Theta, \sin\Theta\, v)$$
$$|v| = 1$$
$$\ln(q) = (0, \Theta v)$$

and, inversely for the pure quaternion (zero scalar part):

$$q = (0, \Theta v)$$
$$\exp(q) = (\cos\Theta, \sin\Theta\, v)$$

Finally, in order to illustrate the principles underlying this discussion on the parametrization of orientation, we return to our block letter 'R' and apply the various interpolation techniques that we have discussed. Because all orientations take place about a fixed point, R effectively moves over the surface of a sphere (Figure 15.25).

Using the principal rotations of an x-roll followed by a y-roll followed by a z-roll, the animator sets up an orientation key represented by the rotation matrix $R(\Theta_{1i}, \Theta_{2i}, \Theta_{3i})$. This rotation matrix is then lifted into quaternion space to give the quaternion key q_i. The animator specifies three such keys. As we have discussed, interpolation to generate the inbetweens can be carried out by:

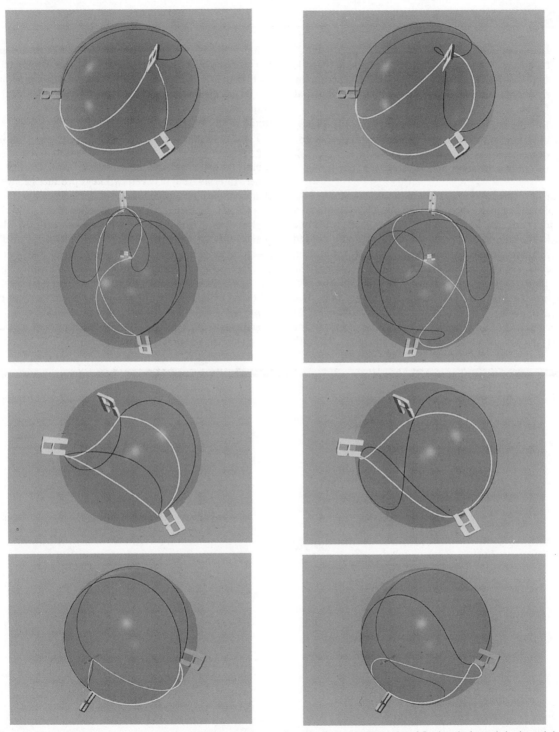

Figure 15.25 Shows how R moves through the three keys. In all cases the white line tracks the motion of R when the interpolation is carried out in quaternion space; the black line tracks the motion of R when Euler angles are interpolated. In each row the left illustration compares linear interpolation of Euler angles with spherical linear interpolation of quaternions. In each row the right illustration compares a cubic spline interpolation of Euler angles to the spherical cubic spline interpolation of quaternions (using squad( )).

1. Using the Euler angle keys $(\Theta_{1i}, \Theta_{2i}, \Theta_{3i})$, $i = 0,1,2$, to produce an interpolated Euler angle $(\Theta_1(t), \Theta_2(t), \Theta_3(t))$ at time t which is used to generate the rotation matrix $R(\Theta_1(t), \Theta_2(t), \Theta_3(t))$ for that frame.

2. Moving into quaternion space and using the quaternion keys q_i, $i = 0,1,2$, to produce an interpolated quaternion key $q(t)$ at time t, which is then converted to a rotation matrix $R_q(t)$ for that frame.

In all cases periodic interpolation modulo 3 is employed to give a closed loop. Figure 15.25 shows how R moves through the three keys. In all cases the white line tracks the motion of R when the interpolation is carried out in quaternion space; the black line tracks the motion of R when Euler angles are interpolated. In each row the left illustration compares linear interpolation of Euler angles with spherical linear interpolation of quaternions. In each row the right illustration compares a cubic spline interpolation of Euler angles to the spherical cubic spline interpolation of quaternions (using squad( )). In both columns quaternions come out better than Euler angles, the motions being far more direct and less convoluted. Note that if we change the coordinate axes and regenerate the image, the black lines will change shape whereas the white lines will stay constant. Going down the rows, the initial set of key orientations is varied in each case.

Finally, we mention a potential difficulty when applying quaternions. Quaternion interpolation is indiscriminate in that it does not prefer any one direction to any other. Interpolating between two keys produces a move that depends on the orientations of the keys and nothing else. This is inconvenient when choreographing the virtual camera. Normally when moving a camera the film plane is always required to be upright – this is usually specified by an 'up' vector. By its very nature, the notion of a preferred direction cannot easily be built into the quaternion representation. Thus the advantages afforded by quaternions as applied to objects cannot be exploited when setting up camera moves. In fact, specification of an up vector is problematic whatever way we choose to parametrize orientation.

16 Animating articulated structures

Introduction

Articulated figure animation has become popular in recent years because of the desire to use human beings as synthetic actors in three-dimensional computer animation environments. Notable among the attempts at this is the film *Tony de Peltrie* [BERG86b] and *Rendezvous à Montréal* [THAL87]. *Tony de Peltrie* is a three-dimensional caricature of a jazz pianist directed by P. Lachapelle, P. Bergeron and P. Robidoux. Bergeron describes his character in the following terms '. . . that sings, talks and moves as a normal human being. Although his face is highly caricatured his facial expressions are natural and suggest feelings and emotion'.

The Thalmann film features attempts to model real people – Marilyn Monroe and Humphrey Bogart. They describe it in these terms: '. . . The idea behind the film is that two legendary stars live in some other world beyond the grave, and they long to return to Earth. First Bogart appears and calls Marilyn and begs her to come to Earth.' In assessing the film the directors say: 'It is not important (and not possible) with image synthesis to render an actor completely. What we wanted to do was portray these great stars emotionally – to reconstruct Marilyn's and Humphrey's personalities as most people know them.'

Comparing these two well-known productions, it is our opinion that the highly caricatured film is far more successful than the Thalmanns' attempts at realistic imitation of the actors' personae. *Rendezvous à Montréal* has a curious feel to it; the obvious synthetic devices tend to predominate and are unmediated by caricature and humour. Notwithstanding the impressive technical achievements of the Thalmann team, their claims and self-assessments are somewhat arrogant and sometimes absurd. 'Actors will soon be out of a job . . . film makers will be able to create characters so lifelike that members of the audience will not be able to distinguish them from real actors.'

As a profession we need to think about the utility and the contexts in which articulated figure animation will be used. It is surely pointless to pursue the goal of precise animation of 'celebrities'. (In this connection a bizarre aside. In 1986 a strange creation became popular on British and subsequently on American TV. Max Headroom was a counterfeit computer graphics character. Such was the perceived demand for computer graphics animation simulating human beings, that an actor was filmed and, by using heavy makeup and postproduction information reduction techniques, it appeared that the character had been created by a computer graphics system. The effect was enhanced by frame-to-frame processing such as frame reduction. Perhaps the popularity of this character is an apt comment on the public's perception of television celebrities.)

Both the aforementioned films use articulated structures or skeletons on which to base the movement animation; the control of such structures is the topic of this section.

Although animation involving 'clothed skeletons' is now a research topic, much work has been done on animation involving 'naked' articulated structures. And anyway, most animation of clothed structures is controlled by animating an underlying skeleton of some description and then rendering the final images with flesh or clothes.

An early example is the work of Zeltzer [ZELT82] who designed a hierarchical control system that enables a user to control the movement of a skeleton (that is, an actual visualization of a human skeleton rather than an elementary stick figure). High-level control of, for example, a walk simply requires parameters specifying the speed of the walk and the number of steps to take. This involves a walk controller that controls a structure with 22 degrees of freedom (DOF) including ankles, knees, hips and pelvis; wrists, elbows and shoulders; counter-rotation at the base of the spine; and the support rotations about the heels and balls of the feet.

16.1 Articulated figure animation techniques

We commence this section necessarily with some definitions of terms that are particular to articulated figure animation. Moreover, since many results from robotics have proved useful in this field we also include several robotics terms.

Kinematics
This is the specification or study of motion independent of the underlying forces that produced the motion. In this respect it includes position, velocity and acceleration, that is, all the geometrical and time-related properties of the motion.

Articulated figure
An articulated figure is a structure that consists of a series of rigid links connected at joints. Although other joints exist in robotics, computer animation is usually restricted to revolute or rotary joints.

Degrees of freedom (DOF)
The number of degrees of freedom of an articulated structure is the number of independent position variables

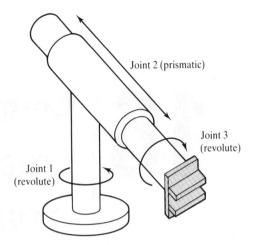

Figure 16.1   A manipulator with three degrees of freedom.

necessary to specify the state of a structure. An example illustrates the concept of DOF. Figure 16.1 shows a manipulator that consists of two revolute joints and one prismatic (sliding) joint. This structure has three DOF.

End effector
Most industrial manipulations are so-called open chains and the free end of such a chain of links is called the end effector.

State vector
Let us define the vector space of all possible configurations of an articulated figure to be the state space of the figure. A set of independent parameters defining the positions, orientations and rotations of all joints constituting the figure, that is, a set of basis figures spanning the state space, forms a basis of the state space. We say that the figure in a particular configuration is described by the state vector:

$$\theta = (\theta_1, \ldots, \theta_N)$$

The dimension of the state space in general is equal to the DOF of the articulated structure. For example, any unconstrained rigid body has six DOF, three translational and three rotational. Thus its state vector is:

$$\theta = (x, y, z, \mu, \phi, \Phi)$$

In the special case of a planar manipulator, the state vector reduces to a set of joint angles.

In these terms finding an animation of an articulated figure reduces to finding an N-dimensional path in its state space.

16.2 Forward versus inverse kinematics in computer animation

Kinematic animation of articulated structures usually falls into one of two categories:

1. *Forward kinematics*

   $$X = f(\boldsymbol{\Theta})$$

   The motion of all joints is specified explicitly by the animator. The motion of the end effector (in the case of a figure, the hands and feet) is determined indirectly as the accumulation of all transformations that lead to that end effector, as the tree of the structure is 'descended'. This, in the case of a figure's foot, would be the combined effect of the transformations at the hip, knee and ankle. That is, given $\boldsymbol{\Theta}$, derive X.

2. *Inverse kinematics*

   $$\boldsymbol{\Theta} = f^{-1}(X)$$

   Sometimes called 'goal-directed motion', the animator defines the position of the end effectors only. Inverse kinematics solves for the position and the orientation of all joints in the link hierarchy that lead to the end effector. Given X, $\boldsymbol{\Theta}$ is derived.

A simple example will illustrate the difference between the two approaches. Consider the simple two-link structure shown in Figure 16.2. One end is fixed and both links move in the plane of the paper. The forward kinematics solution $X = (x, y)$ is given by:

$$X = \left(l_1 \cos \Theta_1 + l_2 \cos (\Theta_1 + \Theta_2),\ l_1 \sin \Theta_1 + l_2 \sin (\Theta_1 + \Theta_2) \right)$$

By applying elementary trigonometry the inverse solution is:

$$\Theta_2 = \cos^{-1} \frac{(x^2 + y^2 - l_1^2 - l_2^2)}{2 l_1 l_2}$$

$$\Theta_1 = \frac{-(l_2 \sin \Theta_2)x + (l_1 + l_2 \cos \Theta_2)y}{(l_2 \sin \Theta_2)y + (l_1 + l_2 \cos \Theta_2)x}$$

Both techniques become harder to use as the complexity of the articulation increases. Each addition of a joint in the hierarchy adds at least one more DOF to the figure and so at least one more dimension to the state vector $\boldsymbol{\Theta}$.

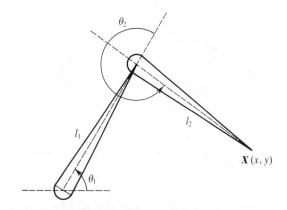

Figure 16.2 A simple two-link structure.

In the case of forward kinematics the animator has more and more transformations to control, which, while lending more freedom to achieve a more expressive animation, may prove to be too complicated and intricate to achieve in practice. A balance has to be struck and the animator can use a scripting language to help reduce the complexity and workload. A library of prespecified animations may be used for well-defined tasks; for example, ease-in and ease-out curves (Section 15.3) and sections of animation, such as the walk cycle in legged figure animation, may be used repeatedly.

In the case of inverse kinematics, as n increases the problem of finding $\boldsymbol{\Theta}$ for a given X becomes underdefined and the system is said to be redundant. A whole subspace $\{\boldsymbol{\Theta}_x\}$, defined by:

$$\boldsymbol{\Theta}(\Theta_1, \ldots, \Theta_n) \in \boldsymbol{\Theta}_x \quad \text{if} \quad f(\boldsymbol{\Theta}) = X$$

maps onto the solution X.

The problem is approached by attempting to reduce the subspace of possible solutions. We do this by adding constraints to the system. Each constraint itself forms a subspace, and the intersection of these constraint subspaces with $\boldsymbol{\Theta}_x$ gives us the set of possible solutions. The difference between the number of DOF and the number of constraints is said to be the degree of redundancy. Typical constraint criteria may include energy minimization, momentum conservation and so on.

Consider Figure 16.3 that shows a two-link manipulator in two configurations, both of which satisfy the constraint that the end effector is positioned at X. If we specify the joint between the two links to be an elbow in a human articulated structure, then one solution would be impossible and the subspace of the solution consequently halved.

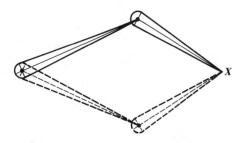

Figure 16.3 Two solutions for a two-link mechanism to position the end effector at *X*.

In robotics, manipulators are said to have a large 'dexterous workspace' in the plane through the joints. A system controlling a manipulator has to choose a single solution and this might be accomplished by minimizing the amount through which each joint has to move to reach a new position X' from a current position X.

Generally, a nonlinear set of equations arises out of any system and an inverse kinematics solution has to address the three problems of existence of solutions, multiple solutions and the method used. In robotics it has been shown that all systems with revolute and prismatic joints, having a total of six DOF in a single series chain, are solvable numerically [CRAI86].

In the computer animation of articulated structures, the inverse kinematic method seems attractive. Say, for example, we are interested in making a synthetic actor walk at a certain speed over a particular terrain to reach a given position. An animator should be able to set up this process using high-level, goal-directed motion commands which are satisfied automatically by an inverse kinematics engine.

Although high-level, goal-directed motion control implies, as we have discussed, the use of inverse kinematics, impressive animation can be achieved by using a simple interactive system with forward kinematics. As we pointed out earlier, there are advantages of freedom and simplicity in an animator using a curve-scripted, real-time interactive setup for animation design. A lot of the tedium and workload of scripting an articulated structure offline is removed in an interactive system. The importance of real-time design in animation cannot be overestimated, and the simplicity and low computational requirements of forward kinematics systems make such interaction possible on currently available graphics workstations.

Goal-directed motion is constrained by the workings of the inverse kinematics engine which simply fills in

components of the state vector. The animator has no control over these components, but control is important particularly in television work where storyboards may have to be realized precisely.

The facts that inverse kinematics becomes computationally more expensive as the complexity of the articulation increases, and that it is very difficult to use when specifying naturalistic or particular animation mean that, so far, it has only been useful in a restricted subset of general computer animation. It is used in applications where the movement of the end effector drives the animation part of the hierarchy. Such animations include walking and arm/hand positioning. As we shall see (Section 16.6.1), trying to animate such movements using forward kinematics is completely counterintuitive and tedious to do in practice – thereby ensuring the place of inverse kinematics in the future of computer animation.

The relative freedom and flexibility of forward kinematics mean that of the two techniques it dominates computer animation at the moment, particularly in the entertainment/advertising industry. Moreover, a large body of tricks and principles from traditional classical animation transfers easily into the forward kinematics domain [LASS87].

Of course the inverse/forward kinematics argument is not the only factor involved in considering the animation of articulated structures. Apart from the considerations of forces and dynamics, the motion of rigid links is not wholly appropriate for natural articulated structures. In this discussion, we have considered articulated structures with rigid links, using simple examples of manipulators. Any extension of these ideas to the animation of, say,

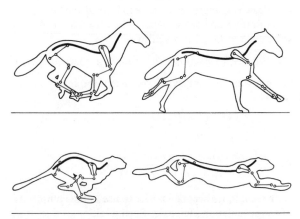

Figure 16.4 Spine flexion in a horse and cheetah (after [GRAY68]).

vertebrate mammals, has to cope with the fact that significant shape change occurs because of the flexing of the spine, which is not a rigid link unless considered at the level of an individual vertebra. Figure 16.4 shows two examples of this effect. We shall see a simple example of flexing in the double bass sequence below (Section 16.5.1). The issue of deforming a model attached to a skeleton is discussed in Section 17.6.

16.3 Representing articulated figures

The first problem in articulated animation is how to represent an articulated figure mathematically, or, put differently: what state basis do we choose to describe our state space? Great care has to be taken in making this choice as it is easy to get bogged down in a clumsy notation. This section describes two useful conventions.

16.3.1 DH notation

To represent the state of an articulated structure notation developed originally for robotic manipulations, the Denavit–Hartenberg (DH) notation [DENA55] can be used. This describes the kinematics of each link relative to its neighbours by attaching a coordinate frame to each link. Four parameters are used to define a linear transfor-

mation matrix between consecutive coordinate systems attached to each joint. These are defined to be the length of the link, a_i, the distance between links, d_i, the twist between links, α_i and the angle between links, Θ_i. Referring to Figure 16.5:

- a_i is the distance from z_i to z_{i+1} measured along x_i – the length of the link.
- α_i is the angle between z_i and z_{i+1} measured about x_i. This is the twist of the link.
- d_i is the distance between the x_{i-1} and x_i axes measured along z_i – the distance between links.
- Θ_i is the angle between x_{i-1} and x_i measured about z_i.

The z_i-axis of coordinate frame i lies along the axis of the joint. The x_i is normal to this axis and points towards joint $i+1$. The origin of the ith coordinate frame is where the common normal to z_i and z_{i+1} intersects z_i.

It is usual to refer to (a_i, α_i) as link parameters and (d_i, Θ_i) as joint parameters. This notation is used to describe linked structures where the joints have a single DOF allowing rotation about a single axis. 'Ball' joints can be represented as multiple, single DOF joints located at the same part in space.

Consider the simple example shown in Figure 16.6. We assign DH parameters to this structure as follows. First, we define a fixed reference or base frame. If we assume the structure can only move in the plane of the paper then all z_i are parallel and normal to the paper and all α_i and d_i are zero and the structure is specified as follows:

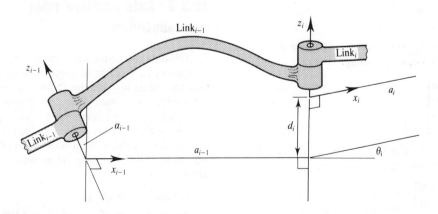

Figure 16.5 DH notation.

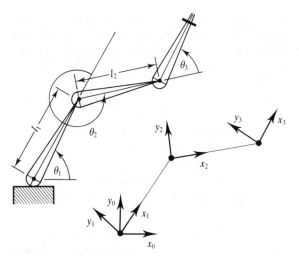

Figure 16.6 A simple example of DH notation.

i	α_{i-1}	a_{i-1}	d_i	θ_i
1	0	0	0	θ_1
2	0	l_1	0	θ_2
3	0	l_2	0	θ_3

Returning to the general case and using forward kinematics on a structure specified in DH notation we need the transformation that relates coordinate frames to neighbouring frames. This is given by the following four transformations:

1. Rotation $R_{z\,\theta}$ of angle θ_i about the z_{i-1}-axis aligning the x_{i-1}-axis with the x_i-axis:

$$\begin{bmatrix} \cos\theta_i & \sin\theta_i & 0 & 0 \\ -\sin\theta_i & \cos\theta_i & 0 & 0 \\ 0 & 0 & 1 & 0 \\ 0 & 0 & 0 & 1 \end{bmatrix}$$

2. Translation T_{zd} along the z_{i-1}-axis of a distance d_i to make the x-axes coincident:

$$\begin{bmatrix} 1 & 0 & 0 & 0 \\ 0 & 1 & 0 & 0 \\ 0 & 0 & 1 & 0 \\ 0 & 0 & d_i & 1 \end{bmatrix}$$

3. Translation T_{xl} along the x_i-axis of a distance a_{i-1} making the two origins coincident:

$$\begin{bmatrix} 1 & 0 & 0 & 0 \\ 0 & 1 & 0 & 0 \\ 0 & 0 & 1 & 0 \\ a_{i-1} & 0 & 0 & 1 \end{bmatrix}$$

4. Rotation $R_{x\alpha}$ of an angle α_{i-1} about x_i finally to make the coordinate frames coincident:

$$\begin{bmatrix} 1 & 0 & 0 & 0 \\ 0 & \cos\alpha_{i-1} & \sin\alpha_{i-1} & 0 \\ 0 & -\sin\alpha_{i-1} & \cos\alpha_{i-1} & 0 \\ 0 & 0 & 0 & 1 \end{bmatrix}$$

The concatenation of these four transformations is a single transformation that relates frame i to frame $i-1$:

$$^{(i-1)}T_i = \begin{bmatrix} \cos\theta_i & \sin\theta_i\cos\alpha_{i-1} & \sin\theta_i\sin\alpha_{i-1} & 0 \\ -\sin\theta_i & \cos\theta_i\cos\alpha_{i-1} & \cos\theta_i\sin\alpha_{i-1} & 0 \\ 0 & -\sin\alpha_{i-1} & \cos\alpha_{i-1} & 0 \\ a_{i-1} & -d_i\sin\alpha_{i-1} & d_i\cos\alpha_{i-1} & 1 \end{bmatrix}$$

All frame-to-frame transformations can be concatenated to form a single transformation that links frame 0 to frame N:

$$^0T_N = {}^0T_1\,{}^1T_2 \dots {}^{(n-1)}T_N \tag{16.1}$$

This transformation is a function of all the joint variables and will give the cartesian position and orientation of the last link and thus the end effector. It is a function of all the joint and link parameters of any articulated system. In robotics the position sensors of each joint can be interrogated and the position of the end effector can be calculated from Equation (16.1). In computer graphics the position and orientation of all links in the world coordinate system can be calculated from Equation (16.1) and the transformation between the base frame and the world coordinate origin.

16.3.2 Axis position joint representation

The DH notation is an economical relative system, where each coordinate frame is specified with respect to the previous. Sims and Zeltzer [SIMS88] introduce a less economical but more intuitive system called axis–position (AP) joint representation. They point out that the DH notation is only really suitable for manipulators that consist of a single chain with one end fixed, and cannot incorporate branching joints and links. Sims and Zeltzer store:

1. the position of the joint;
2. the orientation of the axis of the joint;
3. pointers to the link(s) that each joint is attached to.

This now requires seven parameters (three for position, three for axis orientation and one for joint angle) compared with the four values in the DH notation.

16.4 Inverse kinematics

16.4.1 The Jacobian

The Jacobian is the multidimensional extension to differentiation of a single variable. Given a function:

$$X = f(\Theta) \tag{16.2}$$

where X is of dimension n and Θ of dimension m, the Jacobian J is the $n \times m$ matrix of partial derivatives relating differential changes of Θ, written as $d\Theta$, to differential changes in X, written as dX. We write:

$$dX = J(\Theta)d\Theta$$

where the (i, j)th element of J is given by:

$$J_{ij} = \frac{\partial f_i}{\partial x_j}$$

For our purposes we divide by the differential time element to give:

$$\dot{X} = J(\Theta)\dot{\Theta} \tag{16.3}$$

where $\dot{X}$ is the velocity of the end effector which, most generally, is a vector of six dimensions that includes both the linear velocity V and the angular velocity Ω, and $\dot{\Theta}$ is the time derivative of the state vector. The Jacobian thus maps velocities in state space to velocities in cartesian space. At any given time these two quantities are related through the linear transformation J which itself changes through time as Θ changes. J is best thought of as a time-varying linear transformation.

Why is the Jacobian so useful in inverse kinematics? Recall the inverse kinematics problem as stated in Section 16.2:

$$\Theta = f^{-1}(X)$$

where we solve for the state vector Θ given a position (and orientation) of the end effector X. Now for all but the simplest of articulations the function $f(\ )$ is highly nonlinear, rapidly becoming more and more complex as the number of links increases and so the inversion of this function soon becomes impossible to perform analytically. The problem can made linear, however, by localizing about the current operating position and inverting the Jacobian to give:

$$d\Theta = J^{-1}(dX)$$

and iterating towards the goal over a series of incremental steps. This approach is shown schematically in Figure 16.7. Here we are iterating towards a final goal position, but if our velocity term $\dot{X}$ contains the angular velocity also, dX will contain an incremental angular displacement term, enabling us to iterate towards a final goal orientation as well. This inversion and iteration process will be discussed in greater detail at the end of the section. The first thing we need to do, given an articulation, is to construct the Jacobian.

16.4.2 Constructing the Jacobian

If we know the analytical expression of Equation (16.2) then we can always evaluate the Jacobian through straightforward differentiation. Returning to the articulation of Figure 16.2 (and abbreviating the notation) we have:

$$X = (l_1 c_1 + l_2 c_{12}, l_1 s_1 + l_2 s_{12})$$

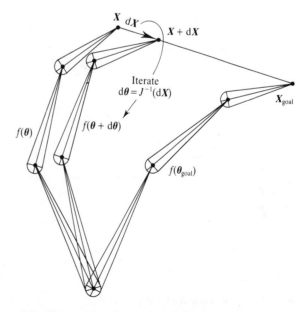

Figure 16.7 One iteration step towards the goal.

differentiating using the chain rule gives:

$$\dot{X} = \left(-l_1 s_1 \dot{\theta}_1 - l_2 s_{12}(\dot{\theta}_1 + \dot{\theta}_2), \; l_1 c_1 \dot{\theta}_1 + l_2 c_{12}(\dot{\theta}_1 + \dot{\theta}_2) \right)$$

$$= \begin{bmatrix} -l_1 s_1 - l_2 s_{12} & -l_2 s_{12} \\ l_1 c_1 + l_2 c_{12} & l_2 c_{12} \end{bmatrix} \begin{bmatrix} \dot{\theta}_1 \\ \dot{\theta}_2 \end{bmatrix}$$

For nontrivial articulations the complexity of the analytical expression makes straight differentiation extremely tedious to perform and an alternative, more geometrical approach must be sought. In robotics formulations of inverse kinematics, the construction is usually based on a notation that is specific for a particular type of link. This is not really appropriate to our needs since the skeletons need not necessarily be connected by mechanical links. What follows is a practical method of construction, derived from first principles, better suited to the more general requirements and mathematical environment of an animation program.

From the example of Section 16.3.1 we have seen that the mathematical representation of an articulation is a hierarchically ordered series of links with coordinate frames attached to each link. Mathematically speaking, the coordinate frames are the links. We shall denote frame/link i as $\{i\}$ and an articulation as a series of $n + 1$ links $\{\{0\}, \{1\}, .., \{n-1\}, \{n\}\}$ as shown in Figure 16.8. Each frame is local in that the position and orientation of $\{i+1\}$ is expressed relative to $\{i\}$, $\{i\}$ relative to $\{i-1\}$ and so on down to the base frame $\{0\}$. If x_i is the six-dimensional vector denoting the position and

orientation of $\{i+1\}$ relative to i then the collection of these vectors $(x_0, x_1, \ldots, x_{n-1}, x_n)$ makes up the state vector of the articulation.

Now Equation (16.3) expresses, via the Jacobian, the velocity of the end of the articulation in terms of velocities in state space. But these state space velocities are simply the collection of local linear and angular velocities of our frames. Hence the Jacobian expresses the velocity of $\{n\}$ in terms of the local velocities of all the intermediate frames $\{1\} \rightarrow \{n-1\}$. Now implicit in Equation (16.3) is the fact that it has to be evaluated in one frame of reference only. Therefore the problems we have to solve in order to construct our Jacobian are twofold:

1. How can the velocity of one frame relative to a given frame of reference be expressed in another frame of reference?

2. How are these velocities starting at $\{n\}$ propagated down to $\{0\}$?

We now address these two points.

Moving axis formula

Consider two coordinate frames $\{i\}$ and $\{j\}$ whose origins are coincident and where $\{j\}$ rotates with an angular velocity $\boldsymbol{\Omega}_{ji}$ with respect to $\{i\}$ as shown in Figure 16.9(a). Consider a point P fixed in $\{j\}$ (denoted by the vector P_j in $\{j\}$) but obviously moving with respect to $\{i\}$. To an observer fixed in $\{i\}$ over an incremental time element dt, $\{j\}$, and consequently P_j, will be rotated by an amount $\boldsymbol{\Omega}_{ji} dt$. Recall the result obtained in Section 15.3.8 which gave the expression for a vector r after it has been rotated by an amount θ around an axis n as:

$$Rr = \cos\theta \, r + (1 - \cos\theta) n (n \cdot r) + \sin\theta \, n \times r$$

Now as $\theta \to 0$, $\cos\theta \to 1$ and $\sin\theta \to \theta$ and we get for incremental rotations:

$$Rr = r + \theta \, n \times r$$

Putting $\boldsymbol{\Omega}_{ji} dt = \theta n$ and $P_j = r$ the incremental change in P_j as seen from $\{i\}$ is thus:

$$\boldsymbol{\Omega}_{ji} dt \times P_j$$

and, dividing through by dt, the velocity of P relative to $\{i\}$ denoted as V_{pi} is given by:

$$V_{pi} = \boldsymbol{\Omega}_{ji} \times P_j$$

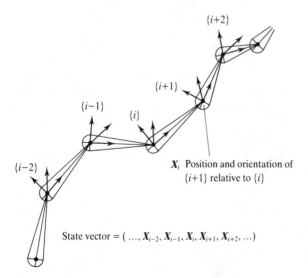

State vector = $(..., X_{i-2}, X_{i-1}, X_i, X_{i+1}, X_{i+2}, ...)$

X_i Position and orientation of $\{i+1\}$ relative to $\{i\}$

Figure 16.8 State vector of articulation.

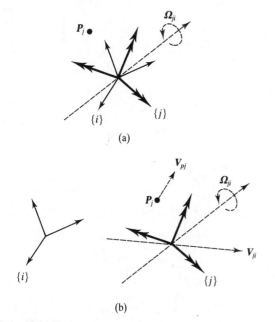

Figure 16.9 Moving axes.

In the most general case the origin of frame $\{j\}$ could be moving with a linear velocity V_{ji} with respect to $\{i\}$ and the point P could be moving with a linear velocity V_{pj} with respect to $\{j\}$ as shown in Figure 16.9(b). Because these velocities are linear they may simply be added to the right-hand side of the above to give, finally:

$$V_{pi} = \mathbf{V}_{ji} + \boldsymbol{\Omega}_{ji} \times P_j + V_{pj}$$

which is our basic equation, sometimes called the 'moving axes formula'. It is important to realize that as this is a vector equation it can be expressed in any frame. Here, by default the frame is $\{i\}$, expressing it in another frame, $\{k\}$ say, just involves rotating each individual vector in the expression by the rotation matrix that rotates the axes of $\{i\}$ into those of $\{k\}$. However, the differentiation in time has to be done with respect to the original frames – any rotations performed must be done *after* the differentiation. A good perception of this point is vital to an understanding of inverse kinematics. In the following derivations we shall not explicitly state in which frame the expression is evaluated as it should be clear from the context but the reader should bear this point in mind. We are now ready to consider how the velocities are propagated from the end of the articulation down to the base.

Velocity propagation across links

Returning to our articulation of Figure 16.8 let the origins of the frames be located by the set of vectors $\{P_0, P_1, \ldots, P_{n-1}, P_n\}$ that is defined relative to a common frame which, without loss of generality, we set to $\{0\}$. Using our moving axes formula we can express the velocity of $\{k\}$ relative to $\{i\}$ via an intermediate frame $\{j\}$ as:

$$V_{pki} = V_{ji} + \boldsymbol{\Omega}_{ji} \times \left(P_k\right)_j + V_{pkj}$$

Notationally this is getting rather unwieldy, but we can simplify by noting that $(P_k)_j = P_k - P_j$ and writing this as P_{kj}, and replacing P_k when it appears as a subscript with just k to give:

$$V_{ki} = V_{ji} + \boldsymbol{\Omega}_{ji} \times P_{kj} + V_{kj}$$

Let's start with angular velocity of the end of the articulation; for this derivation we start at $\{0\}$ and work up. Setting (i, j, k) to be $(0, 1, 3)$ we have:

$$V_{30} = V_{10} + \boldsymbol{\Omega}_{10} \times P_{31} + V_{31}$$

substituting for V_{31} by setting (i, j, k) to be $(1, 2, 3)$ and setting $P_{31} = P_{32} + P_{21}$ gives:

$$V_{30} = V_{10} + \boldsymbol{\Omega}_{10} \times \left(P_{32} + P_{21}\right) + V_{21} + \boldsymbol{\Omega}_{21} \times P_{32} + V_{32}$$

but $V_{20} = V_{10} + \boldsymbol{\Omega}_{10} \times P_{21} + V_{21}$ so:

$$V_{30} = V_{20} + \left(\boldsymbol{\Omega}_{10} + \boldsymbol{\Omega}_{21}\right) \times P_{32} + V_{32}$$

but $V_{30} = V_{20} + \boldsymbol{\Omega}_{20} \times P_{32} + V_{32}$ from which we can deduce:

$$\boldsymbol{\Omega}_{20} = \boldsymbol{\Omega}_{10} + \boldsymbol{\Omega}_{21}$$

By a similar argument we can show:

$$\boldsymbol{\Omega}_{30} = \boldsymbol{\Omega}_{20} + \boldsymbol{\Omega}_{32}$$

and so, by induction, we get:

$$\boldsymbol{\Omega}_{n0} = \sum_{i=1}^{n-1} \boldsymbol{\Omega}_{i, i-1} \qquad (16.4)$$

that is, the angular velocity of the end of the articulation is the sum of all the local angular velocities (not forgetting to evaluate them all in the same frame of course).

For the derivation for the linear velocity of the end of the articulation we start at the end $\{n-1\}$ and work down. Setting (i, j, k) to be $(n-2, n-1, n)$ we have:

$$V_{n, n-2} = V_{n-1, n-2} + \boldsymbol{\Omega}_{n-1, n-2} \times P_{n, n-1} + V_{n, n-1}$$

Now since we want to apply inverse kinematics to articulated figures we can assume that the distance between successive links stays fixed throughout its animation, which corresponds to the fact that the limbs of a figure seldom become detached and move by themselves. If this were the case the figure has probably had a bad accident and won't be moving anyway. This translates in the language of robotics by saying the links are nonprismatic, that is, the linear velocity between successive frames is always zero:

$$V_{i,i-1} = 0 \quad \text{for all } i \text{ in } (1 \to n)$$

and so:

$$V_{n,n-2} = \Omega_{n-1,n-2} \times P_{n,n-1}$$

now:

$$
\begin{aligned}
V_{n,n-3} &= V_{n-2,n-3} + \Omega_{n-2,n-3} \times P_{n,n-2} + V_{n,n-2} \\
&= \Omega_{n-2,n-3} \times P_{n,n-2} + \Omega_{n-1,n-2} \times P_{n,n-1}
\end{aligned}
$$

and so on down to {0} to give:

$$V_{n0} = \sum_{i=1}^{n-1} \Omega_{i,i-1} \times P_{ni} \qquad (16.5)$$

that is, the linear velocity of the end of the articulation is the sum over all intermediate frames of the cross-product of the local angular velocity with the vector from the end of the articulation to the origin of that frame. Physically, this equation has a simple physical interpretation as shown in Figure 16.10. The angular velocities θ_1, θ_2, θ_3 of the links of the arms point out of the plane of the paper (since in this special case they are all pointing in the same direction we don't have to worry about expressing them in a common frame). The vectors V_1, V_2, V_3 are the vectors $\theta_1(0, 0, 1) \times P_{41}$, $\theta_2(0, 0, 1) \times P_{42}$, $\theta_3(0, 0, 1) \times P_{43}$, and their sum by the above gives the velocity of the end of the arm. But V_1, V_2, V_3 are just the instantaneous, tangential velocities of the respective links as seen from the end of the arm. Hence, for nonprismatic articulations, the linear velocity of the end is simply the sum of all the linear velocities of the links as seen from the hand at that instant in time.

Now we have derived these formulae let's see how they are used to construct the Jacobian of an articulation. Once again we return to the articulation of Figure 16.2 where, in our new terminology, the linear velocity X is now written as V_{30} and expanding out for $n = 3$ gives:

$$V_{30} = \Omega_{10} \times P_{31} + \Omega_{21} \times P_{32}$$

where all these vector quantities are to be evaluated in

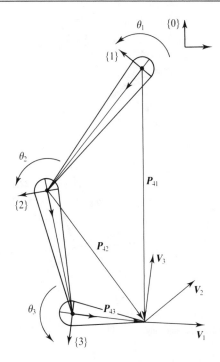

Figure 16.10 Physical interpretation of $V_{n0} = \sum_{i=1}^{n-1} \Omega_{i,i-1} \times P_{ni}$.

{0}. The position vectors are:

$$
\begin{aligned}
P_{31} &= (l_1 c_1 + l_2 c_{12}, l_1 s_1 + l_2 s_{12}) \\
P_{21} &= (l_2 c_{12}, l_2 s_{12})
\end{aligned}
$$

and the angular velocities:

$$
\begin{aligned}
\Omega_{10} &= (0, 0, 1)\dot{\theta}_1 \\
\Omega_{21} &= (0, 0, 1)\dot{\theta}_2
\end{aligned}
$$

Substituting these values into the expression for V_{30} and rearranging terms gives us the same result as was obtained earlier in Section 16.4.2 by straightforward differentiation.

This example is a little contrived – we need to know how to construct a Jacobian for a general articulation within a computer graphics context. As we shall see, this turns out to be quite simple – all the information is readily extracted from transformation matrices that already exist in the graphics pipeline. We make the assumption that at any time the local transformation matrices, $^{i-1}T_i$, that transform points in {i} into {i − 1} are known. This is not such a big assumption since they constitute the building blocks of the articulation – it is difficult to see what could be achieved without them. In order to evaluate (16.4) and (16.5) the information we seek is just P_i and $\Omega_{i,i-1}$ for each $\{i\}$.

Given these matrices (just as in Section 16.3.1) we can concatenate them together to get the global transformation matrix, ^0T_i, of frame i by:

$$^0T_i = \prod_{j=1}^{i} {}^{j-1}T_j$$

Now by definition, the position vector of P_i is the position vector of the origin of frame $\{i\}$ relative to frame $\{0\}$ and so can be obtained, trivially, by multiplying the origin of frame $\{i\}$ by the global matrix ^0T_i:

$$P_i = (0, 0, 0, 1)\,{}^0T_i$$

which is just the first three elements of the fourth row of the matrix ^0T_i.

The derivation for $\Omega_{i,i-1}$ is far more subtle but the result is just as simple. Returning to our formula for incremental rotations:

$$Rr = r + \Theta n \times r$$

and expressing the differential rotation in matrix form gives:

$$\Theta n \times r = (r_x, r_x, r_x, 1)\begin{bmatrix} 1 & \Theta n_z & -\Theta n_y & 0 \\ -\Theta n_z & 1 & \Theta n_x & 0 \\ \Theta n_y & -\Theta n_x & 1 & 0 \\ 0 & 0 & 0 & 1 \end{bmatrix}$$

This result can be interpreted as the product of successive rotations about the three coordinate axes, with the angles small enough so that the order in which the rotations are applied makes no significant difference. The sum of these three incremental rotations gives Θn. To see why this is so take the three rotation matrices for rotations about the three coordinate axes and let the rotated angles of each axis $(\Theta_x, \Theta_y, \Theta_z)$ be small enough so that $\cos\Theta_i \to 1$ and $\sin\Theta_i \to \Theta_i$, for $i = x, y, z$. Now multiply the three matrices together in any order and eliminate second and higher order terms. The result you will get (corresponding to that directly above with $\Theta_x = \Theta n_x$, $\Theta_y = \Theta n_y$, $\Theta_z = \Theta n_z$) will be the same regardless of the order.

In an incremental time dt then, substituting $\Omega_{i,i-1}dt$ for Θn, we can decompose the rotation into three separate rotations about the coordinate axes. The coordinate frame $\{i\}$ can be thought of as having been rotated by an amount $\Omega_{i,i-1,x}dt$, $\Omega_{i,i-1,y}dt$, $\Omega_{i,i-1,z}dt$ about its x-, y- and z-axes. So we can write:

$$\Omega_{i,i-1} = (\dot\Theta_{xi}, \dot\Theta_{yi}, \dot\Theta_{zi})$$

where $\dot\Theta_{xi} = \Omega_{i,i-1,x}$, $\dot\Theta_{yi} = \Omega_{i,i-1,y}$, $\dot\Theta_{zi} = \Omega_{i,i-1,z}$. These quantities are none other than the time derivatives of the Euler angles about the coordinate axes.

Now the Jacobian requires us to express $\Omega_{i,i-1}$ in $\{0\}$, which means we have to transform the axis of rotation in $\{0\}$. Using our decomposition into Euler angles, all we have to do is to transform the three coordinate axes of $\{i\}$ into $\{0\}$. Let these transformed axes be denoted by a_{xi}, a_{yi}, a_{zi}. Trivially:

$$a_{xi} = (1, 0, 0, 1)\,{}^0T_i$$

which is just the first three elements of the first row of ^0T_i. Similarly, a_{yi} can be obtained from the first three elements of the second row and a_{zi} from the first three of the third.

16.4.3 Summary of construction process

Finally, we summarize these results. For an articulation consisting of $n+1$ nonprismatic links $\{\{0\}, \{1\}, \ldots, \{n-1\}, \{n\}\}$ the linear velocity V_{n0} and angular velocity Ω_{n0} of the end of the articulation as seen in frame $\{0\}$ is related to the local angular velocities $\Omega_{i,i-1} = (\dot\Theta_{xi}, \dot\Theta_{yi}, \dot\Theta_{zi})$ about the coordinate axes of frames $\{i\}, i = 1, \ldots, n-1$, through the Jacobian matrix by:

$$\begin{bmatrix} V_{n0} \\ \Omega_{n0} \end{bmatrix}$$

$$= \begin{bmatrix} b_{x1}, b_{y1}, b_{z1}, & \ldots b_{xi}, b_{yi}, b_{zi}, & \ldots, b_{xn-1}, b_{yn-1}, b_{zn-1} \\ a_{x1}, a_{y1}, a_{z1}, & \ldots, a_{xi}, a_{yi}, a_{zi}, & \ldots, a_{xn-1}, a_{yn-1}, a_{zn-1} \end{bmatrix}\begin{bmatrix} \dot\Theta_{x1} \\ \dot\Theta_{y1} \\ \dot\Theta_{z1} \\ \vdots \\ \dot\Theta_{xi} \\ \dot\Theta_{yi} \\ \dot\Theta_{zi} \\ \vdots \\ \dot\Theta_{xn-1} \\ \dot\Theta_{yn-1} \\ \dot\Theta_{zn-1} \end{bmatrix}$$

where the vectors a_{xi}, a_{yi}, a_{zi} are the x, y, z-axes of frame $\{i\}$ transformed into frame $\{0\}$ and the vectors b_{xi}, b_{yi}, b_{zi} are the cross-products of these axes with the vector $P_n - P_i$ where P_n is the position of the end of the articulation and P_i the position of the origin of frame $\{i\}$:

$$b_{xi} = a_{xi} \times (P_n - P_j)$$
$$b_{yi} = a_{yi} \times (P_n - P_j)$$
$$b_{zi} = a_{zi} \times (P_n - P_j)$$

a_{xi}, a_{yi}, a_{zi} and P_i can be obtained from the global transformation matrix ^0T_i that transforms frame $\{i\}$ into frame $\{0\}$ since:

$$^0T_i = \begin{bmatrix} a_{xi}, & 0 \\ a_{yi}, & 0 \\ a_{zi}, & 0 \\ P_i, & 1 \end{bmatrix}$$

The reader will note that the column matrix on the right-hand side which is the rate of change of the state vector of the articulation contains time derivatives of Euler angles only. This is because the positional derivatives are always zero since we have restricted the links to be non-prismatic. The number of columns of the Jacobian represents the number of degrees of freedom – for us this is just three times the number of links since we allow three rotational degrees of freedom at each link.

16.4.4 Inverting the Jacobian and iterating

These final two stages in the process of building an inverse kinematics engine are almost always done numerically and are by far the most problematic. Developing techniques to solve them, however, was a preoccupation of researchers in robotics long before computer graphicists came along and so there is a wide body of literature devoted to them, for example [KLEI83, WHIT72]. (See also [GIRA85, SIMS88] for applications from a computer graphics perspective.) For this reason we shall not go into them in great depth but merely make the reader aware of possible pitfalls.

Numerical error

If the Jacobian is not square, that is, if the dimension of X is not equal to the dimension of Θ then it is rectangular

and so cannot be inverted (this is almost always the case). So-called pseudo inversion techniques are then brought into play. These techniques are approximate and local. Hence the iteration process which, given a desired change in the end effector dX from its current position, tries to calculate the corresponding change in the state vector $d\Theta$ by:

$$d\Theta = J^{-1}(dX)$$

is subject to error. Moreover if dX is already too large then, due to the local nature of the solution, errors will almost certainly occur. These kinds of errors are called 'tracking' errors – the magnitude of these errors is obtained from the norm of the difference between the actual change and the desired change, that is:

$$\|J(d\Theta) - dX\|$$

We now describe a strategy that minimizes these tracking errors. Suppose the tracking error when we iterate over $[X, X_{goal}]$ (that is, when $dX = X_{goal} - X$) is unacceptable, it exceeds a predefined threshold value. The path from X to X_{goal} is subdivided and the articulation is made to iterate towards an intermediate goal position and then, if this iteration produces an acceptable error, to iterate from the resulting intermediate configuration towards X_{goal}. If this error is also too large, however, then the appropriate interval is subdivided and the process repeated. The procedure is shown schematically in Figure 16.11 which shows an iteration towards an intermediate position X_i. We increment i (by following the lower route) until the error is sufficiently small whereupon the articulation is updated (by following the higher route) with the acceptable configuration, that is, $X = X + J(d\Theta_i)$, and the process starts anew. By these means the end of the articulation, in a piecewise fashion, approaches the goal. The reader may note that tracking error minimization was implicit in the drawing of Figure 16.7.

Singularities

The rank of a matrix is defined as the largest number of linearly independent rows (columns) of a matrix. As the articulation moves the Jacobian will change with time and this variation can produce sudden discontinuities in the rank of the Jacobian. These singularities are not caused by any inadequacy of the formulation but are inherent in the transformation from state space velocities to cartesian velocities. Physically, the singularities usually occur when the articulation is fully extended or

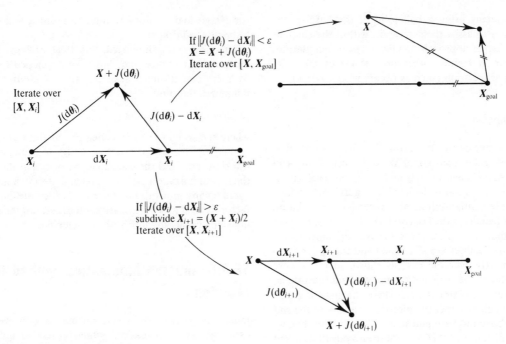

Figure 16.11 Minimizing tracking error.

when the axes of separate links align themselves. Figure 16.12 shows a fully extended articulation – at this instant, changes in either Θ_1 or Θ_2 will both produce changes in the end of the articulation in exactly the same direction, namely perpendicular to the axes of the links. There is no set of state space velocities that will give a cartesian velocity towards or away from the base – one degree of freedom has been lost.

Now texts on linear algebra will tell you that the determinant of a matrix provides a measure of its rank – if the determinant is equal to zero the matrix has lost its rank – so we can use it to calculate the singular configurations of an articulation. We already know the Jacobian of the articulation in Figure 16.2 – it was calculated in Section 16.4.2. The determinant is thus:

$$\begin{vmatrix} -l_1 s_1 - l_2 s_{12} & -l_2 s_{12} \\ l_1 c_1 + l_2 c_{12} & l_2 c_{12} \end{vmatrix} = l_1 l_2 s_2$$

This is 0 when Θ_2 is either 0 or π, which corresponds to full extension or when the second link is completely folded back on the first. There are two alternative approaches to the problem of the singularity at full extension (in robotics language it is said to be a workspace boundary singularity). The first is simply not to allow the articulation to become fully extended – it is enough

simply to push the end back towards the base by a very small amount and thereby retain that degree of freedom. The second is to adopt a different iterative process within the region of the singularity. Sims and Zeltzer adopt the

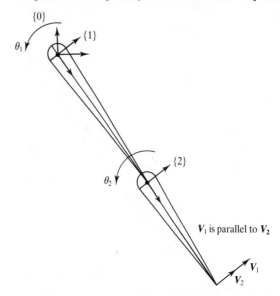

Figure 16.12 Singularity at full extension.

second strategy using a ball joint at the base of the articulation to assist their iteration within the singular region. Neither approach handles interior singularities that occur in regions other than those at the fully extended articulation (such as occurs when $\Theta_2 = \pi$).

Ill conditioning

Ill conditioning occurs at the transition between singular and nonsingular configurations and results in wild oscillations and unacceptably high state space velocities. Just such a situation is depicted in Figure 16.13 which shows three configurations of a three-link articulation where the lengths of the last two links added together are equal to that of the first. There is thus a singularity when the axes of the links are all aligned and the end is positioned directly over the base as shown in (a). Figure 16.3(b) shows the articulation in two configurations, both close to this singularity, where the first links are oriented in almost opposite directions, one with the end slightly above the base and one with it slightly below. Now the distance dX between these end positions at (b) can be made arbitrarily small but the distances traversed in state space between the two configurations, particularly that of Θ_1, are comparatively huge. As $dX \to 0$, $d\Theta_1$ most certainly does not, its behaviour becoming more and more erratic. So determining the required value

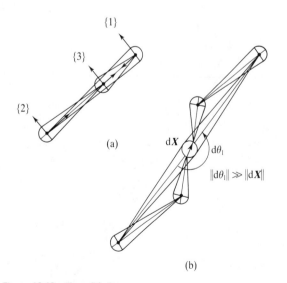

Figure 16.13 Ill conditioning.

for $d\Theta_1$ given dX is not a well-posed problem – it is said to be ill conditioned.

The most commonly used numerical strategy, called damped least square, that has been developed to cope with ill conditioning searches for a solution that minimizes the sum:

$$\|J(d\Theta) - dX\|^2 + \lambda^2 \|d\Theta\|^2$$

where the second term is a measure of the state space velocities. The rationale is thus to try to minimize the tracking error and the state space velocities at the same time; minimization of the second term hopefully avoiding any spurious movement. λ, called the damping factor, is used to set the relative importance of the tracking error versus the norm of the velocities.

16.4.5 Inverse kinematics applied to skeletons

In our development of inverse kinematics so far we have used the term 'articulation' rather loosely. It may not have escaped the reader's notice that all the examples of articulations have been single chains only – there has been no mention of branching links that are typical in skeletal structures. The purpose of this section is to clarify this shortfall – to this end we make two basic generalizations:

1. *Inverse kinematics as an 'attachable engine'* Consider an arbitrary skeletal structure, by which we mean a hierarchical network of nodes, one of which is the root, the rest being descendants of this root, where any node can have any number of children. Travelling down the hierarchy from the root we can reach any node, and, conversely, moving up the hierarchy from any node we always end up at the root. We can apply inverse kinematics between any two nodes in the skeleton; the only rule to be observed is that the node corresponding to the end effector, the end node, is lower down the hierarchy than the node corresponding to the base, the base node. We can think of the inverse kinematics as a numerical engine that can be attached to any part of the skeleton whose purpose is to specify the position and orientation of all the nodes between the end node and base node – we call these types of nodes empty nodes. We can apply more than one engine to the same skeletal structure. Figure 16.14(a) shows one obvious arrangement of engines for the human

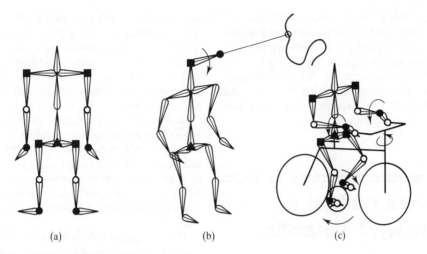

(a)   (b)   (c)

Figure 16.14 Inverse kinematics applied to a skeleton.

skeleton. The root, denoted by the black triangle, is at the pelvis, base nodes, denoted by black squares, are at the hips and shoulders, end nodes, denoted by black circles, are at the hands and feet, and the empty nodes, denoted by outlined circles, are at the elbows and knees. Of course other arrangements are possible; [PHIL91], for example, positions the root at one foot, making the other an end node, in order to animate the motion of a basically standing figure. (Such motions include bending, shifting of weight from one foot to another and turning.) Additional rules must be applied in the case where engines on a skeleton overlap. One obvious rule would be to order them by assigning a priority to each – higher priority engines being evaluated before the lower ones which 'fill in' any remaining empty nodes.

2. *Animating the goal* The notion of independently animating the goal position/orientation that the end node tries to reach is extremely powerful – in this context the goal is usually referred to as a constraint which the inverse kinematics engine tries to satisfy. As we shall see in the examples that follow, constraint animation normally reduces to making the constraint an independently animated entity that is already part of the environment. Thus the skeleton, in a very real sense, can be made to interact with its environment through time. Animation of the constraint must not be confused with the iteration process the end node undergoes in order to reach it – this should never be considered as part of the animation.

At any given moment, the constraint is well defined and, at this time, the end node is iterated until it is satisfied or, when this is impossible, adopts the best possible configuration that minimizes the difference between the constraint and the end node. Note that since the constraint is animated independently the latter case can occur quite easily.

Given these two generalizations, the key to generating skeletal animation successfully is a careful analysis of the context in which it is animated, identifying where to attach the inverse kinematics engines and how to constrain the end nodes. A couple of examples illustrate the power of the method. Figure 16.14(b) shows our figure with an extra segment attached to the top of it. We use this segment to specify the motion of the head and attach an engine across it, attaching the end node to a moving reference point (the shaded circle) which corresponds to, say, a fly buzzing around. Note that here we constrain orientation only, not position. As the fly moves around the head will track it as if it were watching it. Moreover, we can alter the trajectory of the fly and the head will alter its motion automatically. The eyes too, could be similarly constrained. Figure 16.14(c) shows the arrangement of (a) sitting on a bike. The end nodes of the hands are constrained to the handles and those of the feet to the pedals. As the pedals are made to revolve, or as the handlebar turns, then the feet and hands follow accordingly. We can also animate those nodes of the skeleton that are not empty nodes. If, say, we wanted the figure to cycle uphill, we could lift the figure off its seat and bend the torso forwards and, providing this additional motion keeps within certain limits which are no more than the limits that exist in real life, the inverse kinematics engines will keep the hands and feet correctly constrained. This last example is taken from the development work of SoftImage (Montreal) who have pioneered this type of animation.

16.5 A case study of a general forward kinematics system

This section studies the use of a completely general forward kinematics system and its purpose is to give some insight into the underlying system and interface requirements. This is a good example of the power and flexibility of a general-purpose forward kinematics system. In addition, the entire sequence was created by an animator with no software skills, other than use of the systems interface. This means that the creativity is left in the hands of the animator. Constraints in inverse kinematics systems mean that for completely general-purpose creations a deal of flexibility is locked up in the specific nature of the solution of the goals, these goals being supplied and designed by the software writers.

In a general forward kinematics system any movement assigned to a particular node will, by definition, also drive all subsequent nodes beneath it in the hierarchy.

For example, applying rotation at a left shoulder rotates the entire left arm. This implies that, when building up an animation, the animator must start at the top of the hierarchy and work down, successively animating the motion at each node. This need to animate each node is the source of the tedium and the workload in a forward kinematics system.

Animation of a particular sublevel is carried out 'on top of' the animation that it 'inherits' from the upper levels. In this respect, an important principle that animators must observe is to try to perfect the animation at a given level before moving down to the next one, because any subsequent readjustment of animation at this level would imply a change to all animations at levels below it.

The examples now described are taken from a production that provides an initial and link sequence for a rock music program shown on UK Channel 4 in 1988 called *WIRED*. The animation features a band made up of characters that consist of explicitly and implicitly linked structures, and most of the modelling is achieved using cylinders and spheres. It is difficult to convey the visual effect of an animated sequence in words, but the sequence is vital and the paucity of the modelling primitives does not detract in any way from the overall visual impression. The film is at the opposite end of the 'photorealistic' spectrum as exemplified by Pixar's *Tin Toy* (described in Section 15.1) and it is an object lesson on how the composition and dynamics of a sequence are more important than the modelling realism.

In the first example shown (Plate 49) a character called Mad Bastard (subsequently referred to for reasons of good taste by his, or even her, initials – MB) appears in frame and snaps at the screen. The face of this character (Figure 16.15) is an implicitly linked structure that is sub-

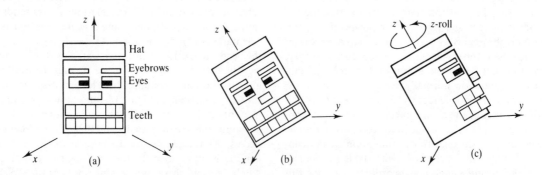

Figure 16.15   MB – an implicitly linked structure – (a) Local coordinates. (b) Global transformation. (c) Local transformation.

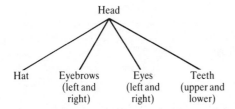

Figure 16.16 The hierarchy of MB.

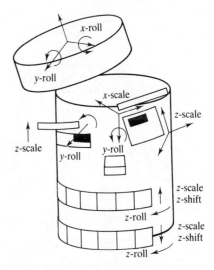

Figure 16.17 MB – local transformations at the bottom of the hierarchy.

jected to local and global transformations. In Figure 16.15 the axis system shown is the local coordinate of the actor and is separate and distinct from the global coordinate system of the scene in which the character sits. So although the head tilts and moves towards the screen (global transformation), rotation of the head about its neck is achieved by a z-roll in its local coordinate system.

The hierarchy of this structure is very simple, being only one level deep (Figure 16.16). The head's global transformations are passed down the tree so that as the character moves around the scene and turns its head, the eyes, teeth and so on follow and turn with it accordingly. Once the head has been animated its features can be animated separately. For example, the eyes and teeth change their size menacingly by applying local z-scale transformations which are applied on top of the head's transformations, and MB is able to frown, rotating the eyes and eyebrows accordingly using a local y-roll transformation. A feature of this particular system is that the axes about which the actors are rotated (usually rotation in either or any combination of the three axes

directions is sufficient) can be specified to pass through any point in space.

Figure 16.17 shows the separate transformations applied to the leaves of the tree in order to arrive at frame 4 of the sequence. As always, the order in which these transformations is applied is important. The pillbox hat is made to tilt forward by applying an x-roll followed by a y-roll. MB's eyebrow is extended (x-scale) before it frowns (y-roll) and his teeth gnash by applying a z-scale followed by a z-shift.

In many instances animation of the lower nodes of the tree occur in order to nullify effects of transformations

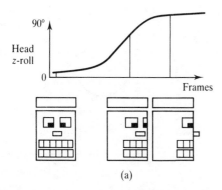

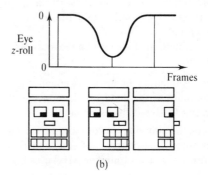

(a)   (b)

Figure 16.18 (a) Rigid and (b) 'elastic' links in a hierarchical structure.

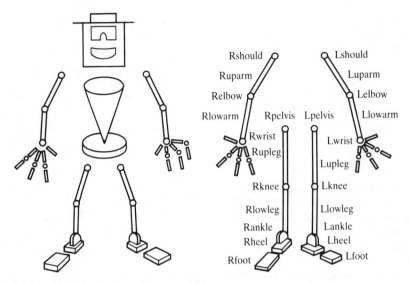

Figure 16.19 Xylophone man.

they inherit from higher parts of the tree. In these cases the lower nodes' animation is said to compensate for the higher node animation. In this way we undo a restriction of the rigid link manipulator paradigm. The model becomes an articulated structure with elastic links where the behaviour of the links can be scripted.

Consider the following example: after MB snaps at the screen the head turns away but the eyes continue to stare at the viewer before turning also. The spline representing the z-roll of the turn is shown in Figure 16.18. Figure 16.18(a) shows what we would see with animation of the top level only. By adding a compensation spline for the local z-roll of the eyes, we can make the eyes lag behind before catching up with the head movement. If compensation curves act over a significant length of the animation, this would imply that too much work is spent cancelling out inherited animation and the hierarchy should be restructured.

So, in general, animation of the lower nodes occurs for one of two reasons:

1. *Refinement* Animating in order to enhance and add to the animation inherited from the upper levels (as in the case of MB's facial expressions).

2. *Compensation* Animating in order to subtract and nullify unwanted components of the inherited animation (as in the case of making MB's eyes lag).

The xylophone man sequence (Plate 50) shows animation of a full figure that has both explicit or rigid links

and implicit links. The figure and the hierarchy are shown in Figure 16.19.

16.5.1 Interaction in forward kinematics systems

MB has a similar articulated structure to xylophone man and is shown in Plate 51 playing the kettle drum. This example illustrates another important feature of articulated structure animation, namely interaction – the effects different actors in the scene have on each other. In this case the interaction occurs between the mallets

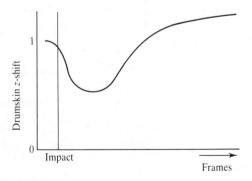

Figure 16.20 Interaction – a z-shift control for mallet–drumskin impact.

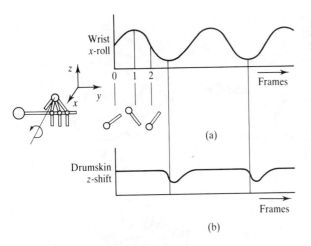

Figure 16.21 Mallet–drumskin interaction timing.

and the drums. As the mallet hits the drum the drumskin is momentarily depressed and then bounces back. On impact the drum will follow a z-shift spline shown in Figure 16.20. The asymmetry in the curve simulates the drumskin depressing quickly, as it absorbs the momentum of the mallet, and returning to its original position more slowly, under natural elasticity.

The animation of MB's hand is done 'above' this animation. The x-roll of the wrist controls how the hand moves the mallet (Figure 16.21a). The animation of the wrist is constructed such that the impact occurs at the minima of the above curve. Armed with this fact the timing of the synchronization between the two actors becomes easy. The drum's z-shift curve is shifted along the frame axis such that it aligns with a minimum of the wrist x-roll. This is duplicated at each minimum point as shown in Figure 16.21(b).

We have discussed the concept of an articulated structure with rigid links and elastic links, where inherited animation at a node can be further refined independently. It is useful to further generalize this concept and allow links to be broken altogether in certain contexts. In this case only particular transformations are passed downwards and other animation can be made to be peculiar only to that node. This enables independent manipulation of nodes in a hierarchy as well as the dependent manipulation of the hierarchy itself.

The double bass sequence (Plate 52) is an example of such as articulated structure. The bass player is shifted relative to the bass and its limbs positioned on the instrument (Figure 16.22a). The bass player is then linked to

the bass so that when the global transformation of the bass occurs the player follows (Figure 16.22b). The following actions are animated using this setup:

1. A y-roll is set up, its axis passing through the instrument spindle. The player is linked to this y-roll so that both player and bass roll together.

2. The bass player spins the bass. This is done by applying a local z-roll, its axis positioned through the centre of the bass, to the bass only. The player does not pick up this z-roll even although it is beneath the instrument in the hierarchy.

3. The player's arms are animated as it strums the strings. Its legs are animated to jump off the bass before the spin and back on after the spin is completed. Additionally, the ribs are enclosed in an FFD box (see Section 17.4.2), which is animated to make the ribcage flex forwards and back.

16.6 Animation of legged figures

Animating a walk cycle has long concerned computer animators. In an early example of bipedal locomotion animation, Zeltzer [ZELT82] uses a high-level system to control a skeleton (that is an anatomical skeleton, not an abstraction such as a stick figure) exhibiting jumping and straight-ahead gait over level unobstructed terrain. This work demonstrates how an organizational hierarchy can be imposed on a forward kinematics system, allowing an animator high-level control and, presumably, access to any of the sublevels when detail needs to be altered.

Inverse kinematic approaches to legged animation can be found in Sims and Zeltzer [SIMS88] and Girard and Maciejewski [GIRA85]. The attraction of inverse kinematics is that such tasks as causing a figure to walk over uneven terrain need not be explicitly animated in detail. The nature of the terrain is defined to the system and the animator need only supply such parameters as direction and speed of walk.

It is useful to start off by consolidating our ideas about bipedal gait cycles. We will then look at how these can be incorporated in a simple forward kinematics system.

There are many ways in which the characteristics of bipedal gait can be described and categorized. Two

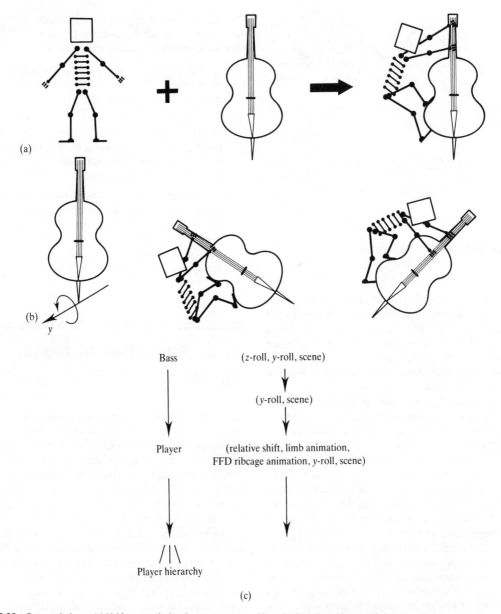

Figure 16.22 Bass and player. (a) Linking an articulated structure to an object. (b) Transformations applied to the object 'carry' the structure. (c) Showing the transformations applied to each actor and the subset of transformations inherited by the player.

aspects are selected here as being of particular interest to designers of animation systems. These are:

- The possible gait modes of a simple articulated structure representing leg and hips, using descriptors due to Saunders *et al.* [SAUN53].

- The definitions associated with the timing of legged animation described in [GIRA85].

Saunders *et al.* define a set of gait determinants (in its nonmathematical sense) that can be used in conjunction with a simple mechanical abstraction to explain the

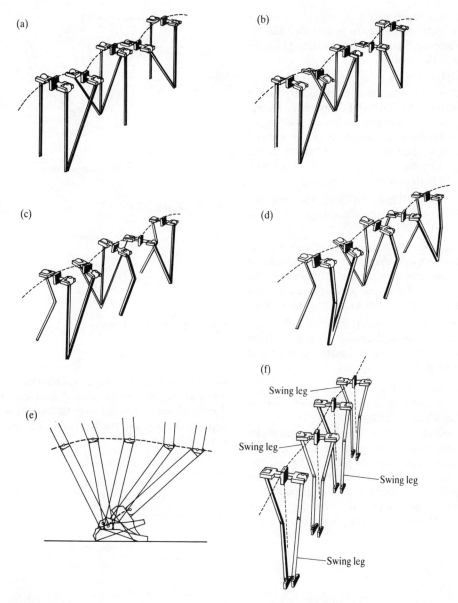

Figure 16.23 Walking gaits. (a) Compass gait. (b) Pelvic rotation. (c) Pelvic tilt. (d) Stance leg inflexion. (e) Plantar flexion. (f) Lateral pelvic displacement. Based on an illustration in Inman *et al.*, *Human Walking*, Williams & Wilkins, Baltimore MD.

kinematic nature of bipedal locomotion. This is done by imposing the determinants, one at a time, on the model, resulting in a definition that builds up in order of increasing complexity. For each leg, a determinant in the sequence depends on a single DOF in a joint. The gait determinants are:

1. Compass gait (Figure 16.23a) The legs remain straight, moving in parallel planes. The pelvis moves in a series of arcs whose radius is determined by the leg length.

2. Pelvic rotation (Figure 16.23b) Allowing the pelvis

to rotate about a vertical axis through its centre enables the length of the step to be increased and the arc to be flattened. Saunders *et al.* quote $\pm 3°$ for the amplitude of this motion.

3. Pelvic tilt (Figure 16.23c) If the pelvis is allowed to tilt as well as rotate the arc of its trajectory can be further flattened. In practice the hip on the 'swing' side of the walk falls below the hip on the 'stance' side. This lowering occurs immediately after the end of the double support phase and the 'toe-off' of the swing leg. Introducing a pelvic tilt necessarily involves a knee flexion of the swing leg.

4. Stance leg flexion (Figure 16.23d) The next elaboration is stance leg flexion where the pelvic trajectory arc is further flattened.

5. Plantar flexion of the stance angle (Figure 16.23e) The transition between the double support phase and the swing phase is made smoother if the angle of the stance leg moves down just prior to toe-off. This means that the foot must flex with respect to the shin.

6. Lateral pelvic displacement (Figure 16.23f) Normal walking involves displacement of the pelvis from side to side, as the weight is transferred from one limb to another.

Having defined an articulated structure on which gait definitions are imposed we now look at useful timing relationships described in [GIRA85].

First, the repetition of a gait sequence is called a gait cycle and the time taken to complete the cycle is called the period. We can then define the phase within a cycle, and the relative phases of legs of quadrupeds are often used to distinguish quadrupedal gaits. For example, the difference between bounding and 'pronking' can be defined in terms of the relative phase of the front and rear limbs:

bound:	front	0.0	0.0
	rear	0.5	0.5
pronk:	front	0.0	0.0
	rear	0.0	0.0

Another parameter, called the leg duty factor, describes the time a leg spends on the ground as a fraction of the gait cycle. This can, for example, be used to distinguish between walking and running in bipedal locomotion. In a biped, by definition, the duty factor must exceed 0.5 – both feet must be on the ground simultaneously for some time during the cycle.

The cyclic events and time periods in the complete gait cycle are shown in Figure 16.24. The time a leg spends

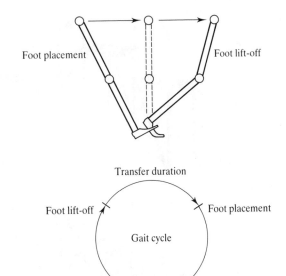

Figure 16.24 Gait cycle definitions.

on the ground during the cycle is called the support duration and the time off the ground the transfer duration. These definitions give rise to simple timing relationships between the legs and the body, that are useful in computer animation:

$$\text{Support duration} = \frac{\text{Step length}}{\text{Body speed}}$$

$$\text{Duty factor} = \frac{\text{Support duration}}{\text{Gait period}}$$

$$\text{Transfer duration} = \frac{\text{Transfer arc length}}{\text{Leg speed}}$$

16.6.1 A case study of legged animation using forward kinematics

This section demonstrates how a simple forward kinematics system can be used for legged locomotion. It also demonstrates that a general forward kinematics system does not deal with legged motion as easily as we would like, and that this particular activity is a prime candidate for inverse kinematics. It is not likely that a

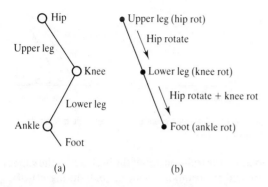

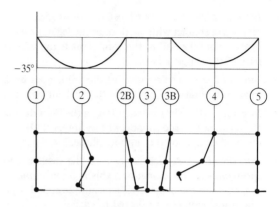

Figure 16.25 (a) A simple articulated structure for a leg. (b) The structure hierarchy.

Figure 16.27 Knee rotation script.

comprehensive hand system, for example, would be accessible, in general, to goal-directed specification. Certainly such activities as grasping can be completely specified with a very few parameters; but unlike legs, hands are used for such a huge variety of spatial gestures that a hierarchical forward kinematics system is likely to be a better approach.

Let us consider animating a walk cycle using a forward kinematics system. Figure 16.25 shows a simple system and the associated hierarchy. The leg is jointed at the hip, knee and ankle, and the links are upper leg, lower leg and foot. For simplicity assume that the leg forms a simple planar link and can only move in the plane of the paper. As always we start at the top of the hierarchy and move downwards.

The upper leg in a walk cycle rotates backwards less than it does forwards and we can define an animation for the hip rotation as a curve between the limits, say, of

$-35°$ and $45°$. This is shown in Figure 16.26. Next we animate the lower leg (Figure 16.27) by rotating this link about the knee joint. This animation is part *compensation* – cancelling out unwanted extremities of rotation inherited from the hip, and part *refinement* – attempting to make the foot appear to be on the floor for some interval of time either side of frame 3, in the interval 2B to 3B, say, the support phase of the gait cycle (and the interval between foot lift-off and foot placement – the transfer phase – when the other leg is in its support phase). 2B corresponds to foot placement and 3B to foot lift-off. We can accomplish this, somewhat crudely, by making the knee rotation zero in that interval. Note that a constraint is that knee rotation can never be positive.

Finally, the foot is animated (Figure 16.28), to imitate plantar flexion, as a refinement of the inherited animation. The refinements are as follows:

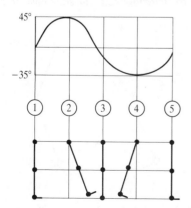

Figure 16.26 Hip rotation script.

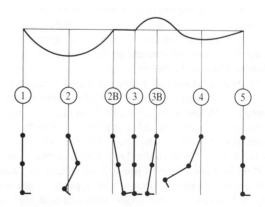

Figure 16.28 Ankle rotation script.

- *Interval 1–2*   The leg lifts off the floor – the foot remains in contact with the floor as the leg notionally pivots about the ball of the foot. This is the lift-off part of the support phase.

- *Interval 2–2B*   The rotation of the ankle goes back to zero to notationally prepare the heel for contact.

- *Interval 3–3B*   The foot stays flat on the floor during the push part of the support phase. Interval 2B–3 is the landing part of the support phase.

- *Interval 3B–4*   A kick is given to the heel to add springiness to the animation. This is an example of exaggeration which in turn is a technique culled from traditional animation referred to earlier.

A figure animated using this approach is shown in Plate 53. It is no accident that there is no floor in this sequence. Although this method of animation produces a result that looks reasonable, its severe limitations can be seen by placing a floor in the scene. The foot will almost certainly penetrate the floor. This is because no consideration has been given to the constraint of foot and floor contact. (There is no guarantee that the joint rotations between 2B and 3B will keep the foot on the ground, and in general the foot will go into the floor.) Furthermore, any attempt to adjust the animation to satisfy this constraint is frustrating and has to be done almost on a frame-to-frame basis. To do this would violate a previously mentioned principle – namely completing the animation of the higher nodes before moving onto the lower ones. It is easy to get into a loop where lower node adjustment requires a subsequent adjustment further up the hierarchy which affects the first lower adjustment . . . .

As we have discussed this is where inverse kinematics comes into its own but we can now note that there is absolutely no guarantee that an inverse kinematics solution would result in precisely the rotation angles and rates that the animator requires – perhaps, for example, to exaggerate a particular aspect in the walk cycle for the purpose of characterization.

An alternative approach that still uses forward kinematics is to recognize that as the foot during the support phase can be seen as 'driving' the animation, the hierarchy should be constructed so that the foot is at the top of the tree. That way we can be sure that the foot behaves correctly with respect to the floor. The sequence shown in Plate 54 is an example of just such an animation. Note that we can now put the floor in with impunity. Here the foot is separated (Figure 16.29) into ball and heel to

Placement   Lift-off

Figure 16.29   Foot used in walking man sequence is itself an articulated structure.

emphasize the rotation about the heel during the support phase and the rotation about the ball during lift-off.

However, we have just moved the problem to the transfer phase of the cycle when the hip should be the top of the hierarchy.

Neither approach, then, is very satisfactory but a combination of the two would be an improvement, that is, animate from the hip down during the transfer phase of the cycle and from the foot up during the support phase.

This implies that a powerful addition to a forward kinematics system would be the ability to redefine the hierarchy of the structure during its animation. The hierarchy usually has its root at the 'centre' of the animation. By 'centre' we mean that node in the articulated structure whose movement has most effect on the remaining structure. If this centre changes during the animation then the hierarchy should be reconfigured, or rerooted so that the root of the hierarchy follows the centre. In the case of a walk, the centre is the foot during support and the hip during transfer. If the walking man were suddenly to swing from a bar, by the right arm say, then the hierarchy would have to be rerooted to the right hand.

In our state space terminology rerooting the tree is equivalent to changing from one state basis to another.

Hip root

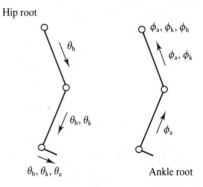

Ankle root

Figure 16.30   Inverting the hierarchy in a forward kinematics system.

Figure 16.30 shows identical leg positions under two different roots (one tree is the reverse of the other) and hence two different bases. Let the two state vectors be:

$$\boldsymbol{\theta} = (\theta_h, \theta_k, \theta_a)$$
$$\boldsymbol{\phi} = (\phi_a, \phi_k, \phi_h)$$

Both the state vectors describe the same configuration at the point of transition. This is written as:

$$X = f(\boldsymbol{\theta}) = g(\boldsymbol{\phi})$$

Note that although θ_h and ϕ_h both describe rotation about the hip (similarly for θ_a, ϕ_a and θ_k, ϕ_k) they will not, in general, be the same. This is because although the mappings $f(\ )$ and $g(\ )$ contain the same transformation matrices, they are applied in the reverse order and, as we know, transformations are not in general commutative.

The problem of rerooting from $\boldsymbol{\theta}$ to $\boldsymbol{\phi}$, then, involves the solution of a set of equations at the point of transition, namely given g, f and $\boldsymbol{\theta}$ find $\boldsymbol{\phi}$ such that

$$\boldsymbol{\phi} = g^{-1}(f(\boldsymbol{\theta})) \tag{16.6}$$

The problem is compounded further. If we consider the animation as a path through state space (referred to earlier) the solution of Equation (16.6) ensures only zero-order continuity of the path at X. Higher order continuities will almost certainly need to be observed if the articulated figure is to move smoothly over this rerooting. This implies solving for the rates of change of $\boldsymbol{\phi}$ given the velocity of X.

16.7 A case study of interacting articulated figures

Finally, we consider an example showing how articulated structures can interact with each other. In the sequence shown as Plate 55 bears interact with each other and with several props. A bear is an articulated structure (Figure 16.31). Consider the animation of bear A to the lower right in the foreground. We shall go through the separate transformations trees that need to be set up to achieve this animation:

1. *Frame F0 to frame F1*   Bear A bends down to pick up a skittle. This is done by applying to the body an

x-roll through axis x_1. As the body is the top of the tree the entire structure picks up this x-roll and the legs are kept attached to the floor by applying a compensatory local x-roll to them, exactly cancelling out the x-roll x_1.

2. *Frame F2 to frame F3*   Bear A picks up a skittle and throws it into the air. This is done by linking the skittle to a local x-roll of the arms about axis x_2. The arms rotate upwards and the skittle follows. At the point of release the skittle becomes unlinked from the bear and is animated independently, proceeding to fall and bounce on the floor. While this is happening the head receives a z-roll about the z-axis as it spots bear B pushing the red box.

3. *Frame F4 to frame F7*   Bear A turns and runs to the red box. This is achieved by applying a z-roll to the body about axis z_1 through the right leg.

4. *Frame F8 to frame F12*   Bear A jumps and rides on the red box. At the point of contact of the bear with the box, the bear becomes linked to the global x-shift of the red box (which is in turn linked to the global x-shift of bear B).

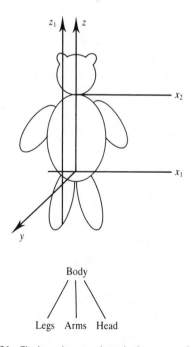

Figure 16.31   The bear character shown in the sequence in Plate 55.

5. *Frame F0 to frame F7*   Bear C runs across the stage carrying a green balloon to bear D who is carrying the three balloons. Carrying a balloon means linking the balloon's position shift to that of the relevant bear.

6. *Frame F8*   Bear C hands bear D the green balloon. The green balloon is unlinked from bear C's hierarchy and linked to bear D's position shift.

7. *Frame F9 to frame F12*   Bear D floats off swaying gently as it does so. Balloons are linked to bear D's global z-shift for floating. The balloons are made to sway by applying a y-roll, about an axis y_1 that passes through the left hand. The bear sways slightly less in the opposite direction (an ad hoc simulation of the conservation of angular momentum) by applying an overcompensating y-roll about y_1 to nullify and oppose the balloon's y-roll.

This example shows how a complicated animation can be built up between articulated structures and/or single actors. These facilities can be described in general terms as:

- Attaching/detaching a single actor to/from an articulated structure (adding/removing a leaf to/from a tree).

- Attaching/detaching articulated structures to/from a leaf to another articulated structure (adding/removing a branch to/from a tree).

17 Soft object animation

Introduction

One of the major motivations of three-dimensional shape animation is to extend the degrees of freedom of conventional computer animation. Compared with traditional animation, the computer animator is restricted to an environment where the virtual camera can be choreographed and objects can be moved. Great efforts are made by computer animators to extract novelty and variety from these somewhat limited aspects. Importing the tricks of traditional animation into computer animation is difficult. One of the most important aspects of Disney-type animation is the ability to give characters a pseudopersonality and, with the possible exception of the landmark film *Luxo Jr.* [LASS87], this aspect, by definition, is not available to three-dimensional computer animators. Another attribute of traditional animation [THOM84] is shape distortion (called 'stretch and squeeze') that is used to highlight dynamic action such as deceleration due to collisions. The artistic domain of three-dimensional animation can be extended by the introduction of shape deformation into the field.

Soft object animation blurs the traditional distinction made in computer graphics between modelling and animating. One can view soft object animation equally as either a modelling process where a different model is created for each frame, or as an animation process where we animate the data that represents the model. The distinction between modelling and animation thus breaks down – the two operations are now intimately linked. Because of this, the methods that are reviewed include work from areas where the original paper may have been

a static graphics technique, but which exhibited a shape animation potential, as well as papers which explicitly claim a shape animation technique.

Whatever method is employed to perform soft object animation we identify two separate processes. These may or may not be explicitly separable depending on the method used:

1. There will be a mechanism or method which facilitates the deformation of the object representation.

2. There will be a method that animates the nature of the deformation as a function of time.

At its most basic, the deformation is usually achieved by moving the vertices of a polygonal model or the control points of a parametric one; the animation is achieved by the choreography of this movement. The organization of this chapter reflects this distinction between deformation and animation. It is divided into the following sections: first, we consider how the representation of the object impacts on the way in which it is to be deformed. Secondly, we cover techniques of deformation that are independent of the object's representation. Finally, we discuss ways of animating deformation.

17.1 Deformation and representation

This section looks at the ways in which the deformation of an object depends on how it is modelled or represented. The representational scheme generally places restrictions on the nature and extent of the deformation that is used. This is best demonstrated by taking the two most common representations, namely polygonal and parametric surfaces, and comparing the consequences of applying an arbitrary deformation to each (these two representations are also compared, within a purely modelling context, in Section 3.2.1). Generally, a polygonal object is deformed by moving one of its vertices and a parametric surface is deformed when one of its control points is moved.

17.1.1 Deforming the polygonal representation

The vertices in a polygon mesh model cannot be treated as a set of independent particles, each possessing their own animation, because they have an implicit connectivity that must be 'respected' by any deformation. The deformation applies only to the vertices of the model – the newly deformed model is retrieved from the unaltered connectivity between the vertices. Deformational schemes applied to polygonal objects are constrained by these connecting links between vertices. Problems occur if deformations are nonglobal or if the nature of the transformation is such that, for example, edges between vertices cross over when deformations are applied to the vertices. For example, we cannot twist a cube, represented as six surfaces without limit, and retain a structure suitable for rendering.

There is a major drawback in the deformation of the polygonal representation which can generally be thought of as a three-dimensional aliasing problem. Problems occur when the deformation is too complex with respect to the object representation. The vertices can be thought of as sample points in three-dimensional space and the shape change or deformation as a three-dimensional function that has to be adequately sampled by these vertices. Deformations where the vertices, initially planar, are moved far apart and become nonplanar have the effect of reducing the polygonal resolution of the deformed model, giving rise to a degradation in silhouette edge aliasing and so on. The polygonal resolution constrains the nature of the deformation and this can only be overcome by subdividing or increasing the resolution of the polygonal object depending on the 'severity' of the deformation.

17.1.2 Deforming the parametric representation

The most significant advantage the parametric representation enjoys over the polygonal one lies in the fact that it can handle a deformation of any complexity and still appear smooth. This is because in altering the positions of the control points we are merely changing the coefficients of the basis functions, that is, altering the functional description of the surface. The deformed parametric surface is therefore in no sense less well defined than its undeformed counterpart. Whether or not the deformed object is a faithful representation of the deformation itself is another matter – the point is that whatever the deformation a parametrically deformed surface will be immune to the degradation associated with deformed polygonal objects.

The deformation of parametric surfaces is just as prone to three-dimensional aliasing as the polygonal representation in that it may not accurately reflect the deformation we intended to make. Furthermore, this problem is exacerbated in the parametric case since, in general, the control points of a parametric object are more sparsely distributed than the vertices of a polygonal object of comparable curvature. Applying a localized deformation to a parametric object that falls between control points will result in no deformation whatsoever. The work of Forsey and Bartels [FORS88], described below, is particularly relevant in this context.

As remarked in Chapter 3, it is generally a more difficult problem to represent objects parametrically than polygonally. The parametric surface cannot easily represent objects possessing a complicated topology. This is because by far the most established type of parametric surface is the rectangular bicubic patch – consequently only objects with a rectilinear topology can be represented. Research has been conducted into alternative patch shapes, such as the triangular patch, but have so far yielded little success [REEV90].

The restrictions placed upon the type of deformation applicable to the parametric representation arise mainly from the properties of the basis functions used and the need to maintain continuity across adjacent patches. We illustrate this point by considering the deformation of Bézier and B-spline patches; obviously these considerations are closely related to the issue of continuity across patches in a modelling context. This issue is dealt with in detail in Chapter 3.

17.2 Deformation of Bézier patch representation

Although a composite Bézier surface can be constructed from a number of patches, each of which can be individually controlled, there are continuity constraints between patches that constrain the movement of the control points. A cubic Bézier patch is given by:

$$Q(u,v) = \sum_{i=0}^{3} \sum_{j=0}^{3} p_{ij} B_i(u) B_j(v)$$

For our purposes, we consider this expression as a set of 16 bivariate functions formed from the tensor product of the two sets of four univariate basis functions. These functions are scaled or weighted by p_{ij}, the network of control vertices, to form the surface patch. Controlling the position of the control points facilitates the shape change of the object that the patch represents.

As explained in Section 3.3.8, to maintain continuity between Bézier curve segments, control points cannot be moved in isolation. They have to be moved in groups of three. C^1 continuity implies that the boundary point between two segments, the point to the left and the point to the right of the boundary point must all be collinear.

Going up a dimension, the constraints on deforming a Bézier patch are even more restrictive. Again as described in Section 3.3.8, observing continuity constraints means that groups of 3×3 control points have to be maintained as coplanar points. Figure 17.1 shows a deformation of a single Bézier curve which is achieved

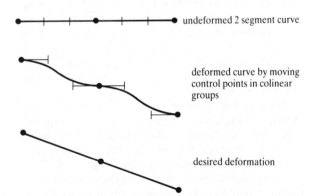

undeformed 2 segment curve

deformed curve by moving control points in colinear groups

desired deformation

Figure 17.1 The formation of plateaux by moving control points in colinear groups.

by splitting the curve into two segments and moving the control points of the segments, observing the above continuity constraint. The continuity constraints introduce two unfavourable consequences. First, they introduce unnatural plateau effects into the deformation. Secondly, it is not possible to have a localized deformation that, by definition, affects only a small part of the surface, since the continuity constraint may well propagate this change further afield.

17.3 Deformation of B-spline patch representation

For precisely the same reasons that B-splines are preferable to Béziers in a modelling context they are superior within the context of deformation. To recap, the reasons are:

1. Up to C^2 continuity across patches is guaranteed automatically as this is a property of the B-spline basis function. Therefore there is no need for continuity constraints.

2. The absence of continuity constraints, together with the locality of the B-spline basis functions, enables us to perform true localized deformations on the B-spline surface leaving the rest of the surface unchanged.

17.3.1 Hierarchical B-spline deformation

The work of Forsey and Bartels [FORS88] represents an important development in the manipulation of B-spline surfaces. One of the problems they identified was the difficulty in varying the scale of the deformations applied to the surface. Moving a given control point produces a change in those patches that share the control point. The scale of this change is thus related solely to the size of the patches. Should a deformation be required that is much finer than the patch resolution then the standard solution is to represent the surface by breaking up the cubic segments into smaller cubic segments and a correspondingly larger number of control points. The patches are correspondingly smaller so that movement of one of these control points produces a deformation on a correspondingly smaller scale.

Mathematically the process is as follows. We define the original surface as:

$$Q(u, v) = \sum_{i=0}^{n} \sum_{j=0}^{m} p_{ij} N_{i,k}(u) N_{j,l}(v)$$

where $N_{i,k}(u)$ is the blending function of degree k for the nonuniform B-spline (Section 3.5.5). Recall that the blending function is nonzero on only k spans. Consequently the act of moving a control point p_{ij} will affect $k \times l$ patch segments only. Using procedures based on the Oslo algorithm, that enables via knot insertion arbitrary refinements of the surface, we can re-express the surface as:

$$Q(u, v) = \sum_{i=0}^{N} \sum_{j=0}^{M} q_{ij} N_{i,k}(u) N_{j,l}(v)$$

and the $(n + 1) \times (m + 1)$ array of control points p_{ij} is replaced by the $(N + 1) \times (M + 1)$ array q_{ij} where, obviously, $N > n$ and $M > m$. Full details on deriving the new set of control points q_{ij} from p_{ij} is given in [FORS88]. Although $k \times l$ patches are still affected by a single control point, the parametric range of the individual curve segments has been reduced so the degree of influence of the control point has effectively been decreased.

Now this operation is global in that the entire surface is represented, that is, there is a large-scale replacement of ps by qs. If one wishes to have fine control over only a small region of the surface the entire surface has to be refined. ps that have no influence on the region to be edited are changed along with those that do have influence, thereby generating more q control points than we have any intention of moving.

Forsey and Bartels point out that, in terms of storage, this process is very wasteful. A more desirable state of affairs would be to retain only those qs that interest us, discarding the rest and retaining the unedited portion in its p definition. In order to do this, we define the minimal surface of the control point that we wish to move as follows. The minimal surface is the smallest section of surface that satisfies the following two conditions:

1. Movement of the control point produces deformations that are localized to this surface.

2. Regardless of the movement of the control point the derivatives at the boundary of the surface remain unchanged.

The second condition ensures that the minimal surface will always coincide with the larger surface from which

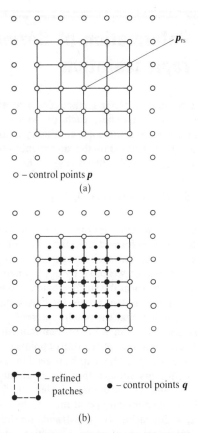

Figure 17.2 (a) Sixteen patch minimal surface with 49 control points. (b) Central 4 patches refined to 16 patches (after [FORS88]).

it is derived. In the cubic case the minimal surface is 16 patches made up of the square grid of 7×7 control points centred at the control point to be moved. Figure 17.2(a) shows schematically the minimal surface of the control point p_{rs}. In the general B-spline case the minimal surface is made up of a square grid of $(1 + 2k) \times (1 + 2l)$ control points centred at the control point to be moved.

Now suppose that the movement results in a deformation too coarse in nature. We therefore subdivide the surface to give us the next minimal surface, centred at p_{rs}, at the next level of refinement. In the bicubic case this is done by splitting the central 4 patches to give us the 7×7 grid of q control points constituting the minimal surface of 16 smaller patches. This is shown in Figure 17.2(b) where the q control points are represented by the black dots and the smaller patches by the dashed lines.

These minimal surfaces are stored hierarchically as a series of overlays. Each level of the hierarchy corresponds to a different level of refinement. At the root there is the original undeformed surface. If, at a given level, overlays have control points in common then they are replaced by a composite overlay made up of the union of their control points. The user can operate on the surface at any desired level of refinement by moving control vertices at that level. The user can traverse the hierarchy in either direction and coarse refinement will 'carry'

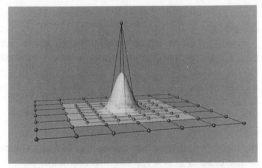

(a)

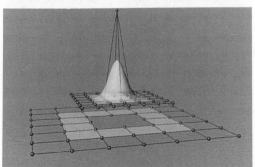

(b)

(c)

Figure 17.3 Hierarchical B-spline refinement. (a) Minimal surface of a B-spline surface at a certain level of refinement. (b) The effect of splitting the central four control points at the next level of refinement. (c) The two surfaces in (b) separated as they would be in a hierarchy of overlays.

previous fine refinements, in the same region, due to the representation of control vertices in terms of offsets relative to a local reference frame.

The refinement process is shown in practice in Figure 17.3. Figure 17.3(a) shows the minimal surface of a B-spline surface at a certain level of refinement. The black spheres correspond to our p control points. The central control point is displaced vertically by a given amount. Figure 17.3(b) shows the effect of splitting the central four control points at the next level of refinement to give us our q control points. The central control point has again been displaced vertically by the same amount and you can see that the resultant deformation is more localized than that of Figure 17.3(a). In Figure 17.3(c) we have separated the two surfaces just as they would be separated in a hierarchy of overlays.

17.4 Deformation independent of representation

This section covers two developments in deformation techniques that are particularly useful in that they are independent of representation. In practice, this means they can be applied equally to both the polygonal and the parametric representation. The first represents a generalization of the standard modelling operations facilitating nonlinear global deformations of objects [BARR84]. The second is a unique and powerful approach that deforms objects by deforming the space in which the object is embedded [SEDE86].

17.4.1 Nonlinear global deformation

Suppose we wish to perform a standard modelling operation, such as scaling, on an object. The operation, usually in the form of a transformation matrix, is applied to each of the vertices (or control points) in turn. Throughout this procedure the transformation matrix does not change. The innovation behind Barr's approach is to alter the transformation *while* it is being applied to the object. The way in which the transformation is altered becomes a function of the position at which it is applied. It is as if the transformation itself undergoes a transformation before it is applied to the object. Three of Barr's transformations are now described. They are:

tapering, twisting and bending. Barr uses a formula definition for the transformations:

$$(X, Y, Z) = F(x, y, z)$$

where (x, y, z) is a vertex in an undeformed solid and (X, Y, Z) is the position of the deformed vertex. Using this notation the standard scaling transformation, for example, is:

$$(X, Y, Z) = (s_x x, s_y y, s_z z)$$

where (s_x, s_y, s_z) are the scaling coefficients along the three axes. Tapering is easily developed from scaling. We

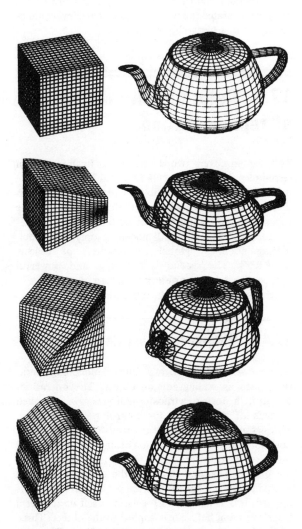

Figure 17.4 Structure-deforming transformations.

choose a tapering axis and differentially scale the other two components. In effect we are scaling a scaling transformation. Thus to taper an object along its z-axis, we just scale the scaling along the x- and y-axes as a function of z:

$$(X, Y, Z) = (rx, ry, z)$$

where:

$$r = f(z)$$

is a linear or nonlinear tapering profile or function.

Global axial twisting can be developed as a differential rotation just as tapering is a differential scaling. In effect, all we are doing is scaling the rotation angle of a rotation transformation. To rotate an object through an angle θ about the z-axis we apply:

$$(X, Y, Z) = (x \cos \theta - y \sin \theta, x \sin \theta + y \cos \theta, z)$$

Now if we allow the amount of rotation to vary as a function of z the object will become twisted. This is done by setting:

$$\theta = f(z)$$

where $f(z)$ specifies the rate of twist per unit length along the z-axis.

Finally, a global linear bend along an axis is a composite transformation comprising a bent region and a region outside the bent region where the deformation is a rotation and a translation. Barr defines a bend region along the y-axis as:

$$y_{min} \leqslant y \leqslant y_{max}$$

the radius of curvature of the bend is k^{-1} and the centre of the bend is at $y = y_0$. The bending angle is:

$$\theta = k(y' - y_0))$$

where:

$$y' = \begin{cases} y_{min} & \text{if } y \leqslant y_{min} \\ y & \text{if } y_{min} < y < y_{max} \\ y_{max} & \text{if } y \geqslant y_{max} \end{cases}$$

The deforming transformation is given by:

$$X = x$$

$$Y = \begin{cases} -\sin \theta (z - k^{-1}) + y_0 & y_{min} \leqslant y \leqslant y_{max} \\ -\sin \theta (z - k^{-1}) + y_0 + \cos \theta (y - y_{min}) & y < y_{min} \\ -\sin \theta (z - k^{-1}) + y_0 + \cos \theta (y - y_{max}) & y > y_{max} \end{cases}$$

$$Z = \begin{cases} \cos\Theta\left(z-k^{-1}\right)+k^{-1} & y_{\min} \leqslant y \leqslant y_{\max} \\ \cos\Theta\left(z-k^{-1}\right)+k^{-1}+\sin\Theta\left(y-y_{\min}\right) & y < y_{\min} \\ \cos\Theta\left(z-k^{-1}\right)+k^{-1}+\sin\Theta\left(y-y_{\max}\right) & y > y_{\max} \end{cases}$$

Figure 17.4 shows an example of each of these three transformations in turn. The deformation on the cube is an intuitive reflection of the effects and the same transformations are applied to the Utah teapot. More general shape change can be achieved by using a combination of these transformations. Plate 56 shows the effect of a tapering operation followed by a twisting operation applied to an initial primitive best described as a corrugated cylinder to achieve a conch shell-like shape.

To summarize, Barr extends the range of modelling transformations by allowing the transformations themselves to be modified according to where they are applied in space. In the case of twisting and tapering this modification is achieved by the use of a profile curve $(f(z))$ that weights the scaling or rotation angle, respectively. We shall see later (Section 17.5.2) that a generalization of this technique, which takes a transformation and modifies it according to when it appears in *time*, is very useful in that it provides us with a powerful and flexible tool for animating deformation.

17.4.2 Free form deformation

The second representational-independent deformation technique we shall look at is the Free Form Deformation (FFD). Where Barr's deformations are restricted to particular transformations, this technique, developed by Sederburg [SEDE86], is completely general. In this respect it is the more flexible of the two and eminently suitable for soft object animation.

The unique aspect of the method is that instead of deforming the object directly, the object is embedded in a space that is then deformed. Sederburg uses the physical analogy of a parallelepiped of clear flexible plastic, in which is embedded one or even a number of objects. The plastic is deformed and the objects change shape in a manner that Sederburg describes as being 'intuitively consistent'.

Another useful analogy of the process is the deformation of two-dimensional space using a bicubic surface patch. Let us represent two-dimensional space as a grid of squares that are mapped onto an initially planar, square surface patch. If we move the control points of this surface patch arbitrarily then the grid of squares and hence two-dimensional space become distorted. More-

Figure 17.5 Two-dimensional deformation of grid textured onto a patch: a two-dimensional analogy of the FFD process.

over, we can track how a point distorts by substituting its u, v-coordinates into the patch definition to find its new position. This process is shown schematically in Figure 17.5. The control points of a hyperpatch are used to control the deformation of three-dimensional space in a manner entirely analogous to this situation; we simply add an extra dimension.

A single tricubic Bézier hyperpatch is defined as:

$$Q(u, v, w) = \sum_{i=0}^{3} \sum_{j=0}^{3} \sum_{k=0}^{3} p_{ijk} B_i(u) B_j(v) B_k(w) \quad \textbf{(17.1)}$$

where $B_i(u)$, $B_j(v)$ and $B_k(w)$ are the Bernstein polynominals of degree 3 (see Section 3.3). The hyperpatch is specified by a three-dimensional grid of 64 control points p_{ijk} and defines a volume of space parametrized by the three parameters u, v and w where u, v, $w \in [0, 1]$.

Hyperpatches can be connected together to form a piecewise Bézier volume. We shall call this composite of hyperpatches an FFD block. The undeformed FFD block consists of a rectangular lattice of control points arranged along three mutually perpendicular axes. Let the three sides be represented by the vectors (S, T, U). We defined the FFD block to be an array of $(3l + 1) \times (3m + 1) \times (3n + 1)$ control points, or, equivalently, a stack of $l \times m \times n$ hyperpatches. The steps involved in deforming an object embedded in this FFD block proceed as follows (we assume, for simplicity, that the object is polygonal – for parametrically defined objects substitute the words 'control point' for the word 'vertex'):

1. *Determine the positions of the vertices in lattice space.* We set up a local parametric coordinate system of the FFD block, termed 'lattice space', given by:

$$X(s, t, u) = X_0 + sS + tT + uU$$

where X_0 is the origin of the local coordinate system (a corner of the FFD block) and S, T and U lie along the edges of the volume. Since the magnitudes of these vectors reflect the dimensions of the volume, it follows that any point interior to the volume has lattice space coordinates (s, t, u) where $s, t, u \in [0, 1]$. Control point locations are thus given by:

$$p_{ijk} = X_0 + \left(\frac{i}{3l}\right) S + \left(\frac{j}{3m}\right) T + \left(\frac{k}{3n}\right) U$$

where $0 \leqslant i \leqslant 3l$, $0 \leqslant j \leqslant 3m$, $0 \leqslant k \leqslant 3n$. Since it would be perverse to do otherwise, we assume the object space is defined using coordinate axes parallel to (S, T, U). For a vertex within the FFD block, then, its lattice space coordinates are easily found from its object space coordinates (requiring the solution of three linear equations only). All vertices are assigned their (s, t, u) triples which stay with them unchanged throughout the deformation. At this stage the only difference between the lattice parameter space and object space is one of scale.

2. *Deform the FFD block.* This is achieved by moving the control points p_{ijk} from their undisplaced, lattice positions. As in the case of Bézier curve and surface patches there are meaningful relationships between the deformation and the placement of control points. The lattice space coordinates of a point now record only its parametric position within the FFD block. Varying u, say, now moves us along a Bézier curve (whereas undeformed we would have moved along a straight line) and similarly varying, say, s and t moves along the surface of a Bézier patch (whereas undeformed we would have moved along a plane).

3. *Determine the deformed positions of the vertices.* After the deformation, object space and lattice space are obviously very different. Now the transition from lattice space to object space is nontrivial since this transition amounts to the deformation itself. Given the lattice space coordinates (s, t, u) of a vertex, we find the relevant hyperpatch within which it is located and convert to the local (u, v, w) coordinate system of the hyperpatch. The location of the hyperpatch is indexed by the integer part of (ls, mt, nu), which we write as (is, it, iu), and the conversion from lattice space to its local coordinates is given by, trivially:

$$(u, v, w) = (ls - is, mt - it, nu - iu)$$

The final step is to substitute the value of (u, v, w) into Equation (17.1) to get the deformed position of the vertex $Q(u, v, w)$.

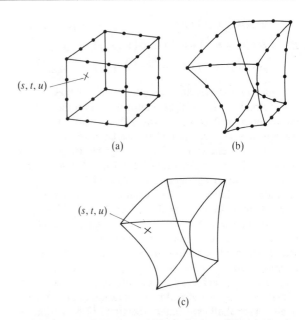

(a)   (b)

(c)

Figure 17.6 The FFD process. (a) Determine (s, t, u) for point interior to hyperpatch. (b) Deform hyperpatch by moving control points. (c) Find deformed positions of point from (s, t, u).

These steps are shown schematically in Figure 17.6 for an FFD block consisting of one hyperpatch only with control points on the edges of the block shown as dots. Figure 17.7 shows the effect a single hyperpatch (rendered black) has on objects embedded within it (rendered white). The 64 control points of the hyperpatch are represented by the black spheres, the control points that are not interior to the hyperpatch are connected together. Figure 17.7(b) shows the effect of moving a few control points. The white lattice structure within the hyperpatch is made up of cylinders that run along isolines of constant u, v or w. Undeformed they run along straight lines, deformed they run along Bézier curves and provide a·sense of how the space within the hyperpatch becomes warped. The deformation of the sphere (Figures 17.7(c) and (d)) shows how a more typical object becomes deformed within this space.

Although objects themselves can be represented as hyperpatches (some CAD systems use tricubic representations, for example, [CASA85]), important advantages result from distinguishing between the hyperpatch as a deformable space and points which are embedded within it. The method can be applied locally to deform just part of a space, containing, say, a single object or part of an object, or it can be applied globally to the whole scene. If applied locally derivative continuity can be maintained

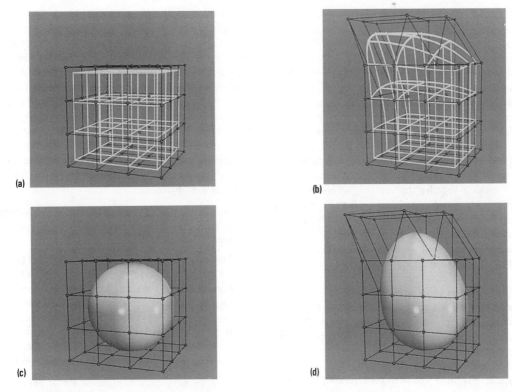

Figure 17.7 FFD deformation. (a) A single hyperpatch coloured black. The 64 control points are shown as black spheres. The white structure is a representation of the hyperpatch space. (b) Moving the control points distorts the space. For example, planes of constant *w* now become Bézier patches. (c) A sphere in the hyperpatch space. (d) The sphere deformed by moving the control points in the same way as for (b).

between the deformed and undeformed regions by not deforming that part of the FFD block connected to the undeformed region. Also, two or more FFDs can be defined in a piecewise manner to provide for complex deformations beyond the power of a single FFD. Again, cross-boundary continuity can be maintained by maintaining continuity constraints across the two FFD blocks in a manner completely analogous to preserving continuity across two surface Bézier patches.

If the FFD mesh is comparable in complexity to the object it is deforming then the previously mentioned three-dimensional aliasing problem can arise. A good rule of thumb is that the 'curvature' of the deformation introduced should not approach the maximum curvature of the undeformed object. Plate 57 shows the wireframe and rendered versions of a spoon and its FFD blocks. Note that the polygonal resolution of the spoon is a lot higher than that of the FFD block. If problems do arise then they can be dealt with by subdividing the polygon mesh. An animated sequence of the spoon deforming is shown in Plate 58 and is discussed in detail in Section 17.5.1 which also contains other instances of FFD blocks used to animate deformation.

Finally, the disadvantage of the FFD method is that it is really a global deformation method in that it takes a space and bends it. It works well for the examples given, but falls down when complex, subtle, local deformations are required over a surface, such as would occur when modelling facial expression. The number of FFD blocks that would have to be used would render the technique unworkable.

17.4.3 Extended free form deformation

A development of the FFD method appears in the work of Coquillart [COQU90] as the so-called Extended Free Form Deformation (EFFD). Coquillart points out that the intrinsic parallelepiped shape of the FFD block constrains the shape of the deformation. In order to remove this restriction nonparallelepiped lattices are introduced. An EFFD block differs from an FFD block in that it allows such lattices to be part of its structure; the FFD block definition becomes a subset of the EFFD block definition which can be made up of any number of any type of lattice.

One of these lattices, the cylindrical lattice, turns out to be particularly useful. Its construction is shown schematically in Figure 17.8. An FFD block consisting of a row of six hyperpatches is shown in lattice space in Figure 17.8(a). The control points are arranged circularly, as shown in Figure 17.8(b). The two ends of the block are welded together by merging corresponding control points in the two end planes $s = 0$ and $s = 1$. The cylindrical lattice is obtained by merging control points that lie along the u-axis, more specifically, all control points satisfying $u = 0$ and $t = 0$ are made coincident, as are all control points satisfying $u = 1$ and $t = 0$ (Figure 17.8(c)). This is an example of an elementary EFFD block; more complex cases can be designed by welding such elementary blocks together. Care must be taken when merging control points from separate blocks to ensure continuity by also merging the corresponding tangents. Specific examples of this design process are discussed in more detail in [COQU90].

Once the EFFD block has been constructed, it is used to deform an object in a manner largely similar to that

for the strictly parallelepiped FFD block detailed in the previous section. You will recall that this proceeded in three stages: first, the coordinates of the object in lattice space are determined by solving three linear equations; secondly, the FFD block is deformed; and finally, the position of the deformed vertex is derived. For EFFD blocks the first stage is different. Previously, the fact that the axes of the FFD block and the axes of object space were aligned made the transformation from object space to lattice space trivial. For EFFDs, by definition, we cannot assume such a simple connection between the two spaces. The calculation proceeds in two steps, for a given point on the object:

1. We use the convex hull property of the hyperpatch to find the relevant hyperpatch within which the point is located.

2. The local u, v, w-coordinates of the point $Q(u, v, w)$ are found by performing Newtonian iteration on Equation (17.1) where the P_{ijk} are the *undeformed* control points of the hyperpatch. Coquillart reports that simply using a starting point for the iteration at $(u, v, w) = (0.5, 0.5, 0.5)$ usually results in convergence. For divergent cases she suggests subdividing the hyperpatch and repeating the exercise.

So far we have only considered FFDs being applied more or less globally to an object. Coquillart considers EFFDs applied locally to the surface of an object. In this way the EFFD and the object become disassociated from one another, enabling the introduction of a modelling tool paradigm, where the object is deformed with an EFFD block that can be taken from a 'toolkit' of EFFD blocks, each of which can be applied in a variety of contexts over more than one object.

The technique is simple and powerful. Plate 59(a) shows a cylindrical EFFD block attached onto a surface. Plate 59(b) shows the EFFD block being deformed and Plate 59(c) the result that this has on the surface. Plate 60(a) shows a similar cylindrical EFFD block, again with two hyperpatches extending in the radial direction, applied to an entire surface. Plate 60(b) shows the deformation applied to the block and the result – Plate 60(c) – a convincing tablecloth.

17.5 Animating deformation

Since most deformation is achieved by the movement of either vertices or control points, the problem of ani-

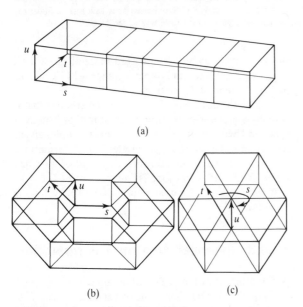

(a)

(b)   (c)

Figure 17.8 Construction of cylindrical EFFD. (a) Hyperpatches in lattice space. (b) 'Welding' end control planes. (c) Merging control points on u-axis.

mating deformation reduces to how to choreograph and orchestrate the movement of these points. The deformation schemes enumerated above are low level in that they work well when a few, simple deformations are required. For more complex animations, such as a large number of interacting local deformations acting on an object containing a large number of vertices, however, it becomes hopelessly impractical to animate using these tools. The need for higher level control (discussed in general in Section 15.1) is just as great when animating deformation as it is in other areas of animation. Now the control hierarchy not only has to manage the purely kinetic details, it also has to drive the modelling procedures to effect the shape change itself.

Other considerations outlined in other areas of animation need to be adhered to here. For example, easing-in and easing-out are just as relevant in starting and stopping a deformation as they are in the motion of a rigid body.

17.5.1 Animating deformation and characterization control

The most exciting application of soft object animation is in the extension of traditional two-dimensional character animation into three dimensions. This process is still in its very early stages but no one can deny that the goal of being able to produce three-dimensional character animation of the same quality and quantity as those produced by Disney, say, is worth pursuing. As remarked in the general introduction to animation in Chapter 15, there are major difficulties in trying to bring characterization into an environment of solid rigid bodies. Soft object animation is one of the few areas of computer animation that is powerful and general enough to give animators of three-dimensional computer models sufficient shape control to enable some degree of character or personality control.

One of the most fundamental principles of traditional animation is that of squash and stretch. When an object is moved, the movement should reveal the rigidity of the object. Only the most rigid of inanimate objects remain so during motion. Anything composed of living flesh will show considerable distortion in its shape during an action. The standard example given for this is a bouncing ball. The ball, represented by a circle (Figure 17.9) is 'squashed' on impact, and stretched prior to, and after, impact. Obviously, deformation techniques are extremely relevant in this context and later on in this sec-

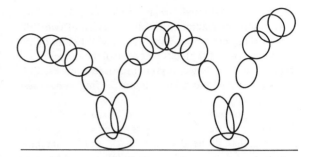

Figure 17.9 The standard example of 'squash and stretch': the bouncing ball.

tion we shall see specific examples of their application to produce squash and stretch sequences.

17.5.2 Factor curves

A simple but powerful technique for the animation of deformation follows from a generalization of Barr's method of nonlinear deformation. You will recall that central to the method was the notion of *weighting* the parameters of a transformation that is being applied to an object by an amount that is a function of the position at which the transformation is applied. In the case of tapering this was achieved by weighting a scaling transformation acting in the x, y-plane as a function of z.

We shall call this function that modifies the parameters of a transformation before it is applied to the object a 'factor curve'. Barr defined factor curves that are functions of space only; we extend the definition of factor curves to include the time domain. This enables us to modify transformations according to *when* they are applied, as well as *where* they are applied. Factor curves, when used to weight parameters, are used multiplicatively; we also allow factor curves to be used additively to add or subtract values from parameters. The basic methodology is as follows. The animator breaks down the problem of animating a deformation into two components:

1. A set of transformations that, taken together, can accomplish the range of deformation required along with a parametrization of these transformations.

2. A set of factor curves in both space and time that modify the parameters of the deforming transformations according to where and when they are applied.

An understanding of the method is best done through example. The animated sequence (Plate 58) shows a spoon jumping through the air then landing. The animation is done by animating the deformation of two FFD blocks that control the upper and lower halves of the spoon and two FFD blocks that control the shapes of the arms. These are shown as grey transparent blocks. FFD blocks are also deployed to animate the fingers but these are not shown.

We will consider the animation of the upper half of the spoon in detail. Just as a human figure, when jumping, has its head thrown back and on landing, has its head then brought forward by momentum, then so has the upper half of the spoon been animated. Emulating the motion of a human figure in this way has the effect of imparting to the spoon a degree of characterization.

The deformation is applied along the vertical axis of the FFD block which is made up of $3 \times 3 \times 7$ hyperpatches – the higher resolution along the axis subject to the deformation. It will be convenient to work in the lattice space of the FFD block. You will recall that points within the block are specified by (u, v, w) where $u, v, w \in [0, 1]$. The animation of the block, shown schematically in Figure 17.10, breaks down as follows:

1. The transformation is simply a rotation about the v-axis. The parameter is just the rotation angle θ about this axis.

2. The space factor curve $f_{\theta w}(w)$ is aligned along the w-axis, and increases with increasing w. Applied to θ this will bend the FFD block away from the vertical. The higher a point within the block the greater its value of w so the more it gets bent. Note that $f_{\theta w}(0) = 0$ implies that the bottom of the block will remain undeformed, ensuring that the surface of the spoon will be continuous across the bottom of the block. The time factor curve $f_{\theta t}(t)$ is set up with a large negative value at the start, corresponding to the upper spoon being bent backwards, moving through zero, where the block will be undeformed, to a smaller positive value as the head gets thrown slightly forwards.

Given an initial value for θ, say θ_0, the deforming transformation for a point (u, v, w) is thus a rotation about the v-axis of an amount given by:

$$\theta = \theta_0 f_{\theta w}(w) f_{\theta t}(t)$$

This expression represents a powerful overall parametrization of the animation. The factor curves $f_{\theta w}( )$ and $f_{\theta t}( )$ could be specified analytically, but far greater

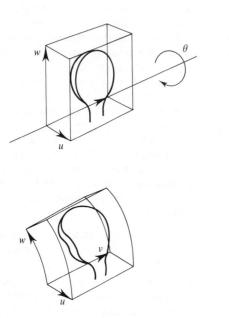

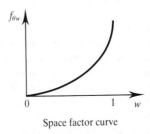

Space factor curve

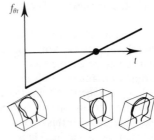

Time factor curve

Figure 17.10 Factor curves and resultant deformation.

Figure 17.11 Stick figure jumping.

flexibility is afforded if the animator can construct them interactively using, say, cubic splines. The use of these curves to control the animation is highly intuitive and their modification gives the animator easy access to a wide range of artistic possibility.

This example shows the use of factor curves to deform FFD blocks which, in turn, deform the object embedded in the block. The factor curve method is not restricted to animating FFD blocks, however; there is no reason why it could not be applied directly to the object itself as the next example illustrates.

The animated sequence (Plate 63) shows an environment-mapped kettle jumping into the air. Reference to Plate 64, which places the kettle *in situ*, shows, in terms of the storyboard, that the kettle is actually situated on a cooker and leaps excitedly into the air, emitting a whistle, as the spoon and cartons of yoghurt fly past.

Once again, in order to endow the kettle with character we emulate the actions of a jumping human figure. A standing figure about to jump will crouch downwards bending its legs as it does so. The energy required for the jump comes from pushing against the ground which will straighten the legs. Just after the point of lift-off the legs are maximally extended. The jumper will then bring its legs up underneath it in order to gain height. These steps are shown in the stick figure sequence of Figure 17.11 and are drawn to more or less correspond with the frames from the animated kettle sequence.

In the absence of an FFD block, the coordinate system used to apply the transforms is simply the normalized bounding box of the undeformed kettle; a point within the bounding box is specified by (u, v, w) where u, v, $w \in [0, 1]$. Just as in the case of lattice space coordinates, these coordinates are assigned to the points before any deformation occurs and are carried around unchanged throughout subsequent deformations. The animation of the kettle, shown schematically in Figure 17.12, breaks down as follows:

1. The transformations needed are a vertical translation, required to achieve the squashing and stret-

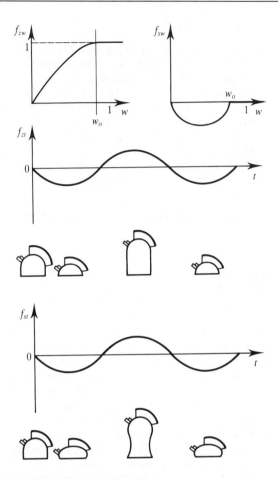

Figure 17.12 Effect of vertical deformation followed by combined effect of vertical and horizontal deformation.

ching of the kettle parametrized by z, followed by a scaling in the x, y-plane parametrized by s. The purpose of the scaling transformation is to augment the vertical deformation, making the kettle bulge out when it is being squashed and contract when it is being stretched. This will imply the kettle has constant volume – an important principle established from the traditional animator's experience of squash and stretch.

2. As in the previous example the parameters are modified by space factor curves aligned along the vertical axis w. The expression for the vertical deformation of a point (u, v, w) is given by a vertical shift by an amount z, where:

$$z = z_0 f_{zw}(w) f_{zt}(t)$$

It was felt that the deformation should occur mainly within the body of the kettle, as far as possible the handle and spout should remain undistorted. This is why the space factor curve for z, $f_{zw}(w)$, is set to unity for $w > w_0$. All points above the plane $w = w_0$ therefore receive identical vertical shifts given by $z_0 f_{zt}(t)$ and so remain undistorted throughout the animation. Below the plane $w = w_0$ the weighting of z decreases down to zero, $f_{zw}(0) = 0$ ensuring that the base of the kettle stays in the plane $w = 0$.

The expression for the horizontal scaling parameter is given by:

$$s = 1 + s_0 f_{sw}(w) f_{st}(t)$$

Note that this is an instance of a factor curve being used additively. For $w > w_0$, $f_{sw}(w)$ is zero and hence s is unity so the top part of the kettle is unaffected throughout the animation. For $w < w_0$ the coefficient s_0 is weighted negatively by $f_{sw}(w)$. This factor curve is constructed thus to highlight the basic similarity between the two time factor curves $f_{zt}()$ and $f_{st}()$, the only difference between them being one of scale. In general, this is not an uncommon occurrence: when two or more transformations are used in combination to create a single animated deformation they are usually highly synchronized. An experienced animator is well aware of this and, where appropriate, will use copies of a single time factor curve as starting points for others.

Finally, from the same storyboard in which the kettle appeared, Plate 65 shows an animated sequence of yoghurt cartons taking off and flying out of a fridge and provides another good example of the applicablity of factor curves when squashing and stretching. Plate 66 shows the yoghurt cartons *in situ*.

17.5.3 Independent animation of deformation and object

The FFD and EFFD methods, originally presented as modelling techniques, readily extend themselves to animating coordinates. In the previous section we saw how a classical approach to animating deformation can be applied to FFD blocks by animating the control points of the FFD blocks – the animation propagating to the object itself in an obvious way. In an interesting extension to previous work, Coquillart and Jancene [COQU91] allow the deformation and the object to be animated *independently* of each other, rather than associating a deformation with an object or part of an object and keeping this association fixed throughout the animation. For the animation two FFD blocks are employed, one being the deformed counterpart of the other. The animation is achieved simply by animating the undeformed object relative to the undeformed FFD block. The lattice space coordinates of the object are thus no longer fixed – as was the case for static deformations. The deformation proceeds automatically as you would expect: the lattice space coordinates of the object, frame for frame, are plugged into the deformed FFD block.

Plates 61 and 62 illustrate the method: in the former the undeformed FFD block is made to move with respect to the object, whereas in the latter the FFD block stays fixed and the object moves. In the case of the cylinder, the undeformed (green) FFD block is translated along the axis of the cylinder. The deformed (red) FFD block then undergoes the same translation. Plate 61(b) shows in a wireframe a side view of six frames of the animation as specified by the animator, and Plate 61(c) the resultant deformation as the swelling travels along the cylinder.

Plate 62(a) simulates the path of a sheet of paper as it moves through a photocopier. This time the FFD block is fixed and the paper simply moves through it as shown in Plate 62(b), Plate 62(c) showing the resultant deformation as the lattice space coordinates of the paper are plugged into the deformed FFD block. This example perhaps illustrates the power of the method – it is difficult to see how such an animation could be achieved more simply.

Coquillart and Jancene also compare their method of animating deformation with that of inbetweening through key deformations which they refer to as metamorphosis. Plate 61(d) shows the animation resulting from specifying two key deformations (corresponding to the first and last frames of Plate 61(c)) and applying a linear interpolation through them to get the deformations for the intermediate frames. Plate 62(d) shows the inbetweening approach applied to the photocopier animation. In this case, three key deformations of the paper were specified and spline interpolation was employed. The blue curve represents the path the paper should have followed. It is clear that in these two contexts at least, the inbetweening approach produces inferior results. Inbetweening key deformation is discussed in more detail in Section 17.8.

17.6 Deformation of animated articulated structures

The kinematic aspects of animating articulated structure is covered in Chapter 16. If the structure is not just a trivial stick figure, that is, if it is 'fleshed out', then as the links move relative to each other, there will be deformation at the joints of these links. The accurate physical simulation of fatty tissue requires complex viscoelastic, anisotropic models which are expensive to compute and hard to control. A more fruitful approach is to take advantage of the sculptural flexibility of the FFD to deform the surface of the structure.

Plate 67 shows partially overlapping FFD blocks being used to control finger bending. Here the deformation of one FFD block occurs after the deformation of another. Where FFD blocks overlap points are deformed twice.

The galloping sequence of Plate 68 shows the method controlling a more elaborate model. This is based on the photographs of E. Muybridge [MUYB99] who photographed, for his classic work *Animals In Motion*, the cycle of limb movements characteristic of a wide variety of tetrapod mammals moving at different speeds. FFD blocks are used to control the deformation across joints in the legs, neck and tail. In this particular example, our somewhat crude method of overlapping FFD blocks is approaching the limits of its usability; some frames show the horse in very peculiar attitudes indeed.

Although useful in simple cases, the problem with this approach is twofold: first, it is difficult to control or predict the deformation in the region where the FFD blocks intersect; and, secondly, the method does not really incorporate within its working the underlying articulated structure.

A far more rigorous approach to this problem is presented by Chadwick *et al.* [CHAD89] with their Critter system. This is a good, working example of a nontrivial control hierarchy (or, as it is referred to in the work, animation in layers) that controls both the kinematic and modelling details. The animator need only specify the motion of the underlying skeleton – consistent yet expressive shape change is generated automatically.

The lowest three layers in the control hierarchy from top to bottom are:

1. The skeletal layer, which is just the underlying articulated structure.

2. The muscle layer: a muscle is modelled as an FFD which is attached to the skeletal structure.

3. The skin layer, which is the polygonal skin of the skeleton and acted upon by the muscle layer in the obvious way.

The control of the muscle layer by the skeletal layer is of particular interest. The muscle is represented as an FFD block consisting of two connected hyperpatches orientated along the axis of the link which gives seven planes of control points orthogonal to the link axis (Figure 17.13). The function of the two control planes at either

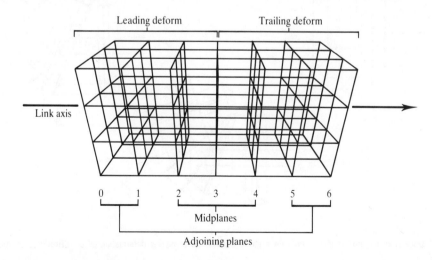

Figure 17.13 Two connected hyperpatches oriented along the link axis (after [CHAD89]).

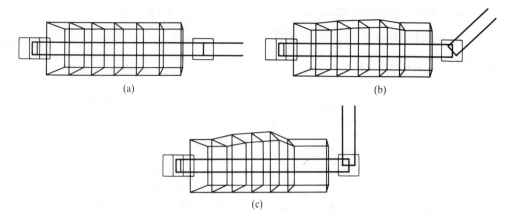

Figure 17.14 FFD block straddling the joint connecting two links (after [CHAD89]). (a) Joint angle zero, no deformation; (b) Joint angle less than threshold continuous deformation; (c) Joint angle greater than threshold creasing.

end is to preserve continuity across the skin. Chadwick *et al.* use procedures based on the underlying positions of the links to orientate and scale these planes separately – full details of these procedures appear in the work.

The bending of the joint is managed by the tendon muscle which is simulated as an FFD block straddling the joint connecting two links. Each tendon muscle has a threshold angle beyond which creasing occurs. The angle between the two links is passed down the hierarchy from the skeletal layer and drives the configuration of the seven planes. Figure 17.14 shows three configurations for three different angles.

The flexor and extendor muscles are also simulated to give the visual effect of muscle contraction – such as would occur to your bicep when you bend your elbow. Each flexor muscle is placed along a link and is assigned a coefficient, the displacement ratio, which scales the shortening of the FFD block proportional to the angle of the joint. In order to preserve volume, or at least its implication, the central control planes are scaled outwards, orthogonal to the link. Figure 17.15 shows three different configurations for three different angles.

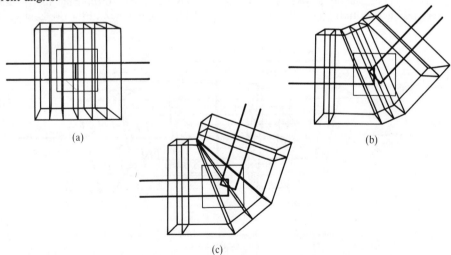

Figure 17.15 FFD block is scaled proportional to the joint angle to simulate flexor muscle deformation (after [CHAD89]). (a) Angle 0°; (b) Angle $\pi/4°$; (c) Angle $\pi/2°$.

17.7 Animating facial expression

In 1987 Keith Waters published an intriguing study [WATE87] for the animation of facial expressions. This consisted of a parametric muscle model that controlled the deformation of a polygon mesh representation of a human face using muscle vectors. The model is based on a notational system called Facial Action Coding System (FACS) [EKMA77] and work by Summerfield [SUMM83] and Badler [BADL81]. The model features muscle processes controllable by a limited number of parameters and is nonspecific to facial topology. Thus his parametrization deals with the 'motivators of the action' and the model can be applied to a model of any face.

Particular parameter values are assigned to muscle models that are consistent between faces. The parameters are abstractions and do not attempt to model underlying physical or neuro–physiological mechanisms.

The vertices, or control points, of models of different faces are controlled by parametric muscle models attached to these points. Thus individual facial topography is maintained in the model of the object, while dynamic movement of the object to form different

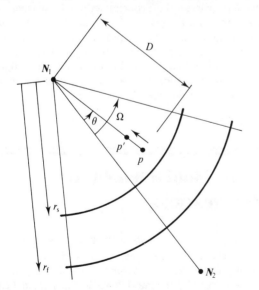

Figure 17.16 Waters' muscle vector model. Points inside the angular zone are displaced towards N_1 when the muscle is activated.

expressions is controlled by the underlying muscle model. Waters produces convincing expressions for happiness, fear, anger, disgust and surprise. The 'signature' of the model is visible in the final animation in a rather intriguing way. This is presumably because we have the facial topology of known individuals all being driven by exactly the same muscle model.

Two types of muscle models are used: linear or parallel muscles that pull and sphincter muscles that squeeze. Waters models a linear muscle as an entity centred on a node, that when 'excited' generates a pull that affects neighbouring nodes. The linear muscle is defined by two points N_1 and N_2 corresponding to the muscle's attachment to the bone and skin respectively. The bone attachment point N_1 remains stationary, the displacement increasing towards the skin attachment point N_2. The vector $N_1 - N_2$ defines the direction of the muscle vector. The remaining parameters of the model define the zone of influence of the muscle and ensure a smooth dropoff in displacement from the point of maximum displacement, N_2, down to zero at the edge of the zone.

The model used is shown in Figure 17.16 for two-dimensional space. This shows a zone of influence around points N_1 and N_2 (an angular region between 150° and 160°). A muscle pull along the vector $(N_1 - N_2)$ moves a point in the zone of influence (in practice a point on the model) from p to p'. A displacement is dissipated throughout the skin in the region of this muscle vector, both along $(N_1 - N_2)$ and radially on either side of this vector. Waters defines a start and finish for the displacement falloff as r_s and r_f and defines a displacement on a two-dimensional grid from (x, y) to (x', y') as:

$$x' \alpha f(karx)$$
$$y' \alpha f(kary)$$

where:

k is a muscle spring constant
a is the angular displacement modelling factor, given by:

$$a = \cos\left(\frac{\theta}{\Omega}\frac{\pi}{2}\right)$$

where Ω limits the angular displacement of the model. r is the radial displacement modelling factor given by:

$$r = \begin{cases} \cos\left(\frac{(r_s - D)}{r_s}\frac{\pi}{2}\right) & (x,y) \text{ inside the inner zone} \\ \cos\left(\frac{(D - r_s)}{(r_f - r_s)}\frac{\pi}{2}\right) & (x,y) \text{ inside the outer annulus} \end{cases}$$

Waters produced impressive, but somewhat quirky, animation sequences using a fairly coarse polygon mesh model of heads controlled by 10 implanted muscle models. Subsequently, the computer graphics community as a whole enthusiastically took up the notions central to Waters' paper and now the subject of facial animation is sufficiently well established to warrant its own course at SIGGRAPH.

The baby in the recent Pixar Oscar-winning animation *Tin Toy* is a good example of the capabilities of facial animation. Around 50 muscle models were employed to choreograph the movement of around 3000 control points of a parametrically modelled face. Reeves [REEV90] describes the imposition of a further, higher level of control in the form of macromuscles. A macromuscle is a collection of low-level muscles each of which is assigned an individual scaling parameter, or weight. Contraction of the macromuscle would translate down to the lower level where the muscles would undergo contractions weighted by the appropriate amount. The rationale behind such a control mechanism is that for certain commonly used expressions groups of muscles behave in a coordinated, synchronized fashion. Indeed, it has been demonstrated that the expressions of happiness, anger, fear, surprise, disgust and sadness can be generated from a limited set of muscles.

The application of facial animation to character animation is obvious and, as to be expected, a lot of principles established in the field of traditional character animation [THOM84] are equally applicable here. These principles provide useful guidelines as to what works and what doesn't, and anyone wishing to create a successful animation sequence should always bear them in mind. The most salient of these rules are enumerated below.

The closer the facial model resembles that of an actual human head the more critical is our perception of it. In general, the complexity of the facial model is secondary, and in some cases obstructive, to creating a successful sequence. The power of a character lies in its animation and not its form - very convincing characters can be built out of the simplest of geometric primitives (a good example is Plate 49).

It is more important to animate certain features than others for expressing emotion. High-priority features are the eyes, mouth, eyebrows and eyelids. Low on the list are the cheeks, nose, tongue, ears and hair. By far the most important are the eyes - they play an important role in tracking the action of the story and directing the gaze of the audience to look in the same place. Also, a surprising degree of expression can be achieved simply by animating the dilation/contraction of the pupil. Walt Disney once said to his animation team that the audience watches the eyes and this is where the time and money must be spent if the character is to act convincingly. Animation of the head itself, however minimal, is also crucial and must not be forgotten - no matter how expressive the animation of the face it will tend to look wooden if the head itself does not move.

Animating the features symmetrically will produce lifeless, unconvincing results and should be avoided. This is a general principle of traditional animation, not just restricted to faces, where it is called the avoidance of 'twins', a twin being an instance of a pair of features either side of the body doing exactly the same thing at the same time. A good example of this occurs when blinking the eyes, the blink of one eye should precede the blink of the other by a few frames.

A rigidly observed, phonetically driven, automated approach to synchronizing the movement of lips to speech is difficult to do and disappointingly mechanical in its results. Generally, the importance of lip syncing should be played down, it being far easier and more effective to capture the dynamics of the dialogue - to go for plausibility rather than exactitude. Witness the animation of Snow White in Walt Disney's film *Snow White and the Seven Dwarfs*. She probably represented one of the most demanding examples of a talking head the Disney studios had to face. Close inspection of the character will reveal the coarsest level of lip syncing that, combined with the highest degree of coordination between gesture and dialogue, produces a very convincing result. The action of the character is phrased in terms of the phrases of dialogue and if these actions are properly conceived in relation to the dialogue then the mouth shapes become far less critical.

17.8 Inbetweening key deformations

In the film *Tony de Peltrie* [BERG86], Bergeron and Lachapelle used inbetweening for facial expressions. Twenty facial expressions were sculpted then digitized (these included phonemes) from a real human being. From this relatively small set of expressions, keyframes were created by using any linear combination of these expressions. The keyframes were also used to facilitate lip synchronization, peaks on the soundtrack being synchronized with keyframe generation.

A drawback to this approach is its inflexibility. We are unable to model an expression that cannot be constructed as a linear combination of the digitized expressions. The multitudinous nuances of expression defy cataloguing. Any subtle, localized movement of the face requires the construction of the face as a complete model, where most of the data is not different from adjacent key expressions. Waters' method of using local muscle models interactively seems far more flexible. These considerations extend to inbetweening key deformations generally; in many instances the action may be confined to a small part of the total shape thereby introducing a good deal of redundancy into the inbetweening approach.

Figure 17.17 shows a shape change from the letter 'E' to the letter 'Z' which is done by inbetweening between the two letters. The letters are modelled using piecewise Bézier curves with appropriate continuity constraints imposed throughout the animation. This example reveals further inadequacies when interpolating through key deformations for anything but the simplest of shapes – the inbetweens look messy, bearing little resemblance to the keys. Some segments rotate faster than others and may cross each other, causing the Bézier curves to loop back on themselves, thus creating an apparent discontinuity in the curve. In general, when working with a complex model, inbetweening key deformations directly gives rise to unpredictable results. The path of action may generally be incorrect and objects may well intersect themselves or one another. It is more advisable to interpolate the key parameters that cause the deformation.

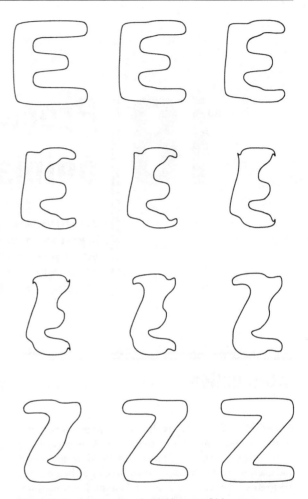

Figure 17.17 Inbetweening using multisegment Bézier curves.

18 Procedural animation

This chapter should be read in conjunction with Chapter 7. Both chapters use Fourier synthesis: the treatment in Chapter 7 is more general, in this chapter we deal with the special case of water waves. Fourier theory is also used in Chapter 4. The procedural animation of turbulence (specifically a flame) is dealt with in Chapter 7.

Introduction

Procedural animation is an area where computer graphics animation comes into its own. At its most basic level, procedural animation means building an object and then using a procedure to control or animate some attribute of the object. Procedural animation sometimes involves shape changes. We distinguish between the material in this chapter and that in Chapter 17 (Soft object animation) by the fact that the shape changes that come out of procedural animation usually have some bearing on the real world and are based on underlying principles or mathematical models taken from the physical sciences. In soft object animation, as we have defined it in Chapter 17, the shape changes are completely arbitrary and under the control of an animator rather than a mathematical model.

The simplest form of procedural animation is where a mathematical model specifies the geometry of an object as well as its movement or shape change as a function of time. The classic example of this is wind-perturbed water waves (see Section 18.3.2). Fourier synthesis is used to model the shape of the waves and their movement as a function of time.

Another category of procedural animation that has recently emerged is where objects, modelled conventionally, have their behaviour in collisions, say, modelled using a mathematical model. Prominent in this category is the work of Terzopoulos *et al*. [TERZ87, TERZ88] where elasticity theory and dynamics are used to predict the deformation of colliding flexible objects. This approach integrates motion and shape deformation, but suffers from the disadvantage of specificity and complexity of the model.

It is obvious that procedural animation is applicable in ViSC applications (Chapter 13) and some impressive work in this field has been carried out in computational fluid dynamics.

Finally, we mention methods that do not involve object modelling at all. In this approach – stochastic or particle set animation – an object is a 'fuzzy' cloud of particles. Each particle may be animated individually and the visibility of individual particles in the cloud will depend on the application area. Either a fuzzy object will be perceived, in which case individual particles are not visible, or the behaviour of individual particles will be apparent. Although in Chapter 15 we introduced stochastic animation and behavioural animation as separate categories (because of their diverse application areas), they can both be considered as forms of procedural animation and we will treat them as such here.

By its nature, procedural animation is not a coherent topic and because of this, the chapter consists of a list of prominent and popular examples.

18.1 Particle set animation

The pioneer in this field is Reeves, who published a paper in 1983 [REEV83] that used particle sets to model fuzzy objects such as fire and clouds. In this work an object is represented by a set of particles, each of which are born, evolve in space and die or extinguish, all at different times depending on their individual animation. In this method scripts can be written that control not only the position and velocity of the particles, but also their final appearance parameters – attributes such as colour, transparency and size. Thus the dynamic behaviour of the particles and their appearance, as a function of time, can be merged into the same script. Stochastic processes can be used to control both these aspects of particle behaviour.

Reeves describes the generation of a frame in an animation sequence as a process of five steps:

1. New particles are generated and injected into the current system.
2. Each new particle is assigned its individual attributes.
3. Any particle that has exceeded its lifetime is extinguished.
4. The current particles are moved according to their scripts.
5. The current particles are rendered.

From this it can be seen that the overall shape of the particle cloud, as a function of time, is controlled by any or all of the first four processes.

The instantaneous population of a particle cloud is controlled or scripted by an application-dependent stochastic process. For example, the number of particles generated at a particular time t can be derived from:

$$N(t) = M(t) + \text{rand}(r)V(t)$$

where $M(t)$ is the mean number of particles perturbed by a random variable of variance $V(t)$. The time dependency of this equation can be used to control the overall growth (or contraction) in cloud size. Reeves used a linear time dependency with constant variance in the examples given, but he points out that the control can incorporate quadratic, cubic or even stochastic variations.

The number of particles can also be related to the screen size of the object – thereby allowing the amount of computation undertaken to be controlled efficiently.

Although this mechanism will clearly contribute something to shape evolution of the cloud, this is also determined by individual particle scripts. The combination of these two scripting mechanisms was used to animate phenomena such as an expanding wall of fire used in the motion picture *Star Trek II: The Wrath of Khan* and multicoloured fireworks. Individual particle scripting is based on the following attributes:

1. initial position,
2. initial velocity and direction,
3. initial size,
4. initial transparency,
5. shape,
6. lifetime.

Velocity and lifetime scripts can be based on dynamic constraints. An explosion, for example, may cause a particle to be ejected upwards and then pulled down under the influence of gravity.

Associated with both the attribute script and the population script is a 'generation shape' – a geometric region about the origin of the particle cloud into which 'newly born' particles are placed. For example, an exploding firework might have a spherical generation shape.

Although the applications Reeves described are generally growing phenomena, which the population of the particle cloud tends to increase, the method is general enough to model phenomena where, say, the population remains constant, while the shape of the cloud perturbs or where the population decreases or implodes.

As we have already pointed out, the final object appearance is determined from the net effect of individually rendering all the particles. Rendering is carried out by simply treating each particle as a single light source and using the final value of the appearance parameters.

In a later paper [REEV85] Reeves and Blau further develop particle systems. Moving away from using particles to model amorphous and continually changing shapes, they use them as 'volume filling' primitives to generate solid shapes whose form then remains generally constant, but which have the ability to change shape in different situations, such as blades of grass moving in the wind.

These techniques were used in the film *The Adventures of Andre and Wally B.* [LUCA84] to generate the three-dimensional background images of a forest and grass.

The primary significance of particle systems in this context is not their ability to model shape-changing objects, but rather the property of 'database amplification' – the ability of a simple database to describe the general characteristics of an object that can then be modelled to the required level of detail. Objects are modelled with a resulting complexity that is far higher than that obtainable by conventional techniques. For example, in a forest scene, Reeves states that typically well over a million particles will be generated from basic tree descriptions.

The other advance described in this paper is the shading model used. This is a technique that lies between the two extremes of treating each particle as a self-luminous source (see above) and extracting a surface from a particle cloud and using a conventional renderer (see Section 18.2). Reeves develops a method for shading particles as light-reflecting objects that uses ambient, diffuse and specular components as well as self-shadowing, external shadows and coloured light sources. A unique geometric model is given for the calculation of reflected light and a stochastic scheme is used for self-shadowing.

Particle systems were also used by Peachey [PEAC86] and Fournier [FOUR86] to model spray and foam in the animation of wind driven waves (see Section 18.3.2). Peachey uses a sinusoidal profile as a basic model that presupposes that the underlying water motion (as opposed to the wave motion through the water) is a circular or elliptical motion. The average orbital speed of the water in such a model (Figure 18.1) is given by:

$$Q = \frac{\pi H}{T} = \frac{\pi H C}{L} = \pi S C$$

where:

T is the period of the wave
C is the wave speed
H is the diameter of the orbit
L is the wavelength
$S \ (= H/L)$ is the 'steepness' of the wave

Spray caused by breaking waves occurs when the orbital speed of the water exceeds that of the wave:

$$Q > C$$

or

$$S > 1/\pi$$

(Peachey modifies Q to correct the coarse assumption of uniform circular motion, based on the observation that the maximum value of S does not exceed 0.1). This model is used as the basis for a particle system for foam. Initial position of a particle is the crest of a wave and its initial velocity is given by Q. Spray particles can then be assigned a trajectory and their initiation perturbed to prevent visual uniformity.

Peachey also employed a particle system to simulate the spray that results from waves crashing into an obstacle. Particles are generated from an obstacle at a rate that depends on the position of the crest of the wave with respect to the position of the point of impact (that is, maximum when the peak of the crest collides with the

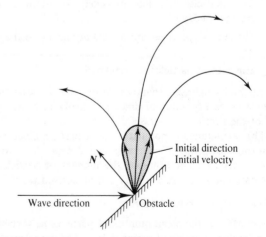

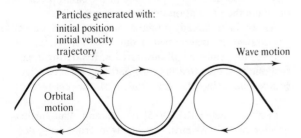

Figure 18.1 Model used to initiate a particle system for breaking at the crest of a wave.

Figure 18.2 Initiating a particle system when a crest strikes an obstacle.

object, and zero at some point when the crest has passed the obstacle).

The initial velocities can be chosen from a distribution centred on the orbital speed Q and the initial direction taken by perturbing about the reflected directon for an ideal elastic collision (Figure 18.2).

18.2 Behavioural procedural animation

A particle-related method was developed by Reynolds [REYN87] to simulate the flocking phenomena in birds, fish and so on. Although the obvious goal in this case is to render each particle (now a flock member) separately, the flock itself can be considered as a fuzzy object (particularly when a densely populated flock is viewed from a distance that enables the entire flock to be seen). The method differs from Reeves' method in two respects:

1. The particles are not independent but interact with each other to simulate various flocking mechanisms that give the group its characteristic behaviour.
2. Of less importance is the fact that the individual particles are now specific objects rather than point light sources. They now possess a particular orientation/attitude in space (as well as position).

Consider the geometric factors first. Reynolds defines 'geometric flight' based on incremental translations in the direction of the flock members' local z-axis. Pitch and yaw (rotations about the local x- and y-axes) are allowed and course changes imply realignment of the z-axis. The dynamic behaviour of a flock member is determined by a flock simulation or behaviour model that determines the way in which individuals react with each other. The sum total of the movements of all flock members results in a fuzzy object that exhibits the dynamic appearance of a flock with its characteristic direction changes, wheeling and general shape change.

This global behaviour of the flock is controlled by supplying global positions or global direction vectors. The flock is led around by animating a 'goal point' along a path ahead of the flock.

Reynolds points out that flocking behaviour consists of two opposing factors – a desire to stay close to the flock and a desire to avoid collision within the flock. This

behaviour is implemented as three rules which, in order of decreasing precedence, are:

1. Collision avoidance: avoid collisions with nearby flockmates.
2. Velocity matching: attempt to match the velocity of nearby flockmates.
3. Flock centring: attempt to stay close to nearby flockmates.

The behaviour of the model is summarized by Reynolds as follows:

> The flocking model described gives birds an eagerness to participate in an acceptable approximation of flock-like motion. Birds released near one another begin to flock together cavorting and jostling for position. The birds stay near one another (flock centring) but always maintain prudent separation from their neighbours (collision avoidance), and the flock becomes quickly 'polarized' – its members heading in approximately the same direction at approximately the same speed (velocity matching); when they change direction they do it in synchronization. Solitary birds and smaller flocks join to become larger flocks, and in the presence of external obstacles, larger flocks can be split into smaller flocks.

Many systems exist in the biological sciences that could be modelled by particle systems. For example, biologists have for many years studied the life cycle of the cellular slime mould (*Dictyostelium discoideum*). This mould starts life as a set of cells that first aggregate together in 'two-dimensional' space and then grow upwards in three-dimensional space to form a body that eventually produces spores. Biologists have long considered this to be an example of a rudimentary system formed by cells that are initially unconnected but that come together and cooperate [BONN67].

18.3 Animating analytical models

This category is arguably the most popular and diverse area of procedural animation. We illustrate it by using three case studies: animating cloth, animating water waves and snake locomotion. In the case of water waves

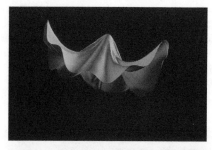

Figure 18.3   Animating shape in cloth: frames from a sequence that depicts a ghost flying around a room.

the procedural scheme is used both to model the original geometry of the object and to animate it; with the cloth and snake examples the model is used to animate the shape changes of an object that has been modelled manually.

18.3.1 Animating shape in cloth

Weil describes a method [WEIL86] for computing the surface formed by a piece of cloth when it hangs over 'constraint' points in three-dimensional space. The method is ideally suited to animation as frames can be computed by animating the constraint points. Figure 18.3 shows frames taken from a sequence that depicts a ghost flying around a room. The cloth also ripples as it moves around in three-dimensional space.

Weil's method provides a solution to the way in which the cloth will hang from the constraint points and he points out that simply determining a smooth surface for the cloth is insufficient because, in general, the cloth will contain folds.

The method is divided into two stages: the first approximates a solution and the second stage applies certain cloth constraints to the first stage providing a more realistic or 'cloth-like' solution.

The first stage is calculated by considering the shape a thread (or chain) makes when it hangs under its own weight. This is a catenary given by:

$$y = c + \cosh\left(\frac{x - b}{a}\right)$$

where the coefficients a, b and c are derived from the end points of the catenary and its length. The full derivation is given in [WEIL86].

The technique takes an original undeformed cloth – in this case a square of 80 points by 80 points centred at the origin and lying in the x,y-plane – and forces all its points to lie on catenaries.

First, we need to distinguish between the world coordinate system in which the cloth moves and its own coordinate system – the cloth coordinate system – where the cloth is rectangular, undeformed and is represented as a two-dimensional array. Point (j, k) is thus the (j, k)th element of the grid array.

Initially, the cloth is divided into four triangles. The overall animation of the cloth is driven by animating only the four corners and the centre. As these are moved around, the position of the interior points are calculated algorithmically. This is done by recursively subdividing the triangles until all grid points have been moved.

The first stage is to position the four corners and the centre as required for the basic ghost shape, and to hang catenaries between them. This forms four triangles which are then pushed onto a stack. Then, for each triangle popped from the stack:

1. Split the triangle by hanging a catenary between one of its corners and the midpoint of the opposite side. The arclength of the catenary is defined to be the length between the points on the original undeformed cloth.

2. Move all points that lie between these two points so that they lie on the catenary. We do this by defining these points lying between points (i, j) and (l, m) to mean those points given by drawing a rasterized line between (i, j) and (l, m) on the grid. We then count the number of points on the line and uniformly divide the catenary along its arclength. Points on the line are then moved to their corresponding points on the catenary (Figure 18.4).

3. If either of the subsequent two triangles contains interior points then push it onto the stack.

In this way each triangle is treated as a separate entity

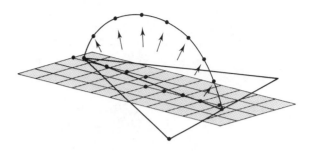

Figure 18.4 Subdividing a triangle and moving the rasterized line points onto the catenary that is hung from the vertex of the triangle and the midpoint of the opposite side.

that is repeatedly subdivided until all interior points have been positioned on a catenary.

This part of the algorithm, as specified by Weil, does, however, exhibit a certain problem in animation applications. The triangles can be split in one of three ways depending on which vertex is chosen to hang the catenary from. A criterion has to be established to decide which vertex to choose. Weil suggests picking the catenary which has the lowest height. However, as the vertices of the triangle move relative to each other, a different vertex may be chosen from one frame to the next. Consequently, the shape of the cloth within this triangle may suddenly change. This 'snapping' effect over the animation is overcome only by using a criterion that is *independent* of the world position of the triangle's points.

At this stage, we have created an intermediate approximate model that requires further refinement. This model is used as the basis for a relaxation algorithm that produces the final cloth model. This is done to ensure that all points lie within a given distance, their original thread distance, L, from their neighbours (thereby making the crudest of approximations to the fact that in general cloth maintains a constant surface area regardless of deformation). This also has the additional advantage of smoothing out discontinuities introduced in the first stage.

The algorithm proceeds by constructing a displacement vector for all points on the grid (Figure 18.5), between a point and one of its neighbours. The magnitude of the displacement vector is proportional to the distance between these two points and its direction is given by the direction of the neighbour relative to the point. The constant of proportionality between the magnitude and the distance is the relaxation factor. The *resultant* displacement vector is the sum over all neighbours of

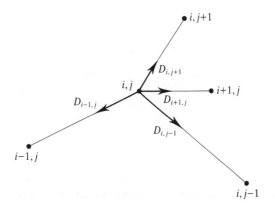

Figure 18.5   Displacement vectors used in relaxation method.

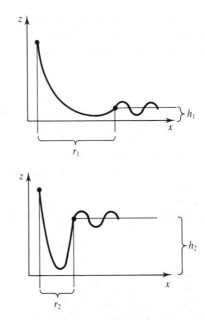

Figure 18.6   Animating the cloth, $h_2 > h_1$, so $r_2 < r_1$.

each individual displacement vector. The point is then displaced before going on to the next relaxation (a process that uses the latest available information as in the Gauss–Seidel method for solving sets of linear equations – see [WATT89]).

This process is repeated over the grid in several passes. Each pass produces a maximum distance, d_{max}, between any two neighbouring points within the grid. The algorithm terminates when:

$$d_{max} < L + \epsilon$$

where ϵ is a tolerance factor.

Figure 18.3 was rendered directly from the triangular mesh produced by the algorithm. Weil claims that using a standard rendering technique will only suffice for certain materials; for fabric, where, for example the weave is coarse, a more elaborate rendering technique is required, particularly for closeups.

Weil used ray tracing which treated the cloth as a collection of line segments, where each line segment had the spatial extent of a cylinder. Clearly the justification for the considerable expense of this method depends on the application.

The idea of the ghost animation (Figure 18.3) was to show a ghost drifting around a room. The animation consists of moving the constraint points around in world coordinate space *and* animating the cloth so that it flutters as the constraint points move. This kind of example where a completely ad hoc procedural construction is used to create an effect is endemic to production driven animation. Moving the constraint points globally is just a normal path specification (Section 15.3).

The animation was embellished by controlling the relative position of the corner points. The four corners were animated by varying the height of a corner sinusoidally, and making the distance, r, from the centre of the cloth, a simple function of this height. The further the point's altitude departs from its original height in the flat cloth, the closer it is pushed towards the cloth centre (Figure 18.6).

Another enhancement found to be visually effective was to send a sine wave along the hem of the cloth, vertically perturbing the catenaries. The sine wave was driven by the angular distance, in the x,y-plane, from the cloth centre. This is done on the hem edges of the first four triangles before they are pushed onto the stack and the effect propagates through the entire model. This gave the effect of the ghost rippling in the wind (Figure 18.7).

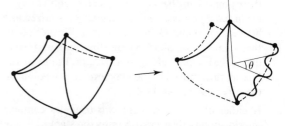

Figure 18.7   Propagating a sine wave along the hem by perturbing the outer edges of the initial four triangles.

18.3.2 Animating water waves

A simple but effective way of simulating water waves is to synthesize a function by superimposing sinusoidal waves. Animated effects are easily achieved by making such parameters as amplitude, phase and displacement a function of time. This is one of the easiest parametric models to set up and it produces convincing results.

Fourier synthesis is described in more general terms in Chapter 7. Here we look at a special case. Water waves fall into various categories depending on their motivating force. The waves that are modelled in computer graphics are 'surface gravity waves' or 'wind waves' which result from the action of the wind. These are the waves that we notice when looking at the sea from a beach.

Fourier synthesis, as the technique is known, can be used in either a two-dimensional or a three-dimensional domain as a basis for generating many natural phenomena. Two-dimensional waves were first used in computer graphics to provide texture patterns for terrain [SCHA80, SCHA83] in flight simulators. Here a two-dimensional cosine function was used to modulate the colour of a flat plane in perspective, providing economical depth cues for scenes that would otherwise consist of large flat shaded polygons. Gardener [GARD84, GARD85] has used three-dimensional Fourier waves to models clouds, trees and terrain.

Water waves can be modelled by using parallel waves – sinusoidally corrugated surfaces in three-dimensional space. These are sometimes called 'long-crested' travelling waves and, for example, a single sine wave would be specified by a function of a single spatial variable and time:

$$z(x, t) = A \cos(k(x - ct))$$

where:

A is the wave amplitude
k is the wave number given by $k = 2\pi/L$
L is the wavelength
c is the velocity given by $c = (g/k)^{1/2}$
g is acceleration due to gravity

The formula for the velocity is an approximation for small amplitude water waves and makes the assumption that the force due to gravity overrides that of surface tension. It is important to note that we are specifying the motion of waves propagating through water and not the motion of the water. As discussed in Section 18.1 with relevance to breaking waves, a simple sinusoidal wave

model presupposes that the net water motion is zero. Water at the crest of the wave moves in the same direction as the wave, while water in a trough moves in the opposite direction, giving rise to circular or elliptical water motion.

Extending this to two variables for a surface in three-dimensional space gives:

$$z(x, y, t) = A \cos(k \cdot (x - ct))$$

where:

k is the wave vector $(u, v, 0)$
c is a velocity vector and both vectors lie in the direction of the propagating wave
x is the vector $(x, y, 0)$

Such a wave and its Fourier representation is shown in Figure 18.8. A static wave in three-dimensional space is a sinusoidal corrugation whose contours of constant height are the lines:

$$k \cdot x = \text{constant}$$

(Figure 18.9). The peaks and troughs of the corrugations face a direction that makes an angle:

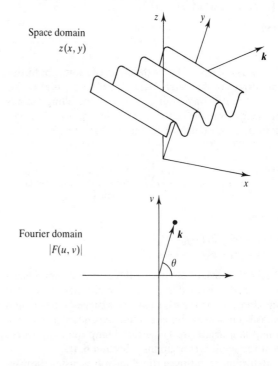

Figure 18.8 A single sinusoidal corrugation and its Fourier amplitude spectrum.

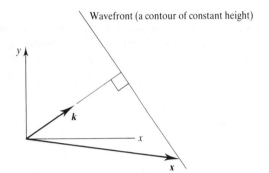

Figure 18.9 Illustrating **$k.x$** = constant.

$$\Theta = \tan^{-1}\left(\frac{v}{u}\right)$$

with respect to the x-axis, and the wavelength is:

$$\left(u^2 + v^2\right)^{-\frac{1}{2}}$$

Similarly, we can define radial waves where each wave is radial with a centre C:

$$z(x, t) = A \cos\left(k\left(|r| - ct\right)\right)$$

where:

$$r = x - C$$

This is useful in simulating the effect of raindrops hitting the surface of the water. Here we define a radial packet as a concentric wave train of length, l, travelling radially outwards from the centre at start time t_0, say. We only deform those points r in the annular region $(r_a(t),$ $r_b(t))$. That is:

$$z(x, t) = 0 \qquad \text{for } r < r_a, \text{ and } r > r_b$$
$$z(x, t) = A \cos\left(k\left(|r| - ct\right)\right) \quad \text{for } r \text{ within the annular region } (r_a, r_b)$$

where:

$$r_a(t) = |r| - c\left(t - t_0\right)$$
$$r_b(t) = |r| - c\left(t - t_0\right) + l$$

Due to the obvious discontinuities across the boundaries $r = r_a$ and $r = r_b$, this method works best when the amplitude of the wave is small. This suggests the method is easily implementable as a frame-dependent procedural bump map (since we know that bump mapping works well for small perturbations – Section 6.4).

Returning to the linear travelling waves, using the principle of linear summation we can state that the effect of

several waves together is just the sum of their separate contributions. The undisturbed water is represented as a flat polygonal mesh lying in the x, y-plane. It is displaced by a height field $z(x, y)$ given by:

$$z(x, y, t) = \sum_i A_i \cos\left(k_i\left(x - c_i t\right)\right) \qquad \text{(18.1)}$$

It would be a tedious task to assign wavelengths, amplitudes and so on individually to each separate wave, so upper and lower bounds are set for each parameter and a random number generator is used to choose numbers from within these bounds. Tuning the numbers to achieve the best result then consists simply in shifting these bounds around to find the best domains and choosing the optimum time interval to be incremented over frames. In the example shown (Plate 69) there are two separate wave groups: one of low amplitude, long wavelength and the other of much shorter wavelength.

In frequency domain terms this corresponds to a group of points with low energy clustered at low frequencies and a separate group in a high-frequency region. The frequency domain could be used as an alternative interactive design domain. Spatial frequencies are specified by positioning a single point (complex valued if phase is included) and a reverse FFT (Fast Fourier Transform) used to generate Equation (18.1).

If you have a reasonably powerful workstation the Fourier domain can be used interactively. We may, for example, operate on the Fourier transform of white noise, $N(u, v)$, with a filter $H(u, v)$ and control the shape of the filter H until a satisfactory (static) wave model results. Each time H is altered the product:

$$H(u, v) N(u, v)$$

where:

H is either 0 or 1 over the Fourier domain

is injected into a reverse FFT to produce $z(x, y)$. Figure 18.10 shows such a filter. This will produce a long-crested wave synthesis whose peaks and troughs will tend to be normal to the direction given by Θ in the space domain. The angular spread of the filter, ϕ, determines the spread of the sinusoidal corrugations about this predominant direction in the space domain and the radial depth of the annular region controls the bandwidth of the contributions. This is a special case of the technique suggested in Chapter 7, Figure 7.9.

Once an amplitude/frequency distribution producing the right visual effect has been decided upon, all that

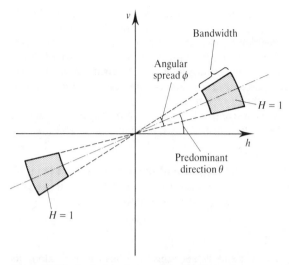

Figure 18.10 Synthesizing long-crested wave models in the frequency domain by using a 'zero–one' filter $H(u, v)$ operating on the spectrum of white noise.

remains is to control the speed at which the waves travel. Since our formulation for water waves includes a term that specifies the speed in terms of the frequency, this simply reduces to tuning the time interval over consecutive frames.

In order to avoid the aliasing problems referred to above, it is sufficient that the distance between points in the polygon mesh be less than half the shortest wavelength.

More sophisticated wave models exist, reflecting more accurately the physical process involved. In a paper entitled 'Fourier Synthesis of Ocean Scenes' [MAST87] Mastin *et al.* use a model based on the work of Pierson and Moskowitz who use wind-driven sea spectra, derived from observed data, to describe the motion of deep ocean waves in fully developed wind seas [PIER64]. Wave animation is invoked by manipulating the phase of the Fourier transforms.

Mastin *et al.* point out that ocean waves are not simple spectra but complex waveforms that are influenced by momentum transfer from the wind, and that energy is transferred between spectral components in a nonlinear fashion, making linear superposition models an approximation. In their model, seas are constructed in the Fourier domain. Mastin *et al.* use a formula based on the Pierson and Moskowitz model.

This method means that we specify a particular empirical shape in the Fourier domain for a spectrum and then use a reverse FFT to generate $z(x, y)$ as previously discussed. The spectrum is used to filter a set of frequency components that have been generated from uniform white noise. The Pierson and Moskowitz model is defined as a univariate spectral function:

$$F_1(f) = \frac{\alpha g^2}{(2\pi)^4 f^5} \exp\left(-\frac{5}{4}(f_p/f)^4\right)$$

where:

f_p = peak frequency
α = Phillip's Constant (0.0081)
g = gravitational constant

This is extended into a two-dimensional frequency spectrum specification (suitable for the generation of $z(x, y)$) using a suggestion due to Hasselmann *et al.* [HASS80]:

$$F_2(f, \theta) = F_1(f)\, D(f, \theta)$$

$D(f, \theta)$ is a directional spreading factor given by:

$$D(f, \theta) = N_p^{-1} \cos^{2p}\left(\frac{\theta}{2}\right)$$

where:

$$p = 9.77\left(\frac{f}{f_p}\right)^{\mu}$$

$$\mu = \begin{cases} 4.06 & f < f_p \\ -2.34 & f > f_p \end{cases}$$

N_p is a normalization constant

This gives a two-dimensional frequency spectrum whose maximum (along the line $\theta = 0$) is aligned in the wind direction.

Advanced wave effects

Fourier synthesis is only adequate for a very basic deep-water shape. Our experience tells us that wave profiles are not, in general, single-valued stationary profiles, but multivalued continuously changing shapes. A sea exhibits a bewildering variety of shapes in a continuum whose extremes we describe as calm and angry. Factors that mathematical models exist for are:

1. *Propagation speed of the waves depends on the current water depth* This effect is predicted by the Airy

model [KINS65] and has been implemented in computer graphics by Peachey [PEAC86] and Fournier [FOUR86]. The consequence of the model is that waves slow down in shallow water. This produces a refractive effect causing the waves to align themselves with the shoreline. This model is detailed in the next section.

2. *Wave profiles*   A cross-section through a wave in the direction of propagation will not reveal a sine wave. Wind-driven waves have shapes that are a function of wind speed. As wind speed increases, the crests become more sharply peaked and the troughs shallower. This is predicted by the Gerstner–Rankine model [KINS65] which gives a trochoid as the ideal profile. The sine wave shape occurs only for small amplitude waves under certain conditions. Fournier [FOUR86] also models shape change in the wave profile due to wind at the crest of the wave.

3. *Spray and foam*   Both Peachey [PEAC86] and Fournier [FOUR86] employ a classic computer graphics model to simulate spray and foam. A particle model (see Section 18.1) is used for both phenomena. Spray is given a lifetime and a trajectory, foam is sent sliding along the wave surface. Interestingly this is the least convincing of the effects implemented by Fournier.

Animating waves approaching the beach

We now describe the implementation of wave refraction, using a simple Fourier synthesis approach to specify the wave profile, that simulates the way in which wave fronts change as they approach shallow water. This technique was used to produce Plate 69. As we have discussed this will model a gentle (low wave amplitude) sea approaching a gently curved beach. The Airy model predicts the following dependence of wavelength and wave speed on depth:

$$L = T \left(\frac{gL_\infty}{2\pi} \tanh \left(2\pi \frac{h}{L_\infty} \right) \right)^{\frac{1}{2}} \qquad (18.2)$$

where:

g is acceleration due to gravity
h is the depth of the water at the point of interest
L is the wavelength
L_∞ is the wavelength in deep water
T is the period of the wave

This gives the instantaneous wave speed and wavelength for a given depth h where the period, T, of the wave tends to remain a constant. The depth of the water will vary along its direction of propagation, and the speed of the wave at the point of interest will depend on its 'history' as it passes over a height-varying sea bed from its origin to the point of interest.

We can control the animation of waves approaching a beach by constructing a table of phase values:

$$\theta(x, y, t_0)$$

that describe the phase of the wave at a fixed time, t_0, over the complete surface. If the depth of the water is constant then the phase is simply given by:

$$\theta = \frac{x}{L}$$

where x is the distance the wave has travelled along its direction of propagation. In practice the phase function is evaluated by taking the rate of change of the phase function $\theta'(u)$ with respect to the distance travelled, u. That is:

$$\theta(x) = \int_0^x \theta'(u) \, du$$

where $\theta'(u)$ for an instantaneous depth is given by $1/L$ (Equation 18.2).

A grid of phase values can be constructed where the phase is found by numerically integrating the above along the direction of propagation over the sea bed. Phase for points within the grid is obtained by bilinear interpolation. This phase table is constructed only once for one wave and one sea bed. Assuming that phase change is constant in time makes animating the model simply a matter of incrementing the phases in the grid table by a fixed amount frame for frame.

Rendering waves

In all of the water illustrations, the surface of the water was rendered using a 'chrome' mapping technique (see Chapter 6), indexing into the texture maps shown. Advantage was taken of the fact that water always faces upwards, that is, the z-component of the normal to the surface is always greater than zero, to build a customized water chrome mapping.

Recall (see Section 6.3.1) that chrome mapping is mapping from R^3 to R^2 of the reflected view vectors at the vertices of the polygon to the texture coordinates of the texture map, that is:

$$(R_x, R_y, R_z) \rightarrow (u, v)$$

Since the normal to the surface is always greater than zero, it follows that $R_z > 0$ also. Now a standard chrome mapping function will effectively stretch a map over the entire surface of the sphere (see Figure 6.8). In this particular case, since we know the lower hemisphere will never be hit by a reflected vector, we can restrict the mapping function to project onto the upper hemisphere only. Thus the map is now effectively stretched over a hemisphere only – more detail is packed into a smaller area. This has the effect of increasing the level of detail, or resolution, of the reflection at the water surface thereby producing a visually richer image. The reflected vector is assumed to be normalized and $u, v \in [0, 1]$. The water chrome mapping is defined thus:

$$(R_x, R_y, R_z) \rightarrow (\Theta, \Phi) \rightarrow (u, v)$$

where:

$$\Theta = \tan^{-1}\left(\frac{R_x}{R_y}\right) \qquad 0 \leqslant \tan^{-1}\Theta \leqslant 2\pi$$

$$\Phi = \cos^{-1}(R_z) \qquad 0 \leqslant \cos^{-1}\Phi \leqslant 2\pi$$

$$u = \frac{\Theta}{2\pi}$$

$$v = \frac{\Phi}{\pi}$$

because $R_z > 0$ it follows $0 < \Phi < \pi$ and hence $0 < v < 1$.

Plate 70 shows a surface with a sinusoidally distributed height field, and Plate 71 shows the effect of adding radial packets as bump maps. The chrome map used is shown in Plate 72.

Plate 69 shows two frames of a sequence showing the refraction of waves over a gently curving beach. The height field used was taken from Fournier's work and consists of two parallel waves, initially set obliquely to the shoreline. Two phase tables, one for each wave, were calculated.

In order to increase the amount of detail, to make these images richer visually, a group of nonrefracting linear travelling waves, of much smaller amplitude and higher frequency than the two parallel refracting waves, were added. Now, because the frequencies were an order of magnitude larger than the refracting waves, if they were simply added to the height field, the resolution of the polygonal mesh would have to increase by a corresponding order of magnitude to ensure no aliasing occurred. This would have made the compute frame times unaccep-

tably long. To get round this problem the group of smaller amplitude waves were added as a frame-dependent bump map.

The position and orientation of the camera, relatively close to the water and looking across it, threw up another problem. The polygons closest to the camera were quite large in screen space. This led to large regions of screen where nothing much was happening visually as only four normals were being used to get the colour from the chrome map and only four height values were accessed to determine the orientation for a polygon which was projected over several pixels. What was needed was a fractal-like approach, where more detail was generated where it was needed. The polygons were subdivided in screen space using a technique similar to that used in generating fractal terrains by subdivision (Section 17.1). This works in conjunction with a scan line renderer as follows.

In a scan line renderer, you will recall, we need to determine the maximum y-height of each polygon in screen space in order to decide which scan line to hang the polygon from. If we use a fractal terrain type subdivision technique to increase the polygonal resolution of the height field then polygons are, in general, perturbed out of their original (unsubdivided) plane, and the projection of the vertices into screen space no longer gives the required value. To overcome this we use a bounding box technique. Each polygon is enclosed in a box which represents the maximum and minimum z-displacement (Figure 18.11). In this case, since the height field consists of a sum of waves of known amplitude, and the undisplaced water surface is at $z = 0$, the maximum displacement is the sum of all amplitudes (maximum constructive interference) and the minimum the negative sum (maximum destructive interference). These values are constant and are a function of the wave synthesis only. Wherever the polygon is in world space its position is always bounded by this box.

The bounding box is projected onto the screen and the polygon is 'hung' from the highest scan line of this projection. As a polygon is picked off a scan line it is subdivided into four. The bounding box of each separate polygon is calculated and each in turn is projected onto the screen and the polygon then hung on the relevant scan line. This process is repeated until the bounding box has a screen space projected area of less than one pixel. The polygon within it is then assigned its true height field z-value and then put on the relevant scan line of its projection (guaranteed to be less than or equal to the one that it is already on) and processed in the normal way.

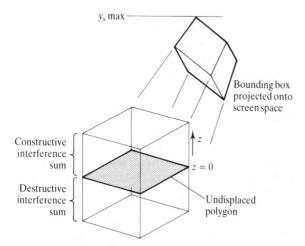

Figure 18.11 Bounding box for a polygon in a height field.

Finally, Plate 74 shows frames from an animated sequence that uses a combination of techniques described in the text:

1. FFD blocks were used to control the movement of the ducks' necks. (Chapter 17)

2. Long-crested wave model with raindrop perturbations added as bump map packets. The water surface is chrome mapped.

3. Selective ray tracing for the reflection of the ducks in the water (see Chapter 9). The water surface was tagged to be ray traced.

4. Coalescing raindrop models. This film was for a credit card commercial – the typically banal script using water as an analogy for money. The line 'Money can be taken out in drips and drops' was storyboarded as negative raindrops. So negative gravity was employed to make the negative raindrop decoalesce and rise vertically upwards. A sequence of models generated by the 'surface of revolution' or 'potter's wheel' technique was used to model the raindrops separating from the surface.

5. The ducks were texture mapped using the 'reverse projection' technique described in Chapter 6.

18.3.3 Scripting animal movement procedurally

An example of procedural animation that involves a procedural model to control or script parameters is given by the movement of certain reptiles. For example, consider Figure 18.12, based on an illustration from [GRAY68] which shows the paths followed by the head, middle and tail of an *Anguilla* (glass-eel). Such data could be used directly to drive a polygonal model of the animal. This example illuminates an important modelling point. This particular context has been procedurally animated from two different approaches or levels. On the one hand, an observational kinetic model has been used to simulate movement as we describe. On the other hand, a more complex dynamic model, involving springs, has been used to simulate the forces that produce the motion [MILL88].

Note that in this case the motion is sinusoidal (more or less) with different amplitudes. In this particular case an analytical model could easily be set up and the parameters experimented with to give different effects.

Sinusoidal functions also determine the motion of snakes (at least as far as the visual appearance of the animation is concerned) and a more elaborate example (also taken from Gray's prodigious work) is now given.

The progression of snakes has been characterized as consisting of four basic motions:

1. Serpentine movement – which appears as a travelling sinusoidal wave. The whole of the body forms a sinusoidal function that progresses in the direction of travel.

2. Concertina movement – a wave that actually travels along the body of the snake as it progresses.

3. Sidewinding – the direction of progression does *not* coincide with the axis of the wave.

4. Rectilinear movement – progression where there is no wave and the snake progresses with its body aligned in the direction of travel.

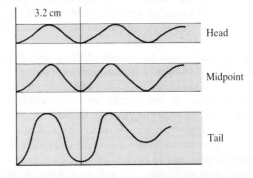

Figure 18.12 Observed data showing the paths followed by the head, midpoint and tip of the tail of a glass-eel (after [GRAY68]).

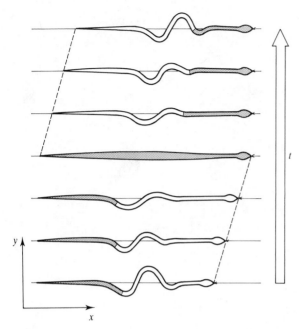

Figure 18.13 Concertina movement of a snake (after [GRAY68]).

Most snakes exhibit any one of the first three modes. The fourth is confined to such species as boas.

Concertina movement is shown in Figure 18.13 in which it can be seen that the model could be controlled by a travelling wave packet:

$$y = d(t) + \sin(ax) \exp(-b(t)x)$$

that is, a sine wave modulated by an exponential decay, where both the displacement of the deformation, d, along the long axis and the damping factor, b, are functions of time.

This example of animating a snake by imposing a kinetic model on a polygonal object contrasts with a recent animation described by Miller [MILL88]. In this paper, snakes are modelled as a mass–spring system. Muscle contractions are simulated by animating the spring tensions. Friction is also included.

It is an open question whether this physical model is capable of producing better animation. One of the advantages of the suggested scheme is that it is derived from visually observed data and we would assume that the model is more closely or directly coupled to the actual visual appearance of the motion.

References

ABRA85 Abram, G. and Westover, L., Efficient Alias-free Rendering using Bitmasks and Lookup Tables, *Computer Graphics*, **19**(3), 53–9, (Proc. SIGGRAPH '85).

ABRA90 Abram, G.D. and Whitted, T., Building Block Shaders, *Computer Graphics*, **24**(4), 283–8, (Proc. SIGGRAPH '90).

ADLE67 Adler, C., Shadow-Sausage Effect, *American Journal of Physics*, **35**(8), 774–6, Aug. 1967.

AMAN84 Amantides, J., Ray Tracing with Cones, *Computer Graphics*, **18**(3), 129–36, (Proc. SIGGRAPH '84).

APPE68 Appel, A., Some Techniques for Machine Rendering of Solids, *AFIPS Conf Proc.*, **32**, 37–45, 1968.

ATHE78 Atherton, P., Weiler, K. and Greenberg, D., Polygon Shadow Generation, *Computer Graphics*, **12**(3), 275–81, (Proc. SIGGRAPH '78).

ARVO86 Arvo, J., Backwards Ray Tracing, Developments in Ray Tracing, *SIGGRAPH Course Notes*, **12**, 1986.

ARVO87 Arvo, J. and Kirk, D., Fast Ray Tracing by Ray Classification, *Computer Graphics*, **21**(4), 55–64, (Proc. SIGGRAPH '87).

BADL81 Badler, N.I., Animating Facial Expression, *Computer Graphics*, **15**(3), 245–52, (Proc. SIGGRAPH '81).

BADO90 Badouel, D., An Efficient Ray-polygon Intersection, *Graphics Gems*, A.S. Glassner, ed., pp. 390–6. Academic Press, N.Y., 1990.

BARN78 Barnhill, R., Brown, J. and Klucewicz, I., A New Twist in CAGD, *Computer Graphics and Image Processing*, **8**, 78–91, 1978.

BARR84 Barr, A.H., Global and Local Deformations of Solid Primitives, *Computer Graphics*, **18**(3), 21–30, (Proc. SIGGRAPH '84).

BARR86 Barr, A.H., Ray Tracing Deformed Surfaces, *Computer Graphics*, **20**(4), 287–96, (Proc. SIGGRAPH '86).

BARS83 Barsky, B. and Beatty, J.C., Local Control of Bias and Tension in beta-Splines, *ACM Trans. on Graphics*, **2**(2), 109–34.

BART87 Bartels, R., Beatty, J. and Barsky, B., *An Introduction to Splines for use in Computer Graphics and Geometric Modelling*, Morgan-Kaufmann, 1987.

BAUM89 Baum, D.R., Rushmeier, H.E. and Winget, J.M., Improving Radiosity Solutions through the use of Analytically Determined Form Factors, *Computer Graphics*, **23**(3), 325–34, (Proc. SIGGRAPH '89).

BECK63 Beckmann, P. and Spizzichino, A., *Scattering of Electromagnetic Waves from Rough Surfaces*, Macmillan, 1963.

BERG86 Bergeron, P., A General Version of Crow's Shadow Volumes, *IEEE Computer Graphics and Applications*, **6**(9), 17–28, 1986.

BERG86 Bergeron, P., Techniques for Animating Characters, *SIGGRAPH Course Notes*, **22**, 240–65, 1986.

BERG86 Bergman, L., Fuchs, H., Grant, E. and Spach, S., Image Rendering by Adaptive Refinement, *Computer Graphics*, **20**(4), 29–38, 1986.

BERR80 Berry, B. and Upstill, H., Catastrophe Optics: Morphologies of Caustics and their Diffraction Patterns, *Progress in Optics*, **18**, 1980.

BERR83 Berry, B. and Hajnal, U., The Shadows of Floating Objects and Dissipating Vortices, Optica Acta, **30**(1), 23–40, Jan 1983.

BEZI72 Bézier, P., *Numerical Control: Mathematics and Applications*, Wiley, Chichester, UK, 1972.

BIER86 Bier, E.A. and Sloan, K.R., Two-part Texture Mapping, *IEEE Computer Graphics and Applications*, **6**(9), 40–53, Sept. 1986.

BISH86 Bishop, G. and Weimar, D.M., Fast Phong Shading, *Computer Graphics*, **20**(4), 103–6, (Proc. SIGGRAPH '86).

BLIN76 Blinn, J.F. and Newell, M.E., Texture and Reflection in Computer Generated Images, *Comm. ACM*, **19**(10), 542–7, Oct 1976.

BLIN77 Blinn, J.F., Models of light reflection for Computer Synthesised Pictures, *Computer Graphics*, **11**(2), 1977, (Proc. SIGGRAPH '77).

BLIN78a Blinn, J.F., Simulation of Wrinkled Surfaces, *Computer Graphics*, **12**(3), 286–92, (Proc. SIGGRAPH '78).

BLIN78b Blinn, J.F., Computer Display of Curved Surfaces, *PhD Thesis*, University of Utah, 1978.

BLIN82 Blinn, J.F., A Generalization of Algebraic Surfaces, *ACM Trans. on Graphics*, **1**(3), 235–56.

BLIN82 Blinn, J.F., Light Reflection Functions for Simulation of Clouds and Dusty Surfaces, *Computer Graphics*, **16**(3), 21–9.

BLIN88 Blinn J.F., Me and my (Fake) shadow, *IEEE Computer Graphics and Applications*, **8**(1), 82–6.

BLIN89 Blinn, J.F., Return of the Jaggy, *IEEE Computer Graphics and Applications*, **9**(2), 82–9, March 1989.

BLOO85 Bloomenthal, J., Modeling the Mighty Maple, *Computer Graphics*, **19**(3), 305–11, (Proc. SIGGRAPH '85).

BÖHM82 Böhm, W., On Cubics: A Survey, *Computer Graphics and Image Processing*, **19**, 201–6.

BONN67 Bonner, J.T., *The Cellular Slime Molds*, Princeton University Press, Princeton, NJ, 1967.

BORN64 Born, M. and Wolf, B., *Principles of Optics*, Pergamon Press, London, 1964.

BOUK70a Bouknight, W.J. and Kelley, K., An Algorithm for Producing Half-tone Computer Graphics Presentations with Shadows and Moveable Light Sources, *Proc. SJCC*, AFIPS, **36**, 1–10.

BOUK70b Bouknight, W.J., A Procedure for the Generation of Three-dimensional Half-toned Computer Graphics presentations, *Comm. ACM*, **13**(9), 527–36.

BRAC86 Bracewell, R.N., *The Fourier Transform and its Applications*, McGraw-Hill Book Co., New York, 1986.

BROT84 Brotman, L. and Badler, N., Generating Soft Shadows with a Depth Buffer Algorithm, *IEEE Computer Graphics and Applications*, **4**(10), 71–81.

BU89 Bu, J. and Deprettere, E.F., A VLSI System Architecture for High Speed Radiative Transfer in 3D Image Synthesis, *The Visual Computer*, 5, 121–33, 1989.

BUIT75 Bui-Tuong, Phong, Illumination for Computer-generated Pictures, *Comm. ACM*, **18**(6), June 1975.

CABR87 Cabral, B., Max, N. and Springmeyer, R., Bidirectional Reflection Functions from Surface Bump Maps, *Computer Graphics*, **21**(4), 273–81, (Proc. SIGGRAPH '87).

CARP84 Carpenter, L.C., The A-buffer, an Anti-aliased Hidden Surface Method, *Computer Graphics*, **18**(3), 103–8, (Proc. SIGGRAPH '84).

CASA85 Casale, M.S. and Stanton, E.L., An Overview of Analytic Solid Modelling, *IEEE Computer Graphics and Applications*, (2), 45–56.

CATM74 Catmull, E., Subdivision Algorithm for the Display of Curved Surfaces, *PhD Thesis*, University of Utah, 1974.

CATM78 Catmull, E., A Hidden Surface Algorithm with Anti-aliasing, *Computer Graphics*, **12**(3), (Proc. SIGGRAPH '78).

CHAD89 Chadwick, J.E., Hauemann, D.R. and Parent, R.E., Layered Construction for Deformable Animated Characters, *Computer Graphics*, **23**(3), 243–52, (Proc. SIGGRAPH '89).

CHAT87 Chattopadhyay, S. and Fujimoto, A., Bi-directional Ray Tracing, *Proc. of CG International '87*, pp. 335–43, Springer-Verlag, Tokyo 1987.

CHIY88 Chiyokura, H., *Solid Modelling with DESIGNBASE*, Addison-Wesley, Wokingham, UK, 1988.

CLAR76 Clark, J.H., Hierarchical Geometric Models for Visible Surface Algorithms, *Comm. ACM*, **19**(10), 547–54, Oct 1976.

CLAR79 Clark, J.H., A Fast Scan Line Algorithm for Rendering Parametric Surfaces, *Computer Graphics*, **13**(2), 289–99.

CLAR82 Clark, J.H., The Geometry Engine: A VLSI System for Graphics, *Computer Graphics*, **16**(3), 127–33, (Proc. SIGGRAPH '82).

COHE85 Cohen, M.F. and Greenberg, D.P., A Radiosity Solution for Complex Environments, *Computer Graphics*, **19**(3), 31–40, (Proc. SIGGRAPH '85).

COHE86 Cohen, M.F., Greenberg, D.P. and Immel, D.S., An Efficient Radiosity Approach for Realistic Image Synthesis, *IEEE Computer Graphics and Applications*, **6**(2), 26–35, March 1986.

COHE88 Cohen, M.F., Chen, S.E., Wallace, J.R. and Greenberg, D.P., A Progressive Refinement Approach to Fast Radiosity Image Generation, *Computer Graphics*, **22**(4), 75–84, (Proc. SIGGRAPH '88).

COOK82 Cook, R.L. and Torrance, K.E., A Reflectance Model for Computer Graphics, *ACM Trans. on Graphics*, **1**(1), Jan 1982.

COOK84 Cook, R.L., Shade Trees, *Computer Graphics*, **18**(3), 223–31, (Proc. SIGGRAPH '84).

COOK84 Cook, R.L., Porter, T. and Carpenter, L., Distributed Ray Tracing, *Computer Graphics*, **18**(3), 137–44, (Proc. SIGGRAPH '84).

COOK86 Cook, R.L., Stochastic Sampling in Computer Graphics, *ACM Trans. on Computer Graphics*, **5**(1), 51–72.

COOK87 Cook, R.L., Carpenter, L. and Catmull, E., The REYES Image Rendering Architecture, *Computer Graphics*, **21**(4), 95–102, (Proc. SIGGRAPH '87).

COQU90 Coquillart, S., Extended Free-Form Deformation: A Sculpturing Tool for 3D Geometric Modelling, *Computer Graphics*, **24**(4), 187–96, (Proc. SIGGRAPH '90).

COQU91 Coquillart, S. and Jancene, P., Animated Free-Form Deformation: An Interactive Animation Technique, *Computer Graphics*, **25**(4), 23–7, (Proc. SIGGRAPH '91).

CRAI86 Craig, J., *Introduction to Robotics: Mechanics and Control*, Addison-Wesley, Reading, MA, 1986.

CROW77 Crow, F.C., Shadow Algorithms for Computer Graphics, *Computer Graphics*, **11**(3), 242–8, (Proc. SIGGRAPH '77).

CROW81 Crow, F.C., A Comparison of Anti-aliasing Techniques, *IEEE Computer Graphics and Applications*, **1**(1), 40–8, Jan 1981.

CROW84 Crow, F.C., Summed-area Tables for Texture Mapping, *Computer Graphics*, **18**(3), 207–12, (Proc. SIGGRAPH '84).

DAVI54 Davies, H., Reflection of Electromagnetic Waves from Rough Surfaces, *Proc. Inst. Elec. Engrs* (London), 101, pp. 209–14, 1954.

DENA55 Denavit, J. and Hartenberg, R.S., A Kinematic Notation for Lower-pair Mechanisms Based on Matrices, *J. Applied Mechanics*, June 1955, 215–21.

DERO88 DeRose, T. and Barsky, B., Geometric Continuity, Shape Parameters and Geometric Spline Constructions for Catmull–Rom Splines, *ACM Trans. on Graphics*, **7**(1), 1–41, Jan 1988.

DIPP85 Dippe, M.A.Z. and Wold, E.H., Anti-aliasing through Stochastic Sampling, *Computer Graphics*, **19**(3), 69–78, (Proc. SIGGRAPH '85).

DOCT81 Doctor, L.J. and Torborg, J.G., Display Techniques for Octree Encoded Objects, *IEEE Computer Graphics and Applications*, **1**(3), 29–38, July 1981.

DREB88 Drebin, R.A., Carpenter, L. and Hanrahan, P., Volume Rendering, *Computer Graphics*, **22**(4), 65–74, (Proc. SIGGRAPH '88).

DUFF79 Duff, T., Smoothly Shaded Renderings of Polyhedral Objects on Raster Displays, *Computer Graphics*, **13**(2), 270–5, (Proc. SIGGRAPH '79).

DUFF86 Duff, T., Splines in Animation and Modelling, *SIGGRAPH Course Notes*, **15**, 1986.

EKMA77 Ekman, P. and Friesman, W., Manual for the Facial Action Coding System, *Consulting Psychologist*, 1977, Palo Alto CA.

FARI90 Farin, G., *Curves and Surfaces for Computer Aided Design* 2nd edn, Academic Press, Boston, 1990.

FARR83 Farrell, J., Colour Display and Interactive Interpretation of Three-dimensional Data, *IBM J. Res. Develop.*, **27**(4), 356–66.

FAUX79 Faux, I.D. and Pratt, M.J., *Computational Geometry for Design and Manufacture*, Ellis Horwood, Chichester UK, 1979.

FEIB80 Feibush, E.A., Levoy, M. and Cook, R.L., Synthetic Texturing using Digital Filters, *Computer Graphics*, **14**(3), 294–301, (Proc. SIGGRAPH '80).

FIUM83 Fiume, E.L. and Fournier, A., A Parallel Scan Conversion Algorithm with Anti-aliasing for a General-purpose Ultracomputer, *Computer Graphics*, **17**(3) (Proc. SIGGRAPH '83).

FIUM89 Fiume, E.L., *The Mathematical Structure of Raster Graphics*, Academic Press, San Diego CA, 1989.

FOLE89 Foley, J.D., van Dam, A., Feiner, S.K. and Hughes, J.F., *Computer Graphics – Principles and Practice*, Addison-Wesley, Reading MA, 1989.

FORS88 Forsey, D.R. and Bartels, R.H., Hierarchical B-spline Refinement, *Computer Graphics*, **22**(4), 205–12, (Proc. SIGGRAPH '88).

FOUR82 Fournier, A., Fussell, D. and Carpenter L., Computer Rendering of Stochastic Models, *Comm. ACM*, **25**(6), 371–84.

FOUR86 Fournier, A., A Simple Model of Ocean Waves, *Computer Graphics*, **20**(4), 75–84, (Proc. SIGGRAPH '86).

FOUR88 Fournier, A. and Fiume, E., Constant Time Filtering with Space Variant Kernels, *Computer Graphics*, **22**(4), 229–38, (Proc. SIGGRAPH '88).

FUCH80 Fuchs, H., On Visible Surface Generation by a priori Tree Structures, *Computer Graphics*, **14**, 124–33, (Proc. SIGGRAPH '80).

FUCH85 Fuchs, H. *et al.*, Fast Spheres, Shadows, Textures, Transparencies and Image Enhancements in Pixel-Planes, *Computer Graphics*, **19**(3), 111–20, (Proc. SIGGRAPH '85).

FUJI86 Fujimoto, A., Tanaka, T. and Iwata, K., ARTS: Accelerated Ray Tracing System, *IEEE Computer Graphics and Applications*, 6(4), 16–26, April 1986.

GALL89 Gallager, R.S. and Nagtegaal, J.C., An Efficient 3D Visualization Technique for Finite Element Models and Other Coarse Volumes, *Computer Graphics*, **23**(3), 185–94, (Proc. SIGGRAPH '89).

GANA82 Ganapathy, S. and Dennehy, T.G., A New General Triangulation Method for Planar Contours, *Computer Graphics* **16**(3), 69–75, (Proc. SIGGRAPH '82).

GANG82 Gangnet, M., Perny, D. and Coueignoux, P., Perspective Mapping of Planar Textures, *Proc. EUROGRAPHICS '82*, pp. 57–71, North-Holland, Amsterdam, 1982.

GARD84 Gardener, G.Y., Simulation of Natural Scenes using Textured Quadric Surfaces, *Computer Graphics*, **18**(3), 11–20, (Proc. SIGGRAPH '84).

GARD85 Gardener, G.Y., Visual Simulation of Clouds, *Computer Graphics*, **19**(3), 297–303, (Proc. SIGGRAPH '85).

GARD88 Gardener, G.Y., Functional Modelling of Natural Scenes, *SIGGRAPH Course Notes*, **28**, 44–76, 1988.

GIRA85 Girard, M. and Maciejewski, A.A., Computational Modelling for the Computer Animation of Legged Figures, *Computer Graphics*, **19**(3), 263–70, (Proc. SIGGRAPH '85).

GLAS84 Glassner, A.S., Space Subdivision for Fast Ray Tracing, *IEEE Computer Graphics and Applications*, **4**(4), Oct 84.

GLAS89 Glassner, A., *An Introduction to Ray Tracing*, Academic Press, 1989.

GLAS90 Glassner, A. (ed), *Graphics Gems*, pp. 539–47, Harcourt Brace Jovanovich, Boston, 1990.

GOLD71 Goldstein, R.A. and Nagel, R., Three-Dimensional Visual Simulation, *Visual Simulation*, **16**(1), 25–31.

GOLD86 Goldfeather, J., Hultquist, J.P.M. and Fuchs, H., Fast Constructive Solid Geometry Display in the Pixel-Powers Graphics System, *Computer Graphics*, **20**(4), 107–16, (Proc. SIGGRAPH '86).

GOME87 Gomez, J.E., Comments on Event Driven Animation, *SIGGRAPH Course Notes* **10**, 1987.

GORA84 Goral, C., Torrance, K.E. and Greenberg D.P., Modelling the Interaction of Light between Diffuse Surfaces, *Computer Graphics*, **18** (3), 212–22, (Proc. SIGGRAPH '84).

GOUR71 Gouraud, H., Illumination for Computer Generated Pictures, *Comm. ACM*, **18**(60), 311–17.

GRAY68 Gray, J., *Animal Locomotion*, Weidenfeld and Nicolson, London, 1968.

GREE86a Greenberg, D.P., Cohen, M.F. and Torrance, K.E., Radiosity: A Method for Computing Global Illumination, *The Visual Computer* **2**(5), 291–97, Sept 1986.

GREE86b Greene, N. and Hechbert, P.S., Creating Raster Omnimax Images Using the Elliptically Weighted Average Filter, *IEEE Computer Graphics and Applications*, **6**(6) 21–7, June 1986.

GREE86c Greene, N., Environment Mapping and Other Applications of World Projections, *IEEE Computer Graphics and Applications*, **6**(11), 21–9, Nov 1986.

GREE87 Greenberg, D.P., The 1987 Steven A. Coons Award Lecture, *Computer Graphics*, **22**(1).

GUEN90 Guenter, B. and Parent, R., Computing the Arclength of Parametric Curves, *IEEE Computer Graphics and Applications*, **10**(3), 72–8, May 1990.

HAHN88 Hahn, J.K., Realistic Animation of Rigid Bodies, *Computer Graphics*, **22**(4), 299–308, (Proc. SIGGRAPH '88).

HAIN86 Haines, E.A. and Greenberg, D.P., The Light Buffer: A Shadow-Testing Accelerator, *IEEE Computer Graphics and Applications*, **6**(9), Sept 1986.

HAIN89 Haines, E., Essential Ray Tracing Algorithms, in *An Introduction to Ray Tracing*, Glassner, A., ed. Academic Press, 1989.

HALL83 Hall, R. A. and Greenberg, D.P., A Testbed for Realistic Image Synthesis, *IEEE Computer Graphics and Applications*, **3**(8), Nov 1983.

HALL86 Hall, R., Hybrid Techniques for Rapid Image Synthesis, *SIGGRAPH Course Notes*, **16**, 1986.

HALL89 Hall, R. A., *Illumination and Color in Computer Generated Imagery*, Springer-Verlag, New York, 1989.

HANR83 Hanrahan, P., Ray Tracing Algebraic Surfaces, *Computer Graphics*, **17**(3), 83–90, (Proc. SIGGRAPH '83).

HANR90 Hanrahan, P., Three-pass Affine Transform for Volume Rendering, *Computer Graphics*, **24**(5), 71–6, Nov. 90.

HANR90 Hanrahan, P. and Lawson, J., A Language for Shading and Lighting Calculations, *Computer Graphics*, **24**(4), 289–98, (Proc. SIGGRAPH '90).

HARR88 Harrison, K., Mitchell, D. and Watt, A., The H test – a Method of High Speed Interpolative Shading, *Proc. CG International '88*, pp. 106–16, Berlin, Springer 1988.

HASS80 Hasselmann, D.E., Dunckel, M. and Ewing, J.A., Directional Wave Spectra observed during JONSWAP 1973, *J. Physical Oceanography*, pp. 1264–80, Aug. 1980.

HECK84 Heckbert, P.S. and Hanrahan, P., Beam Tracing Polygonal Objects, *Computer Graphics*, **18**(3), 119–27, (Proc. SIGGRAPH '84).

HECK86 Heckbert, P.S., Survey of Texture Mapping, *IEEE Computer Graphics and Applications*, **6**(11), 56–67, Nov. 1986.

HERM79 Herman, G.T. and Liu, H.K., Three-dimensional Display of Organs from Computed Tomograms, *Computer Graphics and Image Proc.*, **9**(1), 1–21.

HIBB89 Hibbard, W. and Santek, D., Interactivity is the Key, *Chapel Hill Workshop on Volume Visualization*, 39–44, ACM (No. 429892).

HOCK71 Hockney, D., *Pool with two figures*, painting 1971.

HÖHN89 Höhne, K.H., Bomans, M., Pommert, A., Riemer, M., Schiers, C., Tiede, U. and Wiebecke, G., 3D Visualization of Tomographic Volume Data using the Generalized Voxel-Method, *Chapel Hill Workshop on Volume Visualization*, pp. 46–51, ACM (No. 429892).

HÖHN90 Höhne, K.H., Bomans, M., Pommert, A., Riemer, M., Schiers, C., Tiede, U. and Wiebecke, G., 3D Visualization of Tomographic Volume Data using the Generalized Voxel Model, *The Visual Computer*, **6**, 28–36.

HOTT67 Hottel, H. and Sarofirm, A.F., *Radiative Transfer*, McGraw-Hill, New York, 1967.

ILM90 Industrial Light and Magic, *SIGGRAPH Course Notes*, Appendix C, **17**, 1990.

IMME86 Immel, D.S, Cohen, M.F. and Greenberg, D.P., A Radiosity Method for Non-diffuse Environments, *Computer Graphics*, **20**(4), 133–42, (Proc. SIGGRAPH '86).

JACK80 Jackins, C.L. and Tanimoto, S.L., Octrees and Their Use in Representing Three-dimensional Objects, *Computer Graphics and Image Processing*, (14), 249–70, 1980.

JOHN89 Johnson, E.R. and Mosher, C.E., Integration of Volume Rendering and Geometric Graphics, *Chapel Hill Workshop on Volume Visualization*, pp. 1–8, ACM (No. 429892).

JOY86 Joy, I.K. and Bhetanabhotla, M.N., Ray Tracing Parametric Surfaces Utilizing Numeric Techniques and Ray Coherence, *Computer Graphics*, **20**(4), 279–86, (Proc. SIGGRAPH '86).

KAJI82 Kajiya, J.T., Ray Tracing Parametric Patches, *Computer Graphics*, **16**(3), 245–54, (Proc. SIGGRAPH '82).

KAJI83 Kajiya, J.T., New Techniques for Ray Tracing Procedurally Defined Objects, *Computer Graphics*, **17**(3), 91–102, (Proc. SIGGRAPH '83).

KAJI84 Kajiya, J.T. and von Herzen, B.P., Ray Tracing Volume Densities, *Computer Graphics*, **18**(3), 165–74, (Proc. SIGGRAPH '84).

KAJI85 Kajiya, J.T., Anisotropic Reflection Models, *Computer Graphics*, **19**(3), 15–21, (Proc. SIGGRAPH '85).

KAJI86 Kajiya, J., The Rendering Equation, *Computer Graphics*, **20**(4), 143–50, (Proc. SIGGRAPH '86).

KAJI89 Kajiya, J.T. and Kay, T.L., Rendering Fur with Three-dimensional Textures, *Computer Graphics*, **23**(3), 271–80, (Proc. SIGGRAPH '89).

KAPL85 Kaplan, M.R., Space Tracing, a Constant Time Ray Tracer, *SIGGRAPH '85 Tutorial*, San Francisco, July 1985.

KAY79 Kay, D.S. and Greenberg D., Transparency for Computer Synthesised Objects, *Computer Graphics*, **13**(2), 158–64, (Proc. SIGGRAPH '79).

KAY86 Kay. T.L. and Kajiya, J.T., Ray Tracing Complex Scenes, *Computer Graphics*, **20**(4), 269–78, (Proc. SIGGRAPH '86).

KELL46 Kellaway, G.P., *Map Projections*, Methuen, London, 1946.

KEMP89 Kemp, M., ed., *Leonardo on Painting*, Yale University Press, New Haven and London, 1989.

KEMP90 Kemp, M., *The Science of Art: Optical Themes in Western Art from Brunelleschi to Seurat*, Yale University Press, 1990.

KINS65 Kinsman, B., *Wind Waves*, Prentice-Hall, 1965.

KLEI83 Klein, C. and Huang, C., Review of Pseudoinverse Control for use with Kinematically Redundant Manipulators, *IEEE Trans. on Systems, Man and Cybernetics*, **SMC-13**(3), 245–50.

KOCH84 Kochanek, D.H.U., Interpolating Splines with Local Tension, Continuity and Bias Control, *Computer Graphics*, **18**(3), 33–41, (Proc. SIGGRAPH '84).

LANE80 Lane, J.M., Carpenter, L., Whitted, T. and Blinn, J., Scan Line Methods for Displaying Parametrically Defined Surfaces, *Comm. ACM*, **23**(1), 23–34.

LASS87 Lasseter, J., Principles of Traditional Animation Applied to Three-dimensional Computer Animation, *Computer Graphics*, **21**(4), 35–44, (Proc. SIGGRAPH '87).

LEE85 Lee, M.E., Redner, R.A. and Uselton, S.P., Statistically Optimized Sampling for Distributed Ray Tracing, *Computer Graphics*, **19**(3), 61-7, (Proc. SIGGRAPH '85).

LEVO88 Levoy, M., Display of Surfaces from Volume Data, *IEEE Computer Graphics and Applications*, **8**(3), 29-37.

LEWI89 Lewis, J.P., Algorithms for Solid Noise Synthesis, *Computer Graphics*, **23**(3), 263-70, (Proc. SIGGRAPH '89).

LIND68 Lindenmayer, A., Mathematical Models for Cellular Interactions in Development, *J. Theor. Biol.*, **18**, 280-315, 1968.

LOPE90 Lopes, M.A., Generating Images of a Biological Species, B.Sc Dissertation, 1990, Dept of Comp. Sci., University of Sheffield.

LORE87 Lorensen, W.E. and Cline, H.E., Marching Cubes: A High Resolution 3D Surface Construction Algorithm, *Computer Graphics*, **21**(4), 163-9, (Proc. SIGGRAPH '87).

LUCA84 Lucasfilm Ltd, Computer Graphics Div., *The Adventures of Andre and Wally B.*, (film 1984).

LUDE87 Ludeman, L.C., *Fundamentals of Digital Signal Processing*, J. Wiley & Sons, New York, 1987.

MAGN85 Magnenat-Thalmann, N. and Thalmann, D., *Computer Animation: Theory and Practice*, Springer, Tokyo, 1985.

MAMM89 Mammen, A., Transparency and Antialiasing Algorithms Implemented with the Virtual Pixel Map Technique, *IEEE Computer Graphics and Applications*, **9**(4), 43-55.

MAND77 Mandelbrot, B., *Fractals: Form, Chance and Dimension*, W.H. Freeman, San Francisco, 1977.

MAND82 Mandelbrot, B., *The Fractal Geometry of Nature*, W.H. Freeman, San Francisco, 1982.

MARR80 Marr, D. and Hildreth, E.C., Theory of Edge Detection, *Proc. Royal. Soc. Lond.*, B207, pp. 187-217.

MAST87 Mastin, G.A., Watterberg, P.A. and Mareda, J.F., Fourier Synthesis of Ocean Scenes, *IEEE Computer Graphics and Applications*, **7**(3) 16-23.

MAX81 Max, N., Vectorized Procedural Models for Natural Terrain: Waves and Islands in the Sunset, *Computer Graphics*, **15**(3), 314-17, (Proc. SIGGRAPH '81).

MAX86 Max, N., Atmospheric Illumination and Shadows, *Computer Graphics*, **20**(4), 117-24, (Proc. SIGGRAPH '86).

MAX86 Max, N., Shadows for Bump Mapped Surfaces, in *Advanced Computer Graphics*, T.L Kunii, ed., pp. 145-56, Springer-Verlag, Tokyo, 1986.

MCOR87 McCormick, B.H., DeFanti, T.A. and Brown, M.D., Visualization in Scientific Computing, *Computer Graphics*, **21**(6), (Special Issue on Visualization in Scientific Computing).

MEAG82 Meager, D., Geometric Modelling using Octree Encoding, *Computer Graphics and Image Processing*, (19), 129-47.

MEYE86 Meyer, G.W., Rushmeier, H.E., Cohen, M.F., Greenberg, D.P. and Torrance, K., An Experimental Evaluation of Computer Graphics Imagery, *ACM Trans. Graphics*, **5**, 1986, 30–50.

MEYE88 Meyer, G.W., Wavelength Selection for Synthetic Image Generation, *Computer Vision, Graphics and Image Processing*, **41**, 57–9, 1988.

MILL84 Miller, G.S. and Hoffman, C.R., Illumination and Reflection Maps: Simulated Objects in Simulated and Real Environments, *SIGGRAPH '84: Advanced Computer Graphics Seminar Notes*, July 1984.

MILL86 Miller, G., The Definition and Rendering of Terrain Maps, *Computer Graphics*, **20**(4), 39–49, (Proc. SIGGRAPH '86).

MILL88 Miller, G., The Motion Dynamics of a Snake, *Computer Graphics*, **22**(4), 169–78, (Proc. SIGGRAPH '88).

MITC87 Mitchell, D.P., Generating Antialiased Images at Low Sampling Densities, *Computer Graphics*, **21**(4), 65–72, (Proc. SIGGRAPH '87).

MITC90 Mitchell, D.A.P., Fast Algorithms for 3D Computer Graphics, *PhD Thesis*, University of Sheffield, July 1990.

MOOR88 Moore, M. and Wilhelms, J., Collision Detection and Response for Computer Animation, *Computer Graphics*, **22**(4), 289–98, (Proc. SIGGRAPH '88).

MUYB99 Muybridge, E., *Animals in Locomotion*, London, 1899.

MYER84 Myers, W., Staking out the Graphics Display Pipeline, *IEEE Computer Graphics and Applications*, July 84, 61–5.

NEWE72 Newell, M.E., Newell, R.G. and Sancha, T.L., A New Approach to the Shaded Picture Problem, *Proc. ACM National Conf. (1972)*, pp. 443–50.

NEWM73 Newman, W. and Sproull, R., *Principles of Interactive Computer Graphics*, McGraw-Hill, New York, 1973.

NISH85 Nishita, T. and Nakamae, E., Continuous Tone Representation of Three-Dimensional Objects taking account of Shadows and Interreflection, *Computer Graphics*, **19**(3), 23–30, (Proc. SIGGRAPH '85).

NISH87 Nishita, T., A Shading Model for Atmospheric Scattering Considering Luminous Intensity Distribution of Light Sources, *Computer Graphics*, **21**(4), 303–10, (Proc. SIGGRAPH '87).

OPPE75 Oppenheim, A.V. and Shafer, R.W., *Digital Signal Processing*, Prentice-Hall, Englewood Cliffs NJ, 1975.

OPPE86 Oppenheimer, P.E., Real Time Design and Animation of Fractal Plants and Trees, *Computer Graphics*, **20**(4), 55–64, (Proc. SIGGRAPH '86).

PEAC85 Peachey, D.R., Solid Texturing of Complex Surfaces, *Computer Graphics*, **19**(3), 279–86, (Proc. SIGGRAPH '85).

PEAC86 Peachey, D.R., Modelling Waves and Surf, *Computer Graphics*, **20**(4), 65–74, (Proc. SIGGRAPH '86).

PEAC88 Peachey, D.R., Anti-aliasing Solid Textures, *SIGGRAPH Course Notes*, **28**, 13–35, 1988.

PERL85 Perlin, K., An Image Synthesizer, *Computer Graphics*, **19**(3), 287–96, (Proc. SIGGRAPH '85).

PERL89 Perlin, K., Hypertexture, *Computer Graphics*, **23**(3), 253–62, (Proc. SIGGRAPH '89).

PHIG88 PHIGS+ Committee, Andries van Dam, Chair, PHIGS+ Functional Description – Revision 3.0, *Computer Graphics*, **22**(3), 125–218.

PHIL91 Philips, C.B. and Badler, N.I., Interactive Behaviour for Bipedal Articulated Figures, *Computer Graphics*, **25**(4), 359–62, (Proc. SIGGRAPH '91).

PHON75 Bui-Thong, Phong, Illumination for Computer-generated Pictures, *Comm. ACM*, **18**(6), June 1975.

PIER64 Pierson, W.J. and Moskowitz, L., A Proposed Spectral form for Fully Developed Seas based on Similarity theory of S.A. Kilaigorodskii, *J. Geophysical Research*, Dec. 1964, pp. 5181–90.

PIXA88 Pixar Corporation, *The RenderMan Interface*, Version 3.0, Pixar Corporation, San Rafael CA, May 1988.

PIZE86 Pizer, S.M., Fuchs, H., Mosher, C. *et al.*, Three-dimensional Shaded Graphics in Radiotheraphy and Diagnostic Imaging, *NCGA '86 Conf. Proc.*, pp. 107–13, Anaheim CA, 1986.

PLAT88 Platt, J.C. and Barr, A.H., Constraint Methods for Flexible Models, *Computer Graphics*, **22**(4), 279–88, (Proc. SIGGRAPH '88).

POTM81 Potmesil, M. and Chakraverty, I., A Lens and Aperture Camera Model for Synthetic Image Generation, *Computer Graphics*, **15**(3), 297–306, (Proc. SIGGRAPH '81).

POTM83 Potmesil, M. and Chakravarty, I., Modelling Motion Blur in Computer Generated Images, *Computer Graphics*, **17**(3), 389–99, (Proc. SIGGRAPH '83).

PRUS88 Pruinkiewicz, P., Lindenmayer, A. and Hanan, J., Developmental Models of Herbaceous Plants for Computer Imagery Purposes, *Computer Graphics*, **22**(4), 141–50, (Proc. SIGGRAPH '88).

PURD70 Purdue University, *Thermophysical Properties of Matter*, Vols. 7,8 and 9, 1970.

REEV83 Reeves, W.T., Particle Systems – A Technique for Modelling a Class of Fuzzy Objects, *Computer Graphics*, **17**(3), 359–76, (Proc. SIGGRAPH '83).

REEV85 Reeves, W.T. and Blau, R., Approximate and Probabilistic Algorithms for Shading and Rendering Structured Particle Systems, *Computer Graphics*, **19**(3), 313–22, (Proc. SIGGRAPH '85).

REEV87 Reeves, W., Salesin, D. and Cook, R., Rendering Antialiased Shadows with Depth Maps, *Computer Graphics*, **21**(4), 283–91, (Proc. SIGGRAPH '87).

REEV90 Reeves, W.T., Simple and Complex Facial Animation, State of the Art in Facial Animation, *SIGGRAPH Course Notes* **26**, 1990.

REFF88 De Reffye, P., Edelin, C., Francon, J., Jaeger, M. and Puech, C., Plant Models Faithful to Botanical Structure and Development, *Computer Graphics*, **22**(4), 151–8, (Proc. SIGGRAPH '88).

REIL87 Reilly, P. and Halbert, A.R., *Using Computer Graphics to Analyse Archaeological Survey Data from the Isle of Man*, IBM Report UKSC 153.

REYN82 Reynolds, C.W., Computer Animation with Scripts and Actors, *Computer Graphics*, **16**(3), 289–96, (Proc. SIGGRAPH '82).

REYN87 Reynolds, C.W., Flocks, Herds, and Schools: A Distributed Behavioural Model, *Computer Graphics*, **21**(4), 25–34, (Proc. SIGGRAPH '87).

RHOD88 Rhodes, M.L. and Kuo, Yu-Ming, Simple Three-dimensional Image Synthesis Techniques for Serial Planes, *SPIE Medical Imaging II*, **914**, 1286–9, 1988.

ROCK89 Rockwood, A., Heaton, K. and Davis, T., Real-time Rendering of Trimmed Surfaces, *Computer Graphics*, **23**(3), 107–16, (Proc. SIGGRAPH '89).

ROGE85 Rogers, D.F., *Procedural Elements for Computer Graphics*, McGraw-Hill, New York, 1985.

RUBE81 Rubenstein, R.Y., *Simulation and the Monte-Carlo Method*, J. Wiley, New York, 1981.

RUBI80 Rubin, S.M. and Whitted, T., A Three-dimensional Representation for Fast Rendering of Complex Scenes, *Computer Graphics*, **14**(3), 110–16, (Proc. SIGGRAPH '80).

RUSH90 Rushmeier, H.E. and Torrance, K.E., Extending the Radiosity Method to Include Specularly Reflecting and Translucent Surfaces, *ACM Trans. Graphics*, **9**(1), 1–27, Jan. 1990.

SABE88 Sabella, P., A Rendering Algorithm for Visualizing Three-dimensional Scalar Fields, *Computer Graphics*, **22**(4), 51–8, (Proc. SIGGRAPH '88).

SAUN53 Saunders, J.B., Inman, V.T. and Eberhart, H.D., The Major Determinants in Normal and Pathological Gait, *J. Bone Joint Surgery*, (35A), 543–58.

SCHA80 Schachter, B.J., Long Crested Wave Models, *Computer Graphics and Image Processing*, **12**, 187–201.

SCHA83 Schachter, B.J., *Computer Image Generation*, J. Wiley, New York, 1983.

SCHM86 Schmitt, F.J.M., Barsky, B. and Du, W., An Adaptive Subdivision Method for Surface Fitting from Sampled Data, *Computer Graphics*, **20**(4), 179–88, (Proc. SIGGRAPH '86).

SCHU69 Schumaker, R.A., Brand, B., Guilliland, M. and Sharp, W., *Applying Computer Generated Images to Visual Simulation*, Tech. Report AFHRL-Tr-69, US Airforce Human Resources Lab.

SEDE86 Sederburg, T.W., Free-Form Deformation of Solid Geometric Models, *Computer Graphics*, **20**(4), 151–60, (Proc. SIGGRAPH '86).

SHAN87 Shantz, M. and Lien, S., Shading Bicubic Patches, *Computer Graphics*, **21**(4), 189–96, (Proc. SIGGRAPH '87).

SHEP78 Shepperd, S.W., Quaternion from Rotation Matrix, *J. Guid. and Control*, **1**(3), 223–4.

SHIN87 Shinya, M., Takahashi, T. and Naito, S., Principles and Applications of Pencil Tracing, *Computer Graphics*, **21**(4), 45–54, (Proc. SIGGRAPH '87).

SHOE85 Shoemake, K., Animating Rotation with Quaternion Curves, *Computer Graphics*, **19**(3), 245–54, (Proc. SIGGRAPH '85).

SHOE87 Shoemake, K., Quaternion Calculus and Fast Animation, *SIGGRAPH Course Notes*, **10**, 101–21, 1987.

SIEG84 Siegel, R. and Howeol, J.R., *Thermal Radiation Heat Transfer*, Hemisphere Publishing Corp., Washington DC, 1981.

SILL89 Sillion, F., A General Two-pass Method Integrating Specular and Diffuse Reflection, *Computer Graphics*, **23**(3), 335–44, (Proc. SIGGRAPH '89).

SIMS88 Sims, K. and Zeltzer, D., A Figure Editor and Gait Controller for Task Level Animation, *SIGGRAPH Course Notes*, **4**, 164–181, 1988.

SIMS90 Sims, K., Particle Animation and Rendering using Data Parallel Computation, *Computer Graphics*, **24**(4), 405–13, (Proc. SIGGRAPH '90).

SIMS91 Sims, K., Artificial Evolution for Computer Graphics, *Computer Graphics*, **24**(4), 319–28, (Proc. SIGGRAPH '91).

SMIT78 Smith, A.R., Color Gamut Transform Pairs, *Computer Graphics*, **12**(3), 12–19, (Proc. SIGGRAPH '78).

SMIT84 Smith, A.R., Plants, Fractals, and Formal Languages, *Computer Graphics*, **18**(3), 1–10, (Proc. SIGGRAPH '84).

SPEE85 Speer, L.R., DeRose, T.D. and Barsky, B.A., A Theoretical and Empirical Analysis of Coherent Ray Tracing, *Computer-Generated Images*, **27**(31), 11–25, (Proc. of Graphics Interface '85).

SPER90 Speray D. and Kennon, S., Volume Probes: Interactive Data Exploration on Arbitrary Grids, *Computer Graphics*, **24**(5), 1–12.

SPRO68 Sproull, R.F. and Sutherland, I.E., A Clipping Divider, *Fall Joint Computer Conference*, pp. 765–775, 1968.

STAR77 Stark, H., Diffraction Patterns of Non-overlapping Circular Grains, *J. Optical Society of America*, **67**(5), 700–3.

STEI84 Steinberg, H.A., A Smooth Surface Based on Biquadric Patches, *IEEE Computer Graphics and Applications*, **4**(6), 20–3.

STEK85 Steketee, S.N. and Badler, N.I., Parametric Keyframe Interpolation Incorporating Kinetic Adjustment and Phrasing Control, *Computer Graphics*, **19**(3), 255–62, (Proc. SIGGRAPH '85).

SUMM83 Summerfield, Q., *Analysis, Synthesis and Perception of Visible Articulatory Movements*, Academic Press, 1983.

SUTH63 Sutherland, I.E., Sketchpad: A Man–machine Graphical Communications System, in *Proc. of the Spring Joint Comp. Conf.*, Spartan Books, Baltimore MD, 1963.

SUTH74a Sutherland, I.E. and Hodgman, G.W., Reentrant Polygon Clipping, *CACM*, **17**(1), 32–42.

SUTH74b Sutherland, I.E., Sproull, R.F. and Schumacker, R.A., A Characterization of Ten Hidden Surface Algorithms, *ACM Computing Surveys*, **6**(1), 1–55.

TERZ87 Terzopoulos, D., Platt, J., Barr, A. and Fleischer, K., Elastically Deformable Models, *Computer Graphics*, **21**(4), 205–14, (Proc. SIGGRAPH '87).

TERZ88 Terzopoulos, D. and Fleischer, K., Modelling Inelastic Deformation: Viscoelasticity, Plasticity, Fracture, *Computer Graphics*, **22**(4), 269–78, (Proc. SIGGRAPH '88).

THAL87 Thalman-Magnenat, M. and Thalman, D., The Directions of Synthetic Actors in the Film *Rendezvous à Montréal, IEEE Computer Graphics and Applications*, Dec. 1987, 9–19.

THOM84 Thomas, F., and Johnston, O., *Disney Animation: The Illusion of Life*, Abbeyville Publishers, NY, 1981.

TIED90 Tiede, U., Hohne, K.H., Bomans, M., Pommert, A., Riemer, M. and Wiebecke, G., Investigation of Medical 3D rendering Algorithms, *IEEE Computer Graphics Applications*, **10**(2), 41–53.

TODD91 Todd, S.J.P. and Latham, W., *Mutator, a Subjective Human Interface for the Evolution of Computer Structures*, IBM UK Scientific Centre Report 248, 1991.

TORR67 Torrance, K.E. and Sparrow, E.M., Theory for Off-specular Reflection from Roughened Surfaces, *J. Opt. Soc. Amer.*, **57**(9), 1105–14.

TSO87 T'so, P.Y. and Barsky , B., Modelling and Rendering Waves: Wave Tracing using Beta splines and Reflective and Refractive Texture Mapping, *ACM Trans. Graphics*, **6**(3), 191–214.

UPSO88 Upson, C. and Keeler, M., V-Buffer: Visible Volume Rendering, *Computer Graphics*, **22**(4), 59–64, (Proc. SIGGRAPH '88).

UPST89 Upstill, S., *The RenderMan^{TM} Companion*, Addison-Wesley, Reading MA, 1989.

WALL87 Wallace, J.R., Cohen, M.F. and Greenberg, D.P., A Two-pass Solution to the Rendering Equation: A Synthesis of Ray Tracing and Radiosity Methods, *Computer Graphics*, **21**(4), 311–20, (Proc. SIGGRAPH '87).

WALL89 Wallace, J.R., Kells, A.E. and Haines , E., A Ray Tracing Algorithm for Progressive Radiosity, *Computer Graphics*, **23**(3), 315–24, (Proc. SIGGRAPH '89).

WARD88 Ward, G.J., Rubinstein, F.M. and Clear, R.D., A Ray Tracing solution for Diffuse Interreflection, *Computer Graphics*, **22**(4), 85–92, (Proc. SIGGRAPH '88).

WARN69 Warnock, J., *A Hidden-Surface Algorithm for Computer Generated Half-Tone Pictures*, Univ. Utah Computer Sci. Dept, TR 4–15 (NTIS AD-753 671), 1969.

WARN83 Warn, D.R., Lighting Controls for Synthetic Images, *Computer Graphics*, **17**(3), 13–21, (Proc. SIGGRAPH '83).

WATE87 Waters, K., A Muscle Model for Animating Three-dimensional Facial Expression, *Computer Graphics*, **21**(4), 17–24, (Proc. SIGGRAPH '87).

WATK70 Watkins, G.S., *A Real-Time Visible Surface Algorithm*, Univ. of Utah Comp. Sci. Dept Tech. Report, UTEC-CSC-70-101, June 1970.

WATT89 Watt, A., *Fundamentals of Three-dimensional Computer Graphics*, Addison-Wesley, Wokingham UK, 1989.

WEGH84 Weghorst, H., Hooper, G. and Greenberg, D.P. Improved Computational Methods for Ray Tracing, *ACM Trans. Graphics*, **3**(1), 52–69.

WEIL77 Weiler, K. and Atherton, P., Hidden Surface Removal using Polygon Area Sorting, *Computer Graphics*, **11**(2), 214–22.

WEIL86 Weil, J., The Synthesis of Cloth Objects, *Computer Graphics*, **20**(4), 49-54, (Proc. SIGGRAPH '86).

WEIS68 Weisskopf, V.F., How Light Interacts with Matter, *Sci. Amer.*, Sep. 1968 (Special Issue on Light), 60-75.

WEST90 Westover, L., Footprint Evaluation for Volume Rendering, *Computer Graphics*, **24**(4), 367-76, (Proc. SIGGRAPH '90).

WHIT72 Whitney, D.E., The Mathematics of Coordinated Control of Prosthetic Arms and Manipulators, *Trans. ASME., J. of Dynamic Systems, Measurement and Control*, 122, 303-9.

WHIT80 Whitted, T., An Improved Illumination Model for Shaded Display, *Comm. ACM*, **26**(6), 342-9.

WILH87 Wilhelms, J., Towards Automatic Motion Control, *IEEE Computer Graphics and Applications*, **7**(4), 11-22.

WILL78 Williams, L., Casting Curved Shadows on Curved Surfaces, *Computer Graphics*, **12**(3), 270-4, (Proc. SIGGRAPH '78).

WILL83 Williams, D.R. and Collier, R., Consequences of Spatial Sampling by a Human Photoreceptor Mosaic, *Science*, **221** July 22, 1983, pp. 385-7.

WILL83 Williams, L., Pyramidal Parametrics, *Computer Graphics*, **17**(3), 1-11, (Proc. SIGGRAPH '83).

WOLF90 Wolff, L.B. and Kurlander, D.J., Ray Tracing with Polarization Parameters, *IEEE Computer Graphics and Applications*, **10**(6), 44-55.

WOO90 Woo, A., Poluin, P. and Fournier, A., A Survey of Shadow Algorithms, *IEEE Computer Graphics and Applications*, **10**(6), 13-32.

WYLI67 Wylie, C., Romney, G.W., Evans, D.C. and Erdhal, A.C., Halftone perspective Drawings by Computer, in *Proc. Fall Joint Computer Conf.*, 1967, pp. 49-58, Thompson Books, Washington DC.

WYVI86 Wyvill, B., McPheeters, C. and Wyvill, G., Data Structure for Soft Object, *The Visual Computer*, **2**(4), 227-34.

WYVI86 Wyvill, B., McPheeters, C. and Wyvill, G., Animating Soft Objects, *The Visual Computer*, **2**(2), 235-42.

YAMA84 Yamaguchi, K., Kunii, T.L., Fujimura, K. and Toriya, H., Octree Related Data Structures and Algorithms, *IEEE Computer Graphics and Applications*, **4**(1), 53-9.

YELL82 Yellott, I., Spectral Analysis of Spatial Sampling by Photoreceptors: Topological Disorder Prevents Aliasing, *Vision Research*, **22**, 1205-10.

ZELT82 Zeltzer, D., Motor Control Techniques for Figure Animation, *IEEE Computer Graphics and Applications*, **2**(9), 53-9.

ZHU88 Zhu, Y., Peng, Q. and Liang, Y., PERIS: A Programming Environment for Realistic Image Synthesis, *Computer and Graphics*, **12**(3/4), 299-307.

Index